American Labor Struggles and Law Histories

American Labor Struggles and Law Histories

Edited by

Kenneth M. Casebeer

CAROLINA ACADEMIC PRESS
Durham, North Carolina

Library of Congress Cataloging-in-Publication Data

American labor struggles and law histories / [editor] Kenneth M. Casebeer.
    p. cm.
 Includes bibliographical references and index.
 ISBN 978-1-59460-930-5 (alk. paper)
1. Labor laws and legislation--United States--History. 2. Labor--United States--History. I. Casebeer, Kenneth M., 1949-
 KF3319.A8 2011
 344.730109--dc23
                              2011020196

Carolina Academic Press
700 Kent Street
Durham, North Carolina 27701
Telephone (919) 489-7486
Fax (919) 493-5668
www.cap-press.com

Printed in the United States of America

To the mentors who have given me so much,
James J. Unger, Roberto Mangabiera Unger, Soia Mentschikoff,
Morton J. Horwitz, and Laurence H. Tribe,
To the hero of my lifetime, and one before,
Rev. Martin Luther King and Eugene V. Debs,
And to all people who continue to engage in collective action fighting oppression.

Contents

Editor's Preface

Historians, like the rest of us, tend to "find what we see," rather than the more aspirational claim to "see what we find."

As the editor of this book, what I personally "see" over the course of post-revolution American History is: the importance of the labor question — the place of all those who directly produce the wealth of the society by the expenditure of their time and energy (lives) in relation to the social use of their products, and their welfare; the importance of struggle by workers in collective actions contesting power exercised to reduce their social and economic position and security in society; and the involvement of law and legal institutions in constructing the context of those struggles. This Preface is therefore written from my point of view, and should be distinguished by readers from the Introduction, which will be written from the point of view of the book as a collection of authors. Many "points of view" are represented in approaching the past and in the histories of labor they partially tell.

The shared premise of all the contributors, however, is that the History of labor in the United States cannot be captured without acknowledging the ubiquity and centrality of the struggle of workers to gain power otherwise denied to them to achieve the independence allowed by an adequate and just standard of living, and often as importantly, to create the kind of democratic society that included their equal voice and dignity. These struggles have not been uniform, or continuous, or isolated from the aspirations of others for similar aims. But these worker struggles were constant and quite self-conscious. These struggles also met with organized opposition as vicious any other conflicts in America. Finally, it is striking, that workers' ideas, interests, goals, and achievements almost always took the form of "collective actions." Collective actions did not always involve unions, or unions of a particular type, or involve politics toward parties, independent or not, or toward the State. This book is about how this range of collective actions intersected with law and legal practices. It therefore addresses power as exercised in American society.

Much can be learned from studying labor struggles — not least is their relevance to workers today as they confront tremendous membership declines in unions, and receding identification with a labor movement. Paradoxically, at the same time, workers experience increasing labor class consciousness of the insecurity of globalized markets, and unprecedented inequalities of income and wealth in America. For the labor movement, experience gained should not be lost. Both lessons of militancy and avoidance of self-defeat can be learned. Based on what did not occur, the generation of new strategies becomes possible, and these lessons expose remarkable continuing, repetitive repressions of labor in the name of capital and the undermining of democracy by capitalism. Collective actions are more necessary for workers than ever before. Workers do win. The losses, while painful, are not lost.

Recovering and investigating labor struggles form all the justification needed for this book. I should stop here. At the risk of becoming too academic, however, I want to put the book's focus in an ongoing intellectual literature. Why this book now? I believe that what was actually experienced by American workers has increasingly been overshadowed in contemporary academic disputes more concerned with privileging particular narratives and historiography. I personally hope this book will provide something of a corrective balance.

First, as a labor law professor, too much legal writing, including labor law histories, proceed from an unexamined assumption of the legitimacy and State protection of "business unionism"[1] within a social organization reflecting "industrial pluralism."[2]

I would view Labor Law more broadly. First, American workers have been and are less than unanimous about business unions and their usually top-down and only semi-democratic organization, and their institutional distance from the rank-and-file. Second, unions or not, American workers have engaged continuously in other forms of collective actions than simply collective bargaining, including less tamed struggles for power: rebellions, politics, boycotts, picketing, labor and social movements, and especially strikes. Third, Labor Law as Collective Bargaining regulation thus shortchanges not only the range of collective activities of workers, but recognition of the wide range of legal rules and practices brought to bear on labor struggles—criminal law, antitrust, property law, legislation, court injunctions, petty arrests, murder and treason prosecutions, police and military suppression, vigilantes, and more. Labor Law is much more than the law of collective bargaining.

Second, as a legal history academic, there has been increasing call for a *New* "New Legal History," rejecting the "Law & Society" distinction, the basis of the academic cocoon of the Law & Society Association, which had promulgated the "social science" rejection of progressive or whiggish histories prevailing in legal histories before 1970. Law & Society sought in empirical and ideological study of consciousness and conditions of society a critical purchase on the study of law. The more sophisticated studies acknowledged the reciprocal interdependencies of these two spheres of action, law and society, but critical rationality still depended on at least conventional separation. The *New* New histories deny separation, "seeing" law as just another, although often central, discourse in constructing the "meaning" of society through which all persons understand their acts. The conceptual non-distinction, following post-modernism, is text/context. Power is lodged and deployed in the specialized discourse of legal practices from which in part social, and more specifically cultural, relations emerge. The historiographical problem is still one of "critical purchase," but the historical problem now is that of "imaginings of alternative practices." The former battleground of agency is backgrounded within the dominance of cultures contested between subalterns and empires. Among many problems with this lens on Law, an exclusive study of legal texts (most often court opinions) and the contexts of their deployment, is in a sense, while sometimes shifting, always a "winners" history. Where are the losers accounted? Particularly in labor law history, where are the workers and their consciousness?

The implicit response of the *New* "New Legal" Historians is the necessity of abolishing reductionist, instrumentalist, functionalist, institutionalist, or any other form of determinist explanation of law or any other discourse, or of thought. Historiography must now be indeterminate, discontinuous, contingent, contextual, multi-dimensional, and meaningfully discursive. I don't believe it. History, what actually "happened," is actions. Actions are not imaginings. Actions depend on conditions prevailing in some sense at a

---

1. *See,* Victoria Hattam, *Labor Visions and State Power: The Origins of Business Unionism in the United States* (Princeton University Press, 1992).

2. *See,* Katherine Van Wezel Stone, "The Post-War Paradigm in American Labor Law," 90 *Yale Law Journal* 1509 (1981).

given point in time, of course including discourse. Workers who have been crushed and live in dismal conditions have not just lost an argument. Sticks and stones do break and have often broken their bones. Gravestones and funeral processions of more than 30,000 marchers, while symbolic, are still marking acts.

Third, as a labor historian, the broadest intellectual context is post-modernism in its increasing prominence in labor histories. Labor history in its classical period almost exclusively focused on the institutional and political history of labor unions, and trade unions at that.[3] The new labor history, under the clear influence of E. P. Thompson, turned to discovery of the working class, and thus the forces of culture, politics, and ideology in shaping working class experience and opportunities.[4] This led in two sub-disciplinary directions, incorporation of the new social histories of largely local studies,[5] and the relation of class to social relations at the point of production.[6] Most recently, labor historians have taken their social histories toward the independence of culture by emphasizing worker consciousness and discursively inscribed limitations of alternative opportunities.[7]

The intellectual and strategic problem posed to the relevance of historical work for labor by this turn by historians is an old one — the priority of structure and agency — do conditions determine social relations necessary to production, or does choice determine what social relations are permitted and thus the provisioning conditions required by them.? Marxian reductionism, the priority of the material base generating its ideational superstructure, has been completely marginalized as vulgar within historiography.[8]

To my mind, the content of law (and histories) is of course historically contingent, and relatively indeterminate; the production of ideas is in principle no different than the production of goods, services, technologies, knowledge's, indeed social relations, a continuum rather than categories. Following Thompson, law is both an arena and form of social struggle. But this does not mean that the ideational realm and/or the discursive context has no particularized dependence whatsoever on material conditions at any given moment.

---

3. John R. Commons, et al., *History of Labour in the United States* (1918–26), Selig Perlman, *The History of Trade Unionism in the United States* (1922).

4. E. P. Thompson, *The Making of the English Working Class* (London: Vintage Books, 1963), Herbert Gutman, *Work, Culture, and Society in Industrializing America* (New York: Vintage Books, 1976).

5. *See e.g.*, Sean Wilentz, *Chants Democratic: New York City & the Rise of the American Working Class, 1788–1850* (New York: Oxford Univ. Press, 1984).

6. David Montgomery, *The Fall of the House of Labor: The Workplace, the State, and American Labor Activism, 1865–1925* (New York: Cambridge Univ. Press, 1987), David Brody, *Workers in Industrial America: Essays on the Twentieth Century Struggle* (1985).

7. "A predominant theme has been the discovery of alternative cultural meanings or distinctive subjectivities in working class expression and behavior," Leon Fink, "The New Labor History and the Powers of Historical Pessimism: Consensus, Hegemony, and the Case of the Knights of Labor." *In Search of the Working Class: Essays in American Labor History and Political Culture*, 89 (Urbana: Univ. of Illinois Press, 1994). Emphasizing the role of American culture in restraining labor, *see* Philip Yale Nicholson, *Labor's Story in the United States* (Philadelphia: Temple Univ. Press, 2004).

8. The vulgar reductionist is a straw Marx. E. P. Thompson replies: "In *Capital* ... Marx repeatedly uses the concept of the circuit of capital to characterize the structure of the capitalist economy — and, more than that, of capitalist society more generally. But historical materialism (as assumed as hypothesis by Marx, and as subsequently developed in our practice) must be concerned with other "circuits" also: the circuits of power, of the reproduction of ideology etc., and these belong to a different logic and to other categories. Moreover, historical analysis does not allow for static contemplation of "circuits," but is immersed in moments when all systems go and every circuit sparks across the other." E. P. Thompson, "Marxism and History," *The Poverty of Theory and Other Essays* (New York: Monthly Review Press, 1978).

What the post-modern, or linguistic turn, has somewhat dictatorially done is in some sense simply flip Marx. Instead of structure determining discourse, discourse now determines what can be known of the material structure. In its vulgar form this is reverse reductionism—even if the content of discourse at any given moment is perceived as indeterminate, contingent, and afunctional.[9] As Leon Fink observes, "The yellow-dog contract, criminalization of the boycott, the antistrike injunction, and the gleam of militia bayonets ... were not the tools of consent."[10] Recovering as histories the deeds to which these legal enactments responded is emphatically not sentimentality as charged by newer critics of labor histories.

This book aspires to offer a corrective to all three academic limitations. The book serves to provide law professors a supplemental reader to provide the contexts of collective actions to decisions in labor law texts, to also provide historians a chronology of case studies to illustrate a trajectory of legal history that can accompany thematic American History courses, and finally, above all, to reassert the interconnectedness of the material world and law and consciousness in relation to the possibility of agency (once again fore grounded) in histories. This book re-centers struggles undertaken in collective actions of workers, and experienced in some ways also as legal actions.

The history of actual people is not that of the hegemony of individualism, the taxonomy of Paternalism, or the discourse of the bayonet. That is not the way we live our lives. To my knowledge, workers in American history have not yet given their consent to domination, or accepted their share of the value of what they produce as just, and workers continue to fight to enact alternative social relations in reproducing their society. They have often lost. They have often been beaten, many literally. Many have died. Triumph and Anguish are words but they do not represent discourse, and the past carries memory in deeds that are much more than words. Both old and new labor law histories have a lot to learn.

I want to express particular appreciation to Jim Pope, who has offered important and sage advice throughout, and encouraged the participation of many in this project; and to my assistant, Shannon Maharajh who cheerfully makes appear all I need; and to my partner, Marnie Mahoney, who tired of hearing my complaints about the literature, and challenged me to stop talking and write a book about it, and has been a constant consultant. Marnie has always in her writing and ideas reminded us of the twin couplets—Power and Control, Oppression and Resistance ...

Kenneth M. Casebeer
Asheville, North Carolina
May, 2011

---

9. "The history of meaning has successfully asserted the reality and autonomy of its object. At the same time, however, a new form of reductionism has become evident, the reduction of experience to the meanings that shape it. Along with this possibility, a new form of intellectual hubris has emerged, the hubris of word-makers who claim to be makers of reality," John E. Toews, "Intellectual History After the Linguistic Turn: The Autonomy of Meaning and the Irreducibility of Experience," 92 *American Historical Review* 879, 906 (1987).

10. Leon Fink, *supra* note 8, at 103.

Authors

Eric Arnesen: Professor of History, The George Washington University, is the foremost scholar of the intersection of labor and civil rights history. His seminal books include *Brotherhoods of Color: Black Railroad Workers and the Struggle for Equality* and *Waterfront Workers of New Orleans: Race, Class, and Politics, 1863–1923*. He is engaged in a biography of A. Phillip Randolph.

James B. Atleson: SUNY Distinguished Teaching Professor of Law, Emeritus, University of Buffalo Law School, authored the acclaimed *Values and Assumptions in American Labor Law* and *Labor and the Wartime State*.

Eileen Boris: Hull Professor and Chair, Department of Feminist Studies, University of California Santa Barbara. Eileen Boris cuts across disciplinary boundaries as if never there. Of her many books are *Caring for America: How Home Health Workers Became the New Face of Labor* (co-authored with Jennifer Klein; *The Practice of US Women's History: Narratives, Dialogues, and Intersections*, edited by S.J. Kleinberg, Eileen Boris, and Vicki Ruiz; *Major Problems in the History of American Workers*, Second Edition, edited by Eileen Boris and Nelson Lichtenstein; *Home to Work: Motherhood and The Politics of Industrial Homework in the United States*—Winner of the 1995 Philip Taft Prize in Labor History. Prof. Boris and Prof. Klein have a book forthcoming, *Organizing Home Care*.

Kenneth M. Casebeer: Professor of Law, Director, Employment, Labor, and Immigration certificate at the University of Miami Law School, is co-author with Gary Minda of *Work Law in American Society*. His recent scholarship focuses on recovering lost voices as part of Critical Labor Law History.

Thomas Dublin: SUNY Distinguished Professor of History, Co-director, Center for the Historical Study of Women and Gender SUNY Binghamton. He is author of the classic, *Women at Work: The Transformation of Work and Community in Lowell, Massachusetts, 1826–1860*, and numerous other books on labor, immigration and women.

Leon Fink: University of Illinois Chicago Distinguished Professor of History, Director of WRGUW (History of Work, Race, and Gender in the Urban World), Editor, *Labor: Studies in Working-Class History of the Americas*. He is author of *Workingmens' Democracy: The Knights of Labor and American Politics* and *The Maya of Morganton: Work and Community in the Nuevo New South*, among other books.

Philip S. Foner: Prof. of History, Lincoln University, now deceased. Prof. Foner was a distinguished and prolific materialist historian, author of the ten-volume *History of the Labor Movement in the United States*, among many other books.

William E. Forbath: Lloyd M. Bentsen Professor of Law and History, University of Texas—Austin, is one of the foremost legal historians working today. He is author of *Law and the Shaping of the American Labor Movement*.

James Green: Professor of History and Labor Studies at the University of Massachusetts—Boston. Jim Green is a past President of the Labor and Working Class History Association and an editor of its Journal, *Labor: Studies of Working Class History in the Americas.* He has authored six books, most recently, *Death in the Haymarket: A Story of Chicago, the First Labor Movement and the Bombing that Divided Gilded Age America.*

Michael K. Honey: Fred T. and Dorothy G. Haley Endowed Professor of the Humanities, Professor, Labor and Ethnic Studies and American History, University of Washington — Tacoma, Past President, Labor and Working-Class History Association. Michael Honey is an author of breathtaking scholarship, ten years of which culminated in *Going Down Jericho Road: The Memphis Strike, Martin Luther King's Last Campaign.*

Jennifer Klein: Professor of History, Yale University, is the author of *For All These Rights: Business, Labor, and the Shaping of America's Public-Private Welfare State.* She is also on the Editorial Board of the journal *International Labor and Working Class History.*

Sidney Lens: Labor leader, activist, and author of many progressive books, including *The Labor Wars.*

Kari Lydersen: A journalist who writes for the *Washington Post, The New York Times, In These Times,* and other publications, Kari authored, *Revolt on Goose Island: The Chicago Factory Takeover and What it Says About the Economic Crisis.*

Staughton Lynd: Attorney, Legal Services of Youngstown, Ohio, formerly Professor of History, Yale University. A well-known pacifist and labor activist, he is the author of numerous books, including *The Fight Against Shutdowns, Solidarity Unionism,* and with Alice Lynd, *Rank and File.*

Martha R. Mahoney: Professor of Law at the University of Miami, is co-author with Stephanie Wildman and John Calmore of *Social Justice: Professionals, Communities and Law.*

David Montgomery: Farnam Professor of History Emeritus, Yale University. Professor Montgomery is the dean of American Labor History. His numerous seminal books include: *Citizen Worker, The Fall of the House of Labor, Workers' Control in America, Beyond Equality,* etc.

Walter C. Nelles: A Professor of Law at Yale Law School, Nelles was the first General Counsel of the American Civil Liberties Union. He died in 1939.

James Gray Pope: Professor of Law and Sidney Reitman Scholar, Rutgers Law School—Newark. James Pope is a former member of the IAM and the Industrial Union of Marine and Ship Builders. A prolific historian of Labor Law, he forcefully argues for the contemporary relevance of the Thirteenth Amendment.

Linda G. Schneider: Professor of Sociology Emeritus at SUNY—Nassau Community College. She is the co-author with Arnold Silverman of *Global Sociology.*

Philip Taft: Professor and Chair, Department of Economics, Brown University. Taft, an old school labor union institutionalist who died in 1976, wrote the two-volume study, *The A.F. of L. in the Time of Gompers,* and *The A.F. of L. from the Death of Gompers to the Merger.*

Kieran Taylor: Assistant Professor of History, The Citadel, specializes in twentieth-century US, Labor, and Civil Rights history. He is Coordinator of the Citadel Oral History Program and co-editor of volumes 4 and 5 of *The Papers of Martin Luther King, Jr.*

Mary Heaton Vorse: Labor Journalist. Vorse, who died in 1966, was everywhere labor was in the 1930s. She wrote *Labor's New Millions* about the formation of the CIO.

Ahmed A. White: Professor of Law at the University of Colorado Law School, specializes in the intersection of Criminal and Labor Law history.

Rebecca E. Zietlow: Charles W. Fornoff Professor of Law and Values, University of Toledo College of Law, writes about the Reconstruction Era and congressional protection of individual rights. Her work includes the book- *Enforcing Equality: Congress, the Constitution, and the Protection of Individual Rights.*

American Labor Struggles and Law Histories

Introduction

Labor Struggles, Collective Action, and Law

Boston Massacre 1770.

Kenneth M. Casebeer

March 5, 1770, British guns sounded in the course of a labor dispute. Those guns signaled the beginning of the insurgency that culminated in the American Declaration of Independence and American Revolution. During the Boston Massacre, the first to fall was a black man, Crispus Attucks, a sailor. The other four killed were also workers involved in a collective protest: James Caldwell, ship's mate; Patrick Carr, journeyman leathermaker; Samuel Gray, ropemaker; Samuel Maverick, apprentice ivory turner.

British troops supplemented their poor wages by seeking casual labor, and in doing so were willing to accept lower wages for the jobs available. At a time of high unemployment, Boston workers resented this competition. On March 2, Patrick Walker of the 20th Regiment entered upon John Gray's ropewalk. Ropemaker William Green confronted him, responding vulgarly to Walker's job inquiry. Ten to twelve ropeworkers dissuaded Walker from fighting at that time. Walker instead rounded up a number of fellow soldiers for an ensuing series of brawls with workers in the vicinity of the ropewalk, resulting that day in the soldiers eventually being driven away. A few nights later, the smarting soldiers again ventured forth, beating random citizens. A crowd formed at the Custom's House, objects were thrown, and the soldiers fired. Among others, the shots killed Sam Gray, a jour-

3

neyman involved in the first fights.[1] It was an event mourned annually in Boston the next thirteen years, marking a hatred of the citizenry toward the violent and arbitrary force of the Crown.

The Labor Question, the relation of owners of property to others engaged in production utilizing such private resources, from the advent of the United States, has been the central issue linking democracy to maintenance of a stable society and legal reinforcement of the social relations necessary to reproducing American society. At the same time, the history of the Labor Question in America has not been peaceful. Owners battled workers economically, often to the point of worker's starvation and impoverishment, condemned as "wage slavery." In this battle, law was almost never neutral. It upheld the power of owners of enterprise, often to the point of military suppression of workers. Thousands died. This book is most of all about the workers in those labor struggles—struggles intensely engaged and about the material conditions of life in America. American workers have not ever "consented" to the prevailing rules of the Labor Question. The frequency, intensity, indeed violence, and heroism of American labor struggles cry out for acknowledgement and priority in reconsidering American history at our own potential turning point.[2]

Labor struggles must effectively take the form of collective actions. The extent of power brought to bear against workers could not conceivably be countered individually. Workers had to act collectively, and when they did, they mutually experienced a consciousness called solidarity, a consciousness the law did not reinforce or celebrate.[3]

Law channeled, shaped, and mostly reacted to labor's collective actions in negative forms. American law self-consciously served the instrumental interests of employers and legal elites, but it did more than that. American law, conceptualized ideologically in terms of liberal individualism and implemented through property rights of increasing generality and scope, hostilely repressed the aims and consequences of collective action. As a Harlan County, Kentucky mine woman put it during the early 1930s, when asked what the "law" meant to her, "The law is a gun thug in a big automobile."[4] Workers thus continuously fought both economic and legal authority.

The entire trajectory of American Labor Law and American Labor Struggles yields too few studies.[5] This book, taken as a whole and not just a collection, tells the stories of law

---

1. Richard B. Morris, *Government and Labor in Early America*, 190–92 (New York: Harper & Row, 1965).

2. The editor locates the labor question initially in the Constitution of the United States. Others have traced its explicit formation to the politics of the Progressive era, or its prominence in twentieth century labor discourse. Nelson Lichtenstein uses the labor question from the Progressives forward to frame his book on the development of the twentieth century labor movement, its organization and politics, Nelson Lichtenstein, *State of the Union: A Century of American Labor* (Princeton: Princeton Univ. Press, 2002).

3. "Solidarity has often been an organic product of worker collective experience existing prior to and then alongside the law." David Abraham, "Individual Autonomy and Collective Empowerment in Labor Law: Union Membership Resignations and Strikebreaking in the New Economy." 63 *N.Y.U. L. Rev.* 1268, 1273 (1988).

4. Theodore Dreiser, et al., *Harlan Miners Speak*, 35 (Lexington: Univ. of Kentucky Press, 2008).

5. Many fine local studies of law and labor interaction have been produced, only some of which obviously appear in this book in modified form. Notable exceptions to local studies of law and labor include; David Montgomery, *The Fall of the House of Labor: The Workplace, the State, and American Labor Activism, 1865–1925* (New York: Cambridge Univ. Press, 1987); David Montgomery, *Citizen-Worker: The Experience of Workers in the United States with Democracy and the Free Market During the Nineteenth Century* (New York: Cambridge Univ. Press, 1993); William E. Forbath, *Law and the Shaping of the American Labor Movement* (Cambridge: Harvard Univ. Press, 1991); Christopher L. Tom-

and legal action inevitable to workers in triumph or in anguish over all of United States history. The intellectual structure of this relation of work and law as represented here, is complex, contingent, and manifold. To oversimplify: In the most general conceptual frame, the Labor Question relates production to democracy, as mediated by the material conditions of social organization. In an intermediate framing, labor struggles relate to legitimated power, as mediated by community or communities. At the most specific framing, collective actions relate to legal rules and interventions, as mediated by the point or process of production, and often class and other identities.

Importantly, understanding and entering law as an intervention in collective struggle inevitably requires a view of law from the bottom up. In contrast, entering law initially via Supreme Court opinions and other elite texts tends to record legal activity as winners-only history. Yet law is always constructed as one arena of social struggle. Win or lose: "[V]ictorious events come about as the result of many possibilities ... for one possibility that actually is realized, innumerable others have drowned.... And yet, it is necessary to give them their place because the losing movements are forces which have at every moment affected the final outcome."[6] For workers, there has always been something gained beyond the individual contest, in the knowledge and experience that resistance is possible and the dignity that the fight will come again. As one worker put it, "A strike is never lost."

How did the Labor Question and its contest—labor struggle and legal practices—become central? Go back to the Revolution. Throughout the history of the United States, justification for the exercise of the coercive power by government over persons depended on popular sovereignty. In modern Western societies at the time of the Revolution, used to either divine descent of power to Kings and aristocracy, or the alternative of military dictatorship, this was big news. However popular sovereignty was variously given idea and voice, it rested on the separation of legitimacy and government, the latter limited and subordinate to the people as a whole. Almost unanimously that subordinate role has been taken to mean a social commitment to democracy. Although the form and location of implementing democracy has been fiercely contended, it has usually been cast within the broad umbrella of the representative republic.[7] In turn, the economic organization of American society proceeded on the understanding that individual freedom would be secured by political liberties defined and enforced by laws made by or in the name of such a democratic republic. At the outset, therefore, the constitutional mechanism protected the primacy of liberty, protected in rights of property, as the necessary precondition of the diverse pursuit of diverse interests. Protection of control over resources became simultaneously the first duty of and chief need for strong regulatory government under democratic accountability.[8]

The control of resources as private property as a legalized entitlement was not only a right to use such resources for personal satisfaction, but at the same time a right to exclude others from using that property, unless permitted to others by the owner. Especially when such resources were accumulated by owners, the use of property as means of production were controlled by its owners, subject of course to public regulation consistent with the underlying assumption of private ownership. Christopher Tomlins claims: "the distinctive role occupied by law in the American polity has, from that polity's in-

---

lins, *The State and the Unions: Labor Relations, Law, and the Organized Labor Movement in America, 1880–1960* (New York: Cambridge Univ. Press, 1985).

6. Fernand Braudel, quoted in Herbert Gutman, *Work, Culture & Society*, 67, (New York: Vintage Books, 1976).

7. The Guarantee Clause, Art. IV, U. S. Constitution, 1789.

8. James Madison, *The Federalist Papers*, No. 10, November 22, 1787.

ception, had quite crucial implications for the institutions and ideologies through which laboring people in America have identified and pursued their interests; but also, second, that this intimate interaction between law and labor has taken place because, quite apart from the exigencies of specific occasions, labor has throughout been positioned in legal discourse as the preeminent liability of the polity which the American legal order epitomizes."[9] Workers believed this labor question contested.

The centrality of the Labor Question for economics and politics did not mean that democracy, republican institutions of democracy, the law so produced, the concept of property, or the actions legally or illegally undertaken in the name of property were in any way fixed. What this unavoidable relation between owners and workers did insure as a matter of "fact" for the history and "progress" of democracy was that owners and workers were not identical. Their relations were contested between them, and involved others affected and interested. Indeed, the centrality of the Labor Question insured that all such issues were fought fiercely, and often violently, in both action and ideology. Nothing about constitutional democracy prevented any faction's will to power.

As the scope and scale of production increased and changed, fed by increasing accumulation of resources, the power of owners who were increasingly interested in further wealth required coordination. No longer as individual action, more and more, coordination took the form of informal and then formal collective action, chiefly under the legal authorization of corporations. Long before the understanding of "capitalism" and its supports, American workers realized that their interests would not prevail unless they too undertook collective action, and in turn that collective action most effectively depended upon organization: "Brethren, in order to be able to assume this position, we must organize ourselves, and act in concert. The privileged classes have always prevailed against us, though we are the many and they the few, because they have combined their numbers and acted together. We must not disdain to follow their example, so far as to combine in our own defense. We would, therefore, recommend to our brethren throughout the Commonwealth and the Union, to organize themselves into associations, which, by mutual correspondence, may bring about a concert of action between all the workingmen of the country."[10]

In America from the beginning, collective action was always central to social relations prevailing in the economy and to the actual experience of democracy.[11] Indeed, most often workers acting collectively prioritized democracy in the workplace and/or industrial economy as the precondition to authentic political democracy. Therefore, the Labor Question of the proper place of labor in the society, or what may be termed the relation of those who directly produce the wealth from the total resources available in society to those who own such resources or their uses, likely, perhaps inevitably, commits labor as a whole to the pursuit of material equity, even equality. The society was historically hard pressed to have it both ways: increasing private accumulation and an egalitarian democ-

---

9. Christopher Tomlins, *Law, Labor, and Ideology in the Early American Republic*, xii (New York: Cambridge Univ. Press, 1993).

10. *Third Grand Rally of the Workingmen of Charleston, Mass, Held October 23rd, 1840*, 5–7, 17, 18.

11. Senator Robert Wagner thus defended his proposed National Labor Relations Act, "The principles of my proposal were surprisingly simple. They were founded upon the accepted facts that we must have democracy in industry as well as in government; that democracy in industry means fair participation by those who work in the decisions vitally affecting their lives and livelihood ..." *N.Y. Times*, April 13, 1937, at 20.

ratic public. Law has always been invoked in mediation of private accumulation and participatory democracy,[12] no matter how non-neutral or contingent such mediation.[13]

The strategies of collective action for labor took numerous forms, as did the legal practices invoked by all those interested in the consequences of collective action by labor. The goal of this book is to re-center our attention on labor struggles undertaken in collective action in the histories of labor, and law, and on the inevitable intersection of labor actions and legal practices, and therefore finally on the constitution and deployment of power and the possibility of freedom in American society.

Most people assume labor collective actions are carried out through trade unions, and therefore that the relevant law of labor is the regulation of a particular form of collective bargaining between the representatives of workers (unions) and the representatives of owners (management)—the union of workers bargaining with the union of owners. Neither assumption is accurate. It is striking to discover that most of these key labor struggles started either spontaneously among a group of workers, or at least began out in front of a sometimes unprepared or skeptical national union leadership that had to catch up to their members. Labor has at different times chosen strategies well beyond bargaining backed by strikes: from consumer information (the union label), boycotts, picketing, small scale and ad hoc control over the tools, speed, and process of work, occupation of industrial plants, cooperative ownership, civil rights actions, independent and/or party politics, up to mass exodus, or even rebellion.

Not surprisingly, while sometimes invoked by labor as well as management, an amazing range of legal practices have been used by the State in the protection of employer interest and/or the repression of labor or in thwarting its aims. Frequently, law appeared in protection and expansion of the common law prerogatives of property, antitrust legislation applied to unions but not to trusts, Master-Servant obligations of obedience of workers, mass arrests for petty offenses of trespass, disturbing the peace, disorderly conduct, vagrancy, more serious prosecutions of murder, treason, and criminal syndicalism—prosecuted against workers but not against employers, authorized permanent discharge and replacement of strikers, criminal and civil conspiracy convictions sustained by courts at all levels through sweeping injunctions prohibiting labor activity, and often use of militia or the U.S. Army explicitly to break strikes, or if official force was denied, by public approval of private vigilantes (detectives) to spy, agitate, propagandize against labor or violently intimidate workers.

Even after unionization and collective bargaining became national legal policy, employers increasingly engaged in illegal practices to prevent organization and break unions, on the ground that eventual punishment, often taking years, is well worth the costs of operating union-free.

The histories of labor and law collected in these chapters cover the entire trajectory of American history. This history has not ended. Another important task for this book is making that ongoing labor struggle clear. It is interesting to note how the issues raised even in the distant past of American labor still resonate in our time, how the more things change, the more they remain the same. At the same time these narratives make plain that the outcomes and consequences of labor struggles were and are still contingent on the particular contexts of their point in time. There may be patterns, but the conflicts arose and were shaped, and certainly ex-

---

12. "[W]here the employment contract seeks to combine exchange (property) with subordination (power), the law furnishes organizational opportunities for employees, as well as stipulating formal obligations and suggesting general norms for both parties." David Abraham, *supra* note 3, at 1293.

13. *See, eg., Coppage v. Kansas*, 236 U.S. 1 (1915).

perienced by their participants at the cusp of their own moment. The outcome of the associated legal interventions, indeed the content of law in its relative autonomy, was also contingent. Sometimes workers won, more often they lost, always they adapted and continued.

Virtually all these types of labor action appear at any point in American history. As strategies, however, some very broad and general ideological positions of workers emerge. In colonial and early constitutional times, both skilled and free unskilled workers invoked an "Artisan Republicanism" stemming from Thomas Jefferson and Thomas Paine—a belief that all men by nature were free and deserved to participate in a democracy regulating their community in providing for a good life. This meant that every producing worker required the time and return on work that would support decent living standards necessary to full community participation and mobility. No sharp distinction arose between public and private spheres of life.

The Republican ideal continued for workers through the nineteenth century, although in later years this ideal became increasingly an "Industrial Republicanism." In the cooperative movement of the Knights of Labor, all workers were welcome and mutually interdependent, deserving a participatory role in the management of the enterprises in which they worked and a just share of the fruits of their work. Community was still neither public nor private, although work life denominated an increasingly distinct sphere of activity. Concerns such as the eight-hour day and non-arbitrary treatment at work became prominent. Not completely inconsistently, distrusting an increasingly activist state, The A.F. of L. began its "voluntarist" economic organization of craft workers to control work processes and secure its members' just share of firm income.

By the turn of the twentieth century, the concentration of ownership in factories and trusts, and a constitutional ideology of individualism in the courts, heightened the tension between worker organizations over the need for an independent Labor Party, or on the other hand, the rejection of organized entry into state politics at all. A public versus private distinction was now assumed to exist, but the question remained whether workers would win a formal say against management's assertion of management's right to control investment and work process decisions, and therefore employment relations. Industrial unions fought management of huge factories, and also fought against craft unions in disputes over effective union counters to vast industrial development. The new goal conceded private ownership of the means of production, except perhaps for utilities, but fought for "Industrial Democracy," or at a minimum, co-development, up to the radical industrial syndicalism of the Industrial Workers of the World, both aims including determination of wages as a just share of the enterprise economic surplus.

By the Depression, all workers were concerned with security for their jobs and incomes. Thus they demanded recognition of independent unions that were powerful enough economically through successful strikes to gain higher wages—"Wage Consciousness." Mostly, they would not succeed against violent and entrenched anti-union management that insisted that labor was a commodity, and that like all other commodities, its prices were set by supply and demand. In turn, once a worker sold that labor commodity, management completely controlled its deployment, use, and termination. Anti-union retaliation succeeded until passage of the federal labor statutes of the mid-1930s. But "Collective Bargaining" or "Business Unionism," under government protection came at a price—public regulation of bargaining and institutionalizing of union-management interdependence in the name of "Industrial Peace." The union sphere of "wages, hours, and conditions of employment," seems to insulate management entrepreneurial control over investment decisions. Today, unions have been battered by antagonistic and weak labor laws, global capital mobility, the stagnation of capitalism, and consumerist individualism driven substantially by fear of economic collapse.

Increasingly, the goal of "Worker Voice" competes with wage preservation within an expanding array of non-strike collective actions and individual employment rights.

At the same time as political democracy expanded, economic democracy declined almost continuously. As the ideology of worker demands has responded to the re-characterization of employment by employers, democracy within the economic or "private" sphere has contracted. Artisan republicans had more say over their work and workplace than industrial republicans who, at best, sought institutions of co-management. Late nineteenth-century industrial workers had more say at the point of production than industrialized union members who tried to leverage bargaining power and direct action to gain job rules and job security from employers who had in exchange been ceded management control of the investment and production decisions.[14] Finally, federal recognition of unions confirmed the business of unions was wage procurement through bargaining over "wages, hours, and conditions of employment." At present, with the precipitous decline in union density, most workers have only the rights they can negotiate as individuals in employment contracts—which is to say no democracy at all.

Not surprisingly, the voices of the prominent authors assembled in this book represent many different approaches to their work, many different histories of collective action, and many different levels of narrative. Some involve more law, some involve more labor history. Some will disagree with each other as to their purpose or tools. Some will emphasize ideology and consciousness, some will emphasize prevailing conditions and actions. Taken together they illustrate the potential diversity and richness of what we can learn about history, about workers, and about law. And every bit of it is riveting.

The book begins in New York City in 1712 with a prelude of violent collective action by slaves driven to desperation by the oppressive conditions and relations of chattel slavery. It seems probable that such coordination between slaves of different masters first happened in the North because those slaves witnessed free black laborers and did not live in plantation isolation. Execution of the slaves swiftly followed.

The first full chapter is Walter Nelles's account of the contest over Jeffersonian Republicanism between an association of journeymen shoe and boot makers against an association of master craftsmen. The import and export trade pressured Masters to lower wages relative to new laboring time involved in shoemaking, and reduced individual craftsman production of finished shoes as a control of costs. Even though each individual could work or refuse to work at the offered wage, a group of workers withholding labor together to uphold minimum piece rates was criminally prosecuted as a conspiracy against the public. It was condemned as an act of "private government," an oxymoron, supplanting legitimate authority and thereby injuring non-member craftsmen who wished to work at lower piece rates. A political republicanism found by the judge within the English Common Law trumped the civic republicanism claimed by the journeymen. Judicial legal ideology and injunction defeated worker collective action.

In the first interlude (meant as shorter, more focused, narratives), in 1836, rural women and girls working within the new textile factories/lodgings of large textile manufacturers controlling all aspects of community life, formed the Lowell Factory Girls Association. Thomas Dublin describes the more or less spontaneous "turn-outs" of 1834 and 1836 in Lowell, Massachusetts over wage cuts. The turnouts expanded in the 1840s into protest over regimentation of all the worker's time and activities. At the beginning of factory development,

---

14. David Montgomery, *Workers' Control in America* (Cambridge: Cambridge University Press, 1979).

the new semi-skilled operatives thought more in terms of association for mutual purposes rather than economic unions. The law here appears only as an authorizing back-stop for manufacturers' complete control of the labor force and labor market within towns dominated exclusively by manufacturers.

In a long skip forward, Professor Leon Fink provides another interlude on the incredible rise of the Knights of Labor as the first national labor union. Open to all workers, emphasizing worker dignity and ethic, encouraging cooperatives, and backing strikes on an ad hoc basis, the Knights also promoted labor entry into politics. The Knights created a producer's political ideology, focused on a labor theory of value, as a counter consciousness to the rising legal and political imperative of possessive individualism.

In chapter two, Linda Schneider narrates the Homestead Lockout, then Strike, of 1892. Homestead, Pennsylvania existed solely as a company town of the Carnegie Steel Corporation, yes that Andrew Carnegie. An A.F. of L. union, the Amalgamated Iron, Steel, and Metal Workers Union, had organized a minority of skilled metal workers in the vast plant. Manager Henry Frick was ordered to slash wages and cut labor costs. He built a wall around "Fort Frick," announced the cuts and locked out protesting workers. Union resistance refused to allow strikebreakers into town. Frick hired 300 Pinkertons to float down the river to protect strikebreakers, reopening the plant. Tipped off, the workers armed and drove off the Pinkertons until they eventually surrendered their boats and barely walked out alive. The state militia eventually broke the strike and union members were mostly replaced. As a sociologist, Prof. Schneider describes the community in which the collective action takes place. Regardless of formal company property rights in owning town and stores, Prof. Schneider emphasizes that all workers believed they collectively controlled the community. They lived there, raised families, attended church, intended to stay and work indefinitely as citizen-workers, industrial republicans. Perhaps especially because it was a company town, there was no conception of private rights versus public rights. In consequence, virtually all mill workers walked out and defended the plant, union members or not. Injunction and military power of the state destroyed their reality.

Following closely in time, members of the new industrial American Railway Union formed by Eugene Debs, struck the Pullman Palace Car Company in 1894 in the supposed utopian company town of Pullman, Illinois. Pullman had sharply reduced piece/wage rates while refusing to lower company rents for housing and food prices. Workers' families literally starved. The ARU nationally boycotted any train pulling a Pullman passenger car. Sidney Lens narrates the events of the strike. Prof. David Montgomery then locates the importance of the strike and its breaking in the trajectory of labor and industrial organization in the emerging modern economy. Prof. William Forbath sets the battle between the ARU and the railroad General Managers Council, within an omnibus Federal Court injunction of dubious legality under federal law, enforced by an even more constitutionally dubious use of the U.S. Army to break the strike/boycott, eventually leading to criminal contempt imprisoning of Debs and all strike leaders. The jailing effectively crippled the strike, and broke the by now bankrupt union. While Mine Worker strikes had spread from employer to employer in entire coalfields earlier, this was the first nationwide industrial union collective action. But national power responded to transportation shutdown. Workers would not be permitted to leverage such power. Strikers could now be enjoined against boycotts, picketing, assembling, entering private property, or even organizing workers during a strike, and the U.S. Army would enforce the court order.

An interlude next describes one of the early fights for free speech and assembly on public streets so important to mass or industrial union organizing. Historian Philip Foner describes the 1909 speeches and mass arrests of Industrial Workers of the World members in Spokane, Washington. Seasonal workers who were prey to employment firms, and who having no permanent residences locally, could only be reached in public places. After the first arrests, I.W.W. members would flood into a town provoking arrest by speaking one after another, filling jails and other locations until citizens pressured the police to stop and stem the rising public costs.

The next chapter is a hybrid of two shorter but related articles about racial division of workers in the shadow of law. While the I.W.W. was open to women and African Americans, most craft unions were not, or were officially segregated. Martha Mahoney shows how in 1906 the Supreme Court in *Hodges v. U.S.* interprets the Reconstruction Civil Rights statutes to prevent their application to white-capping, whites driving black workers from jobs coveted by white workers. Restrictive laws preventing worker organization combined with denial of legal protection of black worker access to jobs, thereby structured both white and black workers' attempts at interracial cooperation in labor organizing, making it much more unlikely. *Hodges* is followed in little more than a decade by the Elaine, Arkansas, white riots against blacks. In attempting to organize a union in a black church, African-American tenant farmers were attacked by white policemen, shots were exchanged. Whites in the area rampaged against blacks, killing more than one hundred. Despite the deaths, several African-Americans, but no whites, were convicted of riot crimes and imprisoned. Prof. Kerry Taylor attributes African-American organizing to their experience of military service during World War I, leading to demands for a better life and civic dignity, and intense white reaction due in part to labor market constriction following the war. The two events together demonstrate civic and legal racialization of power with long and destructive consequences for the labor movement and the larger society.

During World War I, the Industrial Workers of the World attempted to organize Arizona metal mines, where the AFL United Mine Workers and the Western Federation of Miners had failed. The One Big Union idea and the I.W.W.'s toughness appealed to the miners, who signed up in large numbers. Philip Taft, an economic institutionalist of the Common's School demonstrates why the I.W.W. had more success but also was perceived as a radical threat by many in the community. With the complicity of local law enforcement and non-resistance of railroad workers, the Anaconda Copper Company and deputized company police in Bisbee, Arizona, rousted miners from their homes, marched over 1500 of them to rail cars, and transported them across state lines into the New Mexico desert, leaving them without food or shelter, with instructions never to return. After a day and a half, U.S. Army units provided shelter but did not escort the workers back to Bisbee. Subsequent prosecutions resulted in trivial punishment and the local was broken.

In the sixth chapter, Prof. Ahmed White describes the Great Steel Strike of 1919. This massive strike from Western Pennsylvania through Ohio to Chicago vented the rank and file anger of more than 350,000 steel workers against the hours, poor working conditions, and low wages imposed by the steel companies led by behemoth U.S. Steel. The feeble support of the AFL under which the organizing drive of the National Committee for Organizing Iron and Steel Workers derived nominal authorization, probably doomed the strike from the beginning. Its leader, William Z. Foster, formerly of the IWW leadership, allowed public opinion to be swayed by a rabid press, and with the steel companies shrieking Bolshevik revolution, paved the way for great violence against strikers. In the end, repression of the workers rank and file efforts to sustain the strike proved too much to prevail against the power of the largest industrial companies in the world.

The seventh chapter is also a hybrid, this time about the attempt to organize southern textile mills in Gastonia, North Carolina, in 1929. Once again a radical union, the National Textile Workers, under communist leadership, entered an area of extreme anti-union hostility and prior failure of AFL organizing. Labor journalist Mary Heaton Vorse was in Gastonia reporting on events: the company fired the strikers and evicted their families from company houses, many of whom worked in the mill as family units including young children. The union formed a tent colony that was shortly entered by police without a warrant. A gun battle erupted and the local sheriff died. Seventeen union leaders were arrested and prosecuted for conspiracy to commit murder, seven convicted, with organizer Fred Beal sent to prison for ten years even though he had not been seen at the shooting and did not have a gun. The Harvard Law Review reported the case of *State v. Beal*, critically describing legal irregularities. In contrast, the killing of a woman mill worker was never prosecuted. Where labor was concerned, justice was not blind, just available only to one side.

A series of chapters involve the critical period of the 1930s and the Great Depression. Aside from the Pullman strike, most collective actions mirror local communities. Not so the Coastwide Dock and general strike in San Francisco in 1934. The strike began as a rank and file movement by longshoremen protesting the anti-union company organization of workers under the "Blue Book." Only Blue Book members were chosen in the daily shape-ups at the docks. While many accounts of the strike and violent police battles, including the killing of two worker bystanders, have been written, little in them views the strike and union organizing exclusively from the bottom up, the perspective adopted by Ken Casebeer. Harry Bridges, longshoremen, and the rank and file Joint Strike Committee involved the seamen of the various maritime unions in San Francisco and the strike spread almost instantly to similar groups on the entire West Coast docks and ships. The International Longshoremens Unions' leadership attempted frequently to sell the workers out to the shipping companies. The companies induced multiple injunctions and arrests. The police violently attempted to move strikebreakers to the docks and goods from the docks. But the rank and file in the Teamsters union refused to cross picket lines and forced the Central Labor Council to call a general strike. Settlement of the strike produced somewhat ambiguous results for the strikers, but the militant International Longshoremen and Warehouseworkers Union was firmly established.

During the Depression, the automobile industry collapsed. Even with work sharing, employment dropped by two-thirds. Toledo in 1934 suffered thousands of workers unemployed in the auto plants. Again working with radicals, socialists led by A.J. Muste among the unemployed, and within the federated union formed by the AFL, the United Auto Workers struck Auto-Lite and other companies there. Professors Pope and Zeitlow show how a coalition of the employed and unemployed, usually in desperate competition with each other for dwindling jobs, united in refusing to obey local court injunctions, engaging in mass picketing barring both police and strikebreakers from entering the Auto-Lite plant. Working class conscious organization supported by aggressive leadership sustained the workers and fostered solidarity within the community. The mass mobilization made the strike.

In the early 1930s, millions of workers in core heavy manufacturing and mass production industries were crying out for help in organizing. While paying lip service to their efforts, the skilled craft AFL unions opposed the threat of industrial unions competing for members, and looked down upon the unskilled workers and semi-skilled operatives employed in the core industries. In steel, the by now entirely incompetent Amalgamated accomplished less than nothing, alienating many steel workers. When John L. Lewis sundered the old AFL by forming the Congress of Industrial Organizations, the new Steel Workers Organizing Committee was established by the United Mine Workers. Ken Casebeer describes the social history of the company town of the Jones & Laughlin Steel Company, the setting of the discharge of union members that culminates in the strike and test case of the Wagner Act's constitutionality. Are the ten firings a purely local affair or could the dispute bring down the entire national economy? Called "Little Siberia," Aliquippa, Pennsylvania, was controlled dictatorially by the company, economically, socially, politically, all ways. Anyone entering the steep valley did so by train, and was met at the station by company police, who put anyone they found undesirable back on the train. Company police charged into homes on motorcycles, arrested and beat suspected union sympathizers. The company recruited ethnically-divided workforces for separated jobs to inhibit communication. But when the Supreme Court upheld the NLRA, J. & L. settled the strike and the entire community of over 10,000 people marched in the streets, declaring, "Now we are free."

The Interlude of Mary Heaton Vorse reminds us that not all industrial organization in Steel ended in victory. The "Little Steel" strikes were bloody, culminating in the Memorial Day Massacre outside Chicago. Newsreels recorded police opening fire on unarmed workers and their families in an open field as they approached a Republic Steel plant. The upholding of numerous unfair labor practices of the company squelching the unions could not erase the killing of ten workers left to bleed to death in paddy wagons, or the scores who were shot in the back as they attempted to flee. Just a day earlier, a court had upheld the workers' First Amendment right to picket during the dispute. Justice did not protect them.

CIO unions almost accidentally discovered the collective action that brought millions into the CIO: the sit-down. Workers arrested for violating court injunctions, replaced by strikebreakers running their former machines, beaten by police attacking picket lines maintained in freezing weather, found they could avoid all of that if they just stopped working and sat at their machines. Production shut down completely, and strikers were hard to dislodge. Injunctions followed, but how could they be enforced? Jim Pope describes these strikes in rubber and then in the famous sit-down at G.M.'s Flint, Michigan, Fisher Body in 1937. In vertically-organized industries of geographically-dispersed plants, shutting any link in the production of finished goods shortly shut the whole colossus. Workers learned they could win not just contracts, but control of the shop floor. No one knew whether these tactics were legal or illegal. Eventually reaching the Supreme Court in 1939, in a small company context, *Fansteel Metallurgical Corp.*, the court held that the protection of collective actions provided under the NLRA did not outbalance the near absolute property right of possession by employers. Increasingly, the federal courts would find the most effective tools of unions to be unprotected against employer retaliation and government suppression: sit-downs, boycotts, sympathy strikes, and mass picketing, among others.

Shortly thereafter, the Supreme Court in *Southern Steamship Company* ruled a withholding of labor aboard ship, despite no interference with ship movement or Captain's discipline, nonetheless constituted a serious crime, mutiny, at one time punishable by death. As Ahmed White puts a shipboard strike in the context of the industrializing of shipping and removal of sailor custom, the Court rules that no ceasing of work no matter how draconian ship rules or routine, can take place. This is despite the fact that sailors have a right to collective action and at the same time that there are no sidewalks at sea from which to lodge a protest. When judges read this hardly believable policy into labor law, they encouraged the workers to take the only recourse that remained—mass desertion of the ship at the next port!

Eric Arnesen describes the context, legal strategy, court decision, and limited effectiveness despite hailed promise, of *Steele v. Louisville and Nashville Railroad Company*, in 1944. The Railroad craft unions, the Brotherhoods, had always prohibited African-American membership in their unions. They contracted with the railroad corporations to squeeze out all black employment on the rails. In *Steele*, the Supreme Court reversed precedents creating a union's "duty of fair representation" of all members and non-members over jobs within their collective bargaining domain. Black workers could no longer be silenced and ignored in their own demands, or contracted out by all-white unions, but they could also not yet get in, until finally the passage of the Civil Rights Act of 1964.

As the collective bargaining system begins to mature, other collective actions attempting to control or alleviate shop floor production did not disappear. Often these actions were wildcats of small groups of rank and file workers, often opposed by their unions or prohibited under a collective bargaining contract. Professor Jim Atleson narrates the story of a slowdown by workers loading railroad cars at a lumber mill in Oregon in 1950. When the company switched from piece rates (cars loaded) to hourly wages, pay dropped more than 30%. The aggrieved workers adjusted the rate at which they were willing to load cars accordingly. They were fired, which was upheld by the National Labor Relations Board on the ground that workers were not permitted to set the conditions under which they worked or determine the adequacy of their pay while remaining on the job. If unhappy with new rules set by management, they could strike if not contractually prohibited, and then likely be replaced permanently under slack labor market conditions. *Elk Lumber* was one of a series of NLRB decisions following the Taft-Hartley amendments of the NLRA failing to accord protection to collective actions of workers amounting to direct action by employees to resist employer practices or act in sympathy to other employees. The apparent intent despite the language of Section 7 was to channel all worker actions through collective bargaining even as leveraged by the limited utility of strikes.

Given decreasing legal protection of strikes, such actions became less and less effective as the 1960s approached the Seventies. In the cities, public employee unions mushroomed, although public employees were not protected under the NLRA. Yet a landmark strike of African-American public sanitation workers over horrid work conditions and poverty pay spontaneously broke out in the Mississippi Delta in Memphis, Tennessee, in early 1968. A white supremacist mayor refused to recognize or negotiate with the new union local of AFSCME, calling all public employee strikes illegal and obtaining an injunction the workers refused to heed. All the garbage collectors were black, the city population 40% black, but the city brought in strikebreakers who kept the white neighborhoods clean and ignored garbage in black neighborhoods. Historian Michael Honey describes how the strike transformed from a labor strike into a civil rights struggle in Memphis. With limited white worker support and no white craft support, African-American churches became the necessary buttress for the sanitation workers. Workers and ministers were maced and beaten. The ministers reached out to the Reverend Martin Luther King who had increasingly advocated civil rights and labor unity as "civil rights unionism" in order to transform the South, economically and politically. On March 18, King electrified a mass meeting calling for a one-day general strike. He returned March 28 to lead a mass march on city hall. Organization broke down, looting by non-marchers erupted, the police charged indiscriminately into the march, brutally gassing and clubbing workers even into their church sanctuary. King's movement tried to regroup for another attempt. On April 3, King gave one of the greatest speeches in the twentieth century, vowing not to abandon the sanitation workers, proclaiming "I have been to the mountaintop." The next day Martin Luther King was murdered in Memphis. Civil Rights and Labor unity did not die.

Rank-and-file lawyer, activist and historian Staughton Lynd relates how steel workers and their union locals used unconventional legal tactics in trying to prevent steel mill closures in Youngstown, Ohio, from 1977–1980. U.S. Steel had promised on many occasions not to close the Youngstown mills as long as they were "profitable," indeed publically acknowledging several times that thanks to worker sacrifices, the mills made profits. When U.S. Steel decided to close anyway, the USWA locals offered to buy the plants and keep working. U.S.S. refused, arguing that it did not want workers to compete with U.S.

Steel's remaining mills. The union locals sued the company arguing the equity doctrine of promissory estoppel. The union could not contractually stop closure under labor law, but the company had pledged to remain open and the workers relied. Alternatively, the union argued for a community property right to prevent the laying of economic waste upon the community. Finally, they charged the company with violating the anti-trust statute. While sympathetic, a federal court of appeals panel found factually that the company was not showing real profits despite their talk so no reliance was justified and that there was no legal property right for the community.

Memphis demonstrated first that unions needed new tactics, and second, no strike could henceforth succeed without widespread community support. Historian Jim Green chronicles a strike forced on the United Mine Workers in Appalachian Virginia in 1989 when the Pittston Coal Company withdrew from the Bituminous Coal Operating Agreement, and slashed wages and terminated contributions to pensioners' health insurance. The union could not survive without field wide agreements, and workers in America's most hazardous industry would not contemplate union give-backs on pension issues. To prevent strikebreaking and mine shifting, the Mine Workers adopted massive civil disobedience, in part learned from the Civil Rights Movement. Mass meetings were conducted daily in the parks, families were recruited into the strike, the uniform of strike supporters became surplus army fatigues, mine communities in the mountain hollers were at war with absentee owned mines. Convoys of workers clogged highways, creeping along to frustrate coal trucks from hauling for mines still operating. Workers sat or lay in front of huge coal trucks on the roads, or blocked mine entrances until limp bodies were dragged away by police. Hundreds of mine families were arrested, jamming jails and overwhelming small town facilities. A working mine was briefly occupied by miners that just walked through the open gates. State and Federal judges went berserk, issuing multiple injunctions, eventuating in nearly $65 million in contempt fines. As union leaders were jailed, the international union sent in top leaders as replacements, men with long terms in the mines themselves. The miners won this community strike, but only a Supreme Court decision, years later, procedurally struck down the assessed fines preventing union bankruptcy.

Chapter sixteen by feminist historians Eileen Boris and Jennifer Klein chronicles the conditions of women home care workers who by definition work in other people's homes, not a factory. Originally home care workers were considered domestic workers excluded from NLRA protection, then later they were characterized as independent contractors, also excluded. However, welfare reform stimulated employers to organize home care work in companies contracting with local government recipients of federal grants. The State and localities in California won a federal court of appeals decision in the early Nineties, declaring home care workers to still be independent contractors given the location of their work despite being employees of the contractors. After long public campaigns of AFSCME and the SEIU unions, at times including the worker's clients, the organizing succeeded in changing state law and forming unions at least in the larger cities. The chapter describes events in San Diego, where the Court of Appeals decision applied. Women have long been critical to successful collective action even if not union members. But, as women-dominated service jobs expand and more substantially all-women union locals form, and women earn leadership positions in national unions, women articulate important issues relating work and family conditions.

Two chapters highlight contemporary labor market developments. Ken Casebeer reports on a strike over unfair labor practices in 2006 by housekeepers and groundskeepers working at the University of Miami. The largest private employer in the county, the University, contracts out its service employment with the employee leasing company,

UNICCO. The strike was against UNICCO, the direct employer, but the workers believed they were really fighting the end-user of their labor, the University. The University washed its hands, claiming to be the innocent neutral, but publically supported management's position. Here was the new economy, low wage immigrant service workers whose labor market had been organized by employee leasing contractors—the gang boss or patrone writ large. The workers maintained only token picketing at the remote gate the University set aside for UNICCO. Instead, they held marches through campus and the nearby community and demonstrated at the airport and City Hall. They joined with student activists and religious leaders, at one point sitting down with ministers in the middle of a mass thoroughfare intersection until arrested, creating a diversion during which students packing kitty litter for their eventual needs occupied the admissions office. After a tense sixteen hour stand-off with police, the students agreed to leave when the University promised joint talks with the union and company. Faculty moved many classes off campus to honor the virtual picket line. Then the workers decided themselves, against private SEIU advice, to create a tent city under the mass transit tracks and go on a hunger strike lasting seventeen days, requiring several hospitalizations. Facing rising public and community outrage, UNICCO agreed to card checks, and were surprised within a week by 70% worker sign-up.

The final chapter by journalist Kari Lydersen follows the plant occupation in 2008 by UE workers in Chicago at Republic Windows and Doors. When workers discovered the company moving out production equipment in the middle of the night in preparation to close the plant, they organized a planned occupation of the plant. The company's precipitous closing violated the federal WARN act requiring sixty days notice before closing or sixty days' severance pay in the alternative. Outside supporters of the union occupation ignored the former owner and began a corporate campaign against the banks who they said refused to extend credit to the company even to pay the WARN obligations. The largely Latino/a immigrant membership of the Local, supported by local elected officials, demanded that since Bank of America received $25 billion in bailout funds, it should put up the money due the 250 workers. Elected officials threatened to stop doing business with the banks involved. President-elect Obama offered support, and the banks agreed to pay the workers if they ended the occupation. A buyer was found, who is still struggling to keep the business going in tough times for the construction industry and rehire the former employees. The end for these workers and all American workers beset by globalization and world economic depression is yet to be written.

As a Postlude, Kenneth Casebeer notes the Wisconsin government services crisis that was meant to serve as a Tea-Party blueprint following the 2010 elections for breaking Public Workers' Unions and privatizing cut government services.

What will be the future options to be invented by American Labor? Will it be occupational or regional unions facing multi-employer associations, independent grassroots solidarity unions without a national umbrella or bureaucracy, new community alliances supported by reinvigorated central labor councils, worker owned cooperatives, or worker centers supporting individual workers and living wage movements, or something not yet foreseen? What new law will be required? One thing is certain, The Labor Question has not gone away or become less important to the reality and possibility of democracy in American society.

Prelude

The Slave Rebellion in New York City of 1712

Slave Rebellion New York City 1712.

Kenneth M. Casebeer

Depending on definition, it is hard say when the first collective action of labor happened in the territory to become the United States. In 1526, in a small Spanish colony on the South Carolina coast, 100 African slaves killed their masters and sought refuge with local Native Americans during Native conflict with the Spanish. The Spanish survivors shortly thereafter left for Haiti. Artisan Polish Glass Blowers refused to work in 1619 at Jamestown, Virginia, because they had not been enfranchised to vote by a new colony enactment of the Council. Several labor unions consider the first strike to be a mutiny of fisherman in 1636 in Richmond Island, Maine, over unpaid previous season's wages. Others characterize the action more as a boycott of new contracts where the unhappy workers simply left for another fishing port. During the seventeenth and eighteenth centuries, associations of master craftsmen sometimes jointly refused to finish contracted work for less than their own published scale of prices. In the first collective action of workers that drew a legal response, carters refused to move material owned by New York City to the wharves. The carters, however, worked more like present-day independent contractors than as workers regularly employed in service to specific firms. They were charged with criminal contempt, initially discharged from city service, fined, which they as individuals paid, and were reinstated. None of these examples fit perfectly with organized collective activity by workers that in some way depend on an employer over time, to protest or bargain over aspects of their work.

Such is not the case with the slave revolt of New York City in 1712.[1] The midnight of April 6, 1712, twenty-five to thirty African slaves and two Native-American slaves gathered, armed with guns, hatchets, and swords, and by blood oath pledged their secrecy and their lives to each other. Their gathering was probably facilitated by the small area of New York City, and the daily access to the streets shared with other slaves and freemen occasioned by errands for their several masters. The claimed precipitation of their action was the "hard usage" of them by their masters. The slaves targeted a storage building of one master named Vantilburgh, on Madison Lane near Broadway, and set it on fire. The slaves, marching in formation, attacked Whites who rushed to contain the blaze, killing nine and injuring six. The following day, militia from New York and Westchester arrested seventy slaves; six committed suicide, twenty-seven were swiftly prosecuted, twenty-one convicted, two women spared and the rest executed, one by being drawn on a wheel, one was hanged from chains, the rest burned at the stake, one over a period of eight hours.[2] Thereafter, strict laws passed prohibiting more than three Africans from congregating at any time and creating severe criminal penalties for violence by slaves.

1. Robert J. Steinfeld, in *Coercion, Contract, and Free Labor in the Nineteenth Century* (Cambridge: Cambridge Univ. Press, 2001), describes various types of slave resistance to work discipline as including strikes. The cite is to Mary Turner, *From Chattel Slaves to Wage Slaves: The Dynamics of Labour Bargaining in the Americas* (London: James Curry Ltd., 1995). There is no doubt Turner makes this claim, however there is no instance of a strike in the United States described or noted in the book. Probably more appropriate is Eugene Genovese's claim, *Roll, Jordan Roll* 620–21 (New York: Random House, 1974) of strike-like activity: temporarily running away, ubiquitous slowdowns, possible tool breaking, feigned illness, purposeful accident, even suicide. While such actions became customary, there is little evidence that they were organized in advance by slaves in concert. Genovese does cite one source for a strike, U. B. Philips, *Life and Labor in the Old South*, 303–04 (New York: Appleton & Co., 1918) (somewhat discredited by its racism), a letter relating another master's complaint of a reaction to indiscriminant whippings after which the slaves ran away temporarily. The most frequently cited source on slave resistance, Raymond A. Bauer and Alice H. Bauer, "Day to Day Resistance to Slavery," 27 *The Journal of Negro History* 388 (1942), does not describe any strikes.

2. All accounts appear to rest on the Letter of Governor Robert Hunter to the Lords of Trade, in E. B. O'Callahan, *Documents Relative to the Colonial History of the State of New York, 1707–33* (Albany, 1855).

President Thomas Jefferson

The earth is given as a common stock for man to labour and live on. If, for the encouragement of industry we allow it to be appropriated, we must take care that other employment be furnished to those excluded from the appropriation.

It is the mark set on those, who not looking up to heaven, to their own soil and industry, as does the husbandman, for their subsistence, depend for it on the casualties and caprice of customers. Dependence begets subservience and venality, suffocates the germ of virtue, and prepares fit tools for the designs of ambition.[1]

Thomas Paine

All accumulation, therefore, of personal property, beyond what a man's own hands produce, is derived to him by living in society; and he owes on every principle of justice, of gratitude, and of civilization, a part of that accumulation back again to society from whence the whole came. This is putting the matter on a general principle, and perhaps it is best to do so; for if we examine the case minutely it will be found that the accumulation of personal property is, in many instances, the effect of paying too little for the labour that produced it; the consequence of which is that the working hand perishes in old age, and the employer abounds in affluence.[2]

Adam Smith

… workmen desire to get as much, the masters to give as little as possible. The former are disposed to combine in order to raise, the latter in order to lower the wages of labour.

It is not, however, difficult to foresee which of the two parties must, upon all ordinary occasions, have the advantage in the dispute, and force the other into a compliance with their terms. The masters, being fewer in number, can combine much more easily; and the law, besides, authorizes, or at least does not prohibit their combinations, while it prohibits those of the workmen. We have no acts of parliament against combining to lower the price of work; but many against combining to raise it. In all such disputes the masters can hold out much longer. A landlord, a farmer, a master manufacturer, a merchant, though they did not employ a single workman, could generally live a year or two upon the stocks which they have already acquired. Many workmen could not subsist a week, few could subsist a month, and scarce any a year without employment. In the long run the workman may be as necessary to his master as his master is to him; but the necessity is not so immediate.

We rarely hear, it has been said, of the combinations of masters, though frequently of those of workmen. But whoever imagines, upon this account, that masters rarely combine, is as ignorant of the world as of the subject. Masters are always and everywhere in a sort of tacit, but constant and uniform combination, not to raise the wages of labour above their actual rate. To violate this combination is everywhere a most unpopular action, and a sort of reproach to a master among his neighbours and equals. We seldom, indeed, hear of this combination, because it is

---

1. Thomas Jefferson, "Query XIX: Manufactures," *Notes on the State of Virginia*, William Peden, ed., (Chapel Hill: Univ. of North Carolina Press, 1982).

2. Thomas Paine, Agrarian Justice, in Michael Foot & Isaac Kramnick, eds., *The Thomas Paine Reader*, 485 (London: Penguin, 1987).

the usual, and one may say, the natural state of things, which nobody ever hears of. Masters, too, sometimes enter into particular combinations to sink the wages of labour even below this rate. These are always conducted with the utmost silence and secrecy, till the moment of execution, and when the workmen yield, as they sometimes do, without resistance, though severely felt by them, they are never heard of by other people.[3]

3. Adam Smith, *The Wealth of Nations*, 98–99 (1776).

I

Organization as Criminal Conspiracy

Early Cordwainers Shop.

The First American Labor Case (1806)

Walter C. Nelles[*]

[*]The first case arose from a cordwainers' strike at Philadelphia in the fall of 1805.

The on-coming of the Industrial Revolution seems in this country to have been first felt in the foot-wear industry. Before the end of the eighteenth century master cordwainers at Philadelphia and other eastern cities had passed from manufacture only for people who "bespoke" boots or shoes for their own wear to comparative quantity production of stocks for their retail stores. Thenceforth counter-organizations of masters and journeymen were in intermittent conflict.[1]

The journeymen's standard of living was not luxurious. As a matter of course, as in all manual employments, the work-day was from sun-rise to sun-set, and was often protracted by candlelight. A slow workman testified that he could not earn ten dollars a week

* This article was first published as Walter C. Nelles, "The First American Labor Case," 41 *Yale L. J.* 165 (1931–1932). The article has been edited, and a few quotations added from the record of the case as printed in Commons, *infra* note 1. It is printed here by permission of the Yale Law Journal.

1. My attempt to explain the development of friction in the foot-wear industry leans heavily upon Professor Commons' Introduction to volume iii of John R. Commons, *Documentary History of American Industrial Society* (Cleveland: Arthur H. Clark Co., 1910), and upon Part I (by David J. Saposs) of Commons and Associates, *History of Labour in the United States* (1918).

at the piece-work rates paid in 1805 if he should work all the twenty-four hours of the day.[2] One first-rate workman, making only the finest shoes at the highest rate, averaged six or seven dollars a week; another averaged nine or ten.[3]

Since journeymen worked at their own speed in their own houses with their own tools, their only direct object of pressure was to maintain or advance piece-work wages. Their success was at first considerable. They maintained the closed shop; "scabbed"[4] masters and workmen, though they might hobble along for a time, had ultimately to make their peace with the society. The society seems to have been sensitive to the limit within which masters could advance wages, and sale prices, without curtailing production and, consequently, employment. Governing its wage demands by this limit, and so controlling the labor supply that submissive masters could not be hurt by open-shop competition, it won consistently until 1805.

But with the passing of the industry beyond the stage of manufacture for a local market, the society's strategic position was impaired. During the Napoleonic wars, even before Non-Intercourse and Embargo, it became possible for Philadelphia manufacturers to sell boots in the South in competition with boots made in England. The journeymen were not far-sighted enough to perceive the menace of this trade. They helped it grow by accepting—initially doubtless by way of special favor to masters in what seemed exceptional cases—a twenty-five cent reduction of the regular piece work rate when boots were made for export.[5] That both masters and journeymen should become increasingly dependent upon the export trade was inevitable. In 1805, aware too late that it was regular instead of occasional, the society conjoined demands for a higher regular rate for boots and for discontinuance of the rebate of wages for export or "order" work.[6]

That the masters could not have conceded or compromised these demands without loss of export trade does not appear—unless from their agreement to resist, or from evidence that several years earlier a master had had to cancel export orders which he could not fill before wages had been jumped.[7] The journeymen "turned out." They were weakened not only by their impotence to affect the price of competitive English boots but also by internal disharmony; the vote to turn out was sixty to fifty.[8]

The best workmen, being employed exclusively upon fine footwear for the local market, saw no benefit to themselves. They turned out only to avoid being "scabbed," and it seems likely, though there was no such testimony, that the growth of the export trade had made room for inferior workmen who feared that to win the demands might kill the export trade and throw them out of employment. Both classes of unwilling strikers stood out, however, for several weeks. But after the arrest of eight leaders on a charge of criminal conspiracy they went back to work at the old rates, and the strike ended in total failure.[9]

---

2. 3 *Doc. Hist.* 118.

3. *Ibid.* 83, 123.

4. The word "scab" was already in common use, carrying its full modern connotation. A spectator at the cordwainers' trial was fined five dollars for his contempt in exclaiming in court, "A scab is a shelter for lice." *Ibid.* 83.

5. *Ibid.* 124

6. *Ibid.* 117. The demand was for the same wages that prevailed at New York and Baltimore. *Ibid.* 129.

7. 1 *History of Labor, supra* note 1, at 64–5.

8. 3 *Doc. Hist.* 139. On the failure of the strike forty members left the society. *Ibid.* 90.

9. *Commonwealth v. Morrow.* The indictment against the eight was not found until January, 1806, after the strike was over. *Ibid.* 61. This fact has sometimes been so stated as to imply that the prosecution had nothing to do with the failure of the strike. But a journeyman testified that while the strike was

The trial of the eight for the supposed common law crime of "conspiracy to raise their wages" was in the following spring. The legal controversy, both out of court and in, was part of the major political controversy of the time—then still usually expressed as between "aristocracy" and "republicanism" (which meant Jeffersonian democracy).

The interests, feelings and convictions which had sought to "tone the new government as high as possible" were naturally outraged by efforts of journeymen to control their masters. The "aristocratic faction" included such men as John Adams, whose humanitarianism was as deep as Jefferson's, but who were convinced of the incompetence of the masses to know and secure their own good. Hamilton, however, who seems to have been indifferent to mass welfare, represented a larger constituency; it was in his view an excellence of manufacturing establishments that they would provide dawn to dark employment for the wives and young children of the poor.[10]

The essence of Jeffersonianism was humane concern for "the security of each and the welfare of all," and conviction that those ends were, for the time being, best served by a maximum of individual freedom and a minimum of law and government. Jeffersonian freedom was not a sterile dogma; it meant freedom to obtain as well as to pursue a fair degree of happiness. It was obviously not possible for the journeymen cordwainers to obtain such happiness as better wages could confer if the only effective way to raise their wages was closed to them. It was natural, therefore, that Jeffersonian feeling should rally to their defense. The Jeffersonian newspaper, *Aurora,* edited by William Duane, published their initial protest.[11] And it is clear, from the fact that their own counsel felt professionally obliged to echo to the jury his adversaries' admonition to disregard the newspapers,[12] that Duane himself was fulminating on their behalf before, if not during, the trial.

The *Cordwainers' Case* fell neatly into place in the line of Federalist common law holdings over which Jeffersonianism had been boiling for years. Jefferson himself felt that his "revolution" would not be complete until it had republicanized the law as judicially declared.

The case was tried in the Mayor's Court of Philadelphia. Recorder Moses Levy presided. The prosecution was conducted by two of the ablest members of the brilliant Philadelphia bar of that period: Joseph Hopkinson and Jared Ingersoll.

In 1805, Hopkinson had been a prominent member of the corps of distinguished lawyers, headed by Luther Martin, that defended Chase from impeachment. John Quincy Adams appointed him to the Federal bench. Jared Ingersoll had been a member of the Constitutional Convention of 1787. He seems to have been a man of extraordinary sophistication, sagacity, and good nature; "He glided into the affections, and disregarding the passions, he captivated, by the strength and simplicity of his appeals, the reason and the judgment of his hearers."[13]

---

still on the society had "collected sums of money to meet the expenses of this prosecution." *Ibid.* 85. The strikers' protest that the prosecution was invasive of their right to pursue their own happiness was published in Aurora for Nov. 28, 1805. 1 *History of Labor, supra* note 1, at 141–2. The inference that while the strike was still on the eight strikers were arrested on a preliminary complaint seems strong enough to be stated as a fact. How much the arrests had to do with the failure of the strike is of course conjectural; the natural tendency of the division of interests among the strikers was probably hastened.

　　10. Hamilton, *Report on Manufactures*, 3 *Works* (ed. Lodge 1885) 331; and see generally 1 Parrington, *Main Currents in American Thought*, 292–320 (1927).

　　11. *Supra* note 9.

　　12. 3 *Doc. Hist.* 173.

　　13. David Paul Brown, *The Forum*, 471 (1856).

Caesar A. Rodney had been imported from Delaware by the majority faction of Pennsylvania Republicans to prosecute the attempted impeachment of the Supreme Court justices in 1805. Rodney, as one of the managers for the House of Representatives, had taken part in the prosecution of Justice Chase. In 1806 he was brought again to Philadelphia to defend the journeymen cordwainers, with Walter Franklin as his junior. Though Rodney was a wind-bag, he was by no means an empty one; but his florid professional artistry often overreached itself. Probably he was as competent an advocate as, in the conditions of time and place, the journeymen could have got. Within the year Jefferson appointed him Attorney-General of the United States.[14]

The practice of arguing law as well as fact to juries in criminal cases was still universal at the time of the cordwainers' trial. There was no controversy as to the facts. The question of law involved was novel in the United States. It would have been rash, therefore, for the court to undertake to prevent counsel from appealing to the jury on grounds of public policy as well as by citation of English authorities.

The major premise of the prosecution's case was that unlimited expansion of manufactures is beneficial to the community. It is therefore proper, said Hopkinson, "to support this manufacture. Will you permit men to destroy it who have no permanent stake in the city; men who can pack up their all in a knapsack, or carry them in their pockets to New York or Baltimore?"[15] The journeymen's confederacy, said Ingersoll, will destroy the industry, to the ruin, not of the masters, who could stand the shock, but of the journeymen themselves.[16]

Another of the prosecution's scare-crows may have seemed to the jury more perturbing: if the masters pay higher wages, "you must pay higher for the articles." From this was drawn the inference, perhaps plausible if the export trade had not yet become important to the masters, that the masters "have no interest to serve in the prosecution ... They, in truth, are protecting the community."[17]

Rodney, for the defendants, speciously denied that higher wages meant higher prices: "If you banish from this place (as it is morally certain you will) a great number of the best workmen, by a verdict of guilty, can you reasonably expect, that labour will be cheaper? Will it not rise in value, in exact proportion to the scarcity of hands, and the demand for boots and shoes, like every other article in the market?"[18] It followed, he argued, that it was not the journeymen's society but the prosecution that endangered the export trade and the prosperity which "must be the sincere wish of us all."

"The best method to accomplish this desirable object is to secure to workmen the inestimable privilege of fixing the price of their own labour.... No person is compelled to give them more than their work is worth, the market will sufficiently and correctly regulate these matters. If you adhere to our doctrines ... I venture to predict ... that scarcely a breeze will blow, but what will waft to our shores, experienced workmen from those realms, where labour is regulated by statutable provisions; not a wave of the Atlantic, which will not bear on its bosom to this country, European artificers, by whom the raw materials furnished from our extensive regions, will be wrought in the greatest perfection. Give me leave, however, frankly to declare, that I would not barter away our dear bought rights and American liberty, for all the warehouses of London and Liverpool, and

---

14. Jefferson to Rodney, Jan. 17, 1807, 9 *Jeff.* 12.
15. 3 *Doc. Hist.* 136.
16. *Ibid.* 214.
17. *Ibid.* 137.
18. *Ibid.* 198.

the manufactures of Birmingham and Manchester: no; not if were to be added to them, the gold of Mexico, the silver of Peru, and the diamonds of Brazil."[19]

That the prosecution was subversive of American freedom was the main contention of the defence. Even if it were conceded (as of course it was not) that at English common law the cordwainers' society would be a criminal conspiracy, that common law was not American common law. In support of this, counsel argued, relying upon Tucker's Blackstone,[20] that if a doctrine of labor conspiracy had been used in this country during the colonial period—which it had not—it could not survive as law in one of the United States, even under a constitution or statute which continued "the common law" in general terms. For it would be in derogation of the natural and unalienable rights of man, and inconsistent with democracy.

The anomalies of freedom were, however, as striking then as now. To associate for betterment is an exercise of freedom. And the associates may claim freedom of collective action. The power of the association serves generally the substance of the freedom, which is economically conditioned, of its members. But efficient service may involve a variety of coercions of unwilling individuals—to join, or to conform with its regulations, or to concede its demands.

So Ingersoll had also freedom points, with which, disclaiming emulation of Rodney's "appeals to passion," he could play more effectively than Rodney upon the feelings of both judges and jury.

"The defendants formed a society, the object of which was ... What? That they should not be obliged to work for wages which they did not think a reasonable compensation? No: ... they may legally and properly associate for that purpose. But when we allow the rights of the poor journeymen, let us not forget those of the rich employer, with his wedges of gold, his bars of silver, and his wings of paper stock, mentioned by Mr. Rodney."[21]

The object of the society was not freedom, but compulsion: "We charge a combination, by means of rewards and punishments, threats, insults, starvings and beatings, to compel the employers to accede to terms, they the journeymen present and dictate."[22]

In repeated instances the society had substituted compulsion for freedom of contract in fixing wages. A turn-out in 1798 had forced wages above the contract rate; and when, in 1799, the masters combined to restore the contract rate, another turn-out kept them up.[23] The evidence—which had not been confined to the events of 1805, but had ranged back into the eighteenth century—was full of concrete hardships suffered by individuals. Ingersoll adroitly, without heightening or cumulation of details, refreshed the jury's sense of the moving quality of this evidence as it had come from the lips of the witnesses.

---

19. *Ibid.* 179–181.

20. *Ibid.* 240–242. St. George Tucker (1752–1828) was successively a soldier of the Revolution, judge of the General Court of Virginia, professor of law at William and Mary College, President Judge of the Virginia Court of Appeals, and United States District Judge. His poems and satires rank high in the meager American literature of the period. His edition of Blackstone (Philadelphia, 1803) "containing the first legal commentaries on the Federal Constitution which appeared in the United States" was one of the first important American law books. Warren, *History of the American Bar*, 336 (1913). His views were very close to those of Madison.

21. 3 *Doc. Hist.* 207

22. *Ibid.* 221.

23. *Ibid.* 216–218.

Job Harrison had joined the society in 1794 for fear of being scabbed: "if I did not join the body, no man would set upon the seat where I worked, ... nor board or lodge in the same house, nor would they work at all for the same employer." Most of the turn-outs were for wages on boots; he, making only fine shoes, had nothing to gain:

> "In a little time there came a turn-out to raise the wages upon boots; knowing I had my full terms for my own work and that I had no interest in the turn-out upon boots, that I have everything to lose but nothing to gain; I remonstrated with the society at large, of which I was still a member. I stated that they ought not to include me with them, in the turn-out, as I worked altogether upon shoes, and their measure, was, to raise the wages on boots. I mentioned that I had a sick wife and a large young family, and that, I knew I was not able to stand it: they would grant me no quarters at all, but I must turn-out."

During the turn-out of 1799, having "a sick wife and a large young family," he scabbed secretly for Mr. Bedford until, having been detected by the "tramping committee" and roused to indignation by the strikers' rejection of the tearful plea of one Dobbin for leave to support his children, he resolved to scab openly.

> "John M'Curdy, John Waltar, and one Cooke, were a tramping committee, that I know ... their business was to watch the Jers that they did not scab it. They go round every day, to see that the Jers are honest to the cause."

Mr. Bedford promised to protect him, and kept him on after the strike had been won. Mr. Bedford's shop was therefore scabbed; his force, which before the strike had been twenty, was for a year and a half reduced to four or five journeymen, of whom only two were competent. While his shop was scabbed his shop window was broken with potatoes which had pieces of broken shoemakers' tacks in them — "at least the one had they aimed at my person, and was near hitting me in the face." Harrison having finally been readmitted to the society on payment of a fine, Mr. Bedford could get workmen again.

> "the members told us on their return that the sense of the body had been taken and that they fined me twenty dollars, for being a hypocrite, tho' my work did not belong to what they had been contending for: they fined Logan but eighteen dollars although he was a boot-maker and consequently interested in the event."

He went South and secured many customers; but soon after his return, business becoming a little brisk, his new force compelled him to raise their wages and demand higher prices of his Southern customers—with the result that he lost trade to the amount of $4,000 a year.[24] Mr. Blair testified: "At the turn out in 1798, I had six men working for me; who were willing to continue notwithstanding the turnout. These men were kept up in a garret, but sometimes after dark, they would venture out to Mrs. Finch's, next door but one, to get a drink of beer; one Sunday evening ... I found them hid away in the cellar; they had been beaten, and the girl was crying, and had been beaten also. I was very angry, and determined next day to buy a cow-skin, and whip the first that came near the house. Their clerk, Nelson, was the first, and I fell foul and beat him; he sued me for it, and my men sued them afterwards; we dropped the whole and squared the yards.... I afterwards had to pay fines for my men, to get them into the body again."[25] A journeyman testified:

---

24. *Ibid.* 73–85, 99–101.
25. *Ibid.* 97–98.

"The name of a scab is very dangerous; men of this description have been hurt when out at nights. I myself have been threatened for working at wages with which I was satisfied. I was afraid of going near any of the body: I have seen them twisting and making wry faces at me, and heard two men call out scab, as I passed by. I was obliged to join, for fear of personal injury...."[26] There was no evidence, however, of any violence within five years of the 1805 turn-out, or that any of the defendants had ever done more than take part in strikes and live up to the no-association-with scabs rule of the society.

As to the events of 1805, Harrison testified,

"Q. Did they scab any shops the last turn-out? A. No: there was a division in the body, and they were forced to go to work at the old price; therefore it was impossible to scab any one: they did not gain the cause; they stood it out six or seven weeks, but they found it impossible to get their wages advanced, and they went to work again."

However,

"At a meeting of the employers, master cordwainers, October, 30th, 1805. Resolved unanimously that we will not give any more wages than we have given for some time past.

Wm. M'Culley, president, Lewis Ryan, Presly Blackiston, John Bedford, William Blair, Thomas Rimer, [40] John Conyers, Fred Errenger, secretary, John Wharton, Casper Souders, William Stokes, George Falker, John M'Curdy, Robert Murphey, William Montgomery, Daniel Kossack, John Thompson, William Green, Jacob Bechtel, Robert Taylorson, William Harkins, William Niles, Charles Justis, Adam Walter, John Hallman, John Owen, Peter Sturgis, John Yeager, Robert Christy, Robert Millikin, George Kemble, Jacob Malambre, Leonard Shallcross, George Abel, St. Lawrence Adams, James Newton, Stephen Clayton, Thomas Amies, Daniel Pierson, George Rees, Samuel Logan, Nicholas Crap, L. Keating for Joseph Baldwin, James Alexander, Lemuel Franklin, Richard Miles."

Whether the journeymen cordwainers were guilty of crime depended, not upon the English authorities which Recorder Levy purported to find controlling, but upon whether a Jeffersonian or a Tory judgment of tendency with respect to the prosperity and happiness of people, standing in thought as *the* people, should prevail.

Since journeymen's societies were clearly obstructive of rapid increase in manufacturing wealth, they were obstructive of both public and private security and prosperity.

The jury was composed of one merchant, three inn-keepers, three grocers, a bottler, a watch-maker, a tailor, a hatter, and a tobacconist.[27] If, for non-inclusion of persons dependent upon wages, it was not fairly representative of the economic interests of all the people of Philadelphia, it represented a probable majority. All such as those jurors, having a head-start upon the competitors who would be sure to arise, stood to fatten their pocket-books through increase in the total amount of money to be spent in Philadelphia. Export manufacture would clearly bring to town much money; there would be more employers with more money to spend before there would be fewer, with still more; and however low the wages of manufacturing labor, their aggregate would be enormous. Manufacturing wage-earners then present in Philadelphia would

---

26. *Ibid.* 93.
27. 3 *Doc. Hist.* 61.

obviously suffer loss, but opportunities to re-coup were many and hopeful. If their wages became unsatisfactory, it was true that a good many could pack their all in a knap-sack and better themselves at New York or Baltimore, or by going West, or by changing occupation.

A weighty other side to the case could, however, be seen or felt even in 1806. Economic factors are not the sole factors in human welfare, and wealth is neither an equivalent of happiness nor its necessary condition. Our twentieth century-preoccupation with economics tends to make thinking lop-sided. The pendulum has swung from extravagant denial of the heresy of economic determination to counter-extravagance of affirmation.

The eighteenth century produced men who, like Jefferson and Madison, saw things in better proportion. Candid though they were in recognition of economic motives and values, they did not deem it soft-headed to perceive that economic gains may be human losses, even to their gainers.

It was obvious to Jefferson that somewhat autonomous work (whether or not stimulated by gain or need) in which main attention is upon excellence of product—whether tobacco leaves, a civilization, poetry, or tables and chairs—develops more satisfactory human animals than work whose doing fails to shut from view a gain or need which prompts it.[28]

Jefferson seems never to have expressed himself with direct relation to any cordwainers' conspiracy case. In 1806, as a practical politician, he was rigorously shutting his lips against expression upon any question that was dividing his party in Pennsylvania, anxious that both factions should continue to call themselves Republicans, support his foreign policy, and vote for his Republican successor in 1808.[29] Our buffetings by combatants in the Napoleonic wars convinced him that domestic manufacture of necessities was desirable, and he himself stimulated them, not only by his foreign policy but also privately, setting an example of ordering cloth for clothes from Connecticut.[30] For all his abhorrence of the effects of industrialization upon people, he would not, even had it been possible, have invoked the power of outlawing manufactures which he conceived government to have. But neither would he have regarded the desirability of their stimulation as justifying legal restriction of workmen's possibilities of self-help. Had he let himself look closely at the Philadelphia case, there can be little doubt of his reasoning or conclusions.

Freedom had not become, for most, a sterile right of fruitless seeking. It was substantial, enabling men rather generally, if meagerly, to obtain and enjoy both economic goods and goods ulterior.

While it is reasonable to suppose that the individually weaker may by collective self-help somewhat better themselves without, in the large, reducing to insubstantiality the goods enjoyed by their competitors, government and its law would best neither help nor hurt them.

At the very beginning of quantity production of foot-wear for the local Philadelphia market, the bargaining power of the individual journeyman became insufficient to enable him to keep his head up in society. The same principle that forbade legal interference with the masters' enlargement of their business equally forbade interference with the equally natural self-advancement of the journeymen through the only means open to

---

28. 533 *Jeff.* 268–9; 4 *ibid.* 87 ff., 105; *cf.* 10 *ibid.* 143–6.
29. 9 *ibid.* 102, 103n, 129n, *of.* 313.
30. 9 *ibid.* 373; 10 *ibid.* 225–6.

them—collective pressure. And so long as advances in wages could be passed on to the local public, there was no thought of a law against such pressure. Both masters and journeymen, in spite of occasional hot friction, were on the whole reasonably satisfied—as was also the public. For if it paid the advanced wages when it bought shoes, it got them back again when they were spent. If the principle of *laissez faire* required that the masters be free to undertake an adventure, pregnant with dangers as well as benefits to the local community, into remote markets whose power to pay wage advances was doubtful or non-existent, it required correlatively that the journeymen be free to refuse to take part save on satisfactory terms. If the adventure failed in consequence, it would be renewed. It could not "naturally"[31] succeed until there should be a substantial body of journeymen as well as of masters whose interests would be served by its success. If that was not already the case in 1806, immigration and the birth-rate would quickly bring it to pass. Union or no union, no appreciable number of journeymen who would be condemned to unemployment unless boots were manufactured for export would long hold out for a wage prohibitive of such manufacture; and their own losses from a mistaken strike would sufficiently deter repetition of their blunder. The law of a free society has no business to punish mere blunders, or to aid in an economic subjugation which it might properly intervene to prevent.

But the counter pressures of employers and workmen never come naturally to rest in failure. Mr. Bedford could normally, in the absence of closed shop conditions effective throughout the industry, find three Dobbins who were willing to make his boots for the wages he was willing to pay. If their freedoms and A's, B's and C's are equal, they have a "right" to do so. Mr. Bedford has in consequence a coercive power to which A, B and C must surrender, unless they can by association with others organize a coercive power superior to Mr. Bedford's. To coerce Mr. Bedford the association must coerce the cooperation of many Dobbins. It may also have to coerce Job Harrison, who makes. shoes, not boots, at satisfactory wages; for even if he is not likely to be persuaded to turn from shoes to boots if he stays at work, his participation in a turn-out may be essential to a solidarity sufficient to break down the resistance of the Dobbins or Mr. Bedford. Unless the association may resort to the minimum of coercion essential to its efficiency—a minimum which is not susceptible of definition precise enough clearly or always to exempt Job Harrison[32]—the "right" of journeymen to refuse to work for unsatisfactorily low wages is as barren as Mr. Bedford's "right" to refuse to pay unsatisfactorily high wages would be if he had not also a "right" to hire Dobbins.

The question is which coercive power (not of course *right* in any strict sense) will result in more peace, freedom and happiness. But it was attempted for a century to settle it by individualist dogma. Mr. Bedford's power to hire Dobbins was easily reconcilable with dogma, simply by not calling it a right to coerce. All attempts to reconcile a coercive "right of association" with individualist dogma end, however, in dilemma or paradox. And while the sanctity and adequacy of dogmatic individualism were unchallenged, the rising industrial Toryism was able to make tremendous use of this irreconcilability.

---

31. In question-begging uses of the word "natural" and its derivatives I am trying to connote the values for whose cultivation the sages of the eighteenth century-Enlightenment endowed Nature with benign authority. Their baptism as "natural" of what they thought desirable was often, of course, somewhat arbitrary. See Becker, *the Declaration of Independence* (1922) and his Storrs Lectures at Yale, 1931, delivered under the title, *The Heavenly City of the Eighteenth Century.*

32. In 1806, of course, no glimmering of the notion that a boycott of any sort might be unlawful had yet dawned. Rodney could argue without fear of contradiction that it would be "perfectly lawful ... for two or more persons to agree not to purchase dry goods or groceries at a particular store." 3 *Doc. Hist.* 176.

The *Cordwainers' Case* involved no claim for the defendants of unequal rights or special privileges or immunities in a strict sense of those words.[33] It did involve, however, upon the artificial assumptions that freedom is a right instead of an end to be furthered and that freedoms are equal and include equal and absolute immunities from coercion, the principle of equality of "rights." The stress of the prosecution was upon the coercions incident to the activities and objects of the association, without regard to whether they were brought home either to the defendants or the association, and without distinction between whether they were effected by acts then recognized as unlawful (beating of strike-breakers) or by acts which were not (refusal of association). The question may be stated in two ways: it was between Mr. Bedford's power, through his "right" to hire Dobbins, to coerce his own workmen on the one hand, and his workmen's power, through coercion of Dobbins, to coerce Mr. Bedford on the other; it was between temporary impairments of the freedoms of a few individuals in a few instances and the service which the efficient existence and activity of the association would render to the freedom of journeymen generally. Decision either way would result in one side's practical immunity to coerce.

The power of the journeymen's association, if let alone by law, would encounter natural checks. It could not long or often maintain solidarity for wages which the industry was not prosperous enough to pay, or which would result in substantial curtailment of production and, consequently, of employment. If it tried to do so, it would destroy itself—as it perhaps had done in 1805, irrespective of the prosecution, since almost half the members had turned out unwillingly.

A different position, however, was taken by Recorder Levy. In his charge to the jury such sensitiveness as he showed to considerations which have been here adduced was not catholic.

> "Mr. Levy. This laborious cause is now drawing to a close after a discussion of three days; during which we have had every information upon the facts and the law connected with them, that a careful investigation and industrious research have been able to produce. We are informed of the circumstance and ground of the complaints, and of the law applicable to them. It remains with the court and jury, to decide what the rule of law is; and whether the defendants have, or have not violated it. In forming this decision, we cannot, we must not forget that the law of the land is the supreme, and only rule. We live in a country where the will of no individual ought to be, or is admitted, to be the rule of action. Where the will of an individual, or of any number of individuals, however distinguished by wealth, talents, or popular fame, ought not to affect or controul, in the least degree, the administration of justice.

---

33. It may be necessary to repeat that there was no claim or evidence that anything which an individual might not lawfully have done had been done in the 1805 strike. The defendants might therefore have claimed that they were denied equality of right. Since there is no wish to palliate the fact that instances of violent and intimidatory coercion such as had occurred in 1798 are naturally incident to collective labor pressures, especially to an initial establishment of a closed shop, the fairness of trying the defendants for the whole past history of their organization is not discussed. No claim of legal immunity for the instigators or perpetrators of violent coercions is involved in the argument that in spite of the likelihood of occasional incidents of lawlessness if the society survived, membership in the society would better not have been held unlawful. Occasional lawlessness is incident to many lawful activities.

There is but one place in which to determine whether violation and abuses of the law have been committed ... it is in our courts of justice: and there only after proof to the fact: and consideration of the principles of law connected with it."

"The law is the permanent rule, it is the will of the whole community."

It was proper, he said, to consider whether the journeymen's combination was injurious to the public welfare. It interferes with the "natural" regulation of wages and prices by supply and demand. If journeymen may combine to exact "artificial" wages "dependent upon the will of the few who are interested," it follows that the masters may combine to exact artificial prices for boots. "If they could stand out three or four weeks in winter, they might raise the price of boots to thirty, forty, or fifty dollars a pair, at least for some time.... In every point of view this measure is pregnant with public mischief and private injury tends to demoralize the workmen, destroy the trade of the city, and leaves the pockets of the whole community to the discretion of the concerned." No merchant can do business if, after he has contracted to deliver articles, his journeymen may arbitrarily jump their wages. Consider, moreover, the effects upon the journeymen themselves. "The botch, incapable of doing justice to his work," is put on a level with the best workman. Indigent workmen, with families to maintain, "however sharp and pressing their necessities, were obliged to stand the turn-out, or never afterwards be employed." They were not free to use their own good sense and return to work. Does not this tend to lead "necessitous men ... to take other courses for the support of their wives and children? It might lead them to procure it by crimes-by burglary, larceny, or highway robbery! A father cannot stand by and see, without agony, his children suffer."[34]

The laws of the journeymen "leave no individual at liberty to join the society or reject it.... They are not the laws of Pennsylvania." Are we to have, "besides our state legislature, a new legislature consisting of journeymen shoemakers"[35]—an *imperium in imperio?*

"An attempt has been made," he continued, "to shew that the spirit of the revolution and the principle of the common law, are opposite in this case. That the common law, if applied in this case, would operate an attack upon the rights of man. The enquiry on that point was unnecessary and improper. Nothing more was required than to ascertain what the law is."[36] Later in the charge, however, he undertook to refute Rodney's unnecessary and improper contention. "Was it the spirit of '76 that neither masters or journeymen, in regulating the prices of their commodities, should set up a rule contrary to the law of their country? General and individual liberty was the spirit of '76. It is our first blessing. It has been obtained and will be maintained."[37]

"If the purpose to be obtained, be an object of individual interest, it may fairly be attempted by an individual.... Many are prohibited from combining for the attainment of it."

"... a combination of workmen to raise their wages may be considered in a two fold point of view: one is to benefit themselves ... the other is to injure those who do not join

---

34. 3 *Doc. Hist.* 228–230, 234.
35. *Ibid.* 225.
36. *Ibid.* 225
37. *Ibid.* 235.

their society. The rule of law condemns both. If the rule be clear, we are bound to conform to it even though we do not comprehend the principle upon which it is founded.... It is enough, that it is the will of the majority. It is law because it is their will—if it is law, there may be good reasons for it though we cannot find them out."[38]

The sealed verdict signed by the jurors in the *Cordwainers' Case* was as follows: "We find the defendants guilty of a combination to raise their wages."[39] Whatever may have been the intention of the jurors, or some of them, this was entered as a verdict of Guilty.

Counsel for the prosecuting masters had assured the jury that they were concerned only to establish a principle, and were not desirous that the defendants be punished. The court, doubtless anxious to avoid further exasperation of popular feeling, kept their implied promise. The defendants were each fined eight dollars.

Duane published the stenographic report of the trial, dedicated to the Governor and General Assembly "with the hope of attracting their particular attention, at the next meeting of the Legislature." He thus, as paraphrased by McMaster,[40] expressed the majority Republican reaction to the whole case:

> "Among the blessings promised mankind by the Revolution was the emancipation of industry from the fetters forged by luxury, laziness, aristocracy, and fraud.... Of all the barbarous principles of feudalism entailed on us by England, none was left but slavery, and even this would be greatly restricted in 1808. Yet, would it be believed, at the very time when the state of the negro was about to be improved attempts were being made to reduce the whites to slavery.... It was by the English common law that such things became possible."

The importance of authority in the *Cordwainers' Case* was rather formal than real. It would strain credulity to say that Recorder Levy and the Mayor and Aldermen and jurors of Philadelphia were constrained or controlled by authority. The fact that there existed in text-books clear sweeping loose statements as to the common law, even though those statements were not warranted by decisions, counted, however, to this extent in the complex of pressures by which the result of the case was determined: it served all the interests pressing for conviction by making it possible for decision to wear a dress of submission to compulsive legal obligation—a dress which may somewhat have lessened the effective power of objections.

The result was far from an unqualified victory of the pressures which induced the decision. The force of the counter-pressure of wage earners adversely affected was not insubstantial, even before universal male suffrage. And the force of Jeffersonian convictions and values, impaired though it was by the logical obscurity which tended to reduce it to the form of unreasonable sympathy, was tremendous. These counter-pressures sufficed to assure that prosecutions of labor unions would for long be rare; that the rule of law, in spite of Recorder Levy, would not be felt as clear and settled; and that the Recorder's doctrine would not, without verbal qualification, be adopted in later cases.

---

38. *Ibid.* 233.
39. 3 *Doc. Hist.* 236.
40. *Ibid.* 59; 3 McMaster, *supra* note 24, at 512, citing *Aurora* for May 29, 1806.

Interlude

The Lowell Mills

Early Lowell.

"The Oppressing Hand of Avarice Would Enslave Us": Women, Work, and Protest in the Early Lowell Mills (1834–36)

*Thomas Dublin**

In the years before 1850 the textile mills of Lowell, Massachusetts were a celebrated economic and cultural institution. Foreign visitors invariably included them on their American tours. Interest was prompted by the massive scale of these mills, the astonishing productivity of the power-driven machinery, and the fact that women comprised most of the workforce. Visitors were struck by the newness of both mills and city as well

* This interlude is excerpted from an article published as, Thomas Dublin, "Women, Work, and Protest in the Early Lowell Mills: 'The Oppressive Hand of Avarice Would Enslave Us," 16 *Lab. Hist.* 99–116 (1975). It is reproduced by permission of the publisher, Taylor & Francis.

as by the culture of the female operatives. The scene stood in sharp contrast to the gloomy mill towns of the English industrial revolution.

Lowell was, in fact, an impressive accomplishment. In 1820 there had been no city at all—only a dozen family farms along the Merrimack River in East Chelmsford. In 1821, however, a group of Boston capitalists purchased land and water rights along the river and a nearby canal, and began to build a major textile manufacturing center. Opening two years later, the first factory employed Yankee women recruited from the nearby country-side. Additional mills were constructed until, by 1840, ten textile corporations with thirty-two mills valued at more than ten million dollars lined the banks of the river and nearby canals.[1] Adjacent to the mills were rows of company boarding houses and tenements which accommodated most of the 8,000 factory operatives.

As Lowell expanded and became the nation's largest textile manufacturing center, the experiences of women operatives changed as well. The increasing number of firms in Lowell and in other mill towns brought the pressure of competition. Overproduction became a problem and the prices of finished cloth decreased. The high profits of the early years declined and so, too, did conditions for the mill operatives. Wages were reduced and the pace of work within the mills was stepped up. Women operatives did not accept these changes without protest. In 1834 and 1836 they went on strike to protest wage cuts, and between 1843 and 1848 they mounted petition campaigns aimed at reducing the hours of labor in the mills.

These labor protests in early Lowell contribute to our understanding of the response of workers to the growth of industrial capitalism in the first half of the 19th century. They indicate the importance of values and attitudes dating back to an earlier period and also the transformation of these values in a new setting.

The major factor in the rise of a new consciousness among operatives in Lowell was the development of a close-knit community among women working in the mills. The structure of work and the nature of housing contributed to the growth of this community. The existence of community among woman, in turn, was an important element in the repeated labor protests of the period.

The preconditions for the labor unrest in Lowell before 1850 may be found in the study of the daily worklife of its operatives. In their everyday, relatively conflict-free lives, mill women created the mutual bonds which made possible united action in times of crisis. The existence of a tight-knit community among them was the most important element in determining the collective, as opposed to individual, nature of this response.

The mutual dependence among women in early Lowell was rooted in the structure of mill work itself. Newcomers to the mills were particularly dependent on their fellow operatives, but even experienced hands relied on one another for considerable support.

New operatives generally found their first experiences difficult, even harrowing, though they may have already done considerable hand-spinning and weaving in their own homes....

Living conditions also contributed to the development of community among female operatives. Most women working in the Lowell mills of these years were housed in company boardinghouses. In July 1836, for example, more than 73 percent of females employed by the Hamilton Company resided in company housing adjacent to

1. *Statistics of Lowell Manufactures*, January 1, 1840. Broadside available in the Manuscripts Division, Baker Library, Harvard Business School.

the mills.[2] Almost three-fourths of them, therefore, lived and worked with each other. Furthermore, the work schedule was such that women had little opportunity to interact with those not living in company dwellings. They worked, in these years, an average of 73 hours a week. Their work day ended at 7:00 or 7:30 pm, and in the hours between supper and the 10:00 pm curfew imposed by management on residents of company boardinghouses, there was little time to spend with friends living "off the corporation."

In addition to the structure of work and housing in Lowell, a third factor, the homogeneity of the mill workforce, contributed to the development of community among female operatives. In this period the mill workforce was homogeneous in terms of sex, nativity, and age. Payroll and other records of the Hamilton Company reveal that more than 85 per cent of those employed in July 1836 were women and that over 96 percent were native-born.[3] Furthermore, over 80 percent of the female workforce was between the ages of 15 and 30 years old; and only 10 percent was under 15 or over 40 years old.[4]

II

In February 1834, 800 of Lowell's women operatives "turned-out"—went on strike—to protest a proposed reduction in their wages. They marched to numerous mills in an effort to induce others to join them; and, at an outdoor rally, they petitioned others to "discontinue their labors until terms of reconciliation are made." Their petition concluded:

> Resolved, That we will not go back into the mills to work unless our wages are continued … as they have been.
>
> Resolved, That none of us will go back, unless they receive us all as one.
>
> Resolved, That if any have not money enough to carry them home, they shall be supplied.[5]

The strike proved to be brief and failed to reverse the proposed wage reductions. Turning-out on a Friday, the striking women were paid their back wages on Saturday, and by the middle of the next week had returned to work or left town. Within a week of the turn-out, the mills were running near capacity.[6]

This first strike in Lowell is important not because it failed or succeeded, but simply because it took place. In an era in which women had to overcome opposition simply to work in the mills, it is remarkable that they would further overstep the accepted middle-class bounds of female propriety by participating in a public protest. The agents of the textile mills certainly considered the turn-out unfeminine. William Austin, agent of the Lawrence Company, described the operatives' procession as an "amizonian [sic] display." He wrote further, in a letter to his company treasurer in Boston: "This afternoon we have paid off several of

---

2. Statistics are based on linkage between company payrolls and register books of the Hamilton Manufacturing Company. The register books were alphabetically organized volumes in which operatives were signed into and out of the mills. They gave the nativity and local residence of operatives as well as additional data.

3. *Ibid.*

4. These data are based on an analysis of the age distribution of females residing in Hamilton Company boardinghouses as recorded in the Federal Manuscript Censuses of 1830 and 1840.

5. Boston *Evening Transcript*, February 18, 1834.

6. *Lawrence Manufacturing Company Records*, Correspondence, Vol. MAB-1, March 4 & March 9, 1834.

these Amazons & presume that they will leave town on Monday."[7] The turn-out was particularly offensive to the agents because of the relationship they thought they had with their operatives. William Austin probably expressed the feelings of other agents when he wrote: "... notwithstanding the friendly and disinterested advice which has been on all proper occassions [sic] communicated to the girls of the Lawrence mills a spirit of evil omen ... has prevailed, and overcome the judgment and discretion of too many, and this morning a general turn-out from most of the rooms has been the consequence."[8]

Mill agents assumed an attitude of benevolent paternalism toward their female operatives, and found it particularly disturbing that the women paid such little heed to their advice. The strikers were not merely unfeminine, they were ungrateful as well.

Such attitudes notwithstanding, women chose to turn-out. They did so for two principal reasons. First, the wage cuts undermined the sense of dignity and social equality which was an important element in their Yankee heritage. Second, these wage cuts were seen as an attack on their economic independence.

Certainly a prime motive for the strike was outrage at the social implications of the wage cuts. In a statement of principles accompanying the petition that was circulated among operatives, women expressed well the sense of themselves that prompted their protest of these wage cuts:

UNION IS POWER

Our present object is to have union and exertion, and we remain in possession of our unquestionable rights. We circulate this paper wishing to obtain the names of all who imbibe the spirit of our Patriotic Ancestors, who preferred privation to bondage, and parted with all that renders life desirable—and even life itself—to procure independence for their children. The oppressing hand of avarice would enslave us, and to gain their object, they gravely tell us of the pressure of the time, this we are already sensible of, and deplore it. If any are in want of assistance, the Ladies will be compassionate and assist them; but we prefer to have the disposing of our charities in our own hands; and as we are free, we would remain in possession of what kind Providence has bestowed upon us; and remain daughters of freemen still.[9]

At several points in the proclamation the women drew on their Yankee heritage. Connecting their turn-out with the efforts of their "Patriotic Ancestors" to secure independence from England, they interpreted the wage cuts as an effort to "enslave" them—to deprive them of the independent status as "daughters of freemen."

Though very general and rhetorical, the statement of these women does suggest their sense of self, of their own worth and dignity. Elsewhere, they expressed the conviction that they were the social equals of the overseers, indeed of the mill-owners themselves.[10] The wage cuts, however, struck at this assertion of social equality. These reductions made it clear that the operatives were subordinate to their employers, rather than equal partners in a contract binding on both parties. By turning-out, the women emphatically denied that they were subordinates; but by returning to work the next week, they demonstrated that in economic terms they were no match for their corporate superiors.

7. *Ibid.*, February 15, 1834.
8. *Ibid.*, February 14, 1834.
9. Boston *Evening Transcript*, February 18, 1834.
10. Harriet Robinson, *Loom and Spindle*, 72; *Offering*, February, 1841, p. 45.

In point of fact, these Yankee operatives were subordinate in early Lowell's social and economic order, but they never consciously accepted this status. Their refusal to do so became evident whenever the mill owners attempted to exercise the power they possessed. This fundamental contradiction between the objective status of operatives and their consciousness of it was at the root of the 1834 turn-out and of subsequent labor protests in Lowell before 1850. The corporations could build mills, create thousands of jobs, and recruit women to fill them. Nevertheless, they bought only the workers' labor power, and then only for as long as these workers chose to stay. Women could always return to their rural homes, and they had a sense of their own worth and dignity, factors limiting the actions of management.

Women operatives viewed the wage cuts as a threat to their economic independence. This independence had two related dimensions. First, the women were self-supporting while they worked in the mills and, consequently, were independent of their families back home. Second, they were able to save out of their monthly earnings and could then leave the mills for the old homestead whenever they so desired. In effect, they were not totally dependent upon mill work. Their independence was based largely on the high level of wages in the mills. They could support themselves and still save enough to return home periodically. The wage cuts threatened to deny them this outlet, substituting instead the prospect of total dependence on mill work. Small wonder, then, there was alarm that "the oppressing hand of avarice would enslave us." To be forced, out of economic necessity, to lifelong labor in the mills would have indeed seemed like slavery.[11] The Yankee operatives spoke directly to the fear of a dependency based on impoverishment when offering to assist any women workers who "have not money enough to carry them home." Wage reductions, however, offered only the prospect of a future dependence on mill employment. By striking, the women asserted their actual economic independence of the mills and their determination to remain "daughters of freemen still."

While the women's traditional conception of themselves as independent daughters of freemen played a major role in the turn-out, this factor acting alone would not necessarily have triggered the 1834 strike. It would have led women as individuals to quit work and return to their rural homes. But the turn-out was a collective protest. When it was announced that wage reductions were being considered, women began to hold meetings in the mills during meal breaks in order to assess tactical possibilities. Their turn-out began at one mill when the agent discharged a woman who had presided at such a meeting. Their procession through the streets passed by other mills, expressing a conscious effort to enlist as much support as possible for their cause. At a mass meeting, the women drew up a resolution which insisted that none be discharged for their participation in the turn-out. This strike, then, was a collective response to the proposed wage cuts — made possible because women had come to form a "community" of operatives in the mill, rather than simply a group of individual workers. The existence of such a tight-knit community turned individual opposition of the wage cuts into a collective protest.

In October 1836 women again went on strike. This second turn-out was similar to the first in several respects. Its immediate cause was also a wage reduction; marches and a

---

11. The wage cuts, in still another way, might have been seen as threatening to "enslave." Such decreases would be enacted by reductions in the piece rates paid women. If women were to maintain their overall earnings, given the wage cuts, they would have to speed up their work or accept additional machinery, both of which would result in making them work harder for the same pay. Opposition to the speed-up and the stretch-out was strong during the Ten Hour Movement in the 1840s, and although I have found no direct evidence, such feeling may have played a part in the turn-outs of the 1830s as well.

large outdoor rally were organized; again, like the earlier protest, the basic goal was not achieved; the corporations refused to restore wages; and operatives either left Lowell or returned to work at the new rates.

Despite these surface similarities between the turn-outs, there were some real differences. One involved scale: over 1,500 operatives turned out in 1836, compared to only 800 earlier.[12] Moreover, the second strike lasted much longer than the first. In 1834 operatives stayed out for only a few days; in 1836 the mills ran far below capacity for several months. Two weeks after the second turn-out began, a mill agent reported that only a fifth of the strikers had returned to work: "The rest manifest *good spunk* as they call it."[13] Several days later he described the impact of the continuing strike on operations in his mills: "we must be feeble for months to come as probably not less than 250 of our former scanty supply of help have left town."[14] These lines read in sharp contrast to the optimistic reports of agents following the turn-out in February 1834.

Differences between the two turn-outs were not limited to the increased scale and duration of the later one. Women displayed a much higher degree of organization in 1836 than earlier. To coordinate strike activities, they formed a Factory Girls' Association. According to one historian, membership in the short-lived association reached 2,500 at its height.[15] The larger organization among women was reflected in the tactics employed. Strikers, according to one mill agent, were able to halt production to a greater extent than numbers alone could explain; and, he complained, although some operatives were willing to work, "it has been impossible to give employment to many who remained." He attributed this difficulty to the strikers' tactics: "this was in many instances no doubt the result of calculation and contrivance. After the original turn-out they [the operatives] would assail a particular room—as for instance, all the warpers, or all the warp spinners, or all the speeder and stretcher girls, and this would close the mill as effectually as if all the girls in the mill had left."[16]

Now giving more thought than they had in 1834 to the specific tactics of the turn-out, the women made a deliberate effort to shut down the mills in order to win their demands. They attempted to persuade less committed operatives, concentrating on those in crucial departments within the mill. Such tactics anticipated those of skilled mulespinners and loomfixers who went out on strike in the 1880s and 1890s.

In their organization of a Factory Girl's Association and in their efforts to shut down the mills, the female operatives revealed that they had been changed by their industrial experience. Increasingly, they acted not simply as "daughters of freemen" offended by the impositions of the textile corporations, but also as industrial workers intent on improving their position within the mills....

The experiences of Lowell women before 1850 present a fascinating picture of the contradictory impact of industrial capitalism. Repeated labor protests reveal that female operatives felt the demands of mill employment to be oppressive. At the same time, however, the mills, provided women with work outside of the home and family, thereby offering them an unprecedented opportunity. That they came to challenge employer paternalism was a direct consequence of the increasing opportunities offered them in these years. The Lowell mills both exploited and liberated women in ways unknown to the pre-industrial political economy.

---

12. Robinson, *Loom and Spindle,*p. 83; Boston *Evening Transcript*, October 4 and 6, 1836.

13. *Tremont-Suffolk Mills Records*, unbound Letters, Volume FN-1, October 14, 1836.

14. *Ibid.*, October 17, 1836.

15. Hannah Josephson, *The Golden Threads: New England's Mill Girls and Magnates*, 238 (New York, 1949).

16. *Tremont-Suffolk Mills Records*, unbound Letters, Volume FN-1, October 10, 1836.

Lowell Factory Girls Association Constitution (1836)

Preamble.

Whereas we, the undersigned, residents of Lowell, moved by a love of honest industry and the expectation of a fair and liberal recompense, have left our homes, our relatives and youthful associates, and come hither, and subjected ourselves to all the danger and inconvenience, which necessarily attend young and unprotected females, when among strangers, and in a strange land; and however humble the condition of Factory Girls, (as we are termed,) may seem, we firmly and fearlessly (though we trust with a modesty becoming our sex,) claim for ourselves, that love of moral and intellectual culture, that admiration of, and desire to attain and preserve pure, elevated and refined characters, a true reverence for divine principle which bids us to render to every one his due; a due appreciation of those great and cardinal principles of our government, of justice and humanity, which enjoins upon us "to live and let live"—that chivalrous and honorable feeling, which with equal force, forbids us to invade others rights, or suffer others, upon any consideration, to invade ours; and at the same time, that utter abhorrence and detestation of whatever is mean, sordid, dishonourable or unjust—all of which, can alone, in our estimation, entitle us to be called the daughters of freemen, or of Republican America.

And Whereas, we believe that those who have preceded us have been, we know that ourselves are, and that our successors are liable to be, assailed in various ways by the wicked and unprincipled, and cheated out of just, legal and constitutional dues, by ungenerous, illiberal and avaricious capitalists—and convinced that "union is power," and that as the unprincipled consult and advise, that they may the more easily decoy and seduce—and the capitalists that they may the more effectually defraud—we, (being the weaker,) claim it to be our undeniable right, to associate and concentrate our power, that we may the more successfully repel their equally base and iniquitous aggressions.

And whereas, impressed with this belief, and conscious that our cause is a common one, and our conditions similar, we feel it our imperative duty to stand by each other through weal and woe; to administer to each others wants, to prevent each others backsliding—to comfort each other in sickness, and advise each other in health, to incite each other to the love and attainment of those excellences, which can alone constitute the perfection of female character—unsullied virtue, refined tastes and cultivated intellects—and in a word, do all that in us lies, to make each other worthy ourselves, our country and Creator.

Therefore, for the attainment of those objects, we associate ourselves together, and mutually pledge to each other, a females irrefragable vow, to stand by, abide by, and be governed by the following provisions: . . .

President Abraham Lincoln

All that harms labor is treason to America. No line can be drawn between these two. If any man tells you he loves America, yet hates labor, he is a liar. If a man tells you he trusts America, yet fears labor, he is a fool.

The strongest bond of human sympathy, outside the family relation, should be the one uniting all working people, of all nations, and tongues, and kindreds.

Annual Address Before the Wisconsin State Agricultural Society, at Milwaukee, Wisconsin, September 30, 1859

The world is agreed that labor is the source from which human wants are mainly supplied. There is no dispute upon this point. From this point, however, men immediately diverge. Much disputation is maintained as to the best way of applying and controlling the labor element. By some it is assumed that labor is available only in connection with capital—that nobody labors, unless somebody else owning capital, somehow, by the use of it, induces him to do it. Having assumed this, they proceed to consider whether it is best that capital shall hire laborers, and thus induce them to work by their own consent, or buy them, and drive them to it, without their consent. Having proceeded so far, they naturally conclude that all laborers are naturally either hired laborers or slaves. They further assume that whoever is once a hired laborer, is fatally fixed in that condition for life; and thence again, that his condition is as bad as, or worse than, that of a slave. This is the "mud-sill" theory. But another class of reasoners hold the opinion that there is no such relation between capital and labor as assumed; that there is no such thing as a free man being fatally fixed for life in the condition of a hired laborer; that both these assumptions are false, and all inferences from them groundless. They hold that labor is prior to, and independent of, capital; that, in fact, capital is the fruit of labor, and could never have existed if labor had not first existed; that labor can exist without capital, but that capital could never have existed without labor. Hence they hold that labor is the superior—greatly the superior—of capital. They do not deny that there is, and probably always will be, a relation between labor and capital. The error, as they hold, is in assuming that the whole labor of the world exists within that relation. A few men own capital; and that few avoid labor themselves, and with their capital hire or buy another few to labor for them. A large majority belong to neither class—neither work for others, nor have others working for them. Even in all our slave States except South Carolina, a majority of the whole people of all colors are neither slaves nor masters. In these free States, a large majority are neither hirers nor hired. Men, with their families—wives, sons and daughters—work for themselves, on their farms, in their houses, and in their shops, taking the whole product to themselves, and asking no favors of capital on the one hand, nor of hirelings or slaves on the other. It is not forgotten that a considerable number of persons mingle their own labor with capital—that is, labor with their own hands and also buy slaves or hire free men to labor for them; but this is only a mixed, and not a distinct, class. No principle stated is disturbed by the existence of this mixed class. Again, as has already been said, the opponents of the "mud-sill" theory insist that there is not, of necessity, any such thing as the free hired laborer being fixed to that condition for life. There is demonstration for saying this. Many independent men in this assembly doubtless a few years ago were hired laborers. And their case is almost, if not quite, the general rule. The prudent, penniless beginner in the world labors for wages awhile, saves a surplus with which to buy tools or land for himself, then labors on his own account another while, and at length hires another new beginner to help him. This, say its advocates, is free labor—the just, and generous, and prosperous system, which opens the way for all, gives hope to all, and energy, and progress, and improvement of condition to all. If any continue through life in the condition of the hired laborer, it is not the fault of the system, but because of either a dependent nature which prefers it, or improvidence, folly, or singular misfortune. I have said this much about the elements of labor generally, as introductory to the consideration of a new phase which that element is in process of assuming. The old general rule was that educated people did not perform manual labor. They managed to eat their bread, leaving the toil of producing it to the uneducated. This was not an insupportable evil to the working bees, so long as the class of drones remained very small. But now, especially in these free States, nearly all are educated—quite too nearly all to leave the labor of the uneducated in any wise adequate to the support of the whole. It follows from this that henceforth educated people must labor.[1]

---

1. *The Complete Works of Abraham Lincoln*, vol. 5. John G. Nicolay and John Hay, eds. (New York: Francis D. Tandy Company, 1894).

Eight Hour Movement and Haymarket Bombing (1886)

We mean to make things over
  We're tired of toil for nought
But bare enough to live on; never
  An hour for thought.
We want to feel the sunshine: we
  Want to smell the flowers
We're sure that God has willed it
  And we mean to have eight hours.
We're summoning our forces from
  Shipyard, shop, and mill
Eight hours for work, eight hours for rest
  Eight hours for what we will!

Now these are my ideas. They constitute a part of myself. I cannot divest myself of them, nor would I, if I could. And if you think you can crush out these ideas that are gaining ground more and more every day, if you think you can crush them out by sending us to the gallows — if you would once more have people to suffer the penalty of death because they have dared to tell the truth — and I defy you to show us where we have told a lie — I say, if death is the penalty for proclaiming the truth, then I will proudly and defiantly pay the costly price! Truth crucified in Socrates, in Christ, in Giordano Bruno, in Huss, in Galileo, still lives — they and others whose number is legion have preceded us on this path. We are ready to follow!

August Spies, Haymarket Martyr

There will come a time when our silence will be more powerful than the voices you strangle today.

August Spies, From the Gallows

Interlude

The Knights of Labor and Cooperative Production

I suppose I am like hundreds of others who a few years ago could look ahead and see nothing but misery, hard work, and starvation, but what a change, when I first heard of the K's of L, I immediately subscribed for a daily paper so as to learn all I could of the K's. It seemed as if the Cloudy Heavens had opened and I could faintly see a little bright clear sky. Finally I became interested and with about forty others we were organized into an Assembly. We now number over three hundred and a good field before us. I have taken more interest in Cooperation than in strikes and if this whole country could be managed on that plan how much better it would be for all. Bro Powderly says that the next five years will see the emancipation of the white slaves. I do not believe that strikes will do it, but think they will assist. Legislation will also be a great help but cooperation must after all do the whole business.

Master Workman Leonard Wheeler

So long as the entire control and management of the public highways of the country—the railways—remains in the hands of private individuals while doing the work of the nation, just so long will the operation of co-operative enterprises be attended with failure. We may manufacture the best quality of goods and be prepared to sell at the most reasonable rates, but we cannot depend on having those goods transported to market so long as the transportation facilities of the nation are controlled by monopoly.

Grand Master Workman Terence Powderly

Consensus, Hegemony, and the Case of the Knights of Labor
Leon Fink*

A combination of affirmation and negation of American culture was reflected in the eloquence of labor radical George E. McNeill in the late 1870s: "We declare an inevitable and irresistible conflict between the wage-system of labor and the republican system of government."[1]

The Knights of Labor as the largest and most representative labor body until its time—and probably the single largest unionizing movement in the Western world during the 1880s—appear as a natural repository of a characteristic and distinctive American labor vision. Propelled not merely by a set of specific group grievances but, as Susan Levine writes, the Knights offered a "counter-vision of cooperation, equality, and social responsibility." At its height the Gilded Age labor movement, argues David Scobey, "would pose alternative productive relations to the marketplace, an alternative conception of the republican polity, even an alternative morality to this 'present system of all for self.'"[2]

Throughout American history, workers, perhaps more or less sincerely, have sought to identify their interests and actions directly with national governmental institutions and political principles. This was especially so in the first century of the new republic, when the contested civic concepts of "independence," "equality," "free labor," and "commonwealth" carried a discrete social, as well as a political, meaning. None, for example, were more zealous than the artisan classes in seeking ratification of the United States Constitution. Similarly, as early as 1810 the Declaration of Independence was used to justify a strike. More generally, worker ideology in the antebellum decades has been defined in recent studies as "artisanal republicanism." Even unenfranchised female workers at Lowell found political sustenance as "daughters of free men."[3] Protests at midcentury in New

---

* This article is substantially reduced from a chapter in Leon Fink, "The New Labor History and the Powers of Pessimism: Consensus, Hegemony, and the Case of the Knights of Labor," 756 *J. of Am. Hist.* 1125 (1988). This edit is reprinted with the permission of the publisher, Oxford Univ. Press.

1. *See* Sean Wilentz, *Chants Democratic: New York City and the Rise of the American Working Class, 1788–1950* (New York, 1984); Alan Dawley, *Class and Community: the Industrial Revolution in Lynn* (Cambridge, Mass. 1976); David Montgomery, *Beyond Equality: Labor and the Radical Republicans, 1862–1872* (New York, 1967); and for the best treatment connecting the earlier labor reform critique to the Knights of Labor, Richard Schneirov, "The Knights of Labor in the Chicago Labor Movement and in Municipal Politics, 1877–1887" (Ph.D. diss., Northern Illinois University, 1984), 14–68. George E. McNeill, "The Problem of Today," in *The Labor Movement: The Problem of Today*, ed. George E. McNeill, 459 (Boston, 1887).

2. My point about the Knights in comparative terms is elaborated in Leon Fink, "Looking Backward: Reflections on Workers' Culture and the Conceptual Dilemmas of the New Labor History," in *American Labor History: Toward a Synthesis*, ed. Alice Kessler-Harris and J. Carroll Moody (DeKalb, 1988). Susan Levine, *Labor's True Woman: Carpet Weavers, Industrialization, and Labor Reform in the Gilded Age*, 103 (Philadelphia, 1984); David Scobey, "Boycotting the Politics Factory: Labor Radicalism and the New York City Mayoral Election of 1886," *Radical History Review*, 28–30 (Sept. 1984), 292. *See also* Gregory S. Kealey and Bryan D. Palmer, *Dreaming of What Might Be: The Knights of Labor in Ontario, 1880–1900*, 278, 275 (New York, 1982); Peter Rachleff, *Black Labor in the South: Richmond, Virginia, 1865–1890*, 192 (Philadelphia, 1984); Leon Fink, *Workingmen's Democracy: The Knights of Labor and American Politics*, 219 (Urbana, 1983).

3. Eric Foner, *Tom Paine and Revolutionary America* (New York, 1976); Charles G. Steffen, *The Mechanics of Baltimore: Workers and Politics in the Age of Revolution, 1763–1812* (Urbana, 1984), 81–101; Wilentz, *Chants Democratic*, 61–103; Thomas Dublin, *Women at Work: The Transformation of Work and Community at Lowell, Massachusetts, 1826–1860* (New York, 1979).

England's shoe factories likewise appealed directly to a political tradition of "equal rights"; not coincidentally the greatest strike up to 1860 occurred on Washington's Birthday. Following the Civil War, a gathering working-class movement again chose the symbols of the Republic as the basis for its critique of corporate capitalism. The written constitutions of the national trade unions also borrowed from the structure and procedure of the nation's federal institutions.[4]

For their part, the Knights of Labor stretched republican idealism to new political limits. Their rhetoric suffused with appeals to community and nation, the Knights sought to regenerate American life and institutions through a radical activation of citizenship. By defining their contemporary enemies as a new "slave power" (thus invoking both the recent Civil War and instinctual American hatred of feudal serfdom), the Knights cast themselves as the last, best defenders of a true republic of individual liberties, which defined the Knights' aims entirely within the tradition of natural rights and human liberty. The "real mission" of their order, affirmed the General Assembly, "is the complete emancipation and enfranchisement of all those who labor. It is imbued with the lofty spirit of the Declaration of Independence."[5]

Stirred by the appeal to equal rights, the Knights generally held the courts and their intricate legal reasoning in righteous, if somewhat ignorant, disdain. Even when attempting a serious defense of the legitimacy of the boycott in 1886, for example, Knights' executive officer George McNeill showed little patience for fine points of legal doctrine:

> Recent decisions of judges upon the question of conspiracy and boycotting are new revelations of an old fact, that the interpretation of law rests largely upon the public sentiment of the wealthy part of the community. The *Dred-Scott* decision was declared infamous by those who were lifted to the level of the spirit of our institutions; yet, nevertheless, that decision was a confession that the controlling classes were under the subtle influence of the slave-power.... So, too, the attempts now made to prevent the working people from using the great power of the boycott will be found to be in contradiction, not only of individual, but of constitutional rights. A man has not only the right to buy where he pleases, but has the right to advise another man to buy or not to buy of friend or enemy; *and whether the exercise of the boycott is judicious or injudicious, justifiable or unjustifiable in certain circumstances,*

---

4. Dawley, *Class and Community*, 80; George E. McNeill, "The Problem of Today," in *The Labor Movement: The Problem of Today*, ed. George E. McNeill, 459 (Boston, 1887); Theodore W. Glocker, *The Government of American Trade Unions*, 140–41, 197, 236–37 (Baltimore, 1913). Although trade-union constitutionalism may have paralleled, rather than copied, governmental constitutionalism, there were also direct influences, although not entirely one way. Glocker, for example, saw the influence of national political traditions in trade-union respect for representative forms of government and in a "federal" approach to national associations, that is, "federations" of labor. The internal judicial systems of the unions mirrored the hierarchical appeals process from lower to higher authority found in the national institutions. American unions more zealously guarded local sovereignty than their British counterparts. However, American unions experimented with the secret ballot system before its adoption by state and municipal governments, and at the turn of the century, labor unions were among the most active advocates of direct-government reforms such as referendum and recall.

5. For elaboration of the theme of the Knights' republicanism, see Fink, *Workingmen's Democracy*, 3–37. See also Barry H. Goldberg, "Beyond Free Labor: Labor, Socialism, and the Idea of Wage Slavery" (Ph.D. diss., Columbia University, 1979). John Swinton, *Striking for Life: or Labor's Side of the Labor Question*, 296 (n.p., 1894). On the changing dimensions of post-Civil War worker republicanism, see Forbath, "Ambiguities of Free Labor," 800–814. *Labor, Its Rights and Wrongs*, 204–206 (Washington, 1886).

the innate right of man to the privilege of exercising his moral power and social influence in the direction of trade, or to withhold trade, cannot be safely denied.[6]

With a simultaneous appeal to the laboring classes as citizens and as producers, the Knights of Labor effectively reached out in the 1880s from a base among artisans and coal miners to a cross-class constituency, including small shopkeepers, even a few manufacturers, and a growing factory proletariat. The occupational inclusiveness of the Knights—who barred only lawyers, stockbrokers, bankers, and saloonkeepers from membership—also permitted the labor body to extend itself beyond a constituency of old immigrants and old-stock Americans toward new-immigrant, Afro-American, and female recruits. The result was an economic and cultural solidarity extending beyond a given class or corporate interest.

A moralistic, republican message sealed the unity of the Knights' heterogeneous constituency. To the Knights' partisans, emphasis on the "labor theory of value" and "the producing classes" went hand in hand with commitment to "independence" and "American citizenship." While "liberal" in its continuing respect for private property and fear of concentrated power in public or private hands, popular labor rhetoric appropriated a "republican" emphasis on the public good and individual moral responsibility to promote it. Indeed, to establish a footing for the practice of good citizenship, the Knights wished to encumber the liberal marketplace with a limitation of working hours, recognition of union shops, and a host of legislative reforms, including abolition of the banking system and nationalization of monopoly power. Asserting a direct link between civic virtue, political democracy, and the economic welfare of the laboring classes, the Knights fashioned a social democratic vision—albeit one without the accoutrement of the administrative state.[7]

The labor movement, likewise, stitched together old and new elements of meaning. The language of labor republicanism itself reflected the internal crisis and attempted restructuring of liberal political ideology. The labor theory of value, for example, underwent a subtle transformation. A mere strand of individualist Jeffersonian thought (and one that disappeared in neoclassical economics), it became a moral pillar of the collective claims of the laboring classes. Similarly, participants in the labor movement used antimonopoly principles, rooted in a free-market critique of mercantilism, to attack the very creations of the marketplace, even as they still attributed the exorbitant powers of banks, railroads, and utilities to governmental favoritism.[8]

Aside from refashioning such bedrock political values, Gilded Age labor drew on what Raymond Williams has called "residual" cultural elements: "certain experiences, meanings, and values ... lived and practiced on the basis of ... some previous social and cultural institution or formation." In particular, the Knights found ample, if informal, wellsprings of communal solidarity and collective discipline inside a society formally

---

6. George E. McNeill, "Declaration of Principles of the Knights of Labor," in *Labor Movement*, ed. McNeill, 488–89. Italics added.

7. I am not taking sides here on the historical debate over the timing of republicanism's subordination to liberal individualism in formal American thought and institutions. For a sample of the debate, see J. G. A. Pocock, *The Machiavellian Moment: Florentine Political Thought and the Atlantic Republican Tradition* (Princeton, 1975); Joyce Appleby, "What is Still American in the Political Philosophy of Thomas Jefferson?" 19 *William and Mary Quarterly*, 287–309 (April 1982); and John Patrick Diggins, *The Lost Soul of American Politics: Virtue, Self-interest, and the Foundations of Liberalism* (New York, 1984). A synthetic and convincing gloss is offered by James T Kloppenberg, "The Virtues of Liberalism: Christianity, Republicanism, and Ethics in Early American Political Discourse," 74 *Journal of American History*, 9–33 (June 1987).

8. Fink, *Workingmen's Democracy*, 3–17.

sworn to individual rights and the logic of self-interest. As Gregory Kealey and Bryan Palmer have documented, ethnic traditions, prior workplace cultures, community parades and celebrations, and the mutualism of voluntary societies were among the borrowings that helped animate the move toward a new solidarity among working people in the 1880s. Workers' newer class identity, David Scobey argues, "redefined older communal loyalties" through a variety of instruments: boycotts, sympathy strikes, cooperatives, unions based on class rather than skills, special support for unskilled workers, reading and lodge rooms, gymnasiums, employment bureaus, and finally, independent labor politics.[9]

As evidenced in their order's name, hierarchy of officers, and elaborate ritual, the Knights of Labor were particularly indebted to the larger culture of nineteenth-century Anglo-American fraternalism. Begun as a secret, oath-taking brotherhood (in 1881 the oaths were discontinued to forestall Catholic opposition), the Knights in many respects bear out Charles W. Ferguson's venerable claim that "class-consciousness, American style ... expressed itself through the characteristic medium of social clubs and secret orders. The native technique of reform is, first of all, to demand three raps and a high sign." If the order's ritual book, the *Adelphon Kruptos*, borrowed heavily from Masonic and Odd Fellows ceremony, however, the emphasis of its own mutualism was original and pointed. Powderly's elucidation of one symbol of the order—the "Great Seal of Knighthood" is instructive. (See illustration.) Looking from the inside out, the equilateral triangle covering the Western Hemisphere was endowed with three layers of meaning— "humanity": or birth, life, and death; the elements of human happiness: land, labor, and love; and the three keys to economics: production, exchange, and consumption (along with the lesson that "no middlemen are necessary to carry on business ... profits are not a necessity"). The lines of the inner pentagon, representing justice, wisdom, truth, industry, and economy, defined the principles of "Universal Brotherhood," while they also symbolized the five senses, the five elements of nature (land, air, light, heat, and water), and the demand for a five-day work week. Powderly's illumination of the pentagon went further to include five mechanical powers, "the lever, pulley, screw, wedge, and hammer." "Though not, strictly speaking, a mechanical power ... the hammer was introduced that the member might be instructed how to weld together the various natures, dispositions, sentiments, feelings, and aspirations by which men are actuated in gaining their ends.... As improvements are being made every day in the machinery of the world, we assert our right, not alone to these powers, but to the results of man's toil while making use of them."

In addition to reinterpreting contemporary political culture, the Knights *politicized* the culture of civil society and everyday life. Harnessing popular values regarding education, temperance, and family responsibility to a critique of the wage system, the "movement culture" of the Knights contested the implications of the most basic American assumptions. While embracing the principle of self-improvement, for example, the Knights incorporated it into a cooperative ethic. As David Brundage has emphasized, their version of the principle "bore little resemblance to self-improvement as conceptualized by the YMCA and its business supporters." Likewise, the Knights made of "domesticity," the Victorian feminine counterpart to male productive efficiency, a moral and political sword to swing at the factory lords. Equal rights, Susan Levine has demonstrated, commingled with domestic idealism in the critical vision of the Knights. A poem emerging from the national carpet weavers' strike of 1885 suggests the interplay of spheres male and female, past and future:

---

9. Raymond Williams, *Marxism and Literature*, 122–23 (New York, 1977); Kealey and Palmer, *Dreaming of What Might Be*, 289–92; Scobey, "Boycotting the Politics Factory," 288–90.

We ask not your pity, we charity scorn.
We ask but the rights to which we were born.
For the flag of freedom has waved o'er our land,
We justice and equality claim and demand.
Then strive for your rights, O, sisters dear,
And ever remember in your own sphere,
You may aid the cause of all mankind,
And be the true woman that God designed[10]

In word and deed, the late nineteenth century thus provided ample evidence of popular opposition to the consolidation of control over economic and political life by a corporate elite. One might still argue that such a contest implied neither conscious rejection of capitalism, nor categorical repudiation of liberal values. But if we limit ourselves to the broad antitheses of capitalism versus socialism, liberalism versus communalism, we are likely to miss the real play of historical possibilities at the time.

The Knights' message to the producing classes, while opposing wage labor in the abstract, tended to deemphasize the conflict between wage workers and employers, resist mass strikes, and ignore mounting class antagonism in favor of visions of an arbitrated world of harmony.

Although the producer culture possessed a critical, even "utopian," thrust, "the same cultural premises also defined republican forms as the only political means for the freeing of the nation from obstructive selfish interests." Such a stance left considerable room for co-optation of labor's cause by party politicians uninterested in radical reform

Employers and their friends in the courts, of course, did not roll over. Labor's urban base was threatened by court decisions declaring the boycott an unfair restraint of trade and invoking automatic injunctions against sympathy strikes. Spreading confrontations on the railroads and in coalfields further polarized laboring communities and the law-and-order alliance of business with state and federal authority. Finally, a brutal setback for the Amalgamated Association of Iron and Steel Workers at Homestead, Pennsylvania, in 1892 offered a catalyst for national political mobilization by the Knights of Labor, now over a million strong. Only with a common, minimal set of rights, local activists realized, could labor survive the corporate reaction. Around the country workers settled on a single national political priority—statutory recognition of labor's rights to organize, strike, and boycott, and crystal-clear prohibition of incursions on those rights by employer police forces, yellow-dog contracts, and injunctions. How to win such protection? By alliance with Populist farmers, who, impressed by labor's political revolt, moved as early as 1890 toward an independent, third-party alternative. Backed by Populist and big city Democratic votes, labor's "Bill of Rights" thus passed the Congress and was signed hesitatingly by President Grover Cleveland in 1893.

Even after Haymarket one promising option still beckoned the embattled general movement of producers. That was the road of independent labor politics, to try to use state power to change the rules of a game that had begun to go badly. In a remarkable display of the depth of the Gilded Age labor revolt, workingmen's tickets sprang up in 1886–1887 in every corner of the country. Yet, although those tickets won in 61 of 189 contested locales, the political moment for united labor power, like the industrial moment that preceded it, soon expired. A declining base of organized constituents, co-optation of labor programs and candidates by the major parties, and the labor culture's own ambivalence

---

10. David Brundage, "The Producing Classes and the Saloon: Denver in the 1880s," 26 *Labor History*, 40 (Winter 1985); Levine, *Labor's True Woman*, 131.

toward state action and party formation dulled the edge of the political challenge. Although class issues continued to break into the political discourse, urban workers by the turn of the century generally found enfranchisement within a political system defined by ethnicity, rather than class.

The "cultural" contribution to labor republicanism's real-life denouement cannot be abstracted from the worsening repression, political disunity, and strategic disaster that ensnared the movement. To be sure, arrest of the Knights' forward momentum did bring to the surface a variety of ideological tensions, as well as personal animosities. Debate over defense of the Haymarket defendants, the order's proper relation to independent trade unions (and the question of craft federation versus 'mixed' assemblies within the Knights themselves), the temperance issue, and electoral options reflected not only confusion of vision among the order's leaders but also a larger uncertainty of purpose among a heterogeneous rank and file. Yes, under the stress of defeat, fear, and the unknown, the edifice of a worker's movement and a labor alternative did crack. Division and contradiction ultimately replaced unity and confident initiative from below.

II

The Homestead Lockout, The Pinkertons, and the Militia

Joseph Pennell, Homestead Works Carnegie Steel.

The Citizen Striker: Workers' Ideology in the Homestead Strike of 1892

*Linda G. Schneider**

Any description of labor's outlook in nineteenth-century America must set union activity in the context of the distinctive American ideology of working-class republicanism. In the Homestead strike of 1892 republicanism both shaped workers outlook in the strike and was itself reinterpreted in the course of militant union action.

At Homestead, the symbols of republicanism were publicly interpreted for steel workers by a group of more than usually articulate workmen who were chosen as lodge correspondents or local union leaders. They were a local, very low-level leadership stratum, often men cast up by the force of events from positions as skilled or semi-skilled workers and returned to obscurity in short order. This minority surely spoke for other skilled men; unskilled workers' ideas may have differed, though there is some evidence of their agreement and unity with the skilled men. Certainly these local leaders represented only

* This chapter first was published in 23 *Labor History* 47 (1982), reprinted by permission of the publisher, Taylor & Francis.

the English-speaking workers at Homestead. The ten to twenty percent of Homestead's workforce who were immigrants from Southern and Eastern Europe and were in later years to play such a large part in the steel industry, found no spokesmen in the labor press in 1892, and there is little record of what they thought or did.[1]

The dramatic industrial conflict at Homestead came into being as the result of a major transformation of the iron and steel industry. As the competitive, innovative steel industry disrupted and replaced iron production, the established labor-management relations of the iron industry were challenged by employers. At the Carnegie Company's Homestead mills the management, under Henry C. Frick's direction, sought to free production from the network of union wage scales and rules established in past contracts with the Amalgamated Association of Iron and Steel Workers. In 1892, as in several previous contract years, the immediate focus of dispute was the Amalgamated Association system of linking pay to tonnage produced (on a sliding scale which tied wages to steel prices).[2] Since mechanization, which increased output, resulted in higher pay on this scale, the Carnegie Company demanded rate reductions. The Amalgamated Association accepted in principle the idea that mechanization necessitated changes in tonnage rates, but bickering over the setting of new rates was usual. At Homestead, the men resisted cuts, contending that increased output was the result of faster and more continuous work, not just new machinery.[3]

There has been no scholarly work produced about Homestead which adequately unifies a narrative of events with discussion of the economic and ideological underpinnings of the strike. Instead several popular labor histories have regaled readers with the dramatic tale of the Homestead battle. They tell us how, when negotiations collapsed on June 28th, 1892, three thousand unskilled Homestead steelworkers rallied behind the Amalgamated Association, recognizing that union recognition and collective bargaining, rather than wages, had become the issue. Fearing strikebreakers, the men, led, by a forty-eight member Advisory Committee, began a series of extraordinary preparations which amounted to a seizure of civil functions in Homestead. Roads were blockaded, saloons shut down, special strike officials patrolled the town. These preparations reached their well-known climax on July 6th in a battle between gathered strikers and two barge-loads of Pinkerton guards attempting to debark on the river bank. Several hours of fighting in which many strikers and guards were injured preceded the Pinkertons' surrender to the Amalgamated men.

Three hundred Pinkertons were to gather at Ashtabula, Ohio, on the morning of July 5 and were to proceed by rail to Youngstown. From there they were to be transported at night by boat up the river to Homestead. Since it might prove il-

1. The data reported here is drawn from the author's unpublished doctoral dissertation, "American Nationality and Workers' Consciousness in Industrial Conflict, 1870–1920: Three Case Studies," (Columbia Univ., 1975), which traces changes in workingmen's usage of political symbols in a series of strikes—a number of the 1873–74 strikes in coal and iron chronicled by Herbert Gutman, the Homestead Strike, and the Great Steel Strike of 1919.

2. David Brody provides a succinct account of American iron manufacture and the early steel industry in *Steelworkers in America: The Nonunion Era* (New York, 1960), see especially 3, 8, 51–52.

3. The conflicts resulting from mechanization are described in Brody, 52; John Fitch, *The Steelworkers,* 104 (New York, 1910); Jesse S. Robinson, *The Amalgamated Association of Iron, Steel and Tin Workers,* 38 *Johns Hopkins Studies in History and Political Science,* 114 (Baltimore, 1920). Workers' reactions may be found in U.S., Congress, House of Representatives, Committee on the Judiciary, *Investigation of Homestead Troubles,* H. Rept. 2447, 52 Cong., 2nd sess., 1892–93, 87, 109; testimony of Hugh O'Donnell, Testimony of W.T. Roberts (hereafter cited as *House Report 2447*); "Statement of the Workers," *National Labor Tribune,* July 16, 1892, 4.

legal to bring an armed force into the state, the rifles, pistols, batons, and ammunition were to be shipped separately in care of the Union Supply Company. The detectives were to be armed after they were within the boundaries of Pennsylvania. Frick agreed to pay $5 per day for each man. In the meantime two barges were fitted up for the Pinkertons, one with bunks as a dormitory, the other with tables as a large refectory, and two steamboats were engaged to tow the barges.

The attempt to introduce the Pinkertons clandestinely failed. The company had evidently hoped that the recent open request for deputies had diverted the attention of the workmen from any other preparations. But the detectives were sighted at 4 o'clock in the morning by a patrol about one mile below Homestead; soon whistles sounded a general alarm throughout the town, and a crowd of men, women, and children lined the river bank.

When the barges pulled up to the company beach, where the wire-topped fence had been brought down to the low-water mark so as to cut off all access by land, and the crowd on shore saw that the Pinkertons intended landing, it tore a gap in the fence and trespassed for the first time on the mill property. The workmen warned the detectives back, but both the Pinkerton prestige and the pay were at stake. A gangplank was shoved out and several Pinkertons started down it. Someone fired a shot. Who fired is unknown, each side later proclaiming its innocence. But it is certain that the Pinkertons then fired a volley into the crowd and brought down several workers. The women and children ran out of the range of the rifles to watch the struggle, while the men barricaded themselves behind ramparts of steel, pig iron, and scrap iron, and opened fire. The Pinkertons retreated into the shelter of their barges. The steamboat which had towed the barges took on board two or three wounded detectives and steamed away, leaving the invaders without means of escape.

This battle lasted from 4 o'clock in the morning of July 6 until 5 o'clock that afternoon; it resulted in three deaths among the Pinkertons and seven among the workers, besides many wounded. The news spread, and at 3:30 P.M. President Weihe of the Amalgamated arrived to stop the bloodshed. At first the workmen were hostile to any suggestion for the release of the Pinkertons. Only after a moving speech by Hugh O'Donnell did they agree to accept a surrender of the Pinkertons, who were to be handed over to the sheriff on charges of murder. But the promise of O'Donnell and the workers was of no avail. As the Pinkertons marched unarmed from the barges to the skating rink of the town, where they were to be kept, they were attacked and badly beaten, chiefly by the women. The advisory committee, in fact, got many bruises and scars in its endeavor to shield the surrendered detectives. The crowd also seized the guns and provisions left behind and burned the barges.[4]

Soon after the battle, which drew national attention to Homestead, the Carnegie Company and the state government successfully took steps to defeat the strike. The state militia called to Homestead on July 10th put a quick end to Advisory Committee control of the town. In succeeding weeks a total of 160 indictments were brought against strikers on charges of murder, conspiracy, aggravated riot, and treason. While none of the men were ever convicted on these charges, bail funding and defense put a heavy strain on strikers'

---

4. Samuel Yellen, *American Labor Struggles*, 84–86 (New York, 1936). This extended quotation has been added to the original article.

energies. Alexander Berkman's attempted assassination of Frick on July 22nd turned public sympathy toward the company. On July 27th, the works were reopened with military protection and with 700 new men. The strikers held out, but finally on November 20th the Amalgamated Association declared the strike over.[5]

There is no doubt that workers at Homestead acted as a class. Therein lies the fame of the Homestead strike: dramatically, militantly, violently, steel workers joined together to oppose their employers and their employers' hired allies. Homestead's strikers overcame major obstacles to achieve their class solidarity. First of all, in the contract negotiations of 1892 the Carnegie Company had acted in such a way as to divide its men, agreeing to contracts for eight of the twelve Homestead mills, while setting unacceptable conditions for the remaining four mills. When the company began to close down these four mills, the men whose contracts had already been won rallied behind the affected men, giving up their security to begin a strike of all the Homestead mills. Furthermore, the Homestead strikers were able to create solidarity between skilled and unskilled, union and non-unionized men. The Amalgamated Association admitted only skilled workers. Even among these, the union's strength was limited; at the start of 1892 fewer than four hundred of the two thousand men eligible were members of the Amalgamated Association at Homestead. A spring organizing drive raised union membership to about eight hundred. But following the closing of the four mills, three thousand men turned out at a mass meeting called by the Amalgamated lodges and began the strike.[6]

The actions of Homestead's workmen rested on distinct class beliefs which they articulated in response to a pressing need to explain their action. They addressed other workers, the public, their employers, the courts and investigatory committees of the U.S. Senate and House. The workers' statements were not limited to the bread and butter issues of the immediate crisis, but linked material interests to issues of principle. Strike spokesmen needed to be eloquent in their cause, to formulate their goals convincingly, and to counter charges made by the press, employers and the courts. Convincing arguments were needed to gain and keep public sympathies; the Homestead strikers benefitted from favorable treatment by the police, storekeepers, and juries.[7] Also, an inspiring statement of goals was important to maintain solidarity among skilled and unskilled, unionized and non-union-

---

5. There are several popularized accounts of the Homestead strike. See, for example: Jeremy Brecher, *Strike* (Cambridge, 1972); Samuel Yellen, *American Labor Struggles* (New York, 1936); Henry David, "Upheaval at Homestead," in Daniel Aaron, ed., *America in Crisis* (New York, 1952). A recent book-length account is Leon Wolff, *Lockout: The Story of the Homestead Strike of 1892* (New York, 1965). For details on the events of the Homestead Strike the writer has also consulted accounts which appeared at the time in the local newspapers—the *Pittsburgh Gazette-Times, Pittsburgh Dispatch, Pittsburgh Post, Homestead Local News, National Labor Tribune,* two contemporary popular accounts of the strike—Myron Stowell, *Fort Frick: Or the Siege of the Homestead* (Pittsburgh, 1893) and A.G. Burgoyne, *Homestead: A Complete History of the Struggle of July 1892* (Pittsburgh, 1893), and a scholarly report published soon after the events of 1892, E.W. Bemis, "The Homestead Strike," 2 *Journal of Political Economy,* 369–396 (1894).

6. There is some indication too of cooperation between English-speaking and "foreign" men. Strike leaders mentioned a "brigade" of eight hundred "Slavs and Hungarians" held in reserve in the watch for strikebreakers. See Testimony of W.T. Roberts, Senate Committee on the Employment of Armed Bodies of Men for Private Purposes, Report 1280, 52nd Cong., 2nd sess., 1892–93, 211 (hereafter cited as *Senate Report 1280*).

7. Herbert Gutman has emphasized the importance of local support for strikers in several small industrial towns during the latter 19th century. See for example, "Class, Status and Community Power in 19th Century American Industrial Cities—Paterson, New Jersey: A Case Study," in Fred Jaher, ed., *Age of Industrialism in America* (New York, 1968); "An Iron Workers' Strike in the Ohio Valley 1873–74," 68 *Ohio Historical Quarterly* 353–370 (1959); "Two Lockouts in Pennsylvania 1873–74," 83 *Pennsylvania Magazine of History and Biography,* 307–326 (1959).

ized, foreign and native workers. It was equally desirable to persuade other workmen of the importance of their fight, for moral and financial support and to keep strikebreakers away. During the confrontation at Homestead, workers thus sought to express their fears and grievances effectively.

Workers at Homestead expressed themselves in republican ideology, a set of ideas with long antecedents in American history. Early notions of American national identity drew heavily on British themes and were influenced as well by European Jacobinism. Republicanism was elaborated through Jeffersonian ideals, further evolved in Jacksonian America, and certainly featured prominently in the altered form of Civil War Republicanism. Interpretations of Republicanism were evident in the antimonopoly, Greenback, and cooperative movements as well. Throughout the nineteenth century in America, the discussion of national virtues and values was the common language of public rhetoric. Workers at Homestead used republican rhetoric in a distinctive way, linking unionism to the preservation of American national values. The cause of the Homestead strike, workers asserted, was the company's determination to defy certain American values—liberty, rights, independence, the rule of law. In so doing, the company posed a threat to the American political system. When they described their situation, workers concentrated primarily upon the Carnegie Company and upon Frick as their enemies. When they looked beyond these immediate actors, which labor editors seem to have done more frequently than the strikers themselves, they saw a growing corporate "plutocracy," a privileged class of corporations. Against this threat they set themselves, speaking not as workers alone, but in the name of the American citizenry as a whole.

The theme of republicanism may be seen in statements by a wide variety of Homestead workers and their supporters. A statement issued by Homestead strikers explained their goal as "those rights which are the principles of organized labor and which are inseparable from their citizenship." For the *National Labor Tribune,* the official organ of the Amalgamated Association, the Homestead struggle was "the Frick conspiracy against workmen's rights and the institutions of freedom"; it was a "contest for the rights of labor."[8] Rank and file workers used similar language. For example, striking mechanics and laborers issued resolutions after a meeting to which none of the skilled men were admitted. In the statement, they pledged to strike with the Amalgamated Association to the end, and declared "that we consider it an injustice to the mechanical department and day laborers and an insult to their manhood to ask them to work under guard, as we believe that in this free land, all men should be free."[9]

An amalgamation of the language of class and an American political vocabulary is notable in these statements. Conflict between the company and its workers appears as a denial of "rights" to labor or workmen. The cause of unionism is identified with the concept of the rights of citizenship.

Various analogies elaborated the idea that the Carnegie Co. wished to deny its men their rights as American citizens, and, in so doing, posed a threat to vital American institutions. The actions taken by the company were often compared to conditions of serfdom and slavery. For example, the Advisory Committee, in an appeal issued to the trades unions of the United States, began,

---

8. Statement of Homestead Employees to the *Pittsburgh Dispatch,* submitted by George Rylands, a strike leader, as part of his testimony before the House investigating committee, *House Report 2447,* 185; *National Labor Tribune,* Sept. 3, 1892, 1, July 23, 1892, 1 (hereafter cited as *NLT*).

9. *Pittsburgh Post,* July 18, 1892, 1.

FELLOW WORKMEN: We are constrained by the force of circumstances to lay before you a matter of vital importance, not alone to us, but one which threatens, if successful, to undermine every trade organization in the United States, and reduce us to the system of serfdom which was the lot of our forefathers in the middle ages.

The *National Labor Tribune* took up historical analogies with relish, raising the question of the growth of aristocracy in America. "The great republic," the editors declared,

is rapidly taking on impositions upon the public that the free Briton would not submit to, and it is getting up a plutocracy which promises to be a stand-off to the British aristocracy, while American corporations form now a privileged class, with privileges hardly less than those held in monarchies, beside which Britain is a free and untrammeled state.[10]

Slavery was also a favored theme. The Vice President of the Amalgamated Association was present at a public meeting of strikers in Homestead on October 1st, and urged them to continue the fight:

The battle is with you; see that you win it. If you lose such conditions as never confronted the slaves in the South will be yours.[11]

The imagery of "citizens' rights" illustrated above enjoyed a widespread appeal; it was by no means limited to steelworkers, to Homestead, or to the early 1890s. This rhetoric was used as early as the 1830s and was still in use, in a much altered form as late as the World War I period, by workers in a variety of crafts and industries. It was used in internal discussions as well as in addressing the public.[12] Evidence that the identification of "citizenship" and unionism was widespread among workers at the time may be found in letters and resolutions of support sent to Homestead by organized workers of different trades and from rather distant parts of the country. Many of these were printed in the *National Labor Tribune*. For example, one Alabama correspondent wrote that

the lockout was originated with a determination to tie the hands of the laboring men of this great, free American country and make a degraded slave with loss of his liberty as a free citizen and voter. It is a bold strike for despotism. (If these things continue) it will be a matter of a short time till American liberty will only be known as a thing of the past.

A mass meeting of miners agreed that the Carnegie Co. was "arrogating to themselves at pleasure of the functions of the state ... outrageously ... to challenge the dignity of our common citizenship." They pledged their support for the Homestead strikers in their

---

10. Quoted in Stowell, 150–151; *NLT*, Aug. 27, 1892, 1.

11. Speech quoted in *Pittsburgh Dispatch*, Oct., 1892, 2.

12. Reading John R. Commons' documentary history, for example, one learns that in their New York trial of 1836, striking tailors convicted of conspiracy denounced the verdict as "utterly at variance with the spirit and genius of our Republican government." The locked-out Johnstown coal miners studied by Gutman, attacked their employers for asking workers "to give up all their citizen rights and make the Cambria Coal and Iron Company lords and rulers over them." In 1919, striking steelworkers accused the steel companies of engaging in "un-American efforts *to* impose the iron will of the autocrat upon their employees." Quoted in John R. Commons, *Documentary History of American Industrial Society* (New York, 1958), vol. 5, 317–319; Herbert Gutman, "Two Lockouts in Pennsylvania, 1873–1874," 320; David Brody, *Labor in Crisis: The Steel Strike of 1919*, 114 (Philadelphia and New York, 1965). Phillip Foner's recent collection, *American Labor Songs of the Nineteenth Century* (Evanston, IL, 1976) records many popular songs which revolve around these same themes. For example, an 1892 version of "When Johnny Comes Marching Home" declaimed, "When labor has come to its own again, Hurrah! Hurrah! We'll live in a real Republic then, Hurrah! Hurrah!"

"struggle for principle and bread." Other groups sent resolutions of support for the strikers in their "endeavor to free themselves and their families from serfdom and despotism" and in the "defense of your just rights."[13]

At Homestead, the idea that the Carnegie Co. posed a threat to American political liberties and to its workmen's independence was developed in an attack on employer's disrespect for the law. Obedience to American law and the proper uses of civil authority became major topics of discussion during the strike. The strikers identified themselves as defending the nation by upholding the law, and accused their employers of defying the laws of the nation. This concern was manifested before the battle with the Pinkertons, but that confrontation put an even greater emphasis on the conflict as a civil, rather than an industrial struggle. On July 9th, the *Homestead Local News* listed the names of workers killed in the battle. The list was titled, "VICTIMS OF A CONFLICT OF WORKINGMEN, NOT WITH THE LAWFUL AUTHORITIES, BUT WITH THE HIRED FORCES OF A GREAT CORPORATION." Later analyses pointed to Frick's disregard of civil authority. For example, the *National Labor Tribune* editorialized in this vein:

> In the first place the Carnegie Company failed to more than touch on the outskirts of the civil law when it applied to the sheriff. Its counsel must have known and probably Chairman Frick knew that in a number of strikes of recent years at Pittsburgh the courts were applied to for injunctions or preliminary restraining orders upon the strikers, and to the credit of the workmen such writ has always been respected. Chairman Frick, however, preferred to take the law into his own hands, and, ignoring the statute of Pennsylvania, now some fifty-six years on the books and in practice committed a criminal act which resulted in the killing and wounding of many men.

An Amalgamated Association lodge wrote the *National Labor Tribune* expressing its support of the strikers and declared,

> it is the sense of our membership and the public at large that it is an outrage on our citizenship and our American manhood for firms to ignore our regularly commissioned officers of the law, and resort to such unprincipled and un-American methods as has been used in this case.[14]

In September, charges for treason against the State of Pennsylvania were brought (under an 1860 statute) against thirty-five Amalgamated men by Pennsylvania's chief justice. These charges spurred renewed debate over the legitimacy of the strikers' and the company's actions. Steelworkers' spokesmen tended to turn the charges of treason around, and apply them to employers: "If there is any treason in connection with the Homestead affair, Frick himself is the guilty party," argued one correspondent to the *National Labor Tribune*. The charges "capped the climax" of the "misuse of civil authority" by the Carnegie Company, that paper charged. If anyone was levying war against the state, the Carnegie Company had done so by its importation of armed men, not the strikers. Frick arranged with Pinkerton

---

13. Manager of the Humming Bird, Gate City, Alabama, to the editor, July 23, 1892, *NLT,* July 30, 1892, 4; Miners of Keystone Hill to the editor, July 14, 1892, *NLT,* July 23, 1892, 5; Major Jones and T. Bentham, Shawnee, Ohio, to the editor (enclosing resolutions adopted at a "mass meeting" of the citizens), *ibid.,*4; Scioto Lodge No. 65, Portsmouth, Ohio, to the Homestead Lodges of the A.A. of I. & S.W., July 12, 1892, *NLT,* July 16, 1892, 4.

14. *Homestead Local News,* July 9, 1892, 2; *NLT,* July 23, 1892, 1; Blue Valley Lodge No. 2, Sheffield, Mo., to the editor, *NLT,* July 30, 1892, 4.

to invade the peace of Pennsylvania with an armed band of 300 men, which armed force the Carnegie Company mustered in the face of state and federal authority. We have our doubts whether this constitutes treason, but there can be no doubt that it comes much closer to that offense than does the allegation of the complaint made at the instigation of the Carnegie Company on September 30.[15]

Looking back upon the political rhetoric of Homestead, one may discern a basic, underlying issue, often expressed in terms of citizens' rights and the rule of law, but conceptually distinct. Homestead's workmen opposed the subordination of the wage laborer to capital. They argued that the company wished to do away with the union in order to force its employees into a state of dependence. Fear of dependence was sometimes directly expressed. For example, one strike leader, William T. Roberts, testified before the Senate Committee that

We look upon the hiring of Pinkerton forces as an unjust and unlawful way of forcing us into submission to the will of people who seem disposed at all times to take advantage of us.

If the struggle were lost, the *National Labor Tribune* declared,

The workmen of all the mills, union and non-union, would be in a position of positive dependence on the 'beck and nod' of their employers, to take what would be given them humbly, and thank the Lord if they and their families have the bare necessities of life as those necessities were understood fifty years ago.

By denying its employees the right to combine, the company wished to

force uncomplaining submission to every imposition that it might be desired to introduce ... in place of the mutual understanding and respectful recognition of the position of each by the other there was to be substituted a management that would let nothing interfere with its will.[16]

The importance to workers of the issue of economic subjection may be seen in the great emotion with which they spoke of it. A feeling of righteous indignation colored their letters and resolutions. As we have seen above, they construed the actions of the Carnegie Company as "insults," as injustices, as attempts to "challenge the dignity" of their "citizenship," to reduce them to slavery. In addition, workers often asserted a further, psychological loss, namely that Company actions "threatened" or "insulted" their manhood, assaulting their very pride and self-respect as independent men. For example, this idea was expounded by several writers in connection with a plan for refusing Carnegie charitable gifts. The Pittsburgh Typographical Union first proposed that

the officers of our city and members of our councils ... recall the acceptance of the recent gift of a public library to the 'workingmen' of this city, ... that we declare that the honest workmen of Pittsburgh cannot, without loss of manhood and self-respect, accept, even in name, a gift that has been purchased in the slightest part by the blood of our fellow workmen.

---

15. D.H. Johnson, Sharon, Pa., to the editor, Oct. 3, 1892, *NLT,* Oct. 8, 1892, 5; "Is Treason A Trump Card," *NLT,* Oct. 8, 1892, 1.

16. *Senate Report 1280,* 207; *NLT,* July 23, 1892, 12; Nov. 26, 1892, 4. There are interesting parallels to this situation in a rather different context, the strike of gypsum workers studied by Alvin Gouldner in 1950. Gouldner also analyzed underlying grievances which were not directly expressed in strike demands. He found that a rationalization of production which required an end to customary privileges was seen by workers as a demeaning threat to their independent status. Gouldner's workers even attacked their new supervisors as "slave drivers" and claimed they were treated as "niggers," as "slaves." Alvin Gouldner, *Wildcat Strike* (Yellow Springs, OH, 1954), see esp. 72–76.

The plan was swiftly taken up by other groups, one of which wrote to the *National Labor Tribune* suggesting that

> justice be done to organized labor before charitable bequests be made to large cities, and that such gifts be rejected as an insult to American manhood.[17]

In expressing their fear of economic dependence Homestead's workmen were implicitly making a point about class relations, about the powerlessness of the worker confronting his employer without a union to back him up. They saw unionism as the force capable of creating and preserving for the worker a status consistent with American ideals of citizenship and independence. Those values were to be achieved by collective action. Unlike their employers, Homestead's workers did not equate independence and individualism, but rather, acted collectively to preserve their liberty by a vigorous defense of unionism.

Thus, in describing their fear of actuation in which employers were overwhelmingly powerful, steelworkers at Homestead employed republican notions of citizenship and American manhood. They crystallized their desires in two ideals of independent status, both focused on the worker situated in the civil community, not his industrial setting. As we have seen, one of these ideals was the worker as independent citizen. The second ideal to which Homestead's workers had frequent reference was that of the worker as homeowner.

Discussions by Homestead strikers often featured a glorification of domestic property. Strikers spoke passionately about the Homestead conflict as a case of homeowner-citizens defending their dwelling place. Homestead's workmen claimed a vested right to live and work in the town because they had laboriously made homes there. They objected to employer control over hiring and wages as undermining domestic security. This theme appears clearly in one of the books about Homestead published locally soon after the strike. The author observed that the people of Homestead had a feeling of considerable ownership in the place:

> Many of them had bought and paid for their homes and were pillars of the borough government. Some were still paying for their dwellings.... It was clearly impossible that men of substance, heads of families, solid citizens of a prosperous municipality could be rooted up, as it were, out of the soil in which they were so firmly planted and beaten to earth by the creature of their labor.[18]

The "defense of home" was also invoked to justify workers' part in the battle with the Pinkertons. To this end, the hated Pinkertons were described as armed invaders stealing by night onto Pennsylvania shores to attack citizens defending their homes. Thus, the Pittsburgh Typographical Union condemned the act in which

> hireling offscourings of our country were mustered and armed to shoot down upright, honorable and peaceful citizens who were standing for their rights and their homes.

Two days after the battle Hugh O'Donnell told the *Pittsburgh Dispatch* that

> our interests are like Mr. Carnegie's here; our homes, our families are here also, and only the presence of unfriendly invaders will force us into a defense position.

Later, he wrote Whitelaw Reid, the Republican candidate for Vice President, in a letter asking his intervention to settle the strike, that

---

17. Resolution of the Typographical Union No. 7, July 10, 1892, *NLT,* July 16, 1892, 4; B.F. Boggess, President, Brotherhood of Painters and Renovators, Louisville, Ky., July 14, 1892, *NLT,* July 23, 1892, 4.

18. Burgoyne, 13.

a majority of the present employees own their own homes. All their interests centre there, and they will never surrender them without the most determined effort.... The trouble will, in my judgment, only begin in earnest when the mills are set going by the men who will take the place of the old employees.... It is not desirable ... that the men who have by years of patient toil acquired a little homestead should be cut off from their employment if it can be prevented in any honorable way.[19]

Similarly, William T. Roberts explained the workers' motivation at Homestead to the Senate investigating committee. He said:

Now the men at Homestead were a peculiar condition. The most of them had started to build their own little homes. Some of them had them about half paid for under the conditions that existed prior to this time. They were allowed to enjoy the privilege of belonging to their association, and they also knew from experience that their organization was the only thing, in the first place, that enabled them to accumulate sufficient to build their homes, ... and then to be denied the privilege of belonging to an organization ... to be forced into accepting a reduction that they didn't think was right or just at that time, and them to be confronted with a gang of loafers and cutthroats from all over the country, coming there, as they thought, to take their jobs, why they naturally wanted to go down and defend their homes and property and their lives, with force, if necessary.[20]

Some evidence indicates that the "defense of home" was a theme genuinely stirring to the steelworkers of Homestead, and not merely an appeal made by their leaders to the sentimental temperament of the time. The theme figured prominently in the most popular song about the Homestead strike, "A Fight for Home and Honor at Homestead, Pa.," published in Chicago on July 16th, 1892. The song "was sung everywhere and old-timers still sing it when a nostalgic mood takes possession of them." Jacob Evansohn, a Pittsburgh folk-song researcher, heard it sung by a retired steelworker, John Schmitt, who learned it during the strike when he was sixteen. The song, one of the most eloquent presentations of the strikers' case, reflects both the older ideal of citizen's rights and liberty and a new emphasis on the protection of homes:

We are asking one another as we pass the time of day,
Why workingmen resort to arms to get their proper pay,
And why our labor unions they must no be recognized,
Whilst the actions of a syndicate must not be criticized.
Now the troubles down at Homestead were brought about this way,
When a grasping corporation had the audacity to say:

19. *N LT,* July 16, 1892, 4; *Pittsburgh Dispatch,* July 8, 1892, 1; Hugh O'Donnell to Whitelaw Reid, July 16, 1892, quoted in Bemis, 384.

20. Testimony of William T. Roberts, *Senate Report 1280,* 210–211. Claims by labor spokesmen that a "majority" of Homestead's steelworkers owned their own homes are difficult to credit, but a more conservative estimate, offered by the American Federation of Labor, the Amalgamated Association and the Advisory Committee, computed that 8–10% of the Homestead workers owned their homes outright, while another 15% had homes under mortgage. Assuming these were all skilled workers, the figure compares favorably with the 11% of skilled workers reported by Thernstrom as owning taxable property (largely real estate) in Boston in 1880, and it is roughly similar to the rates of property-holding for skilled iron workers reported by Daniel Walkowitz for Troy, New York in 1860. Statement by AFL, Amalgamated Association and Advisory Committee officers to the *NLT,* Aug. 20, 1892, 4; Thernstrom's figures are from *The Other Bostonians,* 299 (Cambridge, MA, 1973); Daniel Walkowitz, "Statistics and the Writing of Working Class History: A Statistical Portrait of the Iron Workers of Troy, New York 1860–1880," 15 *Labor History,* 449 (1974).

"You must all renounce your union and forswear your liberty
And we will give you a chance to live and die in slavery."
Now this sturdy band of workingmen started out at the break of day
Determination in their faces which plainly meant to say:
"No one can come and take our homes for which we have toiled
    so long,
No one can come and take our places—no, here's where we belong!"

When a lot of bum detectives came without authority,
Like thieves at night when decent men were sleeping peacefully—
Can you wonder why all honest hearts with indignation burn,
And why the slimy worm that treads the earth when trod upon will turn?
When they locked out men at Homestead so they were face to face
With a lot of bum detectives and they knew it was their place
To protect their homes and families, and this was neatly done,
And the public will reward them for the victories they won.[21]

Homestead's workmen thus made their claims to respect and independence not only as citizens of the nation, but as citizens of the local community. We must note however that in stressing their residence in Homestead, the strikers were laying claim to citizenship in a particular kind of town. Theirs was not a claim to inclusion in a middle-class dominated community. Homestead was very much a working-class town. Feelings of belonging to the town may perhaps be construed as expressing a kind of class solidarity.

There are many indications that a pronounced degree of working-class domination existed in Homestead. The most striking evidence of workers' local power is the ease with which the town was taken over by the strikers, and the way government by the Advisory Committee was substituted for the legal town government. This was only possible because no one in the town with any substantial power was opposed to the action.

The population of Homestead was homogeneously working-class. Eleven thousand people lived in the town; 3800 worked in the mill. Even assuming that some steelworkers lived outside the borough, and that many of the "slav" workers had no families with them, almost every man in the town must have worked at the mill. Because of the town's late foundation and rapid growth, there was no entrenched local elite of landowners, bankers, professionals, etc. In the absence of a resident notability with longstanding control of town affairs, the steelworkers administered the town and determined its social character. The presence of the Amalgamated Association, a strong union, further contributed to worker influence in the town. Steelworkers' importance in the eyes of local tradespeople was assured by their substantial purchasing power and the company did little in this period to counter worker influence. Carnegie was not interested in plans of elaborate paternalism. He donated libraries and the company ran a small savings and mortgage project for the benefit of its employees, and beyond that he did not go. Management in this period was preoccupied with production, and not with the social relations in the town in which production took place.

Thus, John McLuckie, an assistant roller, and member of the Advisory Committee, was Homestead's Burgess (or mayor). The chairman of the police committee, empowered to act as chief of police in any trouble, was David Lynch, a heater, and also a leader of the

---

21. George Swetnam, "Songs of a Strike," *Pittsburgh Press*, Feb. 5, 1967; Jacob A. Evansohn, "Folk Songs of An Industrial City," in George Korson, ed., *Pennsylvania Songs and Legends*, 445–6 (Philadelphia, 1949).

Amalgamated Association. The borough police were also loyal to the strikers. Communal working-class institutions in Homestead gave workers power and perhaps gave the place added significance in strikers' minds.

The importance of "home and Homestead" as a symbol in the strike must also be evaluated in relation to the symbols of craft and work, or their lack. Twenty years earlier, the symbol of home had not figured so strongly in iron and steelworkers discussions. At that time, workers seemed to fasten upon their right to their particular jobs, rather than to a special place of residence.[22] At Homestead in 1892, the sense of possession in jobs stemming from a craft identity was being replaced by a sense of possession in the *place*, a commitment to the town where workers hoped to build the good life of which their jobs were a necessary part. It was perhaps for this reason that the "defense of home" was a symbol with wide appeal despite the fact that not all workers actually owned their homes. The ties of domesticity in a particular locale had wider play than did home ownership.

Changing industrial conditions and a restructuring of the rewards available to steelworkers in industry underlay the new importance of domestic property as a symbol at Homestead in 1892. As the older craft system of iron production was undermined at Homestead, and skilled workers' relative autonomy receded, attitudes toward work also changed. New machinery held out to workers the lure of increased production, which brought with it higher wages on tonnage scales. But the same union rules which supported the craft system of worker-regulated production also limited output; they were increasingly ignored by steelworkers. The new technology offered the men the attractions of higher consumption at the expense of the maintenance of craft regulations.

However, it would be a great mistake to see at Homestead a simple trade-off of craft autonomy for consumerism. While Homestead's workers were willing to modify the union rules which in the past had codified a degree of on-the-job worker control, they still remained very much concerned with wider issues of control. As we have seen, workers' frequent discussion of their dignity and rights as citizens flowed from an intense desire to escape subjection to employers' power. Home life was the focus of desires for a higher standard of living, which in this case served to undercut loyalty to restrictive craft practices. But it must be noted that the home was also a symbol of autonomy, of resistance to the insecurity and indignity of economic dependence. There were conflicting pressures at work. It seems likely that Homestead's strikers were not particularly concerned to defend a concrete set of work rules. Rather, they took their stand in defense of the union, which represented for them the principle of class control over access to jobs and production. Union recognition and union contracts meant respectful treatment and security as workers and as residents of Homestead.[23]

Homestead's strikers forged a radical ideology: a republicanism which opposed wage labor, which viewed home ownership and the independent status of citizenship as collective goals to be achieved through unionism. Steelworkers at Homestead thus expressed genuine work-

---

22. *See* Schneider, chapter 4.

23. Richard Sennett and Jonathan Cobb, in *The Hidden Injuries of Class* (New York, 1972) advance a similar analysis of the home as a symbol of autonomy for today's suburban workers. They discuss interview material with workers who seem to see their homes as an independent refuge from the demeaning and dependent character of their working-class jobs. Clearly, I am here arguing for a broader interpretation of the crisis of craft control that that provided by Katherine Stone. *See*, for example, her article, "The Origins of Job Structures in the Steel Industry," *Radical America*, 7 (Nov.–Dec., 1973). Stone refers extensively to an unpublished paper by David Montgomery, "Trade Union Practice and the Origins of Syndicalist Theory in the United States." A later published article by Montgomery, "Workers' Control of Machine Production in the Nineteenth Century," *Labor History*, 17 (Fall, 1976), deals with similar questions of workers' job control and the institution of scientific management.

ing-class perceptions in the language of republicanism, perceptions of a sense of possession in their town and jobs, of opposition to employers, of unions as a defense against oppression and indignity. These perceptions took concrete form in class actions. The national symbols of republicanism were thus used to create a radical vocabulary of class analysis.

But the strikers at Homestead recognized only some aspects of their oppression. Republicanism expressed what they did not perceive as well as what they did. As a result, the strikers' systems of beliefs, while invoked in a confrontation, functioned as well to aid in circumscribing the bounds of class conflict. This was particularly true with regard to steelworkers' perceptions of the national government. During the strike, Homestead's workers claimed a conservative position, protecting citizens' rights and legitimate authority against destructive actions by employers. Taking this stand, workers identified American government as the embodiment of national ideals. They saw government as a neutral force, not allied with any class, which acted to safeguard the interests of all the people. Adopting the role of the conservers of the true national values and the purity of government, steelworkers committed themselves to support of government agencies. If employers were to be the subversives, the workers must, of necessity, be the guardians of loyalty, and as such, could not criticize the government nor picture it as the agent of any class.

The moderating influence exercised by workers' identification with legitimate authority is particularly apparent in the story of the militia at Homestead. Having made obedience to civil authority the focus of their attacks on the Carnegie Company, the strikers were faced with a dilemma when the governor ordered the state militia to Homestead. They had justified their battle with Pinkertons as resistance to illegitimate power; but how could they justify resisting the state guard? It is apparent from records of strikers' debates that at least some strikers wished to try. At a meeting of striking workers, some men pointed out that the militia would defeat the strike, and called for forceful action against the troops. Moderate leaders successfully opposed this strategy. They argued that the militia represented the people of Pennsylvania, and could not be treated as enemies. If treated as friends, they could not bring harm to the strike. In this fashion, the insurrectionary potential of the strike was restrained by invocation of a commitment to legitimate government and a conviction of its neutrality and justice.[24] Thus, since Homestead's workers equated themselves with the American people and the actions of the state with their own goals, they were not willing to continue their resistance once the state government entered the confrontation. This led directly to their defeat.

This article has analyzed a particular case history of labor conflict. I have sought to portray the Homestead strike in a unified social context, that is, as class action and ideology in its socio-economic setting.

In order to understand the motives and goals of the Homestead strikers, it is necessary to see these men not simply as workers, but as participants in a variety of social contexts: as communities of workers in craft, union and shop, as residents of the working-class town of Homestead, and certainly as citizens of the nation as well. Steelworkers' experience as workers pushed them toward confrontation with their employers. Their political socialization as American citizens shaped their perceptions of class conflict and in some ways constrained it.

The ideal of unionism allowed them to see the national ideals of citizenship and their collective economic interests as inseparable. To force this working class radicalism into an abstract, dualistic mold is to shatter it, losing a distinctive and significant part of American working-class history.

---

24. Reported in Stowell, 115; Burgoyne, 111; *Pittsburgh Post*, July 12, 1892, 1.

III

Industrial Unions, The Pullman Strike, Injunctions, and *In Re Debs* (1895)

The Utopian Company Town, Pullman, Illinois.

The Debs Revolution

*Sidney Lens**

There have been no revolutions in the United States since the first one in 1776. The closest America has come to revolution has been in the labor wars, each one of which has been, in a sense, a revolution-in-microcosm. The strikers in these industrial flare-ups confronted not only the power of their employers but, ultimately, that of the State — the government, courts, police, militia. To succeed, they had to check or neutralize the administrative machinery of government, and in the process there was always the possibility of a widening and escalating of the conflict to a point where it might border on insurrection.

---

* This narrative of the strike is taken from, Sidney Lens, *The Labor Wars: From the Molly Maguires to the Sitdowns*, 88–126 *passim*. (New York: Doubleday & Co, Inc., 1973).

No event illustrates this point more vividly than the Pullman Strike of 1894, or, as it was called by some, the "Debs Rebellion." Each side escalated the war until it was only steps away from an actual revolution—and an actual counterrevolution. On one hand, a relatively small strike of 5,500 men in a single town became a nationwide strike in one industry and almost evolved into a nationwide strike in all industries. On the other hand a single employer was given organized aid by a gargantuan employer association, and through it the fulsome assistance of the federal government, its Army, Attorney General, and courts.

"The Pullman strike," writes Professor Selig Perlman, "marks an era in the American labor movement because it was the only attempt ever made in America of a revolutionary strike on the continental European model. The strikers tried to throw against the associated railways and indeed against the entire existing social order the full force of a revolutionary labor solidarity embracing the entire American wage-earning class brought to the point of exasperation by unemployment, wage reductions and misery ..."

The American Railway Union was an instant success. As a fledgling just a few months old it conducted an eighteen day strike against James J. Hill's Great Northern Railroad and forced the company to restore almost the entire amount of three wage cuts—$16 a month. "That a corporation of so gigantic proportions," said the Salt Lake *Tribune,* "had to yield so quickly to their men indicates that the day has already come when the voice of united labor has to be heard in the matter of wages." Victory against a rail system with 2,500 miles of track, as well as 9,000·employees, was so remarkable, especially in a depression period, that the ARU gained recruits at the rate of 2,000 a day. Within a year it had grown to 465 lodges and 150,000 members—not much smaller than the AFL at that time, and considerably larger than all the old Brotherhoods combined.

In 1880, when it became necessary to build a larger factory, Pullman decided to construct a "model" community for his workshops and workers that, like his sleeping cars, would be the talk of the universe. It would be a town, said a company brochure, where "all that is ugly and discordant and demoralizing is eliminated, and all that inspires to self-respect is generously provided." If it were not entirely eleemosynary—Pullman expected to earn a 6 per cent profit, in fair weather or foul, on its tenements, stores and other facilities—it was to be "so attractive as to cause the best class of mechanics" to seek it out as a place of employment. Not surprisingly, the town would be called Pullman.

The Pullman Palace Car Company operated on the simplistic thesis of all the great corporations of the day that it was permissible to haul in heavy profits in good times, without sharing them with workers, but mandatory to lower wage rates in bad times. Since its formation in 1867 (capitalized at approximately a million dollars) the company had always paid its stockholders a dividend of at least 8 per cent, in addition to which it earned large sums of undivided profits. As of 1894, with a total capitalization of $36 million, the firm had $25 million more in surpluses (which it distributed four years later, incidentally, in the form of a 50 per cent stock dividend and a 20 per cent cash dividend, in addition to the regular one of 8 per cent). Profits for 1892 and 1893, the two years before the strike, were so good they almost approximated the total wage bill. Dividends in 1892 amounted to $2.3 million, plus $3.3 million in undivided profit. Dividends in 1893 came to $2.5 million, with $4 million more in undivided profits, or a total of $6.5 million. The full wage bill for 5,500 workers for the year ending July 31, 1893 was less than a million dollars higher—$7.3 million—and for the year ending July 31, 1894 it was $4.5 million as against $2.9 million in dividends. Admittedly there was a sharp cutback in the building of new sleeping cars after the panic of 1893 got under way, but there was plenty of money in the Pullman exchequer to cushion the shock without cutting wages. Why, asked the *Daily Republican* of Springfield, Massachusetts, could not Pullman "dip back into the surplus of $4,000,000 made in the single previous year and keep up the wages of employees who are so carefully housed and otherwise looked after as so many dependents at Pullman?"

But in the summer of 1893 Pullman and his vice-president, Thomas H. Wickes, began a dual squeeze on their employees. The work force in the model town was trimmed to 3,100 men, and earnings of the remaining workers severely sliced. A table published by Stanley Buder in his book *Pullman* shows the number of journeyman mechanics falling from 2,625 in April 1893 to 1,950 a year later, and average monthly earnings from $59.33 to $40.07 — approximately a one-third loss. Average monthly income in the largest department, car-builders, fell from $60.71 to $39.52; in the second largest, painters, from $59.23 to $44.60. While the average wage cut for all American manufacturing that depression year was 12 per cent, at Pullman's it was 28 per cent — from $51.00 a month to $36.50. Yet, though he cut staff and wages, the car king refused categorically to reduce rents on his tenements or the charges for his utilities.

Lashed from a number of directions, workers fell behind in rent payments in the amount of $70,000. Reverend Carwardine cited the cases of three workers, who after deductions from their semi-monthly earnings, had pay checks of two cents, seven cents and forty-seven cents respectively. All refused to cash their largesse, one stating indignantly: "If Mr. Pullman needs the 47 cents worse than I do, let him have it." Generally, reported Carwardine, pastor of the Pullman Methodist-Episcopal Church, the workers "had only from one to six dollars or so on which to live for two weeks." Theoretically employees could have moved to nearby Kensington or Roseland, where rentals were a fifth to a quarter lower, but in practice the company gave first choice in employment to its own tenants, just as in the coal fields and other company towns. In the stark winter of 1893–94, then, the model town of Pullman was a town of extreme hardship, with children going hungry and laborers not knowing where their next meals were coming from. The mood of the Pullman workers was grim as they formed a central strike committee and placed a cordon of three hundred men around the plant. "We do not expect the company to concede our demands," said their leader, Heathcoate. "We do not know what the outcome will be, and in fact we do not much care. We do know that we are working for less wages than will maintain ourselves and families in the necessaries of life, and on that proposition we refuse to work any longer."

[The Pullman workers joined the ARU and succeeded in persuading the ARU convention to act in sympathy.] The boycott against Pullman vehicles began slowly. On the appointed day trains ran normally, palace cars still coupled to them. At 9 P.M. George Pullman visited the Twelfth Street Station of Illinois Central to watch the *Diamond Special* take off for St. Louis and was elated to see that the boycott was "ineffective." The next shift of switchmen, however, refused to handle the sleepers, and the day crew that followed did likewise. As anticipated, management reacted by firing those who would not switch the Pullman cars, and fellow workers in turn walked off the job. In a nonce 3,500 Illinois Central employees were out of work, and the boycott-strike had spread to fourteen other roads. After two days there were 18,000 railroaders on strike, on the third day 40,000, and on the fourth 125,000. With incredible speed the stoppage had immobilized such giants as the Burlington, Santa Fe, Northwestern and Illinois Central, had closed down the Union Stock Yards and Transit Company in Chicago, had halted the Southern Pacific and Northern Pacific out West, and had caused suspension or curtailment of traffic from the Far West to upper New York. According to the New York *Tribune* of July 3 there were 150,000 men involved in the first truly national strike in U.S. history. In the great expanse from Chicago to the Golden Gate only the Great Northern was able to maintain anything remotely resembling a normal train schedule. Despite open opposition by the old brotherhood leaders, such as P.M. Arthur of the Engineers, who threatened his members with expulsion and discharge, the response to Debs's appeal had far exceeded expectations.

For a strike that engulfed twenty-seven states and territories it produced an unusually small amount of lawlessness in its early stages, particularly and surprisingly, perhaps, in Chicago. Eventually twenty-five proletarians would be killed and sixty seriously injured nationwide, but the first outbreaks were, given the scale of protest, negligible.

What tipped the scales in this stalemate—and aroused popular fury—was the federal government and its actions. It turned on the strikers with a vindictiveness never before seen on the American labor front. President Cleveland's administration identified so thoroughly with the Managers' point of view that it was impossible to tell where the activities of one left off and the other began. It was as if the General Managers Association knew in advance that when its own resources were exhausted it would automatically be able to be resupplied by those of the Attorney-General, the courts, and the troops.

An injunction is a tricky legal gadget whose origins trace back to English law. Ordinarily a man is punished for a crime *after* he has violated a statute. But an injunction is an order which restrains him from committing an allegedly illegal act in advance. The presumption is that it would be too late to punish him afterward, since *irreparable* damage already would have been done. The first important use of such a device in labor disputes was around 1880, involving a financially strapped railroad being reorganized by a court-appointed receiver. The receiver complained that the walkout placed the property entrusted to him in jeopardy and an equity judge promptly issued an order restraining the walkout. Those who violated it did not have to be convicted as guilty by a jury of their peers, but were adjudged guilty of contempt by the judge alone, and packed off to prison without trial. "The whole transaction from strike to jail," writes legal expert Charles O. Gregory, "could be counted in hours rather than in the weeks and months required in actions at law."

The injunction as a handy legal tool was used only sparingly against unions until the Pullman strike, but the triumvirate of Olney, Walker, and the Managers' now adopted it as their primary strikebreaking weapon. On July 2 the Chicago *Tribune* appeared with the headline: Strike Is Now War. On the same day, Walker and Milchrist applied for an injunction, using the strange argument that the strike was a violation of the Sherman Anti-Trust Act and the Interstate Commerce Act—two anti-monopoly bills passed on the initiative of labor and the farmers to curb big business, not unions. Olney never used these laws against big business, but by means of sophistry, his emissaries twisted them to apply to the Pullman strike, which, it was said, constituted a conspiracy "in restraint of trade." The application for an injunction was immediately granted by federal judges Peter S. Grosscup—who weeks before had stated that "the growth of labor must be checked by law"—and William A. Woods—who was much beholden to the railroads for past favors. Without hearing a single witness on the union's side, and solely on the basis of "information and belief" affidavits by the government, offered without proof, the two jurists outlawed the great Pullman strike, and placed 150,000 workers at the mercy of their employers.

Under the omnibus injunction, the most severe ever issued before or since, Debs, George Howard, fifteen other leaders and. "all other persons whomsoever" were prohibited from in any way or manner interfering with, hindering, obstructing, or stopping" any trains entering Chicago, and "from compelling or inducing or attempting to compel or induce by threats, intimidation, persuasion, force or violence, any of the employees of any of said [twenty-three] railroads to refuse or fail to perform any of their duties as employees of any of said railroads, or the carriage of the United States mail by such railroads ..." or "to leave the service of such railroads" engaged in interstate commerce. What this meant was that *any* action to further the strike would be in contempt of court, with the people involved subject to arrest and imprisonment. It thus became illegal for Debs to send wires or otherwise communicate with his local unions. It became illegal for striking workers to picket, raise relief funds or open a strike headquarters. Worst of all it became illegal under the injunction to "persuade" a railroad worker to join the strike or stay on strike, even if the means of persuasion were peaceful and amicable. "It is seriously questioned...," wrote the U.S. Strike Commission in its later report, "whether courts have jurisdiction to enjoin citizens from persuading each other in industrial or other matters of common interest."

How far the courts had to go to tailor legality to the needs of management during the Pullman strike is evident from the decision of the Supreme Court upholding the injunction months later. According to the high tribunal, the government had to establish two criteria for a restraining order, first that the damage to the complainant's property would be irreparable unless checked beforehand, and second, that the alleged criminality was part of an illegal and malicious conspiracy. Now there was obviously no "conspiracy" (all the union's activity was and had been out in the open) and the amount of property damage until the injunction was a scant few thousand dollars. Undaunted, the Court devised a vague definition of "irreparable" beyond its normal meaning. It held that the "expectancy" of *future* business was as much a hallowed property right as a locomotive. So too the "expectancy" of retaining old experienced employees. By this odd logic the high court decided that Debs and his union men were inflicting "irreparable" damage on the helpless railroads. Moreover, it decided that damaging or deflating the "probable expectancies" of management for future business could be deemed "malicious conspiracy." It is interesting that the court never declared—then or later—that "expectancy" of future wages was also a property right, reparable by injunctions against strikebreakers.

Nonetheless, the Grosscup-Woods restraining order—and many others, from Michigan to California, that restated its essentials—stood sacrosanct. Railroaders were arrested, according to George Howard, for refusing to turn switches or fire up a locomotive engine. A fireman in Albuquerque who failed to carry out a company order to climb aboard an engine was held in contempt, and sentenced to fifteen days in prison. The injunctions and arrests derived from them, placed Debs and the ARU in an unenviable quandary. They could abide by court restrictions, in which case the ARU would be eviscerated, the strike lost. Or they could flout the court, go to jail, see the strike smashed by federal troops. They decided to abide the injunction, to risk prison—in the hopes that somehow an infuriated labor movement would rescue them at the eleventh hour.

On July 3, 1894, U.S. Marshal Arnold, as well as Walker, Milchrist and Judge Grosscup wired Washington urging that armed forces be sent to Chicago—to protect federal property, prevent interference with mail and interstate commerce, and generally enforce the judicial edict. President Cleveland ordered troops to Chicago from nearby Fort Sheridan. Eleven companies were on duty in Chicago on Independence Day and 1,936 federal soldiers by July 10.

Cleveland's action, like injunctions, was of doubtful legality. Apart from the fact that he had disregarded the Constitution by bypassing the state governor and state legislature in Illinois, no federal property had been destroyed in Chicago—or even seemed to be in jeopardy. According to the Superintendent of Railway Mail Service, the mail cars were operating, and there was no pileup of mail in the post office. Governor Altgeld protested to Cleveland that the President had been misled, and that the action "is entirely unnecessary, and, as it seems to me, unjustifiable.... So far as I have been advised, the local officials have been able to handle the situation." Altgeld stressed the point that "if any assistance were needed, the state stood ready to furnish a hundred men for every one man required, and stood ready to do so at a moment's notice. Cleveland and Olney were undoubtedly aware of all of this but they also knew while Altgeld, a friend of labor, would alert the militia to keep order, he would not instruct them to actually crush the Pullman or any other strikes.

Similar dissent from Cleveland's actions and similar insistence that the states could handle their own affairs came from the governors of Kansas, Colorado, Texas, and Oregon. The militia had been called out in twenty states and was presumably capable of dealing with any emergency without federal troop support. Debs and James R. Sovereign of the Knights of Labor jointly warned Cleveland that "a deep-seated conviction is fast becoming prevalent that this Government is soon to be declared a military despotism." Reacting further, in fury, Debs cried out that "the first shot fired by the regular soldiers at the mobs here will be the signal for a civil war … Bloodshed will follow, and 90 percent of the people of the United States will be arrayed against the other 10 percent." He was to be proven wrong in his estimate of labor's strength and public support, but as the U.S. Strike commission was to observe there were no serious disorders until the federal troops arrived. Afterward there was a great surge of what Attorney General Olney referred to as "anarchy."

On the evening of July 4 in Chicago, people congregated on railroad tracks, overturned some cars and set some aflame. Amid the explosion of firecrackers, citizens heard the clag of fire engines hurrying to and fro to douse the burning freights. Women and children constituted a large part of the crowds gathered at the rails, as did adolescents who found that the cars were perched on the tracks in such a way that thirty or forty men pushing back and forth could topple them. The next day the situation grew worse. Ten thousand people gathered at the Stock Yards, and as they moved east, on Rock Island property again, turned over and set fire to freights, threw switches, altered signal lights, burned down a signal light, burned down a signal house and tossed rocks. The troops did not use firearms in response to these actions, but they did attack the crowd with bayonets drawn, inflicting some injuries. The crowd, however, could not be dispersed entirely nor could any railroad cars be moved. When two hundred soldiers and three hundred deputy marshals tried to take out a trainload of livestock at Union Stock Yards they were halted by strikers after one mile and had to abandon the effort four hours later. In fact, from July 4 through 10 not a single carload of meat or livestock left these yards, so stubborn was the resistance of Chicago's militants.

July 6, … $340,000. of rail assets [were] demolished or went up in smoke. One of the unique features of the day's events was the outbreak of street fighting for the first time; deputy marshals shot and killed two participants. Not far from Pullman, where freights were being toppled, a deputy shot an innocent bystander a hundred yards away and, in full sight of everyone, pumped a bullet into the victim as he tried to rise—killing him.

There were now 6,000 federal and state troops in Chicago, 3,100 police, and 5,000 deputy marshals, but the fury of the strikers and their supporters could not be checked. A peak of violence was reached on the Seventh when Illinois National Guardsmen fired into a mob trying to stop the movement of a wrecking train at Forty-ninth and Loomis Streets. The Guard, assaulted by the protesters, began to shoot at will when four of its members were badly injured. At least four civilians were killed (one estimate put it at twenty or thirty) and twenty were wounded, including some women.

[Under Federal occupation and the arrests of the ARU leadership, the national strike collapsed within three weeks.]

Federal Troops Ending the Pullman Boycott.

The Pullman Boycott and the Making of Modern America

*David Montgomery**

A hundred years ago the United States, along with the rest of the industrialized world, was in the grip of an economic crisis so profound that it provoked an intense social and political reaction against the regime of free market liberalism by which it was then governed. The Pullman boycott epitomized that conflict. On one side the American Railway Union had organized the collective power of railway workers of all grades over the vast geographic terrain from the northern Appalachian Mountains to the Pacific Coast. Its members imposed an effective boycott across the western portion of the country in a concerted effort to assist the men and women whose incomes had been gutted by the Pullman Company. On the other side were the railway executives (who had bound themselves together in the General Managers' Association), the justices of the highest courts, and President Grover Cleveland.

Cleveland stood like Horatio at the Bridge, prepared to sacrifice his presidency and his party's control of Washington and to endure in secret a painful operation, so that he might slash government expenditures, pare down the tariff, and save the gold standard—to his mind and to his admirers, the ultimate emblem of Euro-American civilization and unfettered global commerce. As the rapid flow of gold out of the United States in 1893 made starkly evident, pegging national currencies to gold imposed a tight discipline on the budgets of every industrialized country. Gunboats and marines were soon to be de-

* This article first appeared in longer form in Richard Schneirov, Shelton Stromquist, and Nick Salvatore, eds., *The Pullman Strike and the Crisis of the 1890's: Essays on Labor and Politics*, 233–243 (Urbana: University of Illinois Press, 1999). It is reprinted by permission of the publisher, University of Illinois Press.

ployed to impose similar budgetary discipline on less developed countries (or, to use the language of Theodore Roosevelt, those who were less "civilized").[1]

The personalities and ethics of the 1890s have receded so far into the past that it is hard to imagine a Gene Debs or a Grover Cleveland among us today. Debs had been but a child and Cleveland a young man when a bloody civil war secured the future of the United States as a unified capitalist republic, in which people related to each other through contractual relationships—marriage, sales, and wages. Both of them had served political apprenticeships as Democrats—devoted to the integrity of the nation and to a government that rested lightly on the self-regulating economic activity and exuberant religious and cultural diversity of civil society. No prominent individual in our current political scene closely resembles either one of them. Yet their dramatic confrontation in the summer of 1894 framed issues involving the most desirable relationship between organized society and what is called the "free market" that haunt our current discussion of the Pullman boycott, not like ghosts of Christmas past but like ghosts of Christmas yet to come.

The issues at stake were concisely formulated by Karl Polanyi in 1943, trying to explain what had produced the bloodiest war that human beings had ever experienced. Polanyi wrote in his book *The Great Transformation* that "the fount and matrix" of nineteenth-century civilization was "the self-regulating market." But, he observed, "the idea of a self-adjusting market implied a stark utopia. Such an institution could not exist for any length of time without annihilating the human and natural substance of society.... Inevitably, society took measures to protect itself, but whatever measures it took impaired the self-regulation of the market, disorganized industrial life, and thus endangered society in yet another way."[2] Looking back at the Pullman boycott over the span of a century of soaring hopes, embattled accomplishments, and crushing defeats for working people may help us assess the promise and the perils of both the free market and society's attempts to protect itself from the social and environmental ravages market freedom has inflicted on us.

By the time of the Pullman boycott the United States added more value to its national income by manufacturing than did any other nation of the world. It also exported unequaled quantities of agricultural products. The American economy had undergone prodigious expansion since the 1850s, but that growth had been spasmodic and vexed by a protracted decline in the selling prices of both manufactured and agricultural wares since the early 1870s. The depression of the 1890s began in mining and commercial agriculture, the major shippers for the vast railway network. The railroads' loss of revenues precipitated the spring 1893 crisis of major investment banks, and that in turn contracted sales, abruptly pitched already deflated prices to levels that precluded profits, and paralyzed manufacturing.

For twenty years before the outbreak of that depression, despite remarkable technological improvements in some industries, the nation's manufacturing output had grown primarily as a result of ever greater inputs of labor—especially the arrival of 6,825,000 immigrants since 1881 (one-quarter of them from Germany, but an ever-increasing proportion from the rural outskirts of European capitalism). Output per worker continued

---

1. Horace Samuel Merrill, *Bourbon Leader: Grover Cleveland and the Democratic Party* (Boston: Little, Brown, 1957); Nick Salvatore, *Eugene V. Debs: Citizen and Socialist* (Urbana: University of Illinois Press, 1982); John Sproat, *"The Best Men": Liberal Reformers in the Gilded Age*, 170–203 (New York: Oxford University Press, 1968); Theodore Roosevelt, "Fourth Annual Message ... December 6, 1904," in *A Compilation of the Messages and Papers of the Presidents*, vol. 15, 7053–54 (New York: published by the authority of Congress, 1914).

2. Karl Polanyi, *The Great Transformation: The Political and Economic Origins of Our Time*, 3 (New York: Farrar and Rinehart, 1944).

to increase steadily, but it did not grow at the spectacular rates that had been evident between 1840 and 1870. The endemic decline in selling prices pushed down the average rate of return to investors in manufacturing, which produced a relentless battle over production costs—and in the 1870s and 1880s that usually meant efforts by employers to hold down wages and especially to reduce piece rates. The great Pullman works in Chicago had been the scene of a running war over piece rates for more than a decade before the conflict exploded in the strike of 1894.[3]

Real incomes of workers had risen considerably since 1850, though the wide gap between the highest and lowest earnings of workers, the insecurity of every worker's income, and fierce competition for jobs and survival made deprivation and want the fighting themes of workers' rhetoric. Those themes appeared not only in the famous speech of Reverend William Carwardine of the town of Pullman to the 1894 convention of the American Railway Union but also in Samuel Gompers's denunciation of "the barbarity of capitalism" the same year.[4]

By the 1880s workers had developed powers of resistance to their employers' wage-cutting efforts that drew strength from familial, gender, ethnic, and community loyalties and especially from the decisive role of craft-workers in the existing relations of production. The contest so pervaded social life that the ideology of acquisitive individualism, which explained and justified a society regulated by market mechanisms and propelled by the accumulation of capital, was challenged by an ideology of mutualism, rooted in working-class bondings and struggles. Contests over pennies on or off existing piece rates had ignited controversies over the nature and purpose of the Republic itself. On one side of that ideological divide stood President Cleveland and Attorney General Richard Olney. On the other stood Debs and the delegates to the ARU's historic convention.

The ARU embodied something new in the labor movement: a style of trade unionism that embraced all grades of workers, that often covered large geographic regions, and that openly opposed the free market economy. The great 1894 strike of bituminous coal miners, which stretched from Ohio to Illinois, exemplified this trend. So did the strike of textile workers in Lawrence, Massachusetts, that summer—a general stoppage of 2,500 workers in all the city's mills, which was the climax of decades of small strikes by groups of textile workers (as well as a futile effort by the Knights of Labor to improve wages through arbitration). Only two years earlier in New Orleans a demand for the closed shop by laborers who handled sugar and molasses products had ultimately brought out on strike forty-two unions with more than 20,000 white and black members—all the city's unions, with the noteworthy exception of the powerful waterfront cotton-handling trades.

---

3. David Montgomery, *The Fall of the House of Labor: The Workplace, the State, and American Labor Activism, 1865–1925*, 44–57, 126–31, 148–54 (New York: Cambridge University Press, 1987); James Livingston, "The Social Analysis of Economic History and Theory: Conjectures on Late Nineteenth-Century American Development," 92 *American Historical Review* 69–96 (February 1987).

4. Montgomery, *Fall of the House of Labor*, 69–70, 171–72; William Carwardine, *The Pullman Strike* (Chicago: Charles H. Kerr, 1894); Samuel Gompers, "The Strike and Its Lessons," in *A Momentus Question: The Respective Attitudes of Labor and Capital*, ed. John Swinton, 314 (Philadelphia and Chicago: Keller Publishing, 1895). On workers' efforts to deal with insecurity, *see* S. J. Kleinberg, *The Shadow of the Mills: Working-Class Families in Pittsburgh, 1870–1907* (Pittsburgh: University of Pittsburgh Press, 1989); August Sartorius von Waltershausen, "Das Hilfkassenwesen in Nordamerika," *Jahrbücher für Nationalokonomie und Statistik*, 10 Neue Folge, 97–154 (1885); and Alexander Keyssar, *Out of Work: The First Century of Unemployment in Massachusetts* (New York: Cambridge University Press, 1986). For an argument that workers' incomes did decline relative to those of the upper classes between 1870 and 1900, *see* Jeffrey G. Williamson and Peter H. Lindert, *American Inequality: A Macroeconomic History* (New York: Academic, 1980), chaps. 10–11.

The New Orleans struggle not only enjoyed the vigorous support of the American Federation of Labor (AFL), which hoped it might open the way to unionization of the South, but also inspired the AFL to devote close attention to the unionization of southern black workers for a few years. Until 1895 it barred the International Association of Machinists (IAM) from affiliating because the IAM allowed only caucasians in its ranks.[5]

All these industrial strikes had foundered on the heavy unemployment produced by the economic crisis. All of them had also triggered the mobilization of military power by state governors to enable scabs to pass through the strikers' lines. Moreover, the Workingmen's Amalgamated Council of New Orleans, which had organized that city's general strike, was successfully prosecuted under the new Sherman Anti-Trust Act. The crime of the New Orleans workers, wrote the district judge, consisted of this: "The combination setting out to secure and compel the employment of none but union men in a given business, as a means to enforce this compulsion, finally enforced a discontinuance of labor in all kinds of business, including the business of transportation of goods and merchandise which were in transit through the city of New Orleans, from state to state, and to and from foreign countries."[6]

Both the enlarged role of the state and the consolidation of organization in the business world, which were evident in the strikes of the early 1890s, deserve our close attention. It is important to keep in mind that although free market policies sharply restricted the scope of governmental activity, leaving major decisions about priorities in social development to private economic and social entities, the free market (and above all the reduction of labor to an unprotected commodity) could never have matured without significant strengthening of the coercive authority of the government. Policing the everyday behavior of working men and women and enlarging the geographic domain encompassed by the industrializing economy—not to mention preserving the United States against secession, destroying chattel slavery, and incorporating rural and urban freed people into the nexus of wage labor—had all contributed to the appearance of uniformed municipal police forces, professional (rather than personal) prosecution of crimes, and draconic legislation against tramps and vagrants (the "wandering unemployed") as well as incessant attempts to regulate popular drinking and public conduct.[7]

In a word, the political order that celebrated freedom of contract as its basic principle had become one in which what the eminent typographer Andrew Cameron called "the cruel law of supply and demand" determined not only the level of people's incomes but even whether they had any income at all. Whatever reciprocal obligations had once bound masters and servants had given way to the commodification of labor, a safety net of abstemious relief for the so-called worthy poor, and police repression of idleness and dissipation. A learned commentary on criminal law written by Joel Bishop in 1892 made the point clear: "There is, in just principle, nothing which a government has more clearly

---

5. Montgomery, *Fall of the House of Labor,* 126–30, 154–70, 198–201; Maier B. Fox, *United We Stand: The United Mine Workers of America, 1890–1990,* 44–47 (n.p.: United Mine Workers of America, 1990); Eric Arnesen, *Waterfront Workers of New Orleans: Race, Class, and Politics, 1863–1923* 114–118 (New York: Oxford University Press, 1991).

6. *United States v. Workingmen's Amalgamated Council of New Orleans et al.,* 54 Fed. 994, 999 (1893).

7. David Montgomery, *Citizen Worker: The Experience of Workers in the United States with Democracy and the Free Market during the Nineteenth Century,* 52–114 (New York: Cambridge University Press, 1993). New state constitutions of the 1870s had narrowed the range of state legislative powers over economic activity. See Morton Keller, *Affairs of State: Public Life in Late Nineteenth Century America,* 110–21 (Cambridge, Mass.: Belknap of Harvard University Press, 1977).

the right to do than to compel the lazy to work; and there is nothing more absolutely beyond its jurisdiction than to fix the price of labor."[8]

The growing coercive power of government was also evident in the development of a small but effective standing army, which had a highly professionalized officer corps, and a National Guard, which placed an elaborate network of volunteer companies and armories at the disposal of governors in every state of the Union. Between 1886 and 1893 state governors called out their units of the National Guard 328 times. In one third of the mobilizations the adjutant generals officially reported the cause as "labor troubles." Numerous other disturbances also arose out of workplace disputes. For example, soldiers were dispatched to return convicts whom miners had set free in Tennessee. General Coxey's Commonweal of Christ and the related Industrial Army of the Far West on their marches to Washington in 1894 were constantly dogged by the National Guard, which was called out nine times against them. No fewer than 91 other guard actions had been caused by lynchings or outbreaks officially described as "race troubles (negroes and whites)." That description usually referred to the suppression of some collective action by African Americans, but it could include anything from evicting black squatters to enforcing laws against gathering oysters.[9]

"Government by injunction," which the Democratic platform of 1896 denounced as "a new and highly dangerous form of oppression," had been born of the marriage of court orders and enforcement by bodies of armed men drilled for action against urban crowds. Precedents for the court orders had two major sources. One was the growing use of injunctions against railroad strikes during the 1880s.[10] The other was court orders against boycotts.

The citywide boycott, by which all residents were mobilized to "leave severely alone" a particular firm that persecuted or defied its workers, had developed by the mid-1880s into the most effective weapon of the Knights of Labor. While workers defended their hundreds of local boycotts as the sort of private arrangement to promote the common welfare that was favored by America's Jeffersonian legacy, courts prohibited them precisely because their motivation was not self-interested but sympathetic. By introducing community moral standards into economic behavior, boycotts represented a particularly flagrant intrusion by society into the hallowed preserve of the market. Judges made and enforced the law by which community boycotts, which Virginia's judges called "combinations of irresponsible cabals or cliques," were proclaimed criminal acts.[11]

The ARU's boycott of Pullman cars was national in scope, and it focused on the railroad system. In response, as William Forbath has written, "Federal judges … turned their courtrooms into police courts by issuing roughly one hundred decrees prohibiting the ARU and other unions from threatening, combining, or conspiring to quit in any fash-

---

8. Andrew Cameron, editorial in Workingman's Advocate, March 25, 1865; Joel Bishop, *New Commentaries on the Criminal Law,* vol. 1, 273–74 (Chicago: T.H. Flood, 1892).

9. Winthrop Alexander, "Ten Years of Riot Duty," 19 *Journal of the Military Service Institution of the United States* 1–62 (July 1896): (quote on 26); Henry Vincent, *The Story of the Commonweal* (Chicago: W.B. Conkey, 1894).

10. The Democratic Platform of 1896, in *National Party Platforms,* ed. Kirk H. Porter, 185 (New York: Macmillan, 1924); Gerald G. Eggert, *Railroad Labor Disputes: The Beginning of Federal Strike Policy* (Ann Arbor: University of Michigan Press, 1967).

11. Norman J. Ware, *The Labor Movement in the United States, 1860–1895,* 334–45 (New York: D. Appleton, 1929), 334–45; William E. Forbath, *Law and the Shaping of the American Labor Movement,* 79–97 (Cambridge, Mass.: Harvard University Press, 1991); *Crump v. Commonwealth,* 84 Va., 927, 946 (1888), quoted in Forbath, *Law and the Shaping of the American Labor Movement,* 84.

ion that would embarrass the railways' operations. They also enjoined refusals to handle the cars of other struck lines."[12]

This escalating confrontation between capitalism and popular liberties sounded alarm bells in the organizations of workers and farmers alike. Although the conference of twenty-four officials of national unions held in Chicago's Briggs House shortly after Debs's arrest on conspiracy charges declined to call a general strike in support of a demand for reinstating all ARU strikers, its official communique saluted the boycott as "an impulsive, vigorous protest against the gathering, growing forces of plutocratic power and corporation rule." Its concluding lines summoned workers to strengthen their unions and prepare to "go to the ballot-box and cast our votes as American freemen, united and determined to redeem this country from its present political and industrial misrule, to take it from the hands of the plutocratic wreckers and place it in the hands of the common people."[13]

A very different interpretation was offered by John Bates Clark, then president of the American Economics Association. Clark, too, saw the decade's social conflict as the birth pangs of a new social and political order, but in his 1894 address to the association he described the current merger movement in industry as the precondition of both greater stability in the business world and a new upsurge of productivity, from which all members of society would benefit. "What productive energies will this process unchain!" Clark exclaimed. Electricity not only would provide cheap "motive power" for machinery everywhere but also would call unimagined "forms of utility and beauty … out of non-existence at the touch of a button!" Clark prophesied that those business leaders whom the trade unionists had denounced as "plutocratic wreckers" would not destroy democracy but would renew and reconstruct it: "The crowning gain of it all is the irrepressible democracy of it. By the processes that others control, and by wealth that others own, the laborer will get, in the end, the most valuable personal gains. Mastership and plutocracy, in a good sense, yield by natural law a democratic result; for it is by the wealth that these ensure that the productive power of man must rise."[14]

As Clark had written six years earlier, "The new era has, in fact, begun, but it has not brought socialism."[15] On the contrary the new era was presaged by the railway executives who sat on the General Managers' Association. Although the largest factories before the 1890s were owned by individuals or partnerships, such as those of Pullman and Carnegie, their major customers were railroads. The consolidated railroad systems themselves were owned by corporations and directed by elaborate managerial bureaucracies. The expanding use of the corporate form of organization in manufacturing and commerce and the widespread formation of holding companies during the waves of business mergers immediately before and after the depression of 1893–97 greatly enlarged the capacity of business executives to administer the markets in which they bought materials and sold finished products, while both the judiciary and Congress concluded a protracted and intense debate over the legality of corporate economic power by ultimately authorizing its exercise,

---

12. Forbath, *Law and the Shaping of the American Labor Movement*, 75.

13. The Briggs House statement is reproduced in Swinton, *Momentus Question*, 308–13 (quotes on 312, 313). For a description of the conference, *see* Almont Lindsey, *The Pullman Strike: The Story of a Unique Experiment and of a Great Labor Upheaval*, 326–29 (Chicago: University of Chicago Press, 1942).

14. John Bates Clark, "The Modern Appeal to Legal Forces in Economic Life," 9 *Publications of the American Economic Association*, 501 (October and December 1894): 501, quoted in Nancy Cohen, "The Problem of Democracy in the Age of Capital: Reconstructing American Liberalism, 1865–1890," 364–65 (Ph.D. diss., Columbia University, 1995).

15. John Bates Clark, *The Philosophy of Wealth*, 291 (Boston: Ginn, 1886).

provided the marketing practices pursued by corporations were "reasonable." As Martin J. Sklar has argued persuasively, the public controversy over governmental regulation of corporate activity, which dominated political discussion during the two decades before 1914, was also the process by which corporate control of economic life was legitimated.[16]

That very process, however, was also part of the development Polanyi had in mind when he wrote that "society took measures to protect itself" against the destructive impact of "the self-regulating market."[17] The era of the trust did not end with "the *nation*" taking "*possession* of the *trusts*," as the Socialist Victor Berger had desired. Nor did antitrust laws fragment economic activity into units governed by market forces beyond their individual capacities to shape. On the contrary a few large enterprises came to dominate most industries and also provide young men and women new careers as office employees. Such regulatory measures as local, state, and federal governments undertook in this turn-of-the-century reshaping of market activities were increasingly entrusted to commissions of professional experts rather than to elected members of legislative bodies.[18]

Hoping to prevent a resurgence of all-grades unionism and sympathetic boycotts on the railroads Congress enacted the first in a series of railway labor acts—the Erdman Act in 1898. That measure, crafted by former Attorney General Richard Olney, who had earlier shaped the injunctions that had smashed the Pullman Boycott, secured the insurance funds of the older craft brotherhoods, prohibited dismissal of a railroad worker for membership in a brotherhood (a provision soon overruled by the Supreme Court), and established machinery for voluntary arbitration of future disputes.[19] Membership in the brotherhoods and shop craft unions swelled from 100,700 in 1897 to 357,800, but with that growth came rank-and-file initiatives to press for regional wage standards and for the eight-hour day, often in defiance of the cautious union leaders, and culminating in a 1916 membership vote in favor of a nation-wide joint strike to secure the eight-hour day for railroad workers. Congress averted the strike by enacting a legal eight-hour day on the railroads through the 1916 Adamson Act two days before the strike deadline. More than two decades of tumultuous labor struggle on the nation's railroads did not bring back the ARU, but they did draw the craft unions into joint struggles for economic demands and increasingly into reformist politics, culminating in the 1922 Conference for Progressive Political Action.[20]

---

16. Alfred D. Chandler Jr., *The Railroads, The Nation's First Big Business: Sources and Readings* (New York: Harcourt, Brace and World, 1965); Alfred D. Chandler Jr., *The Visible Hand: The Managerial Revolution in American Business* (Cambridge, Mass.: Belknap of Harvard University Press, 1977); Naomi R. Lamoreaux, *The Great Merger Movement in American Business, 1895–1904* (New York, 1985); Martin J. Sklar, *The Corporate Reconstruction of American Capitalism, 1890–1916: The Market, the Law, and Politics,* 33–40 (New York: Cambridge University Press, 1988).

17. Polanyi, *Great Transformation,* 3.

18. On Berger, *see* Sally M. Miller, *Victor Berger and the Promise of Constructive Socialism, 1910–1920,* 26 (Westport, Conn.: Greenwood, 1973). On careers and expertise, *see* Sklar, *Corporate Reconstruction of American Capitalism,* 20–33; Dorothy Ross, *The Origins of American Social Science,* 219–56 (New York: Cambridge University Press, 1991); and Ellis W. Hawley, "Herbert Hoover, the Commerce Secretariat, and the Vision of an 'Associative State,' 1921–1928," 61 *Journal of American History,* 116–40 (June 1974). J. Morgan Kousser, *The Shaping of Southern Politics: Suffrage Restriction and the Establishment of the One-Party South, 1880–1910,* 252–62 (New Haven, Conn.: Yale University Press, 1974), argues that deliberate and effective restriction of the size of the electorate was an important part of this process.

19. Gerald G. Eggert, *Railway Labor Disputes: The Beginning of Federal Strike Policy,* 221–2 (Ann Arbor: University of Michigan Press, 1967).

20. Montgomery, *Fall of the House of Labor,* 366–369.

The gold standard *was* retained until the Great Depression of the 1930s. Business leaders, with the noteworthy exception of owners of silver mines, rallied vigorously to its defense with a massive campaign of public education between 1893 and 1896, spearheaded by the Reform Club of New York. As James Livingston has observed, the Reform Club feared that expansion of the currency, through free silver or greenbacks, would reinvigorate small competitors to the emerging corporations and further destabilize the economy. To defenders of the gold standard money was more than a medium of exchange; it was the instrument of expanded production through accumulation and credit—its acquisition the reason for engaging in production. Control of the money supply was a crucial instrument of economic regulation and consequently had to be entrusted to experts who understood its purpose.[21]

In brief neither the political and economic order Debs and Gompers championed nor the one Cleveland defended emerged intact from the depression of the 1890s. Even before the decade ended Cleveland's name had appeared, together with Gompers's, on a futile plea to the U.S. Senate not to annex the Philippines and Puerto Rico. The new business regime, which took shape in the major industrial countries with breathtaking speed during the decade and a half of erratic but vigorous economic expansion after the depression, was accompanied by mounting international tension and armament (especially naval construction in the United States), providing early evidence of Polanyi's point that the measures taken by society "to protect itself ... endangered society in yet another way." For the labor movement neither the merger movement itself nor governmental demands for patriotic service and loyalty ended military repression of strikes, but they did present new opportunities and new perils.[22]

Although most manufacturing and construction firms remained relatively small and privately owned, the average worker in manufacturing now worked for one of the new giant enterprises. By 1909 fully 62.2 percent of all wage earners in manufacturing were employed by only 4.8 percent of the firms (all of them corporations).[23] These firms shaped the cutting edge of new technologies, scientific management, and sometimes company welfare experiments. Unsuccessful strikes in steel, meatpacking, and farm equipment had left large-scale industry overwhelmingly nonunion, even while the trade union movement increased its membership by more than three-and-a-half times between 1897 and 1904. Although workers still hungered for the improved earnings and control over their working lives that only collective action could bring, the new circumstances left their firm imprint on workers' organizations.

In his 1894 reflections on the Pullman boycott Samuel Gompers advocated cautious and deliberate action by working people to secure effective power in their occupations and to improve their own conditions step-by-step.[24] This course of action was heartily approved by the delegates to the AFL's 1895 convention. It emphasized the pursuit of trade agreements with employers or associations of employers to fix the terms of employment for union members. Sympathetic actions were curtailed, and general strikes were anathema

---

21. James Livingston, *Origins of the Federal Reserve System: Money, Class, and Corporate Capitalism, 1890–1913*, 83–99 (Ithaca, N.Y.: Cornell University Press, 1986).

22. Philip S. Foner, *History of the Labor Movement in the United States*, vol. 2, 423–24 (New York: International, 1955); Howard K. Beale, *Theodore Roosevelt and the Rise of America to World Power* (Baltimore: Johns Hopkins University Press, 1956).

23. Livingston, *Origins of the Federal Reserve System*, 57–7. See also Daniel Nelson, *Managers and Workers: Origins of the New Factory System in the United States, 1880–1920*, 3–10 (Madison: University of Wisconsin Press, 1975).

24. Gompers, "The Strike and Its Lessons," 306–14.

to most national union leaders. During the economic upswing between 1897 and 1903 union membership expanded more rapidly than in any other comparable period of time in American history, and sympathy strikes were numerous. But few of those strikes were sanctioned by the international unions. Citywide general strikes that took place later—in Philadelphia in 1910; Springfield, Illinois, in 1917; Kansas City and Billings in 1918; and Seattle in 1919—were all basically sympathetic actions organized by local trade unionists in the face of vigorous opposition from the top officials of the AFL. In 1922, when AFL unions in the railroad shop crafts waged a strike involving far more workers than had engaged in the Pullman boycott and reaching every corner of the land, national unions in the carrying and maintenance trades directed their members not to participate.[25]

Second, the efforts at political alliances between black and white workers and farmers, which had been widespread if hesitant during the decade and a half between Virginia's Readjusters and North Carolina's Populist Republican coalition, crumpled before a new wave of disfranchisement, segregation, and lynchings. The blood-drenched drive to racial segregation was a critically important lineament of the society that emerged from the 1890s, and it imposed its stamp decisively on the union movement and labor politics. It also framed the proposals Progressive Era reformers made for governmental regulation of social life and the market economy. The last attempts in the U.S. Congress to keep alive the possibility of interracial democracy in the South had appeared in 1890, with the demise of Senator Henry Blair's bill for federal aid to primary education and Senator Henry Cabot Lodge's proposal that federal election supervisors be dispatched to every congressional district where a hundred citizens petitioned for such help against electoral fraud and coercion. Both bills went down to defeat under the combined and vehement opposition of southern white congressmen, the Democratic Party, and Republican friends of free silver. In the summer of the Pullman boycott the Democratic majority in Congress repealed the portions of the Enforcement Act of 1870 on which Lodge's proposals had been based. By 1896 the Republicans themselves had dropped from their national platform all mention of fair voting in the South.[26]

Segregation became institutionalized in the trade union movement itself, starting with the railroads, which had long been distinguished by elaborate racial hierarchies. The carrying trades were among the few sectors of employment in the country that were dominated by native-born whites. Brakemen drew their recruits largely from local farm youth. Repair shops and northern switchyards were the domain of northern European immigrants in some regions, native-born whites in others. Track laying varied with the region: Scandinavians in the Northwest, Chinese and Mexicans in the Southwest, African Americans in the Southeast. Union practice both reflected and reinforced those divisions. The

25. Montgomery, *Fall of the House of Labor*, 263–65, 371, 407–10; Fred S. Hall, *Sympathetic Strikes and Sympathetic Lockouts* (New York: Columbia University Press, 1898); Ken Fones-Wolf, *Trade Union Gospel: Christianity and Labor in Industrial Philadelphia, 1865–1915*, 167–70 (Philadelphia: Temple University Press, 1989); Dana Frank, *Purchasing Power: Consumer Organizing, Gender, and the Seattle Labor Movement, 1919–1929*, 34–39 (New York: Cambridge University Press, 1994); Colin J. Davis, *Power at Odds: The 1922 National Railroad Shopmen's Strike* (Urbana: University of Illinois Press, 1997).

26. Kousser, *Shaping of Southern Politics;* Luther P. Jackson, *Negro Office-Holders in Virginia, 1865–1895* (Norfolk: Guide Quality, 1945); James Tice Moore, *Two Paths to the New South: The Virginia Debt Controversy, 1870–1883* (Lexington: University Press of Kentucky, 1974). The abrupt and violent demise of political democracy in North Carolina is described vividly in Glenda Elizabeth Gilmore, *Gender and Jim Crow: Women and the Politics of White Supremacy in North Carolina, 1896–1920*, 1–146 (Chapel Hill: University of North Carolina Press, 1996).

brotherhoods had long excluded any but whites from membership. At its 1894 convention the ARU followed suit. The next year the AFL admitted the International Association of Machinists, whose members were pledged to propose only Caucasians for affiliation. That decision laid out the AFL's welcome mat to numerous other unions that barred black workers from their ranks.[27]

Finally, the socialist movement grew to far greater size, coherence, and influence than it had exhibited during the nineteenth century. The Socialist Party of America, whose resolutions and candidates for AFL offices mustered a third of the votes at federation conventions by 1910–12, called for collective ownership of industrial enterprise and the subordination of all economic activity to the democratically determined needs of working people. The Industrial Workers of the World (IWW) transformed the historic attempts of the Knights of Labor and the ARU to enroll all grades of workers into a campaign to organize both industrial and agricultural workers along lines that flouted historic craft divisions, dispensed with salaried officials (as well as with strike and benefit funds), and rejected the very idea of contractual relations with the bosses. Unlike the ARU, the IWW scorned all racial exclusions. Japanese, Mexicans, African Americans, and all other wage earners were summoned, as Arturo Giovannitti told the jurors in Salem, Massachusetts, to join "the heralds of a new civilization," to diffuse "in every known tongue, in every civilized language, in every dialect … this message of socialism, this message of brotherhood, this message of love."[28]

---

27. Montgomery, *Fall of the House of Labor,* 74–81, 198–201; Shelton Stromquist, *A Generation of Boomers: The Pattern of Railroad Labor Conflict in Nineteenth-Century America,* 48–80, 201–11 (Urbana: University of Illinois Press, 1987).

28. John H. M. Laslett, *Labor and the Left: A Study of Socialist and Radical Influences in the American Labor Movement,* 1881–1924 (New York: Basic Books, 1970); Ira Kipnis, *The American Socialist Movement,* 1897–1912 (New York: Monthly Review Press, 1952); James Weinstein, *Decline of Socialism in America,* 1912–1925 (New York: Monthly Review Press, 1967); Montgomery, *Fall of the House of Labor, 281–329;* Joyce L. Kornbluh, *Rebel Voices: An IWW Anthology,* 193–95 (Ann Arbor: University of Michigan Press, 1968) (Giovannitti's speech to the jury).

Law and the Shaping of the American Labor Movement: Government by Injunction

*William E. Forbath**

By the eve of the Pullman Strike the main elements that composed the federal judicial role in that strike were also in place. Built up over sixteen years of judicial experience, they included: the enjoining of strikes and boycotts on non-receivership lines; the long experience of collaboration with railroad management and attorneys; the precedents for summoning troops over the heads and against the will of state authorities; the preference for summary proceedings over jury trials; and the transformation of the federal courtroom into "a kind of police court," in Judge Taft's words, when railway workers went on strike.[1] The Pullman Strike was extraordinary for its scale and the corresponding scale of judicial involvement, the executive branch's role, and the Supreme Court's imprimatur. The last was a comprehensive endorsement of the federal judicial role in railway strikes and of the new use of equity in industrial conflicts.

The American Railway Union (ARU) called the Pullman Strike.[2] In 1894 the ARU was a fledgling industrial union, created by Eugene Debs and other former railroad brotherhood leaders to overcome the older brotherhoods' often divisive craft boundaries and their exclusion of the railways' masses of unskilled workers. Correctly fearing a showdown for which the new union was unprepared, Debs urged the ARU membership not to take on the cause of the Pullman Company's desperate workers. Swayed by Pullman's ruthless wage cuts and labor policies and his intransigent refusal to confer with his employees, the ARU membership rejected Debs's counsel and voted a boycott of Pullman cars. An eloquent voice of working-class republicanism, Debs then defended the boycott as the "practical exhibition of sympathy," Christian brotherhood, and republican mutualism.[3] However, in the eyes of virtually all of the nation's legal elite, conservative and reformist alike, Debs represented all that was "lawless" in the labor movement, and the web of sympathetic boycotts of Pullman cars that constituted the "Strike" embodied the movement's most threatening developments.

Judge Taft's letters during the strike capture much of the experience and reactions of conservative jurists. Like many Midwestern federal judges in 1894, Judge Taft had ordered a railroad into receivership.[4] "[W]hat has worried me more than anything else," Taft wrote to his wife, "is this railway boycott. I have a force of fifty deputy marshals on one side of the river and of seventy-five on the other. Men are constantly being arrested and brought before me and I am conducting a kind of police court ... Last night ... I was the object of fiery denunciations in many meetings."[5]

---

  * This selection is taken from, William E. Forbath, *Law and the Shaping of the American Labor Movement*, 73–93 *passim*. (Cambridge: Harvard University Press, 1991). It is reprinted by permission of the publisher and the President and Fellows of Harvard College.

1. Letter from William H. Taft to Helen H. Taft (July 1894), quoted in 1 H. Pringle, *The Life and Times of William Howard Taft*, 135 (1939). I owe to Professor Dianne Avery the suggestion that Pringle's biography contains valuable material on Taft's experiences as an injunction judge.

2. The most thorough and insightful accounts of the Pullman Strike include R. Ginger, *The Bending Cross: A Biography of Eugene Victor Debs*, 108–51 (1949), A. Lindsey, *The Pullman Strike* (1942), and N. Salvatore, *Eugene V. Debs*, 114–46 (1982).

3. Debs, "Labor Strikes and Their Lessons," reprinted in J. Swinton, *Striking for Life*, 324 (1894).

4. *See Thomas v. Cincinnati, N.O. and T.P. Ry.* 62 F 803, 804–05 (S.D. Ohio 1894).

5. Letter from William H. Taft to Helen H. Taft (July 1894).

"The situation in Chicago," he observed, "is very alarming and distressing ..."[6] Governor Altgeld of Illinois disagreed. He had vehemently opposed the marshals and troops ushered in by federal decrees. To him, the "situation" was one of mass demonstrations by strikers and their supporters, but there was neither large-scale destruction of railroad property nor significant violence. For the labor-populist governor, the ARU and the Pullman Boycott were vehicles of reform less daunting and dangerous than the huge corporations that opposed them; for the conservative jurist, they were instruments of anarchy and lawlessness that had to be destroyed. Though Taft was a genial man, his solution was savage: "[U]ntil they have had much bloodletting, it will not be better."[7] In another letter, Taft wrote: "They have killed only six of the mob as yet. This is hardly enough to make an impression."[8]

Federal judges "in nearly every large city west of the Allegheny Mountains" responded to the strike as Taft did; they turned their courtrooms into police courts by issuing roughly one hundred decrees prohibiting the ARU and other unions from threatening, combining, or conspiring to quit in any fashion that would embarrass the railways' operations.[9] They also enjoined refusals to handle the cars of other struck lines. Several of the injunctions, including that against Debs and his ARU, also forebade attempts to induce fellow workers to support the strikes or boycotts. "Injunction writs ... covered the sides of cars, deputy marshals and Federal soldiers ... patrolled the yards of railway *termini,* and chancery process [was] executed by bullets and bayonets."[10] The next May in *In re Debs*[11] the United States Supreme Court unanimously lent its sanction to the new equity device, upholding the blanket injunctions that had issued against the Pullman Strike, and the contempt convictions of Debs and other leaders for violating them.

Justice Brewer in *Debs* credited the decrees with prompting a swift and peaceful acquiescence by strikers, ending what had been an unprecedentedly broad and successful sympathy strike. He concluded that the experience affirmed the broad role the federal courts had staked out for themselves in the policing of strikes.[12] Debs made a similar assessment, insisting that it was "not the army, [nor] any other power, but simply ... the United States Courts"[13] that ended the strike. The blanketing of the strike with injunctions and the arrests of scores of leaders for contempt had "demoralized" the strikers.[14]

The broad-based sympathy strikes of the Pullman Boycott crystallized a growing sentiment among railway workers. The strikes were waged to support the hard-pressed employees of the Pullman company, but they also constituted a more general assertion. As the most meticulous recent history of Gilded Age railway strikes observes, the sympathy

---

6. Letter from William H. Taft to Helen H. Taft (1894), quoted in J. Anderson, William Howard Taft: An Intimate History 63 (1981). I encountered Anderson's account of Taft's letters to his wife in Dianne Avery's essay, "Images of Violence in Labor Jurisprudence: The Regulation of Picketing and Boycotts, 1894–1921," 37 *Buf. L. Rev.* 1, 21–22 (1989).

7. Letter from William H. Taft to Helen H. Taft (1894).

8. *Ibid.* In the legal scholarship of the period even reformers described Debs as an "irresponsible vagabond" and a "dictator" who "reel[ed] with the intoxication which springs from the possession of almost unlimited power." Book Review, 28 *Am. L. Rev.* 629, 633–34 (1894) (reviewing T. Cogley, *Cogley on Strikes and Boycotts* (1894).

9. *See* Allen, "Injunctions and Organized Labor," 28 *Am. L. Rev.* 828, 847 (1894).

10. *Ibid.*

11. 158 U.S. 564 (1895).

12. *See ibid.* at 582–600. Then and now, some commentators have been inclined to dismiss Justice Brewer's assessment of the injunctions' impact as puffery.

13. *In re Debs*, 158 U.S. at 598 (quoting Debs's testimony before the United States Strike Commission).

14. *See ibid.*

strike "had taken deep root in the industrial experience of the railroad men."[15] By feder-
ating their separate crafts—frequently under the Knights of Labor—and by wielding
the sympathetic strike, these railroad workers had begun to assert and win "rights" that
craft organizations had failed to gain, even for their narrower constituencies.[16] The workers who rallied to Debs's ARU hoped that thorough organization and the ability to tie up
broad swaths of the nation's railroad traffic would enable them to extend workers' control further, to a fundamental restructuring of work relations, and even to the "operation of the railroads in the general public interest."[17]

By the early 1890s the formidable legal web the courts had spun around the sympathy strike had already led the old brotherhoods' leaders to use the weapon more cau-
tiously.[18] The leadership condemned efforts like the ARU's to create industrial organizations,
and, though tens of thousands of their members participated in the Pullman Boycott,
the brotherhoods' leaders denounced it.[19] In the wake of the federal assault on the boycott, the ARU disintegrated. But the breadth of worker support for both the ARU and
the boycott encouraged leading railroad managers to reconsider their attitudes toward
the old brotherhoods. The brotherhoods "could be enlisted to police a new era of industrial peace in return for a guarantee of their survival."[20]

The participation of the railroad's less-skilled workers had helped fuel the dynamic
power of the Knights of Labor and the ARU. The rise of these industrial organizations did
much to gain the new and undreamed-of security that the brotherhoods now enjoyed. But
the masses of less-skilled workers were left out of the bargain between the brotherhoods
and the managers,[21] and the *Debs* decision and "government by injunction" led to the
scrapping of the only major weapon by which broader organizations of railroad men had
been able to assert the rights of the skilled and unskilled alike.[22]

Despite Debs's urging, Gompers and the AFL leadership had declined to extend beyond the railways the sympathy strike in support of the ARU.[23] Likewise, the "intelligent and generally law-abiding" railroad brotherhoods chose the Pullman Boycott as the
occasion on which to honor Judge Taft's stern suggestion and abandon the boycotting
tradition.

Thus, the Pullman Boycott would mark a sorely divisive moment—persuading Debs
and many of his kin in the labor movement that independent labor politics and public
control over the railways and other industries were indispensable to building broad, inclusive,

---

15. S. Stromquist, *A Generation of Boomers: The Pattern of Railroad Labor Conflict in Nineteenth-
Century America* 39 (1987).

16. The successful sympathy strikes that bulk large in the overall railroad strike statistics of the 1880s
were over such ambitious control issues as the size of crews and the workers' asserted right to demand
the firing of abusive yardmasters and other supervisors. See *ibid.* at 34–38.

17. *Ibid.* at 46. Eugene Debs told the United States Strike Commission investigating The Pullman
boycott that he believed "that if the people owned and operated the railroads in the interest of the
people instead of for private gain and profit, that the service would be greatly improved, the condition of the men infinitely better, and another strike would never come." *Ibid.* at 39, quoting Debs.

18. *See ibid.* at 39.

19. *See ibid.* at 54–98. They threatened boycott supporters with expulsion. Indeed, one brotherhood, the Brotherhood of Railroad Trainmen, purportedly expelled nearly 20 000 men after the strike.
See *ibid.* at 263–64.

20. *Ibid.* at 263.

21. See *ibid.* at 262–65. "Shopmen, switchmen, and track laborers enjoyed little more security
than they had ever had." *Ibid.* at 266.

22. *See ibid.* at 265.

23. *See* J. Swinton, *Striking For Life,* 306–14.

unions, and confirming Gompers and his cohorts in the view that broad, class-based strategies and industrial ambitions were too costly and self-defeating. Such approaches invited brutal repression — now resoundingly endorsed and encouraged by the Supreme Court.

Some students of industrial relations contend that legal repression did not significantly influence the demise of the sympathy strike. They suggest that the tactic was more a protest than a real economic weapon, and argue that it merely impeded the development of "mature" contractual relations.[24]

This criticism falls somewhat wide of the mark. To be sure, such strikes were protests affirming broad commonalities.[25] But many types of Gilded Age and early-twentieth-century sympathetic actions also provided a substantial measure of bargaining strength.[26] Nor were they inherently incompatible with a collective bargaining regime.[27] The result was not to frustrate the development of collective bargaining but rather to hasten employers' acceptance of it.[28] The AFL tried to bring about just such catalytic reactions in the United States. Legislatures were sometimes willing, but for over three decades the judiciary was not.

Just as judges began to condemn boycotts of struck cars on the railways, boycotts of "unfair" goods and shops began to flourish in the cities. In 1885 the business journal *Bradstreet's* conducted a national survey of such boycotts. Taking stock of their "prodigious [growth] within two years past," the journal counted 196 such incidents across the country since 1883. The 75 percent success rate was daunting, and the numbers of boycotts continued to multiply over the next few years. In 1886 the Illinois Bureau of Labor Statistics recorded 50 boycotts in that state alone: the outcome was ascertained in 31 of those cases, 14 of which were entirely successful and 26 of which were partly so. In New York, of the 59 boycotts in 1885, the state's Bureau of Statistics of Labor recorded a success rate of 81 percent.

---

24. *See*, e.g., E. Hiller, *The Strike: A Study in Collective Action* 62 (1928); L. Reynolds, *Labor Economics and Labor Relations*, 645 (1974) (discussing the controversy over secondary boycotts).

25. This is why they recurred after losing their place in labor's official arsenal and also why their demise must be seen as having profoundly affected the culture as well as the clout of the labor movement.

26. *See, e.g.*, D. Bensman, *The Practice of Solidarity: American Hat Finishers in the Nineteenth Century*, 11I–50, 202 (1985) (noting sympathy strikes in the hating industry); D. Montgomery, *Fall of the House of Labor: The Workplace, the State, and American Labor Activism, 1865–1925*, 269 (1987) (noting the use of sympathy strikes by the Chicago Federation of Labor).

27. *See* W. Haber, *Industrial Relations in the Building Industry*, 330 (1930) (describing how the sympathy strike was used to protect weaker unions and thereby strengthen their bargaining position). Union constitutions as well as collective agreements with employers in several trades in the 1880s and 1890s included provisions setting metes and bounds for such boycotts. Particularly in the construction and carpentry trades, it was common practice in highly organized cities and regions around the turn of the century for collective agreements to provide that only union-made goods would be used on the projects under contract. See, e.g., *2 Industrial Relations: Final Report and Testimony Submitted to Congress by the Commission on Industrial Relations*, S. Doc. no. 415, 64th Cong., 1st Sess. 1618 (1916); L. Wolman, *The Boycott in American Trade Unions* 50–51 (1916); "Unions May Boycott," 17 *Am. Federationist* 228 (1910) (citing such provisions in Oklahoma building trades and other unions' constitutions and contracts).

28. *See* G. Friedman, "The State and the Making of a Working Class: The United States and France" 20 (paper prepared for Social Science History Conference, St. Louis, Mo., Oct. 1986). Friedman also argues persuasively that legalization of large-scale strikes in France bolstered the fortunes of broad, inclusive unionism in that country. See *ibid*.

The boycott's aims and the solidarities it established beyond individual workplaces distinguished this weapon from the typical strike. In boycotts, as opposed to strikes, "control" issues — enforcing unions' work rules and standards — predominated over wage demands. In addition, the 1880s boycott was almost always a rich illustration of what treatise writers would soon be calling a "compound" or "secondary" boycott. If a city labor federation, for example, called a boycott against a brewer who persistently hired "unfair" men or spurned union work rules, then it would do more than proclaim his beer "unfair." Representatives would visit saloons and call on them to cease serving his beer or face boycotts and picket lines themselves.[29] Similarly, a boycott against a printer meant notifying all the printer's customers — "hotels, boardinghouses, public schools, railroads and steamships" — that all who continued to patronize the printer would be put on the city labor weekly's "black list."[30] An "unfair" newspaper found its advertising columns filled with blank space as advertisers chose to "leave their space entirely blank, and pay the few cents their contracts called for, [rather] than to jeopardize thousands of dollars of trade that fair labor would be 'compelled to withhold so long as such advertisements appeared.'"[31]

These boycotts provoked courts' anxiety and rage, in part because they mobilized whole working-class populations — broad networks of workers (and their families) not linked to individual workplaces or particular unions. "Their action," as one court remarked, "in the language of the times, was purely sympathetic."[32] They rested on the notion of a moral circulation of goods and money ("keep the money of fair men moving only among fair men,"[33] read a typical circular), a world of exchange relations under the rules and norms of working-class organizations like New York's Central Labor Assembly or the Essex Trades Council, rather than under the norms of the marketplace and the rules of the courts.

Gilded Age trade unionists described their unions' work rules and standards as "laws" or "legislation."[34] Courts found "class legislation" constitutionally intolerable when it emanated from state legislatures. Small wonder that they would assail efforts to enforce such "legislation" when the "laws" and their enforcement both sprang from rival, nongovernmental centers of authority like unions, labor assemblies, and trade councils. Boycotts were proto-political challenges to official authority, as well as to employers. They were waged with a rhetoric not merely of "fair wages" but of "redeeming the republic" from the grasp

---

29. *See People v. Wilzig*, 4 N.Y. Crim. Rptr. 403 (1886).

30. *See Crump v. Commonwealth*, 84 Va. 927, 945 (1888). The Gilded Age saw the invention of modern advertising. See generally S. Ewen, *Captains of Consciousness* (1976). In its newspapers as well as boycott circulars, placards, and banners, the era's labor movement devised a kind of counter-advertising extolling "fair" commodities, see *J. Knights Lab.*, Sept. 10, 1891, at 4, col. 5 ("Ask your dealers for the clothing made by the solidarity co-operative"), and condemning "unfair" ones, see *Crump*, 84 Va. At 945 (quoting boycott circular urging "Away With The Goods of this Tyrannical Firm").

31. *Barr v. Essex Trades Council*, 53 N.J. Eq. 101, 108, 30 A. 881, 883 (1894) (quoting a labor union resolution). New Jersey's high Court of Chancery found that the "various trades unions affiliated in the trades council as is claimed by them, represent a purchasing power amounting to over $400,000 in each and every week.' *Ibid.* The trades council "put on foot" this power to intimidate many of the paper's dealers, purchasers, and advertisers to cease buying and advertising therein.

32. *Ibid.* at 115, 30 A. at 886.

33. *Ibid.* at 107, 30 A. at 883.

34. *See* Forbath, "The Ambiguities of Free Labor Labor: Labor and the Law in the Gilded Age," 1985 *Wis. L. Rev.* 787–90.

of "money power judges."[35] Judges saw in the boycott an assault not only on marketplace freedom but on the courts and the state. As a result one New York trial judge dubbed boycotting an odious, "socialistic crime."[36] Another judge declared that "if [boycotts] can be perpetrated with impunity, by combinations of irresponsible cabals or cliques, there will be the end of government."[37] In this mood, courts resolved doctrinal dilemmas, loosened inherited restraints, and extended the labor injunction beyond the railways.

In an effort to shore up the doctrinal obstacles to anti-boycott decrees, boycotters' attorneys would argue that insofar as the plaintiffs sought to enjoin more than peaceful communication they were seeking to enjoin garden-variety crimes.[38] True, equity often enjoined people from using their property in a way that amounted to a nuisance, even though the use was also a crime.[39] But that practice lay worlds apart from enjoining thousands of union members and "whomsoever" would aid or abet them from committing any of an indefinite catalogue of criminal offenses such as assault, battery, or trespass. In boycotts, as in railway strike cases, courts candidly justified this innovation on instrumental grounds. Criminal prosecutions, they said, were inadequate to control or deter such "vast conspiracies as these."[40]

Equity judges also had to contend with the unions' argument that boycotts worked no injury to employers' "property." To answer it the courts changed equity's very definition of that term. In place of the inherited view limiting property rights primarily to tangible objects, they adopted the definition that held property to be anything that had "pecuniary" or "exchangeable value" including a man's business or labor. Because boycotts and strikes injured employers' profit-making activities, and therefore their "pecuniary interests," they trenched on employers' "property."

Judges found support for this view of property in a number of contexts. For centuries, the common law had recognized the property interest of "masters" in the labor of their "servants." As late as the 1820s, the common law, in order to guarantee this property right, continued to allow specific performance in certain categories of master-servant relationships: "laborers," and "journeymen" as well as "apprentices."[41] Economic change and anti-slavery ideals brought about the demise of specific performance of service contracts. Even then, however, the view that an employer could have a "property" interest in

---

35. *See* Scobey, "Boycotting the Politics Factory: Labor Radicalism and the New York City Mayoral Election of 1884," 28–30 *Radical Hist. Rev.* 280 (1984). The same labor-republican rhetoric—as well as the trope of "boycotting the politics factory"—attended the election campaigns that hundreds of cities' central labor assemblies also orchestrated in these same years. *See ibid.* at 287–95. The citywide labor assemblies and their boycotts were likened in the press and before grand juries to the Paris Commune—to insurrectionary workers' governments. *Ibid.*

36. *Wilzig*, 4 N.Y. Crim. Rptr. at 425.

37. *Crump v. Commonwealth*, 84 Va. 927, 946 (1888).

38. Invoking the principle that equity would not enjoin a crime, they ignored equity's willingness to assert its power to protect property from irreparable injury, even if such injury stemmed from a crime. But until the Gilded Age that power had been extremely sparingly exercised, and the maxim against enjoining crimes or trenching on trial by jury was frequently invoked by equity judges themselves.

39. "Developments in the Law—Injunctions," 78 *Harv. L. Rev.* 994, 1013–19 (1965).

40. T. Cogley, *The Law of Strikes, Lockouts, and Labor Organizations,* 342–46 (1894); see also *Arthur v. Oakes*, 63 F. 310, 327–29 (7th Cir. 1894); *Thomas v. Cincinnati, N.O. and T.P. Ry.*, 62 F. 803 (C.C.S.D. Ohio 1894).

41. *See* R. Steinfeld, *The Disappearance of Indentured Servitude and the Invention of Free Labor in the United States* (Univ. of North Carolina Press, 1991).

his workers' toil continued to inform the old common law tort action for enticing away another's servants.[42] In the 1870s, courts extended the enticement action to cases involving organized labor.[43] Treating unions' "interferences" with employers' labor supplies as invasions of property rights may have been hard to reconcile with the liberal individualist zeitgeist.[44] However, the goodwill cases in equity, the enticement action at common law, as well as the centuries-old habit of treating servants' labor as masters' property, meant that there were many familiar mental grooves into which the new notions of property could comfortably fit.[45]

But even more often than to these equity and common law precedents, judges turned to recent constitutional cases for the proposition that a "poor man's labor" as well as his employer's "business or enterprise" was "property."[46] By the latter half of the 1880s a handful of state high courts, commencing with the New York Court of Appeals in *Jacobs*, had begun to declare than an entrepreneur's or worker's right to pursue his calling or business was a constitutional property right. The analogy seemed clear and compelling: just as much recent labor legislation had sought without justification to exploit "the force of mere numbers" to "dictate" to employers how they might "use their property" or conduct

---

42. *See ibid. See* also Orren, "Organized Labor and the Invention of Modem Liberalism in the United States," 2 *Studies in Am. Pol. Dev.* 317, 329–31 (1987). In the latter half of the eighteenth century, courts gradually rearticulated the enticement action in contractual terms: the master's property right was now said to rest in the contract and its fulfillment rather than in the services of the laborer as such. See Note, "Tortious Interference with Contractual Relations in the Nineteenth Century: The Transformation of Property, Contract, and Tort," 93 *Harv. L. Rev.* 1510, 1522–23 (1980) (authored by Nockleby).

43. In *Walker v. Cronin*, 107 Mass. 555 (1871), defendant, a shoemaker and fledgling union organizer, persuaded a number of plaintiff's employees "to leave and abandon" plaintiff's employment. The court held that plaintiff could collect damages for the injury to his business. "Everyone has a right to enjoy the fruits and" advantages of his own enterprise, industry, skill and credit," the court declared. *Ibid.* at 564. The specific right infringed by the defendant organizer was plaintiff's property right "derived from the [at will] contract[s]" between him and his striking workers. *Ibid.* at 567.

44. One equity judge, rejecting an 1880 employer's petition for an anti-strike decree based on the enticement right of action, declared: "[T]he origin of this kind of actions was at a time of the substantial enslavement of domestic servants, and at the outset it proceeded upon the theory that such servants had not freedom of action which is conceded to that class at the present day ... [T]he person enticed is a free agent to come and go as he will, responsible only, like other persons, for the violation of his contract or his duty." *Johnston Harvester Co. v. Meinhardt*, 9 Abb. N. Cas. 393, 400 (1880), *aff'd*, 31 N.Y. Sup. Ct. 489 (1881).

45. I differ somewhat, then, with those who treat the "propertyization" of labor relations in the late nineteenth century as a dramatic shift in legal thought. *See* Hurvitz, "American Labor Law and the Doctrine of Entrepreneurial Property Rights: Boycotts, Courts and Juridical Reorientation of 1886–1895," 8 *Indus. Rel. L. J.* 307, 313–16 (1986); Vandevelde, "The New Property of the Nineteenth Century: The Development of the Modern Concept of Property," 29 *Buff. L. Rev.* 325 (1980).

46. Above all, they cited the *Slaughter-House Cases*, 83 U.S. (16 Wall.) 36, 116, (Bradley, J., dissenting), which noted that "a calling, when chosen, is a man's property and right"; *ibid.* at 110 (Field, J. dissenting); and *In re* Jacobs, 98 N.Y. 98 (1885). The anti-boycott injunctions relying on these two substantive due process cases include *Barr v. United Essex Trades Council*, 53 N.J. Eq. 101, 30 A. 881 (1894); and *Brace Bros. v. Evans*, 5 Pa. C. 163 (1888). Similarly, in *Pierce v. Stablemen's Union*, 156 Cal. 70, 103 P. 324 (1909), the California Supreme Court cited to *Ex parte Jentzsch*, 112 Cal. 468, 4 P. 803 (1896), for the proposition that "constitutional liberty means ... among other rights ... the right freely to labor and to own the fruits of [one's] toil." *Pierce*, 156 Cal. at 78, 103 P. at 328. The classic liberal marketplace definition of "property" as anything with "exchangeable value" including the "poor man's labor" and his employer's "firm" found its first constitutional expression in Field's and Bradley's *Slaughter-House* dissents, but one can find common law dicta in the same year in earlier employment contract cases.

their businesses, so too did the new boycotts.[47] Believing that the right to pursue one's calling was a natural right that the common law had protected ever since it broke free from "feudal fetters," many Gilded Age jurists did not find it anomalous to borrow precedent from public law in determining a private law right. The new constitutional right seemed to them merely a constitutional recognition of long-standing—and inviolable—common law protections.[48] In both contexts, the same new "movement of coercion" justified court-imposed boundaries beyond which such interferences with "the rights of property" by force of numbers became illegal.

Whereas the constitutional cases were rather general and terse in their new definition of property, injunction suits led to a more elaborate redefinition—a kind of refeudalization—of work and employment relations.[49] Where a mid-nineteenth-century employer had been merely at liberty to do business with such customers or suppliers as he chose, he was now found to have a property right in these business relations defensible by injunction against boycotters' pressures. Where he had been merely free to run his shop, and use his machinery, as he willed, he now was found to have a property right to do so that was protected from interference created by a boycott or strike pressing for adherence to union work rules and standards. Where previously he had been merely free to hire whomever he liked, now he had a property interest in his employment relations and in the "natural flow" of labor to his shop or factory.[50]

Because this vision of property allowed virtually any strike to be cast as an interference with an employer's property rights, judges reasserted a set of limiting principles that marked off a realm of legitimate strikes. Judge Taft again took the lead, first on a state and then on a federal bench.[51] Relying on criminal conspiracy doctrine, he suggested that one could identify enjoinable strikes by dint of their objects or motives. The general rule was that strikes seeking no immediate gain for the strikers—defined in narrow terms which,

---

47. *See Essex Trades Council,* 53 N.J. Eq. 101, 30 A. 881; see also Taft, "The Right of Private Property," 3 *Mich. L. J.* 215, 227–28 (1894); D. Brewer, *Report of the New York Bar Association Proceedings* 37–47 (1893).

48. *See, e.g., Essex Trades Council,* 53 N.J. Eq. 101, 30 A. 881; *Slaughter-House,* 83 U.S. (16 Wall.) 36, 93 (Field, J., dissenting); id. at 111 (Bradley, J., dissenting). The notion that a unitary right was involved and had determinate implications across broad public and private doctrinal domains also reflected the habits of mind of a distinctive era in the history of legal thought. *See* Kennedy, "Toward an Historical Understanding of Legal Consciousness: The Case of Classical Legal Thought in America, 1850–1940," 3 *Res. L. and Soc.* 3 (1980).

49. Gilded Age trade unionists did not need legal historians to remind them of the old law of master and servant and its recognition of property rights in labor. That history was part of their common culture, and they accused the Gilded Age judges of refeudalizing the law of industrial relations with the labor injunction, just as the judges accused them of refeudalizing it with hours legislation. For the courts', see Forbath, "Ambiguities of Free Labor," *supra* note 14, at 800. For a provocative argument that American labor law remained "feudal" until the New Deal, *see* K. Orren, *Belated Feudalism: Law and Liberal Development in the United States.*

50. *See, e.g., Oxley Stave Co. v. Coopers' Int'l Union,* 72 F. 695 (C.C.D. Kan. 1896); *Casey v. Cincinnati Typographical Union No. 3,* 45 F. 135 (C.C.S.D. Ohio 1891); *Jersey City Printing Co. v. Cassidy,* 63 N.J. Eq. 759, 53 A. 230 (1902); *Matthews v. Shankland,* 56 N.Y.S. 123 (1898); *Brace Bros. v. Evans,* 5 Pa. C. 163, 166–67 (1888). These developments are well chronicled in Hurvitz, *supra.* note 42, at 338–44.

Without judicial protection of these "property rights," one anti-boycott decision declared, the country's industrial and transportation systems would "become dependent on the paternalism of the national government, and the factory and the workshop subject to the uncertain chances of cooperative systems." *Essex Trades Council,* 53 N.J. Eq. at 113–14, 30 A. at 885.

51. See *Moores v. Bricklayers' Union,* 10 Ohio Dec. Reprint 665 (1889); *Casey v. Cincinnati Typographical Union,* 45 F. 135 (C.C.S.D. Ohio 1891). For detailed analyses of these two cases and Taft's role in forging new doctrine, *see* Hurvitz, *supra.* note 42, at 328–32, 337–39.

until the early 1900s, did not transcend wages or working conditions—were deemed to be prompted by malice. Within this conceptual framework, many control and work-rule strikes, strikes for union recognition or for closed shops, and all sympathy strikes and producer or consumer boycotts could be categorized as illegal.[52] As with the sympathy strike, the demise of the citywide boycott was brought on by its legal repression. In 1886, in New York City alone more than one hundred trade unionists were sentenced to state penitentiary terms in conspiracy and injunction suits. Over the new two years boycotts became less aggressive and scored fewer victories. Trade unions, the state's Commissioner of Labor observed, were no longer resorting to "the boycott … as frequently … as in former years."[53] It had lost much of its potency "as a war measure." Judicial decisions had "thrown impediments" in the boycotters' path.[54] By the late 1880s the number of reported citywide boycotts everywhere had dwindled substantially, and after 1890 virtually all the state bureaus of labor statistics stopped reporting them. The diminishing numbers can partially be explained by union and assembly reluctance to report on outlawed activities for state publication. There seems little doubt, however, that the particular form of boycotting that flourished in the mid-1880s, rich with political and cultural significance, with its emphasis on active community mobilization, largely died away under a judicial ban.

---

52. For cases on union work rules and standards, *see Benito Rovira Co. v. Yampolsky*, 187 N.Y.S. 894 (1921), which held illegal a strike to enforce union work standards and work rules; *Hopkins v. Oxley Stave Co.*, 83 F. 912 (8th Cir. 1897) (same); *Folsom Engraving Co. v. McNeil*, 235 Mass. 269, 126 N.E. 479 (1920) (same); But cf *Davis Mach. Co. v. Robinson*, 41 Misc. 329, 84 N.Y.S. 837 (N.Y. Sup. Ct. 1903) (same); and *Jaeckel v. Kaufman*, 187 N.Y.S. 889 (1920) (same). But cf. *National Fireproofing Co. v. Mason Builders' Ass'n*, 169 F. 259 (2d Cir. 1909) (holding legal a strike to enforce union work standards); *Pickett v. Walsh*, 192 Mass. 583, 78 N.E. 753 (1906) (same).

For cases condemning strikes for union recognition, *see Michaels v. Hillman*, 112 Misc. 395, 183 N.Y.S. 195 (1920), which held a strike for union recognition illegal; *Tunstall v. Stearns Coal Co.*, 192 F. 808 (6th Cir. 1911) (same); *Reynolds v. Davis*, 198 Mass. 294, 84 N.E. 457 (1908) (same); and *In re Higgins*, 27 F. 443 (C.C.N.D. Tex. 1886) (same).

For cases condemning strikes to force employer to adopt a union, *see Folsom v. Lewis*, 208 Mass. 336, 94 N.E. 316 (1911), which held a strike for closed shop illegal, and *Erdman v. Mitchell*, 207 Pa. 79, 756 A. 327 (1903) (same). But cf. *National Protective Ass'n of Steamfitters v. Cumming*, 170 N.Y. 315, 63 N.E. 369 (1902) (holding a strike to force discharge of nonunion workers legal).

For cases condemning boycotts of "unfair" materials or shops, *see Gompers v. Buck's Stove and Range Co.*, 221 U.S. 418 (1911), which held that workers may not strike or threaten to oppose working for companies producing "unfair" goods; *Aikens v. Wisconsin*, 195 U.S. 194 (1904) which held as unlawful under a state statute a combination of newspaper managers demanding advertisers pay their papers the same rate as the "injured" party newspaper; *Burnham v. Dowd*, 217 Mass. 351, 104 N.E. 841 (1914), which enjoined the Bricklayers and Plasterers Union from keeping the plaintiff's business on the "unfair list" of the union; and *Auburn Draying Co. v. Wardwell*, 227 N.Y. 1, 124 N.E. 97 (1919), which enjoined a boycott by butchers, bakers, plumbers, and others of an "unfair" draying firm. But cf. *Bossert v. Dhuy*, 221 N.Y. 342, 117 N.E. 582 (1917), which held that carpenters may refuse to work on "unfair" wood trim where work conditions surrounding manufacture of the "unfair" material directly affect members of the same union.

For cases condemning unions urging consumer boycotts, *see Gompers*, 221 U.S. 418 (1911), which held union urging of consumer boycott illegal; *Loewe v. Lawlor*, 208 U.S. 274 (1908); *Brace Bros. v. Evans*, 5 Pa. C. 163 (1888). But cf. *Robison v. Hotel and Restaurant Employees Local No. 782*, Idaho 418, 207 P. 132 (1922) (holding that workers may urge the public to participate in a boycott with a legal purpose); *Rosenberg v. Retail Clerks' Ass'n Local 428*, 27 Cal. App. 769, 177 P. 864 (1918) (same).

53. *See 1887 Annual Report of New York State Bureau of Statistics of Labor*, 521.

54. *Ibid.* By 1892 the number of boycotts reported to the Commissioner had fallen to less than half of those reported in 1890. Compare *1890 Annual Report of New York State Bureau of Statistics of Labor*, vol. 2, at 1170, with 1892 *Annual Report of New York State Bureau of Statistics of Labor*, vol. 2, at 230.

Interlude

Industrial Unionism

Eugene V. Debs circa 1895.

Eugene V. Debs

Speech at Chicago, November 25, 1905

The unity of labor, economic and political, upon the basis of the class struggle, is at this time the supreme need of the working class. The prevailing lack of unity implies lack of class consciousness; that is to say, enlightened self-interest; and this can, must and will be overcome by revolutionary education and organization. Experience, long, painful and dearly bought, has taught some of us that craft division is fatal to class unity. To accomplish its mission the working class must be united. They must act together; they must assert their combined power, and when they do this upon the basis of the class struggle, then and then only will they break the fetters of wage slavery.

We are engaged today in a class war; and why? For the simple reason that in the evolution of the capitalist system in which we live, society has been mainly divided into two economic classes—a small class of capitalists who own the tools with which work is done and wealth is produced, and a great mass of workers who are compelled to use those tools. Between these two classes there is an irrepressible economic conflict. Unfortunately for himself, the workingman does not yet understand the nature of the conflict, and for this reason has hitherto failed to accomplish any effective unity of his class.

It is true that workers in the various departments of industrial activity have organized trade unions. It is also true that in this capacity they have from time to time asserted such power as this form of organization has conferred upon them. It is equally true that mere craft unionism, no matter how well it may be organized, is in the present

91

highly developed capitalist system utterly unable to successfully cope with the capitalist class. The old craft union has done its work and belongs to the past. Labor unionism, like everything else, must recognize and bow to the inexorable law of evolution.

The craft union says that the worker shall receive a fair day's pay for a fair day's work. What is a fair day's pay for a fair day' work? Ask the capitalist and he will give you his idea about it. Ask the worker and, if he is intelligent, he will tell you that a fair day's pay for a fair day's work is all the workingman produces.

While the craft unionist still talks about a fair day's pay for a fair day's work, implying that the economic interests of the capitalist and the worker can be harmonized upon a basis of equal justice to both, the Industrial Worker says, "I want all I produce by my labor."

If the worker is not entitled to all he produces, then what share is anybody else entitled to?

Does the worker today receive all he produces? Does he receive anything like a fair (?) share of the product of his labor? Will any trade-unionist of the old school make any such claim, and if he is bold enough to make it, can he verify it?

The student of this question knows that, as a matter of fact, in the capitalist system in which we live today the worker who produces all wealth receives but enough of his product to keep him in working and producing order. His wage, in the aggregate, is fixed by his living necessities. It suffices, upon the average, to maintain him according to the prevailing standard of living and to enable him to reproduce himself in the form of labor power. He receives, as a matter of fact, but about 17 per cent of what his labor produces.

The worker produces a certain thing. It goes from the manufacturer to the jobber, from the jobber to the wholesaler, and from the wholesaler to the retailer—each of these adding a profit, and when it completes the circle and comes back to the worker who produced it and he stands face to face with the product of his own labor, he can buy back, upon the average, with his paltry wage but about 17 per cent of it. In other words, he is exploited, robbed, of about 83 percent of what his labor produces. And why? For the simple reason that in modern industry, the tool, in the form of a great machine with which he works and produces, is the private property of the capitalist, who didn't make it, and could not, if his life depended upon it, use it.

The evolution is not yet complete.

By virtue of his private ownership of the social tool—made and used by the co-operative labor of the working class—the employer has the economic power to appropriate to himself, as a capitalist, what is produced by the social labor of the working class. This accounts for the fact that the capitalist becomes fabulously rich, lives in a palace where there is music and singing and dancing, and where there is the luxury of all climes, while the workingmen who do the work and produce the wealth and endure the privations and make the sacrifices of health and limb and life, remain in a wretched state of poverty and dependence.

The exploiting capitalist is the economic master and the political ruler in capitalist society, and as such holds the exploited wage worker in utter contempt.

No master ever had any respect for his slave, and no slave ever had, or ever could have, any real love for his master.

The capitalist papers know that there is such an organization as the Industrial Workers, because they have lied about it. Just now they are ignoring it. Let me serve notice on them through you and the thousands of other who flock to our meetings everywhere, that they will reckon with the Industrial Workers before six months have rolled around.

There are those wage workers who feel their economic dependence, who know that the capitalist for whom they work is the owner of their job, and therefore the master of their fate, who are still vainly seeking by individual effort and through waning craft unions to harmonize the conflicting interests of the exploiting capitalist and the exploited wage slave. They are engaged in a vain and hopeless task. They are wasting time and energy worthy of a better cause. These interests never can and never will be harmonized permanently, and when they are adjusted even temporarily it is always at the expense of the working class.

It is no part of the mission of this revolutionary working class union to conciliate the capitalist class. We are organized to fight that class, and we want that class to distinctly understand it. And they do understand it, and in time the working class will also understand it; and then the capitalist class will have reason to understand it better still. Their newspapers understand it so well even now that they have not a single favorable comment to make upon it.

When the convention of delegates was in session here in June last for the purpose of organizing the Industrial Workers, every report that appeared in a Chicago paper — capitalist paper I mean; every single report was a tissue of perversion, misstatement and downright falsehood. They knew that we had met for a purpose, and that that purpose was to fight the class of which they are the official mouthpieces. Now, it seems to me that this uniform hostility of the capitalist press ought to be significant to even the unthinking workingman. Capitalist papers are, as a rule, quite friendly to the craft unions. They do not misrepresent them; do no lie about them; do not traduce their representatives. They are exceedingly fond of them, because they know enough about their own interests to know that the craft unions are not only not a menace to them, but are in fact bulwarks of defense to them. And why? Because, chiefly, craft unions divide and do not unite the working class. And I challenge contradiction.

There was a time when the craft union expressed in terms of unionism the prevailing mode of industry. That was long ago when production was still mainly carried on by handicraftsmen with hand tools; when one man worked for another to learn his trade that he might become its master. The various trades involved skill and cunning; considerable time was required to master them. This was in the early stages of the capitalist system. Even at that early day the antagonism between employer and employed found expression, although the employer was not at that time the capitalist as he is today. The men who followed these trades found it necessary in order to protect themselves in their trade interests to band together, form a union, so that they might act together in resisting the encroachments of the "boss." So the trade union came into existence.

The mode of production since that time has been practically revolutionized. The hand tool has all but disappeared. The mammoth machine has taken its place. The hand tool was made and used by the individual worker and was largely within his own control. Today the machine that has supplanted the old tool is not owned nor controlled by the man, or rather the men, who use it. As I have already said, it is the private property of some capitalist who may live at a remote point and never have seen the machine or the wage slaves who operate it.

In other words, the production of wealth, in the evolution of industry, from being an individual act a half century ago has become a social act. The tool, from being an individual tool, has become a social instrument. So that the tool has been socialized and production has also been socialized. But the evolution is yet to complete its work. This social tool, made socially and used socially, must be socially owned.

In the evolution of industry the trade has been largely undermined. The old trade union expresses the old form of industry, the old mode of individual production based upon the use of the individual tool. That tool has about disappeared; that mode of production has also about disappeared, but the trade union built upon that mode of production, springing from the use of the hand tool, remains essentially the same.

The pure and simple trade union, in seeking to preserve its autonomy, is forced into conflict with other trade unions by the unceasing operation of the laws of industrial evolution. How many of the skilled trades that were in operation half a century ago are still practiced?

At the town where I live there used to be quite a number of cooper shops. Barrels were made by hand and a cooper shop consisted wholly of coopers. The coopers' union was organized and served fairly well the purposes of the coopers of that day, but it does not serve the purposes of the workers who make barrels today. They do not make barrels in the way they used to be made. Today we want a union that expresses the economic interests of all the workers in the cooperage plant engaged in making and handling barrels. But a few coopers still remain, a very few. It is no longer necessary to be a cooper to make a barrel. The machine is the cooper today. The machine makes the barrel, and almost anyone can operate the machine that makes the barrel.

You will observe that labor has been subdivided and specialized and that the trade has been dissipated; and now a body of men and boys work together co-operatively in the making of a barrel, each making a small part of a barrel. Now we want a union which embraces all the workers engaged in making barrels. We lose sight of the cooper trade as evolution has practically disposed of that. We say that since the trade has completely changed, the union which expressed that trade must also change accordingly. In the new union we shall include not only the men who are actually engaged in the making of barrels directly, but also those who are placing them upon the market. There are the typewriters, the bookkeepers, the teamsters, and all other classes of labor that are involved in the making and delivering of the barrels. We insist that all the workers in the whole of any given plant shall belong to one and the same union.

This is the very thing the workers need and the capitalist who owns the establishment does not want. He believes in labor unionism if it is the "right kind." And if it is the right kind for him it is the wrong kind for you. He is more than willing that his employees shall join the craft union. He has not the slightest objection. On the contrary, it is easily proven that capitalists are among the most active upholders of the old craft unions.

The capitalists are perfectly willing that you shall organize, as long as you don't do a thing against them; as long as you don't do a thing for yourselves. You cannot do a thing for yourselves without antagonizing them; and you don't antagonize them through your craft unions nearly as much as you buttress their interests and prolong their mastery.

You are a workingman! Now, at your earliest leisure look yourself over and take an inventory of your resources. Invoice your mental stock; see what you have on hand.

You may be of limited mentality; and that is all you require in the capitalist system. You need only small brains, but huge hands.

Most of your hands are calloused and you are taught by the capitalist politician, who is the political mercenary of the capitalist who fleeces you, you are taught by him to be proud of your horny hands. If that is true he ought to be ashamed of his. He doesn't have any horns on his hands. He has them on his brain. He is as busy with his brain as you are with your hands, and because he is busy with his brain and you neglect yours, he gets a goodly share of what you produce with your hands. He is the gentleman who calls you the horny handed sons of toil. That fetches you every time. I tell you that the time has come for you to use your brains in your own interest, and until you do that you will have to use your hands in the interest of your masters.

Now, after you have looked yourself over; after you have satisfied yourself what you are, or rather, what you are not, you will arrive at the conclusion that as a wage worker in capitalist society you are not a man at all. You are simply a thing. And that thing is bought in the labor market, just as hair, hides and other forms of merchandise are bought.

When the capitalist requires the use of your hands, does he call for men? Why, certainly not. He doesn't want men, he only wants hands. And when he calls for hands, that is what he wants. Have you ever seen a placard posted: "Fifty hands wanted'? Did you ever know of a capitalist to respond to that kind of an invitation?

President Roosevelt would have you believe that there are no classes in the United States. He was made president by the votes of the working class. Did you ever know of his stopping over night in the home of a workingman? Is it by mere chance that he is always sheltered beneath the hospitable roof of some plutocrat? Not long ago he made a visit here and he gave a committee representing the workers about fifteen minutes of his precious time, just time enough to rebuke them with the intimation that organized labor consisted of a set of lawbreakers, and then he gave fifteen hours to the plutocrats of Chicago, being wined and dined by them to prove that there are no classes in the United States, and that you, horny handed veteran, with your wage of $1.50 a day, with six children to support on that, are in the same class with John D. Rockefeller! Your misfortune is that you do not know you are in the same class. But on election day it dawns upon you and you prove it by voting the same ticket.

Since you have looked yourself over thoroughly, you realize by this time that, as a workingman, you have been supporting, through your craft unions and through your ballots, a social system that is the negation of your manhood.

The capitalist for whom you work doesn't have to go out and look for you; you have to look for him, and you belong to him just as completely as if he had a title to your body; as if you were his chattel slave.

He doesn't own you under law, but he does under the fact.

Why? Because he owns the tool with which you work, and you have got to have access to that tool if you work; and if you want to live you have got to work. If you don't work you don't eat; and so, scourged by hunger pangs, you look about for that tool and you locate it, and you soon discover that between yourself, a workingman, and that tool that is an essential part of yourself in industry, there stands the capitalist who owns it. He is your boss; he owns your job, takes your product and controls your destiny. Before you can touch that tool to earn a dime you must petition the owner of it to allow you to use it, in consideration of your giving to him all you produce with it, except just enough to keep you alive and in working order.

Observe that you are displaced by the surplus product of your own labor; that what you produce is of more value under capitalism than you who produce it; that the commodity which is the result of your labor is of greater value under capitalism than your own life. You consist of palpitating flesh; you have wants. You have necessities. You cannot satisfy them, and you suffer. But the product of your labor, the property of the capitalist, that is sacred; that must be protected at all hazards. After you have been displaced by the surplus product of your labor and you have been idle long enough, you become restive and you begin to speak out, and you become a menace. The unrest culminates in trouble. The capitalist presses a button and the police are called into action. Then the capitalist presses button No. 2 and injunctions are issued by the judges, the judicial allies and servants of the capitalist class. Then button No. 3 is pressed and the state troops fall into line; and if this is not sufficient button No. 4 is pressed and the regular soldiers come marching to the scene. That is what President Roosevelt meant when he said that back of the mayor is the governor, back of the governor the President; or, to use his own words, back of the city, the state and back of the state the nation—the capitalist nation.

If you have been working in a steel mill and you have made more steel than your master can sell, and you are locked out and get hungry, and the soldiers are called out, it is to protect the steel and shoot you who made the steel—to guard the men who steal the steel and kill the men who made it.

I am not asking you to withdraw from the craft unions simply because the Industrial Workers has been formed. I am asking you to think about these matters for yourselves.

I belonged to a craft union from the time I was nineteen years of age. I can remember the very evening I first joined the Brotherhood of Locomotive Firemen. I can recall with what zeal I went to work to organize my craft, and it was the pride of my life to see that union expand. I did what I could to build it up. In time I was made to realize that that union was not sufficient unto itself. I next did what I could to organize other branches of the service and then establish a federation of the various unions of railroad employees, and finally succeeded; but soon after the federation was formed, on account of craft jealousies, it was disrupted. I then, along with a number of others who had had the same experience and had profited by it, undertook to organize the railway men within one organization, known as the American Railway Union. The railroad corporations were the deadly enemies of that organization. They understood that its purpose was to unify all the railroad employees. They knew that the unity of the working class meant their end, and so they set their faces like flint against the American Railway Union. And while they were using all their powers to crush and to stamp out the American Railway Union, they were bestowing all their favors upon the several craft brotherhoods, the engineers and the firemen, the conductors and the brakemen. They knew that so long as these craft unions existed there could be no unification of the men employed in the railway service.

Are the railroad men of this country organized today? No! Not nearly one-half of them are organized at all. And when the railroad corporations from motives of good policy make a concession to the engineers or the conductors, it is gouged out of the poor devils who work for a dollar a day and are compelled to submit.

There are a great many engineers who are perfectly willing to be tied up in a contract. They think they can save themselves at the expense of their fellow-workers. But they are going to reap, sooner or later, just what they have sown. In the next few years they will become motermen.

While we are upon this question, let us consult industrial history a moment. We will begin with the craft union railroad strike of 1888. The Brotherhood of Engineers and the Brotherhood of Firemen on the C., B. & Q. system went out on strike. Some 2,000 engineers and firemen vacated their posts and went out on one of the most bitterly contested railroad strikes, the rest of the employees, especially the conductors, who were organized in craft unions of their own, remained at their posts, and the union conductors piloted the scab engineers over the line. I know whereof I speak. I was there. I took an active part in that strike.

I saw craft union pitted against craft union, and I saw the Brotherhood of Engineers and the Brotherhood of Firemen completely wiped from the C.,B. & Q. system. And now you find these men, seventeen years later, scattered all over the United States. They had to pay the penalty of their ignorance in organizing a craft instead of organizing as a whole.

In 1892 a strike occurred on the Lehigh Valley; the same result. Another on the Toledo, Ann Arbor & North Michigan. Same result. The engineers have had no strike from that time to this. Every time they have had a strike they have been defeated.

The railroad corporations are shrewd enough to recognize the fact that if they can keep certain departments in their employ in a time of emergency they can defeat all the rest. A manager of a railroad who can keep control of 15 per cent of the old men can allow 85 per cent to go out on strike and defeat them every time. That is why they have made some concessions to the engineers and conductors and brakesmen, and now and then to the switchmen, the most militant labor union of them all.

A year and a half ago the telegraph operators on the Missouri, Kansas & Texas went out on strike. The engineer remained at his post; so did the fireman; the conductor at his; and the brakeman at his. And they hauled the scabs that flocked from all pats of the country to the several points along the line, and delivered them in good order to take the places vacated by the strikers; worked all round them and with them until they had mastered the details of their several duties; and having done this, the strike was at an end, and the 1,300 craft unionists out of jobs. You will find them scattered all over the country.

Now, were not these other craft unions scabbing on the telegraphers just as flagrantly as if they had stepped into their positions and discharged their duties? They were acting with the corporation against their union fellow workingmen, helping the corporation to defeat and crush them. Without their aid the corporation could not have succeeded. With their aid it was very easily done.

Is it possible that a craft unionist can see such an object lesson as this so plainly presented to him and still refuse to profit by it? Still close his eyes and, as it were, shut up his reason, and absolutely decline to see that this is suicidal policy and that its fruit must always be disruption and disaster?

This world only respects as it is compelled to respect; and if you workingmen would be respected you must begin by respecting yourselves. You have had enough of this sort of experience. You have had more than enough of it right here in Chicago.

Why didn't the steel trust annihilate the Amalgamated Steelworkers? Only two years ago they defeated them completely. The trust had its iron heel upon the neck of the Steelworkers' Union, and could have, had it chosen, completely crushed the life out of it. But Morgan was too wily. Schwab was too wise. They used to oppose trade unions. They don't oppose them any longer. They have discovered that a union can be turned the other way; that it can be made useful to them instead of being useful to the working class. Morgan now says he is in favor of trade unions, and Schwab agrees. They didn't crush out the Steelworkers' Union because they knew that another and a better one would spring from its ruins. They were perfectly willing that the old craft union should grow up again and block the way to real union.

You have had a machinists' strike here in Chicago. You are well aware of this without my telling you. There is something pathetic to me about every strike.

I have said and say again that no strike was ever lost; that it has always been worth all it cost. An essential part of a workingman's education is the defeats he encounters. The strikes he loses are after all the only ones he wins. I am heartily glad for myself that I lost the strike. It is the best thing that ever happened to me. I lost the strike of the past that I may win the strike of the future.

In this barbarous competitive struggle in which we are engaged, the workers, the millions, are fighting each other to sell themselves into slavery; the middle class are fighting each other to other to get enough trade to keep soul and body together, and the professional class are fighting each other like savages for practice. And this is called civilization! What a mockery! What a sham! There is no real civilization in the capitalist system.

Today there is nothing so easily produced as wealth. The whole earth consists of raw materials; and in every breath of nature, in sunshine, and in shower, hidden everywhere, are the subtle forces that may, by the touch of the hand of labor, be set into operation to transmute these raw materials into wealth, the finished products, in all their multiplied forms and in opulent abundance for all. The merest child can press a button that will set in operation a forest of machinery and produce wealth enough for a community.

Whatever may be said of the ignorant, barbarous past, there is no excuse for poverty today. And yet it is the scourge of the race. It is the Nemesis of capitalist civilization. Ten millions, one-eighth of our whole population, are in a state of chronic poverty. Three millions of these have been sunk to unresisting pauperism. The whole working class is in a sadly dependent state, and even the most favored wage-worker is left suspended by a single thread. He does not know what hour a machine may be invented to make his trade useless, displace him and throw him into the increasing army of the unemployed.

And how does labor live today? Here in Chicago you may walk along a certain boulevard, say 18th street, and you will find it lined with magnificent palaces. Beyond that you will find a larger district where the still complacent middle class abide. Beyond that is a very much larger territory where the working class exist; and still beyond that, to complete the circle, you see the red lights flickering in the distance.

Prostitution is a part, a necessary part, of capitalist society. The department store empties in the slums.

I have been here enough to know that when the daughter of a workingman is obliged to go up the street to look for employment, when she is fourteen or fifteen years of age, and ought to be in the care and keeping of a loving mother, and have all of the advantages that our civilization makes possible for all—when she is forced to go to a department store, to one of those capitalist emporiums, and there find a place, if she can, and work for a wage of $3 a week, and have to obey a code of cast-iron regulations, appear tidy and neatly dressed and be subjected to a thousand temptations daily, and then takes a misstep, the first, as she is more than apt to do, especially if she has no home in any decent sense of that term—the very instant this is added to her poverty, she is doomed—damned. All the doors of capitalist society are closed in her face. The coals of contumely are poured upon her head. There is for her no redemption, and she takes the next step, and the next, until at last she ends a disgraceful career in a brothel hell.

This may be your child. And if you are a workingman, and this should fall to the lot of the innocent blue-eyed child that you love more than you do your own life—I want you to realize that if such a horror be written in the book of fate, that you are responsible for it, if you use or misuse your power to perpetuate the capitalist system and working class slavery.

You can change this condition—not tomorrow, not next week, nor next year; but in the meantime the next thing to changing it is making up your mind that it shall be changed.

That is what we Industrial Unionists have done. And so there has come to us a new state of mind, and in our hearts there is the joy of service and the serenity of triumph.

We are united and we cannot be disunited. We cannot be stampeded. We know that we are confronted by ten thousand difficulties. We know that all the powers of capitalism are to be arrayed against us. But were these obstacles multiplied by a million, it would simply have the effect of multiplying our determination by a million, to overcome them all. And so we are organizing and appealing to you.

The workingman today does not understand his industrial relation to his fellow-workers. He has never been correlated with others in the same industry. He has mechanically done his part. He has simply been a cog, with little reference to, or knowledge of, the rest of the cogs. Now, we teach him to hold up his head and look over the whole mechanism. If he is employed in a certain plant, as an Industrial Unionist, his eyes are opened. He takes a survey of the entire productive mechanism, and he understands his part in it, and his relation to every other worker in that industry. The very instant he does that he is buoyed by a fresh hope and thrilled with a new aspiration. He becomes a larger man. He begins to feel like a collective son of toil.

Then he and his fellows study to fit themselves to take control of this productive mechanism when it shall be transferred from the idle capitalist to the workers to whom it rightfully belongs.

In every mill and every factory, every mine and every quarry, every railroad and every shop, everywhere, the workers, enlightened, understanding their self-interest, are correlating themselves in the industrial and economic mechanism. They are developing their industrial consciousness, their economic and political power; and when the revolution comes, they will be prepared to take possession and assume control of every industry. With the education they will have received in the Industrial Workers they will be drilled and disciplined, trained and fitted for Industrial Mastery and Social Freedom.

Interlude

The IWW and Free Speech Fights

IWW Poster.

Elizabeth Gurley Flynn

The working class of Spokane are engaged in a terrific conflict, one of the most vital of the local class struggles. It is a fight for more than free speech. It is to prevent the free press and labor's right to organize from being throttled.

Between three and four hundred men have now been sentenced for speaking on the street.

Those who repeated the crime of saying "Fellow Workers" on the street corner were given thirty days, one hundred dollars' fine and costs. The trials have given additional proof to our much-disputed charge that justice in the United States is a farce. Fellow Worker Little was asked by the Judge what he was doing when arrested. He answered "reading the Declaration of Independence." "Thirty days," said the Judge.

Every day men have gone upon the streets in numbers ranging from six to twenty-five and thirty, have said "Fellow Workers" and have been railroaded for thirty days with a hundred dollars fine and costs. Ordered to work on the rock pile, and refusing, they have been given only bread and water in meager rations. Bread and water for a hundred and thirty days means slow starvation, means legal murder, yet even on Thanksgiving day, the only exception made to the rule was to give smaller portions of more sour bread. The good, Christian Chief of Police Sullivan sneeringly remarked, when asked if the turkey and cranberry dinner applied to all: "The IWW will find the water faucet in good order." As a result of this diet the boys have become physical wrecks and are suffering with the scurvy and other foul discases.

Spokane, 1909–10

*Philip S. Foner**

"The I.W.W storm center for the West just now appears to be Spokane, Wash.," the *Industrial Union Bulletin* of February 20, 1909, reported. Here in the largest western center of the migratory workers, the I.W.W. was conducting its most successful membership drive, and building the biggest local union in the organization. One reason for the success was the campaign it was leading to remedy the most pressing grievance of the "floaters" shipping out of Spokane—the fraudulent employment agencies, or as the Wobblies bitterly labeled them, the employment sharks. The sharks, in alliance with unscrupulous employers, fleeced the "floaters" of thousands of dollars by sending applicants to jobs that did not exist. Not only did the men lose the fee, paid in advance, but the railroad fare to and from the place where they had been sent, and, of course, the time spent. In cases where a job was landed, it usually turned out to last only long enough for the foreman to collect the fee which he split with the employment sharks. The vicious system provoked the grim joke that the sharks had discovered perpetual motion—"one man going to a job, one man on the job, and one man leaving the job." One Wobbly reported that a single firm employing only 100 men at a time hired and fired 5,000 men during the season.[1]

Late in 1908, I.W.W. speakers began to attack the system on streets in Spokane near the employment agencies, exposing their practices and citing evidence of hundreds of cases of workers who were fleeced by their trickery. The I.W.W. called for a boycott of the agencies and demanded that the employers hire through the union. The "Don't Buy Jobs" campaign of the I.W.W. so frightened the sharks that they formed the Associated Agencies of Spokane, and at its instigation, the City Council passed an ordinance in October 1908 prohibiting "the holding of public meeting on any of the streets, sidewalks or alleys within the fire limits" after January 1, 1909.[2] The ostensible reason for the ordinance was to prevent traffic congestion. The I.W.W. was informed that the Wobblies could hold their meetings in the public parks and vacant lots, but these were blocks away from the scene of the struggle against the sharks.

During the winter months the I.W.W. violated the ordinance, again holding meetings in front of the employment agencies. But the organization actually won commendation from the press for preventing indignant workers from violently venting their rage against the sharks. A report in the Spokane *Spokesman-Review* of January 18, 1909, described how two to three thousand workers were about to wreck the offices of the Red Cross Employment Agency "when James H. Walsh, organizer of the Industrial Workers of the World, mounting a chair in the street, stemmed the rising tide of riot and pacified the multitude. In the opinion of the police had it not been for the intervention of Walsh a riot would surely have followed.... Walsh discouraged violence and summoned all workers to the I.W.W. hall where he warned the crowd against any outbreak." This report is significant in view of the fact that when the recently enacted ordinance was amended to exempt religious bodies, like the Salvation Army, from its application, the I.W.W. was refused

---

    * This excerpt is taken from, Philip Foner, *History of the Labor Movement in the United States*, Vol. 4, 177–185 (New York: International Publishers, 1965). It is reprinted by permission of the publisher.
    1. Testimony of William D. Haywood before Industrial Relations Commission, *Senate Documents*, vol. XX, No. 415, Washington, 1916, vol. XII, p. 10573; Elizabeth Gurley Flynn, *I Speak My Own Piece*, pp. 95–96; *Industrial Worker*, Feb. 12, 1910.
    2. Fred W. Heslewood, "Barbarous Spokane," X *International Socialist Review*, 711 (Feb. 1910).

exemption on the ground that it encouraged "violence and riots"[3] This rank discrimination touched off the free-speech fight.

On the evening of November 2, 1909, when James P. Thompson, local organizer for the I.W.W., took the platform at a street-corner meeting, a policeman yanked him down, arrested him on a disorderly conduct charge, and hauled him off to jail. Other Wobblies swarmed up to take his place on the stand. One hundred and fifty, including three women, were arrested and jailed for defying the ordinance from the soapbox. Late in the evening, the police raided the I.W.W. hall, arrested four I.W.W. leaders, closed the offices of the *Industrial Worker,* and proclaimed that they had eradicated the source of "violence and conspiracy" in the city.[4]

But the Wobbly tactics, worked out in the skirmish with the authorities of Missoula, were apparently unknown by the law-enforcement agents in Spokane. Before the arrested men had been fully locked in their cells, the following message was leaving Spokane for all parts of the Pacific Coast and as far east as Chicago: "Big free-speech fight in Spokane; come yourself if possible, and bring the boys with you !"[5] I.W.W. unionists' answered by throwing down their shovels and pitchforks and axes and catching the next freight for Spokane. The evening of November 3 saw the I.W.W. tactics bearing fruit. The next morning's Portland *Oregonian,* which gave the battle complete coverage, told how a police officer had arrested the first "red-ribboned orator.... No sooner had the officer placed the first man under arrest than another took the stand. It was necessary to arrest nine of the offenders before the crowd quieted down. The prisoners were led to the city jail without giving resistance."[6] Thirty new arrivals talked their way into jail the second evening, and the press reported 1,000 men were on their way to Spokane in empty freight cars to join their I.W.W. brothers. By November 5, the city jail was filled to overflowing. "Still they come, and still they try to speak," the local press wailed.[7]

In an effort to halt the mounting conflict, delegates from the A.F. of L. and the Socialist Party petitioned the City Council to repeal the ordinance and permit unrestricted use of the streets. A hearing was held on the petition. An old soldier and the president of the Fidelity Bank testified in support of the ordinance, and their testimony "apparently outweighed that of the labor and Socialist witnesses because the Council did not repeal the ordinance." Later, the discriminatory part of the ordinance which permitted the Salvation Army to use the streets was abrogated by the State Superior Court. However, the Court upheld James Thompson's conviction in municipal court, thus giving the police the signal to proceed with the arrests and jailings.[8]

And proceed they did! The city jails overflowed, even though the crowding of the prisoners in the cells was characterized by one reporter as "monstrous." (Twenty-eight men were forced into a cell seven by eight feet in size.) On November 10, Mayor Pratt wired Governor M.E. Hay for state aid: "The police have so far been able to handle the proposition, but we have no room for prisoners." Governor Hay denounced the I.W.W. as com-

3. "Barbarous Spokane," LXVIII *Independent,* 330 (Feb. 10, 1911); Elizabeth Gurley Flynn, "The Free Speech Fight at Spokane," X *International Socialist Review,* 484 (Dec. 1909).

4. Spokane *Spokesman-Review,* Nov. 3, 1909; Portland *Oregonian,* Nov. 3, 1909.

5. Portland *Oregonian,* Nov. 3, 1909; Spokane *Spokesman-Review,* Nov. 3, 1909.

6. Portland *Oregonian,* Nov. 4, 1909.

7. *Ibid.*

8. Spokane *Spokesman-Review,* Nov. 5, 12, 1909; Tyler, "Rebels of the Woods and Fields," *op. cit.,* p. 29.

posed of "illiterate hoboes" who were unfit for citizenship, and praised the authorities in Spokane as "clean, honorable, upright men." But he did not offer material aid to the city.[9]

The Spokane authorities put the overflow prisoners into the unused, unheated Franklin School building. Still the Wobblies poured into town on every freight, mounted the soapboxes, got arrested, and were hauled off to the city jails or the temporary cells in the school building. The Wobblies carried on the struggle even though imprisoned. Night and day they sang songs from *The Little Red Song Book.* "The singing and shouting service of the I.W.W.'s in jail continues at night; a veritable bedlam being created," the *Oregonian* reported.[10]

The police attempted to stop the flood of prisoners with brutality, bread-and-water rations, and atrocious jail conditions. William Z. Foster, who spent almost two months in jail with the free-speech fighters,* wrote that prisoners "were clubbed and packed into cells so closely they could not sit down. When they protested, the hose was turned on them, drenching them with icy water." Packed into small cells, prisoners were "sweated" by turning up the steam heat, many fainted during this treatment, and only the pressure of closely-packed bodies kept them from falling to the floor. After the "sweating," the guards returned the prisoners to their cold cells.[11]

Food at the Franklin School was "one-third of "a small baker's loaf twice a day." The prisoners went on a hunger strike, but the authorities refused to change the bread-and-water diet. Three times a week the police shuttled the prisoners from the school, eight at a time, over to the city jails for baths. One free-speech fighter, not a member of the I.W.W., recalled later what usually happened on the way:

"When we started back to the school house they marched us in the center of the street and on the sidewalks people had gathered with all kinds of tobacco, fruit, bread and everything in the line of eatables, but the police held them back and would not let them get near us so that the people began to throw tobacco, fruit and everything they had brought. Those who were lucky to get some of those things found themselves unlucky, for no sooner had they caught them when the police knocked them out of their hands. In one case one man had just caught an apple and had started to take a bite when the police struck at the apple and hit the poor fellow on the nose and broke it. This is only one instance of which there are many more."[12]

The Portland *Oregonian* sneered at the prisoners for protesting against the baths in the city jails, denouncing them as hoboes and tramps, and quoting Chief of Police Sullivan as saying that "he never saw such a filthy crowd of men." But it failed to report the reason for the prisoners' objections. Guards stripped the prisoners; pushed them under a scalding spray, then into an icy rinse, and then brought them back to their unheated,

---

9. Portland *Oregonian,* Nov. 11, 1909, Spokane *Chronicle,* Jan. 10, 1910.

10. Spokane *Spokesman-Review,* Nov. 12, 1909; Portland *Oregonian,* Nov. 7, 11, 1909·

* Foster came to Spokane to report the free-speech fight for *The Workingman's Paper* of Seattle (formerly *The Socialist*). He was picked out of "the thick of the crowd" while listening to the soapboxers and arrested. He was sentenced to 30 days in jail, $100 fine and costs, to be worked out on the rock pile. Foster described how he was "loaded with ball and chain (15-pound ball attached to ankle), and shackled by the leg to another man, and then marched to the rock pile, where I was told to work or freeze." (*The Workingman's Paper* Jan. 1, 8, 15, 22, Feb. 12, 1910.)

11. William Z. Foster, *Pages From a Worker's Life,* New York, 1939, p. 145; Elizabeth Gurley Flynn, "The Shame of Spokane," X *International Socialist Review,* 613 (Jan. 1910); Flynn, "Free-Speech Fight at Spokane," *op. cit.,* p. 485.

12. Robert Rose to the Industrial Relations Commission, Sept. 19, 1914, in "Letters, Etc. Addressed to Vincent St. John, by various writers," Department of Labor Files, MNC. II-IO-I4, Serial No. 763, *NA.*

freezing quarters in the school. Three Wobblies died in the completely unheated Franklin School. Many prisoners developed pneumonia and other ailments. One month saw 334 prisoners in the hospital lists, another month, 681. William Z. Foster had his feet frozen while lying in jail. One of the prisoners, a veteran of the Civil War, declared that conditions in the School reminded him of Libby and Andersonville prisons.[13]

Still the Wobblies came. "Riding through blizzards on 'the rods,' 'on top' and on the 'front end' of every freight train, these traveling 'salesmen of an idea' poured into town to face pick handles and jails that awaited them at their journeys end."[14] On November 17, 1909, Spokane *Spokesman-Review* carried the headline: "I.W.W. Man Hurt, Yearns for Jail. 'Martyr' Spurns Proffered Freedom and Begs to Suffer With 'the Boys.'" The morale of the prisoners did not slacken. Weak and sick from hunger and cold though they were, they had enough strength to adopt a resolution denouncing the imprisonment of "Fellow Workers Preston and Smith" who had been "railroaded to the Nevada State Penitentiary on a trumped-up charge of murder,"* and pledged themselves "when liberated to use every means in our power to secure their release."[15]

"The members of the I.W.W. confined in the city jail have organized themselves in a temporary organization, and hold regular meetings twice a week," William Z. Foster wrote to *The Workingman's Paper* of Seattle. "... Monday night is devoted to propaganda work, and that this is not without effect is evidenced by the large number of non-I.W.W. prisoners who have declared their intention of joining the organization on securing their release.* Wednesday night is business night, and it certainly is surprising the amount of business we have to transact. We have established 10:30 P.M. as the time when 'lights out' shall sound, have elected a secretary and a propaganda committee that has charge of the Sunday programs.... There are dozens of other rules and regulations that we have established."[16]

The free-speech prisoners served 30 days, and when "liberated," immediately attempted to speak again. Two youth of 18 years, arrested a second time, were offered a suspended sentence by Judge Mann if they would promise not to speak again and leave town. Both refused and were sentenced to another 30 days in jail and $100 fine, to be worked out on the rock pile.[17]

On November 16, the press reported the arrival on the scene of "Elizabeth Gurley Flynn [who] addressed a meeting in the Municipal Courtroom and after roasting the newspapers, police judges and city authorities, took a collection of $25."[18] Since she was pregnant, the Wobblies decided that the "rebel girl" should not speak on the forbidden streets, but only in I.W.W. halls, clubs, and organizations willing to give her a hearing to raise defense funds. But the condition of "the beauteous, black-haired" girl did not concern the police. On November 31st the police arrested the second group of I.W.W. leaders, among them Gurley Flynn, and threw them in jail.[19] The Wobbly press flashed the news of the imprisonment of "Joan of Arc of the I.W.W." in flaming headlines, and circulars were issued announcing that "Eliz-

---

13. Portland *Oregonian,*. Nov. 7, 14, 1909; Flynn, "The Shame of Spokane," *op. cit.,* pp. 611–12; Flynn, *I Speak My Own Piece,* p. 97; Ralph Chaplin, *Wobbly,* p. 150; *Solidarity,* Dec. 18, 1909.

14. *Industrial Worker,* Jan. 8, 1910; Spokane *Spokesman-Review,* Jan. 3, 10, 1910; Ralph Chaplin, *Wobbly,* p. 150.

 * The incident referred to occurred during the Goldfield strike led by the I.W.W. in Nevada.

15. *Industrial Worker,* Jan. 8, 1910.

 * Foster himself joined the I.W.W. after his release.

16. "From Foster in Jail," *The Workingman's Paper,* Jan. 22, 1910.

17. Flynn, *I Speak My Own Piece,* p. 97.

18. Portland *Oregonian,* Nov. 16, 1909.

19. Flynn, *I Speak My Own Piece,* p. 98.

abeth Gurley Flynn, a girl organizer only 19 years old, soon to become a mother, was arrested, charged with criminal conspiracy, confined in jail with prostitutes and insulted by an officer of the law."* The Wobblies west of the Mississippi, now more aroused than ever, poured into Spokane in increased numbers. "Logging crews of pine camps deserted in a body to Spokane." In a special circular, the Spokane I.W.W. Free Speech Committee set March 1, 1910, as the day "to begin again new full scale invasions to fill Spokane jails and bull-pens. We will never surrender until we gain our constitutional right to speak on the streets of Spokane. The right to organize must be protected."[20]

It was becoming too much for the citizens of Spokane. With between 500 and 600 Wobblies in jail, all of whom announced that "we will serve 30 days bread and water, and when we get out we will immediately be rearrested," with 1,200 arrests on the books, and with fresh delegations arriving from points as far as McKees Rocks, Penna., Canada, Mexico, and Skowhegan, Maine, it was obvious that the town was licked. Moreover, the I.W.W. had brought damage suits to the amount of $150,000 against the city and individual officials, and threatened to carry them to the Supreme Court if necessary.[21]

On March 5, 1910, the city officials surrendered and made peace with the I.W.W. on the following terms (1) Street speaking would permitted; (2) all I.W.W. prisoners would be released; (3) the I.W.W. hall would reopen and remain undisturbed; (4) the *Industrial Worker* would be free to publish;* (5) all I.W.W. damage suits against the city would be dropped; (6) the I.W.W. would refrain from speaking on the streets until the prohibitive ordinance was officially repealed. The City Council unanimously repealed the law on March 9, 1910. This great victory was made complete shortly thereafter by the City Council's revocation of the licenses of 19 of the city's 31 employment agencies and the promise to repay some of the losses suffered by defrauded workers. Subsequently the Washington State Legislature passed a law forbidding employment agencies from charging fees. An effort was made to install a matron in the city jail to reform conditions publicized by Gurley Flynn, but although the City Council passed a resolution authorizing the appointment, the finance committee tabled it. However, two prison guards, especially denounced by the Wobblies for brutality, were discharged.[22]

On June 28, 1910, the Spokane *Inland Herald* carried this historic report: "For the first time in two years police-sanctioned street speaking occurred Saturday night. The free speech advocates could be heard for blocks, while nearly 1,500 gathered to listen to the contesting orators." "The free speech fight," a Wobbly wrote from Spokane, "has brought the I.W.W. so clearly before the working class of the Northwest that before another year has elapsed all of the workers in the lumber woods, the sawmills, shingle, sash and door factories will be organized."[23]

---

* The reference was to Gurley Flynn's charge that an officer approached her in her cell and attempted to take improper liberties with her. (*See* Solidarity, Dec. 23, 1909.) Miss Flynn was not the only woman subjected to such treatment. Agnes Theela, a Spokane Socialist imprisoned for participating in the free-speech fight, wrote a description of attempts to rape her while in prison which, when published in *The Workingman's Paper*, almost shut it out of the mails. (*See* issue of July 2, 1910.)

20. I.W.W, Circular, copy in *AFL Carr.; Solidarity*, Feb. 26, 1910.

21. *Industrial Worker*, Feb. 5, 3:910; Elizabeth Gurley Flynn, "Latest News from Spokane," *op. cit.*, pp. 828–29; Tyler, "Rebels of the Woods and Fields," *op. cit.*, p. 34.

* In all, eight successive editors of the *Industrial Worker* were jailed after getting out eight successive issues, finally, the office of the paper was raided, and it was decided late in December 1909 to transfer the paper — masthead plates and all — to Seattle. It was returned to Spokane in May 1910.

22. *Industrial Worker*, Feb. 5, 1910.

23. Spokane *Inland Herald* reprinted in *The Workingman Paper*, July 2, 1910; *Solidarity*, March 19, 1910; New York *Call*, Jan. 6. 1910.

IV

The Racial Division
in the Labor Movement

White-Capping, Poinsette County, Arkansas, Resettlement Administration, Ben Shahn.

What's Left of Solidarity?
Reflections on Law, Race, and Labor History (1906)

*Martha R. Mahoney**

Law hides the prescriptive power of the state so well that sometimes even lawyers and historians fail to see it. Legal rules helped make class-based interracial organizing difficult in labor history. Judges developed doctrines that made it hard for workers to organize and strike and prevented states from giving workers effective protection in joining unions.[1] Courts struck down most attempts by legislators to enact labor-protective regulation.[2] The rules that made interracial work difficult went beyond the direct regulation of labor. Judges also limited or struck down Reconstruction civil rights

---

* This entry has been edited from a small portion of the article, Martha R. Mahoney, "What's Left of Solidarity? Reflections on Law, Race, and Labor History," 56 *Buf. L. Rev.* 1515 (2009). It appears here with the permission of that law review.
    1. *See generally* William E. Forbath, *Law and the Shaping of the American Labor Movement* (1991).
    2. *Ibid.*

statutes that should have protected equality.[3] Taken together, these decisions fostered racial division, promoted insecurity among workers, and placed burdens on class-based organizing.

In most theories of class, solidarity among workers is an actual or potential unifying interest. The term "class" includes more than identification of the position in society of an individual or group. Class involves the work people do; the understandings they form about themselves, their lives, and the people with whom they live and work; economic and social relations between groups; and the actions they take to pursue their interests.[4]

Legal rules on both labor and race facilitated racial discrimination and repressed shared organizing. While many economic and social forces affected interracial organizing, the ideology of white supremacy treated privilege and oppression as reflections of a natural order, and the impact of racial hierarchy affected class mobilization. Background rules helped run a system of inequality without acknowledging the importance of state power to social outcomes.

Even when labor organizations did not exclude workers by race, the availability of exclusion as a choice affected both the direction of the labor movement and the challenges of interracial class-based organizing. The Court created constitutional barriers against restraints on racial exclusion while it struck down most legislation that protected labor.

At a practical level, legal obstacles made collective organization and action difficult. Union victories were difficult to consolidate. Interracial organizing had to overcome further vulnerability to division as well as the challenges imposed by the lack of legal protection for labor. As William Forbath has explained, legal obstacles also affected the strategy and ideology of the labor movement.[5] Injunctions and judicial hostility to labor-friendly regulation pushed labor leaders toward voluntarism[6] and away from the political process and reliance on the state.

Legal decisions on race and civil rights also affected class consciousness and labor organizing. Congress passed the Civil Rights Act of 1866 under its power to enforce

---

3. *See, e.g., Hodges v. United States*, 203 U.S. 1 (1906) (reversing convictions of white defendants who attacked a sawmill to drive black workers from their jobs and holding that the Civil Rights Act of 1866 did not reach private conspiracies to deprive African Americans of work because of their race), *overruled by Jones v. Alfred H. Mayer Co.*, 392 U.S. 409 (1968); *The Civil Rights Cases*, 109 U.S. 3 (1883) (holding the Civil Rights Act of 1875 unconstitutional).

4. The relationship between how people understand their situations and how they act moves in both directions: action affects consciousness, and consciousness affects action. E.P. Thompson described class as a *happening*, not a thing. E. P. Thompson, *The Making of the English Working Class* 10 (1964). Quoting Thompson, Ira Katznelson described the relationship between class and consciousness: "Class formations ... arise at the intersection of determination and self-activity: the working class 'made itself as much as it was made.' We cannot put 'class' here and 'class consciousness' there, as two separate entities, the one sequential upon the other, since both must be taken together—the experience of determination, and the 'handling' of this in conscious ways. Nor can we deduce class from a static 'section' (since it is a *becoming* over time), nor as a function of a mode of production, since class formations and class consciousness (while subject to determinate pressures) eventuate in an open-ended process of *relationship*—of struggle with other classes—over time." Ira Katznelson, "Working Class Formation: Constructing Cases and Comparisons," in, *Working Class Formation: Nineteenth-Century Patterns in Western Europe and the United States* 3, 8 (Ira Katznelson & Aristide R. Zolberg eds., 1986) (quoting E.P. Thompson, "The Poverty of Theory," in *The Poverty of Theory & Other Essays*, 193, 298 (1978)).

5. *See generally* Forbath, *supra.* note 1.

6. Voluntarism was the philosophy and strategy that committed labor to relying on its own resources rather than relying on the state for systemic reform and protection for labor. *See, e.g.,* Forbath, *supra* note 1, at 1–2 n.3.

the Thirteenth Amendment. That historic statute gave every citizen the same rights as white citizens to make and enforce contracts, and to purchase, lease, hold, and convey property.[7]

In 1906, the Supreme Court held in *Hodges v. United States* that the Thirteenth Amendment did not give Congress power to reach discrimination by private actors except in situations of slavery or involuntary servitude.[8] More than sixty years later, the Supreme Court finally held in *Jones v. Mayer* that the Civil Rights Act of 1866 had barred private discrimination in the sale of property and in contracts.[9] The intervening decades had seen the passage of the National Labor Relations Act and a wave of organizing that reached the highest percentage of union membership in United States history.[10] Steel mills had been built, organized, and begun to rust. Around urban neighborhoods, suburbs had spread by streetcars and sprawled further through cars and highways. Meanwhile, *Hodges* had protected the privilege of employers, workers, unions, developers, lenders, and homeowners to exclude African Americans from workplaces and neighborhoods.

Hodges involved an attack in August 1903 on a new sawmill in Poinsett County, Arkansas. The mill had hired eight African-American workers.[11] At least fifteen white men with guns and torches converged on the mill, demanding that the owner fire the workers[12] and threatening the workers if they did not leave.[13] The mill owner "went to [the] Justice of the Peace, ... [who] 'not only refused to help keep the peace, but joined the mob.'"[14] The mill owner then gave in and fired all the African-American workers.[15]

---

7. The Thirteenth Amendment banned slavery and "involuntary servitude, except as a punishment for crime whereof the party shall have been duly convicted ... within the United States ..." and authorized Congress to enact legislation to enforce the amendment. U.S. Const. amend. XIII.

8. 203 U.S. 1 (1906), *overruled by Jones v. Alfred H. Mayer Co.*, 392 U.S. 409 (1968).

9. 392 U.S. at 441–43 n.78 (overruling *Hodges* as inconsistent with the history and purpose of the Thirteenth Amendment); *Johnson v. Railway Express Agency*, 421 U.S. 454 (1975) (stating that in *Jones v. Mayer*, the Court concluded "that Congress intended to prevent private discriminatory deprivations of all the rights enumerated in s 1 of the 1866 Act, including the right to contract," and applying that holding to discrimination in employment.).

10. Union membership reached its highest point at 25.4% of the workforce in 1954, with a total of 17,022,000 union members; the highest total number of union members was 22,809,000 in 1974. *See* Michael Goldfield, *The Decline of Organized Labor in the United States* 10–11 (1989). For 2008, there were 16,100,000 union workers, at 12.4% of the workforce. U.S. Dep't of Labor, Bureau of Labor Statistics, Union Members Summary: Union Members in 2008 (Jan. 28, 2009), http://www.bls.gov/news.release/pdf/union2.pdf.

11. *See* 203 U.S. at 2 (naming eight workers); *see also*, Jeannie M. Whayne, *A New Plantation South: Land, Labor, and Federal Favor in Twentieth Century Arkansas*, 70 (1996) (describing attack at sawmill).

12. Whayne, *supra* note 11, at 50 (noting that fifteen were arrested and three of the fifteen later convicted); Hon. Gerald W. Heaney, Tribute, *Jacob Trieber: Lawyer, Politician, Judge*, 8 U. Ark. Little Rock L.J. 421, 442 (1985–86) (noting that there were "at least fifteen" whitecappers and that indictments were sought that fall against "fifteen of the whitecappers").

13. According to the indictment, the defendants appeared at the mill on August 17, 1903 and intimidated the black workers "'with the purpose of compelling them by violence and threats and otherwise to remove from said place of business, to stop said work and to cease the enjoyment of [the right and privilege of contracting for their labor],' in violation of sections 1977 and 5508 of the Revised Statutes." Pamela S. Karlan, "Contracting the Thirteenth Amendment: *Hodges v. United States*," 85 B.U.L. Rev. 783, 786 (2005) (alteration in original) (quoting Transcript of Record at 4, *Hodges*, 203 U.S. 1 (No. 14 of Oct. 1905 Term).

14. Heaney, *supra* note 12, at 442 (quoting Arkansas Gazette, Mar. 17, 1904); *see also* Whayne, *supra* note 11, at 50. The report about the justice of the peace joining the attack appeared in the newspaper during the trial, a year after the attack, and therefore was probably based on trial testimony.

15. Heaney, *supra* note 12, at 442.

This "whitecapping" attack was part of a wave of terrorism across the South that fell between the organizational periods of the Ku Klux Klan but involved similar nightriding and terror tactics.[16] Whitecapping reflected overall economic instability as well as racial hatred and competition.[17] Attacks in nearby states in the same period attempted to move black citizens completely out of some counties in Texas and Mississippi.[18]

In the months before the attack on the sawmill, whitecappers had posted notices on farms throughout Poinsett County warning all black residents to leave the county "or else" and simultaneously warning white planters against selling to blacks.

The U.S. Attorney brought federal prosecutions against the whitecappers under the Civil Rights Act of 1866 in both the Cross County tenant farming case, *United States v. Morris*,[19] and the Poinsett County sawmill case that became *Hodges*.[20] The defendants challenged the constitutionality of the statute, but the district judge ruled that the Thirteenth Amendment gave Congress the power to protect the right to earn a living:

> That the rights to lease lands and to accept employment as a laborer for hire are fundamental rights, inherent in every free citizen, is indisputable; and a conspiracy by two or more persons to prevent negro citizens from exercising these rights because they are negroes is a conspiracy to deprive them of a privilege secured to them by the Constitution and laws of the United States, within the meaning of section 5508, Rev. St. U.S.[21]

In *Hodges*,[22] the Supreme Court held that the Thirteenth Amendment did not authorize Congress to protect of equal right to contract against interference by private actors unless those actions amounted to slavery or involuntary servitude.[23] Justice Brewer's opin-

---

16. Whayne, *supra* note 11, at 48 (describing whitecapping as "almost commonplace" across parts of the South during the expansion of the plantation system); Heaney, *supra.* note 12, at 439 n.53 (describing whitecapping as a continuation of Klan activity during the period after the organization had been officially disbanded in 1868 and before it reorganized in 1915).

17. At the time, the African-American population in the area was increasing. Both white and black farmers were losing their land, and relatively few landowners remained stable across the ten year periods of the census. Whayne, *supra* note 11, at 72. Economic insecurity persisted over subsequent years. *Ibid.* at 47–56.

18. *See, e.g., Negroes Driven from Texas: Whitecaps Active and Cotton Planters Fear Crop Cannot Be Picked*, N.Y. Times, Aug. 4, 1904, at 7 ("If the exodus of negroes from the state continues there will not be enough labor to pick the immense cotton crop ... the army of cotton pickers from other states has been cut off by the treatment of blacks, who are warned not to return."). Some employers said that they could not get any workers because labor was scarce and whites would not work their jobs no matter how much they paid. *Texans Drive Out Negroes; Whitecappers in Orange County Active and Industries Suffer*, N.Y. Times, Aug. 9, 1904, at 1 (stating that white labor was not available even at high wages).

19. 125 F. 322.

20. *Hodges v. United States*, 203 U.S. 1 (1906), *overruled by Jones v. Alfred H. Mayer Co.*, 392 U.S. 409 (1968). The *Hodges* case was initially captioned *United States v. Maples*. Karlan, *supra* note 13, at 786.

21. *Morris*, 125 F. at 331. The opinion sustaining the indictment in *Morris* was the only opinion published by the district court in these cases. In *Jones v. Mayer*, the Supreme Court cited the holding in *Morris*, stating: "The only federal court (other than the Court of Appeals in this case) that has ever squarely confronted that question held that a wholly private conspiracy among white citizens to prevent a Negro from leasing a farm violated § 1982." 392 U.S. at 419.

22. *Hodges v. United States*, 203 U.S. 1, 1 (1906), *overruled by Jones v. Alfred H. Mayer Co.*, 392 U.S. 409 (1968).

23. *Ibid.* at 17. The opinion also noted that a slave was defined as "held in bondage to another" and servitude was "the state of voluntary or compulsive subjection to a master." *Id.* The meaning of the Amendment was "as clear as language can make it." *Ibid.* at 16. Congress was given power to enforce the prohibition on slavery and involuntary servitude. "All understand by these terms a condi-

ion relied on Webster's definition of slavery as "the state of entire subjection of one person to the will of another."[24] Even though "one of the disabilities of slavery, one of the *indicia* of its existence" was the inability to make or perform contracts, and even though the defendants had subjected the workers to their will in forcing them to leave their jobs, "no mere personal assault or trespass or appropriation operates to reduce the individual to a condition of slavery."[25] The only reference to intent ignored the question of denial of contract or property rights on the basis of race, asserting that "it was not the intent of the Amendment to denounce every act done to an individual which was wrong if done to a free man, and yet justified in a condition of slavery, and to give authority to Congress to enforce such denunciation."[26]

Thirty years after the *Hodges* decision, the founding meeting of the Southern Tenant Farmers Union (STFU) took place in Poinsett County.[27] By the 1930s, conditions had changed. New Deal relief flowed to landowners rather than sharecroppers or tenant farmers, and evictions increased.[28] Planters were discharging both whites and blacks.[29] Eighteen men—eleven white and seven African American—met to found the organization; both whites and blacks spoke to the need for an integrated union.[30] A white farmer "rose to the question and, admitting that his own father had been a Ku Klux Klan member who had helped drive black Republicans from Crittenden County in the 1890s, insisted that black and white tenants and sharecroppers had to stand together."[31] A black sharecropper had survived a bloody race riot and the destruction of an all-black farmers' union in Elaine, Arkansas in 1919; he spoke to the need to work together and the danger that planters would divide blacks and whites by exploiting racism.[32] The union worked on an interracial basis, and locals were interracial in most areas.[33]

---

tion of enforced compulsory service of one to another. While the inciting cause of the Amendment was the emancipation of the colored race, yet it is not an attempt to commit that race to the care of the nation." *Ibid.* at 16.

24. *Ibid.*

25. *Ibid.* at 18.

26. *Ibid.* at 19.

27. *See* Whayne, *supra* note 11, at 198.

28. *See* Alex Lichtenstein, "The Southern Tenant's Farmer's Union: A Movement for Social Emancipation, Introduction" to Howard Kester, *Revolt Among the Sharecroppers*, 15, intro. 30–31 (Univ. of Tenn. Press 1997) (1936) (describing AAA program that caused evictions to increase); *id.* intro. 32 (describing complete suppression and disappearance of report that documented conditions in Arkansas including "pilfered AAA payments"); *see also* Kester, *supra*, at 27–33 (describing process in which AAA payments for crop reduction went to landlords; tenants should have received payments but did not; tenants should have lived without rent on lands for which government had paid compensation but were charged rent or evicted by landlords).

29. Whayne, *supra* note 11, at 199 (describing evictions and diminishing income for black and white tenants and sharecroppers); *ibid.* at 217 (concluding that interracial organizing succeeded in part because planters were evicting without regard to race and in part because blacks were a declining percentage of the county population, increasingly impoverished, and less threatening as competition for whites).

30. *Ibid.* at 198–99.

31. *Ibid.* at 198.

32. *Ibid.* He said, "For a long time now, the white folks and the colored folks have been fighting each other and both of us have been getting whipped all the time. We don't got nothing against one another but we got plenty against the landlord." He concluded with a powerful call for unity: "The same chain that holds my people holds your people too. If we are chained together on the outside we ought to stay chained together in the union." Kester, *supra* note 29, at 56. For details of the Elaine massacre, see Kieran Taylor, This chapter, *infra* at 113.

33. In Marked Tree, Arkansas, the union began with separate locals for blacks and whites; the locals grew together after whites were invited to join meetings of the black local. Lichtenstein, *supra*

Even when workers organized together, they worked with the consequences of bad decisions that protected white privilege, weakened class-based organizing in the United States, and helped conceal the importance of law to inequality.

Hodges held that the Constitution did not give Congress the power to reach actions by private parties to deprive others of rights in property or contract on the basis of race. That rule affected lived experience and organizing options for workers, the legality of excluding minorities from work, the extent of shared interest in collective organizing, the establishment of widespread residential segregation, and the increased danger of private violence to enforce exclusion. Although the property rule in the Civil Rights Act of 1866 did not govern seniority rights directly, residential segregation in the twentieth century affected access to employment.[34] That background law therefore affected the contract rights that were disputed in later cases on seniority, layoffs and recalls.

---

note 77, intro. 35–36; *see also* Donald H. Grubbs, *Cry From the Cotton: The Southern Tenant Farmers' Union and the New Deal*, 66–68 (2000) (describing separate organization in Marked Tree and increasingly shared work); Woodruff, *supra* note 60, at 163. Lichtenstein describes "the union's racial egalitarianism [as] far more radical than its initial economic program"; rather than merely rearranging social relations, "in bringing the 'disinherited' of both races together, the STFU sought to overturn the entire southern economic and political structure of which racism was an integral part." Lichtenstein, *supra* note 29, intro. 33.

34. The interaction of these rules also affected property: exclusion from work, which would have been covered by the right to contract in section 1981, affected the ability to purchase homes that would have been protected under section 1982 and the neighborhoods in which people lived.

Tenant Farmers Taken Prisoner.

"We Have Just Begun": Black Organizing and White Response in the Arkansas Delta (1919)

Kieran Taylor*

On the last night of September 1919, Phillips County deputy sheriff Charles Pratt and two assistants traveled twenty miles south out of Helena, Arkansas, in apparent pursuit of a bootlegger. Shortly after stopping—reportedly to repair a flat tire—in front of a small church at Hoop Spur, just north of the town of Elaine, a shot rang out, followed quickly by a volley of gunfire. Inside the church, a group of black farmers was meeting to consider plans to demand a better price for their cotton and a fairer settlement from their landlords. Many had recently joined the Progressive Farmers and Household Union of America, a local group that had organized chapters of black workers in several Phillips County communities. Interrupted in their discussions by the shooting and believing their union to be under attack, the men hastened to the windows, loaded their weapons, and joined the fray.[1]

After receiving news of the initial clash at Hoop Spur, public officials, local businessmen, and plantation owners in Helena organized a campaign to crush the black union. Their efforts, aided by the intervention of more than five hundred federal troops, marked

---

* A version of this article first appeared in *Arkansas Historical Quarterly,* Vol. LVIII, Autumn 1999, 264. It appears courtesy of Arkansas Historical Quarterly.

1. According to the official version, either someone within the church or the armed guards posted outside the meeting fired on Pratt and his deputies. Union members later maintained that Pratt had shot into the church intending to provoke a larger conflict. For the best accounts of the Elaine riot, *see* Grif Stockley, *Blood in Their Eyes: The Elaine Race Massacres of 1919* (Fayetteville: University of Arkansas Press, 2001); Arthur Waskow, *From Race Riot to Sit-In, 1919 and the 1960s: A Study in the Connection between Conflict and Violence* (Garden City, NY: Doubleday and Company, 1966); B. Boren McCool, *Union, Reaction, and Riot: A Biography of a Rural Race Riot* (Memphis: Memphis State University, 1970); O. A. Rogers, "The Elaine Race Riots of 1919," 19 *Arkansas Historical Quarterly,* 142–50 (Summer 1960. For a defense of the white response, see J. W. Butts and Dorothy James, "The Underlying Causes of the Elaine Riot of 1919," 20 *Arkansas Historical Quarterly,* 95–104 (Spring 1961).

the bloodiest clash of a tumultuous year of racial violence and labor strife in the United States.[2] Joining armed posses from three states, the troops raided homes, chased share-croppers into the woods, jailed and interrogated hundreds of black men and women, and forced hundreds more back to work in the fields and sawmills. Army reports acknowledged twenty-five African Americans were killed. Unofficial reports place the death toll much higher.[3] In the aftermath of the "Elaine Race Riot," sixty-seven African Americans were hur-riedly sentenced to prison terms for their participation in a purported rebellion and twelve were condemned to death for the murder of five white people who died in the fighting. All the sentences were overturned after a highly publicized five-year legal battle that reached the United States Supreme Court.[4]

Looking back across eighty years, the attempt by African American workers to orga-nize a union in the Arkansas delta might appear foolhardy, even self-destructive, given the overwhelming political, social, and economic power of the white elites. It would be easy to fall back upon popular stereotypes of black southerners in explaining the surprising up-surge of militancy in Phillips County. Their efforts might be dismissed as the tragic result of the assumed rural isolation, ignorance, and naivete of black delta farmers. Similarly, it would be easy to rely on popular representations of white southerners to explain the mur-derous reaction of Phillips County whites. Most contemporaneous press accounts of the conflict and some historical treatments have considered the events in such a way. The southern press presumed that gullible sharecroppers had been duped into a money-mak-ing scheme by either Robert L. Hill, a charismatic African American union organizer, or U. S. Bratton, a white attorney who had provided legal assistance to some of the union members.[5] The national black press and liberal magazines emphasized the viciousness of the posses and law enforcement officials, but offered little to explain the motivations of Phillips County whites. Attempting to build popular support for the legal defense of the accused sharecroppers, these publications downplayed or ignored the existence of the Union and described the black men as simple and guileless victims of a racist hysteria.[6] Much of the subsequent scholarship on Elaine, including several books and a half-dozen articles, has not proceeded much beyond these characterizations. The black farmers are por-trayed as passive victims while whites remain a monolithic mob of racist reactionaries.

The stereotypes, however, obscure the very distinctive conditions shaping the actions of both blacks and whites in Phillips County in 1919. At the end of the First World War,

---

2. At least twenty-five U.S. towns or cities experienced violent racial conflicts during 1919, in-cluding Washington, Chicago, Omaha, Baltimore, and Millen, Georgia. Violent labor disputes af-fected dozens of other cities.

3. Walter White, investigating for the NAACP, reported that as many as one hundred African Americans may have been killed (White, "'Massacring Whites' in Arkansas," *The Nation,* December 6, 1919, 715–716). Arkansas writer L. S. Dunaway suggested an even more shocking figure of 856 (Dunaway, *What a Preacher Saw Through a Key-Hole in Arkansas,* 102, 108–109 (Little Rock: Parke-Harper, 1925)). While a strong case can be made that the events represented more of a white rout than a riot, the latter term is not entirely inappropriate considering the evidence of black resistance, however limited in the face of the U.S. Army.

4. Richard Cortner's *A Mob Intent on Death: The NAACP and the Arkansas Riot Cases* (Middletown, CT: Wesleyan University Press, 1988) offers a thorough account of the NAACP-led legal battle to free the sharecroppers and the case's importance in the development of American criminal law.

5. *See,* for example, "Deliberate Plan to Murder Whites of Arkansas," Jackson *Daily Clarion Ledger,* October 7, 1919, and Halbert B. Phillips, "Phillips County Uprising Halted; Six More Slain," Mem-phis *Commercial Appeal,* October 3, 1919.

6. White, "'Massacring Whites,'" 715–716; Scipio Jones, "The Arkansas Peons," *The Crisis,* De-cember 1921, 72–76 and January 1922, 115–117; Walter White, "Truth Comes to Light When Unprejudiced Report is Given," *Chicago Defender,* November I, 1919.

county residents confronted radically changing economic and social conditions. Under these circumstances, blacks and whites developed conflicting visions of Phillips County's future and their role in it. Drawing on the resources of their communities, they fashioned responses to the changing conditions in order to effect these competing visions. Their respective strategies—the establishment of a union and the mounting of an effective counter-revolt—should be seen as neither naive on the one hand nor irrational on the other, but as a measure of how deeply black and white consciousness had changed in Phillips County during the war era.

Before the First World War, African American families had few options for confronting the repression that they faced in the neighborhoods, cotton fields, sawmills, and stores of Phillips County. Though blacks outnumbered whites three to one, whites owned the factories, a majority of stores, and most of the farmland. They controlled the local government. Overt resistance to white power invited the possibility of a long jail sentence, almost certain unemployment, and possible physical harm. Fraudulent employment practices by which planters kept their laborers in perpetual debt often made emigration to the North—the most common strategy for resisting white oppression in the South—difficult.[7] Yet after the World War, African Americans embraced collective and overt action to defend their economic interests and preserve their dignity, most notably through the formation of the Progressive Farmers and Household Union of America.

This shift in strategies that led to the establishment of the union was primarily an attempt by African Americans to advance their interests amidst a rapidly changing local economy. Wartime conditions expanded the range of options for black workers in the Mississippi Delta. The opportunity of factory work in the North and the call for military service encouraged black sharecroppers to leave the plantations. The ensuing labor shortage left those remaining in a better position to bargain over wages, settlements, and working conditions. The rising price of cotton during the war only heightened black expectations. Locally, cotton that sold for eleven cents a pound in 1915, earned twenty-three cents in 1916, twenty-eight cents in 1917, and forty cents by 1919. With more money in their pockets, African Americans began purchasing farms. Black farm ownership increased forty percent in Phillips County between 1910 and 1920, offering tenants an alternative to plantation exploitation or northern emigration. The existence of this group of new farmers, freed from planter control, facilitated the emergence of autonomous black organizations. Of the men who were later sentenced to die for their role in the union, several of them likely farmed their own land, and at least one of them, Ed Ware, owned an automobile.[8]

The war affected black consciousness in other ways. African American men who entered the military (of 1,680 inductees in Phillips County, as many as 1,218 may have been black) were well fed and may for the first time in their lives have had some spending money.[9] Shortly after his induction, a black soldier from Helena wrote home excitedly to tell his mother of military life at Camp Sherman, Ohio: "I can go to Cleveland every Sat-

---

7. For discussions of the working conditions of Arkansas tenant farmers, see John William Graves, *Town and Country: Race Relations in an Urban-Rural Context, Arkansas, 1865–1905*, 70–96 (Fayetteville: University of Arkansas Press, 1990); White, *Chicago Defender,* November 1, 1919; "The Real Causes of Two Race Riots," *The Crisis,* December 1919, 56–62.

8. U.S. Bureau of the Census, *Fourteenth Census of the United States: 1920 Agriculture* (Washington: Government Printing Office, 1922) vol. 4, pt. 2, Table 10; Nan Elizabeth Woodruff, "African-American Struggles for Citizenship in the Arkansas and Mississippi Deltas in the Age of Jim Crow," 55 *Radical History Review* 36–37 (Winter 1993); "Street Car Smashes Ford," *Helena World,* July 15, 1919 and "Municipal Report," *Helena World,* July 18, 1919.

9. McCool, *Union, Reaction, and Riot,* 8.

urday if I want to. We have shows and all kinds of music and games for a good time. We play football and have prize fights here at the camp. We do not have to buy anything but stamps."[10]

While induction might well improve their material circumstances, young black men in Phillips County did not uniformly greet the war with enthusiasm. The Reverend Dr. E. C. Morris, longtime pastor of Helena's Centennial Baptist Church and the president of the National Baptist Convention since the group's founding in 1895, did, like many middle-class African Americans, regard the United States' entrance into the war as an opportunity to advance the cause of the race. Believing African Americans' full rights as citizens would be restored in exchange for their support of the war, Morris offered sermons and speeches encouraging registration, the purchase of war bonds, and food rationing.[11] Yet only one in three African Americans in Arkansas responded to their draft notices and the problem was likely more acute in the rural delta.[12] While the *Helena World* attributed this lukewarm support of the draft not to disloyalty but to ignorance and illiteracy, Nan Elizabeth Woodruff suggests that tenant farmers' refusal to support the war effort was a deliberate response to the existing system of power relations. Woodruff argues that by not enlisting, black deltans resisted the efforts of planter-dominated local defense councils to control their labor and their cultural lives.[13]

Whether or not African Americans supported the war, though, it undoubtedly affected the way they understood their situation. Even those who did not register surely noted the pro-democratic rhetoric emanating from Washington, D.C., and understood the contrast between that rhetoric and the conditions that they faced on the job and in the community. African Americans who ended up in the army and traveled to Europe may have encountered an unprecedented measure of equality. When they returned home they expected to be rewarded with less discriminatory treatment and new opportunities for advancement in return for their service and sacrifice. As one leader of the Progressive Farmers and Household Union explained after the Elaine riot: "We helped you fight the Germans, and are ready to help you fight the next fellows that get after you, but we want to be treated fairly."[14] A military report issued soon after the Hoop Spur shootout claimed that most of the leaders of the union and its most aggressive members were ex-servicemen.[15] The report was never substantiated, but it suggests—at very least—that whites recognized that wartime service was a factor in shaping the new, more militant black consciousness. White people of all classes suffered a particular phobia of returned African American veterans. It was even rumored locally that black veterans had received "letters from French girls urging them" to rise up against the white population and secure their rights."[16] No such letters ever materialized, but the rumor illustrates the mixing of new anxieties whites felt over the return of the black veterans with old fears of miscegenation.

If the First World War expanded black opportunity and steeled black determination, Nan Elizabeth Woodruff has described how it also accentuated planter power by placing

---

10. "Helena Negro Is Pleased With Army," *Helena World,* December 21,1917,
11. *Helena World,* October 30, 1917; Fon Louise Gordon, *Caste and Class, the Black Experience in Arkansas, 1880–1920,* 128 (Athens: University of Georgia Press, 1995).
12. Woodruff, "African-American Struggles," 38.
13. *Ibid.;* "Not Real Slackers," *Helena World,* October 6, 1917.
14. Robert L. Hill to *Arkansas Gazette,* December 11, 1919, reprinted as "Alleged Note Received From Robert L. Hill," *Helena World,* December 17, 1919.
15. McCool, *Union, Reaction, and Riot,* 13.
16. "Race Riot Excites Phillips County; Ten Are Killed," Memphis *Commercial Appeal,* October 2, 1919.

delta elites in control of local boards that implemented federal mobilization policy.[17] Yet the federal government involved itself in other ways in southern life during this decade —ways that may have suggested to African Americans that Washington might once again be the ally and provider it had been during Reconstruction. In the spring of 1916 the Department of Agriculture sent its first black demonstration agent to Phillips County to interest African American farmers in the government's "safe farming campaign."[18] Also in 1916 federal agents investigated sharecropping in Arkansas and uncovered instances of peonage and other abuses of tenants. Their report discovered an "acute unrest ... developing among the tenants" and warned of "clear indications of the beginning of organized resistance which may result in civil disturbances of a serious character."[19] Though the government apparently failed to act on these findings, the investigation may have served as a symbol of hope for African Americans by providing a new platform for their grievances, while lending official authority to their conviction that they were being treated unjustly. Certainly, organizers of the Progressive Farmers and Householders Union strategically capitalized on the hopes that federal authorities had raised and on the historic identification—dating from emancipation—of the black community with the federal government. Organizer Robert Hill identified himself in union literature as an agent of the federal government. Applicants to the union pledged to "defend this government and her constitution at all times."[20] Also, the union constitution claimed the group was "first organized under the act of Congress 1865," and membership registration forms bore various federal symbols, including the stamp: "Orders of Washington, D.C. The Great Torch of Liberty."[21]

The war and its aftermath played yet another role in shaping events in Phillips County. The formation of the union, though typecast as a response to local racial tensions, should not be divorced from the postwar mobilization of labor in 1919, a year in which one in five American workers spent some time out on strike. A present-day visitor to Elaine cannot help but notice the seeming isolation of the community. The town sits just west of a two-lane highway nearly twenty miles south of Helena. A driver from Helena winds through acres of cotton fields, small patches of uncleared woods, and, as the road veers toward the Mississippi River, marshy wetlands upon which sits an occasional home. But it would be a mistake to confuse Elaine's physical separation with intellectual or social isolation either now or eighty years ago. In 1919 just one unpaved road ran between Helena and Elaine, but many people traveled on the daily Missouri Pacific train that stopped at the foot of town. Others shuttled back and forth by boat down the Mississippi River. An informal network of black trainmen, dock, and river workers served as an important channel of information from Memphis, St. Louis, Chicago, and New Orleans. They also passed along news about working and housing conditions in northern industrial centers. Assuredly, local African Americans heard eyewitness accounts of the "race riots" in East St. Louis in 1917 and in Chicago in July 1919, as well as reports on the campaign for fair employment by black railroad workers in Memphis.[22]

17. Woodruff, "African American Struggles," 37, 46.

18. "Movement to Aid the Negro Farmers Here," Helena World, March 23, 1919.

19. Waskow, From Race Riot, 122.

20. White, "'Massacring Whites,'" 715; McCool, Union, Reaction, and Riot, 13.

21. The United States Constitution and By-Laws of the Progressive Farmers and Household Union of America, reprinted in Bessie Ferguson, "The Elaine Race Riot" (M.A. thesis, George Peabody College for Teachers, 1927), xiii–xviii; McCool, Union, Reaction, and Riot, 14.

22. Eric Arnesen, "Charting an Independent Course: African American Railroad Workers in the World War I Era," in Labor Histories: Class, Politics, and the Working-Class Experience, Arnesen, Julie Greene, and Bruce Laurie eds., 295–303 (Urbana: University of Illinois Press, 1998).

Along with their own information, these workers delivered copies of the *Chicago Defender* to Phillips County's black community. This African American newspaper was likely the community's most important source of printed information.[23] Throughout the late 1910s, a loyal correspondent from Helena's black middle class had sent a society column to the *Defender* for publication. Printed along with dispatches from a dozen other southern towns, these reports featured family news, health updates, and the travel plans of community members. But the *Defender* circulated outside the urban middle class as well. According to shipping lists, the area within a ninety-mile radius of Phillips County had among the highest number of subscribers in the South. The paper's circulation in 1919 was one hundred and thirty thousand, but its audience was far larger. Readers shared copies of the *Defender* in barber shops, stores, and taverns.[24]

In Phillips County as elsewhere in the South, the *Defender* undoubtedly played a crucial role in shaping black consciousness during and after the war. It vehemently denounced Jim Crow and southern racist violence while heralding the achievements of individual African Americans. Arkansas governor Charles H. Brough was so convinced that the *Defender* aroused black sentiment that in the wake of the Phillips County riot, he petitioned the postmaster general to have the newspaper banned in the state.[25]

The *Defender's* posture toward labor organization may also have been influential. Since its beginning in 1905, the *Defender* had taken an ambivalent stance toward trade unions and strikes.[26] At times the paper advocated strikebreaking, recognizing it as the only means for African Americans to break into some industries. The 1918 Chicago packinghouse workers strike, a multi-racial effort, and the attempt to organize the nation's steel workers in 1919, however, caused the *Defender* to tentatively embrace the union cause. This shift in sentiment would not have gone unnoticed in Phillips County. And the black community would have had that message reinforced by examples of organizing closer to home. Less than two months before the shootout at Hoop Spur, the railroad employees of the Missouri Pacific shops in Helena struck for higher wages.[27]

It was out of this volatile mix—the new possibilities and expectations bred by war and a renewed federal presence in the South, the return of black veterans, the example of labor militancy, the threats being posed to black communities across the nation by white violence—that the Progressive Farmers and Household Union was formed. Emerging most strongly from the rich cotton land south of Helena, several hundred African Americans joined the union, organizing lodges in the towns of Mellwood, Ratio, Hoop Spur, Elaine, Old Town, Countiss, and Ferguson. Black workers rallied to the union cause hoping to combat their landlords by striking for higher wages, withholding cotton in hopes of a more equitable settlement, and suing corrupt plantation owners. The secret phrase to gain entrance to the meeting at Hoop Spur was reportedly "we have just begun."[28] Affirming the essentially economic foundations of the union, Robert Hill later described the conditions faced by local sharecroppers: "It was a fact that the people could not get statements of their accounts and their cotton was being shipped and the custom in that section was the landlord would take the cotton and seed and ship them away and didn't ask them no odds and the people had decided to put their money together and get legal

---

23. James R. Grossman, *Land of Hope: Chicago, Black Southerners, and the Great Migration* (Chicago: University of Chicago Press, 1989), 78–82.
24. *Ibid.*, 77, 79–80.
25. "To Investigate Negro Sheet," *Helena World*, November 4, 1919.
26. Grossman, *Land of Hope*, 231–236.
27. "Local Shopmen Are Now Out," *Helena World*, August 6, 1919.
28. "Deliberate Plan to Murder Whites of Arkansas," Jackson *Clarion Ledger*, October 7, 1919.

help and somehow up about Elaine, Arkansas, the white people had ordered the Negroes to stop meeting and from that the trouble came up."[29]

Denied fair treatment, these black unionists readily embraced militant measures to protect their interests. Possibly nothing indicates this more clearly than the sharecroppers' willingness to fight back though heavily outnumbered and outgunned by the U.S. troops. Newspaper accounts from the trials of the leaders described the union's military strategy and featured statements the leaders allegedly made encouraging black farmers to retaliate against the white forces.[30] Though much of this testimony must remain suspect, given the apparent use of force, even torture, to extract evidence against black defendants, it does suggest an acknowledgment of the determination with which blacks acted and the specters that their wartime military experience conjured up among the white community. According to one account, union leaders barked commands as men marched in formation: "Moore gave most of the orders. But Ed Hicks and Knox helped him. Moore walked in front of us. Hicks walked along the middle and Knox at the rear threatening to kill anybody who broke ranks."[31]

Others in Phillips County's heterogeneous black community pursued their economic interests in other ways that were surely less threatening to whites. Many in Helena's black middle class had participated in Booker T. Washington's National Negro Business League since that organization's founding in 1900. In keeping with Washington's philosophy, the League sought to promote community self-sufficiency through the development of black-owned businesses.[32] Though the tone of the League differed from that of the Progressive Farmers, some in Helena's black middle class likely sympathized with the goals of the union. Early in the war, the Reverend E. C. Morris, who had good relations with the white community, had "humbly" recommended that white employers either raise wages to meet inflation or expect black workers to continue to move north.[33] Among those in attendance at the national convention of the National Negro Business League in Little Rock in 1911 had been a Helena dentist, D. A. E. Johnston, whose mysterious death eight years later during the Elaine riot may have stemmed from his support of the sharecroppers.[34] During the fighting, Phillips County officials intercepted Johnston and three of his brothers, who had been traveling in an automobile purportedly loaded with weapons. The *Arkansas Gazette* portrayed Johnston as a ringleader of the black insurrection, and the official version of the story contended that Johnston was killed with his brothers after he shot one of the men who was taking him into custody. Contemporaneous black accounts, as well as African American oral tradition in Phillips County, suggest, however, that Johnston was uninvolved in (and perhaps even unaware of) the fighting and was armed simply because he had been hunting. Some believed that whites used the riot as a

---

29. Hill to NAACP, November 26, 1919, Arthur Waskow Papers, State Historical Society of Wisconsin, Madison, Wisconsin.

30. Hill specifically denied the allegations that the union planned to murder plantation owners. In a letter to the NAACP he maintained his ignorance of such a plot suggesting that "it would be awful foolish for me to go to Phillips County only to plan killing whites of that county" (*Ibid.*).

31. As suspect as this testimony is, the white casualties do suggest that, at the very least, blacks did offer meaningful resistance to the assault (Moss E. Penn, "Six Negroes Found Guilty," *Helena World*, November 4, 1919).

32. *Records of the National Negro Business League* (Bethesda, MD: University Publications of America, 1994), pt. 1, First Annual Conference Proceedings 1900, 221.

33. Morris appealed unsuccessfully to the planter's patriotism, arguing that the war effort demanded that black field laborers remain in the South to produce food (*Helena World*, May 27, 1917).

34. *Records of the National Negro Business League*, Pt. 1, Twelfth Annual Conference Proceedings 1911, membership lists.

pretext for murdering Johnston, who had a reputation as a champion of racial equality.[35] If he was in some manner connected to the union, Johnston may have been unique among Helena's middle-class African Americans. Other members of the community demonstrated their support, however, by later raising money for the legal defense fund of the twelve union men who were condemned to death.

Still, there were distinct limits to the collaboration between the black working and middle classes in Phillips County. This might best be illustrated by a letter written by leaders of the newly formed Helena Colored YMCA and published in the Helena World a week before the riot. The Colored YMCA representatives were distraught. A vicious rumor traveling through the community linked their organization with the union. The authors denied any connection between the Y and the crowd of men who had been visiting the black section of town, "chastising" the residents and urging them to stand up for their rights. While the YMCA leaders admitted problems existed in Phillips County, they suggested that education and recreation for African American youth held out the best hope for improving the race. The leaders added that change would only be achieved through cooperation with the "best white people" of Helena.[36]

If the Phillips County black community was not a monolith, neither was its white community. But white people of all sorts saw their postwar expectations confounded by local African Americans' aggressive pursuit of their own interests. During the war, Alvin Solomon, the twenty-year-old son of a Jewish tailor, began making plans to get rich in the rapidly growing town of Helena.[37] He had held several menial jobs, including a stint toting beer buckets for alcoholic tailors, Solomon began to earn a respectable living as a clerk in a downtown bank in 1916. But following his father's example, and recognizing the financial opportunities Helena offered, Solomon dreamt of launching his own business.

The war intervened, however, and Solomon quickly found himself in France. Solomon's dream remained with him through two years of service and was with him still on his first night back in Helena when a neighbor summoned him to the courthouse. There, law officials issued shotguns to Solomon and hundreds of recently returned white veterans, and sent the men south to Elaine to put down an uprising of black sharecroppers. He went without thinking twice.

In taking up arms against his black neighbors in 1919, Alvin Solomon — and hundreds of other whites in Phillips County — made a deliberate choice to defend a vision of a postwar economy that anticipated increased profits and growth but assumed the continued subjugation of black labor. To be sure, the white response to the union was conditioned by years of racism, concretized in Arkansas by the passage of state laws mandating segregation, disfranchising black voters, and enforcing unfair labor contracts. Racism was a constant, stretching back many decades and forward several more. But ascribing the white community's reaction solely to its racial ideology obscures factors that triggered that reaction and shaped the complex motivations of the white rioters of 1919: the changing local economy, the growing presence of the federal government in Phillips County, and the failure of paternalism to control black labor.

---

35. Cortner, *Mob Intent on Death,* 9, 31; C. Calvin Smith, "Serving the Poorest of the Poor: Black Medical Practitioners in the Arkansas Delta, 1880–1960," 57 *Arkansas Historical Quarterly* 301–302 (Autumn 1998).

36. *Helena World,* September 23, 1919.

37. Alvin Solomon's story is taken from a recorded interview in the author's possession. The interview was conducted at Solomon's Helena home on March 25, 1996, one week after his 100th birthday.

Just as the union developed as an attempt to advance black economic interests, the response of the white community sought to thwart a perceived threat to their livelihoods. Ambitious white storekeepers, farmers, and clerks like Alvin Solomon feared the prospect of an economic and social order disrupted by the successes of a militant black sharecroppers' union. Elite whites understood even more acutely the threat of black organization. Recognizing both the opportunity for Helena to exploit its location on the Mississippi River and the need to modernize the town, a group of progressive farmers, bankers, and businessmen had organized the Business Man's League in early 1916. Over the next three years the League, headed by E. M. Allen, an officer of the area's largest corporate plantation, championed crop diversification, paved roads, rail construction, and a downtown drainage system.[38] Coming off a poor year in which the cotton crop was destroyed by bad weather, there was a great deal of optimism looking toward the fall of 1919. In February, several hundred prominent Phillips County white men, many of them Business Man's League members, organized to reduce cotton acreage in an attempt to elevate prices for the coming fall. The *Helena World* cheered the group's efforts, noting that the larger cotton plantation owners had never before heeded the calls for acreage reduction and diversification.[39]

The powerful group realized, though, that the mobility of black laborers endangered their anticipated high profits for the fall. Employing a tactic they had used successfully the year before, many cotton planters delayed payment to their laborers for several months and defended the practice by maintaining that they were holding on to the cotton until the price peaked. The workers, however, understood the move as a deliberate attempt to restrict their mobility. Other planters offered sharecroppers only fifteen cents a pound for their cotton, less than half the going price and local merchants collaborated with the planters by charging tenant farmers much higher prices for goods purchased on credit. A survey of a dozen items at Dowdy and Longnecker, an Elaine grocery store, shows the markup for goods bought on credit ranged from thirty-three percent to sixty percent. Alvin Solomon remembers abusive planter-tenant relationships as the norm: "Most of these tenant farmers didn't get a break. They kept the books on them and they were always in debt. They'd give them what they wanted to give them. There were some exceptions to that, but the exception was just against the rule."[40] These were precisely the sorts of practices that the union organized against and threatened litigation over.

The white response to the union was further sharpened by the existing anxiety over the implications of the war and the expanded federal role in the South, coupled with the realization that Phillips County was not immune to the radical ferment that had swept the rest of the nation. Unlike Helena's black community leaders, local white elites remained ambivalent about the war effort. Many southern planters and politicians had initially opposed the war because the British blockade closed access to continental markets and hurt cotton exports. Eventually, planters and businessmen benefited from the booming cotton prices, but were nervous about the potential effects of the federal government's de-

---

38. While the Business Man's League worked publicly during the day for the economic development of Phillips County, at night the same men made many of the most important decisions in secret, in the halls of fraternal orders. At least ten fraternal societies operated in Helena during 1919, including the Odd Fellows, the Masons, the Woodmen of the World, and the Elks. According to Alvin Solomon, the Elks in particular were powerful and included most of the town's government officials and the men who controlled much of Helena's vice industry. Membership in the Elks provided access to precious city contracts and prime Cherry Street real estate (Solomon interview).

39. *Helena World*, February 20, 1919.

40. *See The Crisis*, December 1919, 57. Ferguson, "The Elaine Race Riot," 17, and Solomon interview.

mocratic rhetoric upon their African American labor force. Despite the authority they exercised over various local wartime mobilization boards and agencies, they were rightly fearful that the wartime upheaval would increase the mobility and militancy of their laborers. In the fall of 1917, an agent from the U.S. Department of Labor ventured into Phillips County to contract several hundred black laborers to work on the construction of an army base near Little Rock. The Department maintained it recruited only idle workers, but the hiring caused such labor scarcity that the lumber mills employed women to sustain production. While assuring the public of its patriotism, the Business Man's League lodged a complaint with the Department of Labor. Within days, the federal contractor released the black laborers from work and "encouraged" them to return to their Phillips County employers. In the wake of the events, the Business Man's League suggested that area employers "warn their employees that labor conditions in the North are certainly far from being ideal, that Negroes in the South especially in this particular locality are not being victimized, but rather to the contrary, are as well treated as are laborers anywhere else in the world."[41]

Just three weeks after the Business Man's League's clash with the Labor Department, sheriff's deputies arrested organizers Red Wiggins and Roy Dramer for encouraging black railroad workers near Helena to join a union. A Helena municipal court judge found the two men guilty of "threatening and intimidating" the workers, fined them five hundred dollars, and sentenced them to twelve month jail terms.[42] In delivering the sentence the Helena municipal court judge declared that "in the present crisis of the country it was a most unpropitious time for creating dissension in the ranks of labor." If the response to these incidents seems extreme, it was only because whites well understood that social changes threatened to mobilize the inert black labor force upon which their livelihoods depended.

By the summer of 1919, the *Helena World* began regularly reporting news of the strike wave sweeping the nation and editorialized against the rise of Bolshevism and anarchy.[43] As early as November 1917 the *World* had alerted local factory and mill owners to the alleged presence of a radical union, the Industrial Workers of the World, in Phillips County: "It is said that explosives have been found in a trunk at a local railway station, and that the trunk was shipped to Helena by an I.W.W."[44] The regularity of stories about strikes and social upheaval and the alarmed tone of the coverage assuredly exacerbated whites' anxieties approaching the fall of 1919 when they began hearing rumors of a revolt among their black tenant farmers. Alvin Solomon remembers that such rumors circulated widely among the white community well in advance of the incident at Hoop Spur. According to Solomon, black servants disclosed to their white employers that the farmers were organizing, and this created a climate of severe mistrust and fear between the races. Similarly, union leader Robert Hill later suggested that "lying negroes carrying tales back and from the whites caused the whites to say hard things about the union" and eventually provoked the attack on the union.[45]

The dramatic response of the white community was a measure of the failure of the usual, less disruptive and violent methods for controlling black labor in Phillips County. Like the local employers whose interests it represented, the *Helena World*, in its coverage

---

41. "Protests Against Labor Deportation," *Helena World,* August 7, 1917; "Army Posts Will Use No More Negro Labor," *Helena World,* August 10, 1917.

42. "Negroes Feared Threats of Men" and "A Risky Business," *Helena World,* August 30, 1917.

43. *See* the coverage and editorials following the May Day riots of 1919; *Helena World,* May 1–15, 1919.

44. "Plans of Helena found on I.W.W.," *Helena World,* November 16, 1917.

45. Hill to U.S. Bratton, December 4, 1919, Waskow Papers.

of race issues, precariously balanced the need to subjugate black labor while not becoming so strident as to encourage out-migration. In an editorial declaring war on bootleggers who sold denatured alcohol, the paper suggested that while whites harmed by drinking the poison should know better, "the ignorant Negro" should be protected by strict laws against still operators: "He is an asset which the community can ill afford to lose or abuse or neglect. He is a producer, and occupies a place in our economic life which cannot be easily filled by others."[46] The paper condemned lynching and mob violence, though it featured stories of such violence in other parts of the South, as a warning to local blacks to adhere to social norms.

But as Phillips County's black community mobilized in the fall of 1919, whites surrendered their commitment to paternalism and embrace irregular and extreme modes of behavior, including the hiring of spies and detectives before the riot and, later, the resorting to mob law, federal intervention in the shape of the U. S. Army, and the orchestration of show trials. Because they were unaccustomed to organized challenges to paternalism, whites were caught off-guard by the union as rural black preachers, women, and senior citizens joined the young black men who made up the group's core. As one white observer noted: "One of the remarkable things that I have observed is that I did not see among them more than one hundred prisoners what I could consider a bad negro. They are all that peaceable working class type."[47]

Though the business and planter interests of Phillips County ultimately prevailed by defeating the union, their hopes for a return to the pre-war work arrangements were not entirely fulfilled. As soon as the riot subsided, Phillips County planters and businessmen set out to secure workers to pick the cotton and man the mills. The *Helena World* urged black laborers to forget about the uproar and return to work: "Go back, then, to the fields, the lumber camps, the sawmills and other employments in which you were formerly engaged and take up the implements of honest industry which you threw away at the instance of the most disreputable set of scoundrels that ever breathed the air of a free country."[48] Hundreds of black tenants, though, had already left Phillips County. When Frank Carruth of Elaine visited Greenwood, Mississippi two weeks after the riot, he told friends of the terrible labor shortage caused by the violence. The *Greenwood Commonwealth* reported:

> With a splendid cotton crop in the field and no prospect of getting it gathered, that is the problem confronting the planters of near Helena, Arkansas.... Mr. Carruth told Mr. Bonner that outsiders had no idea of the serious conditions confronting the people there as a result of the race riot. He said many of the negroes were in jail while the riot was being investigated and scores of others had left the county. He stated labor was scarce and that few negroes could be secured to gather the cotton crop. White people will have to be brought in from the outside if they are able to save the crop, he declared. He told of one planter who had 300 acres of fine cotton and not a negro on his plantation.[49]

By 1925, there were 592 fewer black tenants than in 1920 while the number of white tenant farmers increased by seventeen.[50] Between 1920 and 1930 the county lost 5,660 African

---

46. "More Agitation," *Helena World,* May 14, 1919.

47. Report, Major Robert O. Poage, October 14, 1919, Abraham Glasser Files, Records of the Department of Justice, Record Group 60, National Archives and Records Administration, Washington, DC.

48. "Honest Work the Remedy," *Helena World,* October 6, 1919.

49. "Tells of Labor Scarcity at Helena," *Greenwood Commonwealth,* October 15, 1919.

50. U.S. Bureau of the Census, *United States Census of Agriculture: 1925. The Southern States* (Washington: GPO, 1927), vol. 2, 920.

Americans, or almost one in every five black residents—at the same time as the white population grew fifteen percent.[51]

Living in very separate worlds, both the black and white communities of Phillips County emerged from the World War with clear but ultimately incompatible agendas. African Americans, emboldened by their wartime experience and mobilized by rising cotton prices and opportunities in northern factories, developed militant strategies to counter racial and economic injustice. These black workers were neither ignorant nor isolated, misled nor manipulated. Nurtured by the national black press, their churches, and a union, Phillips County African Americans forged a consciousness that offered an alternative to acquiescence and white supremacy.

Among Phillips County whites, rising cotton prices bred high expectations for the postwar period. But the increased mobility and militancy of their black laborers stood in their way and reminded them of their economic dependence on tenants and black workers more generally. That they were driven to such extreme levels of brutality to stop the Progressive Farmers Union is a testament to the depth of black organization. The less drastic and disruptive methods of controlling black labor that delta whites had developed over the years were no longer sufficient. Phillips County whites skillfully drew on the full range of institutions that comprised the core of their power—the press, the military, the courts, their fraternal clubs, and the mob—to crush the insurgent workers.

---

51. U.S. Department of Commerce, Bureau of the Census, *Fifteenth Census of the United States: 1930. Characteristics of the Population for Counties, Cities, Townships, Alabama-Missouri* (Washington: GPO, 1932), vol. 3, pt. 2, 180.

V

The IWW, Western Radicalism, and Deportation

Loading Men for Deportation in Bisbee.

The Bisbee Deportation (1917)

*Philip Taft**

Bisbee in 1917 had a population of about 8,000 people. It was the seat of Cochise County and the center of the Warren mining district, which had a population of about 20,000. The city is built near a canyon, about six miles long, called Mule Pass Gulch. Bisbee's chief producers in 1917 were the Copper Queen Mining Company, the Calumet and Arizona Company, and the Shattuck-Arizona. The community was dominated by the Phelps-Dodge Company, which controlled the Copper Queen and owned Bisbee's largest hotel, hospital, department store, library, newspaper, and other enterprises as well. Understandably, Phelps-Dodge was referred to as "The Company" by admirers as well as critics.[1]

Unions in Arizona in 1917

The regular or major union in the metal mining industry was the Western Federation of Miners, which changed its name in 1916 to the International Union of Mine, Mill and

---

* This article originally appeared in 13 *Labor History* 3 (1972). It is reprinted in edited form with permission of the publisher, Taylor & Francis.
1. *Arizona A State Guide,* 173 (New York, 1940).

Smelter Workers. One of the more militant labor organizations to appear on the American scene, its early militancy reflected the spirit of violence common to many Western mining camps. Ideological influences appear to have been of only moderate importance, even though the Western Federation was the chief sponsor of the Industrial Workers of the World, and many of the former's leaders were socialists. The Federation soon withdrew from the I.W.W., but it furnished the latter with two of its outstanding leaders, William D. Haywood and Vincent St. John, as well as with a number of lesser ones. Periodically, the Federation and the I.W.W. competed for members, and both rivalry and animosity existed between the leaders if not between the members of the two organizations.

Organizing the miners and gaining recognition was always difficult for both unions because the policy of the large copper producers was adamantly against dealing with unions. At the 1903 convention of the Federation an organizer reported that the membership of the Jerome, Arizona, local had diminished from 600 to 203.[2] In 1907, the Federation called a strike in Bisbee, and, according to Joseph D. Cannon, the leader of the walkout, it was the culmination of twenty-seven years of effort. He reported that 1,600 men had been discharged in the Bisbee area by the various corporations.

> ... for belonging to the Western Federation of Miners ... the companies had made a move ... by discharging every man they found to belong or suspected of belonging to it or even those whom they thought sympathized with the Western Federation of Miners. They even went so far in their discrimination that whenever it was possible to get the date a man joined the union, or even the hour and minute, they told the men at the collar of the shaft that they did not need them, that they had joined the union at such an hour on such a day and there was no further use for them.[3]

Cannon believed that unless Bisbee was organized, little progress would be made in the other Arizona mining camps. In this respect, mining camps were much the same everywhere; and so were mining companies. As the official biographer of the dominant company noted: "In the Phelps-Dodge scheme of things, there was no place for labor union supremacy or domination."[4] It might have been more accurate. Phelps-Dodge and other companies in Arizona, as elsewhere, were more opposed to the Western Federation of Miners than to other unions. Not that they would have greeted a more conservative union with greater enthusiasm. But the Federation's militancy, the individualism of many of its members and of its lower echelon leaders posed problems, and there is some evidence that opposition to it was greater. The mining companies, for example, settled the 1915–1916 strike in the Clifton-Morenci district by recognizing grievance committees of their employees who were ultimately represented by the Arizona State Federation of Labor.

Discontent was widespread in the Arizona copper mines in 1917. The Mine, Mill and Smelter Workers had begun to organize in Bisbee early in 1916, and by Labor Day had enrolled an estimated 1,800 members in the Warren district. Before the 1917 strike, the district was producing about fifteen million pounds of copper per month and, given the importance of copper, the growing dissatisfaction was a serious concern to the government once the United States became involved in the war. The dissatisfaction among the workers antedated America's entry into the European conflict, however,

---

2. *Official Proceedings of the Eleventh Annual Convention of the Western Federation of Miners*, 95 (1903).

3. *Official Proceedings of the Fifteenth Annual Convention of the Western Federation of Miners*, 194 (1907).

4. Cleland, *op. cit.*, 111.

and had little connection with it. Simultaneously, with the rising discontent among the miners, there was a resurgence of I.W.W. activity in the copper mining areas. How much of it was the result of the silent support the I.W.W. received from the copper companies, as claimed by Mine, Mill and Smelter Workers Union leaders, is difficult to determine. There are, however, independent reasons which account for the Wobblies' revival.

The growth of I.W.W. activity resulted, at least in part, from the drive that it made annually, beginning in 1914, in the Middle Western grain belt. These campaigns were a source of new members and considerable finances which could be used in attempts to organize other industries. The I.W.W. Metal Mine Workers Industrial Union No. 800 was established in January 1917, and held its first mass convention in Bisbee on June 15, 16, and 17, 1917. Delegates came from a number of mining camps in the West, but individuals could also attend. The conference confirmed the selection of Grover H. Perry as secretary-treasurer and elected a seven-man executive board.[5]

Demands and Strike

William D. Haywood, Secretary-Treasurer of the I.W.W., was of the opinion that the Bisbee conference had agreed to "... discourage local strikes and agitate for a universal, or at least a statewide strike and the demands passed upon by the convention were to be uniform demands presented at that strike."[6] Gradually the older Miners' Union lost its following among the miners in the Warren district to the I.W.W. Wobbly gains and the loss of members of the Miners' Union was attributed by Fred W. Brown, a voluntary organizer for the American Federation of Labor, to the re-election of Charles H. Moyer as president of the International Union of Mine, Mill and Smelter Workers, and also to the failure of the latter to improve working conditions.[7] On June 24, the Bisbee branch of the I.W.W. Metal Mine Workers Industrial Union, No. 800, at a meeting attended by between 400 and 500 members, elected an executive committee which drew up the demands that were presented to the companies. These called for improvements in safety and working conditions, no discrimination for membership in any labor organization, and six dollars a day for underground work and five dollars and fifty cents for above-ground work. The companies refused to answer the demands, and the I.W.W. called a strike on June 26, 1917. It was, at first, about eighty to ninety percent successful. The heads of the three major companies each issued a statement explaining the reasons for their unwillingness to negotiate with an I.W.W. organization. The chief executive officer of the Phelps-Dodge Copper Queen reiterated the "... policy of his company of direct dealing with its own employees will be continued, and any demands by this organization will be refused, even though such refusal may result in shutting down its mines for an indefinite period." John C. Greenway, general manager of the Calumet and Arizona plant, denounced the I.W.W. as disloyal, and stated that his company "intends to continue its present policy of operations unchallenged." L. C. Shattuck, general manager of the Shattuck Arizona Company, believed "... that the demands of this I.W.W. organization are unreasonable and are the plans of a nationwide conspiracy by enemies of the United States government to restrict or cut off the copper output required to prosecute the war."[8]

---

5. Testimony of A.S. Embree in *Haywood v. United States*, in The Supreme Court of the United States, October term 1920, No. 760, 1439. On the influence of the agricultural workers, see Philip Taft, "The IWW in the Grain Belt," *Labor History*, Vol. I, No. 1.

6. Letter of Haywood, July 10, 1917, to executive committee of Bisbee local. (Letter is in the special collection of the University of Arizona Library).

7. *President's Mediation Commission*, sessions at Bisbee, Arizona, November 1–5, 1917, 27.

8. The full statements are found in *The Bisbee Daily Review*, June 27, 1917.

When the strike was called, Moyer was asked if the Western Federation of Miners considered those who continue to work in Bisbee as scabs. Moyer replied that they would not, as the strike was not called by an "International Union or any bona fide organization of labor."[9] President Moyer, then, was opposed to the cooperation of locals of his union with the I.W.W. Nevertheless, Bisbee Local 106 passed a resolution criticizing the contract and dues checkoff as "detrimental to the workers wherever it has been in operation," and charging that whenever the mine workers have signed a contract, the operators controlled the union. These sentiments reflected long-held views of the I.W.W. The resolution further resolved "to oppose the contract and checkoff system and refuse to support any move to obtain one." When Moyer learned of this resolution, he revoked (on July 6) the charter of the Bisbee local.[10] He never recognized the Bisbee strike as legitimate, but his local lost most of its members to the Wobblies. Many of those who so transferred their allegiance were not conversant with I.W.W. principles; they simply believed that Moyer's organization was ineffective.

The leaders of the Mine, Mill and Smelter Workers' Union tended to attribute these membership losses to the machinations of private detective agents employed by the copper companies to promote differences and suspicions among the members and their unions. Indeed, letters in the office of the "defunct miners' local" in Bisbee showed that James A. Chapman, who had served as secretary of the Mine, Mill and Smelter Workers' local in Bisbee, was on the payroll of a private detective agency. He became active in the I.W.W. and was one of the more radical leaders around the area.[11]

Consequently, there appears to be some truth in these claims, but Moyer never conceded that there existed, rightly or wrongly, deep distrust of his policies.

Of course, the companies were very hostile to granting the Mine, Mill and Smelter Workers' Union recognition. They believed that this militant organization would make it difficult to follow their customary policies, and they were even more confident that they could rally the community against the I.W.W.

The Western Federation of Miners had been a militant organization, but the I.W.W., which espoused a type of syndicalism, was presumably a critic of the war as well. Its views and the statements of its spokesmen could be used by employers and state as well as federal officials to inflame public passions — already aroused by the war — and to justify actions which were in fact designed to defeat the strike. The I.W.W. had also advocated direct action and sabotage (both of which doctrines were never clearly defined), though its strikes were generally peaceful. Moreover, Wobbly leaders were not as skilled in manipulating public opinion, not as willing to go through the ritual of ostensible bargaining, as the regular unions. A larger percentage of I.W.W. members and leaders were likely to be from outside the community than other unions, including the Western Federation of Miners. Consequently, it might be easier to arouse public feeling against them, especially during wartime when a strike for wages and job improvements could be transformed into an unpatriotic attack upon the government.

Nevertheless, *The Bisbee Daily Review* noted the peacefulness of the community on the first day of the strike:

---

9. *President's Mediation Commission,* sessions at Bisbee, 243.

10. *Arizona Daily Star,* July 6, 1917, *President's Mediation Commission,* Globe hearings, 139.

11. *See* the reference in *President's Mediation Commission,* Bisbee, Arizona session, Nov. 1–5, 1917, 537–538. *See* also *ibid.* Globe Sessions, 21–22. Joseph Cannon, general organizer of the Mine, Mill and Smelter claimed members of his union were discharged while members of I.W.W. were retained on the job.

No trouble of any kind was experienced last evening on the streets of Bisbee or Warren and the officers gave it as their opinion that none was expected. The streets were as quiet as usual last evening. They appeared calm and gave no evidence of untoward events pending or otherwise.[12]

This view was corroborated by Sheriff Harry Wheeler, of Cochise County, who arrived in Bisbee on the first day of the strike and set up headquarters. He nevertheless asked the Governor that President Wilson be requested to send troops to the city. The Governor submitted the request, on his own behalf, to the White House. A War Department investigation concluded troops were not needed, and the request was denied.[13] Instead, President Wilson appointed Governor George P. Hunt, who was temporarily out of office and was subsequently restored to the governorship by the courts, as special strike mediator in the hope that he could aid the parties to reach a settlement.[14] This appointment aroused the displeasure of the Tucson Chamber of Commerce, which forwarded a protest of the appointment to the President.[15] The protest reflected both the strained political relations within Arizona, and suspicions about Hunt's labor views. Hunt had, during the 1915 Clifton-Morenci strike, refused to allow strikebreakers from outside to enter the community, and issued a proclamation "pursuant to the plain dictates of humanity," calling for donations of "food, fuel and clothing" to strikers, the "penniless families in this time of industrial trouble."[16]

Conditions in Bisbee were generally peaceful during the strike; at least so witnesses attested, as did the daily newspapers, which were hostile to the strikers. Sheriff Wheeler noted several incidents, such as threats to women working in a laundry, but he failed to arrest any of those allegedly involved because he "could not prove they made them."[17] In the opinion of Police Judge Frank A. Thomas:

> The strikers were exerting themselves to be peaceful. They were peaceful. There were no violent acts or anything like that, and the only thing they did was picketing and large mobs of them would gather on the street and there would be congestion of traffic, and public speaking at the park, and a large crowd would gather there, but as far as any fist fights or anything like that was concerned why it was unusually good.

He also said the men working were pestered and the pickets swore at them, but "these things are incidental to every strike."[18]

Judge Thomas was of the opinion that the strike would have soon ended without the deportation. "This strike was dying a natural death," he said, "when this thing was pulled off, and the men flocking back to work, because things had been most excellent.... I

---

12. *The Bisbee Daily Review*, June 28, 1917.

13. *President's Mediation Commission*, Bisbee Sessions, 477–499, contains the discussion on this point. Felix Frankfurter, counsel of the Commission, insisted that the War Department had opposed sending troops.

14. President Woodrow Wilson to Hunt, July 2, 1917 in Conciliation Service files, Maryland Record Center.

15. L.H. Hoofmeister, President of Tucson Chamber of Commerce, to President Wilson, July 6, 1917, (Conciliation files, Maryland Record Center).

16. Proclamation of Governor Hunt: *Appealing to the People of Arizona for Generous Cooperation in Relief of Suffering Families in the Clifton-Morenci Mining District*, Oct. 27, 1915; *New Republic*, June 22, 1916, 304–306; *The Survey*, May 6, 1916, 145–146.

17. Testimony of Sheriff Wheeler, in *President's Mediation Commission*, 147.

18. Testimony of Police Judge Frank A. Thomas, *ibid.*, Bisbee, 61.

would say it was unpopular among the men.... They were getting the highest wages ever paid and the conditions were very good."[19]

J. McDonald, Deputy United States Marshall, testified: "... it was more peaceful than ordinary ... the strikers, through their organization, had instructed bootleggers whom they knew not to sell any liquor to the men or they would turn them in to the Sheriff, and for that reason there was practically no liquor sold in the district, as far as I know, and that, of course, made the town much more peaceful."[20] The President of the A.F.L. painters' union was of the same opinion. He said "the district was very orderly, more so than any other time."

Edward Massey, State Mine Inspector, testified that the "only thing that I saw, during the strike, was the pickets here at the depot and also up in front of the Copper Queen store, just milling back and forth." When Massey went through the picket line "one morning, and some fellows told them who I was and the pickets said to me, 'Make it safe for them scalies over there.'"[21]

The Legal Rights Committee of the Arizona State Federation of Labor in its statement claimed that between eighty and ninety percent of the underground men were out, and that:

> Large and continuous picket lines were maintained by the strikers, which, with possibly a very few individual exceptions, were conducted in a peaceable and orderly manner and in strict observance of the laws of the State. An investigation of the police records will show that acts of violence, unfortunately common to strikes, were very rare and it is admitted that the voluntary action of the strikers in suppressing the illicit traffic in liquor was much more effective than that of the regular peace officers.[22]

This report challenged the claim of Sheriff Wheeler and the Loyalty League that the pickets were engaging in "wholesale intimidation and threats to kill men who were working, but not a single arrest was made for these alleged crimes." It also questioned the Sheriff's views that a plot to kill and drive out the men working in the mines existed. "No evidence to substantiate this charge has ever been offered to the public and it seems strange that if the Sheriff had in his possession sufficient evidence ... that not a single man was charged with the serious crime of conspiracy to incite this proposed riot and place on trial therefore."[23]

Such a view is corroborated by the Bisbee newspaper, *The Bisbee Daily Review,* which noted in its Sunday edition:

> One of the most striking features of the Bisbee walkout has been the absence of trouble. It is entirely unlike former strikes and particularly where I.W.W. have been involved. Only one construction can be placed upon the peace which has prevailed: the strike leaders realized that any effort to stir up trouble would be met with the mailed fist.[24]

One day before the deportation, the same paper noted:

> In spite of the continued presence of the pickets no trouble of any kind has resulted in the District since Sunday morning. For a time, yesterday, it appeared

---

19. *Ibid.,* 72–73.
20. *Ibid.,* Bisbee, 21.
21. *Ibid.,* 56.
22. *President's Mediation Commission,* Bisbee Sessions, 104.
23. *Ibid.,* 104.
24. *The Bisbee Daily Review,* July 8, 1917.

likely that the pickets would precipitate trouble when the Copper Queen employees came off the day shift yesterday. The miners came off in a body and passed in front of the post office. A hurry call was sent to the union headquarters and a number of I.W.W.'s rushed to the scene. The miners, however, went quietly on about their business and the pickets realizing the hopelessness of their cause made no offer of trouble.[25]

The peacefulness of the strike did not affect the views of some employers. Walter Douglas, the general manager of the Phelps-Dodge Corporation in the district, announced, "There will be no compromise because you cannot compromise with a rattlesnake. That goes for both the International Union and the I.W.W.'s," he added quickly. "This is part of a nationwide propaganda and the alleged grievances are only talking points for that propaganda.... I believe the government will be able to show that there is German influence behind the movement...." The way for the I.W.W. organization to be handled, he also declared, was for the individual communities "to run them out."[26]

Preparing for the Bisbee Deportation

The views of Douglas, the most powerful man in Bisbee, probably affected events, since his strong opinions very likely reflected the sentiments held by many Bisbee businessmen and professionals at the time. Nor was the deportation in Bisbee or the much lesser one in Jerome the product of spontaneous anger generated by violence and disorder on the part of the strikers or pickets. It was carried out as a result of a well-organized program by the Citizens' Protective League, established in 1916 during the boycott campaign of the English Kitchen (which eventually led to the decision in *Truax* v. *Corrigan*, 257 U.S. 312), and the Workers Loyalty League, organized in the last days of June 1917 with Miles W. Merrill, a working miner, as president. The Loyalty League was made up of privates under the command of captains and majors, and the members and others were to be deputized by Sheriff Wheeler for the occasion.[27]

A joint meeting of the Citizens Protective League and the Workers Loyalty League was held on July 11 at the Copper Queen dispensary. Merrill presided and asked for suggestions on the course to pursue during the strike. Present at the meeting were G. H. Dowell, Manager of the Copper Queen, John C. Greenway, head of the Calumet and Arizona, and about fifty leading businessmen as well as fifty captains in the Loyalty League who were company employees. Greenway suggested that they "get a train and run the strikers to Columbus, where," he said, "Uncle Sam would take care of them."[28] His suggestion had the support of G. H. Dowell and Dr. N. C. Bledsoe, chief surgeon for the Calumet and Arizona, each of whom spoke in surgical terms. It was George Kellogg's view that "when they talked about a cancerous growth and surgeons that they meant deportation."[29] The vote to deport was unanimous.

George Kellogg, manager of the Bisbee office of the Bell Telephone Company, had been invited so that he could direct the mobilizing of the armed deputies by telephone. Kellog was opposed to the plan, but believed it would be better if the deportation were

---

25. *Ibid.*, July 11, 1917.

26. The interview is reproduced in *President's Mediation Commission*, Globe sessions, 105–106.

27. Testimony of Merrill, 219; testimony of Sheriff Wheeler, 142–143, in *President's Mediation Commission*, Bisbee sessions. The U.S. Supreme Court, in *Truax,* invalidated a clause in the state constitution forbidding the issuance of injunctions in labor disputes.

28. Testimony of George E. Kellogg, in *President's Mediation Commission, ibid.*, 6.

29. These words were used by Felix Frankfurter in the form of a question, and Kellogg agreed to them.

carried out peacefully, which would only be possible if the strikers and their sympathiz-ers were unaware of the project. "I felt [he said] that as long as the vote was taken and as long as the boys were going to do it that the less chance there was for bloodshed the bet-ter, and right today I am tickled to death at the way things were working on that board, and by keeping the girls from losing their head everything went right."[30]

Kellogg and the operators he directed called members of the Citizens Protective League and the Loyalty League to tell them to be at a certain mobilization point which Merrill had given to Kellogg. Sheriff Harry Wheeler was called into the meeting and "was sim-ply obedient to that viewpoint" — namely, deportation.[31]

The Deportation

At 6:30 A.M. on July 12, Sheriff Wheeler posted a proclamation "with a warning on top of it to women and children to keep off the streets," which announced that a Sher-iff's Posse of 1,200 men "had been formed in Bisbee and one thousand in Douglas ... for the purpose of arresting on charges of vagrancy, treason and being disturbers of the peace of Cochise County all those strange men who have congregated here from other parts and sections for the purpose of harassing and intimidating all men who desire to pursue their daily toil." The proclamation recited that threats had been made daily. "We cannot longer stand or tolerate such conditions. There is no labor trouble — we are sure of that — but a direct attempt to embarrass and injure the government of the United States."

The proclamation urged that "no shot be fired throughout the day unless in necessary self-defense." It warned that strike leaders would be held responsible for injuries "inflicted upon any of my deputies while in performance of their duties as deputies of my posse," and promised humane treatment to the arrested, including examination of their cases "with justice and care."[32]

The Bisbee Daily Review greeted the deportation with an enthusiastic outburst on the front page:

> No longer does a blot remain on the escutcheon of Bisbee. "Wobblyism" has passed into the labyrinth of things discarded; as a coat is shaken from the back; as a boil is lanced and cleansed of its contents.... Without precedent in this or any other country, or any other age, was the occurrence of yesterday. It marked a golden date on the calendar; a date when the law-abiding people of the com-munity ... drove from their midst the "Wobbly."[33]

The deportation was carried out by about 2,000 armed men on foot and on horseback wearing white arm bands for identification. Men were seized in their homes, on the street, in restaurants and stores, and asked if they were working or willing to work. If they an-swered "no," they were forced into line and taken to the railroad station which served as a temporary detention point, and finally marched to the ball park. One of the deportees, A.S. Embree, described how two women, watching the men standing in the hot Arizona sun, brought a tub of water and dippers so that the prisoners could have a drink. Before a drop passed through the lips of a single man, several guards approached the tub, kicked it over and declared: "The sons of bitches don't get a drink."[34]

---

30. *Ibid.*, 8.
31. *Ibid.*, 11.
32. Proclamation in *ibid.*, 137.
33. *Bisbee Daily Review*, July 13, 1917.
34. Testimony of A. S. Embree, *Haywood* v. *United States*, 1449–1450.

People were picked up at random. A deportee who returned to Bisbee told Judge Thomas that he had no part in the strike and that "he had been doing assessment work and came in that night and a man asked him if he was working and he said no, and he told him to get in line."[35] Another witness, Thomas N. English, was not a member of any organization. He said:

> On the morning of the 12th, about seven o'clock in the morning, somebody knocked on the door and I told them to come in, and there were three men came in and asked me if I was working, and I said, "No, sir," and they said "Well, come out of there right away and dress; we want you." And I said, "What is this for?" and they said, "Get in line with the rest of them." That was all the information I could get. There was another man rooming with me by the name of Swanson, and they made him get out at the same time and they taken us down to the line and then into the Ball Park, and I was loaded into a stock car about eleven o'-clock in the morning.[36]

While the deportation was going on, the telegraph and telephones were censored. "Captain" Stout, superintendent of the Copper Queen smelter, requested the manager of the Douglas telephone office to censor the toll lines. Kellogg told Stout it would not be done, but Stout insistently stated that the "Bell System in New York will stand behind you both." Calling his superior, Kellogg was informed that, while being diplomatic, he should not withhold messages. Western Union, however, agreed to shut down its outside service in Douglas and in Bisbee, and refused service to an Associated Press correspondent.[37]

A twenty-four car train was provided by the El Paso and Southwestern Railroad at the direction of Walter Douglas, the head of Phelps-Dodge and a vice president of the road.[38] There was little violence in the gathering up of 1,300 men.[39] One man, refusing to be taken, fired from behind a door and killed a deputy, and was in turn himself killed by another. Otherwise, the round-up was peacefully carried out. Those seized were offered a chance to leave the line. They could go to work in the mines or take up a rifle and help round up their friends and fellow workers. Those rounded up, 1,186 in all, were marched in single file between two lines of armed men, who in testimony were referred to as "gunmen," and loaded in the railroad cars. Their first stop, of about twenty minutes, was at Douglas where, according to one deportee, "both sides of the tracks were lined with gunmen" who had left Bisbee in motor cars. A mounted machine gun was also visible. The train then moved on to Naco, a water stop, where the men were allowed to go out of the cars and stretch. At the next stop, Hachita, the engines were changed and the men were again allowed out; and some of the guards offered them crackers and bread. The train rolled on to Columbus, New Mexico, but the constable there would not allow the men or the guards to remain. He insisted that they return by train. Consequently, they went back to Hermanes, seventeen miles from Columbus, on the Bisbee side. The guards left the train at this point, and the men got off. They had been abandoned without food or adequate water. Fred Brown, a voluntary organizer for the American Federation of Labor, then wired to Gompers. William Cleary, a radical lawyer who was also deported, sent telegrams to the Arizona Governor and to President Woodrow Wilson.[40]

---

35. Testimony of Judge Thomas, 74, *President's Mediation Commission.*

36. Testimony of Thomas N. English, *President's Mediation Commission,* Bisbee, 80.

37. Testimony of Kellog, 14, 19; testimony of Sheriff Wheeler, 161 in *ibid.* Captain Stout was only a captain by courtesy. He was called by that title because it was customary among *"Cousin Jacks"* to call a supervisor "captain."

38. *The New York Times,* July 13, 1917. Also *President's Mediation Report,* 98.

39. *President's Mediation Commission,* 198.

40. Testimony of Fred W. Brown, *ibid.,* Bisbee sessions, 36–37.

The men, leaving the cars, went about foraging for food. It was late July 13, and the humane treatment promised by Sheriff Wheeler obviously referred to the absence of actual bodily harm. None of the men had been fed except those who were able to grab a few crackers or a piece of bread. A collection was taken by A.S. Embree and two men were sent to Columbus. They grabbed a freight train to that point and returned on a passenger train with food. It was distributed at 11 P.M., July 13. The men then found places on the ground or on railroad ties to sleep. At daylight they were taken back to Columbus by a military guard, fed, provided with tents in which to sleep, and allowed to stay in town or depart.[41]

A United States Army survey showed that out of the 1,386 deported men, 520 owned property in Bisbee; 472 had registered for the draft; 433 were married with families; 205 had purchased Liberty Bonds; and sixty-two had served in the armed forces of the United States: Only 426 had been members of the I.W.W.[42] Governor Thomas Campbell's reaction to these events was simply to ask President Wilson that federal troops be sent to several Arizona mining camps, including Bisbee. The President then directed Secretary of War Newton D. Baker to investigate and, in acknowledging the request of the Governor, added:

> May I not respectfully urge the great danger of citizens taking the law into their own hands, as your report indicated having done. I look upon such actions with great apprehension. A very serious responsibility is assumed when such precedents are set.[43]

John C. Greenway, General Manager of Calumet and Arizona Mining Company, saw no need for troops. As one of the original promoters of the Bisbee deportation, Greenway was "... confident if there is any trouble the officers and citizens of the district will again prove that they are patriotic enough to see that the government is not hampered by an interference with her mining interests."[44]

In his testimony before the President's Mediation Commission Sheriff Wheeler was asked for evidence of danger which would justify the deportation. His answer was that:

> ... good reliable men have said that many have told them, "Well, you beat us to it a few days," and it is well understood that they had a plan on foot when they were to be permitted to go down in the mines to get their clothing on Friday night they were to block those tunnels and keep the men down at work in the mines. I am told these things; I cannot vouch for them.[45]

Secretary Wilson's reply did not please the Sheriff:

> And on the strength of rumors of that kind you directed the picking up of twelve hundred people here, some only here for a brief time, and some, as we are informed, for a long time, and under the authority to use whatever power is necessary you undertook to use that power not only within your own bailiwick, but outside of your own bailiwick and take them into the bailiwick of another, where you had no authority and where you were not directed or authorized to use power, wasn't that the situation?[46]

---

41. Testimony of Brown in *Ibid.*, 36–40; Embree in *Haywood v. U.S.*, 1451.
42. Figures, except the numbers of the I.W.W., were read by Felix Frankfurter at the Bisbee hearings. The employers and their lawyers who were present challenged them, but presented no evidence to the contrary, *President's Mediation Commission*, Bisbee Session, 154. The figures on I.W.W. membership came from the message to the legislature by Governor Hunt, cited above. The number deported is found in the *Report of President's Mediation Commission*, November 6, 1917.
43. *The New York Times*, July 14, 1917.
44. *Arizona Daily Star*, July 13, 1917.
45. *President's Mediation Commission*, Bisbee, 157–158.
46. *Ibid.*, 158.

The Sheriff made an emotional answer in which he conjured up dangers of riots and bloodshed, with him alone left to protect the community. He said: "If I hadn't done it, and these people had been murdered and killed, as well as my own, you would still have asked me, "why did you permit it?"[47]

A kangaroo court was then organized. Anyone seeking to enter Bisbee was stopped outside the city limits, brought before the court which then decided whether he could remain in Bisbee, be allowed to leave "voluntarily," or go to jail. Passports were issued by the Douglas Chamber of Commerce and Mines, and those who came into the Warren district had to have them in order to remain unmolested.[48] Hundreds of men were hauled before this court by the Sheriff and his deputies.

> Trials were secret and verdict of deportation was promptly and forcibly executed by deputy sheriffs. At the same time the Sheriff established "guards" at all entrances to the district who examined every person attempting to enter the camp. The reported object of these "guards" was to exclude from the camp any stray "wobbly" that might drift in and endanger the peace and safety of the community. The definition of this term "wobbly" was apparently left to the discretion of the individual guards and all "wobblies" were promptly and forcibly denied the right to enter the camp, and unless removed in the past few days, a reduced number of these "guards" are still on duty.[49]

Judge Thomas informed the Commission that the court ordered many men deported because they were union men. Those who returned from Columbus were arrested for vagrancy and brought before Judge Thomas, and between 300–400 men "were encouraged to leave town"; otherwise, they would be convicted and held in jail.[50] These illegal acts continued, Sheriff Wheeler ignoring a request from Governor Campbell that Fred H. Moore, the attorney for two deportees and I.W.W. counsel, be given "all privileges of the Warren District, which are due as a law-abiding citizen." The Governor's letter was unable to save Moore himself from forcible removal from his hotel after which he was pushed into a car, taken to Osborne Junction, and placed on a train. His plea to the Governor for protection had been to no avail.[51]

The character of the justice meted out by this court is illustrated by the case of A.S. Embree. Returning to Bisbee after the Columbus camp had been disbanded, he was arrested and refused to leave. He was then held in jail for three months, granted a change of venue, tried in Tucson, and was freed by a jury minutes after testimony was closed.[52]

Bisbee remained a community dominated by armed men who arbitrarily decided who could enter its precincts. A committee of six representatives from the Arizona State Federation of Labor sent to investigate conditions there were denied access to the city by Loyalty Leaguers. Informed of this denial of rights, the Governor finally undertook an investigation. He reviewed the lawless acts of officials and private parties, and belatedly noted: "In the Warren District since July 12th, the constitutional rights of citizens and others have been ignored, by processes not provided by law: viz., by deputy sheriffs, who refused persons admittance into the district, and passing of judgment by a tribunal with-

---

47. *Ibid.*, 158.
48. *Bisbee Daily Review*, July 19, 1917.
49. *President's Mediation Commission*, Bisbee. The quotation is from a statement of the Legal Rights Committee of the Arizona State Federation of Labor, 105.
50. *Ibid.*, 69.
51. *The Bisbee Daily Review*, July 31, August 4, 1917.
52. Testimony of Embree, *Haywood v. U.S.*, 1476.

out legal jurisdiction, resulting in further deportations."[53] He then ordered that the kangaroo court be disbanded and directed that all persons charged with an offense be given a proper trial before a regularly constituted body. Upon learning that the kangaroo court intended to continue its deportations and denial of entry, he threatened to use the armed power of the State or the Federal Government to "overcome these unlawful deportations as well as denials of entry into Bisbee as now conducted."

The deportees were left in Columbus, New Mexico, as charges of the United States Government. On July 21, they organized their own police force, and elected an executive committee to represent those who stayed on, initially some 1,168 in number. These deportees also asked for federal protection so that they could return to their homes in Bisbee,[54] to which they were free to leave. On August 12, the executive committee wired Attorney General Wesley E. Jones:

> The sentiment of men deported from Bisbee is that they wish to return to their homes immediately, but they are aware that their arrival may cause acts similar to those of July 12. We wish to avoid any breach of peace, and so respectfully suggest that you incorporate in your report some method by which we will be able to return to our homes with adequate protection.[55]

The men gradually drifted away, and by September 8, when the government cut their ration to one-half, about 450 deportees remained at Columbus. Protests were wired to Secretary of Labor William B. Wilson and Presidential secretary Joseph Tumulty, but the reduction was not rescinded and the camp was disbanded on October 19, 1917.[56] There were, however, peaceful reactions which disturbed the leaders of Bisbee's mining industry. A serious labor shortage was reported due in part to the general stringency of mining labor, but also because of "the fear of further trouble by the more timid men led to a shortage of workmen and curtailment of copper production."[57] The managers of the major companies complained to the President's Mediation Commission that Bisbee was receiving a bad name, and the General Manager of the Copper Queen called on the Commission to put out the information that Bisbee is "safe." He was answered by Secretary Wilson who informed him that the Commission:

> ... could not put out any statement of facts, any statement that such is not the fact; that they are safe here unless a change in conditions takes place or a change in evidence is presented to us. Thus far the evidence indicates that these twelve hundred men were deported and the evidence indicated that men are stopped on the highways coming in here and that they are questioned, that men are still being arrested for vagrancy although they are not vagrants, and the kangaroo court has [not] been eliminated according to the evidence we have.[58]

---

53. The Report of the Governor is in *President's Mediation Commission,* Bisbee sessions, 109–112.

54. *The Bisbee Daily Review,* July 21, 1917.

55. The telegram was also sent to Governor Campbell. It was signed by A.S. Embree, Chairman, Sam Brooks, M.C. Sullivan, Jack Normas, and J. G. Payne, and read into the record by A.S. Embree during his testimony at the Chicago I.W.W. Federal trial. It appears in *Haywood* v. *U.S.,* 1466.

56. *Bisbee Daily Review,* September 9, 1917, reported reduction of ration, and in its September 12 issue, printed the protest signed by Embree as Chairman of the executive committee of the deportees. Statement of Fred Brown, a deportee and organizer for the A.F.L. in the *Arizona Daily Star,* July 15, 1919.

57. *The Mineral Industry Statutes, Technology and Trade.* Edited by G. A. Rush and Allison Butts, 149 (New York: McGraw-Hill Book Company, Inc., 1917).

58. Statement of Secretary Wilson, *Presidents Mediation Commission,* Bisbee, 169–170.

Secretary Wilson, on behalf of the Commission, asked Sheriff Wheeler to respect the right of entrance to Bisbee. Furthermore, he insisted, the "right of all persons to move about the Warren district or to continue to reside within it must be scrupulously respected, except in so far as such is restricted by the orderly processes of law."[59]

The President's Mediation Commission recommended that a system for handling grievances be established, and that committees for this purpose be organized on the facilities of each company. Grievances that could not be settled directly would be carried to a federal administrator, appointed by the Department of Labor, whose decision would be final. But the companies were opposed to any changes. The Commission, however, did not direct that grievance committees must be set up: "... we simply provide that if they do and when they do and have grievances to present that they will be recognized in presenting them."[60] The proposal also called for the re-employment of all men who went on strike on June 27, except those "who have been guilty of utterances disloyal to the United States or who are members of any organization that refuses to recognize the obligation of contracts, or who have heretofore demonstrated their unfitness to work in the mine, or whose employment for any reason is contrary to the best interests of the operations. The facts in such cases, if questioned, shall be determined by the administrator."[61]

The companies objected to the grievance committees and to the appointment of an administrator, but most vehemently to reference to the strike of June 27, which was stricken from the Commission record. Expressing the opposition of all employers, W. B. Gohring, Superintendent of the Calumet and Arizona Company, despairingly stated:

> I personally feel as Mr. Dowell has expressed it that it is not necessary and if I agree with that thing, why, it will be because I must. I don't think the men in the mine want that thing. I feel I owe it to them not to, but if it is essential to get things straightened up to suit you gentlemen, I might have to agree to it.[62]

After the above discussions, a procedure providing for the election of grievance committees, with a final appeal to an administrator appointed by the Secretary of Labor, was adopted. Members of the grievance committees were to be employed in Bisbee at least six months. At the close of the hearing Sheriff Wheeler — stubborn and unrepentant — reappeared "through the courtesy of Mr. Dowell,"[63] and the Secretary of Labor had to explain to him "that there is a wide difference between refusing a man employment and refusing to permit the man to be in the community." Felix Frankfurter, counsel to the Commission, after a company lawyer sought to soften the attitude toward the Sheriff, said: "I think it is fair to the Sheriff to make clear to him that an I.W.W. as such is not a federal crime, and I haven't a particle of doubt if he consulted you (reference is to E.H. Ellinwood, attorney for the Copper Queen) in a professional capacity you would so advise him."[64]

When the directives of the Commission were issued, the operating heads of the three major companies "protested to the end against the imposition of official regulations with our employees, which relations we believe to be satisfactory." The companies reiterated their support of the open shop, and requested the cooperation of employees in carrying

---

59. William B. Wilson to Sheriff Harry Wheeler, November 6, 1917, in *President's Mediation Board* (file in National Archives).
60. Suggestions made by Secretary Wilson, 551.
61. *Ibid.*, 561.
62. Statement of Gohring in *ibid.*, 585.
63. *Ibid.*, 606.
64. *Ibid.*, 609.

out the directive.[65] Subsequently, a staff member of the War Labor Policies Board, Max Lowenthal, called attention to the failure of the Commission's proposals to work in the Arizona copper mines. The dispute machinery had broken down, mediation was not being accepted by either side, and the bitterness and militancy of both miners and operators made settlements difficult.[66]

The employers had their way. None of the Arizona mining camps established a union. It is doubtful if the I.W.W.—or the Mine, Mill & Smelter Workers, for that matter— would have succeeded in gaining concessions from Bisbee's operators or from those elsewhere in the State. It simply lacked the strength; and many of those who became Wobblies around Bisbee appeared to have done so only because of their dissatisfaction with the Mine, Mill & Smelter Workers. Conversely, many who were not sympathetic to the I.W.W. nevertheless disapproved of the deportation, believed that it had been inspired and directed by the copper companies, and that there had been no danger of violence.[67]

In its report to the President, *The President's Mediation Commission Report* confirmed this state of affairs. It found "conditions in Bisbee were in fact peaceful and free from manifestations of disorder or violence in the testimony of reputable citizens, as well as of officials of the city and county who are in a position to report accurately and speak without bias." Reviewing events in Bisbee, it noted that they had "been made the basis of an attempt to affect adversely public opinion among some of the people of the Allies." While seeking to avoid recriminations over the past, the *Report* observed: "… it is impossible to make for peace in the future unless the recurrences of such instances as the Bisbee deportations are avoided. The future cannot be safeguarded against such recurrences unless a candid and just statement is made of the facts surrounding the Bisbee deportation and an understanding is had of the conditions which brought it about." The Commission explained that no machinery for adjustment of grievances existed in the Bisbee mines, that many of those who joined the strike did not favor the walkout, but went out "because of their general loyalty to the cause represented by the strikers and their refusal to be regarded in their own estimation, as well as in the minds of their fellow workers, as 'scabs'". It reviewed the deportations and recommended "that the responsible law officers of the state and county pursue appropriate remedies for the vindication of such laws." The Commission also called the attention of the United States Attorney General and the Interstate Commerce Commission to the possible violations of Federal law. In addition, the Commission recommended "that such occurrences hereafter be made criminal under the Federal law to the full extent of the constitutional authority of the Federal Government."[68]

Former President Theodore Roosevelt, a friend of the man who proposed deportation, John Greenway, the General Manager of the Calumet and Hecla Mining Company in Bisbee, found the report "as thoroughly misleading a document as could be written on the subject." In his opinion, "No officials, writing on behalf of the President, is to be

---

65. G.H. Dowell, Arthur Hule, and W. B. Gohring to William B. Wilson, November 6, 1917, in *Miners Magazine,* December 2, 1917, 2.

66. Max Lowenthal to Felix Frankfurter, August 28, 1918.

67. Moreover, the operation was costly to Bisbee's citizens. In "The Truth About Bisbee," a typewritten manuscript, with an introduction by Samuel Morse, the amount spent by the community in behalf of the families of deportees was set at $80,000.

68. The three last quotations are from *Report on the Bisbee Deportations.* Made by the President's Mediation Commission to the President of the United States, Bisbee, Arizona, Nov. 6, 1917. The report was signed by Secretary of Labor, William B. Wilson, Chairman; E.P. Marsh, John H. Walker, J.L. Spangler, and Felix Frankfurter, counsel to the Commission. It had no listed publisher, and appeared to have been printed in Bisbee.

excused for failure to know, and clearly to set forth, that the I.W.W. is a criminal organization.... No human being in his senses doubts that the men deported from Bisbee were bent on destruction and murder."[69]

The attack upon Wheeler was only the opening gun directed against the leaders of the deportation. There was, after all, considerable feeling that the removal of the Bisbee strikers was illegal and reflected upon the reputation of Arizona. Governor Hunt, who had been restored to office, in a message to the legislature denounced the

> ... mob of nearly two thousand men—directed by county authorities whose sworn duty it was to suppress such lawlessness organized not as mobs are wont to do under the spur of justifiable indignation or self-righteous anger, but with Indian-like stealth, under cover of darkness, calmly, premeditatedly, deliberately, swooped down at dawn upon the homes of unsuspecting, unoffending miners who had committed no violence, nay, much more, who had threatened no violence but who had every reason to feel secure as citizens under guarantees vouchsafed by the Constitution of the United States and the State of Arizona.... In this execrable manner, without a justification or legality nearly twelve hundred unarmed workingmen were driven at the point of a gun from their homes to the public square, later to be herded, like so many beasts in the field, to the public square, later to be herded ... into freight cars into the desert of an adjoining State. During the enforced journey, the hapless victims of copper company vengeance were virtually without food or drink, notwithstanding the heat of an Arizona summer, and stood so long in a position on the floor of jolting cars that their feet were sore and bleeding from the ordeal.[70]

Civil and criminal suits were also started by the State and Federal Governments and by the deportees. Two attorneys, one of whom had been deported in the July 12 sweep, filed suits on behalf of 272 deportees against the El Paso and Southwestern Railroad, the major copper companies, and a number of persons. Each individual sued for $20,000, except William B. Cleary, a practicing lawyer, who sued for $75,000.[71] The cases were never brought to trial. A compromise agreement was reached under which each married man with a child was awarded $1,250; married men received $1,000 each; and single men, $500.[72] *The Survey,* a liberal monthly published in New York, estimated that the total award came to over one million dollars.[73]

Simultaneous with the launching of the civil suits came an investigation by the Federal Government which led to the indictment of Sheriff Harry Wheeler and twenty-four others: the heads of mining operations and other businesses, professional men, as well as government officials. They were charged with violating the constitutional rights of the deportees by conspiring "to oppress, threaten or intimidate any citizen in the free exercise in the enjoyment of any right or privilege by the Constitution or laws of the United States."[74]

The case was not tried on its merits since Circuit Judge Morrow found that the offenses could not be reached by Federal law. He questioned whether the existence of prej-

---

69. Theodore Roosevelt to Felix Frankfurter, Dec. 19, 1917, in *The Letters of Theodore Roosevelt,* selected and edited by Elting E. Morison (Cambridge: Harvard University Press, 1954), VIII, 1264.

70. *Journal of the Senate,* Third Legislative, First Special Sessions, 1918, 11.

71. *Bisbee Daily Review,* July 7, 10, 13, 28, 1910; *The Arizona Daily Star,* July 8, 1919.

72. *The Arizona Daily Star,* July 8, 1918.

73. *The Survey,* June 21,1919.

74. In the United States District Court for Arizona, *United States* v. *Wheeler.* Unreported and in the library of the University of Arizona.

udice warranted *a certiorari* when the cases actually belonged in the state, not the federal, courts, The government appealed to the Supreme Court, and the defendants engaged Charles Evans Hughes to represent them. He argued that the rights allegedly violated were left by the United States Constitution "to the protection of the several states having jurisdiction."[75] Furthermore, an individual is not protected against the acts of individuals but "at the hostile action of the State."[76] On December 13, 1920, Mr. Chief Justice Edward White spoke for the Court and noted the indictment charged twenty-five persons with criminally conspiring "to injure, oppress, threaten ... citizens of Arizona of rights and privileges secured to them by the Constitution or laws of the United States."[77]

The indictments were struck down "on the ground that no power had been delegated by the Constitution of the United States to forbid and punish wrongful acts complained of, as the right to do so was exclusively within the authority reserved by that instrument to the States." Elaborating on this theme, Chief Justice White found:

> no basis is afforded for contending that a wrongful prevention by an individual of the enjoyment by a citizen of one State in another of rights possessed in that State by its own citizens was a violation of the Constitution. This is the necessary result of Article IV, Section 2 which reserves to the several States authority over the subject, limited by the restriction against state discriminatory action, hence, excluding federal authority except where invoked to enforce the limitation, which is not here the case.

Although those responsible escaped from Federal prosecution as a result of the quashing of the Federal indictments, they faced an attack on the state level. R.N. French was elected to serve as district attorney from Cochise County in 1919 and he announced on July 7, 1919, that complaints had been filed against the participants in the Bisbee deportations.[78] The Phelps-Dodge Company and 224 persons, among them the most prominent members of the community, were arrested on the "information of the crime of kidnapping." The character of the indicted is attested by Bisbee's local journal, which noted, "If you are on the selected list of the county attorney's Monday party, it has been arranged for your convenience that when Sheriff McDonald greets you, walk over to the Commercial Club with him, and your bond will be waiting for you. No dealings, no waits. Get your Liberty Bonds early."[79]

Two days later, the same newspaper noted: "The warrant itself resembled a directory of the pioneer residents of the district, practically every man who has taken any active interest in the affairs of the district for the last twenty-five years being included in the charge."[80] It was an accurate statement, for among those who appeared and posted bond were the heads of the three largest copper mining operations in the Warren area, lower officers of the copper companies, heads of banks, merchants, public officials, and ordinary folks.[81]

The defendants were all released on bond, and defense counsel early revealed its strategy; to shift the issue from kidnapping to the character and principles of the I.W.W. De-

---

75. In the Supreme Court of the United States, October 1920, *United States* v. *Wheeler*, Brief for Defendants in Error, 9.

76. *Ibid.,* 291.

77. *United States* v. *Wheeler*, 254 U. S. 281 (1920).

78. *The Arizona Daily Star*, July 8, 1919.

79. *The Bisbee Daily Review*, July 7, 1919.

80. *Ibid.,* July 22, 1919.

81. In the Superior Court of the County of Cochise, *State of Arizona, State of Arizona* v. *Phelps-Dodge Corporation, A corporation, et al.*

positions were taken from a number of United States Marshals and other government officials on the Chicago Wobbly trials, the heads of the printing company which had dealt with the Wobblies testified, and persons were interviewed in Butte, Montana. These depositions were taken, beginning on November 10, 1919, and the State, after formal objections, refused to cross examine. Witnesses testified that I.W.W. headquarters had been searched and that Wobblies had been tried.[82] The deposition of the deputy clerk of the United States Court of Appeals, Seventh Circuit, was obtained with the aim of demonstrating the violent character of the organization, and the fact that its leaders had been convicted on charges of violating the Espionage Act.

It was obvious during the preliminary hearings that the defense would seek to shift the issue from the charge of kidnapping to the theories and practices of the I.W.W. In an exchange with William H. Burgess, chief defense counsel, R.N. French stated, "The I.W.W. has nothing to do with the issue in the trial." He was "a reactionary Democrat," he exclaimed; so much so, in fact, that he was "often accused of being a Republican." But he was "determined … to do his duty as a county attorney, regardless of party."[83]

The number of defendants were reduced to 219 when the trial of H. E. Wooton, hardware merchant, who had been responsible for the deportation of Fred Brown, began. The trial was shifted to Tombstone, and the judge of the Superior Court of Cochise County disqualified himself. Judge Samuel L. Pattee, of the Superior Court of Pima County, presided in his place. It took six weeks to impanel the jury, but the outcome may have been decided on the first day in which testimony was presented.

The Judge refused to strike testimony, including the depositions obtained in Chicago and elsewhere, on the revolutionary character of the I.W.W.[84] Since it was impossible to deny that Mr. Wooton, as well as other defendants, had participated in the deportation, the defense lawyers ingeniously based their brief on two propositions: The "right of self defense and the law of necessity." In discussing the right of self defense, Mr. William H. Burges, the chief counsel, offered the following proposition: "The right is in no way abridged because two are jointly or severally attacked and jointly and severally defend themselves, nor three, nor four, nor five, nor any number, nor can the point be found at which the right of self-defense ceases simply because the number of those whose rights are involved and whose rights call for defense."[85]

Counsel then drew the inference that "the right of self-defense is perfectly valid in behalf of the community as well as an individual."[86] The second essential principle for the defense was based on the law of necessity,

> that law that justifies by virtue of necessity the invasion of another's rights. Both exist and have been applied many times. Both find their origin in the primal instinct of man to defend his life and what is his own whether it be his family or his property; a law stronger than any other in the world; a law before which everything else gives away when the occasion presents itself, excepting the supreme necessity that comes to a man of sacrificing his own life for family or community or country. In addition to this firm basis of fundamental instincts and impulses of the human heart upon which the law of self-defense is founded, the law of necessity is further buttressed by the maxim that the safety of the public

---

82. Materials are in the files of the library of the University of Arizona.
83. *The Bisbee Daily Review,* August 29, 1919.
84. *The Arizona Daily Star,* April 17, 1920.
85. *Argument of William H. Burges of Counsel for Defense,* 10.
86. *Ibid.,* 10.

is the supreme law, a maxim peculiarly applicable to the facts of this case as they will be manifested to Your Honor during the progress of the trial.[87]

Having presented "the law of necessity" as justification for the deportation, the argument was then made that the community was in danger from assault by the strikers. Proof of the existence of such danger was based almost entirely upon Wobbly views and publications, and upon depositions of the I.W.W. trials. The trial records were not available at the Cochise County courthouse, and the information on testimony had to be obtained from the newspapers, which had not given the prosecution's case too much attention.

Six weeks were required to obtain a jury. The selection of Wooten for trial was influenced by the fact that he had personally directed the deportation of Fred Brown, an organizer of the A.F.L. who had, at one time, withdrawn the union poster from Wooton's store because of a dispute with a retail clerks' organization; consequently, there was no question that both men knew one another. The defense announced it would prove that an I.W.W. conspiracy existed since 1908, and it would introduce evidence to this effect. It also inferred that Bisbee was only one link in the conspiracy. The prosecution fought this attempt to shift the case from the issue of deportation to the views, theories, and practices of the I.W.W. When the Judge held that evidence about Wobbly behavior would be admitted, the prosecutor, R.N. French, threatened to dismiss the case; however, he did not do so.[88]

Aside from the evidence of I.W.W. attitudes, which could be used to influence the jury, the defense did not appear able to prove the existence of conspiracy. For example, the superintendent of the Copper Queen described conditions at that mine. He claimed the I.W.W. demands for wages and changes in working conditions were already part of company policies; only the demand for nondiscrimination in hiring was not. "He saw," he testified, "dinner pails taken from two or three men and heard of the assault upon Tony Peralta."[89]

A number of miners testified they were threatened and that members of the I.W.W. threw lighted papers against a house. A woman whose husband was a Wobbly testified that he and other members of the organization told her the demands upon the operators were only a subterfuge.[90] When the defense objected to the introduction of pamphlets on sabotage and other I.W.W. literature, Judge Pattee held it was proper to show what kind of men the Wobblies were. "For instance," said the Judge, "Mr. French, you have a right to show that the leading men of the organization were men of letters."[91]

The State was able to introduce witnesses who testified they were not members of the I.W.W., and that conditions were peaceful,[92] and it sought to have the testimony about Wobbly doctrines as well as the information in the deposition stricken; but Judge Pattee rejected these motions.[93] In his charge, the court asked the jury "to lay aside any question of self-defense in this case for the simple reason that the evidence does not warrant you in considering that subject. There is no self-defense involved." But the court also stated: "If the so-called deportation, including the taking and carrying of Brown from this County and State into the State of New Mexico, is excusable it is only under a rule of law which

87. *Ibid.*, 11.
88. *See Bisbee Daily Review,* February 6, March 13, 16, 26, 28, 1920.
89. *Ibid.,* April 7, 1920.
90. *Ibid.,* April 8, 1920.
91. *Ibid.,* April 14, 1920.
92. *The Arizona Daily Star,* April 17, 23, 1930.
93. *Ibid.,* April 17, 1920.

has been referred to by counsel and for want of a better designation will be here referred to as the Law of Necessity."[94]

Judge Pattee turned to an "eminent writer" who said "Necessity is a defense when it is shown that the act charged was done to avoid an evil both serious and irreparable, that there was no means of escape and that the action was not disproportionate to the evil."[95]

The court instructed the jury that the rule "can be rarely invoked and only success-fully invoked under extreme circumstances." He also informed them that they

> ... must find from the evidence that the impending danger feared by the defen-dant was actually present and in operation and the necessity must be based upon the reasonable belief that no other remedy was available under the circumstances.

> A person [he continued] may not be deprived of his property or forcibly re-moved from his place of abode under the plea of necessity unless the threatened danger is so great and immediate as to actually require that such course be taken in order to avert the threatened peril and such threatened peril is of a character not out of proportion to the invasion of the rights of the citizen.[96]

> ... if the jury believed [he then declared] that at the time of the so-called deportation there actually existed a real, threatened and actual danger of immediate de-struction of life and property or that the appearance were such as to create a be-lief to that effect in the mind of a reasonable man and that the defendant and those associated with him honestly entertained that belief and acted thereon and in so doing and acting upon such belief invaded the rights of others and deprived oth-ers of liberty then a case is presented which calls for the application of the rule of necessity and so far as they invaded the rights of others who were responsi-ble for the creation of such condition or apparent condition and in so far as they only went to the extent of what was actually necessary to avert the threatened peril their acts are in law excused.[97]

The court then told the jury that strikes are permissible, and that picketing is legal even in wartime. Moreover, "the rights of citizens are the same in time of war as in time of peace so far as everyone except the government is concerned and no expression of dis-loyalty, no treasonable utterances, no failure to measure up to that standard of patriotism that is the duty of every good American citizen could itself justify such deportation."[98]

However, the Judge believed that the jury should consider the character of those engaged in the strike as shown by the evidence, and for that purpose, he claimed, the court had

> ... admitted the teachings and doctrines of the organization known as the Indus-trial Workers of the World.... The law does not justify the deportation of members of that organization because they are such. The organization and its doctrines are not on trial and the deportation of any member of that organization, irrespective of other conditions would be as unlawful as that of a non-member. The only pur-pose for which the evidence can be considered is in determining what was the sit-uation in the Warren District at and immediately preceding the so-called deportation.[99]

---

94. Judge Pattee's charge to the jury was made available by the Special Collections Division of the University of Arizona.
95. *Ibid.*, 94.
96. *Ibid.*, 95.
97. *Ibid.*, 96.
98. *Ibid.*, 98.
99. *Ibid.*, 99.

Summarizing the charge to the jury, the Judge defined the issues as follows: "Was Brown forcibly carried from this County and State into the State of New Mexico or did he go voluntarily? If he did not go voluntarily but was forcibly taken into New Mexico, was the act excused by reason of the law of necessity?"[100] While it dealt with the criteria for determining the law of necessity, the charge did not contain an analysis of the evidence about conditions in Bisbee. This avoidance of discussion of life in the town and in the Warren District was noticed by Wooton and the others who admitted "that Brown, the person named in the information, was actually taken from this County and State into New Mexico."[101] Defending the rights of Wobblies, the Court nonetheless instructed the jury that I.W.W. doctrines and views were to help determine the character of the plaintiff. Nowhere in the charge was the *behavior* of Wobblies dealt with. And what about Brown, the man who was deported by the defendant, Wooton? He was not a Wobbly, nor were the great majority of the deportees.

Without the complete court record, the evidence presented at this trial cannot be discussed. Yet an examination of three daily newspapers which reported the testimony scarcely reveals evidence of a situation which would reasonably justify the conduct of Wooton and others. Indeed, lawyers for the copper companies and for those public officials who appeared before the President's Mediation Commission presented little evidence of violence. It is for the court to define the law and for the jury to weigh the evidence, but an observer is struck by the absence of any assessment of the reasonableness of the belief and feeling that the community faced "an evil both serious and irreparable." Can a group led by public officials deport men from their homes and families because they believed conditions of imminent danger existed? No test of reasonableness, no basis for action, except feelings, was given by the court.

The verdict, given the charge, was inevitable; and the twelve men only took sixteen minutes to reach the decision of "not guilty."[102] J.O. Calhoun, the jury foreman, stated:

> The verdict of the jury is a vindication of the deportation, if not in the legal sense, at least in the moral sense. No man could listen to the evidence adduced during the trial without feeling that the people of Bisbee were in imminent danger, and that if their fears were ungrounded, yet they were apparently real and pressing.

> The essence of the law of necessity, as explained and laid down to the jury by Judge Pattee, is that it protects a man in his invasion of the rights of others when his fear for his own safety or welfare is great enough to force him to a drastic step, and this fear does not have to be of really existing dangers, but only of apparent danger when the appearance of that danger is so compelling as to be real to him who views it.[103]

The rest of the jurors echoed these sentiments. John Jones, a juror, stated, "After listening to the evidence in the Wooton case I feel that what happened there was fully justified by the law of necessity."[104] Juror opinions are interesting, especially those of the foreman. None referred to evidence of violence or even to threats, but to the law of ne-

---

100. *Ibid.*, 101.

101. *Ibid.*

102. *The Bisbee Daily Review,* May 1, 1920.

103. *The Law of Necessity As Applied in State of Arizona v. H.E. Wooton.* (The document is in the Special Collections Division, University of Arizona Library and is not dated. It appears to have been written soon after the trial.)

104. *Ibid.*, 5.

cessity. The foreman interpreted the charge accurately when he declared that even if public fears were "ungrounded," as long as belief of danger existed men could take action to defend themselves. Consequently, the only test of the reasonableness of an action is the subjective view of the person who feels impelled to act.

Ultimately, the charges against the other defendants were dismissed. Even without the "law of necessity," it is doubtful if a jury would have convicted its leading citizens for deporting hundreds of miners and their sympathizers. The trial failed to convict, but it demonstrated that the violations of rights would not go unchallenged. One cannot read Judge Pattee's charge without a feeling that despite his efforts to be fair, he was timid and unwilling to speak out against injuries to hundreds of innocent men. In contrast, R. N. French emerges as a courageous lawyer. He had undertaken a herculean task and in carrying it out he was following in the highest traditions of the bar.

VI

Open Shops

Steel Strikers Marching in Cleveland 1919.

The Open Shop Tested:
The Great Steel Strike of 1919

Ahmed A. White*

More than any labor dispute before, the "Great Steel Strike" of 1919 highlighted the unsettled and deeply contradictory state of labor relations in the steel industry. The strike and the drive that preceded it demonstrated the potential to successfully organize the vast army of angry and exploited workers who worked in steel. Yet the strike also revealed the enduring power of the steel companies and the formidable impediments that still hindered efforts to build effective union representation on a foundation of workers' discontent. These conflicting realities emerged in a bitter struggle that culminated in the fall and early winter of 1919. Part of a wave of worker protests that year, including a general strike in Seattle early that same year and a massive coal strike later in the year, the steel strike began to unfold on September 21, when the steel companies, led by U.S. Steel, refused to bargain with the *ad hoc* National Committee for Organizing Iron and Steel Workers (the National Committee), which AFL reformers set up to organize the drive. The companies rejected out of hand a set of demands centered on an eight-hour day, abolition of the dreaded "long turn" (bi-monthly twenty-four hour shift), better wages, a se-

* This chapter is excerpted from a forthcoming book by Ahmed A. White, *The "Little Steel" Strike, The Struggle for Labor Rights, and the Limits of New Deal Reform.*

niority system, standardization of work rules, and the reinstatement of men who had earlier been fired for union activities.[1] The next day, September 22, workers began walking off the job in huge numbers. By the time the strike was finally broken the following January, at least twenty people, eighteen of them unionists, had been killed and hundreds injured in clashes concentrated in western Pennsylvania, eastern Ohio, and the Calumet Region along the southern shores of Lake Michigan.[2]

The exceptional violence and disorder that accompanied the breaking of the strike inspired a sustained investigation by the Interchurch World Movement (or IWM), a creature of the liberal Federal Council of Churches. The IWM's published report on the strike documents an extraordinary campaign, led by U.S. Steel's "Judge" Elbert Gary (after whom the great steel center, Gary, Indiana was named), to use organized violence in concert with blacklisting, discriminatory discharges, and a system of espionage to undermine union organizing, disrupt protests, demoralize the strikers, and ultimately crush the strike.[3] The extent of these efforts was quite amazing. The report found that discharges were widespread during the drive that preceded the strike. Some of these involved mass firings of hundreds of pro-union workers at once. In fact, the frequency of the discharges and the impunity with which they were imposed was one of the factors that pushed the rank-and-file to demand that organizers launch the strike.[4] Just as commonplace was espionage. An IWM investigator obtained some 600 separate espionage reports from one steel company.[5] These were styled as dossiers on dangerous radicals, but were in fact concerned with union people of all political persuasions. They served the more prosaic purposes of abetting intimidation tactics and blacklisting, and compiling other information useful to thwarting the drive and the strike.[6] During the strike itself, one hired detective firm, Corporations Auxiliary Company, claimed to have over 500 spies at work among the strikers.[7]

The drive and the strike were industry-wide and involved dozens of firms, large and small. But in 1919, U.S. Steel dominated the industry and shaped the policies of other companies, including their labor policies surrounding the drive and the strike. The companies' repressive practices were all the more remarkable for the way they were justified by resort to an increasingly refined—and contradictory—ideology of the open shop. In keeping with a rhetorical stratagem honed by Judge Gary and other top managers at U.S. Steel, company representatives continued to claim they had no problem with union membership and that they were as fully committed to the interests of their workers as they

---

1. David Brody, *Steelworkers in America: The Nonunion Era*, 236-40 (Cambridge: Harvard, 1960); William Z. Foster, *The Great Steel Strike and its Lessons*, 76-85 (Arno, 1969); Steel Strikers' Chief Fight is on Long Hours, *Chicago Daily Tribune*, Sept. 25, 1919, p. 4; Gary Declines to See Labor Men, Aug. 27, 1919, p. 2; Gary Stands Firm for the Open Shop, *N.Y. Times*, Aug. 28, 1919, p. 17. See also Steel Strikers' Chief Fight is on Long Hours, *Chicago Daily Tribune*, Sept. 25, 1919, p. 4; Twelve Demands of Steel Workers on Eve of Strike, *Chicago Daily Tribune*, Sept. 19, 1919, p. 2.

2. Foster, *The Great Steel Strike*, *supra* note 1, at 99-101. On the number killed, see *id.* at 222-24. On the strikers' demands, *see* Steel Strikers' Chief Fight is on Long Hours, *Chicago Daily Tribune*, Sept. 25, 1919, p. 4; Twelve Demands of Steel Workers on Eve of Strike, *Chicago Daily Tribune*, Sept. 19, 1919, p. 2.

3. Interchurch World Movement of North America, *Report on the Steel Strike of 1919*, 23-28, 235-42 (New York: Harcourt, Brace, and Howe, Inc., 1920). [hereafter Interchurch Report].

4. Interchurch Report, *supra* note 3, at 170-72, 209-21. *See also* David Brody, *Labor in Crisis: The Steel Strike of 1919*, 87-90 (Urbana: Univ. of Illinois Press, 1965).

5. U.S. Senate, Committee on Education and Labor, Labor Policies of the Employer Associations: The "Little Steel" Companies, Report No. 151, 77th Cong., 1st Sess., 44 (1941). [hereafter The Little Steel Companies].

6. *Id.*

7. David Brody, *Labor in Crisis*, supra note 4, at 159.

were to the quest for profits. It was instead only the attempt by unions and their agents to impose a "closed shop"—by which they would represent and bargain for all their workers and insist on union membership as a condition of employment—and to engage in disruptive agitation within the mills that the industrialists opposed.[8] The essence of this argument is reflected in a passage from a May 1919 letter from Judge Gary to, Michael Tighe, the president of the main AFL union in steel, the Amalgamated Association of Iron and Steel Workers (the AA), in which the Judge rationalized the company's position:

> As you know, we do not confer [with], negotiate with, or combat labor unions as such. We stand for the open shop, which permits a man to engage in different lines of employment, whether he belongs to a labor union or not. We think this attitude secures the best results to the employees and to the employers.[9]

On the eve of the strike, Judge Gary again invoked the open shop to rebuff the organizers' request to negotiate.

> As heretofore publicly stated and repeated, our Corporation and subsidiaries, although they do not combat labor unions as such, decline to discuss business with them. The Corporation and subsidiaries are opposed to the "closed shop." They stand for the "open shop," which permits one to engage in any line of employment whether one does or does not belong to a labor union. This best promotes the welfare of both employees and employers. In view of the well-known attitude as expressed above, the officers of the Corporation respectfully decline to discuss with you, as representatives of a labor union, any matter relating to employees. In doing so no personal discourtesy is intended.[10]

Nor were these appeals to the open shop the companies' only rhetorical foils. The IWM's report also charged the companies with widespread resort to red-baiting propaganda to discredit the strikers, justify the companies' own repressive measures, and distract the public from reflecting on the union's rather modest demands.[11] Together with their allies in Congress, which investigated the strike as it unfolded, the companies made a point of using strike leader William Z. Foster's radical background to tar the strike as a Bolshevik, IWW, or anarchist conspiracy. The unearthing of an obscure, out-of-print IWW pamphlet, that Foster had coauthored in 1911, titled *Syndicalism*, and redolent with radical anti-capitalist rhetoric and militant exhortations, provided a convenient anchor for these efforts. Although the tract was not once found in the possession of any striker, and not otherwise shown to have influenced the strike in any way, it was reprinted and widely distributed in the strike zone by the steel companies to create such impressions.[12] Foster and other union people were also grilled at great length about the pamphlet, and other supposed evidence of the strike's radicalism, by the Senate Committee on Education and Labor.[13] Among the particular charges leveled at the strikers was that they aimed

---

8. *Id.* at 22-28, 87-89, 120-26.

9. William Z. Foster, *The Great Steel Strike*, supra note 1, at 71-72.

10. *Id.* at 80-81.

11. Interchurch Report, *supra* note 3, at 20.43; William T. Hogan, *Economic History of the Iron and Steel Industry in the United States*, 456-61 (Lexington: Univ. of Kentucky Press, 1971).

12. Interchurch Report, *supra* note 3, at 34.35. On the Congressional investigation of strike and Foster's role in it, see U.S. Senate, Hearings Before the Committee on Education and Labor, Investigation of Strike in Steel Industries, 66th Cong., 1" Sess. (GPO 1919); U.S. House, Hearings Before the Committee on the Judiciary, Sedition, Syndicalism, Sabotage, and Anarchy, 66th Cong., 1" Sess. (GPO 1919).

13. Senate Hearings on the Great Steel Strike, supra note 12, *passim*.

to seize control of the basic steel industry as a means of strangling the entire economy and eventually toppling the industrial order in furtherance of a revolutionary program.[14]

Besides being promoted in Congress, these charges were abetted by the press, which used the most intemperate language to excoriate the strikers and their leaders. The reactionary *Chicago Daily Tribune*—long known as the city's "businessman's paper"—fulminated about supposed opposition to the politics and values of "Americanism" on the part of Foster and National Committee co-founder John Fitzpatrick.[15] Fitzpatrick had publically mocked the concept's racist presumptions by describing Indians as the only genuine Americans. To the *Tribune*'s editors, this was nonsense; the true American was not an Indian so much as one who "believes in the institution of private property as an essential expression of freedom." The equally reactionary *Wall Street Journal* likened the organizers to "discontented wolves" seeking to impose the law of the jungle"; and it accused the immigrant steel workers of squandering supposedly generous wages because "they prefer the condition of filth and overcrowding."[16] Later, as the strike wound down, the *Journal* described the strike as a welcome opportunity for the steel companies to rid themselves of troublesome agitators.[17] The *New York Times* was hardly more progressive. Its editors declared the strike a scheme by "radicals, social and industrial revolutionaries" and attributed support for the strike among the "foreign element" to their being "ignorant and easily misled" and altogether less intelligent than their more skilled—and more genuinely American—coworkers.[18]

Revolution may well have been the ultimate aim for Foster, who was soon to lead the Communist Party, and for many other participants in the strike as well.[19] However, as the IMW's report clearly established, and as subsequent studies of the strike have confirmed, the drive and the strike itself remained grounded in the modest aims of the National Committee's stated program. Foster himself harbored no illusions about what the strike might realistically accomplish in the near term. Along with Fitzpatrick, he seemed truly devoted to immediate aims of organizing the workers and realizing the demands communicated to the companies. Nor did Foster enjoy nearly as much control over the organizing campaign as the charges against him implied. The National Committee, staffed mainly by conventional AFL trade unionists, was in actual charge; and the authority of the AFL leadership loomed over all that it did.[20] Nevertheless, the ideological and political assault on the strikers and their leaders was unrelenting, and unrelentingly focused on Foster. Cast as nothing less than a Soviet plot, the strike began to seem to a broad spectrum of elites and many other Americans besides, like a genuine threat to the existing social and economic order—and to their own ideological and material investments in that order. To oppose the strike was then not a distasteful act in defense of capitalist

---

14. On the effort to tar the strike with Foster's views, *see* James R. Barrett, *William Z. Foster and the Tragedy of American Radicalism*, 92-93 (Urbana: Univ. of Illinois Press, 1999); Grill Foster on His 'Red Book', *N.Y. Times*, Oct. 4, 1919, p. 1. On broader recriminations of radicalism in the strike, see "Red" Nests in Gary, *Wash. Post*, Oct. 25, 1919 p. 1.

15. Americanism vs. Radicalism, *Chicago Daily Tribune*, Sept. 28, 1919, p. E4.

16. The Law of the Jungle, *Wall St. J.*, Sept. 8, 1919, p. 1.

17. Steel Freeing Itself from Labor Agitators, *Wall St. J.*, Oct. 7, 1919, p. I.

18. Industrial War, *N.Y. Times*, Sept. 24, 1919, p. 13

19. Foster's purpose beyond building industrial union of steel workers seems to have been, at least at the time, more concerned with a radical reorganization of the labor movement into a powerful block of industrial unions able to challenge capitalist hegemony economically and politically. In this sense, he seemed still very much under the influence of the IWW. James R. Barrett, *William Z. Foster*, *supra* note 14, at 84. See also David Brody, *Labor in Crisis*, *supra* note 4, at 138-46.

20. David Brody, *Steelworkers in America*, *supra* note 1, at 245-46.

avarice—which is apparently how many people were initially wont to perceive opposition to the union's efforts—or a morally dubious subscription to open shop evangelism,
but rather a vital struggle in defense of patriotism and American values.[21]

With their opposition to the strike thus justified, courts, police, and military units
heeded the steel companies' call to deny the strikers to right even to meet freely, let alone
maintain effective picket lines.[22] This was particularly true in the eponymous Gary and
surrounding towns of the Calumet Region, where thousands of state militiamen and regular army troops armed with rifles, machine guns, and field artillery barred strikers from
meeting, picketing, or congregating on the streets and drove many back into the mills.
This use of force led to numerous large clashes and a great deal of the bloodshed.[23] The
authorities played if anything an even heavier hand in the mill towns of western Pennsylvania and bordering districts of New York, Ohio, and West Virginia. Foster estimated that
during the strike, along the Monongahela River around Pittsburg, the steel companies had
some 25,000 armed men in their "service." The sheriff of Allegheny County alone deputized some 5,000 men; and in McKeesport, 3,000 deputies were sworn in.[24] Foster claimed
that throughout Western Pennsylvania the steel companies were able to confront the strikers locally with forces of comparable size, drawing on "State Constabulary, deputy sheriffs, city police, city detectives, company police, company detectives, private detectives,
coal and iron police, ordinary gunmen, armed strikebreakers, vigilantes, and God knows
how many others."[25]

Even before the strike began police in Brackenridge, Pennsylvania shot and killed one
organizer and then shot and beat to death another organizer, a middle-aged grandmother
named Fannie Sellins, as she tried to aid her stricken colleague. Early in September, four
union supporters were killed in Hammond, Indiana, in the Calumet Region. A few days
into the strike, several people were killed and a dozen others shot in clashes in the Pittsburg area.[26] Two strikers were killed at Lackawanna, New York.[27] In some ways as important to the companies' efforts as these actual tragedies were false or grossly exaggerated
reports of other deadly clashes, which were regularly related in mainstream newspapers.
For these gave credence to claims by the companies and their allies that the strike and the
drive that preceded it were indeed a portent of general class upheaval, orchestrated by foreign agents, which needed to be stanched at all costs.[28] However unfounded these claims
were, they effectively converted the companies' own violence and the violence they provoked
into a salient justification for the continued use of force to repress the strikers.[29]

---

21. Robert Justin Goldstein, *Political Repression in Modern America from 1870 to 1976*, 151-54
(Urbana: Univ. of Illinois, 2001). On the argument that antiradical rhetoric eventually overcame sympathy for the strikers, *see* David Brody, *Steelworkers in America, supra* note 1, at 243-44.
22. William Z. Foster, *The Great Steel Strike, supra* note 1, at 110-39.
23. *See, e.g.,* Urge Revolt in Gary, *Wash. Post*, Oct. 14, 1919, p. 1; Halt New Riots at Gary, *Chicago
Daily Tribune*, Oct. 6, 1919, p. l; Steel Strike Situation, *Chicago Daily Tribune*, Oct. 5, 1919, p. l; Gary
Strikers Riot, *Wash. Post*, Oct. 5, 1919, p. l.
24. William Z. Foster, *The Great Steel Strike, supra* note 1, at 97; *see also* James R. Barrett, *William
Z. Foster, supra* note 14, at 93; *see also* Troopers Stop Meetings, *N.Y. Times*, Sept. 22, 1919, p. 1.
25. William Z. Foster, *The Great Steel Strike, supra* note 1, at 119, 132-34.
26. David Brody, *Labor in Crisis, supra* note 4, at 146-48, 172-73; 2 Killed, 12 Shot in Strike Riots,
N.Y. Times, Sept. 23, 1919, p. 1; Troopers Stop Meetings, *N.Y. Times*, Sept. 22, 1919, p. 1; 2 Killed
and 11 Shot in Steel Strike Riots, *Chicago Daily Tribune*, Sept. 23, 1919, p. 1 ; Steel Workers and State
Police Clash Near Pittsburg, *N.Y. Times*, Sept. 22, 1919, p. l.
27. William Z. Foster, *The Great Steel Strike, supra* note 1, at 183.
28. David Brody, *Labor in Crisis, supra* note 4, at 132-34.
29. *Id.* at 145-46.

Violence served the companies' interests in more immediate ways as well. Company-sponsored violence disrupted and frustrated the efforts of organizers, including the top leadership. In the face of repeated threats to his safety, Foster had to be escorted by armed workers as he traveled the strike zones.[30] In early November, he and other organizers were run out of Johnstown, Pennsylvania by police and a crowd of vigilantes. Led by the president of the Chamber of Commerce and the secretary of the YMCA, the mob offered no pretense of lawful authority for its actions; and the public authorities flatly refused to protect the unionists.[31] Foster was arrested several other times besides during the organizing campaign and the strike.[32] In August, Homestead police arrested and jailed Mary "Mother" Jones soon after the aged activist (who claimed to be 89 but was actually 83) gave a rousing speech to strikers in which she challenged Pennsylvania authorities to decide if they supported the cause of "Kaiser Gary or Uncle Sam."[33] Foster and Mother Jones were also arrested, together with several dozen other unionists, at a public gathering in Duquesne, Pennsylvania. When a union man inquired what bail would be required to secure the release of the prisoners, he too was promptly arrested.[34]

The repression of union meetings was relentless. Throughout the whole region mayors and town councils strengthened the policies they had adopted prior to the strike of barring public meetings by labor people, often without legitimate authority to do this.[35] In some places, police attended union meetings and brazenly censored what was said.[36] In Allegheny County, meetings were permitted only at the discretion of the local authorities and on the added condition that they were conducted only in English.[37] In McKeesport this discretion was used to bar all union meetings of all kinds.[38] Weeks earlier, the mayor of nearby Duquesne had rejected a request by liberal New York Rabbi Stephen Wise to speak in that town. When the rabbi proposed to have an intermediary negotiate the issue, the mayor famously responded by declaring that, "It won't do you any good. Even Christ himself could not speak in Duquesne for the A.F. of L."[39]

The aims of company-sponsored repression went well beyond censorship and the persecution of union leaders. Its most immediate function was simply to terrorize strikers, to drive them away from the union, off the picket lines, and back to work. Throughout the region, police "clubbed men and women off the streets, dragged strikers from their homes, abused and jailed them on flimsy charges." In some towns, strikers were arrested by the hundreds, often on charges of "suspicion."[40] In the steel town of Weirton, West Virginia, 118 supposed IWWs were captured by police and "deputies" and then compelled to march to the town square where they were forced to kiss the American flag be-

---

30. James R. Barrett, *William Z. Foster, supra* note 14, at 91-92.

31. David Brody, *Labor in Crisis, supra* note 4, at 164; William Z. Foster, *The Great Steel Strike, supra* note 1, at 188.89; Foster is Driven Out of Johnstown, *N.Y. Times,* Nov. 8, 1919, p. 1; W.Z. Foster Run Out of Town in Pennsylvania, *Chicago Daily Tribune,* Nov. 8, 1919, p. 1.

32. William Z. Foster, *The Great Steel Strike, supra* note 1, at 60, 62-63.

33. David Brody, *Labor in Crisis, supra* note 4, at 93-94.

34. William Z. Foster, *The Great Steel Strike, supra* note 1, at 62-63.

35. *Id.* at 53-60, 111-14.

36. *Id.* at 115-16.

37. David Brody, *Labor in Crisis, supra* note 4, at 148-49.

38. *Id.* at 149.

39. William Z. Foster, *The Great Steel Strike, supra* note 1, at 62; David Brody, *Labor in Crisis, supra* note 4, at 94. *See also* James D. Rose, *Duquesne and the Rise of Steel Unionism,* 32-33 (Urbana: University of Illinois, 2001).

40. David Brody, *Steelworkers in America, supra* note 1, at 249-252.

fore being ejected from town.[41] In other communities, strikers were arrested by the hundreds and then promised release if they renounced the union. Workers who exposed themselves on picket lines were especially vulnerable to being apprehended by police and deputies, and forced back to work by threat of jail. In some instances, unionists claimed, strikers were even visited at home by police and company agents who used threats of blacklisting, beatings, and arrests to pressure them to return to work.[42] Many other strikers were evicted from homes that the companies either owned or held in lien.[43] In many areas, the companies established "citizens groups" under the banner of patriotism and Americanism, which helped agitate and propagandize against the strike; and they also organized "back-to-work" movements, which were presented as proof of mass disaffection.[44] Both types of groups were also vehicles of vigilantism. Indeed, it would have been difficult to say that the thousands of deputies installed in the region during the strike were much more than vigilantes hired for these same purposes. Occasionally strikers responded to these attacks and threats with shootings and bombings. But even such tactics were comparatively rare and did more to inform antiunion propaganda than defend labor rights or visit retribution on the strikers' adversaries.[45] In the end, the strikers were simply unable to realize a meaningful right to picket or even ensure that their pickets would not be run through by police strikebreakers, and scabs.

The strike also highlighted the difficulties labor continued to face on account of their stubborn commitment to craft unionism amidst the many changes that had overtaken the industry and its workforce in the time since the Homestead dispute in 1892. Recognizing from the outset the AA's weakness and the basic obsolescence of its craft-orientated program, the leaders of the campaign had sidelined the AA itself in favor of the National Committee.[46] However, the organizing structure contemplated by the National Committee was not that of a true industrial union. Rather, it represented an effort to organize the industry's many job classifications simultaneously and across the entire industry, but still along craft lines. In essence, the National Committee was committed to a federated model of organizing, of the sort which the AFL had begun to flirt with a few years earlier.[47] By design, the National Committee's program was supposed to temper the parochialism and jurisdictional divisions that had rendered the craft model nearly irrel-

---

41. 118 I.W.W. Kneel and Kiss Flag in Steel Town Raid, *Chicago Daily Tribune*, Oct. 8, 1919, p. 2.

42. William Z. Foster, *The Great Steel Strike*, supra note 1, at 135.

43. *Id.* at 184.

44. David Brody, *Steelworkers in America*, supra note 1, at 258-61; David Brody, *Labor in Crisis*, supra note 4, at 160-65

45. On bombings, *see* Bomb Outrages Cause Terror in Donora, *N.Y. Times*, Nov. 12, 1919, p. 2; Strikers Dynamite Car to Steel Plant, *N.Y. Times*, Nov. 8, 1919, p. 1; Bomb Shatters Mill Roof Near Pittsburg,, *Chicago Daily Tribune*, Oct. 9, 1919, p. 7. On lesser acts of violence by strikers and the way they were dealt with by police and military units, *see* Riots in Canton; Troops Await Call, *N.Y. Times*, Oct. 26, 1919, p. l; Troops Disperse Steel Workers, *Wash. Post*, Nov. 22, 1919, p. 1; Police Clash with Workers in Pittsburg, *Chicago Daily Tribune*, Sept. 22, 1919, p. l. Other reports acknowledged the striker's peaceable conduct. 80,000 Quit Work in Chicago Field, *N.Y. Times*, Sept. 23, 1919, p. l.

46. David Brody, *Steelworkers in America*, supra note 1, at 214.30. *See also* William T. Hogan, *Economic History of the Iron and Steel Industry*, supra note 16, at 456–57. In fact, in the face of dramatic changes in the organization of work, the AFL had been gradually and hesitantly retreating from some of the most rigid aspects of craft unionism for nearly a decade. In 1911, the Federation abandoned the principle of absolute craft autonomy in favor of a more flexible concept that allowed its few industrial unions, like the UMW, the claim of industry-wide jurisdiction. However, the program of "craft industrialism," as described by Christopher Tomlins, *The State and the Unions: Labor Relations, Law, and the Organized Labor Movement in America, 1880-1960*, 69-74 (Cambridge: Cambridge University Press, 1985) proved altogether inadequate.

47. William Z. Foster, *The Great Steel Strike*, supra note 1, at 20.

evant in an industry that had been redefined in the preceding decades by deskilling and an ethos of top-down managerial control; it was supposed to facilitate an industry-wide drive—but without impinging on the jurisdictional boundaries of the existing craft organizations.[48]

An uncertain strategy from the outset, this approach soon revealed its weakness and the continued beckoning of a genuine industrial model. Foster himself was a zealous champion of industrial unionism who, nonetheless, at that point in his career rejected the "dual unionism" which any effort to build an industrial union model alongside the AA would have necessitated. As his successful work in organizing the Chicago stockyards proved, Foster was also a real progressive on questions of race and ethnicity and a gritty and capable organizer to boot. Moreover, the strikers themselves were largely drawn from the ranks of the unskilled and semiskilled. Nevertheless IWM investigators found that the strike's leaders had not sufficiently reckoned with the realities of the steel industry's labor force and the conflicts that skill disparities generated among steel workers during the strike.[49] Jurisdictional conflicts involving the twenty-four AFL unions with toeholds in the industry further impeded organizing and strike activities. In fact, the report implied that however cautious and incomplete the steel workers' half-turn to industrial unionism may have been, it had the effect of limiting the support they received during the dispute from the incumbent craft unions.[50] Consistent with this charge, in many instances AA locals actually *honored* their contracts and continued to work in the struck mills.[51]

The National Committee also failed to organize effective sympathy actions by other workers. Several attempts by the committee to expand the strike to other industries, or mount localized general strikes, were also met with indifference.[52] Of particular importance was the failure to mobilize the railroad brotherhoods, whose men worked both the trunk and switching lines serving the mills, and the United Mine Workers (or UMW), whose members mined the coal that was so vital to the production of steel. In both cases, sympathy action was frustrated by reluctance to break existing labor contracts and by poor coordination and organization among the unions. After the strike, Foster complained that railroad workers who did walk out in sympathy were denied strike benefits and otherwise not adequately supported by the strikers and the National Committee.[53]

In a tone that was as resentful towards the trade union establishment as it was sympathetic to the failures of the steel workers themselves, Foster affirmed the essential truth of the IWM's main criticisms. His book about the strike, which stands today as one of the better and more sober analyses of the conflict, nevertheless positively fumes at the "ignorant blockheads" and "designing tools of the bosses" who betrayed the drive.[54] Scholars like David Brody have confirmed the IWM's criticisms as well, with Brody emphasizing not only the effects of jurisdictional conflicts and lack of solidarity, but also the pathetic level of

---

48. David Brody, *Labor in Crisis, supra* note 4, at 63-66.
49. Interchurch Report, *supra* note 3, at 178.
50. *Id.* at ch. VI.
51. David Brody, *Labor in Crisis, supra* note 4, at 166-69. *See also* Would Widen Steel Strike, *N.Y. Times,* Nov. 15, 1919, p. 2; Amalgamated Acts to Start Up Plants, *N.Y. Times,* Oct. 10, 1919, p. 4.
52. *See, e.g.,* Steel Unions in Last Move for General Strike, *Chicago Daily Tribune,* Nov. 2, 1919, p. 4; Leaders
Urge 25 More Unions to Join Strike, *Chicago Daily Tribune,* Sept. 25, 1919, p. 2.
53. William Z. Foster, *The Great Steel Strike, supra* note 1, at 164-65, 239-41.
54. *Id.* at 106-08, 235-38, 249-54.

political and financial support the AFL unions contributed to the drive and strike.[55] Scandalously, a number of unions, including the AA, actually ended up making money on the drive and the strike, so paltry were their contributions in comparison to their take of the dues collected from new members by the National Committee.[56] According to Brody (as well as Foster himself), the poor financing of the organizing drive was especially debilitating in that it slowed the progress of the campaign, allowing it to be overtaken by the end of the First World War and the advent of less favorable economic and political conditions, and to be met with more potent countermeasures by the companies and their allies.[57]

The IWM report also made a point of blaming the failure of the strike on the AFL's tradition of excluding racial minorities and immigrants. Under Foster's leadership, the organizers of the drive made real efforts to overcome the history of racial and ethnic conflict since Homestead. In at least some instances, organizers appealed directly and earnestly to black workers. Nor were blacks merely the objects of organizing. In the Calumet, a handful of black organizers were able to make real inroads in organizing and helped forge a lasting tradition of interracial unity among the larger community of workers.[58] The work among immigrants was even more substantial, as there were some twenty-five foreign-born organizers (and a fair number of women) among the 100 to 125 or so sent to the mills.[59] Organizers were careful to translate organizing material into the workers' native languages and to reach out to them in their own communities. The organizers had some success turning the anti-immigrant canard of "Americanism" to their advantage by recasting unionism as a means of supporting democracy, liberty, and other ideals central to the effort to propagandize the war.[60]

In fact, the organizers' overall success in recruiting immigrants was impressive. From the outset of the drive through the end of the strike, support among immigrants was consistently stronger than that among Americans.[61] This was a remarkable testament to the organizers' efforts as well as the demographic alignments of craft union morbidity. However, in other respects the committee's efforts proved inadequate. Only in Cleveland, Ohio, Wheeling, West Virginia, and parts of the Calumet, apparently, did really substantial numbers of blacks subscribe to the union cause. Elsewhere, black workers stayed on the job. Worse, as many as 40,000 blacks were recruited as strikebreakers—although to be sure some of them were brought to the struck mills under false pretenses, in some cases in locked boxcars with firearms trained on them to prevent defections.[62] With respect to white ethnics, the union's success in recruiting those on the job was undermined by the frequency with which men of similar backgrounds fell in to serve as scabs and strikebreakers.[63] The IWM's report quite properly saw the AFL's legacy of discrimination

55. David Brody, *Steelworkers in America*, supra note 1, at 216-18; James R. Barrett, *William Z. Foster*, supra note 14, at 85.

56. Interchurch Report, supra note 3, at 230-33.

57. David Brody, *Labor in Crisis*, supra note 4, at 68-69; William Z. Foster, *The Great Steel Strike*, supra note 1, at 181, 235.

58. Ruth Needleman, *Black Freedom Fighters in Steel: The Struggle for Democratic Unionism*, 19-22 (Ithaca: Cornell Univ. Press, 2003).

59. Horace B. Davis, *Labor and Steel*, 245 (New York: International Publishers, 1933); William Z. Foster, *The Great Steel Strike*, supra note 1, at 35.

60. David Brody, *Steelworkers in America*, supra note 1, at 222.24; James R. Barrett, *William Z. Foster*, supra note 14, at 94-95.

61. David Brody, *Labor in Crisis*, supra note 4, at 74.75; William Z. Foster, *The Great Steel Strike*, supra note 1, at 194-205.

62. William Z. Foster, *The Great Steel Strike*, supra note 1, at 207-08; Ruth Needleman, *Black Freedom Fighters in Steel*, supra note 58, at 21-24, 188.

63. David Brody, *Steelworkers in America*, supra note 1, at 223-25.

and derision of blacks and low-status whites as a factor that primed thousands of them to dishonor the picket lines and serve as strikebreakers.[64] As always, the steel companies were not only aware of these racial and ethnic cleavages; they consciously used them to their advantage during the strike. Company spies admitted that they were ordered to foment trouble between the various groups.[65] Among the most shameful and frankly dangerous instances of racial provocation—dangerous not least because the strike began only weeks after one the worst race riots in American history, which occurred in Chicago that July—involved parading black strikebreakers through the streets for all to see.[66] In several instances provocations like this nearly precipitated race riots.[67]

Foster's commitment to egalitarianism and solidarity earned him the reverence of immigrant steel workers. Though clearly frustrated with the reaction of many blacks to the drive, he was explicit in his view that the National Committee's failure to uproot this tradition of conflict surrounding race and to disabuse blacks and ethnics of their suspicions of unionism had doomed the strike.[68] He also faulted the campaign's stubborn adherence to the dictates of craft unionism.[69] Countering these dynamics was not as easy as identifying them, however. In fact, trying to do so presented Foster and his colleagues with a set of dilemmas. For it seems certain that the organizers' efforts to recruit blacks and ethnics, like their commitment to industrial unionism, actually led many Americans and old guard craft unionists to oppose the campaign.[70] Such prejudice reflected a deeply rooted culture of racism. But it also resonated with the established logic of craft unionism. Jealous of their own advantages—however tenuous those may have become—and fearful of employer reprisals, the Americans who predominated in the AA and other craft organizations were generally indifferent to the strike from the outset. To them, the attempt to bring blacks and low-status ethnics into the union fold seemed poised to further undermine what job control and access to wage premiums they still enjoyed. By the logic of the day, workplace democracy, like political democracy, often seemed to the already-privileged like a race to bottom.[71]

The war's end also deprived the War Labor Board, which was abolished in August 1919, of the little power it had to enforce the modest labor standards included in wartime economic regulation.[72] There were unsuccessful attempts to settle the strike by informal mediation. The strike was taken up by an Industrial Conference, which President Woodrow Wilson had convened to address postwar labor issues. But its efforts foundered in the face of the steel companies' intransigence and the Conference's lack of authority.[73] The Conference suffered along with any other hopes for decisive intervention by the federal gov-

---

64. Interchurch Report *supra* note 3, at 176-78. On the AFL's history of indifference to and discrimination against blacks and immigrants in steel, *see* Davis, *Labor and Steel, supra* note 59, at 232-33.

65. Lizabeth Cohen, *Making a New Deal: Industrial Workers in Chicago, 1919-1939*, 40-41 (Cambridge: Cambridge Univ. Press, 2d ed., 2009).

66. Interchurch Report, *supra* note 3, at 177-78.

67. Negro Workers Shoot Picket at Buffington, *N.Y. Times*, Oct. 4, 1919, p. 2; Steel Strike Situation, *Chicago Daily Tribune*, Oct. 5, 1919, p. 1; The Steel War, *Chicago Daily Tribune*, Oct. 6, 1919, p. 2; Negroes Open Fire on Donora Strikers, *N.Y. Times*, Oct. 10, 1919, p. 4.

68. William Z. Foster, *The Great Steel Strike, supra* note 1, at 205-12; James R. Barrett, *William Z. Foster, supra* note 14, at 94-99.

69. William Z. Foster, *The Great Steel Strike, supra* note 1, at 233-54.

70. So salient was the role of racial and ethnic conflict in the union's defeat that the strike has been taken as a case study of this dynamic Cliff Brown, *Racial Conflicts and Violence in the Labor Market: Roots of the 1919 Steel Strike* (Garland 1998).

71. David Brody, *Steelworkers in America, supra* note 1, at 223-25.

72. *Id.* at 228-30.

73. On the War Labor Board and the Wilson Administration concerning the strike, *see* David Brody, *Steelworkers in America, supra* note 1, at 233-34, 238-41. On the administration's desultory

ernment from the President's evident indifference to the strikers. Wilson's already uncertain support for labor rights was probably further muted by a stroke he suffered in October 1919. It also seems that the President had cynically concluded that the companies were simply too strongly positioned to be moved by his office and that it was not worth the political cost of trying.[74] For its part, the Interchurch World Movement also attempted to broker a settlement. Its representatives met with Elbert Gary in early December. The Judge rebuffed the churchmen, couching his obstinacy in platitudes about the threat of radicalism, the virtues of the open shop, and excellent treatment of steel workers.[75]

The strike failed for other, more basic reasons besides repression, ethnic and class conflicts among workers, and political opposition. The National Committee's mounted a well-organized campaign to gather and distribute benefits among the strikers. With the fairly generous support of unions in the clothing industry and mining, they were able to raise enough funds to stave off destitution among the already impoverished strikers. However, this relief campaign was not entirely successful either. Some strikers did suffer greatly; and many were compelled to exhaust their slender savings. These problems were exacerbated as the end of the war eroded the favorable labor dynamics that had helped make the organizing drive feasible in the first place.[76] Even strikers not yet in the grips of need had to reckon with the possibility that, once the strike was lost, they would be either blacklisted or bottom-listed for rehiring back into a shrinking workforce.[77] The steel companies did not suffer. What losses they did incur were easily offset by the accumulated wealth of several years of wartime prosperity as well as the strong support of other industrial capitalists, some of whom vowed to sacrifice their own economic interests if this could help the steel companies defeat the strikers.[78] Obviously, the strike visited no real hardship on the men who led the companies.

Under such conditions, the strikers ran up against the basic difficulty that looms over nearly every strike: they simply could not close a sufficient number of mills and keep them closed long enough to wrest any concessions from the steel companies. For all its concern to show the particular causes of defeat, the IWM report came around to this sobering observation that the companies simply proved too powerful. U.S. Steel in particular was "too big to be beaten by 300,000 workingmen. It had too large a cash surplus, too many allies among other businesses, too much support from government officers, local and national, too strong influences with social institutions such as the press and the pulpit, it spread out over too much earth—still retaining absolutely centralized control—to be defeated by widely scattered workers of many minds, many fears, varying states of pocketbook, and under comparatively improvised leadership."[79]

This resounding defeat notwithstanding, there was still much to appreciate in what the likes of Foster and the National Committee accomplished. If nothing else, the strike

---

efforts to mediate the dispute, *see, e.g.,* David Brody, *Labor in Crisis, supra* note 4, at 102.28; Steel Men Ask Help, *Wash. Post.,* Aug. 30, 1919, p. 1; Wilson to Urge Truce Between Labor and Capital, *Chicago Daily Tribune,* Aug. 10, 1919, p. 1.

74. David Brody, *Labor in Crisis, supra* note 4, at 101-07, 120-21.

75. *Id.* at 172-74.

76. On the overall reasons for the strike's failure, *see* David Brody, *Steelworkers in America, supra* note 1, at ch. X11; Horace Davis, *Labor and Steel, supra* note 59 at 248-50. On the committee's success in raising strike funds, *see* Foster Cheered at Garden Meeting, *N.Y. Times,* Nov. 9, 1919, p. 2.

77. On the nature of the relief campaign, *see* William Z. Foster, *The Great Steel Strike, supra* note1, at 213-22. On the fear of job loss, *see* Interchurch Report, *supra* note 3, at 178-79.

78. David Brody, *Labor in Crisis, supra* note 4, at 110-11.

79. Interchurch Report, *supra* note 3, at 177.

had put the lie to Elbert Gary's boast in the months preceding the strike that the steel workers' universal contentment with the open shop would prevent there being any strike at all.[80] Beyond this, the strike seemed to vindicate its origination in an industry-wide drive, poised to inflict maximum economic damage in a semi-competitive industry characterized by dispersed production while minimizing the ability of these employers to focus their strength on local efforts.[81] Although the strike ultimately failed to bring the companies to their knees, even in failure it was unprecedentedly successful. Perhaps most impressive of all was the National Committee's success in enlisting membership within the mills and in workers' neighborhoods. Despite pervasive harassment, intimidation, and more than a few deaths, organizers managed to enroll about 100,000 employees prior to the strike (Foster estimated even more than this).[82] Still more impressive is that during the strike, organizers were eventually able to bring out at least 250,000—and by Foster's estimate over 350,000—steel workers. Even the lower figure represented a majority of the industry's workforce and a good fraction of the combined number of strikers involved in all other steel strikes in the post-Homestead period.[83] The strikers hailed not only from U.S. Steel but throughout the industry, and across a geographic region stretching from New York to Colorado.[84] Whole regions, such as the Calumet and the Cleveland area, saw production shut down entirely.[85] Against all the odds, the Great Steel Strike managed for a number of weeks to effectively shut down a large part of the steel industry.[86] Even as the strike began to fail, the strikers managed to hold overall steel production to 40 percent.[87] When the strike was called off in early January, the committee still had as many as 100,000 workers out. It is just possible to imagine that the strikers might actually have succeeded in wresting at least some concessions from the steel companies had the postwar economic slump not been so pronounced, or had they been able to stay out a few more months. Considerable credit for this heroic failure belongs to Foster, Fitzgerald, and others on National Committee's staff, who meticulously and proficiently organized the entire campaign; and also to the organizers working under them, who demonstrated extraordinary gumption and skill in infiltrating and working in mills and mill towns teeming with company spies and police.[88] But of course, as Foster himself acknowledged, the greatest tribute must be given to the workers themselves, who showed such determination and courage.[89] The strike demonstrated what the rank-and-file might accomplish if guided by a more ambitious, better-funded program of industry-wide organizing and by a more complete commitment to industrial unionism.[90]

---

80. *See, e.g.*, 82% Oppose Strike, Say Gary Officials, *N.Y. Times*, Sept. 19, 1919, p. 2; 'Open Shop' to Hold Men, Says Gary, *N.Y. Times*, Jul. 23, 1919, p. 19.

81. David Brody, *Steelworkers in America, supra* note 1 at 218.

82. Foster, *The Great Steel Strike, supra* note 1, at 65.67.

83. Brody, *Labor in Crisis, supra* note 4, at 113; The Little Steel Companies, *supra* note 5, at 43-44.

84. The Little Steel Companies, *supra* note 5, at 43.

85. David Brody, *Labor in Crisis, supra* note 4, at 112.

86. William T. Hogan, *Economic History of the Iron and Steel Industry, supra* note 46, at 458; Selig Perlman & Philip Taft, *History of Labor in the United States, 1896-1932*, 465-66 (New York: The Macmillan Co., 1952).

87. Steel Output Cut 40% by Strike, *N.Y. Times*, Oct. 19, 1919, p. 21; The Little Steel Companies, *supra* note 5, at 45.

88. James R. Barrett, *William Z. Foster, supra* note 14, at 86-88; Selig Perlman & Philip Taft, *History of Labor in the United States, supra* note 86, at 466-68.

89. William Z. Foster, *The Great Steel Strike, supra* note 1, at 4-7.

90. William Z. Foster, *The Great Steel Strike, supra* note 1, at 234-65. See also James R. Barrett, *William Z. Foster, supra* note 14, at 100-01; William Z. Foster, *History of the Communist Party of the United States*, 139-40 (Greenwood 1968).

VII

Textiles and Vigilantes in Gastonia

Martyr Ella May Wiggens.

Gastonia and Textiles (1929)

*Mary Heaton Vorse**

Spontaneous uprisings of the people are few. There is some patient quality in man that makes him endure long past the point of actual suffering. Especially is this true of man's economic state. It is appallingly easy to get used to poverty; if one has been poor always one can scarcely comprehend any other way of living.

It was not the number of people who had struck which made this Southern revolt significant. It was the number and variety of communities involved. It was also the fact that those primitive and unorganized workers had struck without union or leaders. There was a shouldering thrust as of a folk movement—of a great many mute, patient people being driven by desperation to revolt. They had moved in almost a score of communities separated by miles. Over the mountains in Tennessee the rayon workers had struck. Far away in Thompson, Georgia, the workers had struck too; and through all the textile towns they were quiveringly awake. One remembered the weavers' revolt of the last century. There was a reverberation of strikes through the textile South. People were talking strike everywhere. Everywhere these "loyal and one hundred per cent American workers" were talking of organization.

---

* The article first appeared in Harper's Magazine in 1929. It is included here by agreement with the Reuther Labor Archives at Wayne State University.

In widely separated mill towns you will find the same reasons for discontent. There are two of equal force—the introduction of the Bedaud efficiency system, which the workers call the "stretchout," and the substantial cutting of wages which has been almost universal during the past two or three years. Through the operation of the stretch-out men and women often do double work while they receive less pay. The mill hands who endured long hours and low pay as their lot, broke down under the burden which was laid upon them. One after another I have heard them say, "We could not do it."

The effect of the stretch-out was explained to me most lucidly by a strike leader in Greenville, South Carolina, named Rochester. He is thirty-seven and has worked twenty-nine years in the mill. He began to work in the mill in 1900 when he was eight years old and did not make a penny his first month. Later he got seventeen cents a week. When he made a quarter a day he "thought he was running into money."

"It amounts to this," he said. "They cut my wages and increased my work. I used to tend forty-eight looms, while under the stretch-out I have to tend ninety looms, and I couldn't do it. Three years ago I was makin' over $19 a week. Now I make $17.70. I ain't a-braggin'. I'm an experienced weaver. I don't believe there's many can beat me. I make a hundred per cent, the most any weaver can make." He hopes again to make nineteen dollars, the highest reward to which he can aspire for a lifetime of unremitting work.

The average weekly wage scale in the great Loray Mill in Gastonia, North Carolina, is less, apparently owing to the parings and cuttings of workers' wages by the management. In 1927, $500,000 was saved on the payroll without cutting production. To make this possible two people had to do the work of three. Piece-work prices were cut. This mighty saving was continued up to the moment of the strike.

The workers in the Loray Mill went out on strike on the same heaving surge of revolt which runs to-day through the Southern mill villages. Their strike was nonetheless a spontaneous demonstration even though a single organizer of the National Textile Workers' Union, Fred Beal, had been laying the foundation of a labor union in that mill. At the beginning of the strike whose tragic climax has been filling the newspapers of the country only a handful had as yet joined the union.

II

The Loray Mill is in West Gastonia. It is owned by the Manville-Jenckes Company, a Rhode Island concern. The mile of road which separates Gastonia from its suburb begins with ample houses surrounded by rose gardens. In West Gastonia the same street which began so pleasantly is lined with brick and wooden stores whose wares tell eloquently of how little people buy.

The great mill dominates the settlement. Behind it is the mill village, a flock of little houses all alike, perched each one on brick stilts. The big mill is like a huge hen with uncounted chicks around it, so obviously do the little houses belong to the mill from which a roar of turning wheels comes night and day. Night and day the men, women, and children from the little houses go into the mill. It is their whole life.

The strikers' lawyer, Tom P. Jimison, outlined for me the course which the strike took. On April 1, seventeen hundred of the twenty-two hundred employees of the mill came out on strike. The immediate cause was the discovery of union activities and the discharge of union members. On April 2 the public street was roped off to prevent the strikers from approaching the mill. The workers pulled the rope from the hands of the police. The Governor was then asked for troops.

During the first days of the strike there were large and orderly picket lines. These picket lines were broken up with increasing severity. Workers were beaten after their arrest and scores were thrown into jail. All the leaders were arrested at one time or another. Gastonia was in a ferment.

As soon as the strike was called, Vera Bush, Ellen Dawson, and George Pershing were sent down as organizers from the headquarters of the National Textile Workers' Union. This is an organization containing Communist elements, which was active in textile strikes in Passaic and New Bedford. The feeling in the town against the Northern organizers ran high. Well-dressed people swore at them when they appeared on the streets of Gastonia. Threatening letters and telephone messages were frequent. Since then Mr. Jimison's life has been threatened for defending them in the murder trial.

The National Textile Workers' Union had rented a small shack on the main street of West Gastonia which it used as strike headquarters. An empty store near-by had been hired as a relief depot, and to it the strikers went daily to get their food supplies. This relief store was supported by the Workers' International Relief, an organization which collects money from labor unions for workers on strike. I speak of these two buildings especially because it was against them, instead of against the strike leaders, that the threats of mob violence materialized. On the night of April 18 a mob of between one hundred and fifty and two hundred masked men descended upon the headquarters and with axes and other instruments almost literally chopped it down. They broke into the relief store, smashed the windows, and threw the supplies of food intended for women and children out into the road and destroyed them. The nine boys who, unarmed, were guarding the headquarters and store were arrested by National Guardsmen. None of the raiders was arrested.

The militia was dismissed at the end of that week. A large number of extra deputies were then sworn in and armed with bayonets. On Monday, April 22, they charged the picket line with bayonets and blackjacks. A reporter was beaten unconscious. Women were beaten. Men and women, their clothing torn, were scratched with bayonets. Large numbers were arrested. The events of that Monday afternoon were a premeditated attempt to terrorize the workers from holding the picket line.

This was the general state of affairs when I arrived. A Grand Jury had already been called to investigate the mob outrage, which was very badly looked upon throughout the State. It failed to bring indictments or to throw any light on who was responsible for the trouble. Two of the nine guards made affidavit that they recognized members of the mill police among their assailants.

III

The first day I was in West Gastonia a striker, guiding me to the open lot where the "talking" was, pointed out the little lamentable wrecked building. Fred Beal was addressing a big crowd from a square platform. It was the first time I had seen an audience of purely American workers at such a meeting and I found the sight of them unexpectedly moving. I got an impression of a people unmistakably American yet of a different flavor from any I had ever known.

Fred Beal is wide-shouldered and heavily built; boyish, red-haired, sunburned, with very blue eyes set far apart. He has absolutely no pose, no "front" whatsoever. He is unassuming and seemingly unconscious that he is a big man hereabouts. He is one of the few young men who can stand the applause of crowds.

He was sweating when he got off the platform. He slumped down in depression beside me. The men didn't want to go on the picket line, he said, without their guns. When the militia had been succeeded by deputies with bayonets, the strikers had gaily said, "We'll get our guns, too!" This they had been restrained from doing by the young organizer from the North. The mountaineers were glum enough about this. Without their guns they felt emasculated, deprived of their manhood.

Beal felt deeply both his responsibility and his isolation in the South. For the moment he was the most conspicuous person in North Carolina. In the eyes of the well-to-do people and the mill owners, he was the "outside agitator," a menace which threatened the peace of the commonwealth. His shoulders, though broad, were not quite broad enough to carry the burden of so much hatred. But if he was the object of fear and hatred of thousands, he was also the spark of hope of thousands more. As Fred Beal walked through the crowd you could see the people loved him. The faces of the gaunt, earnest men and the meagerly clad women broke into smiles at the sight of him.

He and the other Northern organizers were the focus of so much emotion that it was as if they were small incandescent points of radiance made visible by the burden of love and hatred which they carried. There was an apprehensiveness among them that had nothing to do with fear. It was almost as if they, and Beal especially, had a prescience of what was coming. They all agreed that the terrible weight of public enmity oppressed them, this core of white-hot hate which the South visited upon them.

Around these young people were the gaunt mill workers, who are all of them American of the early English migrations. They come from the hills and from tenant farms in the valleys. It is largely upon the cheapness of their labor that the textile South has based its mighty development. Northern capital has poured in to take advantage of the "one-hundred-per-cent loyal American labor," following the advertisements which in the trade journals have read "Avoid labor troubles! Come South! Plenty of American cheap labor!"

The laws requiring children to go to school until they are fourteen have been in effect only a few years. It is not unusual to find mill workers in their late twenties who already have worked twenty years. Such people are, of necessity, illiterate. Yet there is a direct quality, a completeness about them. They do not belong to this century. Their point of view toward the clan, their kin, society, their bosses, is of the seventeenth or eighteenth century. The doubts of our time have escaped them. They are living in another day, when man occupied the center of the universe and communicated directly with his God. And when, moreover, he was the head of the family.

Poverty and lack show in their every line. The old women dress in dark, homemade calicoes as they did in the mountains. They show the effects of malnutrition. Pellagra is common among them and has increased during the last two years. Yet the men have dignity and the women have sweetness. They have not lost their mountain habit of hospitality.

The little girls are often exquisite—many them blonde and blue-eyed and very English in appearance. At forty they are old women. The men are tall and spare and strong looking. One sometimes sees one of the Lincoln type—tall, rangy, and lantern-jawed. Among the women one frequently comes upon that delicate and lovely profile which has made Southern women famous for beauty. The women of forty who look so worn still have heartbreaking moments of evanescent loveliness.

Like all people who read but little, they are great story tellers and they love a political argument. They are law-abiding and have the Jeffersonian jealousy of their constitutional rights. No policeman may enter a house without showing his warrant. They believe that a man should defend his rights as he defends his honor. Among these mill "hands" you will find names that are famous in Southern history; they are many of them descendants of the men who turned the tide of battle at Kings Mountain, which is only a few miles from Gastonia.

IV

I turned from my preoccupation with the strikers and the history of the strike to look at its setting. I spent some time acquainting myself with the look of the city and its surroundings. Nothing I had read prepared me for what I saw. The industrial revolution had here run its completed cycle in thirty years. I found myself in the presence of an industrial development which was so gigantic and had been encompassed in so brief a time, that it had the terror of incalculable energy. There is in North Carolina a sense of ordered direction as though these multitudinous cotton mills had not sprung up for many varied reasons, but as though the whole industrial South was the plan of one. The transformation of North Carolina, within a period of thirty years, from a sleepy agricultural State still struggling with the problems of reconstruction to one of the richest States in the Union, is a miracle. The cities have appeared as if by magic.

North Carolina is so beautiful and so finished, there is such mastery in its great highways, that it seems as though it were the work of some superman—the result of a stupendous, organized plan.

It has beauty enough to make the fortune of a European country. In the springtime red, fertile plowed hillsides overwhelm the eyes with the flame of their color. There is no poet who has sung adequately of the gamut of reds which shout and sing in the Piedmont fields, and which in the evening light are washed with purple.

Among the red fields marches a mighty procession of ordered factories. And again one has the impression that the red earth has blossomed spontaneously and monstrously with red brick and plate glass; as if the God of Machines of the industrial revolution had said "Let there be factories" and there were factories.

Take the city of Gastonia, with its twenty-two thousand inhabitants. It is situated in the southern part of North Carolina in that principality within states known as Piedmont. This is the high red-earth country which begins in Virginia and continues through the Carolinas. It encloses within its confines the richest portion of the textile industry and, therefore, the richest cities, of which Gastonia is one. Thirty years ago Gastonia was a hamlet on the crossroads. It gives the impression of having sprung out of the earth fully equipped. There is a new city hall, a new courthouse, a new county jail, all fine buildings. On an elevation stands a splendid new high school. There is a great orthopedic hospital, where miracles are performed on children and where nearly ninety per cent of the work is done free. The only public building lacking is a library, and this lack, one feels sure, will soon be remedied by Gastonia's public-spirited citizens. There are new churches and new residences everywhere. The city is completely surrounded by fine new mills, of which I was told that the Loray in West Gastonia is the largest.

Few if any of these mills are over thirty years old. It is they which have supported the prosperity of the town and its well-to-do people. The mills created Gastonia, the city of spindles. It is handsome, prosperous, thriving. Here is the cotton-mill population culled from hill settlements and from farms supporting the handsome city. The picture one gets is as complete as an egg. Gastonia tells you its story, loud and clear, the very first day.

The order of these modern factories with their new machines is in strong contrast with the absurd disorder of mob violence: men with stockings pulled over their faces chopping down union headquarters and throwing workers' food into the street; militia called out against these workers; Americans chased by deputies with bayonets on American streets; all the old silly saws printed in the papers about the trouble being caused by outside agitators. How, the visitor asks himself, can a community be so orderly about industry and so disorderly about human life?

The answer was clear. Although other parts of the United States had already accepted the economic theory that short hours and high wages lead to prosperity, this splendid, vigorous, vital South had not yet attacked the human problem.

V

There was no communication, I found, between the mill people and the well-to-do people. When I asked Mr. Jimison if there could not be found at least a few women who would contribute to a milk fund for the babies—for this is one thing for which one can always get a committee in a Northern community, even among people who disapprove violently of unions—he answered bitterly:

"You don't understand. You, in the North, think of workers as human beings. The folks here think of them as hands!"

They can hardly think of them otherwise under the existing system of paternalism. Each factory is surrounded by a settlement of company houses. In East Gastonia, surrounding such factories as the Plymouth, are pleasant streets with rose- and vine-bowered cottages; elsewhere bare dwellings stand in naked and sun-dried earth. There are all grades of villages between the two extremes. The mill village will be bare or flowering according to the will of the factory owner. Within seven miles of Gastonia are to be found villages both better and worse than those within city limits. Cramerton is one of the mill towns where the last word in beneficent paternalism has been uttered. But whether the towns give information concerning a good or bad master, it is always a master of whom they speak.

There are towns in North Carolina which are not incorporated. This means that the very roads belong to the mill owner. He hires the police force, and if the schoolmaster or the minister does not please him he must go. In such towns paternalism becomes a despotic autocracy.

There are many mill owners throughout the South whose paternalism is infused with an ardent desire to do all that they can for the workers. There are few mills within corporate limits today which have not some form of welfare work. There are often women nurses and welfare workers attached to the factory. Some mills have ball fields, recreation grounds, community houses. Frequently day nurseries and rooms are provided where women may nurse their babies, the time they are absent being taken, of course, from their pay. The workers buy their food at the company store. They buy their coal, oil, and wood from the company. If they are ill a company doctor attends them. All this, of course, will be deducted from their pay.

Conscientious mill owners frankly consider their "hands" as children, incapable of taking care of themselves. But whether their conditions are good or bad does not depend upon the workers' joint effort to control hours, wages, and factory conditions. All depends upon the policy of the owners.

Company houses covered with roses still remain company houses. The workers cannot own them. Community activities do not raise the wage scale, which is so low that almost without exception children of fourteen go to the mill as a matter of course. Mothers of young children must work at night.

I heard of these things in terms of human lives. The strikers wanted to talk about themselves. Every day yielded stories like that of Mary Morris, who passed all the young years of her marriage in want because "when I was goin' to have a baby and got so I couldn't work, they'd fire my husband. Lots of mills won't have you unless there's two hands in the family working." Or of Daisy McDonald, who told me she has to support a husband and family of seven children on $12.90 a week.

"My husband lost his leg and has a tubercular bone. What do you think's left to feed my people on when I pay my weekly expenses? My home rent is $1.50, light 50 cents to 85 cents, furniture $1.00, insurance $1.25. What do you think was left the week I paid $2.20 for wood?"

"I used to work in the Myers Mill in South Gastonia, and they wouldn't take my husband unless I worked too, and I had a little baby."

James Ballentyne added another detail. It was a story of police brutality which recurred often in different forms. "I was leading the picket line and I was trying to get through a mob of deputies. They said, 'What do you think you're doing?' I said 'Leading a picket line if I can get through,' and I walked through. They jumped on me and hit me with clubs over the head and in the belly so I was spitting blood and hemorrhaging all night. It was two weeks ago, and I ain't well yet. I was all mashed up inside."

When I had seen some of the sights of Gastonia I went strike-sightseeing with a minister from Greensboro. We were going about strike headquarters getting the addresses of some of the people who had been chased with bayonets by the police, in order to verify to our satisfaction some of the well-nigh incredible stories poured into our ears by strikers and organizers, when Amy Schechter, the relief director, came up saying, "They're evicting people over in the ravine!" We drove to the place, a striker guiding us.

A woman I had noticed at headquarters, a Mrs. Winebarger, was standing in front of a lamentable little heap of household furnishings. Pots, pans, bedding, bureaus were piled helter-skelter. What had been a home of a sort had in a moment become rubbish.

Three yellow-haired children sat solemnly on the heaped-up wreckage. The baby was asleep at a neighbor's. It waked up presently, and the little girl lugged it around. We went into the house, which like most houses in the neighborhood was built without a cellar and stood on little brick pillars. The lumber was of the cheapest. There were knot-holes in the floor through which the wind poured. (This was not a company house but was owned by a private landlord.)

Mrs. Winebarger told us, "It rained in like a sieve. When it rained we had to keep moving our beds around to keep them dry." She had never had the electric lights turned on. "Where'd I get my five dollars for the deposit?" she asked angrily, for she was angry at her house, at the circumstances of her life, and she wanted to go back to the mountains whence she had come. "But it would cost an awful lot to get us back—fifteen dollars." Her husband had pellagra, and she was supporting him and her four children on what she made. She had a venomous feeling toward the house which had finally spewed her forth.

"Look at that chimney! It always smoked! We couldn't have no fire here! We couldn't keep warm. Once, I was buyin' a coal stove for my kitchen and I had $19 paid on it. Then I had to buy medicine for him and I couldn't make my payments and they tuk my stove away."

The furniture of the mill workers is almost inevitably bought on the installment plan. Mrs. Winebarger made $12.50 a week. She paid $1.50 a week for house rent, between fifty cents and a dollar for fuel and light, and more than a dollar a week for medicine. The house was a bungalow of four rooms. It had a fairly wide hall and small shallow fireplaces. Except for its flimsiness it was much better than the tenements of Passaic, New Jersey, or the over-crowded houses of Lawrence, Massachusetts, with their four courtyards.

We went next to the house of Mrs. Ada Howell, an old woman who had been beaten up on Monday, April 22, after the withdrawal of the militia.

Mrs. Howell sat in a rocking chair, her two eyes blackened, her face discolored. It gave one a sense of embarrassment and impotent anger to look at her. She told her story in a detached way. She was curiously without passion as she described something as unbelievable as a nightmare. She had been going to the store for supper on Monday, April 22nd. Policemen came down the street "chasing the strikers before them like rats." A policeman rushed at her with a bayonet.

"He cut my dress and he cut me too, Lawyer Jimison told me I should keep that dress without washing it so I could show it but I didn't have enough dresses to lay those clothes away." Her idea, was that the policeman had gone crazy,

"They acted like crazy men. They was drunk crazed," her son said.

"They had been a-drinkin'," she admitted, "an' they must'a been a-drinkin' to chase women and little kids with baynits. They chased 'em in and out the relief store like dogs huntin' rats.

"An' they hadn't no call to go in that relief store — the laws hadn't. You can't go in any place if you ain't any warrant.

"An' then the policeman came up an' hit me between the eyes with his fist. He hit me more'n twenty times, I reckon. I was all swelled up an' black an' blue."

I had seen photographs of her mutilated face. We didn't say anything. There didn't seem to be anything to say. I suppose when comfortable people read such stories they think, "This can't be true. Why, that just couldn't happen in our town. Such things *don't* happen." No wonder they feel this way.

We went on. Strike-sightseeing is a rather awful thing. There is obscenity in the fact that old women can be beaten for no reason when they are peacefully proceeding on their business; there is equal obscenity in the fact that a mother with four children to support has to work all night for $12.50 a week, and then be evicted because she cannot pay her rent. It does not seem reasonable that such things should happen here in this country, in 1929.

This was not the end of the sights Gastonia had to show that day. In the late afternoon I went out to watch the picket line. Perhaps a hundred men, women, and children walked two by two in orderly fashion. The procession was led by two boys and two gay girls of about fifteen, in overalls. The police whistles shrilled. Two or three automobiles containing police and deputies armed with bayonets speeded after the picketers. The picketers walked away from the mills. The deputies herded them with their bayonets.

I stood on a high bank, watching. A nice-looking woman was rushed to a waiting car by the police. She resisted. I saw a policeman twist the knot of her hair and twist her arms cruelly. She struggled. And still they twisted her arms. Women near me were crying. Murmurs of "Shame !" came from the crowd. One of the village women grasped my arm, trembling. Everyone was saying, "Why don't they do something?"

The arrested woman hadn't been in the picket line. Her little boy had been swept into the procession as it was rounded up by the police, and she had pulled him out. The reason she had struggled so against arrest was that she had a nursing baby. A few hours after her brutal mauling she was set at liberty. Why was she treated this way? There is no answer. Why was Mrs. Howell set upon when she was going to the store to get her evening's supper?

VI

A few days after this a mill company began mass evictions. The fifty people evicted that first day lived in houses distributed through the different sections of the mill village.

"To show the others what's comin' to 'em," a mill official remarked grimly. One official stated frankly that it was intentional that union officials and the most active strikers should be the first to be thrown out.

Accordingly, the house of J.A. Valentine was one of those where the sheriff and deputies stopped first. Mrs. Valentine was sitting on a bench, a little girl in her arms. The child had been in bed when the mill doctor arrived to see if there was sickness in the house. When the doctor was questioned about her, he answered:

"She's convalescing from the smallpox. She's all right now; ain't any temperature. This ain't a smallpox-quarantine state. Compulsory vaccination and compulsory school age is enough without quarantine."

On the next street the deputies were at work taking out the possessions of fourteen people. It was Henry Tetherow's house.

Henry is the head of the family. He is seventeen, and looks fourteen. He and a sister support a family of nine. His father is too sick to work. With them lives the family of William Truitt, the secretary-treasurer of the local union of the National Textile Workers.

"This house has been a hotbed of union meetings," said the company doctor. "The company's been patient to let 'em stay here so long. Let 'em stay five weeks. What's the matter with the little girl in bed? Oh, she's got nothin' but runnin' ears. Might have 'em for weeks."

Men came out, bringing children's beds, a basket of pretty glasses, a tiny old-fashioned organ. A big doll was being evicted.

Henry, pale of face, very small, wandered at random among the swelling mountain of things. Mrs. Tetherow stood as if she would never move again.

At another house in the midst of the immense disorder of eviction a woman sat tranquilly writing a long letter to her husband. Not far from her, tucked into a fold of a featherbed, a little baby lay peacefully sleeping. She was a delicate and beautiful woman, and all her belongings were new and freshly painted.

Only one woman sat crying. The tears slid slowly down her cheeks. She had four small children and expected her new baby to be born any day. Around her were the shards of a home.

The work of eviction continued relentlessly day after day. The mill village became a gypsy encampment. People set up stoves and beds in the lots. The dwellers of two hundred homes were evicted. Over a thousand people must have been homeless.

VII

I went to visit other strike areas, and when I returned the Workers' International Relief, together with the National Textile Workers' Union, had erected a tent colony. Close by was a new union headquarters which the strikers had built with their own labor. The tent colony was picturesquely set among woods near a ravine. There was an air of general happiness and well-being among the strikers and organizers. There were rumors of great discontent among the workers at the mill. The strikers and the organizers talked hopefully of another walk-out.

It was Decoration Day. A band of children with American flags was walking gaily off toward the picket line. They were led by little Sophia Melvin, who had come down recently from the North to teach organized play to the children. Old friends came up and greeted me. Everybody was brown; they looked as if they had gained weight since the early days of the strike. The women's faces were rested.

I was told that there had been prowlers around the tent colony and frequent threats that the new headquarters would be destroyed as the old one had been. Because of this the boundaries were patrolled at night by an armed guard. But this did not seem strange to me, coming as I did from Elizabethton, Tennessee. The place where I had stayed there had been guarded every night by boys peering out of the windows, their fingers on the triggers of their guns.

It did not seem possible that further trouble should occur. Least of all did the Northern organizers expect it. Yet just a week later, during trouble at the tent colony, Chief of Police O.F. Aderholt was killed, and three other policemen and one striker wounded.

Two policemen, after a celebration in Mecklenburg County, chased a man into the Catawba River and playfully shot at him. Two hours later they were at the tent colony. It was nine o'clock. The guard refused to allow the police to enter without a warrant. Another policeman tried to disarm a guard. In the scuffle a gun went off and the shooting began. Each side claims the other fired first. In the next few days seventy persons were arrested. Sixteen people, including three women, were held without bail for first-degree murder, the unfailing penalty for which in North Carolina is the electric chair. The death penalty against the three women was later dropped. Seven others were held for conspiracy. Every Northerner, man or woman, was arrested.

VIII

It is idle to think of Gastonia as a situation peculiar to itself. Edward McGrady, loyal representative of the American Federation of Labor, and Alfred Hoffman of the United Textile Workers were kidnapped in the principal hotel of Elizabethton, Tennessee. In Ware Shoals, South Carolina, George L. Googe, vice-president of the South Carolina Federation of Labor, was threatened by a mob and left town under police protection.

There is no doubt in my mind and in the minds of many other people that had it not been for the Northern organizers and their desire to avoid violence the workers would have shot in what they consider self-defense long ago. Not only would they have shot in Gastonia, but also they would have shot in Elizabethton and elsewhere. Everybody in the Carolinas and Tennessee has a gun. Peaceful citizens going on a long journey take revolvers with them as a matter of course. People think in terms of defending themselves. The trial now in progress will concern itself with the question whether the strikers shot in self-defense or not.

This trial began with a scene of grotesque unfairness, unprecedented in any American court. A life-sized manikin of Chief of Police O.F. Aderholt was rolled into the courtroom dressed in a blood-stained uniform. Conspicuous among the prosecution lawyers sat the widow and daughter of the Chief of Police. Confronted with this unexpected sight they burst into tears. Judge M.V. Barnhill, who throughout the trial was a paragon of impartiality, commanded the figure to be removed. The jury and the appalled audience, however, had filled their eyes with the ghastly effigy.

Three days later one of the jurors went violently insane — from the shock he had suffered at the spectacle of the "ghost," it was claimed. The trial had to be delayed. The defense had not been heard. The principal witnesses for the State had already been examined. Not one of the defendants had been connected with the shooting of the Chief. The released jurors told the press that on the evidence before them they were for acquittal.

At this point of the story the mob reappears. Already on the Saturday before, union organizers going to a meeting in South Gastonia had been surrounded by a mob of two hundred, threatened with lynching, and beaten with blackjacks and bottles. The taxi had plowed its way through the crowd and they escaped with only minor injuries. Apparently as a result of the jurors' statement that they would release the prisoners, an "Anti-Red" demonstration was held in Gastonia on Monday, September 9th, the night the trial came to its abrupt pause. A procession of one hundred cars went to strike headquarters, which was looted. The strike headquarters at Bessemer City, a small town seven miles from Gastonia, was raided.

The mob went next to a house in Gastonia where union organizers lived. A hundred men crowded into the house and kidnapped Ben Wells, an Englishman, and C.D. Saylor and C.M. Lell, local men. They were driven to a wood in a neighboring county where Wells was stripped and flogged. Two 'possum hunters heard his cries. The night riders heard the hunters approaching and thought it was the law and fled, leaving Wells unconscious to be rescued by his companions.

Meantime the major part of the mob had streamed over the twenty miles that separates Gastonia from Charlotte with cries of "Get Beal out of jail and lynch him!" "Let's clean up all the Communists!" "Let's get out Jimison and lynch him!" They went to a hotel where some of the Communists and organizers lived and tore up the hotel register and broke fixtures. They proceeded next to the headquarters of the International Labor Defense, an organization which has been defending the accused men as well as those arrested on charges connected with the strike. The sympathizers and organizers in the office had been warned by telephone from Gastonia and escaped only one minute before the arrival of the mob. After breaking into the International Labor Defense office and finding no one there, the mob went to Tom P. Jimison's house, where they shouted and milled around and finally dispersed.

Two significant facts stand out in this night of terror. One is that no police protection was afforded. The other is that the mob was in nowise a rabble but proceeded along planned lines. It is considered by defense counsel part of the reign of terror which has been in effect throughout the strike, and of which they consider the raid of June 7th an integral part. The better element in North Carolina has been deeply stirred by this lawlessness in which prominent mill people and members of the police took part. An investigation was promptly begun. Fourteen people were arrested including prominent mill men and police officers who were in the tent colony raid. Members of the Gastonia mob have asserted that they will not stop till they have cleaned out every union organizer in their part of the South.

The culmination to mob violence came on September 14th. A truck load of union members were going to an attempted union meeting. The meeting was never held, armed mobs turning away all union members. The truck turned back to Bessemer City, whence it had come, and was followed by a number of cars containing members of the mob. A car swerved in front of the truck apparently to stop it. The truck crashed it, and the car was upset. Immediately rifle fire was opened on the unarmed workers. A woman was shot through the chest and died instantly. She is a widow and leaves five young children. She was especially beloved among the strikers as the composer of the strike songs and ballads. When the Chief of Police was shot, sixteen people were indicted and tried for murder. It will be interesting to see if anyone will be tried for this murder.

Meantime, ever since the arrest of their leaders, the workers have been flowing into the union. This demand of the Southern workers for better conditions, and a union to help them get it, is spreading. The South knows it.

Up to now, mob violence, police brutality, wholesale arrests of workers, ordinances against picketing, intimidation, and the calling out of the militia—a word, repression—has been the only answer the South has made to this movement for economic equality among Southern workers. History shows that repression has always failed. Not all the Inquisitions, not all the Black Hundreds, not all the various spy systems that humanity has devised have ever stopped an idea.

If the Southern industrialists hold to their present policy they face a long and bloody war, bitter and costly. Sooner or later they will have to yield. Political equality cannot exist side by side with industrial feudalism.

The Gastonia Strikers' Case

*Harvard Law Review, 1930**

The decision of the supreme court of North Carolina affirming the conviction of seven defendants for the murder of Chief of Police Aderholt of Gastonia[1] writes the closing words to a bitter chapter in the industrial struggle in that state. Following a disturbance at the Loray mill in Gastonia, where a strike broke out early in April, 1929, Governor Gardner dispatched five companies of militia to the town.[2] On the 18th of April, while the mill was publishing vituperative denunciations of the strike leaders as communists and atheists who were determined to establish racial equality,[3] a masked mob stormed and wrecked the union headquarters, and destroyed the strikers' supplies.[4]

New headquarters were built by the strikers, and an armed patrol was established. On the evening of June 7th, Aderholt was shot and killed, and three other officers and a striker were wounded in an exchange of shots which took place at the union lot.[5] The trial of sixteen defendants indicted for murder was begun in Mecklenburg County, after Judge Barnhill[6]

---

* This article is reprinted with the permission of the Harvard Law Review.

1. *State v. Beal*, 199 N. C. 278, 154 S. E. 604 (1930). The defendants were also indicted and convicted upon separate counts of felonious secret assault upon officers Gilbert, Roach and Ferguson; these charges were tried in the same proceedings.

2. *See N. Y. Times*, 2 (April 4, 1929). By April 21st, the troops had been entirely withdrawn. *Ibid.*, April 22, at 3.

3. *See* the advertisements which appeared in the Gastonia Daily Gazette, reprinted in Blanshard, "Communism in Southern Cotton Mills," 128 *Nation* 500 (1929); *cf.* Tippett, *When Southern Labor Stirs*, 76–108 (1931).

4. *See N. Y. Times*, 2 (April 19, 1929); Lloyd, *Gastonia,* 15 (Prog. Lab. Library, No. 4, 1930); Tippett, *loc. cit. supra* note 3.

5. On the evening of June 7th, a meeting of the strikers was held on the union lot. The defendant Beal was one of the speakers; he told the workers to form a picket line and march to the Loray Mill, and, according to the state's witnesses, urged them to "go into the mill and drag out those at work" and, if anybody bothers, "to shoot and shoot to kill." The defense's witnesses denied that Beal had counseled violence.

The picket line formed and began its march, but was turned back by the police. Chief Aderholt and three of his deputies got into a car and drove to the union lot in answer to a call by one of the neighbors of the union that "If we ever needed protection, we need it now." The officers found the lot dark and quiet. Four of the defendants, Carter, Harrison, McGinnis and McLaughlin, were among those outside the building, guarding it, armed with shotguns. The state's witnesses testified that as the officers approached, one of the guards came toward them with his gun leveled at Gilbert. The latter grabbed the gun and took it away from the guard. Aderholt asked what the trouble was. The guard replied, "None of your ... business." On the chief's order, Gilbert arrested the guard for resisting an officer. The testimony of the defense was that Carter, who was the guard, accosted the officers with his gun under his arm, pointed toward the ground, and asked them for their search warrant; Gilbert replied, "Here is all the warrant I need," as he drew his pistol and flashed it in Carter's face.

Aderholt and Deputy Roach proceeded toward the building; Roach testified that he looked in and saw four men with shotguns raised, one of whom was Beal; then the officers turned back. Meanwhile, as Gilbert held the guard, there were shouts of "Turn him loose, Gilbert," or according to the prosecution, "Shoot them" and "Do your duty, guards." Then three shots rang out, and a volley of firing followed. Whether the guards, or strikers in the building, or the officers fired the first shot is in dispute. When the smoke cleared away, three officers and one of the strikers had been wounded; Aderholt had been shot in the back and, shortly thereafter, he died. See Record of the case *passim.*

6. The conduct of the case by Judge Barnhill, who presided at both trials, was widely commended by observers, who attested to his determination to give the defendants an impartial hearing. See Bailey, "Gastonia Goes to Trial," 59 *New Rep.* 332 (1929); Porter, "Justice and Chivalry in Carolina," 129 *Nation* 160 (1929); *cf.* Nelson, "North Carolina Justice," 60 *New Rep.* 314 (1929); Editorial, *N. Y. Times,* Aug. 3, 1929, at 14. However Judge Barnhill's rulings may have affected the fairness of the proceed-

had granted a change of venue because of prejudice in Gaston County.[7] A mistrial was declared August 16th, when one of the jurors became insane.[8] That night an anti-red mob raided the strikers' headquarters and destroyed their supplies; three of the strike leaders were kidnapped, and one was flogged.[9] Five days later the violence reached a tragic climax when Ella May Wiggins, twenty-nine-year-old "poet laureate" of the strikers, was shot and killed by the anti-communist mob.[10] For the raid, the flogging and the mob murder, there has been no conviction.[11]

From the moment the second trial[12] began the prosecution made persistent efforts to inject into the case testimony relating to communism. These questions to the earlier witnesses were uniformly excluded by the court, but when the defendant Beal, whom the prosecution regarded as the leader of the strikers, was cross-examined the trial judge admitted the testimony to impeach his credibility.[13] After examining Beal concerning his distribution of copies of the communist newspaper, the Daily Worker, the solicitor was permitted to ask Beal whether he advocated the overthrow of the government of the United States and of North Carolina, and had brought his organization to North Carolina to teach the principles of communism to workers' children.[14] Beal's evasions and denials gave little affirmance to these questions.

Then followed the cross-examination of Mrs. Miller, one of the key witnesses for the defense, who had organized the strikers' children into branches of "Pioneer Youth." The state elicited the information that Mrs. Miller had been teaching Gastonia's children that the government and the bosses stand together for the slavery and starvation of the workers; that force is necessary to produce social change, and that in Soviet Russia, as a result

---

ings, the Record in the case, and the charge to the jury reflect a sincere insistence that the defendants be tried for the crime charged, and not for radical beliefs or activities.

7. See N. Y. Times, 8 (July 31, 1929).

8. Ibid., Sept. 10, 1929, at 1.

9. Ibid.; see "Fighting Communism with Anarchy," 102 Lit. Dig. 12 (Sept. 28, 1929); Tippett, op. cit. supra note 3, at 104 et seq.

10. Mrs. Wiggins was killed when the mob fired upon a truckload of union mill workers on their way to a meeting. See N. Y. Times, 1 (Sept. 15, 1929); note 9, supra.

11. The grand jury of Gaston county found the evidence insufficient to indict any of those charged with the killing of Mrs. Wiggins. See N. Y. Times, 24 (Oct. 25, 1929). Governor Gardner thereafter appointed Judge McElroy to investigate the matter. Ibid., Nov. 4, 1927, at 27. After a hearing, he held sixteen defendants for the next term of the grand jury, and five were indicted by that body. Ibid., Jan. 16, 1930, at 47. When the case was tried, the jury, after thirty minutes' deliberation, freed all of the defendants on every count in the indictment. The bail for the defendants had been furnished by the Loray mill. Ibid., March 7, 1930, at 25.

Four persons were indicted for the kidnapping and flogging of the communist organizers on Sept. 9, but all were acquitted at the trial in Concord, N. C. The attorney for the defense was Major A. J. Bulwinkle, counsel for the Loray mill, and a special prosecutor in the Aderholt case. Ibid., Oct. 20, 1929, at 12. Bail had been furnished for the defendants by the mill. Ibid., Sept. 18, 1929, at 22.

12. The state took a nolle prosequi in respect to all but seven of the defendants, and reduced the charges against the remaining seven to second-degree murder and felonious assault. See Record, 3. The prosecution sought to establish a conspiracy on the part of the defendants to resist the police authorities which resulted in Aderholt's death. The court ruled that evidence of the conspiracy would be limited to the events occurring June 7th, the night of the shooting

13. See argument of counsel and court on the point. Record, 1461–71. But cf. ibid., 1656. This Note makes no attempt to treat the numerous exceptions of the defendants and the errors assigned, such as the insufficiency of the indictment, the plea of double jeopardy, the numerous rulings on the admissibility of evidence, the motion to nonsuit, the exceptions to the court's charge. It is limited to the cross-examination into religious and political beliefs and the argument to the jury.

14. See Record 1506–27, 1586–87.

of a revolution, there are no bosses, no private property, and the workers and farmers control the government.[15]

Having disposed of her political beliefs, the state was permitted to examine the witness as to her religious views.[16] The Mecklenburg county jury learned that the witness did not believe in a Supreme Being who controls man's destiny, nor in divine punishment; and that an oath taken on an almanac would be as binding upon her as an oath on the Bible.[17]

The trial court allowed the questions concerning the political beliefs of Beal and Mrs. Miller as evidence affecting their credibility.[18] The upper court apparently regarded the testimony as admissible to prove the charge that the defendants were engaged in an unlawful conspiracy to resist the police.[19] These beliefs may be relevant to prove such a conspiracy on the night of June 7th, although the connection between Mrs. Miller's convictions and the charge against the defendants seems highly attenuated. But the establishment of the testimony's relevancy does not establish its admissibility. The doctrine runs through the whole law of evidence that testimony, though it is relevant, is to be excluded from the jury when it is too prejudicial in character.[20] The probative value of this testimony, whether as direct or as impeaching evidence, seems wholly out of proportion to the dangers with which its admission is fraught. To secure a fair trial of strikers in a community which flogged union leaders, wrecked union headquarters, and refused to indict for crimes against strikers, was at best hardly an easy task. But to link the strikers with "revolution" and "Russia" and "the abolition of private property" was to arouse passions and prejudices likely to result in the conviction of the defendants irrespective of their guilt.[21]

The upper court's answer to the defendants' objections is that the question of the admissibility of the evidence is within the discretion of the trial judge. This proposition is supported by a long line of North Carolina decisions. The tendency to vest wide discre-

---

15. Mrs. Miller testified that she had told the workers' children that the National Guard had been ordered to Gastonia to shoot down workers on the picket line. She had distributed literature showing a child firing at soldiers, and a leaflet urging the support of a children's delegation to the Soviet Union to bring the "message of solidarity of the children of America to the workers' children in Russia." See Record, 1614–31.

16. When Mrs. Miller came to the stand, no objection was made to her testimony on the ground of incompetency. North Carolina has never by statute abrogated the common-law rule of incompetency because of religious disbelief. A law regulating oaths, passed in 1777, is still on the statute books. N. C. Code Ann (Michie, 1927) §§ 3189–91. But decisions have gone far to affirm the admission of testimony when the trial court has found the witness to have a sense of "moral obligation" of the oath. Cf. Shaw v. Moore, 49 N. C. 25 (1856); State v. Pitt, 166 N. C. 268, 80 S. E. 1060 (1914); Lanier v. Bryan, 184 N. C. 235, 114 S. E. 6 (1922); see Biggs, "Religious Belief as a Qualification of a Witness," 8 N. C. L. Rev. 31 (1929); Hartogensis, "Denial of Equal Rights to Religious Minorities and Non-Believers in the United States," 39 Yale L. J. 659; cf. also N. C. Const. § 26.

17. See Record, 1644–56.

18. Mrs. Miller's sympathies had already been shown by her testimony that she was the wife of one of the defendants, and had been sent to Gastonia by the president of the union to organize the children's section. Ibid., 1608–14.

19. In support of its ruling the court relied on Spies v. People, 122 Ill. 1, 12 N. E. 865 (1887), and Commonwealth v. Sacco and Vanzetti, 255 Mass. 369, 151 N. E. 839 (1926). For a criticism of the view taken in the latter case, see Note, 36 Yale L. J. 384 (1927).

20. See 4 Wigmore, Evidence (2d ed. 1923) § 1864; Chafee, "The Progress of the Law," 35 Harv. L. Rev. 428, 433 (1922).

21. The state sought to cross-examine Beal concerning his belief in Negro equality. In spite of the prosecution's vigorous assertion that no "high class respectable white man advocates social equality," and that therefore the testimony should be admitted to impeach the witness, the court ruled against it. See Record 1465–66.

tion in the trial court is a highly salutary departure from the restrictive and confusing rules laid down by some tribunals for the regulation of a trial. But this does not mean that the trial court's discretion is uncontrolled, nor that the appellate court thereby abdicates all duty to prevent an unfair trial resulting from the abuse of discretion. In a recent prosecution growing out of a strike, the New York Court of Appeals, which recognizes wide discretion in allowing impeaching evidence, granted a new trial when the trial court permitted cross-examination into the defendant's communistic beliefs.

The opinion of the court neither approves nor disapproves the examination into Mrs. Miller's religious beliefs. It declares that if there was any error involved, it was not prejudicial.[22] Mrs. Miller, however, was one of the chief witnesses for the defense. And the defendants were convicted by a jury, nine of whom were farmers, living in a community which has been characterized as the most "fundamental Bible-loving people in the world."[23]

The conduct of the prosecution in its argument to the jury was urged as a ground for a new trial. The trial judge struck out the defendants' exceptions to the argument on the ground that when the defendants objected, he stopped the solicitor and warned him to confine his remarks to comment on the evidence, and also because the jury was told to disregard the plea. The upper court refused to order the certification of the record of the argument, taking the position that any prejudice was removed by the court's action,[24] and that thereafter the defendant's failure to continue to object prevented review of the remainder of the argument. If the court means that in fact any prejudice due to a prosecutor's plea is, in the nature of things, removed by a charge and an admonition, its position is untenable; that any jury would, upon the court's instructions, abstract itself from the influence of Solicitor Carpenter's dramatic performance in this case is inconceivable. In numerous instances a new trial has been granted, even though the trial court admonished or stopped the attorney and instructed the jury to disregard the remarks.

Nor should the failure to continue to object prevent reversal. In one case in which the solicitor, after a warning from the court on the defendant's objection, made an improper statement to the jury the North Carolina court itself granted a new trial even though no exception was taken to the final statement. A federal court granted a new trial because of a grossly improper argument of the prosecutor, even though no objection was ever made. The solicitor is duty bound to secure the defendants an impartial hearing. To refuse to consider the fervid appeal of the prosecuting attorney, in reaching a decision that the defendants have been convicted of murder after a fair trial, is hardly jus-

---

22. *State v. Beal, supra* note 1, 154 S. E. at 616–18.

23. *See* Wharton, "Poor White Capitalists," 153 *Outlook and Ind.* 252 (1929); "I have never been in a cotton-mill house whose walls were not littered with cheap, loud-colored prints of Biblical scenes." *Ibid. See* also 129 *Nation* 477 (1929): "To a Southern fundamentalist farmer, a communist or an atheist is a criminal per se."

24. The solicitor knelt and prayed before the jury. Then grasping the hand of the widow of the dead officer, he handed her the shot-torn coat of her husband, and pledged the vengeance of the state. He characterized the defendants as "devils with hoofs and horns who threw away their pitchforks for shotguns, foreign Communists, fiends incarnate, who came sweeping like a cyclone, like a tornado to sink their fangs into the heart and life blood of my community."

"Do you believe in the flag, do you believe in North Carolina, do you believe in good roads? ... Men, do your duty; do your duty, men, and in the name of God and justice render a verdict that will be emblazoned across the sky of America as an eternal sign that justice has been done." *See N. Y. Times,* 2 (Oct. 19, 1929); *ibid.,* Editorial, Oct. 21, 1929, at 26; "The Gastonia Strike-Murder Verdict," 103 *LIT. DIG.* 14 (Nov. 1929); 153 *Outlook and Ind.* 336 (1929).

tified on the ground that the defense counsel failed to continue to interrupt the state's legal representative.

These errors cannot be dismissed as non-prejudicial. Far from revealing the undisputable guilt of the defendants, the record discloses a sharp conflict of testimony upon every important issue in the case. In this state of the facts, the admission of the evidence of nonconformist beliefs and the character of the solicitor's plea make it exceedingly difficult to determine whether the defendants were convicted because of their guilt or because of their radicalism.[25]

---

25. Beal, Miller, and Carter, northerners, and Harrison, a Gastonia resident, were sentenced to prison terms of seventeen to twenty years; McGinnis and McLaughlin of Gastonia received sentences of twelve to fifteen years, and Hendricks, also a local resident, received a five- to seven-year sentence. State v. Beal, *supra* note 1, 154 S. E. at 612. None of the defendants is in jail, however, all having jumped bail. *See N. Y. Times*, 1 (Sept. 30, 1930).

Ella May Wiggins

Mill Mother's Lament

We leave our home in the morning,
We kiss our children good-bye,
While we slave for the bosses,
Our children scream and cry.
And when we draw our money,
Our grocery bills to pay,
Not a cent to spend for clothing,
Not a cent to lay away.
And on that very evening,
Our little son will say,
"I need some shoes, dear mother,
And so does sister May."
How it grieves the heart of a mother,
You every one must know,
But we can't buy for our children,
Our wages are too low.
Now listen to me, workers,
Both women and men,
We are sure to win our union,
If all would enter in.
I hope this will be a warning,
I hope you will understand,
And help us win our victory,
And lend to us a hand.
It is for our little children
That seem to us so dear,
But for us nor them, dear workers,
The bosses do not care.
But understand, all workers,
Our union they do fear,
Let's stand together, workers.

Two Little Strikers

Two Little strikers, a boy and a girl,
Sit by the union hall door.
The little girls hand was brown as the curles
That played on the dress that she wore.

The little boys head was hatless,
And tears in each little eye,
"Why don't you go home to your mama", I said
And this was the strikers reply:

"Our mama's in jail, they locked her up:
Left Jim and me alone,
So we've come here to sleep in the tents tonight,
For we have no mother, no home.

"Our Papa got hurt in the shooting Friday night,
We waited all night for him,
For he was a union guard you know,
But he never came home any more."

Chief Aderholt

Come all of you good people and listen to what I tell;
The story of Chief Aderholt, the man you all knew well.
It was on one Friday evening, the seventh day of June,
He went down to the union ground and met fatal doom.
They locked up our leaders, they put them in jail,
They shoved them in prison, refused to give them bail.
The workers joined together and this was their reply:
We'll never, no we'll never let our leaders die.
They moved the trial to Charlotte, got lawyers from every town.
I'm sure we'll hear them speak again up on the union ground.
While Vera she's in prison, Manville Jenckes in pain,
Come join the textile union and show that you are game.
We're going to have a union all over the South,
Where we can wear good clothes and live in a better house.
Now we must stand together and to the boss reply
We'll never, no we'll never let our leaders die.

The Big Fat Boss and the Workers

The boss man wants our labor, and money to pack away,
The workers wants a union and the eight-hour day.
The boss man hates the workers, the workers hates the boss.
The boss man rides in a big fine car and the workers has to walk.
The boss man sleeps in a big fine bed and dreams of his silver and gold.
The workers sleeps in a old straw bed and shivers from the cold.
Fred Beal he is in prison a-sleeping on the floor,
But he will soon be free again and speak to us some more.
The union is a-growing, the I. L. D. is strong,
We're going to show the bosses that we have starved too long.

Come all you scabs if you want to hear
The story of cruel millionaire.
Manville Jenckes was the millionaire's name,
He bought the law with his money and frame
But he can't buy the union with his money and fame.
Told Violet Jones if she'd go back to work,
He'd buy her a new Ford and pay her well for her work.
They throwed rotten eggs at Vera and Beal on the stand,
They caught the man with the pistol in his hand,
Trying to shoot Beal on the speaking stand.
They took Beal to the Monroe jail,
They put him in a dirty cell,
But Beal and the strikers put up a darn good fight,
We'll make the bosses howl and hear old Manville say,
"It ain't no use fighting the union this way."

VIII

Distinctly American Radicalism in the Depression

Bloody Thursday, Rincon Hill, Library of Congress.

Distinctly American Radicalism and the Coastwide and General Strike in San Francisco of 1934
Kenneth M. Casebeer

I know who wrote the history of this union. It was the people down there facing the guns and doing a few other things.

The rank and file made the decisions. It wouldn't be buffaloed, browbeaten or divided, and therefore it couldn't be licked.

Harry Bridges[1]

Law and law-in-action are sites of struggle over power, as well as law in action is power at the sites of struggle. American workers in the 1930s did have a distinct and radical political agenda in their struggles at the time, an agenda that did not strongly distinguish between worker interests as individual interest as opposed to as working class interests. Their radicalism was "bread and butter" or "porkchop" radicalism, but this was not apolitical and did aim to reshape power in society. Worker politics in this era responded to

---

1. *The Dispatcher*, 10, 6 (Nov. 23, Dec. 20, 1994).

both the particular forms of oppressive conditions and legal regimes that they faced, and the opportunities open for resistance, and that also contributed to the difference in their radicalization. American workers were different, but not so "exceptional" as portrayed by the lack of a strong socialist or labor party. This movement did have considerable impact on the New Deal legislation that was passed even as much of the prevailing legislation was meant to diffuse support for more radical working class alternatives. This movement also at the same time, in many ways served to catalyze the craft/mass production organizational schism of the union movement. The 1934 West Coast dock strike provided a signal moment for this American radicalism.

The narrative of the Coastwise Dock Strike will be familiar to labor historians, prominently in work by Nelson,[2] Selvin,[3] Markholt,[4] Quinn,[5] and Bernstein;[6] the controversy over Harry Bridges and the Communist Party, better documented in Kimeldorf,[7] Larrowe,[8] Cherny,[9] and Klehr.[10] However, the lenses have been skewed in two ways in the literature as a whole. First, while almost unanimously sympathetic to workers, much reliance is placed on the descriptions of the strike and its contexts from management side publications, or by labor leaders.[11] Second, the obsession with American exceptionalism into the Thirties often slides into equating radicals with communists, from both detractors and supporters.[12] It is as if the mantra of the shipowners and politicians of the time enthralled the labeling of radical ideas. Labor historians thus discount a more generic radicalism.

Even given the wildest estimates of Communist Party membership in San Francisco during the strike, the numbers of active strikers joining in resistance and solidarity dwarfs the C.P., and does so even within the rank and file leadership. The San Francisco Call-Bulletin overenthusiastically projected the strikers to include "1,200 acknowledged Communists, and 48,800 workers who were "misled."[13] And even a substantial presence in

---

2. Bruce Nelson, *Workers on the Waterfront: Seamen, Longshoremen, and Unionism in the 1930's,* (Urbana: Univ. of Illinois Press, 1988).

3. David F. Selvin, *A Terrible Anger: The 1934 Waterfront and General Strikes in San Francisco,* (Detroit, Wayne State Univ. Press, 1996).

4. Otillie Markholt, *Maritime Solidarity: Pacific Coast Unionism, 1929–1938* (Tacoma: Pacific Coast Maritime History Committee, 1998).

5. Mike Quin, *The Big Strike* (Olema: Olema Publishing Co., 1949).

6. Irving Bernstein, *The Lean Years,* (Boston: Houghton Mifflin, Inc., 1966).

7. Howard Kimeldorf, *Reds or Rackets?: The Making of Radical and Conservative Unions on the Waterfront,* (Berkeley: University of California Press, 1988).

8. Charles P. Larrowe, *Harry Bridges: The Rise and Fall of Radical Labor in the U.S.,* (New York: Lawrence Hill and Co., 1972).

9. Robert W. Cherny, "The Making of a Labor Radical: Harry Bridges, 1901–1934," *Pacific Historical Review* 63 (1995).

10. Harvey Klehr, *The Heyday of American Communism: The Depression Decade,* (New York: Basic Books, Inc., 1984).

11. *See eg.,* Selvin. However, Selvin's narrative is also the most complete on the San Francisco strike events.

12. Klehr and Markholt are the most explicit, although Markholt offers little evidence for sweeping conclusions of influence, but Kimeldorf and Nelson while speaking more generically about radicalism mostly document Communist activity in measuring radicalism. Yet significantly, Nelson concluded, "The fact is that the Big Strike was an authentic rank-and-file rebellion that had long been waiting to happen. It drew upon deep wellsprings of discontent that required leadership and direction, but did not submit easily to manipulation. There was a spontaneous impulse toward solidarity and discipline that was quite evident in the Battle of Rincon Hill, in the stirring funeral march for Sperry and Bordaise, and in other events where masses of workers flowed together "like cooling lava" in uncanny demonstrations of self-direction and self-discipline that left even their own leadership amazed." Bruce Nelson, *supra* note 2, at 145.

13. *San Francisco Call-Bulletin,* July 17, 1934.

San Francisco does not explain why the strike ran in parallel developments throughout the Pacific Coast where Communist activity was far weaker, and why the weakest port in the strike was San Pedro despite the second largest Party membership on the West Coast in Los Angeles. The issue of Communism also slights the long presence of the I.W.W., particularly in the Northwest and the cross employment of former loggers on the docks there, with influence extending South even to San Pedro via Wobbly Seamen.[14] "Whatever the reasoning, many ex-Wobblies helped to build the ILA during the early 1930s, bringing with them the conviction that militant economic action was the surest way to gain union demands."[15] From Portland, "there is little evidence that these [left-wing] groups were of any importance in the strike. They were not a direct cause of the strike nor did they have any substantial effect on the course or the conclusion of the strike."[16]

George Hedley, an outsider associated with a church organization, who witnessed two weeks of strike activity during the climactic two weeks leading to "Bloody Thursday," recorded, "I have heard no Communist theorizing, and no planning of sabotage. I have seen and heard American working men who want a square deal for themselves and their families; and I have seen them abused, chased, beaten, gassed and shot by the duly constituted defenders of the public peace."[17] According to labor organizer Grace Mettee, "Contrary to stories in some papers, the Communists are taking almost no part in the strike outside of holding street meetings attended by a dozen people or so."[18] Thus, a very different account of radicalism emerges from the grass roots of labor. That lens will be as much as possible used exclusively here. This topic may not be new, but the particulars when collected here are perhaps news, and that too is interrogation that speaks to power, winners, and their records. And Law was always there shaping and reflecting the conflicts — The federal National Recovery Act catalyzing independent union membership, recognition by the Labor Disputes Board of both the ILA and the hated company union, the Blue Book, under the NRA, attempts to manipulate local relief agencies for strikebreakers and against strikers, close collaboration between the Mayor, city newspapers, and the Waterfront Employers Association, constant police violence, illegal arrests and trials, dismissal of union lawsuits and appeals, suppression of civil liberties, and bayonet equipped militias — all interconnected.

Ambiguous Ubiquity of the A.F. of L. Rank & File Committee

One proxy for the recovery of worker voice and radical politics in the 1930s follows the activities of a group called the AFL Rank & File Committee for Social Insurance (originally, Unemployment Insurance). The group, admittedly started as a communist sponsored group in New York City, unexpectedly catalyses a large following of workers, locals, and non-working class supporters nationwide, that in turn gives the larger group life of its own. This larger group is continually marked by the insistence of local activists that they are not communists, that they are only demanding fair treatment and some prospect of the "American Dream" — a refrain often repeated by Harry Bridges. He and they (American workers) could not help it if the communists concurrently held some good ideas and offered support organizationally and monetarily to push those proposals for their own agenda.

---

14. Howard Kimeldorf, *supra* note 7, at 26–27.

15. Otillie Markholt, *supra* note 4, at 62.

16. Roger B. Buchanon, *Dock Strike: History of the 1934 Waterfront Strike in Portland, Oregon,* 43 (Everett: The Working Press, 1964).

17. George P. Hedley, "The Strike As I have Seen It," 9, Address Before the Church Council for Social Education, Berkeley, California, July 19, 1934.

18. Grace Mettee, "Zero Hour on the Coast," 139 *Nation* 102, 102 (July 24, 1934).

At the turn of the 1930s, Louis Weinstock, a painter and a member of the Communist Party, had been leading a rank and file movement to unseat a powerful, but racketeering, local president of the painters union in New York City who was nonetheless supported by the International's leaders. Weinstock used the issue to help organize Black painters in Harlem, and succeeded in ousting the corrupt local leadership. He was then given the task of organizing a rank and file movement in NYC in the wake of the Communist inspired Hunger March on Washington led by Herbert Benjamin, in which part of the demands included a social wage as the solution for unemployment and wage/profit disparities.[19] The NY City Rank & File Committee for Unemployment Insurance was founded in 1931. Quickly gaining national support, the group became the AFL Rank & File Committee for Social Insurance. Rand social scientist (a U.S.S.R. sympathizer, but maybe not more) Mary Van Kleeck drafted the legislative form of the Workers' Unemployment Insurance Bill, introduced by Wisconsin Congressman and later Senator Ernest Lundeen of the Farmer-Labor party. The issue of unemployment, largely avoided by the craft dominated leadership of the AFL and its commitment to voluntarism in social welfare, accelerated the growing discord with existing production workers, such as the Mineworkers, and the call to move unionism into growing mass production industries. R & F Committee delegates to the 1932 AFL convention fought in committees and from the floor for consideration of unemployment insurance, thwarted by the program committee. In 1933, the group crashed the convention when their credentials were denied, and then held a rump convention across the street.

At its height in 1934, the Committee was supported by over 3,000 local unions, six international unions, and scores of central labor unions. The group had moved into general mass production union building, and attacked AFL union corruption. The group was active in the western Pennsylvania steel strikes[20] and active in the Coastwise Strike of 1934. The group's publication, *AFL Rank and File Federationist*, had run articles on the strike, praising Bridges' leadership in the rank and file control of the strike. Weinstock as National Secretary, AFL Trade Union Committee for Unemployment Insurance and Relief, with many other active members in the Unemployment Insurance fight, sponsored in Union Square the largest demonstration supporting the San Francisco General Strike in New York, July 19, 1934. In turn, Bridge's Albion Hall group supported the Workers' Unemployment Insurance Bill, a part of radicalizing dock workers who suffered chronic unemployment under the casual hiring of the shape-up. With the CIO schism in 1935, the AFL R & F group lost much of its reason for being. But in 1935 and 1936, its President was Harry Bridges with Louis Weinstock as Secretary. Much later, in the 1950s, Harry Bridges was chairman of the dinner honoring Weinstock upon his retirement.

Harry Bridges — Rank and File Leader

In 1933, Bridges, himself a winch driver, moved to leadership of rank and file discontent over the industry control of those who worked and lived by the San Francisco docks. Fighting to regain control of hiring halls, boosted by National Industrial Recovery Act, Section 7(a), spurred union membership in the International Longshoremens Association past the resistance of local and international leadership. As a leader of the

---

19. *See generally*, Kenneth M. Casebeer, "Unemployment Insurance, American Social Wage, Labor Organization and Legal Ideology," 35 *Boston Coll. L. Rev.* 259 (1994). Also, Louis Weinstock Papers, Tamiment Archives, New York University.

20. *See* Kenneth M. Casebeer, "Aliquippa: The Company Town and Contested Power in the Construction of Law," 43 *Buffalo L. Rev.* 617, 650–658 (1995).

strike and the proponent of generalizing the successful strike, Harry Bridges later became union president, moving the International Longshoremens and Warehousemens Union into the CIO and becoming its Western director.

However close or not to the communist party apparatus, Bridges refused to distinguish between communist and other workers supporting the strike. In a fight over the city's most important industry, and the largest number of workers in the city, workers had little difficulty identifying friend and foe, and the enemies were not defined by party niceties. It was a working class strike, a partial general strike, and a strike for social justice and control over working conditions by controlling work. In this context, the communists were welcome fighters for the cause of union and worker empowerment. Party members, such as West Coast organizer Sam Darcy, were close friends and strategists of Bridges; the local communist labor newspaper at points during the strike provided virtually the only daily source of information and coordination of the strikers, given the hostility and misinformation in the news industry dominated by William Randolph Hearst. As Bruce Nelson argues, lines were blurred by the fact that under Darcy, West Coast organizing began a united front strategy, supporting the I.L.A. far in advance of the national Party apparatus.[21] While the dual communist union, the Maritime Workers Industrial Union, had strength among seamen, Darcy reports, "Unfortunately, however, our Marine Workers' Union, although having as many as four, and sometimes six, full time functionaries in San Francisco alone, had not a single worker on the docks."[22]

During one of his deportation trials, Bridges was asked if he knew Louis Weinstock, represented to be a member of the Communist Party's Central Committee. Bridges recalls two meetings where they shared podiums. Once, in July, 1935, Bridges spoke to a rally about the importance of unemployment insurance to a rank and file group where Weinstock also spoke (the AFL R&F Committee was the sponsor), and again in 1936. Transcripts show Bridges denied knowing that Weinstock was a communist at the time, and that Weinstock had not identified himself as one. In his first deportation hearing in 1939, Bridges testified, "I have been a member of a trade union since 1916.... So sometimes I get a little irritated when my views are ascribed to the Communist Party, because I had them even before the Communist Party came into being."[23] Irving Bernstein notes, "Bridges was a firm and undeviating believer in conflict between workers and the employers. 'The class struggle is here'.... He did not need [to read] Das Kapital."[24]

Rank & File Committee in San Francisco/Oakland/San Pedro

The West Coast Dock Strike was a rank & file strike. It was also briefly a general strike, and it was always a joint strike of all maritime unions. Both identities made this labor struggle unusual, ultimately dangerous and discrediting of political and business leadership beyond the goals of the strike itself. It was an important victory for labor, and contributed subsequently to solidifying the CIO by giving industrial unions greater importance in Western America.

---

21. Bruce Nelson, "Unions and the Popular Front: The West Coast Waterfront in the 1930's," 30 *International Labor and Working Class History*, 59, 61 (1986).

22. Charles P. Larrowe, "The Great Maritime Strike of 1934," 11 *Labor History* 403, 421 (1970).

23. Joyce M. Clements, "The San Francisco Maritime and General Strike of 1934 and the Dynamics of Repression," D. Crim. Diss. Univ. of California, Berkeley, note 3 at 103, 1975.

24. Irving Bernstein, *supra* note 6, at 259.

The Oakland A.F. of L. R&F Committee pamphlet[25] opens with a frontispiece from the San Francisco A.F. of L. R&F Committee. The manifesto linked the Coast maritime workers with general R&F themes specifically:

> The San Francisco Bay General Strike of July 16–20, 1934, brings home to all of us major and vital lessons for Labor of "life and death" importance.

> First, that to the extent we have real rank and file control, within the unions, or in the governmental setup for that matter, to that extent only do we have real democracy and social and economic security in our lives. For the unions this is illustrated very well by the strength of rank and file control in the I.L.A. local of San Francisco. The I.L.A. local strike committee, together with the Joint Maritime Strike Committee of Fifty, was the spear-head of the fight against the Employer's Open Shop, union smashing program.

> Second, that all employing class organizations—all they set up or control—are united to keep wages down and moreover lower wages and speed up the work, solely for the sake of "protecting profits". These organizations are the Chamber of Commerce, Industrial and Merchant's Associations, "Better America" and "National Civic Federations" and not least, Government Labor Boards and such bodies as Mayor Rossi's Citizens Committee.

> Third, that one of the best ways that our enemies have to exploit labor is to have their "agents" within the trade unions. Some of our enemies, among them high-ups in the N.R.A. "New Deal" administration, will even go so far as to speak for "industrial unionism" and use John L. Lewis (U.M.W. of A.) for their ends. This is done just so the will of the union memberships and rank and file can be choked and held back from struggles for decent and better wages and working conditions. Yet how well do we know that our fight is as natural as sunrise because of failure of the N.R.A. to improve the lot of the employed and jobless workers, and because we will never accept the Hitler call to "Do Without."

> Fourth, the main "tragedy" for labor, a blow at our vitals, is that traitors to Labor are tolerated as "our" leaders, some on "strategy" committees, some in central and state labor councils, some as international union officials. That these inside "agents" (Green, Woll, Berry, Ryan, Tobin, Sharrenberg, Casey and company) are against strikes, especially against SYMPATHY strikes, has been shown very clearly. The **"business"** of people of this sort is only to collect dues (the higher the better), get big salaries and elevate themselves into the ranks of the big-shot business and "Tammany Hall" politics. (Did Vandeleur, O'Connell, Sharrenberg, Casey, Howard, Spooner and Company 'make good' with the **powers-that-be** or not?).

> Fifth, that organized and sympathetic work on the part of all honest union members, on a rank and file control basis, did and can achieve tremendous results for labor, win immediate gains for working people, and change the entire course of development of the labor movement in its battle for a **real** "new deal" under which the welfare of ALL the workers will come **before** profits.[26]

For the Oakland rank and file, the strike was largely a "sympathetic" strike. It was part of the general strike from July 16–July 20, 1934. The focus of the pamphlet lays blame for

---

25. The A.F. of L. Rank and File Committee of Oakland Calif., "The Lessons of the Bay District 1934 General Strike," 1934.

26. *Ibid.* at 1

the disadvantages facing AFL strikers in the East Bay on the organization and leadership of the craft divisions of the AFL. "We are divided into hundreds of different craft unions and international divisions, making united action of our membership difficult. In the East Bay 106 different unions were on strike."[27]

The cause of the maritime strike, in progress from May 9, the rank and file emphasized was the depression.

> The economic crisis that swept the entire capitalistic world during the past five years has had the effect of driving down the American standard of living and working conditions, for which we have paid dearly during the last decade. The full burden of the crisis has been placed on the shoulders of the workers, both organized and unorganized.[28]

In Oakland, a total of 45,000 men went on strike. Unlike in San Francisco, the Building Trades Council voted to take all their unions out too.

However, the strike committee appointed by the Central Labor Council failed to coordinate with their counterpart in San Francisco. While the general strike ended with the Presidential intervention of a Longshoremen's Arbitration Board, the longshore and maritime unions remained out until both sets of unions were promised joint control of hiring halls.

The pamphlet left no doubt that this group saw militant economic power as the only answer to state partnership with capital and the press:

> The calling out of the national guard by Governor Merriam to protect scabs and do the dirty work of the employers, leaves no doubt in the minds of organized labor as to the function of State power. These poor deluded youngsters with their machine guns and bayonets, under the leadership of such fascists as Major General David P. Barrows, who has recently returned from a long stay in Germany, were sent into the strike district to break the strike, and terrorize all workers who were preparing to fight back against rapidly worsening conditions.
>
> The memory of that battle and the devotion and courage with which our brothers fought will never be forgotten. **They were fighting our fight.**[29]

The accompanying raids on radical worker organizations were seen as a first attack aimed at all labor following the German experience, warning:

> The force and violence which has been used against the more radical workers, was in reality a method of terrorism against all labor.... Regardless of how conservative an organization may be, they will feel the hand of Fascism if an attempt is made to better the conditions of labor through the strike, our main weapon.[30]

The Rank & File committee formed in San Pedro too, publishing a broadside urging striking maritime workers to follow the example of the San Francisco Local in rejecting the June I.L.A. sellout.

SUPPORT PROGRAM OF RANK AND FILE COMMITTEE AND WIN THE STRIKE. We demand a membership meeting of the Pedro Local 38-82, in which

---

27. *Ibid.* at 2.
28. *Ibid.* at 4.
29. *Ibid.* at 8.
30. *Ibid.* at 14.

the rank and file will have the opportunity of voicing their opinions on Petersen and his fink recommendations. Next we want to set up a rank and file committee representative of all the men on the docks including representatives of the seamen on strike. Third, return to work only when the original demands of the long-shoremen and demands from the seamen are met. Fourth, election of a rank and file negotiations committee of five; any agreements drawn up to be submitted to rank and file vote. Fifth, immediate organization of a mass picket line, calling on all workers in the harbor section and Los Angeles for support to tie up THIS PORT.[31]

Conditions and the "Rank and File Worker"

Conditions on the Docks and ships generated the rank and file mobilization. At the start it needed no leaders, only an occasion. On the first day of the strike, a Stockton long-shoreman bitterly reacted in support of the San Francisco walkout, "But we're through sweat-ing blood, loading cargo five times the weight we should carry, we're through standing morning after morning like slaves in a slave market begging for a bidder. We'll be out, you'll see; it may be a few weeks, a few months, but WE'LL BE OUT, and then hell can't stop us."[32] In San Francisco, conditions generated the feeling among workers that they had to fight for themselves. Leaders were distrusted. Dock work, tough work, became brutal under the Shipping Company's Blue Book union. If your name was not in the book, you could not work on the waterfront anywhere. Removal or absence from the book was itself blacklisting. The Blue Book meant access to "Fink Hall," the daily location of the shape-up where hundreds gathered each morning in front of whatever ships were docked pleading for the company's favor of a day's work. The Joint Strike Committee de-scribed the shape-up,

> In the past, there has been no way for the men to know whether or not they would be given work. Every Morning long lines of men would form at 6 o'clock, and for hours the men would have to remain there, hoping to be given a few hours of work. Most of them, after waiting about for four hours, would have to go home and go through the same disheartening procedure day after day. Those men who did get work were given their work orders through a company hiring hall, and would have to work as many as 18 or 20 hours a day, while the large bulk of the longshoremen went without any employment at all, or at best could get only 2 or 3 hours of work on occasional days.[33]

If one got chosen, work conditions always hazardous were unbearable. Bosses increased the size and weight of loads, reduced gang size, engaged in competitive speed-ups of load-ing, and kept men working until the ship was completely loaded or unloaded—accidents were so frequent that one in twenty stevedores would be injured in every year. Life expectancy of the average longshoreman was only forty years—men just got used up. "While only a few years back 18 to 20 tons was the average for a gang, and 25 tons was considered ex-ceptional, today 60 to 75 tons an hour is common—a three-fold increase."[34] There was only one countervailing advantage: unlike most factory jobs "efficient longshoring ... de-pended to a considerable degree on the dock workers' ability to exercise judgment and ini-tiative while performing their work."[35]

---

31. I.L.W.U. Archives.
32. Tllie Lerner, "The Strike," 1 *Partisan Review* 3, 3 (September–October 1934).
33. Joint Strike Committee letter, I.L.W.U. archives.
34. *Marine Workers' Voice*, 2, June 1933.
35. Herb Mills and David Wellman, "Contractually Sanctioned Job Action and Workers' Control: The Case of the San Francisco Longshoremen," 28 *Labor History* 167, 191, 1987.

San Pedro, a town of 34,000 people at the port of Los Angeles was the equivalent of the company town. Everyone worked the docks or worked for the daily needs of the dock-workers. Living in San Pedro was tough and hard, and work not easily relinquished. Working as a family head meant dock work dependent on the ship owners. Everyone knows everyone became a two-edged sword. With all identities of workers in this small, closely knit community recognizable, during early stages of the strike, strikebreakers were unceremoniously beaten and put out of town.

Following the collapse of the 1919 and 1921 strikes, the company union was supported by the Ku Klux Klan, which raided houses and gatherings of anyone associated with the IWW led strikes. In 1924, two children, 9 and 11, at a wobbly social, had full coffee urns dumped on them, permanently disfiguring the children. The father of one, Frank Sundstedt, later recalled the Klan focusing on the Catholics and foreign born. He also described the working conditions under the company scheme.

> In the 1920s they had a shape up system down here. You just showed up at the dock where the ship was coming in. If they needed you they hired you. If they didn't know you or didn't like you they wouldn't. They had all kinds of little systems. For example, the old timers would wear matches stuck in their hat bands. Three matches were a code. Maybe it meant a duck for the boss, or a chicken or a turkey, or a bottle of wine or whiskey. It was a signal that the longshoreman would take care of the boss if he'd give him a job.[36]

Another longshoreman, Henry Gaitan, reported, "If you had a nice looking sister, and liquor, and a wife that would put out you'd have a job."[37]

Work conditions were brutal. A gang would be hired for each ship and the workers worked straight through until it was loaded, more than 30 hours a stretch (the record according to the ILA, reached 72 hours without sleep). According to Elmer Mevert,

> Nitrate jobs were tough. I did that at Outer Harbor. They'd just hire enough guys. The higher the piles got—they'd go clear to the beams with sacks of Nitrite—the more guys they'd have to hire to keep passing the sacks up.

> It was just a continual operation, and your hands would bleed from that rough burlap. Packing bananas, your shoulders would swell up, your arches would break down. God it was tough. Sesame seed come in great round sacks and they were slick as silk. You couldn't stack those things for the love of money. And they weighed a hundred kilos (220 lbs.). If you had a bum partner who didn't know how to handle them you broke your God damn neck.

> You never worked fast enough. The boss would come around and he would pressure. "Hey, the hook's hanging." Jack Foster, one boss, would stand there by that port. He'd tap you on the shoulder: "Door six, door seven, door three." Once in a while he'd tap a little too hard.[38]

Tough and unsafe according to Ed Thayne:

> You had a lot more accidents in those days. The companies were so greedy and hoggish that they wanted to get every ounce of energy and blood out of you that they could. If you were hurt it didn't mean anything to them. I got hurt several

---

36. Harvey Schwartz, *Solidarity Stories: An Oral History of the ILWU*, 65 (Seattle: Univ. of Washington Press, 2009).
37. Henry Gaitan, *The ILWU Story*, 6, (2004).
38. Elmer Mevert, in Harvey Schwartz, *Ibid.* at 66 (Seattle: Univ. of Washington Press, 2009).

times myself. You'd go down in the hold—you never heard of a safety net before the 1934 strike. The boss just said, "There's the cargo, you work it." A lot of men got hurt because they didn't have something to protect them from falling, or to keep falling objects from hitting them.[39]

Safety conditions and hiring conditions were intensely interrelated. Protesting unsafe loads or slings or undermanned hatches brought immediate dismissal. For every job lost another man waited to step in because the shape-up was in theory open to anyone who showed up. There was no equalization of work or limitation of workers chosen to membership in any organization but the Blue Book. The Blue Book insured both oversupply and casualization of work, and that effectively prevented either independent organization or ability to protest.

The impetus to challenge the Blue Book company union began in 1933 with the staged reduction of wages from 90 cents an hour for hold work and 80 cents for dock work, to a flat 50 cents for all work, no overtime. It accelerated with the passage of the NIRA in 1933 with its section 7a guarantee of the right to organize a union. Harry Hines, President of the Marine Workers Industrial Union, and later first editor of the Waterfront Worker, and Communist Party organizer Sam Darcy, with fellows Emmet Kirby, Jim Branch, and Elmer Hanoff, started making union speeches each morning by the shape-up. They were soon introduced to longshoremen interested in a union, Harry Bridges, Harry Schmidt, Henry Shrimpf, and others. Bridges and the other organizers were determined not to be whipsawed in the manner of past strikes, when longshoremen had struck separately from the seamen, and/or port by port. Bridges also insisted on seeking an ILA charter.

Voice[40]

If conditions generated maritime worker grievances and unfocused demand for change, and Section 7a of the NIRA encouraged organization, mobilization depended upon shared information and vocalization. This crucial role was largely undertaken by a monthly, then bimonthly, mimeographed newspaper, The *Waterfront Worker*. Before the East Coast based International Longshoremen's Association granted a new West Coast charter in 1933, The Communist Party, under Sam Darcy, and the Communist Marine Workers International Union were the only active organizations to challenge the Company Blue-Book Union on the San Francisco docks. In December 1932, the MWIU started the mimeographed newspaper, *Waterfront Worker*, distributing it on the docks for 1 cent per issue. Soon it had circulation of from 1,000 to 2,000, and a much larger readership,[41] copies were passed hand to hand, and family to family.

The initial issue focused on the employer speed-up and the unwillingness of the Blue Book to challenge dock conditions. It also started a practice that was to cement its credibility among workers over time—publishing factual accounts of employer abuses communicated anonymously by workers, not just in San Francisco but in all West and East Coast ports. This circulation immediately communicated to all dockworkers that their own experiences were not isolated or unusual. Early issues highlighted MWIU actions and encouraged membership, but the greatest urging was for individual workers to secretly agree with fellow gang members to mutually support each other on every dock. Such in-

---

39. Ed Thayne, *supra* note 17, at 6.

40. The term "Voice" is used explicitly to distinguish the contemporary statements and writings of workers from the idea of "Discourse" or "Text" subject to long after the fact deconstructions by post-modernist "readers."

41. Mike Quin, *supra* note 5, at 39.

cipient networking created a base for future organization and to support job resistance against boss control. Issue 5 did reject the I.W.W. as being dead, and the new I.L.A. Local as dominated by conservative absentee leadership, and Issue 6 called for representatives to be sent to the MWIU convention in New York. Early criticism of the paper stemmed from its printing of articles on the Mooney case, the 1919 failed strike, international munitions shipments, and trustified industries—in short, failing to devote space to purely local and dockworker issues. But overall it was a hit from the beginning, "it spoke in terms that the guys couldn't help respect. It was their language."[42]

In July, 1933, beginning with Issue 7, the writing and distribution of the paper was shared and then given up by the MWIU under unclear circumstances, to a new group of rank and file workers. In Spring, 1933, Sam Darcy had collected a small group of rank and file dockworkers that would eventually grow to more than fifty as a study/discussion group on labor history and labor policy. The group came to be known as the Albion Hall group after their meeting place. Whatever Darcy's intent, the group early became autonomous and non-sectarian and was immediately led by dockworker and former seaman Harry Bridges. Albion Hall took over the *Waterfront Worker*, Bridges later acknowledging that it was written by himself, Henry Schmidt, John Schoemaker, and B.B. Jones (only Schoemaker was a Party member) among other contributors. Bruce Nelson argues:

> The key to the Albion Hall group's growing success was not only the quality of its leadership, but also the fact that its program expressed the needs of the stevedores and was based on an accurate assessment of the waterfront's harsh realities. The Main thrust of its program aimed at establishing a democratic union structure and an active, militant union presence on the job. The caucus insisted that the ILA's officials should be "men from the waterfront, whom we know well," and that the local should elect a large executive board, with representation from the various docks, "so that the organization will remain in our hands and be kept from the control of a few officials." The caucus also called for the building of dock committees at each workplace so that the union could assist the men in defending their interests on the job."[43]

Starting with Issue 7, the tone and content changed substantially. While the MWIU was occasionally mentioned thereafter, the content shifted almost entirely to the ILA. In part this made sense as the MWIU never achieved more than a couple thousand members, mostly seamen, while by mid-1933, thousands of dockworkers were signing up with the ILA and deserting the Blue Book—nearly 95% shifted to the ILA.[44] From the first page of the issue, the *Waterfront Worker* attacked the appointed leadership of the West Coast Local 38-79, "Like the rest of the stevedores we have signed up in the I.L.A. and paid the 50 c. Like the rest of the stevedores we are fed up with the B.B. and have organized to finally smash it. It is now up to us to make the new union a real fighting weapon of the stevedores able and ready to win better wages and working conditions and to protect all our interests. To do this we ourselves must take control of our organization."[45] The *Waterfront Worker* demanded:

1) A meeting of all men who have signed up be immediately called.

2) That at this meeting the following be done:

    a) A chairman be elected from the floor to insure fair hearing to all.

---

42. Bruce Nelson, "Unions and the Popular Front," *supra* note 21, at 63.
43. Bruce Nelson, *supra* note 2, at 124.
44. Samuel Yellen, *American Labor Struggles: 1877–1934*, 828 (New York: Monad Press, 1936).
45. *Waterfront Worker*, Vol. 1, #7, 1 (July 1933).

b)   The men elect their own officials—these should be stevedores well known to the men on the docks.

c)   That an Executive Board of 24 to 30 be nominated and elected from the floor, its members representing the different docks. Such a board should be made up of trusted rank and file stevedores from the docks.

d)   That this board be instructed to take care of the negotiations with the ship owners and to report to the membership. Men elected by the stevedores themselves should handle the funds and all affairs of the organization. Those are not only our interests but the interests of every other stevedore. We call on them for their cooperation and support in carrying those steps out.[46]

Attention was not limited to the new union local. A typical letter of standard fare reported: "Cushion Foot Olsen at pier 40, McCormick S.S. Co., was out the other day to hire two men. There were some sixty stevedores there and he milled through them for some time before he could make a choice. He would remind you of a stock buyer. The only difference was he didn't feel the muscles or look at the teeth."[47]

In the August 1, 1933, issue, the new editors attacked the Local leadership of the ILA, objecting to President Holman's policy of going to the local Labor Disputes Board seeking reinstatement of discharged members of the ILA (which the Board refused because a shipping code had not been adopted and by holding the Blue Book to be a legitimate union under the N.R.A.). The paper called for direct action on the dock where a discharge occurred, and electing new Local officials. This issue also announces that the local AF of L Rank & File Committee for Unemployment Insurance called for delegates to a national convention in Cleveland. The editors hailed, "The united front proposes a program for struggle for (1) Immediate and substantial wage increases in all industries and for all workers; (2) A fight against all attempts to put over wage reductions under the guise of a minimum wage program; (3) Struggle against relief cuts, evictions, foreclosures, and gas, water and light shutoffs; (4) Against forced labor camps, commissary relief plans, and for payment in cash at full union scale on all public works; and for Federal Social and Unemployment Insurance."[48]

Beginning bi-weekly publication August 15, the *Waterfront Worker* urged attending the Local meeting, electing a meeting chair from the floor, electing new Local officers, electing an executive board of around 24, building dock committees, and immediately developing action against the Blue Book. Now the demands were not just new work conditions, job security, and wages, but also rank and file organization and control of the burgeoning I.L.A. Local. Reports of course continued about conditions—water cans used during breaks were rusted, surfaced with scum, and occasionally contained rats. Safety conditions on the S.S. Brookings provided two ladders for four hatches and no internal bulkheads. At the election September 1, Holman comfortably won the Presidency and old-line leaders all the offices, but Albion Hall won 18 of the 35 executive committee slots.[49]

Rank and file organization turned to direct action September 14 at the Matson Dock. Workers refused to show their Blue Books and were discharged. The Dockworkers walked out and built a bonfire out of their Blue Books. Matson conceded in order to unload the ship. Days later Matson fired four workers who could not provide their books. At this

---

46. *Ibid.* at 2.
47. *Ibid.* at 4.
48. *Waterfront Worker*, 6 (August 1, 1933).
49. Ottilie Markholt, *supra* note 4, at 58.

point while Holman got nowhere with the Company, Harry Bridges asserted leadership of the Matson dockworkers in October, organizing a walkout of the Matson Dock. Replacements feared to cross picket lines and ships were tied up. Matson was forced to accept I.L.A. members and arbitrate the discharges.

Thus, at the same moment, not only did the *Waterfront Worker* encourage direct action by describing a successful event, but it tied Local leadership ineffectuality to inexperience and corruption, in stark contrast to Bridges' working reputation as one of the boys. It also tied strikebreaking to unemployment encouragement of greenhorns and to company recruiting at city relief offices. Casualization and lack of unemployment insurance made strikebreaking feasible if inefficient. Conditions in general and on the docks enabled discrimination against an independent union beyond mere anti-union animus of the Companies. It became clear to dock workers that change depended on mobilized direct action by the rank and file.

Union officials reacted in alarm, "Lund [ship owner] complained that Green and other AF of L officials could not control the rank and file members, saying 'It is clear that a great deal of the organizing effort and agitation resulting from it is the work of men, some of them of very radical beliefs, who pay little attention to those leaders nominally representing them.'"[50]—an admission that the actions were carried out by the workers themselves.

At the same time rank and file leaders made a crucial move to make direct action effective by forestalling strikebreaking by an experienced group important in breaking the 1919 strike: from a letter to the editor by a Negro Stevedore,

> "What is the I.L.A. going to do for the Negroes? If they are going to be a real union why don't they take away the wedge of the bosses which is the Negro longshoremen? The Negro demands are that they should not be discriminated against under any circumstances; that they should carry the same load, the same hours, and the same pay. The gangs should be mixed up, and the Negroes should be allowed to work at all docks instead of just two." The editor's reply, "This stevedore is right. The S.F. stevedores must take warning from past experiences both here in San Francisco, and in other ports, where the Negro stevedores were used to break strikes on the waterfront. There is but one way out. The Negroes must not be discriminated against. They must be mixed with the white gangs, and be given the same opportunities. They must be organized with the white stevedores or else we shall see another 1919 fiasco."[51]

Worker racial unity and social wage insurance were key planks of the Communist Party organizational efforts, and pushed more forcefully by it than by other groups such as the still voluntarist AFL, but these issues were *also* key for organizing the docks against real abuses of safety, security, and wage leverage—non-denominational worker issues if you will.

News of direct resistance appeared from Everett, Washington, the *Waterfront Worker* being exported to other West Coast ports. Action there led to rotational work assignments, spreading depression effects on employment. In the November 1 issue, in addition to old demands, the paper added election of rank and file dock committees which could lead immediate protest walkouts and, most importantly that any collective bargaining agreement between the union and management be submitted directly to the membership for vote. Insistence on union democracy became a watchword for I.L.A. recruitment as well as a basis for resisting any imposed settlement.

---

50. *Waterfront Worker*, 2 (October 18, 1933).
51. *Waterfront Worker*, 2 (October 3, 1933).

Decembers' papers attacked the proposed N.R.A. Shipping code for taking away the right to strike, by now a key component of the direct action campaign of the rank and file in the I.L.A. as the effective existence of the Blue Book withered away. A strike vote had been taken in Seattle. On December 18, the speed up was blamed for high rates of early death and disability of stevedores, and linked once again to the demand for a social wage. Every new report mobilized more militancy and response. "Lazy" Longshoreman wrote, "[ILA] let's do something, either insure our lives for a larger sum, so that our families shall not suffer after our departure from this vale of tears, or still better, take it easy, let the hook hang, and spend a few more years on this earth."[52]

The first January issue called for a Coast wide rank and file convention at which no union officers would be allowed. Harry Bridges and Dutch Dietrich were dispatched to build support along the whole Coast.[53] This would pave the way for a key demand. In the event of a strike in any port, a Coast wide agreement with uniform pay and conditions would prevent circumvention by ship owners by shifting port destinations — an extension of the same principle as racial unity. "What we want is a united Pacific coast. We want the entire coast organized solidly behind a fighting program."[54] The paper voiced a Coast wide wage demand of a six hour day, $1. per hour, $1.50 overtime, and a thirty hour week. The death of a dockworker crushed by a runaway load reinforced anger over safety, fueling another Coast wide demand. Longshoremen's wives began writing in support of husbands' militancy and calling for establishing an auxiliary, a white stevedore called for racially mixed gangs.

In February, Stockton dockworkers refused to work with any but I.L.A. members. In San Francisco, a stevedore had his thumb torn off during a boss competition over a speed-up, bypassing load procedures. At the convention, "coastwise" bargaining was extended to a unity call between shore maritime workers and seamen to the chagrin of Seamen's President Andrew Furoseth. The convention endorsed the Worker's Unemployment Insurance Bill introduced in Congress by Ernest Lundeen. The *Waterfront Worker* called on the convention to adopt work rules on speed, load limits, and gang size, coastwise, enforced by direct action.

Following the rank and file convention, action in San Francisco Local 38-79 proceeded to a head. March 12, the local voted for a coast wide strike. Demands coalesced around I.L.A. recognition, coast wide bargaining, six hour day, thirty hour week, $1. Per hour, $1.50 overtime, and equal distribution of work under a union hiring hall (effectively a closed shop).

Preparations for a strike were proposed: legal defense for arrests, relief support for families, paid up dues, talking against strikebreaking, and most importantly turning dock committees into a de-facto rank and file organization to control the strike. Preparations provided a glimpse into the effect of the shape up on families. In response to a longshore wife, "I am ready and willing to take my place alongside my husband on the picket line and in the fight for relief or in any way in which I can help," the Editor wrote, "Wives have had to suffer thru the system of keeping longshoremen waiting around for hours awaiting orders when to report at work. This system has been very beneficial to the liquor sellers as many longshoremen while waiting are tempted to drink & spend perhaps most of their wages. Another good reason why we must Win our demands for job control and hiring from the I.L.A. hall."[55]

---

52. *Waterfront Worker*, 5 (December 18, 1933).
53. David F. Selvin, *supra* note 3, at 68.
54. *Waterfront Worker*, 2 (January 4, 1934).
55. *Waterfront Worker*, 4 (March 22, 1934).

At a request from President Roosevelt, the strike was postponed to allow for federal mediation. The *Waterfront Worker* immediately warned against a proposed joint ship owner-union hiring hall. Local President Holman left San Francisco after outrage against his proposed mediation led to his suspension by the membership, and ironically Holman became the first prominent personage to publicly brand the radicalizing rank and file as Communist led—a theme gleefully seized upon by the ship owners and their Industrial Association. The owners also wanted to recognize minority unions in order to prop up the Blue Book. The paper called for boycotting lunch wagons being set up in anticipation of feeding strikebreakers. It was clear that the paper would be crucial to disseminating information during the strike. The difficulty was its bi-weekly schedule. The Communist Party daily, the *Western Worker*, would inevitably turn out to be the source of information on fast moving events as the City's established newspapers became practically a tool of the owners and business elite, but it was the *Waterfront Worker* that continued to be smuggled by seamen along the entire Pacific Coast.

By the beginning of May, it was clear that mediation would satisfy neither side with a union controlled hiring hall the largest dividing point. Nonetheless, the Pacific Coast I.L.A. President Lewis urged acceptance of the mediation proposal. Harry Bridges methodically revealed the drawbacks before a final Local meeting and the proposal was rejected with Lewis backing down and nominally supporting the strike. The strike began May 9 in San Francisco. Portland simultaneously voted down the mediation and voted to strike.

The first issue of the paper after the strike's inception, began listing I.L.A. or regular stevedores that were scabbing. A strike committee was established by Local 38-79 controlled by the rank and file, insisting on no ending of the strike without membership vote. On June 12, the *Waterfront Worker* broached consideration of a general strike on the West Coast, amid signs from San Pedro that Local leadership there was undermining picketing, admittedly given great geographical difficulties there. San Francisco Police began limiting picketing effectiveness by removing it from pier entrances. May 30, was dubbed Laceration Day as Police began beating massed pickets. Citizens were arrested for disturbing the peace when walking singly in the area of the Embarcadero. Shoring up picketing became the main theme in the paper.

The rank and file membership became further alienated when the President of the ILA, Joe Ryan, arrived to take over negotiation with the owners, bypassing the rank and file negotiating delegation. Ryan's agreement June 16 was in direct violation of the I.L.A. constitution which granted autonomy to the West Coast District over agreements. Ryan was hooted off the stage when he tried to defend it at the Local 38-79 meeting following, his proposal rejected in secret ballot by 2,404 to 78. Other ports followed suit. A Joint Strike Committee, headed by Bridges, was constituted by five delegates from each of the ten maritime unions on strike. A similar Northwest Joint Strike Committee had been set up based in Seattle, but representing all Washington ports, operated by rank and file democratic ratification of all committee decisions. The rank and file leadership could thus somewhat reasonably be defended from attack by Labor's national leadership and the San Francisco Central Labor Union, both labeling the strike as an action by a minority of "reds," further dividing the striking men on the front from outside advice. If anything, given the distaste of official union leadership, the strike itself became more controlled under Bridge's leadership.

After the repression following Bloody Thursday, July 5, the destruction of the paper's offices prevented publication for the remainder of the strike. In the aftermath of the owner's concession of union direction of a jointly observed hiring hall and agreement to arbitrate all wage and conditions issues, The *Waterfront Worker* continued to report dock specific direct actions for safety and against discharges. If anything, the strike taught the rank and file to be more militant on specific grievances. This accompanied a changed mood on the docks — bosses were more careful and workers happier and felt dignified. A wife reported, "Since returning to work after the strike he is a changed man entirely. He seems different and happier, and even finds time to pay a little attention to his wife."[56] Such an impact of changed work conditions — ending shape ups, regular work, limited hours, greater safety and less fear of disability — on the families in the neighborhoods surrounding the Docks cannot be overestimated. The paper opined, "But after returning to work after the strike things are very different, which is as it should be. Whereas before the strike they were beaten, docile and meek, they are now in a very opposite frame of mind. To state that the men are militant and aggressive would be putting it mildly; in fact, it is hard to realize that the same body of men could produce such a change of attitude in their own ranks."[57] Stevedores heaped praise on "our" Harry Bridges as a union leader, dismissing concern over his radical ideas, "He is not too radical for me now. He is a good trade unionist. A Conservative Longshoreman."[58] At the next election Bridges was elected Local 38-79 President.

Strike

The original strike was called for March 1934, but was postponed by the attempt of the federal government and the President of the AFL Longshoreman, East Coast boss Joseph Ryan, to prevent the strike. When mediation failed, the longshore vote Coast wide was 6619 to 599 for the strike. The maritime and longshore unions walked out 100 per cent on May 9, and the strike continued until all unions had agreed to accept arbitration of all issues except the hiring halls, July 31, 1934. May 9, 12,000 longshoremen walked out — 2,000 in Seattle, 3,000 in San Francisco, 1,100 in Portland, 700 in Tacoma, 1,800 in San Pedro, 250 in Everett and Grays Harbor, and uniformly in smaller ports.[59] "The I.L.A. established picket lines at all ports; in San Francisco 1000 men paraded two abreast with the American Flag at the head of their column. Along the three and one half miles of the Embarcadero the corrugated steel gates to the piers slammed shut and electrified barbed wire blocked the entrances. Police patrolled the docks on foot, in radio and cruise cars, on motorcycle, on horseback."[60]

Ship owners used to dealing with complacent union leaders were unprepared for a unified rank and file strike.[61] Harry Bridges said in an interview, "It's because it's a militant strike that we've been successful so far. They can call them radical tactics but whatever they are they work. You get nowhere at all with the good old legal tactics, all this reliance on arbitration, injunctions, letting the scabs work, and so forth. You've got to do it this way — start right in with mass picketing and relief, and hold the respect of the men by doing things and not just sitting around waiting."[62] Ship owners had counted on the Depression's unemployed to break the strike and unload ships. In Portland, ship owners violated state law by advertising for stevedores without indicating the presence of a labor strike — nothing was done but few applied.[63] Although 300 to 500 strikebreakers worked Coast wide, the amount unloaded was insignificant. In San Francisco alone 174 ships lay at anchor. Ship owners were especially surprised when Teamster drivers all along the Coast refused to move "hot cargo"

---

56. *Waterfront Worker*, 5 (September 14, 1934).
57. *Waterfront Worker*, 4 (October 22, 1934).
58. *Waterfront Worker*, 6 (October 15, 1934).
59. Otillie Markholt, *supra* note 4, at 77.
60. Irving Bernstein, *supra* note 6, at 263.
61. Charles P. Larrowe, "The Great Maritime Strike of 1934," 11 *Labor History* 403, 414 (1970).
62. Evelyn Seeley, "San Francisco's Labor War," 138 *Nation* 672, 673 (June 13, 1934).
63. Roger B. Buchanon, *supra* note 16, at 65.

from the docks even where it could be unloaded. The Teamsters rank and file unity and sympathy became a crucial factor in the strike's success, and in generating the later general strike.

During the first few weeks in San Francisco, violence was mostly limited to isolated incidents between strikers and strikebreakers, 150 strikebreakers needing hospital treatment for beatings. "When they captured a scab they employed two techniques: kicking out his teeth and jumping on his leg laid across a curb."[64] Seattle and Portland witnessed more massed action, "in Seattle ... longshoremen routed a squad of special policemen after taking their riot clubs away from them, sending five to the hospital with broken noses and bruised heads."[65] Seattle's tepid union leadership would be stiffened when six hundred Tacoma and several hundred Everett longshoremen formed flying squads to rush to trouble spots. Two thousand men stormed the piers and stopped the unloading of eleven ships worked by strikebreakers.[66] This mass action became known as "Gauntlet Day" in the Northwest and insured that Seattle would remain substantially closed for the duration of the strike. "In Portland one day twenty-five would be strike-breakers were thrown into the Willamette River."[67] Across the Bay from San Francisco, in Oakland, four hundred strikers drove police from the piers and fought with 72 strikebreakers.[68] But even in the more initially peaceful San Francisco, the first encounter with the police occurred the third day of the strike, May 12, in front of the "Fink hall." "One of the Strikers cried out, "'Stand your ground men! This is a public street! We have a right to stand here!' Immediately he was seized upon by several police and clubbed. Then the battle started in earnest as strikers resisted police clubs with sticks and stones"[69] (throughout the strike these were the only "deadly weapons" used by the strikers). On the other hand, the Waterfront Employers Association paid for more than $100,000. worth of tear and vomiting gas, clubs, and machine and riot guns, in arming the San Francisco Police.[70]

One of Bridges initial organizing group, Henry Schmidt, noted that the police violence against the strike had existed from very early in the strike. On May 28, 800 men formed a march from the International Longshoremen's headquarters to pier #46 and return. John Shoemaker marched between flag bearers of the U.S. and ILA flags.

> Opposite pier #18, as the marchers were swinging onto the sidewalk they were attacked by policemen on horseback, the flag bearers were ridden down, their flags knocked to the street. Shoemaker was singled out by the police. Three or four cops held him while another on horseback beat him over the head with a club for about four or five minutes, until Shoemaker sank to the sidewalk. He then was arrested for inciting a riot. His face and head were a mask of blood.

> Simultaneously, police appeared from all directions and promptly started beating and shooting with revolvers and gas bombs. Bill Christensen, another member of the ILA, was kicked by a police horse and had his head badly beaten in the bargain.... Alfonso Metzgar, a pedestrian who happened to get caught in the maelstrom, was shot through the back in front of the ILA Hall by a policeman.

---

64. Irving Bernstein, *supra* note 6, at 264.
65. *Ibid.* at 422.
66. Bruce Nelson, *supra* note 2, at 129.
67. Evelyn Seeley, *supra* note 64, at 672.
68. Bruce Nelson, *supra* note 2, at 129.
69. *Ibid.* at 9.
70. David F. Selvin, *supra* note 3, at 103.

He has recovered but was also arrested for inciting a riot. He has had two jury trials, the jury disagreeing each time.[71]

May 30th became know as Laceration Day (Decoration Day). Hundreds of injuries occurred after arrest, strikers were routinely Third Degreed on the third floor of the local police substation. Gas guns fired at strikers were discharged close to workers already held by police in order to burn and disfigure their arms and legs. Strikers were arrested for kidnapping on the theory that they were kidnapping the police who threw them in the Black Mariahs in which the workers were being beaten. The law was certainly deployed against the strike, by direct action against the workers.

The precipitate action was taken July 1, 1934, when the shippers announced the port was open and cargo would begin to move, July 3. When the day came, 3,000 workers formed a massed solid wall and no trucks moved. A manager of an employer warehouse admitted that a few trucks later in the day held negligible cargo and were "intended to bring the whole matter to a head. Which it sure as heck did."[72] At 1:27, the pier doors opened,

> the crowd surged forward. Barrages of tear gas opened the way for the trucks. The police moved on the crowd, nightsticks flailing. Slowly, the crowd fell back, breaking into smaller, rock throwing clusters, fleeing in retreat. Sounds of revolver and riot guns echoed over the clash. Pickets fell back to 2nd and Brannon streets, some to Townsend. Bricks and stray bullets crashed windows; one stray bullet penetrated a window of the American Trust Co. at 3rd and Townsend streets, wounding a teller.[73]

The July 4 holiday was dormant. July fifth a war began, the battle of Rincon Hill.

> Seizing upon every object they could find in nearby lots, the pickets threw up a hasty barricade at the foot of Rincon Hill. It did not hold long.

> Royce Brier, *Chronicle* reporter, described: "Then DeGuire's men, about twenty of them, unlimbered from Main and Harrison and fired at random up the hill. The down-plunging mob halted, hesitated, and started scrambling up the hill again: Here the first man fell, a curious bystander. The gunfire fell away. Up came the tear gas boys, six or eight carloads of them. They hopped out with their gasmasks on, and the gas guns laid down a barrage on the hillside. The hillside spouted blue gas like the valley of the Ten Thousand Smokes. Up the hill went the moppers-up, phalanxes of policemen with drawn revolvers. The strikers backed sullenly away on Harrison Street, past Fremont Street. Suddenly came half a dozen carloads of men from the Bureau of Inspectors, and right behind them a truckload of shotguns and ammunition."

> Firing their revolvers and swinging their long riot sticks, the police charged up the hill, driving the men before them up the steep, grassy slope. The tinkling of glass sounded as bullets crashed through the windows of residences at the top, sending inhabitants screaming to the streets. . . .

> Gas and gunfire at last drove the pickets back into the city. Police took command of the hill and surrounded it with guards to prevent recapture.[74]

---

71. Henry Schmidt, "San Francisco Maritime Strike Statement" 1934, at 1, I.L.W.U. Archive.
72. David F. Selvin, *supra* note 3, at 146.
73. *Ibid.* at 144.
74. Mike Quin, *supra* note 5, at 112.

On Bloody Thursday, Henry Schmidt described the scene at the ILA Hall following the deaths, and the day long battle for Rincon Hill.

> Whenever the strikers congregated in groups of five or six, they would be shelled with tear gas bombs which would cause them to run from the poisonous smoke. Police with rifles and buckshot guns would then shoot them in the back....
>
> A sorry scene was being enacted inside the Union Hall. A Doctor was treating the wounded men who were lying on the floor, when a policeman fired a gas shell directly into the Union Hall, making it impossible for the doctor to go on with his work of helping the wounded men. The policemen at the door of the hall would allow no one to leave, compelling everyone to stay in the gas filled headquarters, including a young lady employed by the ILA as a stenographer,[75]

Bloody Thursday as witnessed by a *striker*:

> Y' wanna know how these two guys were shot, eh? Well, it was damned simple. The cops were shooting at us since 9 in the morning. Thirty-two were wounded that day besides the two who were killed. And all we had to fight back with was rocks we could find in the empty lots around the Embarcadero and the ILA headquarters.
>
> The whole business started when a crowd of us came around to picket the Matson dock in the morning. The cops didn't let us get any further than the land side of the Embarcadero, across the street from the docks. Some of us started up the next street going away from the docks. Then the cops drove around and met us at the next corner. Before every damned shooting, new outburst, I mean, the movie cars would come up front, like the cops were giving the movie boys a scoop.
>
> As soon as the cops got to the corner one of them shouted out "All right, give it to the bastards." Then they shot tear gas into the crowd and rode into us on horses and swinging their clubs and nightsticks. A lot of us ran into the freight yards and threw rocks at them and tried to hide behind the cars.
>
> Some of the cops chased us back into the yards, shooting the whole time, like they meant to kill every damn one of us. A lot of the men were wounded there. The rest of us were plenty scared too, especially when we didn't have a rock in our hands to throw at one of those husky bastards. But when we were throwing things and mad as hell it wasn't bad; we didn't have time to be scared.
>
> Well the fighting went on like that for hours and hours it seemed like. We were moving along the whole time and we finally got to the ILA hall. We were on Stuart near Mission and the cops were near Howard. We would get bricks in the empty lot across the street from the hall where they were building a gas station, run towards the cops, hiding behind cars the whole time, throw our bricks, and then run back for more ammunition.
>
> After a while a cop's car came around to the northwest corner of Stuart and Mission—(there were hundreds of people just standing there and watching)—one cop got out and shot these guys, one after the other. Christ, did they bleed. A crowd collected around the men and then the cops came running over and yelled "Get back you sons of bitches or you'll get the same thing." Then a lot of movie and news-

---

75. Henry Schmidt, *supra* note 68, at 3.

papermen came around taking pictures and things, and it was about 20 minutes before they took the guys to the hospital. And you know the rest,—they both died.[76]

In fact, striker Olsen survived. But the deliberate killing of Howard Sperry, and later Henry Bordoise, a block away, were not the only staged violence of the police. Four men at least eventually died from the police assault on Bloody Thursday, tens more would never work again. An affidavit taken by the City and County of San Francisco from James A. Duggar was equally graphic in describing the tear gas shot to the head of James Engle (Engel suffered a fractured skull and brain damage).

I am a resident of San Francisco and a member of Local 38-79, International Longshoremen's Association.

On July 5, 1934, I was an eyewitness to the series of events on the Embarcadero at San Francisco which culminated in the disabling of James Engle. I was among the group of strikers who were driven down the Embarcadero from the neighborhood of Rincon Hill by police gassing. We passed piers 22, 20, and 18 and then in order to escape the gas fumes, some of us took refuge in a liquor store on the Embarcadero opposite pier 18, which we knew as Nealon's. Nealon's is located on the west side of Embarcadero between Folsom and Howard, next door to the Seaboard Hotel, on the north side of the hotel. As many of the strikers as were able took refuge in the shops along the west side of the Embarcadero. The Seaboard Hotel in particular was crowded with refugee strikers.

As a result of the gassing the Embarcadero was clear for several blocks south of Howard Street. I can safely state that there was not a single striker on the Embarcadero between Folsom and Howard streets. From my position in Nealon's store, I was able to see what was going on in the street. I saw three men come down the Embarcadero from south to north, equipped with long range tear gas guns. One of these men was a uniformed policeman. The other two were in civilian clothes. One of them wore a brown suit and the other a gray suit. I believe the man in the brown suit was Sergeant McInerny of the San Francisco police department, at least he was pointed out to me as Sergeant McInerny. The man in the gray suit was short and dark and was referred to by everybody as the "Federal man." He had been engaged in gassing on the waterfront on previous days. Accompanying these men was a truck bearing a motion picture cameraman with motion picture equipment. The three men stopped almost directly across from the Seaboard Hotel and the truck stopped a few yards north on the Embarcadero. The three men previously referred to then went over on the sidewalk on the East side of the Embarcadero, loaded their guns and put on gas masks. They then came in to the street and took positions parallel to each other with the man in the brown suit on the south side, the federal man in the center, and the uniformed policeman on the north. The three of them then raised their guns and pointed in the direction of the Seaboard Hotel. They fired and one of the shells went through the window of the Seaboard Hotel and exploded among the strikers and spectators gathered in the lobby. I am absolutely certain that at this time the Embarcadero was clear of strikers and spectators.

Immediately after the shot through the window of the hotel, I saw James Engle, a member of the International Longshoremen's Association, whom we always

---

76. "Description of Two Strikers Shot on May 5th, 1934, Near International Longshoremen's Association Headquarters, No. 902, July, 1934, I.L.W.U. Archives.

called "Kentucky", appear on the sidewalk in front of the hotel, step off the sidewalk and walk along the south side of a Chevrolet coupe which was parked diagonally in front of the hotel, put his foot on the running board of the car and peer around it into the street. It seemed to me as if he was looking to see whether the officers had left the scene. I am not sure whether Engle came out of the Seaboard Hotel on account of the presence of gas inside, or whether he came from, Steuart Street through the lot adjoining the hotel on the south side. At any rate Engle was the only striker in the street at the moment. As Engle stuck his head around the side of the car one of the three men previously referred to aimed his gas weapon directly at Engle and fired, the shell striking "Kentucky" on the right side of the head. "Kentucky" was knocked down into the street. He half rose to his feet, felt the side of his head with his hand, looked at the blood and then collapsed. His arms and legs flapped like a chicken whose head had been cut off. I thought to myself, "Will, I guess "Kentucky" is gone." Engle laid there several minutes and then some fellow rushed out of the Seaboard Hotel and picked him up.

Although I did not see which of the three men actually shot the shell which struck Engle, I am almost certain from the respective positions of the three that the shell was discharged by the man in the gray suit whom we knew as the Federal man. The position in which these men were standing were such that only the man in the gray suit could have fired the shot which struck Engle on the right side of his head.

I knew "Kentucky" pretty well. It is absurd to state that he was a Communist. As his nickname would indicate, he was from Kentucky. I know to a certainty that "Kentucky" never had any contact with the radical labor groups on the waterfront or elsewhere. He was a loyal union man and a member of the International Longshoremen's Association in good standing, but it is utterly untrue the he was a communist.

I want to conclude this statement by saying that in my opinion the action of this group of three men in firing those shells was absolutely unjustified. There was no commotion or disturbance at the time whatever. There was no crowd of men in the street and positively no demonstration going on. The only explanation which seems to me to make sense is that the whole thing was staged for the benefit of the motion picture camera. My belief is based on experience of many years as a motion picture operator and I know how valuable a negative of this type would be. From the position of the cameraman and from the fact that he was cranking away throughout the shooting, I would say that the whole thing had the appearance of a put-up job.[77]

When World War veteran Howard Sperry was killed, the ILA mimeoed a broadside calling attention to what was now the moral equivalent of a crusade.

On the fifth day of July, Howard S. Sperry's duty is in the relief kitchen on the Embarcadero — helping to feed his brother pickets. The Lunch hour is over. The pickets have been fed — and it is now time for him to go over to ILA headquarters at 113 Steuart Street to have his strike card punched.

WITHIN FIFTY FEET OF HEADQUARTERS DEATH STRUCK AT HOWARD S. SPERRY, DEATH DEALT OUT BY ORDERS OF THE SHIP OWNERS AND THE INDUSTRIAL ASSOCIATION. DEATH TO FORCE HIM TO GO BACK

---

77. James A. Duggar, Affidavit: City and County of San Francisco, State of California, February, 1937, I.L.W.U. Archives.

TO WORK—AND ARBITRATE. DEATH FROM THE HANDS OF A PO-LICEMAN GONE MAD!

HOWARD SPERRY'S STRIKE CARD NEEDS PUNCHING NO MORE!

HIS DUTY IS DONE—HIS STRIKE CARD IS FILED AWAY.... A MARTYR TO THE CAUSE OF LABOR.

BUT WE—THE LONGSHOREMEN OF SAN FRANCISCO—TOGETHER WITH OUR BROTHERS IN OTHER PORTS—WE WILL PUNCH THE STRIKE CARD OF OUR BROTHER. WE WILL ANSWER THE MURDEROUS S.F. IN-DUSTRIAL ASSOCIATION AND THE SHIPOWNERS BY BUIDING OUR UNION STRONGER THAN EVER! BY WINNING OUR STRIKE! WE—AND SHALL—WIN FOR THE WORKERS ON THE WATERFRONT—AND FOR THE REST OF THE WORKERS AS WELL—THE THINGS FOR WHICH HOWARD S. SPERRY STRUCK—AND DIED! A DECENT ILA CONTROLLED HIRING HALL—AND AN END TO THE ROTTEN COMPANY UNION SYSTEM WHICH HAS HELD US IN PEONAGE FOR FOURTEEN YEARS.[78]

As a result of the wanton police killing of two men on Bloody Thursday, July 5, 1934, the Governor called in the National Guard ostensibly to stop striker violence. In contrast, early in May, the Portland Central Labor Council forestalled any call up of the National Guard by promising a general strike if the Oregon Governor did so there.

Two days later, Portland Police shot four strikers in the back from a flat car preceding a train opening the port. Outraged strikers broke into City Council proceedings waiving the bloody shirt of one of the wounded calling for the police chief's dismissal—the Council voted yes, the Mayor refused. A week later, special police fired on a car containing Senator Robert Wagner who was attempting to mediate—the Senator left Portland.[79] The first strikers to die were Dick Parker and John Knudsen shot by special police in San Pedro, May 15, during an attack on a strikebreakers' camp. In Tacoma, May 30, police shot Shelvy Daffron in the back, he later died, and in Seattle, July 10, John Bateman died of his police inflicted gunshot wounds (under orders to shoot to kill). Coastwise, at least nine strikers died. Hundreds were shot or bayoneted, usually in the back. Thousands were arrested.

In a massive funeral march for Howard Sperry and Henry Bordoise in San Francisco, July 9, 30,000 workers marched, a procession over a mile in length. The marchers were silent, heads bared, only the cadence of the feet of the thousands of workers. Hundreds of thousands lined the sidewalk in hushed awe. "They were lonely plain working people, thousands and thousands and thousands of them, sober and resolute, marching in ranks to bury their dead."[80] It was the climax of the strike. No one, not even ship owners, doubted the inevitability of a general strike. Called for July 16, it lasted until July 20, 1934.

Coordination problems for a general strike were prominent. Commercial news was saturated with anti-strike propaganda and red-hunts. Twice the mainstream newspapers proclaimed the strike over, without foundation. The only devices of mass communication for the strikers were out of a broken down mimeograph at strike headquarters, and the *Waterfront Worker*. The general strike itself was ridden with exceptions for public welfare and safety, but over 70,000 marine workers in the Bay area walked out during it. In

---

78. Joint Strike Committee Broadside, I.L.W.U. Archives, 1934.
79. Roger B. Buchanon, *supra* note 16, at 78–79.
80. Robert Cantwell, "San Francisco: Act One," *New Republic*, 280 (July 25, 1934).

a population of approximately 600,000, 250,000 workers stopped work.[81] During the general strike, San Francisco, the city, closed. The public responded, "In addition to the economic pressure provided by the closing of the port, the public felt the social pressure provided by the killings which underscored the affiliation of the police and the state and local governments with the [Waterfront Employers Association.]"[82]

The general strike itself, always under the control of the less than sympathetic Central Labor Council, collapsed after four days. "As long as the strike had been one of seamen and longshoremen the militant group led by Harry Bridges had been in control. When the strike became general, control automatically passed into the hands of the reactionary leaders of the Central Labor Council, and the militant group became a minority opposition ..."[83] The maritime strike went on in force for three more weeks.

Beatings, buckshot, and arrests happened everyday. But the strike hurt the owners too. They were losing $110,000 per day, with 174 ships tied up in San Francisco, and half a million per day coast wide. During the general strike, the San Francisco economy suffered a 65% loss.[84]

The strike forced the arbitration panel set up by President Roosevelt to actually deal with the union demands. Wages were raised to 95 cents per hour, maximum six-hour days, thirty hours per week, joint safety committees that could stop work upon union demand, and effective union control of hiring halls were the result. It would take another strike in 1936, forced by the shipping lines, to keep these gains.

In the end, the strike's effectiveness depended on work and planning and the community: 1. The ability of rank and file organization making possible flying squads to quickly identify meetings and threats to disrupt the resolve of all the maritime unions to stay out until all settled. 2. The Longshoremen lived close to their jobs, the strike and its violence was in the community itself. Fathers and sons fought the vigilante, and police outsiders. 3. The union provided strict duties and food and shelter as if it were supplying troops. Wives, daughters, sisters tended their wounded and manned the commissaries and emergency support for families. The I.L.W.U. has files of hundreds of receipt records for food for families of strikers injured in the battles and unable to shop or buy, clothes and milk for infants, furniture or housing for families evicted from apartments because of a striker in the family group. Each receipt also recorded the striker's role in the strike, and the reason they or their family were now in desperate need. It was a community solidarity and experience that could be galvanized with confidence again in 1936 as the ship owners refused to comply with the arbitration award ending the 34 strike.

Black dockworkers, segregated to one dock, at first were assumed to be anti union but were persuaded to walk out and join the ILA mid-strike. Women were actively recruited in the first month of the strike as logistics became necessary,

TO WIVES, DAUGHTERS & FRIENDS OF ILA MEMBERS

The ship owners are determined not to grant us the closed shop and union hiring hall. This means a fight to the finish until we secure union conditions. It may result in a long drawn battle.

---

81. Richard O. Boyer and Herbert M. Morais, *Labor's Untold Story*, 287 (New York: United Electrical, Radio & Machine Workers of America, 1977).

82. Anne A. Mini, "The San Francisco Maritime and General Strikes of 1934: A Rank and File Movement for Social and Economic Independence." 120 (Thesis, Dept. of Social Studies, Harvard/Radcliffe College, 1988).

83. Robert Cantwell, "War on the West Coast: I. The Gentlemen of San Francisco," *New Republic*, 310 (August 1, 1934).

84. David F. Selvin, *supra* note 3, at 213.

OUR WIVES, DAUGHTERS AND FRIENDS MUST BECOME MORE ACTIVE IN SUPPORTING THE STRIKE.

We are therefore starting a WOMAN'S AUXILLARY to help us secure the widest support for relief.[85]

Law as Police

Ella Winter reported during the midpoint of the strike, that in such circumstances, red-baiting had little credibility when all strike leaders were so labeled and "arrested on charges of vagrancy, kidnapping, robbery, assault and battery, and held on bail as high as $1,000 (which is fairly obvious no longshoreman can afford). Several hundred are in jail. One man found with 7 cents in his pocket, was arrested for robbery." Winter linked police action to fomenting political radicalism:

> To sum up, this strike seems to be a showdown between two cultures. Is labor a commodity or is it a mass of working human beings who have rights? To call the latter idea communism and thus dispose of it is no longer a sufficient answer — not even to the "conservative" rank-and-file members of a "legitimate" American labor union.[86]

During the strike in San Francisco, over 900 persons were arrested in connection with the strike.[87] In San Pedro, another 500 were arrested.[88] Virtually all union members were arrested in the vicinity of the docks, picketing or in street gatherings to hear news of the strike. Of the total in San Francisco, 402 were I.L.A. members, 346 of which had their cases dismissed, 4 were sentenced and 28 fined, 24 ended after a demand for jury trial. There seems little substance to the continuous propaganda of the Industrial Association of anarchy, armed violence by strikers, or property damage, justifying the violent police repression, shootings, and occupation by state militia. Five strikers were arrested under the gun laws, compared with twenty odd strikebreakers. I.L.A. members were charged for violations of anti-handbill ordinances (21), anti-picketing ordinances (18), assault (60), assault with deadly weapons (28), assault with intent to commit murder (2), contempt of court (1), disturbing the peace (199), gun law (5), injuries to railroads (6), kidnapping (3), malicious mischief (8), motor vehicle theft (1), robbery (7), resisting an officer (5), riot (15), vagrancy (23). The four sentences, three of which were suspended, included one each for assault, contempt of court, disturbing the peace, and riot. The total of all fines assessed reached $335. Despite claims of strikers initiating violence no one was convicted of resisting an officer, and of the 199 arrests for disturbing the peace, virtually half of all arrests, 196 were dismissed! Only two strike leaders, Henry Schmidt, a Socialist, and John Shoemaker, an admitted Communist, were arrested and later released. Clearly legal power was primarily employed not against the strike as such, but against the strikers, in order to get them off the streets, and held largely without access to others, and in miserably overcrowded conditions. Strike leadership and organization were unaffected but the strike was somewhat less effective because of the numbers jailed and their length of incarceration without judicial process. However, the chief effect of the arrests was to further radicalize

---

85. Broadside, I.L.W.U. Archives, 1934.

86. Ella Winter, "Stevedores on Strike," *New Republic* 122 (June 13, 1934).

87. Strike statistics are taken from Herbert Resner, "The Law in Action During the San Francisco Longshore and Maritime Strike of 1934, Report # 1950, 18, 19, 22 (Works Project Administration, Berkeley, 1936).

88. Lew Levenson, "California Casualty List," 139 *Nation* 245 (August 29, 1934).

the rank and file strikers—one observer remarking, "If they weren't radicals before, they are now."[89]

These arrests should be compared to the 300 persons arrested in joint vigilante-police raids on Communist organizations and individuals carried out July 16–17. Eventually 211 would be dismissed, but 29 persons were held for deportation and 41 sentenced to jail, eight for six months. No I.L.A. jail sentences were served while all radicals served their sentences. This was the culmination of the red scare. All raids used the same script—non-uniformed "vigilantes" would drive up in unmarked cars, invade the office, destroy all papers, typewriters, and furniture, beat the inhabitants, and leave. Without interruption police would arrive to "investigate" and arrest all victims, throwing them in the back of convenient "black mariahs" just outside.[90] At the Finnish Hall in Oakland a grand piano was smashed. That the raids were police controlled was demonstrated by the fact that at one of the early raids by mix-up the police burst in before the vigilantes had arrived. All the arrests were for vagrancy, most held with $1000. bonds, and many were arrested for vagrancy in their homes! Almost none were arrested outside offices. Police admitted the only criteria for arrest was that they were radicals.[91]

> In the Jackson Street hall of the M.W.I.U., some 80 to 100 men were gathered at the time of the raid. Many of them did not know one another, as they were seamen from widely separated ports, who were present there because of their common interest in the strike. Several of the men had been arrested and convicted at prior times because of petty theft, one man for stealing a loaf of bread. Within the understanding of those authorities who framed the complaints, the fact that a man was in the hall at the same time that another was present who had been convicted of petty theft, even though they were strangers to one another and did not know the other was there, made the former an 'associate of a known thief.'"[92]

There was a division of legal defense between the two mass groups—all the I.L.A. members were represented by two attorneys provided by the I.L.A., while all the Communists were represented by attorneys working for the International Labor Defense organization, a nominally independent group.

Herbert Resner concluded: "the law was used as a strikebreaking agency. We have recorded in chapters of this monograph different phases of the law's operation to achieve this end: unlawful arrests, unlawful searches and seizures, setting of bail in unreasonable sums, unfair trials, convictions without proper or sufficient evidence and in some cases without even a day in court, denial of counsel, deportation of workers, interference with picketing and distribution of strike bulletins, and other devices just as effective in breaking strikes."[93] The police "forgot that they represented the workers as well as the employers."[94] After the May 28 violence and restrictions of picketing, the I.L.A. sought an injunction against Police Chief Quinn's picketing limitations. Although heard in a series of courts, no action was ever taken in the suit.[95] On the other hand, given the skewed press coverage, the anti-handbilling ordinances reduced communication between strikers and with the public.

---

89. *See eg.,* George Hedley, *supra* note 17, at 13.
90. David F. Selvin, *supra* note 3, at 198.
91. Herbert Resner, *supra* note 81, at 21.
92. *Ibid.* at 177
93. *Ibid.* at 2.
94. *Ibid.*
95. Mike Quin, *supra* note 5, at 82.

Even Federal Mediation had to be set in the context of police action:

> It is the first [strike] in which the power of the new Labor Disputes Board has been invoked—arbitration does not mean that the parties involved are to present their cases before a board of review in an effort to effect a settlement. It means that an elaborate stage show is to precede the feature of the evening: the police are to attack the picket lines while the newspapers energetically pummel that famous old punching bag of the editorial offices, the Red Scare; and after enough heads have been broken, enough lies printed and enough bunk spread, the arbitrators are to rush in with their solution. If that routine had occurred only once in this strike we might call it coincidence. If it had occurred twice it might still be a coincidence. But after it has happened every time the authorities have cooked up a settlement, only a wistful determination not to believe the worst can justify an unwillingness to put two and two together.[96]

"Trials" were conducted by elected police magistrates. Judge George J. Steiger sentenced six Communists to sixty days without permitting them to plead or without arraigning them at the bar upon questioning them in their jail cells. A reviewing judge did not believe it could happen and refused to intervene after a habeas corpus petition; no record of a plea could be produced or their absence explained. Phillip Simmons was pointed out to the judge as "an old confirmed red" by a member of the red squad who advised "sixty days." Judge Steiger asked his name and whether he was a seaman, and without more said "sixty days."[97] Another man served 75 of his 60 days before release. Many court trials consisted only of police testimony without plea or any defense allowed. Although charged with vagrancy, no evidence of such was ever introduced in any trial. Those arrested in their homes, indeed none of the radicals arrested, were pursuant to a warrant. M.W.I.U. Local President Henry Jackson was arrested in his home as a "vagrant enroute to Los Angeles," despite his paid job as a union organizer and official. Elaine Black, paid administrator for the International Labor Defense was arrested for the same in an apartment of a co-worker. Known U.S. citizens were admonished by the judges to go back to the countries where they came from. None of the extraordinarily few convictions appealed were upheld.

Coastwise, San Pedro, Portland and Seattle

Other than San Francisco itself, the bloodiest confrontations occurred at the Los Angeles docks in San Pedro. Early in the maritime strike, the first casualties came in San Pedro. There a scab headquarters was set up on the Grace Line steamer Santa Elena. On May 4 a group of pickets marched in front of the pier. A police attack came without warning. 20 year old Dick Parker, shot in the head, died instantly. Another, Tom Knudsen, died from gunshot wounds days later. Twenty other strikers were described as badly mangled by horse and shot.

During the general strike, violence escalated here too. Another affidavit:

> Thomas Sharpe being first duly sworn deposes and says: that he is a marine fireman by occupation and a member of International Seamans Union; that he came into San Pedro, California on March 28, 1934, on the Point Clear; that the strike was called on May 16, 1934; that affiant came back to San Pedro from a trip on July 13, 1934; that affiant registered for picket duty on July 15 and 16, 1934, from 12 noon to 6 pm. That Affiant came off duty about 6 pm. Affiant had been

---

96. Robert Cantwell, "War on the West Coast: I. The Gentlemen of San Francisco," *New Republic*, 308 (August 1, 1934).
97. David F. Selvin, *supra* note 3, at 74–75.

picketing on Terminal Island and went from there to Seaman's Hall; had his card stamped at Seaman's Hall.

That affiant then went to the Anchorage, a restaurant, about a half block away, and ate. Affiant was there about thirty minutes. The Affiant went to Chateau across the alley and was there talking and lounging until about 7:30pm.

Affiant saw a crowd gathered outside on the opposite side of street. It was dark. I walked across the street and saw a man standing with his back against the wall, dressed as a seaman, with white cap, dark coat, and dungarees. Then saw his riot club held down by his side. I crossed the street and was on the same side as the party above described; then a Buick car pulled up on opposite side of street. The man with white cap took me by arm and across street and put me into the Buick car. I didn't resist. He prodded me along but nothing was said.

He took another prisoner there; he put me into front seat with the uniformed driver. He put the other prisoner, a young fellow, into the rear seat.

He drove us to the police station. He walked me in front entrance and past the booking desk. He never booked me at San Pedro. He walked me to a hallway in the rear which was dark. He had my right arm and he pushed me ahead of him into hall. As he did so he hit me on the right shin with his riot club. The club must have been thirty to twenty-four inches long and about one and one-half inches in diameter. When he hit me the first blow, I fell and every muscle in my body went limp. He continued hitting me about the legs and on the right shin. He hit me on the leg about nine times. I was on the floor all this time. Then he caught my right foot and twisted it inwardly until the bones cracked. My leg started to bleed. Some uniformed officer peeped in. He didn't say a word. Then he caught my left arm and twisted and wrenched it, often jerking me to my feet, saying, "Get up on your feet, you red." Then he dropped me and I went down again. Then the uniformed man came in and grabbed my right arm and jerked me up. The other man took my left arm. They lifted me up. Then everything went hazy.

The next thing I remember was lying on a stretcher in a police station, upstairs I believe. They were putting some stuff in my arm and were trying for some time to stop the blood from my right leg. There was an ambulance driver or doctor in a white coat working on me. Then I came to again in an ambulance. Was half asleep with dope.

Next thing I knew they were booking me at the General Hospital, prison ward. This must have been early Tuesday morning. They were taking things out of my pockets. A doctor looked at me about 8:00 am. He looked at it. "I think you'll have a bad leg since you got here too late for surgery." He took an X-ray and said it was a compound fracture of the shin bone. They brought me back. He didn't try to set it. They gave me a shot for tetanus. They put leg in open basket. Then they let me lay until about noon on the nineteenth, Thursday.

There was an open wound on the leg. They put a little gauze over it. They said they'd put a gate in it later, but they never did. Left the hospital on Wednesday following about the twenty-fifth. Was taken directly from the hospital to the bullpen. Was then laying on iron bed with pad from Wednesday noon to Friday, 1:30 am. I was then taken to San Pedro on police patrol wagon. Left San Pedro at 3:00 pm for Los Angeles in overloaded wagon with fourteen people and a police officer. It was a very hot day. They left me in the bullpen. (Lincoln Heights) for eight days, until today, August 14, 1934. I was unable to sit up in bunks. I asked to see a doctor. They repeatedly refused. I saw the doctor once eight days after my first court appearance on the twenty-fifth. Haven't been able to see a doctor since. No further X-rays have been made. No part of the cast has ever been removed.[98]

Seattle Police were not used in the strike for over a month, in part due to the fact that the Police Chief was a former longshoreman. However, bowing to ship owner pressure, Mayor Smith on June 20 vowed to open the Seattle Port. The Police Chief resigned, but the Mayor sent several hundred policemen to Smith's Cove to protect scabbing longshore operations. While local teamsters refused to move the unloaded cargo, a railroad running to the Smith's Cove docks attempted to move cargo. June 21, six hundred strikers from Seattle, Tacoma, and Everett, packed the tracks preventing train progress. When driven away by police tear gas, the strikers greased the tracks preventing movement. The police used horses and clubs from that point on. Burt Nelson recalls that many strikers were arrested, and gave this description, including the striker's politicization of the picketing:

> Most of those arrested were in situations provoked by the police. It was a bad enough situation that I was prompted to stand on a fire hydrant on the water side of the access area between [Pier] 90 and 91. They would bring troops out there every afternoon from Pier 90 and line them up in two ranks. I would stand on the fire hydrant and read them the Bill of Rights. The commander would swear, but none of them ever tried to put their hands on me … There was always a big crowd that would applaud, hoot and holler at the cops. The only thing that is still there is the viaduct … During that same period of time at night nothing stirred. I don't know who got it started, but we would all applaud in unison. Apparently the cops thought there was a meeting and they would march out 4 abreast. Nothing happened. Not a picket in sight. We'd be back under the bridge. So they'd go back in and we'd applaud again. They never came back the second time. They'd go back in after standing around for an hour on the black top.[99]

Police violence surprisingly peaked in Seattle after the "Bloody Thursday" events in San Francisco. Again Burt Nelson describes the "Battle at Smith's Cove":

> The horse cops were after … Huey Reynolds, who was a big raw-boned man, a tough operator, the horse cops beat him rather badly, broke his arm and cut his head up … The cop stood in his stirrups … turned his horse around and rode away after somebody else … The horses came through … and split us at the railroad tracks. Some of us went South and some went out into Elliot Avenue and the horses stopped there for the time being. These guys ran us clear out to Galer and we were trying to get back to the main bunch. Then they rode us down over the bank just like a cavalry charge. All of these cops had tear gas masks on. They ran us up into the trees as far as they could ride the horses. I lay up there half the afternoon coughing and trying to get rid of that tear gas. Made you sick as hell … This cop on the horse was after me personally. I had made eye contact with him earlier when I was reading the Bill of Rights on a fire hydrant. He thought he was Custer at the Little Big Horn with white horse and all.[100]

---

98. Lew Levenson, "The Case of Thomas Sharpe," 139 *Nation* 272 (September 5, 1934).

99. Interview with Burt Nelson by Ronald Magden, January 22nd, 1987, Ronald Magden Collection, University of Washington Special Collections, Acc #5185-1, Box 5, Folder 1.

100. Interview with Burt Nelson by Ronald Magden, April 28th, 1987, Ronald Magden Collection, University of Washington Special Collections, Acc #5185-1, Box 5, Folder 3.

Aftermath for the Rank and File

ILA Local 38-79 published "The Truth About the Waterfront," in 1936.

> Without the powerful new union, the ILA and its new militant leadership, without the courage and solidarity of the aroused waterfront workers and the support they received from workers in other industries, those improvements in conditions could never have been won. And without such an organization, *they could not now be enforced*. Thanks to the ILA the fourteen year period of waterfront slavery is ended. The Embarcadero has been Americanized.[101]

Noting with pride,

> Let any San Francisco citizen walk along the waterfront today ... No longer will he encounter those crowds of shabby men hanging about the piers with desperation written on their faces.... In short, they can afford the luxury of being MEN.

> Today, THERE ARE NO UMEMPLOYED LONGSHOREMEN. All are working and the work is evenly distributed. There are no "preferred gangs" working to the point of exhaustion. And there are *no longshoremen on relief*. Through the collective action of the men themselves, the burden of their support has been removed from the backs of the taxpayers and is placed squarely where it belongs— upon the shipping industry. The men do not want charity from either the taxpayers or the ship owners. They want a decent return from that industry whose profits they help to swell and they intend to get it.... They are better workers because of this. If this is "Communism," then let the ship owners make the most of it![102]

A warehouseman recalled,

> When the strike was settled we'd nearly doubled our wages. Now you had a feeling of dignity. Before you were just a machine, a nonentity. Now you could say you can treat me like a man, not a damned dog. Now they *asked* you to work overtime, they didn't *tell* you to work overtime. And we got a seniority list, which meant you couldn't fire someone indiscriminately.[103]

Building on the experience of organizing the '34 strike, calling the whole machinery into operation again in 1936 to enforce the arbitration order, also supported Bridges's March Inland. Organizing workers eager to be organized, the local became the International Longshoremens and Warehousemens Union. Joe Lynch remembered,

> And the longshoremen in our Mission District neighborhood swore by Harry; they were church-going Catholics, but they didn't buy this red shit....

> See, the organization took part on a very planned, systematic approach. You had commercial warehouses strung along the waterfront from the Hyde Street pier over to Islais Creek; then you had cold storage warehouses; behind those you had mills, feed, flour, and grain; and behind those you had grocery—big grocery, with 15, 000 people—and that's where they organized. Gee, it was terrific. Then came hardware, paper, and the patent drug industry, and then coffee, tea

---

101. International Longshoremens Association, *The Truth About the Waterfront*, 11 (n.d.).
102. *Ibid.* at 12.
103. Brother Hackett, *The Dispatcher*, 6 (July 20, 1995).

and spice in '37, liquor and wine in '38.... 46 different industries in warehouse distribution, production, and processing.[104]

Worker mobilization won a strike in 1934 that had been crushed in 1919. Worker mobilization began spontaneously under horrid work and employment conditions, gained Voice and communication generated by their own co-workers, emboldening an incipient organization from the bottom up, found courage for direct action from the community neighborhoods they shared and family members who had also had enough. Shared conditions Coast wide and across race and ethnic lines, fomented the same pattern of organization, made the strike possible to be won, and not concluded before a democratic ratification. Police violence and rigged legal proceedings brought the strikers together in the end. Spontaneous resistance coupled with a radical form of organization, and thereby gaining solidarity and support from the rank and file of other unions in a union city, all won as much as could be won in San Francisco as the place the rest of the ports watched but also became the situs of their own struggles. It remained to extend the democratic control of the strike into a powerful but democratically controlled industrial union two years in advance of the formation of the C.I.O.

The contested terrain was geographic, as well as community, production, legality, and democracy. From the workers' side all these contests were inseparably about the possibilities of their life and their freedom, and their San Francisco.

Labor, Power and Law.

A Federal statute appeared as the West Coast rank and file of the maritime industry had had all they could take of dangerous conditions made exponentially worse by employer greed, greed that was enforceable through depression and the legal existence of employer controlled unions; a hated target, an incipient solidarity ready to embrace those workers of their own to lead and voice their issues, and resist control from outsiders within and without the new Locals. Law encouraged and emboldened, but it also threatened, to: impose arbitration, recognize multiple unions to be whipsawed by employers, and prohibit the right to strike. Threatening, because the building of the organization and the resistance to dock conditions necessary to rank and file control was self-consciously syndical—direct action. Secret organization, dock to dock, created a ready shadow infrastructure for rank and file extension of direct action on a dock to a Coastwise Longshore Strike under a Joint Maritime Strike Committee and settlement only upon democratic vote by union members. The strike demands of a union hiring hall, dock safety committees for unilateral rank and file enforcement of an agreement, a Coastwise multi-employer contract were not only radical economically in generating worker control and anticipating the birth of the CIO, but politically in depending on a strong coordinated Coastwise worker industrial organization whose members could take their rank and file union democracy to local government power. Depression conditions were made a national issue of interest, the only such radical national interest because unemployment and casualization on the docks, depended on the absence of a social wage. Police violence, relief manipulation, City complicity in a Red Scare that never was real, day after day sent unmistakable messages to the rank and file that they could only depend on themselves, that forces of power were out to break them for all time, that the strike was war. It was rank and file militancy and solidarity that found response in the rank and file of the teamsters and the 160 other locals who voted for a general strike even as the Leadership of the Central labor Council resisted at every turn. Teamster's Local President Mike Casey warned his mem-

---

104. Joe Lynch, *The Dispatcher*, 8 (July 20, 1995).

bership that a sympathy strike was illegal under their contract and that striking Teamsters would receive no strike benefits. They voted 1220 to 271 to join the general strike anyway, "In all my years of leading these men, I have never seen them so worked up, so determined to walk out."[105] Law and resistance, resistance and rank and file radicalism, were deeply intertwined and made visible the reality of worker interdependence, solidarity and mutualism in the work process itself. Solidarity and mutualism produced results just as they created an identity with clear consequences for worker neighborhoods and social life. All of this is the message of the actions collected in focus here.

The voices of the rank and file self-identify culture in their experience. It is distinct as the history of their struggle. It is the voice of the subordinated as the necessary counterparts by which the official histories convey their [re]presentations. In these voices there is the culture of a workers community, there is the culture of the two-tier organization of labor that rank and file power depended upon, there is the culture of the industrial police state, there is the culture of law—legitimate to the mainstream, hypocritical and cruel to the workers.

The same culture of struggle found in the company town of Aliquippa, Pennsylvania, and internally to the international AFL organization on the issue of the social wage, and the Wagner Act. Yes, the same groups were all there, but not because a few, or a few thousand, joined with a foreign radical group. The group appeared because struggles for power occurred—struggles for human decency, for pride, for democracy in America.

---

105. Ottilie Markholt, *supra* note 4, at 173.

IX

Union and Unemployed Together in Mass Movement

Auto-Lite Strike Street Confrontation.

The Toledo Auto-Lite Strike of 1934 and the Fight against "Wage Slavery"

Rebecca E. Zietlow & James Gray Pope[*]

"I think they did a wonderful thing over at the Auto-Lite, and really that is what started the union."[1]

I. Introduction

On May 21, 1934, about one thousand picketers and supporters gathered at the Toledo Auto-Lite plant in defiance of a court injunction. Dominating the scene was a large banner proclaiming on one side "AMERICAN WORKERS PARTY CALLS FOR MASS PICK-

---

[*] This article originally appeared in 38 *U. Toledo L. Rev.* 839 (2006–2007), and is reprinted with the permission of the Toledo Law Review.

1. Interview by Dr. Juliann E. Fleenor with Margaret Byrd, wife of a union organizer, in Toledo, Ohio (Mar. 20, 1980), Toledo-Lucas County Public Library Local History Archives, Toledo, Ohio [hereinafter Toledo Library Archives].

ETING," and on the other "1776, 1865, 1934."[2] The first two dates were obvious references to the American Revolution and the Civil War. In what sense did 1934 belong in such company? Maybe the leaders of the American Workers Party ("AWP"), an avowedly radical organization, hoped that there would be a revolutionary struggle for liberty in 1934, as there had been in 1776 and 1865. If so, they were to be sorely disappointed. There was, however, a peaceful revolution of sorts in the 1930s. Just as the American Revolution led to the Constitution and Bill of Rights, and just as the Civil War led to the Thirteenth, Fourteenth, and Fifteenth Amendments, the popular struggles of the 1930s produced a constitutional revolution in the form of federal statutes upheld by the U.S. Supreme Court in a series of transformative opinions.[3] Historians and political scientists have shown that struggles like the Toledo Auto-Lite strike and the sit-down strikes of 1936–1937 played a major role in bringing about the constitutional revolution of the 1930s.[4] Do the strikers deserve credit for this result? Or were they merely unwitting precipitators of change?

Throughout history, supporters of social movements have risked their jobs, their security, and even their lives for what they believed were fundamental rights, even though the law did not yet recognize those rights.

What about the Toledo strikers? As of 1934, the Constitution had yet to emerge as a major public issue. Unlike the sit-down strikers, the Toledo strikers rarely raised constitutional issues. Nevertheless, we conclude that the Toledo strike was one episode in a long-term popular movement for constitutional change. Despite the ill effects of the Depression on Toledo and an unemployment rate of over 50%, workers at the Auto-Lite transmission plant risked their jobs and the possibility of employment at other factories for what they believed were fundamental rights—the rights to organize into a union, engage in collective bargaining, and strike.[5] They were following in a long tradition of labor activism that traced back to the Reconstruction Era. According to this tradition, the Thirteenth Amendment protected the rights to organize and strike; working without the right to join a union was tantamount to wage slavery. Section 7(a) of the National Industrial Recovery Act of 1933 ("NIRA")—which recognized the rights to organize, to engage in concerted activity, and to bargain collectively—provided a new vehicle for this longstanding belief.[6] When the Roosevelt administration declined to enforce section 7(a), the Toledo Auto-Lite workers set out to enforce it on their own. They demanded that their employer bargain with representatives of their fledgling union. With help from the Toledo Central Labor Union and the AWP, the Auto-Lite workers resisted an injunction and enforced their right to organize on their own through collective action.[7]

Their strike, in turn, provided a catalyst for the transition of these values into a more effective law, the NLRA. During early debates over the Act, its congressional supporters raised the Auto-Lite strike as a reason why the Act was necessary. Members of Congress echoed the strikers' condemnation of wage slavery and the right to organize as a fundamental right; they then enshrined these voices into law with the NLRA.[8]

---

2. "What Is Behind Toledo," *New Republic*, 87 (June 6, 1934). *See also* Philip A. Korth & Margaret R. Beegle, *I Remember Like Today: The Auto-Lite Strike of 1934*, 118 (1988).

3. 2 Bruce Ackerman, *We the People: Transformations* 345–82 (1998).

4. *See infra* notes 63–80.

5. James Gray Pope, "The Thirteenth Amendment Versus the Commerce Clause: Labor and the Shaping of American Constitutional Law 1921–1957," 102 *Colum. L. Rev.* 1, 15 (2002).

6. National Industrial Recovery Act ch. 90, § 7(a), 48 Stat. 195, 198–99 (1933) [hereinafter "NIRA"]. *See also infra* Part II.

7. *See infra* Part III.

8. *See infra* Part IV.

II. The Thirteenth Amendment and Section 7(a) of the NIRA

The belief that the Thirteenth Amendment protected the rights to organize and strike has its roots in the Reconstruction Era and the philosophy of "free soil, free labor" advocates such as Henry Wilson and John Bingham. The Reconstruction Congressmen who held these views anticipated the impact of abolishing slavery on the entire structure of labor relations raising the floor because slaves occupied the bottom rung in the hierarchy of labor status.[9] Wilson and Bingham's vision lived on in the labor movement, where many generations nurtured it. In the twentieth century, Samuel Gompers, the founder of the American Federation of Labor ("AFL"), called the Thirteenth Amendment the "glorious labor amendment." Many labor activists and rank-and-file union members agreed that working without the rights to organize and strike amounted to wage slavery.[10]

Until the 1930s, labor activists invoked the Constitution mainly to keep the federal and state governments out of industrial relations. The AFL declared anti-strike laws and injunctions unconstitutional, and charged every worker with the "imperative duty" to defy them and "take whatever consequences may ensue."[11] But the changed political climate of the 1930s offered the opportunity to obtain affirmative government protection for workers' rights. In 1933, Congress enacted the National Industrial Recovery Act ("NIRA"), which authorized the President to approve industrial codes of fair competition developed by boards composed of representatives from the affected industry. Section 7(a) of the NIRA required that each code guarantee employees "the right to organize and bargain collectively through representatives of their own choosing," and it prohibited employers from coercing employees or requiring them to join company unions.[12] Congress enacted section 7(a) under its power to regulate interstate commerce, but many labor leaders and activists viewed it as an effort to enforce laborers' constitutional rights. "President Roosevelt signed the bill," explained one Pennsylvania coal miner, "which restored your constitutional rights and industrial freedom."[13] AFL President William Green celebrated section 7(a) as a "charter of industrial freedom," while Mine Workers President John L. Lewis declared that it was an "act of economic emancipation."[14]

At first, labor radicals did not join in the celebration of section 7(a). The Socialist Party warned that the new law might serve as an "instrument of capital,"[15] while the American Workers Party, which was to play a central role in Toledo, went further. Far from claiming section 7(a) as a "charter of freedom" or "act of economic emancipation," AWP leaders invoked labor's constitutional vision *against* the new law. Eighty trade union officials affiliated with the AWP and the Communist Party tarred the NIRA as an Industrial Slavery Act because it might lead to the compulsory arbitration of labor disputes—a sys-

9. Lea S. VanderVelde, "The Labor Vision of the Thirteenth Amendment, "138 *U. Pa. L. Rev.* 437, 441–43 (1989).

10. *See* William Forbath, "The New Deal Constitution in Exile," 51 *Duke L.J.* 165, 188 (2001); William E. Forbath, *Law and the Shaping of the American Labor Movement*, 135–47 (1991); Pope, *supra* note 5, at 943.

11. *Am. Fed'n Labor, Report of the Proceedings of the Twenty-Ninth Annual Convention*, 313 (1909); *Am. Fed'n Labor, Report of the Proceedings of the Thirty-Ninth Annual Convention*, 361–62 (1919).

12. NIRA, ch. 90, §7(a), 48 Stat. 195, 198–99 (1933).

13. William F. Donovan, District 5 *Aflame, United Mine Workers J.*, 7 (July 15, 1933).

14. Joseph G. Rayback, *A History of American Labor*, 328 (1966); John L. Lewis, "Appraisal of the Industrial Recovery Act," *United Mine Workers J.*, 7 (July 11, 1933). *See also* "Industrial Recovery Bill, About to Become a Law, Means Emancipation of the Wage Slave," *United Mine Workers J.*, 1 (June 1, 1933).

15. Editorial, "The Fate of the Thirty-Hour Bill," *Advance*, May 1933, at 6–7; Unsigned, "To Create Proper Machinery for Enforcement of N.I.R.A.," *New Leader*, June 24, 8 (1933).

tem condemned by labor conservatives and radicals alike as involuntary servitude in violation of the Thirteenth Amendment. They called on workers and unions to boycott the Act's code-making processes.[16] Before long, American workers made it clear that such fears would not prevent them from using the Act. In the summer of 1933, they streamed into unions, citing section 7(a) as authorization. Even the Communist-led unions were submitting NIRA codes, and radical activists found themselves invoking a law that they had initially labeled an Industrial Slavery Act.[17]

III. The Toledo Auto-Lite Strike

Although labor radicals had lagged behind in perceiving the potential of section 7(a), they soon took the lead in its enforcement. While conservative unionists like William Green and John L. Lewis urged workers to refrain from striking and rely on government enforcement, radicals helped them to enforce the new law on their own. The result was a series of social upheavals that, in the words of historian Irving Bernstein, "ripped the cloak of civilized decorum from society, leaving exposed naked class conflict."[18] Of these upheavals, one of the most historically significant was the Toledo Auto-Lite Strike.

A. Background

In 1934, the Auto-Lite plant was one of the largest factories in Toledo, Ohio. It manufactured transmissions and was a principal supplier of those parts to the surrounding automobile factories. The Great Depression hit the industrial Midwest hard. All of the banks in Toledo except one had gone under, and unemployment surged above 50%. Without an economic safety net, people literally struggled to survive. Toledoans told stories about families eating nothing but apples, and burning their furniture to warm themselves during the harsh upper Midwest winters. These conditions were devastating for those workers without jobs, but they also had a profound impact on employed workers. The managers at industrial plants such as the Auto-Lite plant treated unskilled and semi-skilled workers as fungible and disposable. Safety conditions were deplorable, and "the foreman's exercise of his power to select workers appeared arbitrary ... In virtually every department, a supervisor had the unrestricted power to choose the workers to perform the jobs available that day."[19] Moreover, the president of Auto-Lite, C.O. Miniger, was widely disliked because he owned the Security Home Trust Co., a savings and loan in which most of the workers had invested their money. That bank had closed down suddenly in the early days of the Depression, depriving workers of what little money they had saved.[20]

---

16. "A Call To Action," *Labor Action*, 2 (July 15, 1933) (printing text of statement). For the labor movement's position on compulsory arbitration, see Victor A. Olander, "Compulsory Arbitration," *Shoe Workers J.*, 6 (July 1920); Am. Fed'n of Labor, *Report of Proceedings of the Fortieth Annual Convention* 378 (1920).

17. *See, e.g.*, "What the Blue Eagle Means to the Workers," *Labor Action*, 3 (Aug. 23, 1933) (arguing that "a law written on a piece of paper means nothing," and therefore the workers had better "act, get together, organize" to realize their rights); Hy Kravif, "The Strikebreaking Forerunners of the Recovery Bill," *Daily Worker*, 5 (June 17, 1933) ("The right of 'collective bargaining'... is meaningless, unless the workers themselves fight to enforce it."); Nat'l Miners Union, Statement of the National Miners Union Delegation on the Mining Code, n.d. (on file with the National Recovery Administration, Records of the National Recovery Administration, Record Group (RG) 9, National Archives I, Washington, D.C., NRA Bituminous Code File, Box 889).

18. Irving Bernstein, *Turbulent Years: A History of the American Worker, 1933–1941*, 217 (1970).

19. Korth & Beegle, *supra* note 2, at 48.

20. Robert S. Brown, "Low Pay, Bank Failures, Slump Breadlines Form Toledo Riot Background," *N.Y. World Telegram*, 6 (May 29, 1934). Leaflets distributed by strike supporters often referred to Miniger as "Bank Robber Miniger." *See, e.g.*, American Workers Party & Auto Workers Union Leaflets, Archives of Labor and Urban Affairs, Wayne State University, Detroit, Michigan [hereinafter WSU Archives].

The workers who wanted to protest the conditions and achieve higher wages were highly vulnerable. Congress had declared a right to join a union in section 7(a) of the NIRA, and for the Auto-Lite workers, as for others throughout the country, "the meaning of Section 7(a) was plain: President Roosevelt wanted them to join unions."[21] However, the Roosevelt administration chose not to enforce section 7(a), and companies routinely fired members who openly belonged to a union.[22] Furthermore, once companies knew that a person was a union organizer, it was difficult for him to get a job elsewhere, and some businesses refused to give credit to union activists.[23] Given the high level of unemployment and economic uncertainty, supporters of the union at Auto-Lite were taking serious risks by identifying themselves. During the strike, they depended on donations from friends and neighbors to feed their families.[24]

B. The Strike

The Auto-Lite struggle played out in two phases.[25] The first began in February 1934, when workers at Auto-Lite and two other parts plants struck for a ten-percent wage increase and recognition of their union, Federal Labor Union Local 18384. At Auto-Lite, this phase involved only about fifty workers.[26] Because they were striking in conjunction with workers at several other Toledo plants, these workers won a partial victory. After intervention by federal government officials, the company granted a five percent wage increase and promised to "set up machinery for future negotiations ... on all other issues."[27] Observers interpreted this vague promise as a grant of union recognition, and the workers ratified the agreement. However, by mid April it was clear that Auto-Lite management had no intention of bargaining with union representatives.[28] The intervening month gave union leaders a good opportunity to organize more members.

On April 12, 1934, a considerably stronger and larger Local 18384 staged a second strike. Auto-Lite resorted to the courts to obtain an anti-strike injunction, a common tactic at the time. Its attempt was initially successful. Judge Roy A. Stuart of the Court of Common Pleas issued an injunction limiting union pickets to twenty-five per entrance and barring the AWP-sponsored Unemployed League and other outsiders from participating.[29] Union leaders such as Thomas Ramsey and Floyd Blosser complied with the injunction, and morale soon waned significantly. On May 3, the Toledo Central Labor Union protested the injunction and warned that the threat of employer tyranny might

---

21. 1 James A. Gross, *The Making of the National Labor Relations Board: A Study in Economics, Politics and Law (1933–1937)* 14 (1974). *See also* Korth & Beegle, *supra* note 2, at 15 (discussing how section 7(a) of the NIRA was an inspiration to union organizers).

22. 1 Gross, *supra* note 25, at 11–13. It is often said that the NIRA lacked effective enforcement mechanisms. However, it empowered the President to require that all businesses in an industry obtain a federal license as a condition of doing business in or affecting interstate commerce. Having done so, he could then revoke the license of any code violator — in effect imposing the business equivalent of a death sentence. NIRA, ch. 90, §4(b), 48 Stat. 195, 197–98 (1933). The Roosevelt administration never utilized this provision.

23. Interview by Dr. Juliann E. Fleenor with Margaret Byrd, *supra* note 1, at 11–12.

24. *Ibid.* at 5; Interview by Tana Mosier with Joseph Ditzel, in Toledo, Ohio (Mar. 5–Apr. 16, 1981), Toledo Library Archives, *supra* note 1, at 52.

25. "Spread of Auto Strike Likely," *Toledo Blade*, 1 (Apr. 16, 1934).

26. Korth & Beegle, *supra* note 2, at 81.

27. Bernstein, supra note 22, at 220. *See also* "Spread of Auto Strike Likely," *supra* note 25, at 1.

28. Korth & Beegle, *supra* note 2, at 82.

29. "Wage Dispute Causes Strike at Auto-Lite," *Toledo Blade*, 1 (Apr. 13, 1934); "City Company and Union Heads are Summoned to Hearing over Picket Injunction," *Toledo Blade*, 1 (Apr. 18, 1934). *See also* Sidney Fine, *The Automobile under the Blue Eagle* 275 (1963).

necessitate a general strike of all trades.[30] Two days later, Sam Pollock, Secretary of the Unemployed League, informed Judge Stuart by letter that the League would "deliberately and specifically violate the injunction ... 'We sincerely believe that this court intervention,' he explained, 'is an abrogation of our democratic rights, contrary to our constitutional liberties and contravenes the spirit and the letter of Section 7a of the NIRA.'"[31]

Supporters of the strike, including members of the AWP and the Unemployed League, began mass picketing in open defiance of the injunction. On May 13, Judge Stuart issued an order banning eighty-seven named individuals from joining the Auto-Lite picket line, including James Roland and Sam Pollack. Those people ignored the order and the police arrested them for contempt of court.[32] When they appeared in court, a crowd of strike supporters joined them, making it impossible for the court to function. On May 15, Judge Stuart made the injunction permanent, but Thomas Ramsey, leader of the local union, promptly rose in the back of the courtroom and announced that "our whole union membership is going to picket until we get a contract, and we'll all go to jail if necessary to see that we get it."[33] More arrests followed, and 200 strike supporters stormed the jail in an unsuccessful attempt to free the prisoners.[34]

On May 23, thousands of picketers led by Pollock, Selander, and Budenz blockaded the plant under a huge banner proclaiming "AMERICAN WORKERS PARTY CALLS FOR MASS PICKETING."[35] Sheriff Krieger arrested Budenz and four others. One of his deputies attacked and beat an elderly man as the workers, now 10,000 strong, watched. Local and state leaders began to lose patience, and Governor White of Ohio called in the National Guard to enforce the injunction and restore order. Instead, the Guard's arrival sparked the "Battle of Toledo," in which thousands of workers fought first 900, then 1,350 guardsmen to a standstill for several days. Two protesters were killed and ten injured by gunfire, while at least ten guardsmen were wounded by hurled bricks.[36]

Following the violence, and amidst threats of a general strike by the Central Labor Union, Auto-Lite representatives agreed to negotiate with the union. By early June, Auto-Lite management reached a settlement with the union, in which they recognized Local 18384 as the representative of the workers and agreed to negotiate with the union. On June 2, 1934, a parade of more than 10,000 people marched through downtown Toledo and celebrated the renaissance of the union movement.[37] Toledo became one of the strongest

---

30. Interview by Jack W. Skeels with James A. Roland (Sept. 25, 1960), WSU Archives, *supra note* 24, at 5; Bernstein, *supra note* 22, at 222; Fine, *supra note* 33, at 277.

31. Letter from Sam Pollock, Secretary, Lucas County Unemployed League, to Judge Roy Stuart, Lucas County Court of Common Pleas (May 5, 1934), *reprinted in Labor Action*, 1 (May 15, 1934).

32. *Ibid.* at 6; "Court Grants Injunction to Curb Picketing," *Toledo Blade*, 1 (May 14, 1934); "Forty-Six Taken to Jail Today Following Roundup Tuesday at Auto-Lite for Alleged Violation of Injunction," *Toledo Blade*, 3 (May 16, 1934).

33. Edward Lamb, *No Lamb for Slaughter: An Autobiography* 41 (1963).

34. "Spectators Storm Courtroom Doors," *Toledo Blade*, 1 (May 18, 1934); Fine, supra note 33, at 278.

35. Korth & Beegle, supra note 2, at 118; Louis F. Budenz, "Toledo-A Miniature Rehearsal for the Workers' Revolution," *Labor Action*, 1 (June 15, 1934).

36. Bernstein, *supra* note 22, at 222; "Soldiers Stoned in Gas Attacks," *Toledo Blade*, 1 (May 24, 1934); "Riot District Quiet; Troops Get Control," *Toledo Blade*, 1 (May 25, 1934). *See also* Bernstein, *supra* note 22, at 222–25; Korth & Beegle, *supra* note 2, at 12–13; Fine, *supra* note 33, at 279.

37. "Confidence Gained in Sunday Parleys," *Toledo Blade*, 1 (May 28, 1934); "General Strike Now Is Unlikely," *Toledo Blade*, A1 (June 2, 1934). *See also* Korth & Beegle, *supra* note 2, at 233–34; "Leaders Hail Big Parade of 10,000 Workers as Sign of Toledo Union Labor's Renaissance," *Toledo Blade*, A1 (June 2, 1934).

union towns in the country, and the Auto-Lite union became one of the first locals of the United Automobile Workers ("UAW").[38]

C. The Beliefs of the Auto-Lite Strikers

By the mid-1930s, an increasing number of workers thought labor unions "would bring about a more equitable capitalist society."[39] Their demands were not just economic, but also moral. Labor unions wanted capitalism to be fair to its workers and create a fair working environment. Many of their demands "concerned equity: equal pay for equal work; an end to job discrimination based on age, race, or sex; seniority in place of favoritism."[40] From the determination and conviction of the striking Auto-Lite workers, it is apparent that they believed that more was at stake than simply improving their wages. Indeed, those workers later stressed that it was the deplorable conditions and the way that their employer treated them that led them to strike. While most leaders of the Auto-Lite strike did not mention the Thirteenth Amendment, a number of them invoked opposition to wage slavery in their speeches and leaflets to rally their supporters. The workers on the Auto-Lite picket line carried on labor's tradition of recognizing the right to organize as a human right as well as an economic right.

The AWP used the language of freedom and slavery to inspire the strikers. Its banner equated the end of chattel slavery in 1865 with the end of wage slavery through collective action in 1934. AWP flyers produced at the time made this connection more explicit. One leaflet proclaimed, "Toledo workers will not work at the points of bayonets like craven slaves."[41] Another declared, "The workers of Toledo ... have starved and sweated and cried in their misery while waiting for this hour. Now they have shaken off the chains of their masters."[42] A leaflet produced by the Auto Workers Union Organization Committee agreed, "It now remains the task of completely closing this slave pen of Minniger."[43]

Union leaders used similar imagery to rally their forces. Floyd Blosser, president of Federal Labor Union Local 18384, explained that the strike was necessary because Auto-Lite management refused to bargain with the union. At the outset of the strike, Blosser told a crowd of workers "that there was nothing left for men and women with a spark of Americanism left in their bodies but to strike against a condition that threatened to make of them mere serfs and slaves whose bodies were to be ground into profits."[44] Similarly, AFL leader Oliver Myers "characterized the automotive parts workers as industrial slaves who seldom get a check large enough to meet their debts," explaining "it is better to starve fighting than to starve working."[45] Thus, the leaders of the Auto-Lite strike saw the strike as part of the struggle against wage slavery and for workers' freedom.

The workers on the picket line were the least likely to invoke the imagery of wage slavery. Rather, they spoke in concrete terms and described their negative experience working without the right to organize. They felt that the only way to fight these conditions was to join a union and asserted a fundamental right to do so. As Patrick O'Malley, an organizer of Cleveland automobile parts workers at the time of the Auto-Lite strike, de-

---

38. *See* Bernstein, supra note 22, at 222; Interview by Jack W. Skeels with James A. Roland, *supra* note 34.

39. Lizabeth Cohen, *Making a New Deal: Industrial Workers in Chicago, 1919–1939,* 252 (1990).

40. *Ibid.* at 315.

41. *Workers of Toledo* (1934), American Workers Party Leaflets, *supra* note 24.

42. *On to the General Strike* (1934), American Workers Party Leaflets, *supra* note 24.

43. *To All Strikers of Toledo* (1934), Auto Workers Union Leaflets, *supra* note 24. C.O. Miniger was the president of the Auto-Lite Company. Korth & Beegle, *supra* note 2, at 11.

44. "Auto Strike Settlements Believed Near," *Toledo Blade,* 1 (Apr. 14, 1934).

45. "Striking Union Promised Aid," *Toledo Blade,* 2 (May 11, 1934).

scribed the situation, "Companies ... pushed the workers more and more so that when the union came in and promised some freedom from this slavery, at that time people were just looking to get better conditions."[46]

The strikers' chief concern was the arbitrary and abusive power wielded by the foremen. The foremen had the power to assign work, and they often used that power to extract favors from workers. Further, workers complained that the companies did not consider seniority when handing out work assignments. As one Auto-Lite worker, Steve Zoltan, explained: "Seniority didn't mean anything in those days. You either had to do something for the foreman or you wasn't working."[47] William Lockwood added, "You would go into work and the boss would make you wait around a while before telling you that you weren't needed ... So, you go home and you didn't get paid, even though you were on the premises."[48] Union leader Joseph Ditzel explained:

> Seniority was the big thing. That was the thing that attracted everybody, because they saw what happened previously and they knew that your job just didn't mean anything. Any lay-off, any whim, any caprice and the foreman could let you out and you'd never have to be taken back to work ... That was by far the biggest attraction for the union.[49]

The workers lacked any autonomy while they were on the job. Auto-Lite worker Mary Aberling described what it was like. "Before the strike they had a matron in the restroom, you couldn't even wash your hands when you had to go to the bathroom or you couldn't wash them when you come out. Out, out and she'd time you to see how long you was in there you know."[50] Auto-Lite worker Elizabeth Nyitrai agreed: "Well, good heavens, about 10:00 you'd get starving, you know. You weren't allowed to walk off the job or even eat an apple on the job. Oh no, not with that cranky boss."[51] Union leader, Chester Dombrowski, elaborated: "You couldn't go to the toilet. You couldn't smoke. If you got caught smoking, you would have been fired. If you got caught eating a sandwich, you'd a been fired."[52] Further, Auto-Lite worker Ted Suska, summed it up, "You know, the conditions were bad. It was all company. It was so bad that you were afraid to move or do anything. They just paid whatever they wanted to, and they shoved you around."[53]

Moreover, working conditions at the Auto-Lite factory were extremely dangerous. As Bernice Rigby, wife of union leader Charles Rigby, explained: "Of course in his department they would have their fingers cut off then you could go down the line and almost every man would have a finger or a couple of fingers cut off."[54] In order to improve profits, the company adopted the hated speed-up system, adding to the danger of the job. Said strike supporter James Roland, "It was the working conditions in the plant. The

---

46. Interview by Jack W. Skeels with Patrick J. O'Malley (July 25, 1961), WSU Archives, *supra* note 24, at 3.
47. Korth & Beegle, *supra* note 2, at 57.
48. *Ibid.* at 78.
49. Interview by Tana Mosier with Joseph Ditzel, *supra* note 28.
50. Interview by Dr. Juliann E. Fleenor with Mary Aberling (Feb. 28, 1983), Toledo Library Archives, *supra* note 1, at 16.
51. Korth & Beegle, *supra* note 2, at 53.
52. *Ibid.* at 60.
53. *Ibid.* at 73.
54. Interview by Dr. Juliann E. Fleenor with Bernice E. Rigby (wife of Charles Rigby) (Feb. 21, 1983), Toledo Library Archives, *supra* note 1, at 3.

speed-up, assembly line. When they wanted more they just cranked up the speed and that was the speed it run."[55]

Auto-Lite union leader John Jankowski summarized the cumulative effect of these conditions on the Auto-Lite workers. "You see what they done, the personnel that worked there, the boys that I worked with together … got so riled up about being treated like animals, that that's what caused them to join the union."[56] He continued, "They only wanted to get the recognition of the union and get the conditions for a human being to operate under. That's all we wanted. We didn't give a damn too much about wages … That wasn't it. It was the conditions that you were under."[57] Charles Rigby, charismatic leader within the plant, agreed:

> The strikers were people fighting for their bread and butter, that's what they are—American men, good, honest men, fighting for their liberty, fighting for justice, fighting for just recognition … And when you are recognized as a human being, no matter where you're at, and they say, "We recognize you" with respect to conditions of employment, with respect to teaching rights, with respect to this or that, you are a human being again.[58]

Consequently, Auto-Lite strikers called for basic fairness and an end to the exploitation they experienced as a result of their lack of bargaining power. They believed in the right to organize in a union and made sacrifices to bring it about. These workers saw themselves as part of a national struggle and were open to arguments that working without the right to organize amounted to wage slavery. While few of those workers invoked images of slavery, many responded positively to such imagery in speeches and pamphlets to rally the forces. Most important, the sacrifices of those striking workers created a strong moral force behind the argument that the right to organize was a fundamental right.

D. Popular Constitutionalism in the Auto-Lite Strike

The role of popular constitutionalism in the Auto-Lite Strike can be understood by visualizing two sets of three concentric circles, the first set representing constitutional ideology, and the second representing labor constituencies. Each set of circles has a core, a middle, and a periphery. At the core of the ideological set sits the labor movement's vision of the Thirteenth Amendment. The radical supporters of the Auto-Lite strike invoked this vision. In the middle of this set, the Auto-Lite union leaders invoked the opposition to wage slavery. The outside circle represents the less systematic beliefs of the Auto-Lite strikers that their working conditions were intolerable and that the right to organize was a fundamental right that was necessary for them to improve those conditions. All three belief circles were consistent with each other, and the core, the most concentrated ideology, was a necessary foundation for the convictions of the workers who made the sacrifices on the lines.

The identity of the people occupying the second set of concentric circles, representing constituencies, is the inverse of the first. Here, the strikers occupy the center, forming the strategic and moral core with their capacity to overcome narrow self-interest (in the form of the free-rider problem and other obstacles to collective action) and to halt production. In the middle sit the union leaders who directed the strike. The outermost layer

---

55. Interview by Tana Mosier with James Roland, in Luna Pier, Mich. (Aug. 12, 1981), Toledo Library Archives, *supra* note 1, at 25.
56. Korth & Beegle, *supra* note 2, at 65.
57. *Ibid.* at 66.
58. Interview of Charles Rigby, *in* Korth & Beegle, *supra* note 2, at 226.

of this set of circles is occupied by radical supporters of the strike, such as the AWP and its affiliate, the Lucas County Unemployed League, whose energy and ideological leadership were necessary to the success of the strike. The combination of these constituencies enabled the strikers to succeed in carrying out their goal, an industrial regime shift from employer dictatorship to unionization.

This model corresponds to the intuitive perceptions of employers, organizers, and workers. Typically, employers view organizers as "outsiders" seeking to implant an alien ideology among "their" workers. From the viewpoint of organizers, however, the core constituency of workers is ripe for ideology of labor freedom; it is only fear of the employer that keeps workers from embracing it. Workers often share the employers' view of organizers, but nevertheless feel drawn to their message.

IV. The Response of Congress

Like the Auto-Lite strikers, workers across the country followed the promise of section 7(a) of the NIRA and formed new unions. And like the Auto-Lite corporation, most of their employers refused to bargain with union representatives. The result was a national wave of strikes. Members of Congress took notice. 1934 and 1935 represented the peak of the political power of unionists in this country.[59] On February 28, 1934, Senator Wagner first introduced the NLRA, a bill "to equalize the bargaining power of employers and employees, to encourage the amicable settlement of disputes between employers and employees, to create a National Labor Board, and for other purposes."[60] The preamble of the Wagner Act explained that "inadequate recognition of the right of employees to bargain collectively through representatives of their own choosing has been one of the causes of strikes, lockouts, and similar manifestations of economic strife."[61] Prominent among those strikes was the Auto-Lite strike.

Only days after the National Guard violence in Toledo, Representative William Connery explained on the House floor that events like the Auto-Lite strike had made the Wagner Act necessary. In his speech, Representative Connery stated:

> You have seen strikes in Toledo, you have seen Minneapolis, you have seen San Francisco, and you have seen some of the southern textile strikes, ... but Mr. Speaker, a labor man in whom I have the greatest confidence said to me two days ago, "You have seen Toledo, Minneapolis and San Francisco. That is mild. You have not yet seen the gates of hell opened, and that is what is going to happen from now on unless the Congress of the United States passes labor legislation."[62]

He elaborated:

> Do you think in Toledo today and in Minneapolis and in any place else in the country where they are having strikes—do you think a man with a family of five children goes out there and is chased down the street with bayonets by the National Guard, as I saw in a picture yesterday of the strike in Toledo, does this because

---

59. 1 Gross, *supra* note 25, at 62. In 1934 alone, there were "'1856 work stoppages involving 1,470,000 workers.'" *Ibid.* (quoting Bernstein, *supra* note 22, at 217).
   60. 78 Cong. Rec. 3443–44 (1934).
   61. *Ibid.*
   62. 78 Cong. Rec. 9888 (1934).

he loves excitement? Do you think he goes out there risking his life ... because he likes it? ... No; he is out there fighting for bread for these hungry little mouths.[63]

Similar discussions occurred in the Senate. Senator La Follette agreed:

I realize that there has been serious opposition to the so-called "Wagner bill" but I do not think Congress should be deterred ... Too many American industrialists fail to recognize that without an organized labor market it is inevitable that the industrial process will constantly be interrupted by strikes, by lockouts, by riots, by bloodshed, yes, and even by death. Already we have seen an example in the strike at Toledo.

He continued:

Unless adequate treatment shall be given this subject by the present Congress, I am apprehensive, Mr. President, that a situation which will constitute a grave national emergency will arise, and that thousands of persons perchance will lose their lives in bloody, open conflict. We had a preview of such a picture in the Toledo strike.[64]

In short, members of Congress invoked the struggles of the workers in Toledo as they attempted to enact the legal claims of those workers into law.

Moreover, members of Congress were influenced, not just by the acts of workers like those at the Auto-Lite plant, but also by their beliefs and the intensity of their conviction. Like the strikers at Auto-Lite, members of Congress spoke of slavery and emancipation and expressed the view that the right to organize was a fundamental right. In a speech given to the conference of code authorities a few days later, Senator Wagner echoed the calls of union leaders, explaining that his act was necessary to ensure the equality of freedom lacking when an individual worker has to bargain with an employer that has thousands of workers. Both the House of Representatives and the Senate agreed with Wagner that "the right to bargain collectively, guaranteed to labor by Section 7(a) of the Recovery Act, is a veritable charter of freedom of contract; without it there would be slavery by contract."[65] In both houses of Congress, Wagner's colleagues echoed this view.

As William Forbath has observed, "when political-constitutional actors sought to enlarge the powers of Congress in the 1930s as they did in the 1860s, they did so in the name of a new and enlarged conception of national citizenship."[66] The debates over the NLRA reflect this, where members of Congress repeatedly invoked imagery from the Reconstruction Era, another era in which Congress expanded citizenship rights.[67] Like Louis Budenz on the Auto-Lite picket line, members of Congress drew parallels between the emancipation of the slaves in 1865 and establishing the right to organize in 1934. Representative William Connery explained:

The Civil War was fought over the question whether man should be free or be enslaved. Today, despite the fact that all our people are free in that they have the right to work and live where they please ... there are many who contend that

---

63. *Ibid.* at 9888–89.

64. 78 *Cong. Rec.* 12029 (1934).

65. Sen. Robert Wagner Speech at the Conference of Code Authorities in Washington D.C. (Mar. 5, 1934), *in* 78 *Cong. Rec.* 3678 (1934).

66. Forbath, *supra* note 14, at 169.

67. *See* Zietlow, *supra* note 7, at 38 (noting the congressional measures taken during the Reconstruction Era to ensure the "belonging, protection, and equality" of freed slaves).

our toilers live in virtual economic slavery in that they are denied an income which will provide a decent standard of living for themselves and their families and too often they are denied the right of collective bargaining.[68]

Representative Truax agreed, calling the NLRA "a new bill of rights, a new declaration of independence, if you please."[69] Truax claimed that the Act would bring about "an emancipation for American labor ... As Lincoln freed the blacks in the South, so the Wagner-Connery bill frees the industrial slaves of this country from the further tyranny and oppression of their overlords of wealth."[70]

Other members of Congress invoked broader images of freedom. Representative Carpenter urged his colleagues to support the Act because:

[S]ome remedy must quickly be found for the misery and wretchedness which presses so heavily on the large majority of the laboring class ... A small number of rich men have been able to lay upon the masses of the poor a yoke little better than slavery itself.[71]

Similarly, Senator Walsh explained that "any injunction or any law that prevents a man from striking ... is a law of servitude, and that is the principle we have to keep in mind. It is the difference between freedom and servitude. A man has a right to work or not to work."[72] Representative Cooley said that the NLRA "breathed the true spirit of freedom; freedom from starvation wages, child labor, and unbearable working hours and conditions ... I am for this bill because it is animated by the same spirit of freedom."[73] Representative Vito Marcantonio echoed the complaints of the Auto-Lite workers as he responded to arguments of the Act's opponents that it would violate the "liberty of contract."

How about the liberty of the worker? Unless Congress protects the workers what liberty have they? Liberty to be enslaved, liberty to be crucified under the spread-out system, liberty to be worked to death under the speed-up system, the liberty to work at charity wages, the liberty to work long hours.[74]

Hence, members of Congress invoked labor's constitutional vision as they acted to protect workers' rights.

Over the objections of labor's leading constitutional thinkers, members of Congress also invoked a more conservative constitutional theory—that the workers' rights to organize and strike were necessary to prevent obstructions to interstate commerce. On this view, Congress wanted protection for workers' rights not because they were important in themselves, but because protecting them would help to reduce strikes. The NLRA's statement of findings and policy took this approach.[75] Due in part to this fateful choice, courts have tended to devalue the workers' rights to organize and strike, while emphasizing the con-

---

68. Rep. William P. Connery, Jr., Speech given on radio station WEVO (May 31, 1935), *in* 79 Cong. Rec. 8536 (1935).
69. 79 *Cong. Rec.* 9714 (1935).
70. *Ibid.*
71. 78 *Cong. Rec.* 9060 (1934).
72. 78 *Cong. Rec.* 12034 (1934).
73. 79 *Cong. Rec.* 9704 (1935).
74. 79 *Cong. Rec.* 9699–700 (1935).
75. *See* Zietlow, *supra* note 7, at 79.

servative goal of protecting commerce.[76] Unfortunately, this approach discounts the contributions of workers such as the Auto-Lite strikers and their vision of freedom as a powerful exercise of popular constitutionalism.

V. Conclusion

The passage of time, court interpretations, and pro-management amendments by Congress have greatly weakened the effectiveness of the NLRA. Union membership is down, and an increasing number of workers labor in low wage, no benefit jobs. Nonetheless, the story of the Auto-Lite strike is worth celebrating. The success of that strike contributed to the formation of the UAW,[77] which is still one of the largest and most powerful unions in the country. Toledo became then, and remains today, one of the strongest pro-labor cities in this country. Homer Martin, elected UAW president with the support of Toledo unionists, said of Pontiac, Michigan:

> When I come into a place like [this town] and find a great, thriving union with all of its various phases of activity, I feel a whole lot like Lincoln must have felt when he went into some of the places and found an emancipated group of slaves, living in the same territory as formerly, but under much different conditions.[78]

One could say the same of Toledo.

As Martin's words suggest, the transformation brought about by the Auto-Lite strikers was part of a regime shift extending from the shop floor to the highest reaches of the constitutional order. By asserting and exercising their rights to organize and strike, workers across the country girded Congress to pass the NLRA and induced the Supreme Court to uphold it. Their accomplishment opened the way for the New Deal economic legislation under which several generations of industrial workers shared in America's prosperity.

The Auto-Lite factory was demolished in 1999,[79] but the plant entrance was left standing. Beside the entrance, an inscription reads: "This stone doorway will stand forever as a symbol of the Toledo Auto-Lite workers' commitment, loyalty and solidarity, which enabled them to break with the past, and enter a better future."[80] That future has now receded into the past, and the example of the Auto-Lite strikers affirms to a new generation that with commitment, loyalty and solidarity, a better future can be won.

---

76. *See generally* James Gray Pope, "How Workers Lost the Right to Strike, and Other Tales," 103 *Mich. L. Rev.* 518 (2005).

77. Interview by Jack W. Skeels with George F. Addes (June 25, 1960), WSU Archives, *supra* note 24, at 40–41; Bernstein, *supra* note 22, at 222.

78. Jim Pope, "Worker Lawmaking, Sit-Down Strikes, and the Shaping of American Industrial Relations, 1935–1958," 24 *Law & Hist. Rev.* 45, 68 (2006) (quoting Homer Martin, Speech at Pontiac, Mich. (May 1, 1937), WSU Archives, *supra* note 24, Homer Martin Collection, Box 3, at 1).

79. Jennifer John, *A Promise Kept*, UAW Solidarity, Dec. 2002 (Democracy and Justice side bar), http://www.uaw.org/Solidarity/02/1202.feature08.html.

80. Inscription on plaque attached to the Auto-Lite memorial in Union Memorial Park, Toledo, Ohio.

Senator Robert F. Wagner

There can no more be democratic self-government in industry without workers participating therein, than there could be democratic government in politics without workers having the right to vote.... That is why the right to bargain collectively is at the bottom of social justice for the worker as well as the sensible conduct of business affairs. The denial or observance of this right means the difference between despotism and democracy.

Planning in Place of Restraint

We are beginning to sense that a new economic society has come to its full maturity.... In modern society, the welfare of the individual is embedded in the destiny of the group. No one can stand alone, and in the new harmony which is requisite, legislation must swing the baton. The need for order marks the reign of law....

It may seem paradoxical that the gospel of freedom for business enterprise nurtured a legal system which indulged solely in restraints and prohibitions.... Let us take as an example our constitutional doctrine of freedom of contract, as it operated upon economic affairs in the nineteenth century. It did not tell business men what they might do. It did not provide channels for the flow of activity. Despite the pleasant connotations of the word "freedom," the doctrine did not serve primarily as a guardian of liberties. It operated to perpetuate an idealized competitive system. There was no freedom to cooperate, no freedom to make contracts for industrial coordination, no freedom to adhere to a unified plan, no freedom for the workingman to secure the collective-bargaining without which his liberty is illusory. We bartered away many opportunities for rational action in exchange for a single type of liberty which the law sought to foster purely by imposing a series of narrowing restraints....

Furthermore, the right thing is no longer confined to the mandates of ancient commandments and the benevolent ideas of earlier governments. It includes the abolition of economic exploitation and of the degradation of laborers which results from starvation wages and excessively long hours. It includes all of the measures necessary, in light of present experience, to bring order into industry and to guarantee social justice to all of its participants.[81]

---

81. Robert F. Wagner, "Planning in Place of Restraint," 22 *Survey Graphic* 395 (1933).

Organization of a Company Town

SWOC Headquarters, Aliquippa, Library of Congress.

Aliquippa: The Company Town and Contested Power in the Construction of Law (1935–1937)

Kenneth M. Casebeer*

Little Siberia they called it and with good reason. The A.F. of L. organizers were not even permitted to enter Aliquippa (then called Woodlawn) during the great steel strike of 1919. Friends or relatives of its inhabitants were not allowed to stop for an unauthorized visit. Roads were barred and every stranger alighting from the train was questioned, and if he could not render a good account of himself and his busi-

---

* A longer version of this article first appeared in, Kenneth M. Casebeer, "Aliquippa: The Company Town and Contested Power in the Construction of Law," 43 *Buffalo L. Rev.* 617 (1995). It is reprinted with permission of the Buffalo Law Review.

ness, hustled into jail overnight and then back to whence he came. When the great steel strike was called in September 1919 the cordon sanitaire proved its effectiveness; not a man walked out of the Jones & Laughlin Aliquippa mills.[1]

The big trouble was, we couldn't call our souls our own. We couldn't think unionism. All the swimming pools in town and all the athletic fields and Tom Girdler's man-to-man policy couldn't make up for the fact that we had no job security. We were treated like pig iron. We were just a commodity.[2]

Aliquippa, Pennsylvania, during the 1930s was the company town of the Jones & Laughlin Steel Co. The works of Jones & Laughlin ("J & L" or the "Company") stretch for over three miles along the Ohio River, twenty five miles north of Pittsburgh. They are now largely rusted, scavenged hulks of mills that employed more than 10,000 workers for decades—before the 1980s takeover by the LTV Corporation in the death pains of the industry.[3] Now they are worked by a few hundred. Then and now, if you did not float to the company docks, you dropped out of the ridges on the single road following the bottom of the side valley emptying into the Ohio. Today, storefronts of old buildings, broken and boarded up, line the mile or so of the highway through the old town. One in ten still opens for business, most prominently as liquor stores. The old hotel, where the union organizers stayed, became a warehouse; the company store, a subsidized housing center. On either side of this main street, creeping up the sides of the hills and ridges defining Aliquippa, the Company built, over time, twelve plans of housing, one per hill. The hills determined the number of houses. J & L determined the ethnic groups of workers and townspeople who would populate each plan. The only way to go between plans was to drop down into town before starting up a separate hill.

Main street ended at the entrance of J & L, called the Wye because of the road's abrupt right turn, through a gated tunnel under the rail road embankment of the Aliquippa and Southern Railroad, also owned by the Company, which separated the town from the works. If it was hard to get into Jones and Laughlin without welcome, it was also hard to get out, or to get others in, as the Company would discover in 1937 during the triumphant organizing strike of the Steel Workers Organizing Committee ("SWOC"). Earlier, in Aliquippa, life had been just plain hard.

In and after June, 1935, the Company discharged thirteen men: Domenic Brandy, Angelo Volpe, Harry Phillips, Martin Dunn, William Collins, George Marroll, Royal Boyer, Gulio Iacobucci, Martin Gerstner, Angelo Razzano, Ely Bozich, Ronald Cox, and Marco Lukich. The men were discharged for a variety of alleged causes, including inefficiency and violation of company rules, such as leaving machine keys unattended, failure to answer a whistle call, using a head signal rather than a hand signal, failing to close a door usually left open, and making bad nails.[4]

---

1. *National Labor Relations Act and Proposed Amendments: Hearings on S.1000, S.1264, S.1392, S.1550, S.1580, and S.2123 Before the Senate Comm. on Education and Labor*, 76th Cong., 3d Sess. 4657 (1940) [hereinafter *NLRA Hearings*] (testimony of Philip Murray, vice president United Mine Workers).

2. Spencer R. McCulloch, "Career of Tom Girdler, Steel's #1 Strikebreaker," *St. Louis Post-Dispatch*, 1C (June 29, 1937). [hereinafter McCulloch] (quoting anonymous steelworker).

3. Barnaby J. Feder, "Survival a Struggle in a Town that Steel Forgot," *N.Y. Times*, C1 (Apr. 27, 1993). *See generally* John P. Hoerr, *And The Wolf Finally Came: The Decline of the American Steel Industry* (1988) (discussing the decline of the American steel industry).

4. *In the Matter of: Jones & Laughlin Steel Corporation and Amalgamated Association of Iron, Steel & Tin Workers of North America, Beaver Valley Lodge No. 200*, No. C57, N.L.R.B. Record 33–42 [hereinafter NLRB Record] (incorporated in *NLRB v. Jones & Laughlin Steel Corp.* 83 F.2d 998 (D.C. Cir. 1936)).

The men, working with the Amalgamated Association of Iron, Steel and Tin Workers, AFL ("AA"), brought unfair labor practice charges of retaliation for union activity to the National Labor Relations Board ("NLRB") under the newly enacted Wagner Act.[5] Thus, the Jones & Laughlin case became the test case of the National Labor Relations Act's ("NLRA") constitutionality. With the case won in 1937, the Steel Workers Organizing Committee of the upstart CIO organized the Aliquippa Works following an unexpectedly brief forty-eight hour strike. J & L soon signed a less favorable version of the industry pattern contract first agreed to by U.S. Steel earlier that year.

Such describes the case — *NLRB v. Jones & Laughlin Steel Corp.*[6] — but not the law. To study any case opinion is to study only an artifact of a certain point of decision making within a larger set of institutional actions affecting the parties, with all such action involving legal intervention, invocation, or reliance. In fact, the powers affected by legal adjudication are often minor parts of the contestation of power between the parties, or indeed wider numbers of people not named. To study the law of the discharged men is more accurately to study the construction of power exercised in Aliquippa. Power is what people actually experience as their law. Power rarely turns on specific issues, but rather on a system of social expectations that prevail and define the realm of the possible. The constellation of power deployed in a community results from an ongoing historically specific struggle of the people there over the terms and conditions of social organization.

Thus, while in 1937, organizing J & L and winning reinstatement of the fired men were transparently separate events as NLRB election and Supreme Court decision, as a matter of legal power, the men and women of Aliquippa experienced them together. The relation between the law of *Jones & Laughlin* and the political-economy of the company town in vertically integrated industrial oligopolies makes something different of the constitutional foundation the steel company challenged in an effort to preserve its local control over production in the plant and reproduction of the labor supply. A democratic interpretation of the distribution of constitutional powers would take the political effects from the workers' perspective into account, weaving workers into the fabric of constitutional construction, just as their mode of production had already demonstrated the interdependence of their work with the production of others across the nation. Horace Davis wrote in 1933:

> Steel mills require much land, and they are seldom built in the middle of an existing city. Rather the mill is located outside urban areas, sometimes far from any important center of population. Steel workers come to live by the mill; they form a town. In this town the steel company commonly exercises in fact, if not in law, all the functions of government. The company dominates education and organized religion. It is the state.
>
> The forces that police the steel communities exercise governmental authority but typically are paid by the companies and are responsible directly to them. In time of industrial peace, the mills and company towns are policed by special deputy sheriffs, usually in uniforms — the retainers of the feudal lords of steel. In Pennsylvania these guards were formerly members of the force known as the "coal and iron police." ... All commissions were revoked in 1931, but the legal basis of the system remains unchanged. The United States is the only important industrial country which permits private payment of officers of the law.[7]

---

5. National Labor Relations Act, ch. 372, 49 Stat. 449 (1936) [hereinafter NLRA] (codified as amended at 29 U.S.C. sections 151–169 (1984)). Sect. 8-1 and 8-3 violations were charged.

6. 301 U.S. 1 (1937).

7. Horace B. Davis, *Labor and Steel* 140 (1933).

In 1851, Benjamin Franklin Jones bought a small iron works in Pittsburgh, merging in 1857 with James Laughlin to form the Jones & Laughlin Steel Company.[8] In 1898, when it became evident that the company needed to expand beyond the limits of its Pittsburgh holdings, agents for the company began buying up undeveloped farm land and swamps in and around Woodlawn and West Aliquippa, including the amusement park along the river.[9] In 1905, plans for a fully integrated steel manufacturing mill in the center of seven and a half miles of Company owned riverbank were completed, and in November of 1906, Paul Moore, head of the Company's Woodlawn Land Company subsidiary, began groundbreaking for the first blast furnace. Building the entire plant would last into the twenties. By then, the mills were fully integrated, with open hearth furnaces, Bessemer converters, coking ovens, and tinplate, tubing and wire metal work sub-divisions.[10] In the early 1930s, Jones & Laughlin ranked as the fourth largest steel company in the United States, with gross assets of 181 million dollars and 4.9% of the gross tonnage in the national market. The Aliquippa Works alone would have constituted the nations sixth largest producer by both employment and gross tonnage.[11]

At first the work force consisted of mostly the local population of British and German stock. But as with other Pennsylvania mill towns, substantial immigration transformed the population before 1920.[12] During this time the population increased nearly five fold, from 3140 to 15,426, with 40% of the total being foreign-born.[13] As the industry and J & L grew, the company recruited workers in waves of Italian immigrants, and by the early 1930s, primarily Eastern Europeans, including Poles, Slavs and Ukrainians. When union organizing began in the thirties, larger portions of the work force were at least first generation natives. The total population stayed virtually the same, 27,116 in 1930 to 27,023 in 1940. However, for men 21 years and older in 1930, native-whites totaled 3239; foreign born whites 4713; and African-Americans 906; shifting by 1940 to 4333; 3654; and 1031 respectively.[14] Of the 4708 foreign born men over 21 listed in Aliquippa in 1930, 337 were from Poland, 451 from Czechoslovakia, 241 from Austria, 1218 from Yugoslavia, 217 from Greece, 1276 from Italy and 968 from other countries.[15]

In the 1930s, Jones and Laughlin still controlled the town economically.[16] It employed 10,000 of the town's population of 30,000. 7918 men and 1224 women were classed as workers in 1940, of which 6125 men and 169 women worked in Iron and

---

8. "Family's Fourth," *Time*, 72 (Apr. 13, 1936).

9. Gertrude Hightower, History of Aliquippa, Logstown and Woodlawn 7 (1941) (unpublished manuscript, on file at the B.F. Jones Memorial Library, Aliquippa, Pa.).

10. For the definitive study of the economic and structural development of the steel industry generally, see volumes I and II of Carroll R. Daugherty et al., *The Economics of the Iron and Steel Industry* (1937). For a discussion of the development of the Jones & Laughlin Steel Co., see 1 Daugherty, *supra*, at 22, 339 n.3, 488; 2 Daugherty, supra, at 666–67, 712, 715.

11. 1 Daugherty, *supra* note 10, at 22–24.

12. On immigration and steel generally, see John Bodnar, *Steelton: Immigration and Industrialization, 1870–1940* (1977) [hereinafter Bodnar, Steelton]. On the conditions of steel workers in Pittsburgh early in the century, see John A. Fitch, *The Steel Workers* (1911).

13. Dept. of Engineering and Public Policy, School of Urban Affairs, Carnegie-Mellon University, Milltowns in the Pittsburgh Region: Conditions and Prospects 70 (May 1983) (unpublished manuscript, on file with Labor Archives, Hillman Library, University of Pittsburgh).

14. 2 Bureau of Census, U.S. Dep't. of Commerce, Sixteenth Census of the United States: 1930: Populations, pt. 6, at 163 (1940) [hereinafter Census].

15. *Ibid.* at 489.

16. For a study of life in a typical steel company town, see Charles Walker, *Steeltown: An Industrial Case History of the Conflict Between Progress and Security* (1950).

17. Census, *supra* note 14, at 183.

Steel.[17] J & L owned 700 houses occupied entirely by employees, and it built many of the rest within twelve "plans" on land owned by its subsidiary, the Woodlawn Land Co. (the "Land Company"). Logstown, site of the original settlement, became Plan #2. This area, known as the Borough of Woodlawn, included 767.5 acres, of which 623.5 were owned by J & L. The Land Company's brochure described the future of "Woodlawn on the Ohio."

> Woodlawn nestles in a beautiful valley 19 miles down the Ohio from Pittsburgh, in Beaver County, and spreads out its cozy homes upon the surrounding hills. Its streets are paved with brick in the business section and macadam in the residence section, concrete sidewalks, shade trees, sewere (sic) and electric lighted. It has every modern utility, such as natural gas, electric light, a pure potable water supply, and ample police and fire protection. Its school system is splendidly organized and its opportunities for delightful home and neighborhood life are not equaled in this end of the state. The new works are attracting iron and steel workers of the better class and the new town is designed to give them the very best homes amidst the most beautiful surroundings. The houses put up by the Woodlawn Land Company contain from six to ten rooms and bath, are constructed of brick, cement or frame or combinations of these materials, and are in every respect as attractive and convenient as any suburban town in the district can show, and are above the average city home in point of comfort and convenience.[18]

In 1917, these houses cost between $2200 and $2400, and consisted of a downstairs with a living room, dining room and kitchen, and an upstairs, with three large bedrooms and a bathroom with running water. The houses were being completed at the rate of one per day.[19] Early immigrants with houses rented to boarders to accommodate the overwhelming demand. The three large bedrooms would house up to 25 men, each of whom would have the use of the bathroom and a bed for the duration of one shift. Families could rent a two room makeshift apartment upstairs, which consisted of a one room living room/kitchen, a bedroom, and the use of a shared bath.[20] Women made and sold lunches to the single men on each shift. According to a June 1930 survey, "American employees preferred six room dwellings for their families. Many foreign, and nearly all Negro families found no constraint in houses of four rooms and bath, considering primarily the cheapness of the house, whether for purchase or for rent."[21]

A worker-occupant could buy a home on time, the title remaining with the company. A deed and mortgage would be delivered to the purchaser upon payment of 50% of the purchase price. If the worker voluntarily left J & L employ, the Land Company would refund the payments less three percent. Whether one left voluntarily depended, in part, on what hours were worked, and therefore whether the house payments could be made. One of the plaintiffs, Ronald Cox, was called into the office of the general manager and told "that if he persisted in affiliating with the union, the company would not tolerate his back rents, and would have to put him out of the house; that the local merchants would not extend any credit."[22] In the early 1930s, 40% of Aliquippa families had mortgages controlled by J & L.

---

18. Mill Creek Valley Historical Association, Story of the Woodlawn Land Company 4 (n.d.) [hereinafter Woodlawn] (unpublished manuscript, on file at the B.F. Jones Memorial Library, Aliquippa, Pa.).

19. Cheryl W. Beck, ed., *The Twentieth Century History of Beaver County*, 41 (1989).

20. *Ibid.* at 42.

21. Woodlawn, *supra* note 18, at 8.

22. NLRB Record, *supra* note 6, at 208 (testimony of Ronald Cox, March 2, 1936).

Only the Woodlawn Land Co. sold lots to merchants along Franklin Avenue, Aliquippa's main street. The Pittsburgh Mercantile Co., the company store, was the only outlet for clothing and sundries, which it would sell on credit, with payments to be deducted from paychecks.

> This benevolent system of credit has the effect of keeping men within the company town, within control of the mill officials. And it assures always a surplus of labor which can be drawn upon whenever needed.... In Aliquippa, as pay envelope deductions, the workers are allowed only enough cash to buy food and meet such bills as can be taken care of in no other way. The average workman with a family to support and a normal debt owed the company, is allowed not more than $10 a week in cash. All of his earnings above that sum, [Plant Superintendent] Saxer said, are credited against his obligations to the company.[23]

The company owned the railroad, the water company, the bus company, and the trolleys. The town newspaper, the *Aliquippa Gazette*, while nominally independent, was tied to its revenue sources, and therefore maintained an extremely pro-company and anti-union editorial policy, frequently warning residents in front page, boxed stories about specific outside agitators sighted in the area.

By 1934, some observers were not reading the brochures:

> An ugly main street of squatty, dingy business buildings sprawled over the ravine between hills, leading to the fortress like entrance to the steel mill. On the steps of the hills rising from either side of the main street are the homes of the mill hands — dingy, dirty-looking frame shacks built by the company. The typical house has five small rooms crowded into two floors, the dwellings built close together. So steep are the hills sloping down to the main street that in heavy rains, tin cans, and the litter from the slopes gush into the main street of the borough. Beyond the area of the main thoroughfare the streets are unpaved cinder paths. Fumes from the mills and the coke plant have had their effect on vegetation. The original verdure of the hills is gone.[24]

Land ownership also allowed the company to control community development. As former Aliquippa resident, Donald Thompson, put it, "You can call it ruthless segregation or common sense, but the company carved up its community into plans and assigned each incoming nationality to its own — Italians to Plan 11, Anglo-Saxons to Plan 12 across the valley, Serbians to Plan 7, and Plan 6, the highest hill, reserved for management."[25] The planned geographical barriers became, in a sense, law. Many of the steel workers,

> when asked, will tell the story of a Negro who was killed by a Jones & Laughlin policeman about a year and a half ago for breaking into a house in the

---

23. Mac Parker, "Steel and its Men — Battle of Giants," *Philadelphia Rec.*, June 27, 1934, section 2, at 1. Consider the experience of workers in the more open Pittsburgh Works. "As early as 1929, nearly half of the workers in the Pittsburgh plants of the J. & L. had accounts at the company store, and their debts to the store were regularly checked off their wages. Since the depression, the proportion has vastly increased, so that nearly all the workers are being "carried" to a greater or less extent at the store, until they are laid off entirely. This "carrying" puts the workers more than ever in the company's power." Davis, *supra* note 26, at 144.

24. Parker, *supra* note 45, at 1, 2.

25. Interview with Donald Thompson, *quoted* in Eric Leif Davin, The Littlest New Deal: SWOC Takes Power in Steeltown, a Possibility of Radicalism in the Late 1930s (n.d) (unpublished student paper, on file with the University of Pittsburgh Labor Archives). *See also* Harold Ruttenberg, "Steel Town," *Nation*, 623, 624 (Nov. 28, 1934).

"white plan," the section where only bosses and officials live and where by an unwritten law no Negro, Italian, or Slovene is allowed. Many doubt whether the Negro was really breaking into a house, but the incident served to intimidate the workers.[26]

By 1916, when Bert Iacobucci arrived from Italy, Plan 11 was virtually entirely occupied by Italians from the Southern Province of Patrica. Ninety percent of Plan 11 were Patricans. Bruzzes' moved to West Aliquippa. The Music and Politics of Italy Club was split almost equally between the provinces. This high concentration of immigrants from two small areas in Italy resulted from a pattern of immigration. Immigrants would pretend to already have a job lined up in America when they were simply following familial word of earlier settlement.[27] This tended to replicate the tight geographic concentration preferred by the company and encouraged by the terrain. This isolation by plans perched on steep hills was compounded by economic circumstances. There were one or two households with a telephone on all of Plan 11.

Ethnic customs also allowed for greater police control. Italian families made wine. Who made wine was easily known by observing who bought crates of grapes at the freight station. As long as wine was not sold during prohibition, home consumption was left alone. However, it served as a convenient excuse to harass those who found themselves on the bad side of the police. Police would break into houses to search ostensibly for liquor and take union papers while smashing the wine barrels. The automatic fine for possession was $11.45. Some activists paid this fine on a weekly basis.[28]

Geographic immobility matched social immobility. During the 1920s, Aliquippa's population approximated 25,000, but only 50 to 75 students graduated from high school. To get jobs at J & L, boys who were under the minimum age of sixteen obtained false age certificates from certain local officials for a small fee. Many immigrant and black children were assigned to work for the summer quarter and given the winter quarter off. In the three out of four quarters attendance system, students often dropped out of school to help their families work the garden plots which provided their margin against hunger. Almost all of the J & L jobs went to men. The only viable opportunity for young women seemed to be marriage to a millworker, a depressing prospect given the much smaller number of eligible males within the tightly knit and segregated ethnic communities.

Of course, the police exerted the most direct form of social control. The borough police were in reality an arm of the Jones & Laughlin company police, and their police chief had been employed by J & L. The company supplied men to become policemen, and antiunion operations were run out of the office of the J & L police chief, William Mauck. Prior to 1935, no public hall would issue a license to hold any open union meeting in Aliquippa. Workers soliciting authorization cards were followed, arrested on suspicious person charges, taken to the city jail, searched and, if union cards were found, fined or beaten. When people were taken into police custody, "they third degreed everyone who came down there."[29] Fines were simply deducted from the monthly paycheck along with rent and debts owed to the company store.[30] Records were kept of all persons entering and leaving any hotel where union organizers stayed.

---

26. Ruttenberg, *supra* note 25, at 624.

27. Interview with Bert Iacobucci 3–4 (Dec. 5, 1979), *in* Beaver Valley Labor History Society Papers [hereinafter Iacobucci Interview] (on file in Labor Archives, Univ. of Pitt.).

28. *Ibid.* at 18–19.

29. *Ibid.* at 20.

30. *NLRA Hearings, supra* note 1, at 4179 (testimony of Clifford Shorts).

What happened in the streets, served as object lessons against protest in the plant. New men recruited from other regions were publicly fired and evicted in front of other workers for gathering socially in each others' houses. A young electrical worker protested his treatment to his foreman, who called the mill police. Four policemen began pushing the electrician around. He tried to escape the property by climbing over a coal pile. The police dragged him back to the mill, severely beat him in front of the workers, a general foreman bound him with haywire around the hands and feet, and they threw him into a police car.[31]

Political organization and social control became a seamless web. "In T.M.'s [Girdler] day you would report for work in the morning. The foreman would say: 'Up kind of late last night weren't you?' When you asked why you would be told: 'The light was burning in your room at 2 a.m.'"[32] Similar control extended to electoral politics.

> On one occasion a small shopkeeper pointed to the fact that members of the governing council of Aliquippa were at the same time continuing to receive salaries as J. & L. officials, in violation of Pennsylvania state law. At the next election these men were replaced with others not openly in the company's pay but equally satisfactory to it. "The company ought to have something to say about the way the town is run," said an official of the J. & L. housing subsidiary, describing the incident. "The company owns pretty near everything in sight."[33]

During elections in the 1920s, Jones & Laughlin trucked people from the mills to voting places, whether they were naturalized citizens or not. Nino Colonna was taken to vote before he was fifteen and every year thereafter. He voted four letter words on the ballot.[34] Workers were fired for reading anarchist literature, and for belonging to the Democratic Party. Republican Party Chairman, J.A. Ruffner wrote an undated form letter, probably for the 1936 elections.

> Dear Sir: In the opinion of the Central Republican Committee the election to be held next November 6th is of the highest importance to the people of Pennsylvania. Every citizen should exercise his or her right of franchise on that day.
>
> THE RECORDS SHOW THAT YOU FAILED TO VOTE AT THE PRIMARY HELD LAST MAY.
>
> You are strongly urged to vote on November 6th, and the Committee requests that you vote the straight Republican ticket."[35]

Workers were fired especially for attempts at economic self-organization. If there was perceived to be a difference in these posed threats, unionism was the highest sin. Pete Muselin, born in Croatia, arrived in America in 1912, and reported being threatened and arrested numerous times for attempting to hold an organizing meeting. He was told that,

> [w]e make the rules. This is not the United States. This is Woodlawn, and we're going to do what we please because J & L gives bread and butter to all these people.... Every once in a while the cops came to my home and just raided the place—no warrant, no nothing. They would take every book, every periodical,

---

31. *Ibid.* at 4178.
32. McCulloch, *supra* note 4, at 1C (quoting anonymous steelworker).
33. Davis, *supra* note 26, at 141.
34. Interview with Nino Colonna 6–7 (Sept. 9, 1979), in Beaver Valley Labor History Society Papers [hereinafter Colonna Interview] (on file in Labor Archives, Univ. of Pitt.).
35. Letter from J. A. Ruffner (on file in Steel Workers Union file, Historical Collections and Labor Archives, Pattee Library, Penn State Univ.).

every bulletin; they'd just dump them in a pile and throw them in the police cruiser and they would never return them. They were looking for books on Marxism, but they could not distinguish one book from another, in order to make sure they cleaned out the house.[36]

While he was chief of police, Mike Kane would run his motorcycle right into a boarding house kitchen to break up the "Hunkies."

In Aliquippa, attempting to organize a union was punishable by five years in prison. At a fraternal lodge meeting in 1926, Muselin and four other Croats were arrested and indicted on a charge of sedition. The district attorney would not touch the case. The solicitor for Jones & Laughlin, Dave W. Craig, was appointed special prosecutor. The Croats were convicted in 1927 and sentenced to five years in the county workhouse. For any infractions, prisoners were sent to the hole, and given two slices of bread and a cup of water per day. Miles Reseter died in the prison hospital two or three months before the others were released in 1932.[37] Later, former J & L President Tom Girdler denied any coercion against unionists.

I don't recall any steps taken to discourage their activities, except the civil liberties and the freedom of speech that we had at that time, sometimes advising a man that he was better off in attending to his own business and handling his own affairs instead of having someone else handle them for him.[38]

Harry Phillips, the first president of Beaver Valley Lodge 200, Amalgamated Association of Iron, Steel and Tin Workers was followed by J & L police, then beaten by unknown assailants in a dark alley. Phillips told his story to the National Steel Labor Board.

[O]n August 30th I was delivering journals to different men to sign up on Davison Street and the Jones & Laughlin police—Donnelly and Slater and Chief Ambrose of the Aliquippa police—drove up to me and said, "What are you doing?" I said, "Delivering these papers." I give them one and it tells about the big meeting in Ambridge. They started to ask me some questions and I said, "I ain't going to answer questions. I got to be at work at nine o'clock." So I went home and changed my clothes and started down the street, and when I got to the bottom of the hill around the Catholic Church—that is on Main Street beyond Franklin Avenue—they passed me there, and they passed me a little further down the street. I didn't see the Chief in the car the next time they passed me, and the last time they passed me just as I got near the old Rialto Theater. I went to the "Y" and happened to meet a fellow by the name of Robinson at the corner. I talked to him a few minutes, and he said, "I see the Jones & Laughlin police driving around backward and forward." I went to catch up to a man in front of me going to work. He wasn't more than twenty feet in front of me. I was going in the tunnel. There was a man there who said, "Harry." I turned around. I said, "Just a minute." I didn't get a chance to say that before I got planted in the mouth and struck over the head with a blackjack. I was pulled in between two automobiles, and the next blow I got must have hit me on the shoulder because I don't remember going in there. I knew I had to grab so I got hold of them. I had one

---

36. Pete Muselin, *The Steel Fist in a Pennsylvania Company Town*, in Bud Schultz & Ruth Schultz, *It Did Happen Here*, 70 (1989) [hereinafter Muselin, *Steel Fist*].

37. *Ibid.* at 72–73.

38. *Violations of Free Speech and Rights of Labor: Hearings before a Subcommittee of the Senate Committee on Education and Labor*, 74th Cong., 3d Sess. 13787 (1938) (testimony of Tom Girdler to "LaFollette Committee").

man down and the other man half way down. I held them there until some help came. I made a lot of noise—I tried to anyhow. They pulled one man off, and the man they pulled off said, "Let them two fight", so they figured he was going to stand by and let them two fight. Before we could get up this man started after me with a blackjack again. When he started in after me he had a black-jack in one hand and screw driver in the other, and when I started to come up he hooked me on the side of the eye but didn't break the flesh—just scratched me. When I got up he made a swing with the blackjack at me and I ducked out in the open. I was going to run in and kick at the man but when I looked at the man again my head wasn't clear and instead of seeing one I saw four, so I thought the best thing for me to do was get out of the way. They started to run. I couldn't find anything to grab hold of but a piece of slag. I could just barely lift it and I couldn't throw it very far, and he started up the steps. He made a motion to throw the screwdriver back at me and I went to look for a Borough cop. In that location there is generally one or two at all times. We have traffic lights there. It is a pretty bad intersection at that point, and they always need an officer there to watch traffic most of the time. I went all the way from there to the police station.[39]

When requesting police protection from town police he was told, "Get the hell out of here. You don't deserve protection." Later, at the Steel Labor Board proceedings, Phillips recognized one of the attackers at a hearing on Huntington, West Virginia's organizing drive.

Company police broke into Financial Secretary Martin Gerstner's house while he was at work. The police threatened his wife and suggested that he should stop union agitating. Martin Gerstner moved to Ambridge. Royal Boyer, a leader of African-Americans in the plant, also had his wife warned of his activities.

And then there was George Isoski. Isoski worked for J & L until he fell from a scaffold and spent 22 months in the hospital with a broken back. In exchange for waiving any corporate liability, he was promised a job for the rest of his life. Less than a week after his return from recuperation, he was discharged.[40] Isoski was not a union leader, but was active in collecting union cards among fellow workers. One evening in 1933, he was stopped by town police on a public street.

I went up to see Mr. [Martin] Gerstner, 213 Franklin Avenue, Financial Secretary. While going up, I seen two Jones & Laughlin Company policemen standing in front of this building and when I came back down from his house, they still were standing there. So I started for home when a friend of mine came to me and told me to watch myself because there is some cops following me. So I started for home and I got as far as the Laughlin School, and a machine came up and three company police came to me and one of them said, first he pointed his finger at me, and asked me how many cards I signed up and I said, "Its none of your business", and then he said again, "You bastard, how many cards have you", and I said none, when all at once he reached over and started searching me while the other cops watched and he took from the inside of my shirt, about fifty cards.[41]

---

39. In the Matter of Amalgamated Association of Iron, Steel and Tin Workers of North America, Beaver Valley Lodge v. Jones & Laughlin Steel Corp: Hearing before the National Steel Labor Relations Board 85–86 (Nov. 16, 1934) (on file in Labor Archives, Univ. of Pitt.).

40. Bruce Minton, "Steel Towns that Labor Runs," *New Masses*, 7 (Feb. 8, 1936).

41. Statement of George Issosky, Exhibit 5, Steel Labor Board Investigation, *in* Clinton Golden Papers (on file in Historical Collections and Labor Archives, Pattee Library, Penn. State Univ., University Park, Pa.).

Police first arrested him for his own protection, claiming that he was drunk. He was taken to the station, held without contact, questioned and then, by the suggestion of the police chief, the next morning, a Sunday, was committed to the State Hospital for the Insane in Torrence, Pennsylvania. The commitment itself was not preceded by the hearings required by state law or medical procedure. Instead, he was examined by a panel that consisted of the company doctor, the company nurse, and the company real estate agent. His family was not informed of his whereabouts. Isoski spent two months in Torrence before intercession by Governor Pinchot forced his release.

In 1933, workers struck the Spang-Chalfant specialty steel plant across the river in Ambridge. Workers at various factories in Ambridge had voted to join the Steel and Metal Workers Industrial Union. Organizing in Ambridge first started over the depression. The seven steel fabricating plants there adopted a share the work policy. No one was fired, but wages were slashed in 1930 and 1931, and workers worked intermittently during each pay period. Many were without enough money for food. An Unemployed Council[42] grew rapidly to fight evictions and water and gas cutoffs.

> The Council would assemble a large group of people in front of the house or apartment from which a family had been evicted. The members of the group carried the family's furniture back inside the dwelling....
>
> Some landlords tried to force tenants out of the apartments by turning off the heat and taking glass out of the windows. The Council fought this tactic by collecting cardboard and placing it over the empty window frames.... Council activists fought gas and water main shutoffs by using a special rod made by a blacksmith to reopen closed valves. They poured concrete over the reopened valves so that the gas or water company would have a hard time shutting them again.[43]

Experience networking and organizing for the Unemployment Council became a direct basis for union organization.

On October 2, 1933, workers at the National Metal Moulding Works voted a strike. The next morning, the men marched to the mill demanding full recognition of the union. The company asked for a few days to think about it, and a union committee asked the workers whether they wanted to come in or stay out. They decided to stay out. The mill closed and nothing happened. The same events occurred at H.H. Robertson, Central, Wykoff, and Byers Mills. At 3:00 p.m. the same day, a delegation, composed first of Spang-Chalfant workers and followed by other union members, went to the Spang mill. They were met there by company deputies armed with rifles, tear gas guns, and machine guns. On October 4, fifteen men tried to go to work and were forcibly stopped by the pickets. Immediately, tear gas and gun shots came from within the mill, wounding one of the pickets.[44] The following day's events were documented in hearings ordered by Governor Pinchot on "Special Policing in Industry" in Ambridge, March 10, 1934. Sheriff O'Laughlin, chief law enforcement official in Beaver County and formerly head of the Jones & Laughlin Coal and Iron Police, was, in his words, contacted by all the industrial plants demanding protection and offering to pay all expenses of special deputies. Where upon, he

---

42. On the Unemployment Councils and their relation to the CIO, see Roy Rozenzweig, "Organizing the Unemployed: The Early Years of the Great Depression," in James Green ed., *Workers' Struggles, Past and Present: A Radical America Reader* 168 (1983).

43. "The Great Ambridge Strike of 1933," *Beaver Valley Lab. Hist. J.,* 1 (Jan., 1980).

44. League for Social Justice, Report on Ambridge Riot 1–2 (1933) [hereinafter Social Justice Report], *in* Beaver Valley Labor History Society Papers (on file in Labor Archives, Univ. of Pitt.).

got William Shaffer, commander of the American Legion Post in Aliquippa, to provide seventy-five boys with military experience, and added another seventy-five by his own efforts. In all 248 special deputies were sworn in, of which about fifty were J & L employees. The steel companies eventually paid $24,811.40. The men were transported to Ambridge, organized into squads of four with at least one ex-serviceman, given weapons, and placed under the command of four lieutenants. One of these was Mike Kane, who was at that time justice of the peace in Aliquippa and an employee of J & L. The force was accompanied by Burgess (mayor) Caul of Ambridge and the county's prosecuting attorney. They marched military style to the Spang-Chalfant plant on Twenty-third Street, carrying tear gas, shotguns, clubs, revolvers and machine guns, marked with white handkerchief arm bands and some wearing overseas helmets.[45]

> The line halted in front of the Wycoff office. Pickets in the front line there stood silent, grimly clutching clubs. Women's voices behind these men sent vile insults at the long line. From the head of the column came: "Break 'em up.'"
>
> Deputies stepped out of rank. One used his club on a striker, hitting the man across the knuckles to force him to drop a stick.
>
> The hundreds of spectators who had crowded the sidestreets, sensing the danger for the first time, started to run up alleys and between houses. Many strikers joined them. But many stayed and defiantly jeered.
>
> Suddenly I heard an explosion and saw a tuft of white smoke seemingly "bouncing" off the side of a brick house across from the Wycoff office. The tuft spread into a cloud and sent people scurrying down Duss Avenue toward Ambridge. It was tear gas.
>
> Two other bombs were shot from deputies['] guns in the same manner and that part of the avenue was effectively cleared.
>
> The marchers then resumed toward the main body of strikers at the Spang works.
>
> The crowd of pickets, spectators and newspapermen knotted at the plant entrance all realized that identity meant nothing to the deputies, who meant to clear the sector at any cost.
>
> A sedan leading the marchers reached the entrance unmolested, as did the head of the column, which halted Out of the car stepped a well-built neatly-dressed man — Sheriff Charles O'Laughlin of Beaver County.
>
> Mounting the car's running board, he raised his two hands and asked for silence. The crowd quieted down.
>
> "We're here" he said slowly, "to clear open up this entrance and clear these streets and we can do it. I hope you'll go peacefully,"
>
> He stepped to the ground. Before the crowd had time to take up its wild shouting, the Sheriff gave a signal and the deputies deployed through the crowd, shoving and poking anyone without a white armband, toward Ambridge.[46]

---

45. Commission on Special Policing in Industry Report to Governor Pinchot (1934) [hereinafter Governor's Report], *in* Beaver Valley Labor History Society Papers (on file in Labor Archives, Univ. of Pitt.).

46. *Social Justice Report, supra* note 44, at 3. Compare the official report by the Governor's Committee, based on the Sheriff's testimony, "the Sheriff crossed the street by himself and made a last effort to persuade the pickets to withdraw. The strikers retorted defiantly and the Sheriff told his men to take the strikers' clubs away. Within a few seconds tear gas was fired, clubs began to fly, and then buckshot was fired." Governor's Report, *supra* note 45, at 12.

When the shooting started, most of the men began to run. Approximately one hundred were injured, most of them shot in the back. A stray bullet killed an onlooker on a porch one to three blocks away. However, the union identified the victim as a picket named Adam Petrasuski. Mother Bloor spoke at the funeral. Police violently interfered with people going to the funeral of the man killed, and two women, Edith Brisker and May Ecker, were arrested when they tried to speak to the crowd.[47]

Abuse was not limited to pickets, a bread delivery man showed the extent of municipal control.

> I was near Twenty-fourth Street. There were no pickets or strikers there. A bunch of deputies, not among those who came in from the outside but from those who were inside shot at me. They were stationed on the railroad tracks. I did not know what for. I had no stick or anything. I was just watching from a distance what was happening when the fellows from the railroad tracks shot at me hitting me in the back....

> When I first came to the hospital I had to hang around in the waiting room. I was very sick, so I found a bench and lay down. Pretty soon someone came to me, I don't know whether he was a doctor or who, I was too sick to look up. He asked me "where you work?" I was too sick to reply.

> The same evening Dr. F.C. Forcey who is on the staff of the Sewickley Valley hospital and who is also the company physician of the Spang-Chalfant Company said to me "You are a red." I said "Sure, can't you see all the blood from my wounds." Then he said "You ought to be shot."

> Then Dr. Boruku, the second day when he went to take the bandage off the wounds, asked me whether I cry. I said no. Then he tore the bandage off my arms, tearing the hair with it. "You must be tough," he said. Then when he started taking the bandage off my head he said "We're going to have fun now." He tried to tear it off. It hurt terribly, tears were rolling down my eyes, but I said nothing. He could not tear the head bandage off, so he took the scissors and cut my hair.

> When the hospital was built a few years ago every worker in the factories of this valley gave three days wages towards it.[48]

Other injured men were also interrogated about their work before treatment.

The next day, three carloads of police patrolled the streets breaking up groups of three or more at gun point, even on the steps of their homes. Many were routinely searched. Police raided the offices of the strikers to arrest several leaders of the strike, carrying off records and cash, without warrants. Leaders spent days in jail until released on habeas corpus.[49] More than twenty men were fired at Spang-Chalfant. J & L officials approved of this "lesson" in law enforcement for its own community. In May, 1934, J & L paid Federal Laboratories Inc. $1,925.60 for riot guns, long range tear gas projectiles, grenades, and ammunition.

Once the organizing campaign began having an impact in 1935, social control was exercised more concertedly and less openly. A civic group known as the Committee of 500 was established with company funds and the participation of many management personnel for the purpose of preventing the anti-American, foreign influences of unionism.

---

47. "The Massacre in Ambridge 1 Dead, 100 Wounded," *Steel and Metal Worker*, 3 (Nov. 1933).
48. *Social Justice Report, supra* note 44, at 5–6.
49. Governor's Report, *supra* note 45, at 13.

The committee was formed at a meeting at which the main speaker was F. E. Feiger, Vice-President of J & L, and which included in attendance Harry Saxon, Superintendent of the Aliquippa works.[50] When asked if he thought it was a good thing to preserve law and order as in Ambridge, where workers were shot, the organizer of the committee, J. A. Ruffner, also county Republican Chairman, owner of the *Aliquippa Gazette*, and vice president of the J & L land company, said, "That's the finest thing that was ever done in this valley."[51] Ruffner added, "Why, they were picketing! Men who wouldn't work! Whenever three or four people gather together and make remarks that could be resented by another person, they are inciting to riot."[52] On July 14, 1935, the same day the Committee of 500 was announced, the *Aliquippa Gazette* ran a page one, boxed reproduction of one of the Committee's pamphlets.

> My name is John L. Lewis.... I am a bloodsucker.... I must stir up hatred and violence ... I will have in my employ many communists. They are good at violence and bloodshed. You cannot be neutral in this hour of strife ... The fight is yours, you cannot evade it ... take your place in the ranks with us, in the movement to show Racketeer Lewis that we have only one answer for him. Mr. John L. Lewis, we do not need you. You are dirty and the town and citizens of Aliquippa are clean.[53]

A company union, the Employee Representation Plan ("ERP"), was established on June 15, 1933. Management distributed the bylaws in the plant and workers were forced to vote for it as the only balloted alternative. Those who refused were disciplined, sent home or threatened with discharge. The men "elected" were allowed to leave work when they wished and turn in whatever time they wanted to be paid. Clifford Shorts estimated his highest monthly take at $900.[54] One man turned in 25 hours one day because of his one hour travel time. The chairman of the ERP was paid the huge sum of $14,000 per year.

The company's efforts were made easier not only by ownership of the company town and access to the town itself by transportation and property ownership, but also by the coincident development of the steel industry in the region of Western Pennsylvania.[55] As each preceding ethnic wave became situated and somewhat organized, a new group could be brought into the plant and at the same time isolated in separate housing locations. In the thirties, southern blacks were recruited often as replacements for more militant workers invoking the inevitable distrust and mixture of race issues.[56]

Geographic ethnic separation mirrored job segregation within the plant's division of labor. The tin department was worked almost exclusively by Welshmen.[57] Italians and Eastern Europeans worked the open hearths and blooming and butt mills.[58] Beginning with a substantial recruitment drive during World War I, the employment office assigned the

---

50. Marguerite Young, "Steel's G.O.P. Vigilantes," *New Masses*, 9,10 (Aug. 4, 1936).
51. *Ibid.* at 11.
52. *Ibid.* at 12.
53. *Ibid.* at 10.
54. *NLRA Hearings, supra* note 1, at 4182 (testimony of Clifford Shorts).
55. On the relationship between work organization and work life in the development of the steel industry, see John Fitch, *The Steel Workers* (1910); David Brody, *Steelworkers in America: The Nonunion Era* (1960); *David Montgomery, the Fall of the House of Labor* (1987); Katherine Stone, "The Origins of Job Structures in the Steel Industry," 6 *Rev. Radical Pol. Econ.* 113 (1974).
56. For the experience of African-Americans in steel, see Dennis C. Dickerson, *Out of the Crucible: Black Steelworkers in Western Pennsylvania, 1875–1980* (1986).
57. Harold Ruttenberg, "Steeltown," *NATION*, 624 (Nov. 28, 1934).
58. Interview with Clark Cobb 15 (May 14, 1980) [hereinafter Cobb Interview], *in* Beaver Valley Labor History Society Papers (on file in Labor Archives, Univ. of Pitt.).

worst jobs in all departments to African-Americans. While comprising 8% of the work-force in the thirties, 13% of the common laborers were black. In the South Coke Works, almost all workers unloading coke from the ovens were black. They had to constantly chew tobacco on the job to clean their mouths of coke fumes and residues. Almost all of the workers in the general labor gangs were black. No blacks worked in the blooming mill or the seamless tube mill. The general superintendent of the seamless mill was ru-mored to have a clause in his personal employment contract that stated that blacks would not be assigned permanent jobs there. He did not want blacks from the general labor gang to use the restrooms when working the seamless mill. The only black job in tin was the "pickler," who prepared rolled steel plates for tinplating by placing them by hand in a foul smelling acid solution. In the thirties, a few blacks moved into higher paying skilled jobs as a last resort when not enough white workers could be found for the most stren-uous positions. For example, they were given the job of wire drawers who were required to move heavy rods on their shoulders.[59] Supervisory jobs were closed to blacks until the union.[60] Clark Cobb worked the same job in the open hearth for twenty three years.

> [T]hey had a few blacks on the lower paying jobs. Cleaning up and the greasy jobs like that. They stayed at one thing. If one would leave, die or quit, he would get replaced with another black, but when a promotion went up, for more money or better working conditions, then that was a white move because we had no rules to be governed by.[61]

Until 1925, the open hearth worked a twenty four hour turn, with a twenty minute break every four hours. Men caught sleeping or eating during work were sent home. Men who did not report were fetched from home by the foreman. In the summer, many passed out. To get through, "some of the old guys would be singing the old hymns, ya know, sing back in the stables, they be singing that, some of them they would go on the side and say a little prayer, the foreman didn't like that."[62]

Segregation was enforced in the town as well as the plant. There were no black teach-ers or store clerks. Some stores kept separate entrances. The movie house had a black balcony. From the beginning of its substantial presence in the twenties, the Woodlawn Land Co. forced the black population to live in Plan 11 Extension. Due to their own insecurity, many foreign born workers supported the twins of job and home segregation.[63] The Klu Klux Klan openly marched and burned crosses during the twenties. They attended church services in white areas, speaking to congregations and making donations. To counter the Klan, in 1923, a former J & L laborer and grocer, Matthew Dempsey, organized a chap-ter of Marcus Garvey's Universal Negro Improvement Association ("UNIA"). Meetings, usually of fifty mostly mill workers, were held secretly behind closed curtains in his gro-cery concealed from the agents of Captain Mauk.[64] Nonetheless, through stool pigeons, some identified members were fired and run out of town, despite the proud claims of Superintendent of the Aliquippa Works, Tom Girdler, that he had run the Klan out of Aliquippa. The harassment of Dempsey and UNIA members was due to a larger effort co-run by J & L Police Chief Harry Mauck and the F.B.I. special agent in charge of the in-vestigation against Garveyism in Western Pennsylvania. The Reverend W. W. Johnson, pastor of the Emmanuel African Methodist Episcopal Zion Church in Aliquippa, com-

59. "Black Workers at the Aliquippa Works," *Beaver Valley Lab. Hist. J.*, 5 (Sept. 1979).
60. Cobb Interview, *supra* note 58, at 15.
61. Cobb Interview, *supra* note 58, at 13.
62. Cobb Interview, *supra* note 58, at 23.
63. *See generally* Dickerson, *supra* note 56.
64. "Matthew L. Dempsey," *Beaver Valley Lab. Hist. J.*, 4 (June, 1979).

plained to the agent that many of the town's 1,500 African Americans, mostly J & L workers, belonged to the congregation, but only about 100 still attended as a result of Garvey's influence. Shortly thereafter, the discharge of UNIA members led to the disbanding of the organization.[65]

In the face of a community so totally organized and rationalized by the needs of the production process, workers established whatever autonomy they could. Each new group took care of its own as much as possible. Initially, this was made necessary by language and housing. Each ethnic group built a hall in its Plan for social occasions, weddings and picnics. The Italians, the largest single group during most of the period, held a huge annual celebration of San Rocco Day. Ethnic organizations flourished, and would later become a highly organized network of communications for the union organizers. The Steel Workers Organizing Committee issued a broadside for a Mass Meeting at the Lithuanian Hall, January 31, 1937, with speakers in Polish, Lithuanian, Russian, Serbian, Croatian and other languages. The meeting was endorsed by the Croatian Fraternal Union, National Slovak Society, Grand Carniolian Slovenian Catholic Union, Slovak Evangelical Union, International Workers Order, Supreme Lodge of Lithuanians of America, Cooperative Distributors, Inc., Slovak Gymnastic Union Sokol, Workmen's Sick and Death Benefit Fund, Federation of Croatian Clubs, Slovak League of America, United Ukranian Toilers, South Slavonic Catholic Union, Association of Lithuanian Workers, Greek Workers Educational Federation, American Lithuanian Workers Literary Association, Workmen's Sick Benefit Association, Lemko Association 5th District, Western Pennsylvania Federation Slovene National Benefit Society, and Russian Brotherhood Association of U.S.A.[66]

Organizing Aliquippa

Sporadic organizing attempts failed until the Depression. The very same isolation that eased the task of social control in flush times and bred community self-organization of workers against local exigency, now served to focus the realities of layoffs, slowdowns and alienation threatening the only real compensation to life in the company town — relative job security and break even debt management with company housing and the company store. By the mid-1930s, workers were sometimes working only two days every fortnight, not enough for subsistence, and certainly the source of outrage when the company played rank favoritism among the men and women competing for such little paid time. The lifeblood of the wage and the security of the community were simultaneously being destroyed and there was no *quid pro quo* available from the company to lead workers to go along anymore. Thus, the relationship of production and community structure again created the conditions for organization that had been so thoroughly opposed and, on necessary occasion, brutally repressed.

Other agencies, outside union organizers with experience in mine work, and a sympathetic state government intervened and were necessary catalysts.[67] But to explain, first, why the shift to organization was so complete within three years in a whole community, and second, how J & L which had escaped the 1919 strike so completely, should now or-

---

65. Dickerson, *supra* note 56, at 82.

66. Steel Workers Organizing Committee Handbill announcing Jan. 31 Mass Meeting, in Beaver Valler Labor History Society Papers (on file *in* Labor Archives, Univ. of Pitt.)

67. On the organizing of the steel industry generally, see Horace Davis, *Labor and Steel* (1933); Harvey O'Connor, *Steel-Dictator* (1935); Robert R.R. Brooks, *As Steel Goes, ... Unionism in a Basic Industry* (1940); Paul F. Clark et al., eds., *Forging A Union of Steel: Philip Murray, SWOC, and the United Steelworkers* (1987).

ganize so quickly as opposed to the bloody summer facing the rest of Little Steel, it seems necessary to focus on what made Aliquippa extreme—its company status.[68]

The isolation of the town made mobility in or out difficult. J & L paid the wages set by U.S. Steel. But jobs were obtained through nepotism or membership in the Republican Party. Some youths got their jobs by displaying sports jerseys of the team sponsored by the J & L police chief.[69] The foremen ran fiefdoms requiring kick backs for continued employment. Finally, in 1929, J & L police arrested Foreman E. K. Griffith for extorting more than $10,000.

> The Griffith's exposure was long delayed because almost all of the men under him were foreigners, many of whom can barely talk English. The majority of them live in company houses which they are either renting or in which they have tied up their savings of years. Being fired by the Jones and Laughlin Company would mean that their only source of income—Aliquippa is a one industry town—would go, and they would be evicted from their homes when the month's rent was up or when the next installment was due.[70]

Griffith pled guilty, was fined $300, and given one year in the county workhouse, but was not required to pay back any money to the men.[71]

When the Great Crash hit, favoritism still prevailed as the company laid off skilled workers and rehired them after a few days as common laborers at $.40 an hour. In one week in May, between 1500 and 2000 were laid off.[72] During the union drive, the company generated much resentment by hiring teenage Republicans when there was so little work for the older men.

Low pay, infrequent work, and favoritism in advancement accompanied labor cost and technological changes. In 1936, steel paid common laborers 47.9 cents an hour, or $3.76 per day, compared to 62 cents per hour for common laborers in mining. The weekly pay of $16.77 ranked twentieth out of twenty-one industries listed by the National Industrial Conference Board.[73] Hourly earnings overall averaged 65.6 cents compared to an average of approximately 80 cents in coal, petroleum, and construction. This amount included two pay increases in steel over the two previous years in order to forestall increased organization. In 1936, a new continuous strip mill replaced 1400 men with 60 to 75 men over eleven months. 150 union member "chippers" were bumped to part time laborers by a new chipping machine. Skilled workers, the old "Aristocrats of Steel" were deskilled. A threading machine operator making $8 to $9 per day on tonnage prior to 1931, made $4.40 per day in 1936, no higher than some laborers on piece rates.[74]

---

68. On the description of the organization campaign and the terrorism of the Company town, subsequent histories have largely relied on Robert R.R. Brooks, *As Steel Goes* 110–29 (1940), including those of Cortner, Bernstein, and T. Brooks. Many of the same events are described in this section, with reliance on Brooks noted.

69. Interview with Nina Colonna, 6 (Sept. 9, 1979) *in* Beaver Valley Labor History Society Papers. (on file in Labor Archives, Univ. of Pitt.).

70. Joseph Dallet Jr., "Swindle Boss Reign Ended," *Federated Press*, May 28, 1929, *reprinted in* Beaver Valley Lab. Hist. J., 6 (May 1980).

71. *Ibid.*

72. *Ibid.*

73. John L. Lewis, *Industrial Democracy in Steel*, 11 (NBC radio address delivered by John L. Lewis, President of the United Mine Workers and Chairman of the Committee for Industrial Organization, on July 6, 1936 reprinted in CIO pamphlet).

74. Letter from Harold Ruttenberg to John Brophy (July 17, 1936), in Ellickson Papers, Box 16, File 17 (on file with the Labor Archives, Reuther Library, Wayne State University).

Laid off workers were at the mercy of the Republican controlled local administration. The town's Republican administration refused to let the Works Progress Administration or Public Works Administration projects into the area. Those who were still on J & L's payroll could report to work for a month or more without receiving one day's work. In Aliquippa, 44% of the city's workforce were in part-time employment in early 1934.[75] Sometimes the foremen would tell men to go to the train station to pick up a bag of government flour. In exchange for food at the rate of $.50 a day, mill workers on the company payroll were placed in public works projects, the main work being the expansion of the superintendent's private golf course and the improvement of the road leading to it. The workers named the road "Hoover Boulevard."[76] Workers put in an eight hour day on the golf course or improving Aliquippa High School's football field. Sometimes 100 to 150 men worked at a time. Frank Kromerich worked three days to pay for a $1.50 prescription for his daughter.[77] J & L also ran a ferry to Cow Island, a small, uninhabited island in the Ohio River, where it allowed under-employed workers and their families to plant small vegetable gardens.

The precursors to union organizing started in the tin mills. Inside the huge building, 32 mills operated with nine man crews. Every 30 minutes a run of 40, 30 pound bars were heated and rolled 12 times to produce 160 long sheets of tin. Considered the hardest work in the plant, each turn lasted only eight hours rather than the 10 to 12 in the rest of the plant. "The heat from the furnaces was so unbearable ... that workers needed special wooden shoes to keep from burning their feet. Fifty-four additional workers, called 'floaters', were needed on each turn to help or replace any of the 288 regularly assigned workers who became weakened or totally incapacitated by the heat."[78] When the tin mills were being staffed in the early 'teens, mostly English speaking workers, Welsh (called goats), English, Irish, and Scottish, were hired. Many had been Amalgamated Association of Iron, Steel and Tin Workers, who had lost their jobs in a fourteen month strike lost in New Castle, Pennsylvania in 1909. These workers signed "yellow dog" contracts, pledging not to join or remain union members. Pay was by the skill of the job. The best jobs of rougher and roller went to English speakers. The foreign born could only hope to rise to the demanding heater job. Blacks were not permitted to work in the tin mills. Only English workers could rent or buy houses on Plan 12.

The first vestiges of organized resistance followed the end of World War I, when tin workers refused to buy company sponsored liberty bonds. The workers complained that their pay had not kept pace with wartime inflation while the Steel companies made huge war profits, and there "was no democracy in Woodlawn." J & L believed this affront to be the result of internal agitation. Agitating in the mill, according to company officials, started with any increase in communication, including the mail received at home. Finns were thought to be pro-union because they were intelligent, visited each other, met in cellars in their own homes and got more mail and newspapers than other "foreigners."[79]

The Company broke this resistance by making an example of Woodlawn's Finnish workers. In the Tin Mill, the general foreman ordered rollers, roughers

---

75. Daugherty et al., *supra* note 10, at 890.

76. "Roots of Beaver Valley Lodge # 200, A.A.I.S. & T.W: Part II," *Beaver Valley Lab. Hist. J.,* 1 (July, 1981). See also Colonna Interview, *supra* note 69, at 8.

77. Interview with Frank Kromerich 1–4 (Sept. 13, 1978), in Beaver Valley Labor History Society Papers (on file in Labor Archives, Univ. of Pitt.)

78. "Roots of Beaver Valley Lodge 200, Amalgamated Associated sic of Iron, Steel and Tin Workers 1909–1929," *Beaver Valley Lab. Hist. J.,* 1 (Mar., 1979).

79. Edward Levinson, *Labor on the March,* 202 (1938).

and heaters to attack Finnish Tin Mill workers as they left the Tin Mill. The Finns were taken to the river banks, stripped naked, and tarred and feathered. Finally, they were told that they were fired and had 24 hours to leave Woodlawn.[80]

No organizing activity took place in Woodlawn during the Great Steel Strike of 1919. During the 1920s, a handful of tin workers secretly belonged to the Amalgamated, but these few told the International's spotters that there was no hope of open activity.

The final union organization drive can be divided roughly into the AFL and the CIO periods. The drive began in 1933 when two veteran UMW organizers, Frank Dobbins and John Mayer, were sent into Aliquippa. Both were beaten, arrested, denied housing in town and gave up without making any progress. Mayer was arrested along with his attacker and fined $5.00, the same as his attacker, by Justice of the Peace J.M. Kane. The Company's attorney, also his representative, paid the attacker's fine. In July 1934, operating out of necessity across the river in Ambridge, AFL and United Mine Workers organizer John Tafelski gathered fifteen supporters of the Amalgamated Association of Iron, Steel and Tin Workers to petition for a charter. The Amalgamated's constitution required that a charter be issued whenever at least ten men as a unit requested affiliation as a lodge. Almost all were workers in the tin mill. Tafelski picked the officers—Harry Phillips, President; Angelo Volpe, Vice-President; B.S. McDonald, Recording Secretary; James A. Dunn, Treasurer; Andrew Smith, Guide; Allen James, Inside Guide; and E.L. Pander, Outside Guide. On August 4, 1934, Joe Dunn drove Harry Phillips to the AA International office to pick up the charter for Beaver Valley Lodge #200. Sergeant Donnelly, a J & L plainclothesman followed them.[81] The day after getting the lodge charter, Phillips was offered a job by Captain Harris of the J & L police if he would quit.

The charter generated action. Two hundred men joined the lodge. As the membership grew to include men from all parts of the plant, the ethnic shape of the union rapidly changed. Still without an office, authorization cards were surreptitiously solicited in the Italian neighborhood meeting places: Tony Ferro's barber shop and Angelo Roma's pool hall. Nino Colonna cut through back streets, doubling back to the bus stop below Plan 11, with signed cards in his underwear, to deliver them to Tafelski in Ambridge.[82] The precautions were not unrealistic. Tafelski's associate, Walter Payne, arrived just before the first open meeting for J & L workers, held in a vacant lot in Ambridge, on September 8th. He noticed plenty of armed plainclothes Jones & Laughlin police attending.[83] After a meeting with Volpe, Brandy, Cox and others at Harry Phillips house, Payne and two others were stopped by a motorcycle borough policeman, and directed to the police station without explanation other than "Drive in; you will soon find out." The car search turned up nothing, so the men were ordered without charge into the station, "Get inside and you will soon find out." Two muscular officers, one plainclothes and one uniformed, took off their coats and shirts, picked up clubs and stood on each side of the prisoners during the questioning by Chief Ambrose. They were eventually released on the ground they had been mistaken for a bald-headed, communistic organizer from Clairton [Tafelski.][84]

---

80. Dallet, *supra* note 70, at 5.
81. "Roots of Beaver Valley Lodge # 200, A.A.I.S. & T.W.: Part II," *Beaver Valley Lab. Hist. J.,* 8 (July, 1981).
82. Colonna Interview, *supra* note 69, at 14.
83. NLRB Record, *supra* note 6, at 75 (testimony of Walter Payne, March 2, 1936).
84. *Ibid.* at 138–39.

The Company was prepared should organization succeed to any extent. Clinton Golden's investigation uncovered a company inspector, who feared his identity would be disclosed, who reported that there

> are enough supplies stored in the J. & L. plant to run for weeks. Arms, ammunition, tear gas bombs, riot guns etc., to equal a U.S. Arsenal. One large bay in the plant is equipped with beds while another is stored with kitchen utensels, all guarded by company police to keep employees away until such time as trouble might arise when the employees would be expected to remain in the plant.[85]

At one of the first meetings, the Lodge elected Albert Atallah to replace Harry Phillips as president. Nothing emerged publicly, for Phillips' courage was highly regarded, but rumors suggested a problem with alcohol.[86] Phillips continued to be active in organizing, becoming one of the discharged workers in the test case. Two weeks later his wife penned a false suicide note and hid at a neighbors, explaining that labor activities "'have made life miserable and I was tired of being an outcast. Every place my children and I went, we were mocked, and I wanted that to end.'"[87]

In the fall of 1934, union activity in Aliquippa became very locally influenced. Organization was not top down. Union ferment occurred throughout the steel and coal valleys of Western Pennsylvania.[88] Some workers had attended meetings of the radical and communist influenced Sheet Metal and Iron Workers Union which had organized the Ambridge Strike, and held meetings during 1933 with dissident AA locals objecting to the quiescent leadership of Mike Tighe. The rank and file steel worker leaders, Clarence Irwin, William Spang, Mel Moore, Roy Halas and Lewis Morris, were part of the Committee of Ten authorized by the AA 1934 convention to coordinate a national strike. Within the AFL generally, a new group, the radical AFL Rank & File Committee for Unemployment Insurance and Relief, appeared nationally and in Pennsylvania.[89] Originally formed to push the voluntarist AFL old guard to support unemployment insurance based on a true social wage administered by worker councils, the Lundeen Bill, the Rank & File Committee expanded its focus to all facets of mass industrial organization. For example, Pittsburgh steel worker and organizer Roy Halas was also involved with Lundeen. The committee, whose president in 1935 was Harry Bridges, constituted a left pressure, pushing organized labor toward what became the CIO schism. Their demands for rank and file organizing of industrial unions appealed to many alienated workers in the company towns. In its paper, the *AFL Rank and File Federationist*, editorial articles urged a break from the AFL. "The steel campaign will be delayed and sabotaged by the A.F. of L. Executive Council because the International officials are out to dismember the steel workers' union into many different craft unions."[90]

Meanwhile, in September, 1934, the National Steel Labor Relations Board investigated charges of intimidation made by Beaver Valley Lodge #200. Clinton Golden compiled re-

---

85. An Inspectors's Story, in Clinton Golden Papers (on file in Historical Collections and Labor Archives, Pattee Library, Penn. State Univ., University Park, Pa.).

86. Interview with Dominic Del Turco 9 (n.d.) [hereinafter Del Turco Interview], *in* Beaver Valley Labor History Society Papers (on file in Labor Archives, Univ. of Pitt.).

87. "Wife, Playing Second Fiddle to Union, Gives Mate a 'Jolt'," *Pitt. Press*, June 9, 1936.

88. On the development of the radical rank and file in steel generally, see Staughton Lynd, "The Possibility of Radicalism in the Early 1930's: The Case of Steel," in James Green ed., *Worker's Struggles, Past and Present: A "Radical America" Reader*, 190–208 (1983).

89. On the history of the AFL Rank and File Committee, and the CIO, see Kenneth Casebeer, "Unemployment Insurance: American Social Wage, Labor Organization and Legal Ideology," 35 *B. C. L. Rev.* 259 (1994).

90. "Labor Must Back Steel Workers," *Rank and File Federationist*, 9 (Mar.–Apr. 1935).

ports for the Board. A number of statements convinced him to report to his superiors of a pattern of police retaliation for union activity.

> From such information as I was able to gather on the 5th and again today, there appears to be plenty of evidence to sustain the Union charges of intimidation and coercion on the part of the Company officials in interfering with the rights of employees to organize as provided for in Section 7A of the NRA. It appears that in addition to the extensive private police force maintained by the Company, there also exists an extensive espionage system whereby practically every move and act of any of its employees whether at work or after working hours, was at once made known to company officials.

> As an instance of this I saw a list of 35 names of alleged stool pigeons in the employ of the company. Of this number 7 were Croatians, 14 Serbians and the balance of various other nationalities. This would seem to indicate that it is the policy to plant informers among each racial or national group.[91]

In one episode, a union member living in Ambridge was continually threatened as he tried to return home from a meeting with several union officers. After several calls to the state police, McDonald was led to a "machine" carrying the Burgess, a police sergeant and another policeman. The ride home was spent persuading McDonald to drop out of the union. Others received less subtle treatment. Captain Harris and Lieutenant Kelly of the company police went to Joe Latone's home and warned: "If he and the rest of the dagoes do not quit organizing the men they will run all the c____ s____ out of town and you rotten s____ of b____s will be the first to go. J & L wants you to get busy among the g____ d____ dagoes and run them g____ d____ rats off"[92] Captain Harris confronted Jack Moses,

> there are about 40 Greek families living in Aliquippa and J & L will chase them out if they attend these meetings.... stay with the company instead of with those s____of b____ robbers and the Company will do more for you than they will.... Get around and talk to the Greeks, Syrians and dagoes and talk against the union.[93]

On August 29, Captain Mauk and Burgess Sohn called a meeting in front of Tony Ferro's Barber Shop, a gathering place for union members. Mauk's first words to about 200 gathered there were,

> [y]ou black handed mothers and s____ b____s I am here to tell you if you don't soon try and bust this association of the Amalgamated we are going to bust you people up.... J & L Co. does not like an outside union and will close their plant before they will recognize them so get busy and drive these grafters out of town. Do you people know that baldheaded organizer [Tafelski] at Ambridge is working hand in hand with those G____ D____ reds that started the riot at Ambridge and you dagoes ought to be thankful that the J & L Co., allows you to remain in this town.[94]

The Company blamed the union for violence. Borough Police Chief Ambrose pointed out to Golden the case of William French, an African-American who claimed that union

91. Letter from Clinton S. Golden (Oct. 6, 1934), *in* Clinton Golden Papers (on file in Historical Collections & Labor Archives, Pattee Library, Penn. State Univ., University Park, Pa.).

92. Report on Joe Latone, *in* Clinton Golden Papers (on file in Historical Collections and Labor Archives, Pattee Library, Penn. State Univ., University Park, Pa.).

93. *Ibid.*

94. *Ibid.*

member Joe Pucci assaulted him with a pipe when he refused to sign a card. Pucci was arrested and fined. Golden had doubts. The six foot French towered over the 120 lb. Pucci. Pucci was drinking with four friends during part of the time the alleged incident took place. Pucci's home had been raided without a warrant while he was gone earlier in the day by borough police who confiscated signed union cards. Pucci was brought into French's hospital room before French picked Pucci out of a police line-up. Judge Walter Stacy, presiding over the Steel Labor Board hearing, struck French's testimony.[95]

In October, J & L workers led by Albert Atallah went to Washington to testify at the hearings of the Steel Labor Board. Fearing for their safety when the proceedings were postponed, they contacted the Democratic governor's office. Eight state police officers were sent to Aliquippa and established headquarters at the Woodlawn Hotel. They came from the Butler Barracks because the brother of Captain Mauck of the J & L police was captain of a nearer barracks. Not coincidentally, the first open union meeting was held October 14, with the governor's wife, Cornelia Byrne Pinchot, speaking.[96] Still, the Company had men with manual machine guns in second floor windows of the hotel.[97] The Steel Labor Board held hearings in Pittsburgh on November 16, 1934. The Board dismissed the complaint in January 11, 1935, acting on assurances by J & L that they would instruct the company police to cease surveillance of union members. J & L President S. E. Sackett declared that "the policy of the company [toward representation] is to receive anyone that wishes to come to talk to us on labor conditions or problems, whether or not he represents himself or is represented by an organization, and it is not the policy of the corporation to keep anybody out of Aliquippa in any way whatsoever." Yet, Phillips, Gerstner, Volpe and Dunn had all testified to harassment by J & L police, and all were fired within the year of 1935, becoming complainants in the NLRB proceedings. The Amalgamated's petition for rehearing generated a document from the Pennsylvania Department of Labor requesting a supervised election. In its documentation, Christopher Cunningham, J & L employee and deacon in the "colored Baptist Church," was visited by Captain Mauk who reportedly said that

> now we want you to get busy on those black bastards and stop them from joining the union. If you black sons of bitches want a job at the J. & L. mill, you will have to help the company break up this organization or we will send all you black bastards back south.[98]

The AFL Rank & File Committee called a mass meeting of steel worker unionists to take place on February 3, 1935, in Pittsburgh. An estimated 100 to 400 representatives attended, including men from 78 lodges of the AA. The AFL reacted swiftly. AFL spokesman David Williams, president of the National Council of Aluminum Workers, issued the following statement on AFL stationary:

> The "rank and file" group which assumes to threaten a strike in the Aluminum as well as other large industries, is just a bunch of Communists acting as agents from Moscow, trying to disrupt the American Labor Movement....

> William J. Spang, expelled member of the Amalgamated Association of Iron, Steel and Tin Workers, has no authority to speak for anyone connected with the American Federation of Labor. He is not entitled to sit in any Central Labor

---

95. *Ibid.*
96. Harold J. Ruttenberg,"Steeltown," *Nation*, 623 (Nov. 28, 1934). 4,000 people attended. *Ibid.*
97. Bodnar, *supra* note 12, at 134.
98. Interference With Unionization, Steel — NSLRB Petition for Re-Hearing (1935), *in* Beaver Valley Labor History Society Papers (on file in Labor Archives, Univ. of Pitt.).

Union as a delegate, nor participate in any union meeting of any Local Union of any International Union while he is an expelled member of the Amalgamated Association of Iron, Steel and Tin Workers.[99]

Michael Tighe, president of the Amalgamated said, "I have nothing for Spang and his followers but silent contempt. We have decided that problem by expelling those insurgents from the union."[100] One of the chief organizers, Clarence Irwin, wrote to Harold Ruttenberg, then a free-lance journalist and early intellectual influence on the rank and file movement, in protest one week before the meeting.

> Now suppose we take up the Communistic business first. I think you know the R & F crowd in the AA well enough to know that we are not Communists. You have been associated quite intimately with us for long enough to know that what we want is a strong Union in the Steel Industry. Imagine calling Mel Moore a "red," he carries "the Red Network" in the same pocket with his Bible, as for Spang you know he doesn't know enough about economics to really know what Communism is....

> There may be some Communists in the A.A. I don't know & really I don't care. What I am interested in is "Unionism." ... Now for the Red Scare & those who instigate them, I think for a labor leader (?) to encourage such a thing is the most contemptible & vicious thing he can do ... I am not a C.P. & the other R. & F. fellows in the A.A. are not. So that's that. Certainly it is no part of my plans to flout the A.F. of L. *I agree that we will need all the help we can get if we are to be even moderately successful.... but we can't afford to simply remain idle in the hope that the A.F. of L. will do something as it is by no means sure that they will.* While I do not want to be expelled from the A.F. of L., let us look at all it means to be in the A.A.... the new lodges have never been in, not in the sense of equality ... Can you imagine Tighe telling the new lodges that it is only a waste of time & money to even present their wage & hour negotiations in the program of business at the Con[vention].[101]

Clarence Irwin and William Spang frequently spoke at lodge meetings in Aliquippa.[102]

The day before the rank and file conference, two of the International's officers came to an Aliquippa Lodge meeting to dissuade attendance. Despite the warnings, Attalah and Lodge #200 members attended the conference.

On February 3, Sergeant Donnelly, and other J & L police watched the loading of two busses of Lodge members going to the Rank and File meeting. He reappeared at the entrance to the meeting. The 78 lodges, including #200, were expelled even though they represented the overwhelming majority of the Amalgamated membership.[103] J & L immediately forgot the Steel Labor Board agreement reached four months earlier. Clinton

99. Steel Misc. Clippings 1934–37 (n.d.) [hereinafter Steel Misc. Clippings], *in* Beaver Valley Labor History Society Papers (on file in Labor Archives, Univ. of Pitt.).

100. Text of Union Leaders Attack on Reds, in Steel Misc. Clippings, *supra* note 99.

101. Letter from Clarence Irwin, labor organizer, to Harold Ruttenberg (Jan. 23, 1935) (on file at Penn. Historical Collections and Labor Archives, Pattee Library, Penn. State University, University Park, Pa.).

102. Interview with Tony Riccitelli 32 (Nov. 9, 1978) [hereinafter Riccitelli Interview], *in* Beaver Valley Labor History Society Papers (on file in Labor Archives, Univ. of Pitt.).

103. Lynd, *supra* note 88, at 201. At the 1934 AA Pittsburgh convention, the expelled lodges held a rump meeting, claiming to represent 50,000 workers in the large plants, while the regular convention represented only the 5000 members in the sheet and tin plate, and puddling mills. Daugherty et al., *supra* note 10, at 967.

Golden, then a state labor mediator while also the regional representative of the Federal Steel Labor Board, reported that,

> Lodge #200 did participate and was represented by a large delegation of members. The charter of the lodge was then revoked. It appears that following public announcement of this action, complaints as to interference, espionage etc., took place. While I have no actual facts at hand, it seems to me that the expulsion of this Lodge was interpreted to mean that its officers and members were more or less dangerous radicals and that they therefore had no rights which they had formerly enjoyed.[104]

Atallah insisted that,

> the only thing we wanted was an organization—no more; no less. Although it may be that among the ranks we had going along with us, there may be Communists, maybe that, but we weren't interested in that.[105] All we wanted was more organization, period. Nothing else. Here I had a large organization and I had nowhere to go. I tried to have a meeting with the company at one time where one of the vice presidents laughed in our faces. Ha! Ha! Ha![106]

On February 10, at an open meeting in the Polish Hall on Plan 11, between 20 to 25 mill foremen from all over the mill stood outside watching all the workers who went into the meeting. Donnelly was also there. Many frightened members were deterred. Similar surveillance took place at district meetings in Ambridge and Braddock. At the same time, Golden reported an increasing number of attacks by "negroes" upon white mill workers, particularly on Plan 11 where the Italian section abutted the Extension built for black workers. If arrested, African-American workers were taken before Squire Hayward, and with company police officers present, the prisoners were discharged. At the Steel Labor Board hearings, Golden noted that few African-American workers had joined the union and that there appeared to be a systematic attempt by the Company to create racial friction.[107] In other areas of Western Pennsylvania, Clarence Irwin was fired, Hank Reamer, the rank and file leader in Massillon was fired, and George Evans, the president of the Weirton locals was fired.[108] Golden later hired Clarence Irwin to run the SWOC campaign at Sharon-Farrell.

---

104. Letter from Clinton Golden, State Labor Mediator, to Clarence Moser, Director, Bureau of Mediation (Mar. 7, 1935) (on file at Penn. Historical Collections and Labor Archives, Pattee Library, Penn. State University, University Park, Pa.).

105. "[S]o-called 'rank-and-file' native white district leaders ... worked with the leftwing unionists, not because they espoused the fundamentals of communism but because the left-wing leaders during those months were the only group with a complete, carefully drawn, hope-inspiring plan for organizing the industry." Daugherty et al., *supra* note 10, at 937.

106. Interview with Albert Atallah 12 (Sept. 20, 1967) [hereinafter Atallah Interview] (on file at Penn. Historical Collections and Labor Archives, Pattee Library, Penn. State University, University Park, Pa.).

107. Letter from Clinton Golden, State Labor Mediator, to Clarence Moser, Director, Bureau of Mediation (Mar. 7, 1935) (on file at Penn. Historical Collections and Labor Archives, Pattee Library, Penn. State University, University Park, Pa.).

108. Ruttenberg reported these developments dispassionately. His own sympathies were anti-communist, reporting, admittedly without evidence, that he believed Irwin to be a party member. This was less than two months after Irwin's denial to him in which Irwin blamed his own reputation on his association with Ruttenberg himself. He wrote of Irwin's pamphlet "The Progressive Steel Worker" that it "now has a section for Negroes and other indications of Communist influence." Letter from Harold Ruttenberg (Mar. 28, 1935) (on file at Penn. Historical Collections and Labor Archives, Pattee Library, Penn. State University, University Park, Pa.). It is true that the Communist Party union efforts, almost exclusively of other organizations, paid great attention to organizing African-American workers in the early 1930s.

When the expelled lodges were denied credentials to the next AA convention, they sued in federal court and were granted an injunction requiring that they be reinstated with all rights and privileges.[109] Whereupon, the AA demanded all back dues for the suspension period. Atallah met with the International Secretary Treasurer Leonard claiming that the lodge records had been lost. An agreement established the arbitrary number of members at 800 for the purpose of reinstating the lodge. Various stories surrounded the disappearance of the books. Some felt that they were hidden from the International. Others believed that they had been stolen by a plant. Eddie Monahan had been elected vice president in the second lodge election. Less than a year later he disappeared after having been seen in the plant in a suit and tie, admitting to a suspicious union member that he worked for Burns or Pinkerton.

Further evidence of the local character of organization during this period comes from the conscious tying of unionism with politics. In late 1934, it was the lodge which set up the Democratic Social Club. An early AA activist, Dominic Del Turco, called it the political arm of the union movement in Aliquippa.[110] Angelo Volpe, vice president of the Lodge was the first president of the club, Mike Kellar was secretary, Dominic Brandy was financial secretary, Tony Riccatelli, assistant financial secretary of the Lodge, was trustee, and other activists occupied key positions. When Kellar became president in 1936, the club moved its offices to the second floor of the Roumanian Hall on Kiehl Street. Individuals who were afraid to walk into the SWOC offices on Hopewell Avenue would hand SWOC pledge cards to Kellar in his Democratic Social Club second floor office.[111] In 1935, Volpe ran for constable, losing closely. Steel workers needed protection to be more effective.

> The burgess and the Council were all appointed by the company. No one dared run against them, so you may as well say they were appointed. They ran the town for the company. Now, if you're going to fight the company on a union basis, the cops in town are going to harass you to stop you from organizing. They'll raid your house and plant moonshine in your house, something of that nature. So we had to go into politics.[112]

In 1936, Aliquippa voted Democratic for president for the first time ever.

During the hearings on the Wagner Act, the J & L ERP sent representatives, led by William Westlake, to testify that 90% of the employees at Aliquippa supported the company union. Albert Atallah, Tony Riccitelli, Tom Bresnin, and Mike Kellar piled into John Fiola's Cadillac and drove all night to reach Washington D.C. When they arrived at the Senate Office Building, they were told the schedule had been filled. But old Tom Bresnin had worked in mines with Philip Murray years before. Murray got them in. Atallah told the senators that the ERP claims were false. When a senator challenged him for proof, Tony Riccitelli opened a suitcase and dumped 9,000 pledge cards on the long hearing table,

---

109. Riverside Lodge No. 164 v. Amalgamated Assoc. of Iron, Steel and Tin Workers, 13 F. Supp. 873 (W.D. Pa. 1935).

110. "The Aliquippa Democratic-Social Club 1934–1936," *Beaver Valley Lab. Hist. J.,* 2 (Mar., 1979).

111. *Ibid.* at 6.

112. Interview with Louis DeSenna, *quoted in* Eric Davin, The Littlest New Deal: SWOC Takes Power in Steeltown, a Possibility of Radicalism in the Late 1930s at 49 (n.d.) (unpublished manuscript on file in Labor Archives, Univ. of Pitt.). Davin believes that political resistance and change preceded and was necessary to unionization in Aliquippa. I prefer to see in his argument the more general struggle, also bottom up from the community, including a conscious tying of elections in the plant and in the town.

proudly telling them, "now you can pick any card you want and you'll find that they're all signed by members of J and L."[113] Westlake was not re-elected as ERP Representative.[114]

The National Labor Relations Board

Despite the passage of the Wagner Act, and indeed the National Industrial Recovery Act before that, J & L increasingly discharged union activists, firing over 100 between June, 1935 and January, 1937. Thirteen of those fired between July, 1935 and January, 1936, became the plaintiffs in the J & L NLRB case, charging unfair labor practices under sections 8(1) and 8(3) of the Wagner Act, interference with organization for mutual aid and protection, and retaliation for engaging in union activities. Following the regional investigation by Clinton Golden and Board Regional Attorney Thomas Kleeb, the NLRB filed charges in January 1936. When the hearings began on March 2, 1936 in Court Room #6 of the Post Office Building in Pittsburgh, counsel for the board began by providing a detailed statistical picture of J & L's vast and far flung operations in order to establish that J & L's labor relations were part of and impacted on interstate commerce. J & L attorney Earl Reed, appeared solely for the purpose of constitutionally objecting to the board's jurisdiction. Reed had prepared a 132 page "brief," entitled "Report on the Constitutionality of the National Labor Relations Act," for the National Lawyers Committee of the American Liberty League, a point group in the legal attacks on the New Deal. Reed counseled that when a lawyer advised a law to be unconstitutional, clients need not obey.[115] After appearing specially on jurisdiction, he took no part in the hearing, and therefore, did not cross-examine any of the Board's witnesses on the unfair labor practices.

> With respect to the specific complaints relating to employees, the respondent takes the position that it is the sole judge of the right to hire and fire, and that it is not subject to the Board in that respect, and, therefore, declines to offer any testimony on that subject and withdraws from the hearing.[116]

The company took the position in their brief that the cases had all been fairly investigated and the men were discharged for cause.

Martin Gerstner, the first financial secretary for Lodge #200, took the stand first among the fired workers. A motor inspector, he had been employed at Jones & Laughlin less than six years. Gerstner's house was watched 24 hours a day. J & L Sergeant Donnelly and Officer Slater followed him everywhere. An employment agent noted everyone who entered or left the house. In September, 1934, Gerstner was evicted from his house for no reason, and J & L policemen followed Gerstner to where he was moving in Ambridge. In the summer of 1935, Gertsner's time was kept down. Gerstner was discharged on Monday evening in December, 1935 because a nut fell off a crane. The nut had fallen off at one o'clock on Sunday afternoon, and three other motor inspectors—Linde, Bevington, and Lang— had their shifts after Gerstner's last duty. None of the others were disciplined.[117]

The first lodge president, Harry Phillips, a motor inspector in the soaking pits, testified second. On July 13, Phillips asked his foreman for a day off to attend the Democratic Social Club picnic. Foreman Walter Gray responded no, but told him that he would have lots of time to go to picnics in the future. On July 20, after fixing three machines, Phillips took his lunch. He then stopped in the wash room to put Vaseline on his hands

---

113. Riccitelli Interview, *supra* note 102, at 35–36.

114. Cortner, *The Jones & Laughlin Case*, 82 (1970).

115. Peter Irons, *The New Deal Lawyers*, 245 (1982).

116. NLRB Record, *supra* note 6, at 129–30 (argument of Earl Reed, counsel to Jones & Laughlin, March 2, 1936).

117. *Ibid.* at 150–51 (testimony of Martin Gerstner).

which were chafed from the heat from the machines where he had been working. The warning whistle blew, but he saw his millwright answer it. When he got there, the man on the pump told him it was okay, they shared a cigarette and Phillips went to check bolts in the shanty. The whistle blew again. This time the day foreman was there at 4:00 a.m. Phillips explained that he did not hear the first whistle and was in the wash room for the second one. Foreman Gray said, "You fellows coming out at night always want the mill-wrights to do all the work around here.... You can get the hell out of here.... You are going to have plenty of time to sell union papers from now on."[118] Phillips had been de-livering Amalgamated papers the night he was black-jacked at the Wye going to work. He had recently been delivering speeches urging men not to vote in the company union elec-tions. Although not participating in the NLRB hearings, the company had replied earlier to a second complaint including the discharging of Phillips, to the National Steel Labor Relations Board. In their view,

> This man was discharged because of inattention to his duties, which occurred on more than one occasion. It was his business to respond to signals when electri-cal equipment was disabled, and on the last occasion he failed to respond to his signals and could not be found. The signals were sounded several times and the work of a large number of men was held up on account of his absence. It was a period of about a half hour before he could be located, and then gave an untrue excuse for his absence. He seemed to feel that his position as President of the Union gave him an immunity from discipline.[119]

No supporting affidavits or specific evidence were presented. Phillips' testimony about his assistant indicates that no time was lost. Phillips was dispossessed from his J & L house shortly thereafter for inability to make his payments. Phillips was married, with four chil-dren. Two weeks before the notice to quit, his wife was warned by Mr. Leslie of the Wood-lawn Land Co. about the union.

Angelo Razzano, one of the leading organizers of the Italian workers, was next to tes-tify. Hired in 1923 or 1924, Razzano drove a tractor hauling material. He was married and had five children. He was a charter member of the union, personally signing up 1500 members and delivering circulars in public. Consequently, the company marked him. On September 17, John Bolger, general foreman in the seamless finishing plant, called Razzano to come in immediately to see Plant Superintendent Fisher. Fisher talked about the union, recalled Razzano,

> He says "Saturday you was in Ambridge at a union meeting?" I says, "Yes." He says, "Well, what for?" I says, "Don't you know I am an American citizen in here and I am supposed to go where I please." He says, "But the Company don's (sic) stand for that."... Well, he said ..."William Green got beautiful home in Wash-ington, sits on soft chair and everything there, and you guys pay for that and he never do anything for you." I says, "Well, I don't know anything about that, but still," I says, "I think this union idea is mighty good thing in the country."[120]

On January 13, 1936, John Bolger sent Razzano to another building to bring back a steel buggy. The route required opening and closing a door, which Razzano did on both the way up and the way down. Nonetheless, Bolger came running up to ask him if he could

118. *Ibid.* at 173–74 (testimony of Harry Phillips).
119. Letter from H.A. Wiley, Chair, National Steel Labor Relations Board, to Albert Attalah 2 (Sept. 10, 1935) [hereinafter Wiley Letter], in Steel—NSLRB Correspondence, 1934–1935, Beaver Val-ley Labor History Society Papers (on file in Labor Archives, Univ. of Pitt.).
120. NLRB Record, *supra* note 6, at 179–80 (testimony of Angelo Razzano).

read the sign, "shut the Door," and if he knew what it meant? "Why didn't you do it?" Razzano replied that he did and Bolger had seen him do it. Ten minutes later, Bolger returned with another foreman asking, "didn't that man say the same thing last week?" Razzanno insisted he had, "Last week was cold weather and if the door was open that man in the mill would freeze to death. Therefore I closed the door because nobody ever complained about it." Bolger told him to go pick up his time.[121] Razzano also testified, however, that it was a common practice for all drivers to leave the door open from time to time.

Ronald Cox, operator of an electrical overhead hoisting crane who started in 1928 as a catcher in the tin mills, believed he had the best safety record among crane men, having received two watch fobs for his three safety awards, one of which was for crane work. Of the 22 cranes in the seamless tube department, Cox was assigned to the hardest one to operate. When he left, the company had to send to another department to get a man to operate it. "Well, it is in the 30 inch round mill, and they allow 90 minutes to change the mill, and they specify something like 85 lifts in 90 minutes. That is almost a lift a minute, and a man has to be very experienced to do that without injuring some one."[122] Cox was a union kingpin in his department. He recruited, sold tickets, passed out literature, and helped at organizing in Midland. He watched himself closely after the first discharges. At the beginning of one shift, the general foreman, usually in his office with daily assignments, showed up on the floor. Cox inspected his crane. As soon as he climbed down, the whistle signaled for him to make a lift. Cox went up and worked his hooks to make a lift, and the foreman who had followed Cox signaled him to come down. "Did you inspect your crane?" he asked. Cox replied, "yes." The foreman then asked, "Did you try your limit stops?" 'No, sir,' Cox answered. Cox was told, "Go back and get your check and go home." The limit stop is an important safety catch to prevent too high a hoist, dropping the load to the floor. An angry Cox changed and went to the office. The turn foreman, Krause, saw him and put his back against the door:

> I just pushed the door open and walked into the office, and Mr. Hussy, the foreman that dismissed me, was talking on the phone, and I got this much of his conversation: He said, "He didn't try his limit stops. Is that enough?" Then he looked up and saw me, and he said, "I can't talk to you now. Mr. Reaves is on his way," and hung up.[123]

The next day, when Cox returned to the same office for his time, the foreman told him, "'Here is your time, Cox. I am going to make an example of you. He said, Now, you can beat it.'"[124]

Earlier, just after the union formed in 1934, the general manager of the plant, Mr. Fisher, called Cox into the superintendent's office for an anti-union talk.

> He told me it was a racket; I was just paying my money to a bunch of big fat guys that sat back and smoked cigars and at the time I was back in my rent of the company's house, and he told me if I was going to persist in affiliating myself with this Union, they could not tolerate my back rents, that they would have to put me out of the house, and the local merchants would not extend any credit, that he would see to that, that Jones & Laughlin had determined to fight this case to the highest court, and that they would close the plant down and throw the key in the river before they would recognize an outside Union; that he had

121. *Ibid.* at 182–84.
122. *Ibid.* at 202–03.
123. *Ibid.* at 205–06.
124. *Ibid.* at 212.

intended to promote me, and by my affiliating myself with the Union I was not helping my standing. All the time he was questioning me, he was writing down something. I couldn't see what he was writing, and he told me, he said, "Cox, any time you change your mind, come in and tell me, and I will tear this up." So I presume it was a black-ball.[125]

When Cox complained before his discharge about being given less time, he was told he could quit. After his discharge, friends and workers were afraid to be seen with Cox on the street, but would stop at his house to tell him he was fighting for the right thing. Cox, married with one child, held no steady work up to the hearing, selling his furniture to buy food. At the hearing, when asked why he wanted the union, he testified,

> I feel that I could be a better workman, for the reason that there would be a better atmosphere in the plant. There would not be all of this dissension that is in there now, and a man could come to work and feel as though he really wanted to do his job.[126]

Fellow crane operator Martin Dunn worked in the sinter plant, starting fifteen years earlier as a mail boy and in the tube and hot mills. He was Harry Phillips' half brother. He was married with one child, and because of that, continually lied to questioning superiors that he did not belong to the union. The Company discharged Dunn for forgetting his keys on a workbench after locking the crane. There was a rule in the plant and a sign on the cab that only cranemen are to enter the crane. All the cranemen left their keys out from time to time. He was given no reason for discharge, except, "Nothing personal." In its response to the National Steel Labor Relations Board, J & L wrote, "This man was discharged for violation of the safety rules in his operation of a crane. The offense occurred on two different occasions. On one of them Dunn's action endangered not only other employees' lives, but his own life."[127] The company did not renew these assertions when discussing Dunn in their brief to the Fifth Circuit Court of Appeals.[128]

Dominic Brandy worked as a jig man and coal washer for fourteen years. He started work at J & L in 1910. He signed up 665 members before an office was opened in Aliquippa, and was a union trustee. He was continually shorted time. After testifying before the NSLRB, two or three stool pigeons always followed him outside the plant. J & L discharged Brandy for a bad sample which was taken from his coal washing. Brandy had worked Saturday, on Sunday there was no washing, and had worked the second shift on Monday. A sample was taken Monday night. An apprehensive Brandy asked the sample man, Charlie Ross, to check the sample. He went to the office and returned saying it was very good. No samples were taken on Tuesday or Wednesday nights. On Thursday, the boss, Mr. Felger, forced the sample man and a millwright, Angelo Sylvester, to sign a sample check without letting them see the contents. Felger then fired Brandy for producing a bad sample. Brandy asked him when the sample was taken, and was told Tuesday night. Brandy replied, "Then I guess that sample ain't mine," He said, "why?" Brandy replied, "Because Tuesday nobody take any sample four to twelve." Felgar responded, "I have to make that change on either Monday or Tuesday, and you go up and get your clothes and get the

125. *Ibid.* at 208–09.
126. *Ibid.* at 215.
127. Letter from attorney for Jones & Laughlin Steel Corporation to H.A. Wiley, Chair, National Steel Labor Relations Board 2 (Sept. 6, 1935), *in* Steel—NSLRB Correspondence, 1934–35, Beaver Valley Labor History Society Papers (on file in Labor Archives, Univ. of Pitt.).
128. Petitioner's Brief, *in* NLRB Record, *supra* note 6, at 16.

Hell out of here."[129] J & L discharged Brandy November 28, 1936, Thanksgiving Day—a working day at J & L.

Croatian laborer Eli Bozich was warned by his foreman for not voting for the company union. The foreman complained that the Croats, Serbs and Slavs never voted in the company union elections.

Royal Boyer, a leader in the African-American community, joined J & L in 1924, working up from the labor gang to making nails. He was fired when a ten pound sample of bad nails turned up in his buggy. Normally a buggy holds 1200 to 1500 pounds. Two men dumped their nails in the same bin, the crooked nails, a single tray's worth, were all found in the same place in the buggy and an immediate inspection of the machinery by the inspector, operator and foreman showed nothing wrong. Bent nails were readily available from a scrap heap. Before his discharge Boyer had been given a Republican sample ballot by Superintendent John Akin and told, "Here is a ballot and I mean for you to put the mark where the mark is, and if you don't you will see the consequences, what it will be." Nail inspector, Chester Hodney, told Boyer's wife, "If I was Royal I would not have anything to do with the union whatever."[130]

The Company instructed George Maroll, machinist helper, to operate a machinist's drill press during the night shift, despite the fact he had no training and no apprenticeship. He was then fired for being "hopeless" in ability, despite the fact the company kept him doing jobs on the press for months, at the helper's pay, not as a machinist. Maroll was married and had three children, so he did not complain at the time.

The final discharged witness, Angelo Volpe, married with four children, was president of the Democratic Social Club, vice president of Lodge #200, and worked for J & L since 1914, a laborer, greaser, rougher, weigh-master, and night foreman in the cold roll department. In 1930, he was busted to a laborer again for refusing to work on Easter Sunday. At that time, he was a crane operator in the tube mill. Management had assigned untrained men to the hookers jobs to save wage rates. An inexperienced man hooked up one of Volpe's loads badly. It was re-hooked and the man gave a head signal to go. A State inspector bawled Volpe out for following a head signal rather than a hand signal. Although head signals were often used, Volpe was discharged. J & L police officers continued to follow Volpe even to the day he testified before the NLRB.

All the men fired in the case were charter members of Beaver Valley Lodge #200; the first president, vice president, financial secretary, the president's half-brother (the first of the group fired), and a trustee. They were leaders of the Italian, Croatian, Black, Slavic and Anglo communities. One was the first president of the Democratic Social Club. The NLRB handed down its decision ordering the reinstatement of these men with back pay, April 9, 1936. It would take a year until the Supreme Court upheld the board's decision.

On July 10, 1936, another fourteen men, fourteen of the eighteen attending the first SWOC meeting, were fired immediately after SWOC entered Aliquippa in June, 1936. The Honor Roll Committee reached 54 members. Pete Cekoric, one of the original fourteen, a year later exclaimed, "When I hear the Wagner bill went constitutional I happy like anything. I say, good, now Aliquippa become part of the United States."[131]

---

129. NLRB Record, *supra* note 6, at 259–60 (testimony of Dominic Brandy).
130. *Ibid.* at 294. (testimony of Royal Boyer).
131. "Pete Cekoric," *Beaver Valley Lab. Hist. J.,* 8 (June 1979).

Atallah had seized upon John L. Lewis's offer of one-half million dollars to organize the steel industry in the face of the reticent Amalgamated, claiming no small role in the schism and the creation of SWOC. Invited by Lewis to the April 14, 1936 meeting of the Committee for Industrial Organization, which Lewis as yet had failed to swing to a direct move on the AA, Atallah was asked by Sidney Hillman, "What can we do when the resolution which was introduced by Mr. Lewis to have the money appropriated by the A.F. of L. is voted against by the Amalgamated?" Atallah replied, "haven't you gentlemen forgotten that within exactly fourteen days from today, the convention of the Amalgamated convenes in Canonsburg, Pennsylvania: Why not make the offer directly to the Amalgamated? And if the Amalgamated fails to accept the offer, then the convention will want to know why." Mr. Dubinsky said, "Are you telling us now that you will be able to deliver the convention?" "I'm not telling you a darn thing. All I can tell you is that I, together with my associate will bring it out and fight it. And if we go down, we will go down fighting—at least the public and the world will know why." Hillman said, "What else can you expect out of a man." Fifteen minutes later Lewis came to the door to shake hands, "Congratulations, you put it over."[132] At the Canonsburg convention, eleven locals, including Lodge #200, were refused seats. When Michael Tighe asked Atallah if he had anything to say, he took the floor from 1:00 p.m. to 5:30 p.m., documenting the whole history of the relationship of the lodge to the international. The convention voted to seat the locals.[133] Five weeks later the Amalgamated agreed to jointly establish SWOC with the CIO.

On June 17, 1936, following the CIO schism with the AFL, John L. Lewis set up the Steel Workers Organizing Committee in Pittsburgh. SWOC took over the cowed and increasingly inactive AA local #200. From approximately 6000 members, the lodge could count on only 72.[134] Veteran UMW organizer Joseph Timko moved to Aliquippa and established a union office at 141 Hopewell Avenue. Timko started in the mines at age fourteen, organized the first boilermakers local, organized Indiana mines as president of UMW District 11, and then was assigned to Harlan County, Kentucky by the International. The organization campaign stepped up as union staff increased. One of the organizers sent to help was Harold Ruttenberg, then head of the SWOC research department. In Beaver Valley, one year later, a central labor council was in place and 51 locals held contracts covering 45,000 employees.

SWOC's regional organization strategy was top down and extremely tightly controlled by Lewis' people, who had undermined the rank and file attempts for a national strike.[135] Whatever hope might have fueled the rank and file strategy when the AA had recruited between 150,000 and 200,000 in 1934–35, that possibility disappeared when, by late 1935 and early 1936, those new members had virtually entirely dropped out. Aliquippa proved no exception.

The SWOC based its strategy on co-opting Employee Representation Plan representatives who had become disenchanted with the corruption of the company unions, and on working through the fraternal organizations of the foreign born. On the former, SWOC

132. Atallah Interview, *supra* note 106, at 13.
133. *Ibid.* at 14.
134. *NLRA Hearings, supra* note 1, at 4180.
135. "SWOC will insist on a centralized and responsible control of the organizing campaign … and will insist that local policies conform to the national plan of upon action which it decides, … Responsibility begins and ends with this Committee." David Brody, "The Origins of Modern Steel Unionism: The SWOC Era," *in Forging A Union of Steel, supra* note 66, at 27 (quoting Philip Murray).

President Philip Murray announced, "Unlike the traditional A.F. of L. policy of calling company union representatives names, we have catered to them with a view to swinging them over."[136] In regard to the latter, SWOC believed it would be very difficult to focus on African-Americans, because the companies had created fear among them of job losses from unionization and actively supported racial division and tension among the workers. This attitude went back to the 1919 strike when African-Americans were brought into mills as strike breakers. An early SWOC position paper closed, "It is our conviction, however, that the organization of the negro steel workers will follow, rather than precede, the organization of the white mill workers."[137]

Yet SWOC did send Ben Careathers almost immediately into Aliquippa. The *Aliquippa Gazette*, July 12, 1936, boxed an announcement, "Information You Should Have" from the Loyalists. "Ben Carreathers, sic Negro Communist organizer, ... is one of the principal leaders, and is connected with the leading Communistic and radical organizations in the Pittsburgh district and adjacent territory. His principle aim is to unite the negroes and whites against the capitalist class."[138] This much was undoubtedly true. However, it did not prevent his effectiveness. He was recognized almost immediately in Aliquippa from his defense of the Scottsboro Boys, and the Communist commitment to unified unions and race equality helped secure union cards among black workers the SWOC thought unsupportive. Careathers was able to organize the National Conference of Negro Organizations, representing 110 groups with a membership of 100,000 in Pittsburgh to pledge support for organizing steel into one industrial union. This became important as, according to one estimate, 80% of Western Pennsylvania's 5235 Black steel workers worked for either Carnegie (U.S. Steel) or J & L.[139]

Ironically, the alliance between the CIO and the National Negro Congress was one avenue through which the national SWOC leadership consciously introduced communist labor organizers into steel and Aliquippa. Philip Murray attributed much of the Aliquippa success to Careathers.[140] The SWOC brought in rank and file activists, including Communists, after the party dropped its dual union strategy and disbanded the Steel and Metal Workers International Union.[141] SWOC used their organizing ability and discharged them when continued employment became a source of outside pressure.

The use of ERP men brought Paul Normile and Clifford Shorts into prominence in organizing in Aliquippa. Normile would later become the first president of Local 1211 of the United Steel Workers of America. In 1936, Normile served as a truck driver and ERP representative (from its inception in June, 1934) in the service department. His assistant, Joe Latone, was active in the AA. In September, Normile and nine other ERP representatives, without company approval, set up a Joint Wage and Means Committee to pressure J & L for higher wages and better working conditions. The Company refused to bargain. Disillusioned, Normile began secret meetings with SWOC supporters. On January 3, 1937, he, Shorts, and three other Joint Committee members signed SWOC cards, with an open letter:

---

136. Philip Murray, *Report to the Steel Workers Organizing Committee* 6 (Sept. 29, 1936) (located in SWOC file, Labor Archives, The Catholic University of America, Wash. D.C.).

137. Untitled document, 1936 (located in Dept. of Archives and Manuscripts, The Catholic University of America, Wash., D.C.).

138. "Information You Should Have," *Aliquippa Gazette*, 1 (July 12, 1936).

139. Dickerson, *supra* note 56, at 146.

140. Philip S. Foner, *Organized Labor and the Black Worker, 1619–1973*, 219 (1974).

141. Lynd, *supra* note 88, at 203. Lynd believed 60 of the approximately 200 organizers were contributed by the Party.

We believe the company union plan of collective bargaining to be equivalent to the age-old custom of writing letters to the mythical Santa Claus.

We are convinced that a majority of the employee representatives are honest and sincere but that they become hopeless prey when confronted with the elaborate series of processes through which each case must pass and the unflinching attitude of the management which acts as both final judge and jury.[142]

When SWOC Local 1211 was officially set up to replace AA Lodge #200, February 13, 1937, sub-regional SWOC director Timko recommended Normile be made president. He was, and Clifford Shorts, another ERP representative, became financial secretary. Both men quit their jobs to work full time for the union. In the local elections of 1937, Normile was one of two of the first Democratic councilmen elected in Aliquippa.

During the Steel Labor Board hearings, the investigator appointed by the board was Clinton Golden. Golden could not convince workers to talk freely with an outsider, so he donned a beaten, old trenchcoat, removed his false teeth, smeared his face and hands and snuck into the Aliquippa beer gardens to eavesdrop.[143] When the CIO formed SWOC, it hired Golden as its regional director for Western Pennsylvania. Golden turned the tables on J & L by infiltrating the main office with his own spy, a man named Malone, who signed his dispatches "M". Initially hired for the labor gang, and having boasted to the employment manager of working for a number of strike breaking detective agencies, M turned in sufficient information on small in plant burglaries to gain the favor of a Captain Nicholson in the J & L police. Nicholson gave M a note for the superintendent of the strip mill, J.B. Carlock:

My dear Mr. Carlock: The bearer, Barry Malone, check #27339, is a very good friend of both Captain Mauck and myself. He is now a laborer and would very much like to improve his position and get something that pays a little better. Anything you can do for him will be greatly appreciated by both myself and Captain Mauck.

Carlock gave M a timekeepers job which offered him the freedom to move around the plant. While M sat in Nicholson's office an open cabinet revealed at least 150 .38 caliber revolvers and three 100 shot drums for Thompson .45 caliber sub-machine guns, among many wrapped packages.[144] M was next assigned to be a weighmaster. His undisclosed college background led him to teaching classes on computations and writing a weighmasters handbook. From there, M was promoted to Supervisor of Weighmasters, worked out of the office of J.W. Murphy, one of the board of strike policy of J & L, and finally moved into the plant's general manager's office where he reported on the will of the corporate management to continue resisting the union. Highest level management never expected to lose the drive. However, they were planting undercover agents in every section of the corporation, encouraging some to join the union in order to maintain surveillance.

The steel industry responded to organizing pressures with sticks and carrots. On the establishment of a SWOC presence in Aliquippa, a J & L spokesman predicted,

Our men do not seek unionization of the type Mr. Lewis and his followers advocate. We are not afraid of the campaign begun by Mr. Lewis. We are not ashamed of our labor record. We have tried, and I think successfully, to be fair

---

142. "Paul Normile," *Beaver Valley Lab. Hist. J.*, 1 (Dec. 1980).

143. Thomas R. Brooks, *Clint: A Biography of a Labor Intellectual — Clinton S. Golden* 129 (1978).

144. Unidentified document, *in* Clinton Golden Papers (on file in Box 7, File 15 of Labor Archives, Pattee Library, Penn. State Univ., University Park, Pa.).

in our relationships with our employees. The employee representation plan has worked out well and we think it will function properly despite what Mr. Lewis and his followers say.[145]

On the other hand, in November 1936, the companies unilaterally raised wages $0.10 per hour, and after SWOC negotiations with U.S. Steel, the industry added another $0.10 per hour in March, 1937. The combined increases raised wages by 33%. But the strategy backfired as workers believed the union to have been principally responsible anyway. Timko argued that the redistribution of profits to wages served the public interest by stimulating business through the greater purchasing power of workers. Then the impact of the totally unexpected U.S. Steel contract triggered increasing membership in Aliquippa. On the afternoon of March 1, a SWOC organizer in Aliquippa phoned Murray at the Grant Building in Pittsburgh to report that he had heard wild rumors. "One of the steel workers just came in and said he heard over the radio that U.S. Steel was meeting with the C.I.O. I told him he was crazy and kicked him out of the office." "Well don't kick him out," Murray chided, "It's true."[146]

On April 12, 1937, the Supreme Court upheld the constitutionality of the Wagner Act. J & L management did not begin to take the law seriously until then. On May 7, 1937, 600 employees met to establish the United Iron and Steel Workers of Aliquippa, an ostensibly independent union, to replace the illegal company union, the ERP. The group elected William H. Turner of the accounting department as chairman.[147] It was too late. One week later on May 12, 1937, J & L workers voted to walk out if an exclusive bargaining contract was not signed with the Steel Workers Organizing Committee. J & L Chairman H.E. Lewis offered to sign a collective bargaining contract with SWOC if it could also sign a similar contract with any other group of non-SWOC members. Philip Murray refused, knowing that men who feared the past would choose to sit out on those terms. Murray also refused an exclusive representation election until union strength could be tested.[148] On May 13, the strike began and on May 15, J & L capitulated. On May 21, the Aliquippa and Pittsburgh Works of J & L voted to establish the United Steel Workers, CIO as their exclusive bargaining representative.

Desperate economic circumstances in the shadow of obscene profits being reaped by J & L led many to seek some new representation and power. In 1936, J & L netted $4,129,600.00 or $7.03 per share.[149] But no one present foresaw the overwhelming solidarity and support of the community for organization now, and desperately now, in 1937. In a sense, a group of steelworkers didn't strike as much as an entire town struck.

Dominic Del Turco, picket captain, worked the 1800 man Welded Tube Department. At fifteen minutes to eleven o'clock, he walked the length of the plant, thumb down, the signal to get ready. At two minutes to eleven he instructed leaders to blow whistles in the noisy Butt Mills. At the end of the plant he and his strong arm men met a 300 lb. worker and Assistant Superintendent Volcher. The worker said, "Who's going to carry me out? I'll tear you apart you little shrimp." Del Turco whistled and five men ran over to carry him out.[150]

---

145. "Labor Board Clash Spurs Steel Union, *N.Y. Times*, 6 (July 11, 1936).

146. Irving Bernstein, *The Turbulent Years* 473 (1970).

147. "Local Union is Formed by J & L Employees," *Aliquippa Gazette*, 1 (May 11, 1937).

148. "[T]he union was by no means sure of its ability to win an election, and it may have wanted the strike as a demonstration of its power, to help convince workers who were on the fence." Walter Galenson, *The CIO Challenge to the AFL* 98 (1960). *See also* Brooks, *supra* note 143, at 123.

149. *The Ambridge Daily Citizen*, 1 (Mar. 25, 1937).

150. Del Turco Interview, *supra* note 86, at 19.

A young organizer, undoubtedly overly enthusiastic, described the strike,

> No one, not even ourselves, believed it possible. It was fantastic to think of. We expected to get the men out, certainly, but not all of them, and not without some opposition from "loyal" groups or from city or company police. But, no, not a bit of it. The walk out was complete, and as far as I can determine 100% effective. For the first time in years, the valley is not brilliant red at night with smoke and fire from the Bessemer furnaces.
>
> It was something of a revolution, too. Aliquippa rose up against a tyranny that had held them in bondage for years. For all practical purposes, the workers took over the functions of government. They were in complete control. Only for less than two hours were city police even in sight. The picket line was absolutely effective. No one got thru (sic), not even the police who tried to force thru (sic) an allegedly empty bus. The cops came with tear gas and guns. They threatened our men if we impeded their progress, but the bus could not get thru (sic). It was pushed back and out. Only once did the police win in a fracas. They were permitted to go in on foot, but when they tried to get out again, they were stopped. They had tear gas and used it to blast their way out.
>
> The strike is a rank and file affair. SWOC may have called it, but it is in the hands of anybody who can lead. It is a mob, not an organization. We organizers have no more control than our lungs can bring us.
>
> There were perhaps one or two thousand at the meeting when the strike call was issued. These men were scattered among the various gates at 9:30. Shifts change at 11. The strike was to begin with the preventing of the night shift from going on duty. First thing we did was to take possession of the tunnel and roads leading thereto. You remember these roads are shaped like a Y and lead directly into the center of town. Our men got American flags and poles and stretched them across the entrance. Behind these perhaps 500 to 1000 people were stationed. Across the street, at the railroad station, at windows, in the parking lot, thousands more assembled. All of these were interested in the strike—J & L is Aliquippa—but few intended to be pickets. Nevertheless, they served that purpose. By the time the second turn came off duty, our active men had increased to a thousand, and in addition to this a good share of those who left the plant remained outside for picket duty. Get the picture. All Aliquippa was there—that is, all except the police. They came later in steel helmets and with guns and tear gas to direct traffic for a short time, but except for what I mentioned above, they played no part in the strike. Fully half the town remained on the scene till after one o'clock, by which time practically all the men were out of the mill.[151]

Women, almost all wives of steel workers, were among the most militant at the gates.[152] Mary Cozzicolli remembered,

> I was at the Wye most of the time and we had quite a few women and elderly women that would stay there night and day and I'm not joking, without no sleep night and day, and I mean they had umbrellas and they were really going to pick up their part because you know, this was their bread and butter to them....[153]

---

151. Letter from Meyer Bernstein (May 13, 1937), *in* Beaver Valley Labor History Society Papers (on file in Labor Archives, University of Pittsburgh). *See also* Brooks, *supra* note 143, at 123–26.

152. "Strike Closes Aliquippa Plant," *Ambridge Daily Citizen*, 1,4 (May 13, 1937).

153. Interview with Mary Cozzicolli 7 (n.d.) [hereinafter Cozzicolli Interview], *in* Beaver Valley Labor History Society Papers (on file in Labor Archives, Univ. of Pitt.). *See also* Interview with Andy

The women alerted pickets to a mail truck they thought to be stuffed with food for the staff still inside, which was halted and overturned with their help.[154] The only police action took place the second day of the strike. Police fired five or six tear gas cannisters at a group of 250 pickets who surrounded Borough Police Chief Ambrose and Burgess William Sohn as they emerged from a tour of the plant. Mrs. Mary Sample, a striker's wife, was arrested for allegedly striking Chief Ambrose with an umbrella.[155] Violence occurred rarely when men tried to force past picket lines, but a handful were severely beaten and a windshield was smashed. One of the tense moments happened when Governor Earle drove through the Wye tunnel to be met by the aimed rifles of Company police who recognized their mistake too late. In general, the heavily outnumbered police, both Borough and Company simply tried to unclog traffic. The bus company had to suspend operations, and with pickets at the train terminal, no trains (all company owned) stopped. Pickets also blocked the end of the Ambridge Bridge. J & L was closed and so was Aliquippa.

The strike lasted 36 hours, ending when J & L Chairman H.E. Lewis agreed to sign an exclusive bargaining contract if the SWOC could win an NLRB election.

> Suddenly a white paper like a flag of truce fluttered above the crowd...."A victory has been won! Jones & Laughlin has signed an agreement with the Steel Workers Organizing Committee. The strike is officially declared over," Joe Timko's voice blared out to the tense waiting crowd ..."I can't believe it's over," one girl said. "They were tear gassin us last night. Yes, last night Turner's vigilantes was bragging they was goin' to shoot us out."[156]

Timko urged the people to go home.

> No one left. Anybody who walked out of the mill was spat upon by the women and attacked by the men. Somehow Timko managed to hire a band and, carrying an American flag, he led a parade of 20,000 people away from the Aliquippa Works. The procession spun out for twelve miles along the Ohio River.[157]

Governor George Earle praised Philip Murray and John L. Lewis for the prompt settlement and conducting the extensive strike with virtually no violence: "Any company which does not want to negotiate as J & L did ought to be ashamed of itself."[158] Formally, the agreement included six points:

1. The men were to return at once pending a Wagner Act election.

2. J & L promised not to interfere or coerce workers in rights of self organization, as guaranteed by the Wagner Act.

3. J & L would facilitate elections at its plants.

4. Pending final determination, conditions then in effect in contract between SWOC and Carnegie-Illinois Steel Corp. would be observed by J & L.

5. "The corporation agrees to negotiate and sign an exclusive bargaining contract with the SWOC in the event a majority of those participating in the election select the SWOC as a collective bargaining agency."

Lopata 48 (July 2, 1979) [hereinafter Lopata Interview], *in* Beaver Valley History Society Papers (on file in Labor Archives, Univ. of Pitt.).
   154. Cozzocolli Interview, *supra* note 153, at 8.
   155. *Beaver Valley Times*, May 14, 1937.
   156. Mary H. Vorse, *Labor's New Millions: The Growth of a People's Power* 116–117 (1938).
   157. Bernstein, *supra* note 174, at 477. The band cost $175. Brooks, supra note 143, at 127.
   158. "Jones & Laughlin Steel Strike is Ended," *Ambridge Daily Citizen*, 1 (May 14, 1937).

6. All employees as of May 12, 1937, will be returned to their former positions without discrimination.[159]

The next week, the workers voted without incident 17,028 to 7,207 for the union, with the vote 7,940 to 3,191 in Aliquippa.[160] The ballot contained a single question: "Do you want the Amalgamated Association of Iron, Steel and Tin Workers of North America through the Steel Workers' Organizing Committee of the Committee for Industrial Organization to represent you as the exclusive representative for collective bargaining?"[161] Broken down by departments, Blast Furnaces workers voted: 443–156; Steel Works, Open Hearth and Bessemers: 479–136; Blooming Mills: 501–264; By-Product Coke Works: 183–192; Fourteen Inch Mill: 112–201; Tin Plate: 1960–642; Wire and Rod Mills: 936–458; Welded Tube: 1100–411; Seamless Tube: 829–381; Electrical: 173–130; Mechanical, Blacksmiths, Riggers and Cranes: 483–301; Carpenters, Bricklayers, Laborers and Motor: 695–622; Misc. 46–136.[162]

The exclusive agency agreement became the first the steelworkers won in the industry; won in the first great industrial election conducted in the country. In an important sense, Murray had staked the future of the SWOC and the entire Little Steel campaign on this victory. Yet one day before the vote, Philip Murray charged Little Steel with a last ditch effort to sabotage the election, the captains of the Republic Steel police forces in Cleveland, Buffalo, Canton, and Warren, with their lieutenants and 30 members of their Cleveland gas pipe gang, were reported in Aliquippa. The underlings and some of the officers had all at one time worked at J & L. Republic responded that the men were just there to observe.[163] William Turner, the president of the former ERP and now independent United Iron and Steel Workers of Aliquippa, gave an affidavit to the NLRB July 25, 1937. Jim Williams, Chief of Republic Steel's police force, met with him in Aliquippa the week of the election. Williams ordered 10,000 handbills printed in English, Serbian, Slavish, and Italian, ostensibly on behalf of the United Iron and Steel Workers, urging a no vote and invoking the mob rule, the beatings and the intimidation practiced by the SWOC and their imported pickets. The cost was $453. for the foreign language versions and $250. for the English. Despite the fact that Williams told the printer that Republic Steel would pay for the former and UISW for the later, Turner denied having any part in the handbilling. At the same time, the broke UISW was assured by Mr. Mays of J & L that Republic Steel would pay the expenses of speakers at anti-SWOC election rallies. Before the strike, Mr. David Craig, characterized as the head of the J & L Republican political machine, assured Turner he would get all the support he would need when they crashed the picket lines.[164]

When Justice Hughes ordered reinstatement of the ten workers remaining in the suit they were given a heroes' parade down mainstreet—Franklin Avenue. When asked what these men would do after the lump sum payment of their back wages, one responded, "The court ordered us back to work"[165] not back to employment—back to work!—a difference not lost on the men. In the early 1930s, when work had been cut to two days a fortnight in many of the shops, the company had run shuttle boats to uninhabited Cow

159. *Ibid.*

160. "2 to 1 at J & L," *Pittsburgh Press*, 1 (May 21, 1937).

161. *Ibid.* at 10.

162. *Ibid.*

163. "Republic Denies Murray's Charges on Steel Elections," *Ambridge Daily Citizen*, 1 (May 19, 1937).

164. Affidavit of William H. Turner (July 23, 1937) [hereinafter Turner Affidavit], *in* Jones & Laughlin Steel Co. Regulatory File (located in NLRB Archives, National Archives Annex).

165. *Beaver Valley Lab. Hist. J.*, 8 (Jan. 1980).

Island in the middle of the Ohio so that workers and their families could clear and farm small patches. Now women stood in open windows along the way crying with joy and chanting "no more Cow Island" as the parade marched by.

At least 42 men from the Honor Roll, fired for union activity between January and July of 1936 (26 in one month from late June) were rehired with seniority and back pay in response to the union and the Supreme Court decision. Their back pay totalled over $26,000. Of the original thirteen men discharged, nine resumed their work at J & L. In the year outside, each had worked some at other jobs, in addition to their back wages: Brandy was paid $973 at the rate of $26 per week, earning $970.48; Volpe $862.21 at $22 per week, earning $1152.16; Phillips — $193.23 at $27.50 per week, but earning $2,446.77; Dunn — $1313.12 at $5.16 per day, earning $1135.75; Maroll — $1329.83 at $24 per week, earning $463.14; Boyer — $1747.38 at $30 per week, earning $451.58; Gerstner — $1171.94 at $27.50 per week, earning $836.; Razzano $1045.61 at $4.80 per day, earning $583.58; Bozich — $367.09 at $15 per week, earning $43.91; and Cox — $342.66 at $34 per week, earning $1332.54. Cox at that time owed the Woodlawn Land Co. $593.11 and the Pittsburgh Mercantile Co. $49.76, almost twice as much as his award. He refused J & L's offer of reinstatement conditioned on the award offsetting his debt. In an important precedent for the NLRB, Associate General Counsel Robert Watts ordered that under no circumstances would the Board agree to any settlement requiring counterclaims and setoffs to back pay awards, arguing that administrative proceedings were neither a suit at law nor a private cause of action. At the time Phillips owed the Woodlawn Land Co. $244.83 and the Pittsburgh Mercantile Co. $24.81, while Maroll, Boyer, and Razzano, owed the latter $113.06, $66.07, and $49.75, respectively.[166] Boyer guessed he would buy a house for his wife and three children in Ambridge, Brandy put his money together with a WWI bonus check to bring his wife and three children from Italy, and Dunn, Maroll, Phillips, Gerstner, Cox Rozzano and Volpe planned to pay bills.[167]

The workers were organized and they had tasted their power, economically and politically. Financial Secretary Clifford Shorts recalled,

> We knew that we were going to have some trouble in carrying out our end of the agreement, perhaps, because for the first time in 30 years some of the people in Aliquippa were feeling their own power, it was the first time that they had ever been allowed or had ever been able to voice their own opinions and do anything really for themselves.[168]

Moreover, as the workers saw it, they had organized themselves from the grass roots. The outside help was appreciated, but given what they had resisted, organization only worked because the workers had revolted. So, if they had struck to organize, they could strike for justice and better treatment in the plant. The rest of 1937 saw a series of wildcat strikes, which Joe Timko had to put down.[169] Steward Andy Lopata wildcatted the first time in the Seamless tube because hot steel would fall down upon the men. When they blew the whistles, the men just stood by their machines. The strike lasted only fifteen minutes when Superintendent Fisher promised an immediate coverplate. The second wildcat over a work clothes laundry forced Timko to call Lopata to his office to tell him that only the Local president could call a walkout. To the men on the floor, it appeared that Timko

---

166. Turner Affidavit, *supra* note 164.
167. "J. & L. Plays 'Santa,' Pays Reinstated Men," *Pitt. Sun Telegraph*, July 22, 1937.
168. *NLRA Hearings*, *supra* note 1, at 4188 (testimony of Clifford Shorts).
169. Lopata Interview, *supra* note 153, at 15–24.

only stopped them from getting their rights.[170] The SWOC had won a contract but management expected discipline in return. Aliquippa steel workers chafed at the apparent cowardice of the national leadership, but no serious work stoppage occurred. J & L attributed success to Timko:

> He is a Dr. Jekyll and Mr. Hyde. While we were fighting him, we thought he was Mr. Hyde—one of the toughest organizers and hardest-fighting strike leaders we had ever come up against. But now that we have been dealing with him for two years, we've found him an able negotiator and responsible union business official.[171]

African-Americans as a group of workers also felt empowered, starting more vigorous civil rights organizations, including leadership from 1920s UNIA organizer Matthew Dempsey and union activist Bartow Tipper. Black workers struck in 1944 protesting J & L's failure to promote them to an equal share of open positions.[172]

Politically, the transformation of Aliquippa was more rapid and complete. In the elections of 1937, the Democratic Party elected union affiliated candidates to the office of Burgess (mayor) and three of seven council seats. The sponsor of the Committee of Five Hundred, a justice of the peace who held office for eight years issuing fines to steel workers, the editor who called John L. Lewis "Mad Dog", J.A. Ruffner, Republican Party Chairman and tax collector since 1914, were swept out of office.[173] Burgess Candidate George Kiefer, a pro-union druggist campaigned,

> We will have but one Chief of Police and one Police Force. Their duties will be to police the town of Aliquippa, keep law and order and meddle with nothing else ... The Police Department will be under the direct supervision of the Burgess with the approval of Council. The entire Police Force will take orders from nobody else.[174]

Local President Paul Normile pledged as Councilman,

> It has been the practice of past and present Councils to be dominated and controlled by men who have no connection with borough affairs in their selection and dismissal of members of the police force. The police force was not selected for the ability of the various members, but consisted of imported persons responsible to special interests not legally having a voice in civic matters ... We pledge ourselves that in the selection of police officers, we will first select local residents.[175]

---

170. *Ibid.* at 21, 24.

171. Brooks, *supra* note 143, at 110. For the SWOC vision of responsible unionism, see Clinton Golden & Harold Ruttenberg, *The Dynamics of Industrial Democracy* (1942). David Brody sees a fit between the SWOC administration of the work force and a more realistic and thus less militant workforce in steel. David Brody, "The Origins of Modern Steel Unionism: The SWOC Era," *in* Paul Clark et al. eds., *Forging A Union of Steel* 14–15 (1987). His view fits Aliquippa uncomfortably given the rank and file activity, the accompanying violent repression of workers, and the wildcats following unionization. While the workers became disciplined, that was not their early inclination. Further, while acknowledging rank and file mobilization as a factor in steel, he provides no explanation for the ability of J & L workers to gain the exclusive representation contract that SWOC could not get from Carnegie-Illinois. The best explanation is the civil uprising nature of the J & L strike, unforeseen by management.

172. Dickerson, *supra* note 56.

173. Levinson, *supra* note 79, at 274.

174. Eric Leif Davin, The Littlest New Deal: SWOC Takes Power in Steeltown, a Possibility of Radicalism in the Late 1930s at 50 (n.d.) (quoting *Union Press*, Sept. 8, 1937, at 2).

175. *Ibid.* at 51. Steel workers documented the origin of the force: Chief Ambrose, previously at the J & L subsidiary Vesta Coal Co.; Lt. Honn, same; Sgt. Bloom, formerly a Ku Klux Klan leader in Jefferson County and a strike breaking policeman at the mines; Sgt. Grosskoff, not a resident of Pa.,

The first battle of the split Council occurred on a motion introduced by the SWOC members to fire six of the most vicious policemen. In subsequent elections, SWOC candidates essentially swept all municipal elections. This secured the streets and public places for a liberty the workers had never experienced before. As one steel worker appraised the victory of the union, "it was "worth twelve dollars a year to be able to walk down the main street of Aliquippa, talk to anyone you want about anything you like, and feel that you are a citizen.'"[176]

True democracy can never be achieved merely through the redistribution of the fruits of production. As we produce wealth to be consumed, we also produce ourselves. True democracy must be part of the distribution of production itself. Much of that distribution is understood and often accomplished through the power constructed by law and by agents claiming the authority of law. The social history of Aliquippa is part of the J & L opinion. It had to be if it was to operate as law. But the town and its people were hidden in the blinders of Justice Hughes. And in this case the workers won! The presence of social struggle as necessary for understanding what happened as law in fact, and in producing the events necessary to legal actions, is documented normally as the presence left unsaid.

When Justice Hughes wrote, "experience has abundantly demonstrated that the recognition of the right of employees to self-organization and to have representatives of their own choosing for the purpose of collective bargaining is often an essential condition of industrial peace,"[177] he was by definition responding through law to social conflict. He could have explicitly connected the law he announced to the struggle over power that a prior regime of constitutional interpretation protecting local control of economic development had anticipated and structured.[178] He could have understood the passion for throwing off the alienation of control fueling the workers to break the peace of the quid pro quo. He could have understood the passion for power to make their own lives of the people of Aliquippa. He could have seen the threat to national prosperity in their iron will for democracy. He could have seen that American promise, because it was there in the law, in the power, in the case.

---

from the Marine Corp.; Tom Elms, local Republican stool pigeon from Beaver Falls; Cole, from Waynesburg; Steel, from Bobtown, a J & L cop; Cook, never a resident, Marine Corp.; Greenley, same; Costlow, former bootlegger and stool pigeon; Bradbury, former state policeman, never lived there; Moraski, former highway patrolman, never lived there; Fuss, U.S. Army, never lived there; Rendos, friend of Sgt. Bloom, from DuBois; Powers, from W. Va. *Ibid.* at 44.

176. Richard Cortner, *The Jones & Laughlin Case* 168 (1971).

177. *NLRB v. Jones & Laughlin Steel Corp.*, 301 U.S. 1, 42 (1937).

178. *See Lochner v. New York*, 198 U.S. 45 (1905) (holding that liberty of contract protected by Due Process prevents bakers from limiting their hours by political contract, when under market conditions individual contracts including limits are unachievable); *Hammer v. Dagenhart*, 247 U.S. 251 (1918) (holding that where the local police powers must include deciding which contractual relations and other voluntary associations are approved as public policy, child labor produced goods are thus protected against national denial of access to the common market). *But cf. West Coast Hotel v. Parrish*, 300 U.S. 379 (1937) (holding that the state is not required to subsidize employers offering below subsistence wages made marketable because of the unemployed surplus labor force resulting from structural failure of domestic market to clear commodity and labor gluts); *NLRB v. Jones & Laughlin Steel Corp.*, 301 U.S. 1 (1937) (holding that when industries vertically organize themselves in response to state choices of what mix of natural and legislated competitive advantages to offer participants in local markets, national regulation must be permitted to allow democratic construction of the national common market, including making possible workers' coalitions access to the construction of local political-economies into their communities).

Interlude

Memorial Day Massacre

Police Fire on Crowd, Memorial Day, Chicago.

Violence in Little Steel — The Chicago Massacre (1938)

*Mary Heaton Vorse**

The workers had won at Jones & Laughlin, but there was trouble ahead. What Philip Murray called an "unholy alliance" had been formed by the Independents of Little Steel. Youngstown Sheet and Tube, which had been negotiating for a long time, now joined Inland Steel, and Republic, in saying it would make a verbal agreement but would sign no contract.

Meantime, Republic fired seventy-five workers, and closed the plant in Massillon where organization was strong. The S.W.O.C. charged unfair labor practices and appealed to the N.L.R.B. In May, the S.W.O.C. organizers met in Pittsburgh and voted to leave a strike call to the discretion of Philip Murray. In Massillon the workers took a strike vote without waiting to hear from Pittsburgh. There was considerable strike pressure in Youngstown. On May 26, the strike with Little Steel was called. It was spread through seven states and a dozen cities and involved 83,000 men. On May 30, the Chicago massacre occurred.

To the majority of employers, Tom Girdler of Republic Steel is a hero. He defied the Steel Workers Organizing Committee. He defied the National Labor Relations Act. Because of this eighteen men are dead.

---

* A longer version of this chapter appears in, Mary Heaton Vorse, "Violence — The Chicago Massacre," *Labor's New Millions*, 118 (New York: Modern Age Books, 1938).

The strike began on the 26th; Wednesday, Thursday, Friday, the picket lines were driven away by the police. There were clubbings and arrests. On Sunday, May 30, the workers assembled at "Sam's Place." The big map of the La Follette Civil Liberties Committee showed Sam's Place far off from the mills, separated by a waste field and a railway track. At Sam's place the meeting was peaceful. Various disinterested spectators testified that the people had come with their families as to a celebration. The women were dressed in their Sunday clothes. Fathers and mothers brought their children.

Leo Krzycki, a well-known organizer for the Amalgamated Clothing Workers was one of the principal speakers. He joked with the crowd. A statement from the Mayor affirming the workers' rights for peaceful picketing was read. Some of the women sang. A vote was taken that the meeting should then proceed across the fields and picket the Republic Mill for the purpose of affirming the workers' rights to picket in accordance with the Mayor's decision.

The audience started out strolling rather than marching, by groups of twos and threes, groups of women marching together, women who laughed and chatted and talked among themselves, as Mrs. Lupe Marshall, the social worker from Hull House, testified.

Probably no group of people ever strolled more casually toward death and wounds. Some of the strikers deployed across the fields, apparently to see what was happening. There is a story of a man's carrying a branch of a tree. Mrs. Lupe Marshall says that she heard someone cry sharply to a worker who picked up a stone, "Drop that, we don't want any of that." There were no guns. The crowd did not even carry clubs. The police, on the other hand, were armed with revolvers, clubs, and tear gas as well as with hatchet handles such as the mill guards carry and which were furnished by the mills.

The testimony showed that the police had been eating in the mills and a platoon of fifty policemen was seen walking out of the mills that morning. The testimony goes to show that this was a planned attack; that the police came out with the intention of shooting down the workers and then arresting them wholesale. The police had planned to make this peaceful picket line seem like a Red plot to capture the mills. The brave policemen were to have warded off the revolution. But their plan failed. There were too many witnesses and too many cameramen.

So the two groups met: the unarmed workers with their two American flags leading them, and the police ready and waiting for the attack. In the Paramount Newsreel which was shown in the high Senate Caucus room you could see the leader of the strikers in the picture arguing peacefully with the police. He is earnest, emphatic, unthreatening. The testimony is that they asked for their rights of peaceful picketing; they begged the police to let them through; that the Mayor had said they had a right to picket. The police testified that they used insulting language and they cried out that they wanted to occupy the factory and that they shot to prevent greater bloodshed in the factory. It is strange that the police defense was so overdone and stupid and that their lawyers should not have advised them better, considering that every steel worker and every thoughtful person in America knows that occupying the factory was not in any worker's mind. Another officer added a touch of the grotesque to the macabre testimony.

"They came along smoking cigarettes like they were doped. I supposed they were smoking marijuana. They seemed to be chanting a long, monotonous chant which seemed to go 'C.I.O., C.I.O.'" "Is that what smoking marijuana does to one?" Senator La Follette asked with sarcasm. The pickets argued with the police.

Suddenly there were shots. Some stones flew through the air. In a moment a heap of people were piled up within a few feet of the police line. This happened so quickly that you could hardly believe your own eyes, but there are stills that also tell the story, and some of these are worse than the Paramount film. There is a terrible picture of Mrs. Lupe Marshall with her hand slightly outstretched, as in a gesture, talking to a policeman (who, she records, called her a foul name), and as she talks, unconscious of what has happened, behind her is a piled heap of the wounded. There is another picture: Lupe Marshall has turned and sees the wounded. In another picture, she bends over them, and in this scene there is a frightful picture of a policeman with his club raised up for a shattering blow. The stills proceed. Now the workers are in full flight, hands up-raised. They face the murderous gunfire, the flailing clubs, the clouds of gas. But for sheer horror, the testimony of the bystanders of what happened on the way to the hospital, of what happened at the hospital, was more terrible.

The story of Mrs. Lupe Marshall is a shocking record. She is a social worker, and the mother of three children, 15, 8, and 4. She is also a distinguished linguist and was helping put on a play at Hull House that very night. She did not put it on because she was arrested.

Tiny Mrs. Marshall weighs ninety-two pounds and is four feet, eleven inches high. You can see her being beaten and see that she has her head broken open by a club. You can see her in the photographs and the Paramount film trying to minister to fallen workers and you can see a policeman twice her size, towering over her and twisting her around viciously as he arrests her and shoves her into the patrol wagon.

Piled on top of each other in this patrol wagon were sixteen dying and seriously wounded. They lay every which way, on top of each other. They couldn't stand, they couldn't sit, they were falling over each other. The blood dripped upon the floor of the wagon.

Lupe Marshall tried to help them. She tried to lift them off each other and straighten out their wounded arms and legs. She pillowed one man's bloody head in her lap. He made a gesture that he wanted to smoke. She searched in his pockets to try to find his cigarettes but they were soaked in blood. Then he said.

"Never mind, you're a good kid," then he shivered, straightened out and died with his head in her lap.

They bounced, rattling, through Chicago streets. She did not know where they went. They seemed to go from place to place. The men were groaning and blood was oozing around her and the dead man lay with his head in her lap. Then at last they got to the hospital.

What happened in the hospital was almost worse than all the rest. The hospital was overwhelmed with the dead and the wounded! There were calls outside for volunteers to help the doctors *but the police tried to keep the volunteers from helping.*

There was a little wounded boy and Lupe tried to help the doctor with him, but the police drove her away. She came back and the police drove her away again. When at last her turn came to have her wounded head dressed she felt very sick from the beating and the gas and the sights she had seen. The nurses wheeled her tenderly upstairs in a wheel chair. She went in the toilet and a policeman followed her there. He grabbed her, saying, "I guess you can walk all right," and dragged her down the stairs into the patrol wagon, to the jail. There they searched her. "What's that in her purse?"

"Communist literature, of course," replied the matron. The "Communist literature" was a handbill with an announcement of a meeting and an advertisement of a post-office auction sale. But every one of the scores arrested that day was booked as a Communist.

This stroll across the fields from Sam's place had to be made into a dark Red plot paid for by "Moscow Gold."

Harry N. Harper, the blinded man, was booked as a Communist. Groping, he had been led in and out of the meetings by his young and pretty wife. Perhaps his testimony was the most horrifying. His voice came out hollow and deep as though he himself had retreated far into the shadows. He told his story slowly, as though each word cost him a painful effort. From time to time Senator La Follette helped him with suggestions.

Harper was a steel worker, a boilermaker and welder employed by Interlake Iron. With his wife he had gone to visit his mother that bright Sunday. They had planned to go to the country. But his mother was ill and she was crying, for Harry Harper's brothers worked at Republic Steel. One was striking and the other was in the mill and she was afraid he was being kept there by force. Disturbed by his mother's grief, Harry Harper, the boiler-maker bound on a holiday, went to Sam's Place, encountered the line of marchers, walked up to the head of it, and begged the officer to let him go to the mill to look for his brother because his mother was sick.

He found himself surrounded by hostile faces. They cursed him. "They seemed" he said, "*to be intoxicated with something I can't explain.*"

There was a blast of a whistle and then hell broke loose.

"Seems as if they were going down, as if you'd taken a scythe."

He was struck on the left side of his head and the blood was running in his mouth. There was a blinding pain in his eye. He fled, blinded by pain and blood. He fell in a ditch. Another man lay groaning beside him.

"The man said, 'Help me, buddy.' I said, 'I am helpless myself.'" A gas bomb like a green ball of fire was sputtering beside him. It went off, affecting his other eye. He said, "A terrible trembling feeling came over me and I went back groping. I lost the vision of my right eye too. I called for help."

You could get a picture of him, his eye beaten out, blood running into his mouth, stumbling and groping and crying for help. He told, too, of his terrible ride in the patrol wagon. He could hear men groaning. He could hear officers saying, "Some of them are breathing yet, but we'll take the others to the morgue," and he knew men were dead or dying beside him. And when he groaned, they said, "Shut up, you damn so-and-so, you got what's coming to you."

He said, and his sightless face did not turn toward the police officers sitting in their uneasy indifference,

"Among those officers there were many of them brought up in my faith, for I am a Catholic, I went to parochial school and I attended Sunday School and Mass faithfully. I think they have forgotten what we all learned there, 'Thou shalt not kill!'"

* * *

There is plenty of other testimony, that for instance of the lawyer, Frank W. McCulloch, Social Relations Secretary of the Council of Social Action of the Congregational Church. The meeting at Sam's place to him was a friendly holiday crowd asserting their rights to organize under the N.L.R.B. He saw a policeman seventy feet away from the marchers empty a gun and reach for another clip.

The Reverend Charles B. Fiske, a Congregational Minister, a minister concerned about civil liberties, had gone down as an impartial observer. He heard the shots, saw the people give way and he took pictures, as he thought, of the whole flight. He took pictures of men being beaten on the ground. In the end he was arrested and thrown into jail and kept incommunicado for nineteen hours and his pictures were taken from him.

There was Meyer Levin's testimony. He is a writer and an editor of *Esquire*. He heard the outbreak of the shooting. He watched workers being shot down and he carried a bleeding child. He was kept by police out of the Burnside Hospital where volunteers had been called for.

Dr. Lawrence Jacques held a mannequin in his hand high up so the crowd could see. He jabbed at this with a pick as he showed where the wounds were made by police bullets in the Chicago Memorial Day massacre. Behind the two investigating Senators of the Civil Liberties Committee, Robert La Follette and Senator Thomas (Utah), were four charts. The chart showing a man's back is peppered with red spots. Each one of these means a gunshot wound. The doctor dropped the doll and moved to the charts. The charts of side views showed scattered wounds. On the chart showing the front view of a man there are no red spots. The dead and wounded were shot in the back as they ran.

The familiar story of the murder of workers was spread out before the people of this country. It was read into the record of the Senate Civil Liberties Committee, before a distinguished Washington audience of five hundred. It is an old story—perjury and Red framing. You can see the dead and wounded dragged like sacks over the ground. You can hear of wounded workers dragged from cars to bleed to death, wounded workers snatched from the hospitals.

It is nothing new. The use of the police by the mills to shoot steel workers asking for their constitutional rights is an old story. The shooting of workers in steel began in Homestead in 1892 and has gone on steadily ever since. In the steel strike of 1919, twenty-one people were killed, including Fannie Sellins who was shot by gunmen as she bent over some children to protect them. They killed steel workers in Ambridge in 1933.

The number of United Mine Workers dead in its long fight for organization is uncounted. The mines of West Virginia are drenched with the blood of workers. The Ludlow massacres are fresh in everyone's mind. Textile workers were killed in 1929 at Marion and at Honea Path, North Carolina, in 1934. The purpose of the killings is always the same. It is to crush the workers' lawful right to organize.

Newsreel Account Paramount Film

A vivid close-up shows the head of the parade being halted at the police line. The flag-bearers are in front.... Behind the flag-bearers is the marchers' spokesman, a muscular young man in shirt sleeves, with a CIO button on the band of his felt hat....

"Then suddenly, without apparent warning, there is a terrific roar of pistol shots, and men in the front ranks of the marchers go down like grass before a scythe. The camera catches approximately a dozen falling simultaneously in a heap. The massive, sustained roar of the pistol shots lasts perhaps two or three seconds.

"Instantly the police charge on the marchers with riot sticks flying. At the same time tear gas grenades are seen sailing into the mass of demonstrators, and clouds of gas rise over them. Most of the crowd is now in flight....

"In a manner which is appallingly businesslike, groups of policemen close in on these isolated individuals, and go to work on them with their clubs. In several instances, from two to four policemen are seen beating one man. One strikes him horizontally across the face, using his club as he would a baseball, bat Another crashes it down on top of his head and still another is whipping him across the back....

"A man shot through the back is paralyzed from the waist. Two policemen try to make him stand up, to get him into a patrol wagon, but when they let go of him his legs crumble, and he falls with his face in the dirt, almost under the rear step of the wagon. He moves his head and arms, but his legs are limp. He raises his head like a turtle, and claws the ground....

"There is continuous talking, but ... out of the babble there rises this clear and distinct ejaculation:

"'God Almighty!'

"A policeman, somewhat disheveled, his coat wide open, a scowl on his face, approaches another who is standing in front of the camera. He is sweaty and tired. He says something indistinguishable. Then his face breaks out into a sudden grin, he makes a motion of dusting off his hands, and strides away. The film ends."

XI

Sit-Downs

Autoworkers Sit-Down, Fisher Body, Flint, Library of Congress.

Worker Lawmaking, Sit-Down Strikes, and the Shaping of American Industrial Relations, 1935–1939

James Gray Pope*

Between 1936 and 1939, American workers staged some 583 sit-down strikes of at least one day's duration. In the latter year, the United States Supreme Court issued its opinion in *NLRB v. Fansteel Metallurgical Corporation*,[1] resolving the official legal status of the tactic. *Fansteel* made it clear not only that a state could punish sit-downers for violating trespass laws, but also that an employer could lawfully discharge them — even if that employer had itself provoked the sit-down by committing serious unfair labor practices in violation of the National Labor Relations Act.[2]

---

* This chapter is an abridged version of "Worker Lawmaking, Sit-Down Strikes, and the Shaping of American Industrial Relations, 1935–1958," 24 *Law & Hist. Rev.* 45–113 (2006). It is reprinted by permission of the publisher, Cambridge University Press.

1. 306 U.S. 240 (1939).
2. Walter L. Eisenberg, "Government Policy in Sitdown Strikes" (Ph.D. diss., Columbia University, 1959), 318; 306 U.S. 240, 251–52 (1939).

This chapter presents a legal history, broadly defined, of the sit-down strike movement in the United States. It covers the legal thought and action not only of lawyers, government officials, and judges, but also of industrial workers and union leaders. It suggests that the sit-down strike enabled workers to engage in five distinct forms of lawmaking. First, mass production workers legislated and enforced unilateral rules directly regulating relations of production, for example restrictions on the pace of work. Second, sit-downers enacted, adjudicated, and enforced rules governing life in the facilities that they had seized. Third, workers claimed and exercised a fundamental right to stage sit-down strikes at their place of work. Fourth, workers used factory occupations to enforce the National Labor Relations Act, thereby pressuring the Supreme Court to uphold the Act in April of 1937. Finally, workers interpreted and enforced collective bargaining agreements directly instead of bowing to management's interpretations while waiting for an official resolution. The chapter concludes by assessing the impact of the Supreme Court's decision on these forms of lawmaking and, more broadly, on the prospects for a democratic industrial order.[3]

I. An Explosion of Worker Lawmaking: Akron and Detroit, 1935–1937

On January 27, 1936, the Firestone Tire & Rubber Company suspended Clayton Dicks for one week without pay. Although the Firestone management recognized no union, members of the United Rubber Workers of America had already established an organization in the Akron plant. Dicks, a union committeeman in the tire building department, had been accused of punching and knocking out a nonunion man. Union tire builders complained that the company had appointed itself "prosecutor, judge, and jury" and demanded "a fair trial before an equal number of union and company representatives."[4] The company refused and the tire builders responded by stopping work in a body. Ruth McKenny penned this account of what happened next:

> Instantly, the noise stopped. The whole room lay in perfect silence. The tire-builders stood in long lines, touching each other, perfectly motionless, deafened by the silence.... Out of the terrifying quiet came the wondering voice of a big tirebuilder near the windows: "Jesus Christ, it's like the end of the world." He broke the spell, the magic moment of stillness. For now his awed words said the same thing to every man, "We done it! We stopped the belt! By God, we done it!" And men began to cheer hysterically, to shout and howl in the fresh silence...."John Brown's body," somebody chanted above the cries. The others took it up. "But his soul," they sang, and some of them were nearly weeping, racked with sudden and deep emotion, "but his soul goes marchin' on."[5]

The tire builders remained at their machines and announced that they would not resume work until Dicks was reinstated. Union leaders labeled the protest a "sit-down" as opposed to an ordinary strike. Although the term had been heard before, the Dicks sit-down marked its entry into the standard vocabulary of industrial conflict. Fifty-five hours after production ceased, the protest ended with Dicks reinstated with back pay at half his normal rate for the period of the suspension and the sit-downers paid at the same rate for the period

---

3. This chapter builds on the work of Karl Klare and Jeremy Brecher. See Karl E. Klare, "Law-Making as Praxis," 40 *Telos*, 123, 124 n.5; (1979): Karl E. Klare, "Judicial Deradicalization of the Wagner Act and the Origins of Modern Legal Consciousness, 1937–1941," 62 *Minnesota Law Review* 265, 321, 324–25 (1978):; Jeremy Brecher, *Strike!* 2d ed. 235 (Boston: South End Press, 1997).

4. *SCLN*, 1 (Jan. 31, 1936).

5. Ruth McKenny, *Industrial Valley*, 261–62 (New York: Harcourt, Brace & Co., 1939).

of the sit-down.[6] A local union leader reported to the CIO that this was "one of the great-est victories ever won by labor" and that it had "done more to build up the Trade Union Movement here than anything we could have even thought of doing."[7] Within days, the Dicks sit-down had sparked similar actions at Akron's other tire-making giants, Goodyear and B. F. Goodrich. Thanks to the sit-down tactic, the legislation and enforcement of work rules—once the exclusive preserve of employers and skilled craft workers—suddenly be-came a realistic possibility for semi- and unskilled workers in mass production industry.

On the Shop Floor: From Wage Slaves to "Men"

Writing in 1923, John R. Commons—America's leading labor scholar—described what he called a "common law of labor springing from the customs of wage earners." This law consisted "in those practices by which laborers endeavor to achieve their ideals through protection against the economic power of employers." To Commons, the workers' com-mon law consisted not of mindless or instinctive adaptations, but of norms consciously "formulated in assemblies or groups while dealing with violations and deciding disputes as they arise." The central norm was that of solidarity among workers, which—unfortunately for them—was "exactly opposite to the ideals and customs of business which the courts have been defining and classifying for some 300 years."[8]

Despite the hostility of courts, workers and unions legislated, adjudicated, and en-forced their own labor laws during Commons's day. For example, an assembly of craft workers might enact a union "law" establishing a minimum wage for the craft. This law would operate directly on workers, with no involvement by the employer. Workers would simply announce to employers that they were bound by union law to refuse any jobs that paid less than the craft's minimum wage. The employer would either pay the min-imum or lose its union workers until the law was repealed or otherwise rendered inef-fective. Such unilateral union laws covered a wide variety of employment conditions and practices including, in some cases, production technology and product design.[9] They often co-existed with joint employer-union collective bargaining agreements, ad-dressing matters not covered under those agreements. Even in non-union shops, groups of workers might combine to regulate on such issues as the pace of production or the obligations of solidarity.[10]

---

6. Alfred Winslow Jones, *Life, Liberty, and Property,* 99 (1941; New York: Octagon, 1964), Daniel Nelson, *American Rubber Workers and Organized Labor, 1900–1941* 181–82 (Princeton: Princeton University Press, 1988).

7. Tom Owens, Firestone Local 7 activist, to Adolph Germer, CIO organizer, Adolph Germer Papers, State Historical Society of Wisconsin, Microform edition [hereafter Germer Papers], reel 3, frame 344.

8. John R. Commons, *Legal Foundations of Capitalism,* 301–05 (1923; Madison: University of Wis-consin Press, 1968). Quotations are at 304, 301–2, and 305.

9. David Montgomery, *Workers' Control in America: Studies in the History of Work, Technology, and Labor Struggles,* 15–18 (Cambridge: Cambridge University Press, 1979); David Montgomery, *The Fall of the House of Labor: The Workplace, the State, and American Labor Activism, 1865–1925,* 9–13 (New York: Cambridge University Press, 1987); Daniel T. Rodgers, *The Work Ethic in Industrial Amer-ica, 1850–1920,* 165–66 (Chicago: University of Chicago Press, 1978); Lloyd Ulman, *The Rise of the National Trade Union,* 526, 541–42, 545–46, 551–52 (Cambridge: Harvard University Press, 1955); Benson Soffer, "A Theory of Trade Union Development: The Role of the 'Autonomous' Workman," 1 *Labor History* 141, 152–53 (1960).

10. Sumner H. Slichter, *Union Policies and Industrial Management,* 1 (Washington, D.C.: Brook-ings, 1941); Carter Goodrich, *The Miner's Freedom,* 58–61 (Boston: Marshall Jones, 1925); Stanley B. Mathewson, *Restriction of Output among Unorganized Workers* (New York: Viking Press, 1931); Montgomery, *Workers' Control,* 13–15; Ronald W. Schatz, *The Electrical Workers: A History of Labor*

Unilateral worker lawmaking thrived mainly in the skilled trades, where the scarcity of qualified workers made it difficult for employers to circumvent union rules by hiring non-union workers. But semi- and unskilled workers also aspired to regulate their work lives. "Whenever they came into regular contact on the job, wherever they recognized a common identity," recounts labor historian David Brody, "factory workers formed bonds, legislated group work standards, and, as best they could, enforced these informal rules on fellow workers and on supervisors."[11] During the 1920s and early 1930s, what Commons called the "common law of labor" had flourished—albeit in crude and fragile forms—in the tire-building rooms of the big-three manufacturers, Goodyear, Firestone, and B. F. Goodrich. Lacking a union, the tire builders forged their own shop-floor culture of resistance. Paid by the tire, they could—at least theoretically—earn more money by producing more tires. In the experience of the workers, however, their employers would lower the piece rate if too many builders were exceeding the expected pace of production. In response, the builders joined together to legislate their own tire quotas, which they enforced through social pressure, slow-downs, and strikes.[12]

Although Akron's tire builders developed tough patterns of resistance during this period, their struggles were brief, small in scale, and conducted as covertly as possible to avoid employer retaliation. As a result, their common law order was limited in scope and crude in definition. They made no attempt to codify their rules or to create formal, rulemaking organizations. This began to change in 1933, when Franklin Roosevelt's election, the passage of the National Industrial Recovery Act, and a mild economic recovery stimulated a wave of union organization. By the end of the summer, AFL organizer Coleman Claherty claimed to have enrolled more than 40,000 Akron rubber workers, 19,000 of them at Akron's big three tire manufacturers.[13]

With union organization came the opportunity for workers to specify their laws in written codes, extend them to cover new situations, and enforce them with formal sanctions. Candidates for union membership were required to "take the obligation" before joining. This entailed pledging to abide by the constitution, laws, and regulations of the union. The principle of solidarity took explicit, legal form in union constitutions and by-laws. The first constitution of the United Rubber Workers (URW), in effect at the time of the events recounted here, barred members from working for "any individual or Company declared in difficulty" with the union. Violators could be fined, suspended, or expelled.[14]

At the same time that union organization offered new opportunities for self-government, it also posed new threats. Many union officials preferred the orderly, hierarchical structure of business organizations to the passion and tumult of rank-and-file democracy. John L. Lewis, for example, viewed his United Mine Workers union as "a business institution" that could best win higher standards for miners through obedi-

---

at *General Electric and Westinghouse, 1923–1960,* 42–44 (Urbana: University of Illinois Press, 1983; Frederick Winslow Taylor, *Scientific Management,* 79–85 (New York: Harper, 1947).

11. David Brody, *Workers in Industrial America,* 205 (New York: Oxford University Press, 1980).

12. *See* John D. House, Birth of A Union, Microform (unpublished book manuscript, Ohio Historical Society), 7–8, 12–14; Mathewson, *Restriction of Output,* 54–56; Nelson, *American Rubber Workers,* 86–87, 93–94.

13. Irving Bernstein, *Turbulent Years: A History of the American Worker, 1933–1941,* 95, 100 (Boston: Houghton-Mifflin, 1971); Nelson, *American Rubber Workers.* 121.

14. First Constitution of the United Rubber Workers of America, secs. 18(b) 2, 18(b)(11), November 7, 1935, *American Labor Unions' Constitutions, Proceedings, Officers' Reports and Supplementary Documents* (Microform) (Ann Arbor: University Microfilms International, 1986) [hereafter *American Labor Unions' Constitutions*], Part II, Reel 120.

ence to his commands.[15] Emulating Lewis, AFL President Green ruled that the members of the newly formed URW were not yet ready to choose their own officers. But the rubber workers insisted on elections despite Green's threat to withhold financial support from their fledgling union. They chose national leaders who, until recently, had labored in the rubber factories.[16] It was not long before this new leadership was put to the test.

In February 1936, the Goodyear Tire & Rubber Company discharged 137 tire builders for staging a sit-down. Within days, the company's enormous Akron plant was shut down, with rotating shifts of pickets manning sixty-three posts around its eleven-mile perimeter. Goodyear obtained an injunction barring mass picketing but a crowd of 5,000 workers faced down the 150 officers who had been assigned to open the plant. When the strike ended on March 21, not only had the 137 sit-downers been reinstated, but the URW had won an agreement limiting Goodyear's discretion to increase hours and granting other concessions without conceding any restrictions on the workers' right to strike.[17] Far from ending the sit-downs, this modest step toward collective bargaining only escalated the struggle for power on the shop floor.

No sooner had operations resumed, than the returning strikers began to enact and enforce their own laws of the shop. The old tradition of informal production quotas emerged into the open in the form of public union legislation. Tire builders limited themselves to fifty-six tires per shift; heater men to eighteen heats. Unionists in the more militant departments imposed a ban on working with nonstrikers.[18] This rulemaking emulated that of the skilled craft workers who had built the first stable unions in the late nineteenth century, but with a narrower scope and a different mode of enforcement. Unlike their skilled predecessors, mass production workers did not attempt to regulate the methods of production themselves; instead, they sought to control the pay and working conditions associated with new technology. And where the skilled workers had drawn on their monopoly of craft knowledge for the power necessary to support effective lawmaking, semi- and unskilled workers drew primarily on their capacity to stage sit-down strikes.

On May 29, 1936, five weeks after the strike settlement, Goodyear issued a detailed "Sit-Down Report" complaining that there had already been nineteen sit-downs in its Akron plants. Of these, six or seven were efforts to enforce production quotas, while one sought to control the pace of work on newly installed machinery. Four aimed at excluding nonstrikers from departments or choice assignments. Three were efforts to share the available work by reducing hours or eliminating overtime work. The remainder sought objectives ranging from pay for work lost during a previous sit-down to the reinstatement of a lead worker. The sit-down movement continued through 1936 as Akron workers staged at least fifty-two between the Goodyear settlement and the end of the year. Reflecting the high level of tension in the plants, these sit-downs were

15. United Mine Workers of America, 2 *Proceedings of the 28th Consecutive and 5th Biennial Convention* 628 (1921); see generally Joseph E. Finley, *The Corrupt Kingdom: The Rise and Fall of the United Mine Workers* (New York: Simon & Schuster, 1972).

16. Bernstein, *Turbulent Years*, 382–83; Jones, *Life, Liberty, and Property*, 86–87; Nelson, *American Rubber Workers*, 164–69.

17. *Akron Beacon Journal*, 1,2 (Feb. 22, 1936); *ABJ*, 9 (March 23, 1936), 9; *ABJ*, 15 (Feb. 22, 1936); Bernstein, *Turbulent Years*, 594; Jones, *Life, Liberty, and Property*, 99; McKenny, *Industrial Valley*, 301–2; Nelson, *American Rubber Workers*, 191.

18. Goodyear Tire & Rubber Co., *What is Happening in Akron* (May 29, 1936) [hereafter *Goodyear Sit-Down Report*], in Germer Papers, reel 26, frame 369, 4–5; *ABJ*, 1, 6 (July 14, 193); *ABJ*, 1 (Aug. 7, 1936).

sometimes accompanied by threats of violence and physical assaults on non-union workers.[19]

Perhaps the most outstanding feature of these early sit-downs was their effectiveness. Of the seventeen whose outcomes were reported by Goodyear, seven produced complete victory for the workers on the spot, three resulted in compromises, and five ended when management promised to meet promptly with the union committeemen; only two failed to achieve any result. "In most instances," the company summed up, "resumption of production has been accomplished only by substantial concessions on the part of management in the interest of peace and continuing production during the present peak period."[20]

The experience of success gave many workers a new self-respect grounded in their identity as producers. "Now we don't feel like taking the sass of any snot-nose college-boy foreman," commented one, while another declared: "Now we know our labor is more important than the money of stockholders, than the gambling in Wall Street, than the doings of the managers and foremen." The sociologist Melvin Vincent observed that the sit-down "makes for greater sociability among the workers," thus creating "a new solidarity among them." After a successful sit-down, the *United Auto Worker* reported "a totally new feeling" among the workers—a feeling that transformed them from "wage slaves" into "men."[21] As we have seen, the Dicks sit-downers expressed this sentiment on the spot, chanting lines from *"John Brown's Body."*

Given the sit-down's impressive rate of success, it is not surprising that the tactic soon spread to other industries and localities—most importantly the automobile manufacturing plants in and around Detroit, Michigan.

In the Occupied Factories: The Most Astonishing Feeling of Order

In early 1936, the automobile industry remained a stronghold of anti-unionism. Even without recognized unions, however, automobile workers were already taking advantage of every opportunity to legislate and enforce rules governing their work lives, especially the pace of production. "We did not have any recognition from the company," observed one activist. "We had our own recognition." Occasionally, auto workers staged brief sit-downs similar to the Akron rubber workers' early actions.[22]

In December 1936, this sporadic activity suddenly gelled into a mass movement. Encouraged by President Roosevelt's smashing re-election victory, auto workers for the first time began to occupy entire facilities and to hold them until a settlement was reached. Along with plant-wide scope came plant-wide demands including union recognition. Week-long factory occupations at three major auto parts manufacturers fell short of winning

---

19. *Goodyear Sit-Down Report*, 4–6; Nelson, *American Rubber Workers*, 209.

20. *Goodyear Sit-Down Report*, 1, 4–6. The quotation is at 1.

21. Louis Adamic, "Sitdown," *Nation*, 654 (Dec. 5, 1936) (quoting workers); Melvin J. Vincent, "The Sit-Down Strike," 21 *Sociology and Social Research* 524, 527 (July–Aug. 1937); *United Automobile Worker*, 5 (Jan. 22, 1937); see also Sidney Fine, *Sit-Down: The General Motors Strike of 1936–1937*, 122 (Ann Arbor: University of Michigan Press, 1969); Herbert Harris, *American Labor*, 289 (New Haven: Yale University Press, 1939).

22. Oral History Interview of Nick DiGaetano by William A. Sullivan, University of Michigan—Wayne State University Institute of Labor and Industrial Relations, April 29 & May 7, 1959, 22. On the auto workers' legislation of production limits, *see* Brecher, *Strike!*, 204–5; David Gartman, *Auto Slavery: The Labor Process in the American Automobile Industry, 1897–1950*, 155–58 (New Brunswick: Rutgers University Press, 1986); Mathewson, *Restriction of Output*, 62, 72, 78–80, 86–88. On the early auto sit-downs, *see* Brecher, *Strike!*, 206; Fine, *Sit-Down*, 116; Roger Keeran, *The Communist Party and the Auto Workers Union*, 155 (New York: International Publishers, 1980); Fred W. Thompson and Patrick Murfin, *The IWW—Its First Seventy Years, 1905–1975*, 166–69 (Chicago: IWW, 1976).

union recognition, but triggered dramatic gains in union membership and influence. Emboldened by these successes, militant workers in Flint, Michigan proceeded to seize and hold two facilities of the General Motors Corporation, bringing on what has been called "the 'most critical labor conflict' of the 1930s and perhaps in all of American history." In January and February, workers in a growing list of industries followed their lead.[23]

Having evicted their bosses, the strikers found themselves in a void of established authority. No sooner did they secure the premises than they began to form committees, make rules, and assign tasks. In every shop for which information is available, workers chose the most direct form of democracy that appeared feasible under the circumstances. In Fisher No. 1, for example, a strike committee of about fourteen to seventeen members was elected on the basis of departmental representation, with a five-member executive board of the strike committee making moment-to-moment decisions. Each day, the strikers met as a body to review the decisions of these committees. This model of an elected strike committee overseen by frequent general meetings became the standard pattern for sit-down governance. At the Dodge Main plant, where a much larger number of strikers were spread out in a huge facility, the supreme governing body was the Chief Steward's Committee.[24]

Instead of relying on ad hoc policymaking, the strikers enacted rules governing virtually every aspect of life in the occupied factories. Rules directed the performance of assigned duties, prohibited sabotage, specified mandatory sanitary practices (no littering; assist in daily clean-up; return dirty dishes to the kitchen; no foreign objects in toilets), provided for safety (no smoking outside cafeteria; no liquor or guns in the plant), set standards of decorum (no yelling; no talking in sleeping areas), and established security procedures (credentials required for all sit-downers; visitors to be searched).[25]

Factory occupations ran up against social norms prohibiting the co-habitation of men and women not married to each other. Because of the need for support from the workers' spouses at home, this stimulated strong rulemaking. Where men made up a large majority of the strikers, they usually enacted total bans on women in the plant. Elsewhere, women and men occupied plants together.[26] On some occasions women strikers nullified men-only rules by refusing to leave.[27] Where women and men resided together in the plant, rules provided for separate sleeping quarters, sometimes with a matron in charge. Although a number of factory occupations were conducted primarily by women, there is no record of women finding it necessary to exclude men. "This is a woman's sit-

23. Walter Galenson, *The CIO Challenge to the AFL,* 134 (Cambridge: Harvard University Press, 1960); see also Edward Levinson, *Labor on the March,* 149 (New York: University Books, 1938); Melvyn Dubofsky and Warren Van Tine, *John L. Lewis: A Biography,* 254 (New York: Quadrangle/New York Times Book Co., 1977); *Monthly Labor Review,* 360–62 (Aug. 1938).

24. *See* Hartley W. Barclay, "We Sat Down with the Strikers and General Motors," *Mill & Factory,* 33, 37, 40 (Feb. 1937); Frank Marquart, *An Auto Worker's Journal: The UAW from Crusade to One-Party Union,* 77 (University Park: Pennsylvania State University Press, 1975); Mary Heaton Vorse, "Detroit Has the Jitters," *New Republic,* 256,257 (April 7, 1937); Fine, *Sit-Down,* 157–58; Keeran, *Communist Party,* 168; Levinson, *Labor on the March,* 177–78; George Morris, "The Sit-Down and How It Grew," *New Masses,* 17–18 (May 4, 1937); Stuart Messan, "The State of Cadillac," *Workers Age,* 2 (Feb. 20, 1937); *Dodge Main News,* 1 (March 14, 1937); Steve Jefferys, *Management and Managed: Fifty Years of Crisis at Chrysler,* 72 (New York: Cambridge University Press, 1986).

25. Fine, *Sit-Down,* 159–60, 165; Kirk W. Fuoss, *Striking Performances/Performing Strikes,* 56 (Jackson: University Press of Mississippi, 1997); Levinson, *Labor on the March,* 124–25, 177–78; Morris, "The Sit-Down and How It Grew," 17, 18.

26. *See* Fine, *Sit-Down,* 156; Keeran, *Communist Party,* 156; *Detroit News,* 1 (Feb. 19, 1937); *DN,* 4 (Feb. 24, 1937).

27. *See DN,* 1 (Mar. 3, 1937); Keeran, *Communist Party,* 169.

down," explained a strike leader at one cigar factory, where five hundred women and thirty men were in residence. "The men are just around that's all."[28]

Factory occupations crossed race as well as gender lines. Although many black auto workers were wary of the UAW, some did join in the sit-downs. Unlike male-female issues, however, black-white problems did not stimulate any recorded lawmaking in the occupied shops. The UAW Constitution called for all auto workers to "unite in one organization regardless of religion, race, creed, color, political affiliation or nationality." On the whole, this principle appears to have been followed. The written record does not reveal any overt racial disputes among the sit-downers, and August Meier and Elliott Rudwick, who interviewed a number of black participants, attributed the lack of black support not to the behavior of white sit-downers, but to generalized, long-term concerns about union racism.[29]

In at least two plants, legislative proposals were challenged on the ground that they violated the United States Constitution. Reading newspapers was an important activity for sit-downers, who received a wide variety of dailies on a regular basis. During both the General Motors and Chrysler sit-downs, strikers introduced proposals to ban the Communist *Daily Worker* from the plants. At Fisher Body No. 1, the assembled strikers voted down the proposal after strike chairman (and secret Communist Party member) Bud Simons argued that to censor the readings would violate the workers' constitutional rights. At Dodge Main, where the Communist presence was weaker, the Strike Executive Committee passed an ambiguous motion after a vigorous debate over free speech.[30]

No sooner would sit-down strikers establish order in an occupied factory than it would begin to unravel. At the Flint Cadillac plant, for example, discipline had eroded by the third day of the strike. "Some workers are doing all the picket duty, others none at all," reported one striker, "and Big Slim has lost his voice pleading, cajoling and threatening."[31] To deal with such problems, the strikers added a judicial branch to their shop government. "Kangaroo courts" adjudicated rule infractions. The sit-downers sought the same distinctively legal capabilities for their courts as were claimed by the official courts. The Cadillac strikers elected a worker who had studied law to be their prosecutor and chose for their judge the "oldest sit-downer, a venerable Scot of 62 combining a ready wit and much dignity." At Dodge Main, an especially skilled departmental court was called upon to try a complicated case that the main court could not handle. After the case "was adjusted satisfactorily to all," the departmental court offered to "gladly assist any department which has no court or which might have a case that is too complicated to try." In at least one plant, juries composed of workers determined guilt or innocence.[32]

---

28. Morris, "The Sit-Down and How It Grew," 17, 18; *DN*, 1 (Feb. 18, 1937) (quoting strike leader); see also *DN*, 1, 4 (Feb. 19, 1937); *DN*, 2 (April 17, 1937).

29. Constitution of the International Union, United Automobile Workers of America, art. 2 (1936), *American Labor Unions' Constitutions* (Microform); August Meier and Elliott Rudwick, *Black Detroit and the Rise of the UAW*, 34–35 (New York: Oxford University Press, 1979).

30. Fine, *Sit-Down*, 162; Keeran, *Communist Party*, 5, 151, 163; "Excerpts from Minutes of Dodge Strike Executive Committee (Official)," *Dodge Main News*, 2 (March 25, 1937). According to Steven Jefferys, the *Daily Worker* was eventually excluded from the Dodge Main plant. Jefferys, *Management and Managed*, 78.

31. Messan, "The State of Cadillac," 2. Similar problems arose at other plants. *See* Henry Kraus, *Heroes of Unwritten Story, The UAW, 1934–39*, 91–92 (Urbana: U. Ill. Press, 1993); *PP* No. 6, n.d. (c. Jan. 27, 1937), 1.

32. Morris, "The Sit-Down," 2; *see also* George Morris, "Sitdown Strategy," *Daily Worker*, 6 (Mar. 3, 1937); Levinson, *Labor on the March*, 177; *Dodge Main News*, 3 (March 19, 1937); *PP* No. 6, n.d. (c. Jan. 27, 1937), 1; Hy Fish, "With the Striking Auto Workers in Fisher Body Plant No. 1," *Socialist Call*, 2 (Feb. 13, 1937); Fuoss, *Striking Performances/Performing Strikes*, 54.

At the sentencing stage, kangaroo courts made an effort to fit the punishment to the crime. Dereliction of duty would be punished with double duty; failure to obey sanitary rules brought "a big clean up job for the culprit." A minor technical infraction might lead to a joke sentence, like making a speech to the assembled body. Interference with the legal process brought prompt punishment. At Hudson two men were sentenced to four hours in the Brig and morning K.P. for "intimidating complaining witnesses against them." Three strikers in Fisher Body No. 2 who failed to carry out their sentences were convicted of contempt of court and lashed with the judge's belt. The capital punishment of the sit-down community was expulsion from the plant.[33]

On the whole, the strikers' legal order appears to have been effective. "The most astonishing feeling you get in the sit-down plants is that of ORDER," enthused one striker. "The plant has been re-administrated." Even hostile observers confirmed that the strikers maintained orderly, smoothly functioning communities in the plants.[34] Officials from the Michigan State Department of Health inspected the Flint factories three times and commended the sit-downers on their condition. Breaches did occur; despite strenuous efforts to prevent sabotage, workers did inflict some damage on company property, including the "mutilating" of some car bodies in Fisher Body No. 1.

Confronting Official Law: Everything Hinges on the Hinges

In the auto parts sit-downs, workers had openly defied management orders to depart the plants. And on one occasion, they had defeated management attempts to infiltrate foremen and nonstriking workers into an occupied factory.[35] The question remained, however, whether they would adopt an equally defiant stance toward legally constituted public authorities.

The answer came on January 11, 1937, when the Flint police assaulted strikers occupying Fisher Body No. 2. The police used firearms and tear gas against the strikers, who retaliated by dousing the officers with a fire hose and bombarding them with a variety of projectiles including two-pound automobile door hinges. Fourteen strikers and supporters were wounded, mostly by gunshot, and eleven officers including Sheriff Wolcott suffered injuries, mostly head wounds from hurled objects. After two hours, the police retired from the field.[36]

This struggle, dubbed "The Battle of the Running Bulls" or "Bulls Run" (the Flint police being the "Bulls") by the UAW, served notice that many sit-down strikers were willing to risk their lives to defend occupied plants and prevent production. They made no pretense of complying with principles of nonviolence. As Victor Reuther quipped, "everything hinges on the hinges." On the other hand, the strikers also declined the *Detroit Labor News*'s invitation to take up firearms.[37] Their implicit rules of engagement—applied with impressive consistency in sit-downs across the country—permitted only the use of non-lethal force in defense against attacks by police or vigilantes on the occupied facilities.

---

33. Messan, "The State of Cadillac," 2; Fuoss, *Striking Performances/Performing Strikes*, 55–56; *see also* Francis O'Rourke, "General Motors' Sit-In Strikers' Thoughts" (diary of Fisher No. 2 sit-down striker), Francis O'Rourke Papers, Wayne State Archives; *Hudson-News*, Mar. 26, 1937, 7; *PP* No. 7, n.d., 2; Fine, *Sit-Down*, 160.

34. *PP* No. 7, n.d., 1. For examples of hostile observers acknowledging orderliness of strikers, see Edwin H. Cassels, Attorney for Bendix Products Corp., to Perkins, Nov. 28, 1936, Office Files of Secretary of Labor Frances Perkins, Records of the Department of Labor, Record Group 174, National Archives II, College Park, Md.; Barclay, "We Sat Down with the Strikers and General Motors,": 33.

35. *See* Nelson Lichtenstein, *The Most Dangerous Man in Detroit*, 70 (New York: Basic Books,1995).

36. *See* Fine, *Sit-Down*, 1–8.

37. Fine, *Sit-Down*, 172; *DLN*, 1 (Dec. 18, 1936); *see also Paper Makers' Journal*, 20, 22 (April 1937); *Seamen's Journal*, 27 (Feb. 1, 1937).

II. Split in the House of Labor

As the sit-downs burgeoned in frequency, scope, and duration, the legitimacy of the tactic came under increasing fire. Unionists divided into three distinct camps over the issue, each corresponding to a broader vision of labor's role in workplace lawmaking. Because each of these visions assigned lawmaking functions to specified institutions, and because each was intended to become operational immediately (without waiting for official recognition by corporations or the state), I call them "constitutions." The first, labor's progressive constitution, treated the sit-down as an unsavory but useful weapon in the struggle for collective bargaining, a form of joint employer-union lawmaking. The second, labor's corporate constitution, actively opposed it as an assault on the older tradition of unilateral craft union lawmaking. The third, labor's freedom constitution, proclaimed and justified a new fundamental right to stage sit-down strikes as a means of enforcing worker-made laws as well as workers' interpretations of official laws.

Labor's Progressive Constitution: The Sit-Down as the Lesser of Two Evils

With few exceptions, the top leaders of the CIO unions portrayed the sit-down as a regrettable but understandable form of worker protest that would disappear once employers accepted the modern regime of collective bargaining established by the Wagner Act. To CIO head John L. Lewis, the sit-down was "the fruit of mismanagement and bad policy towards labor," namely the refusal to respect the workers' legal right to organize. Similarly, President Sherman Dalrymple of the Rubber Workers adopted the pose of a detached observer analyzing "the real reasons and underlying causes" of a phenomenon for which he had no responsibility. "Sit-downs do not occur in Plants where true collective bargaining exists," he asserted and predicted that "the only way these sit-downs can be avoided in the future is through the proper application of all the rules of true collective bargaining in a spirit of fair play." Other CIO officials followed suit, blaming employers for the sit-down tactic, but stopping short of defending its legality or morality.[38] CIO-style unionism was promoted as a form of insurance against sit-downs. "A C.I.O. contract is adequate protection," promised John L. Lewis, "against sit-downs, lie-downs, or any other kind of strike."[39] In short, Lewis and other CIO leaders promoted collective bargaining as a replacement for—not a supplement to—the unilateral worker lawmaking made possible by the sit-down strike.

Labor's Corporate Constitution: Sit-Downs as Trespass on Union Property

While CIO leaders assessed the sit-down in light of its impact on joint employer-union lawmaking, their counterparts in the American Federation of Labor had different concerns in mind. Like the CIO, the AFL promoted collective bargaining as the centerpiece of the industrial order. Unlike the CIO, however, the AFL sought to preserve a continuing role for unilateral labor lawmaking, and it was this consideration that shaped the Federation's position on the sit-down. To the craft unionists who dominated the AFL, the issue of sit-downs was inextricably entangled with the question of craft versus industrial unionism, an issue governed by union law. The AFL considered itself to be *the* House of Labor, lodg-

---

38. *United Mine Workers Journal*, 3 (Jan. 15, 1937); Sherman H. Dalrymple, "Sit-Down Strikes—An Editorial," *United Rubber Worker*, 12 (May 1936), 12; Louis Adamic, "Sitdown: II," *Nation*, 702 (Dec. 12, 1936) (quoting CIO Director John Brophy); Oil Workers International Union, *Proceedings of the Eighth Convention*, 62 (June 7–12, 1937) (quoting CIO organizer Adolph Germer); International Union, United Automobile Workers of America, *Proceedings of the Second Annual Convention*, 131 (Aug. 23–29, 1937) [hereafter *UAW Proceedings 1937*] (quoting ILGWU President David Dubinsky).

39. Galenson, *CIO Challenge*, 145 (quoting Lewis); see also *ABJ*, 19 (April 20, 1936); *UNS*, 1 (April 12, 1937).

ing *all* of the legitimate labor organizations of the United States. The Federation issued each constituent organization a charter specifying its jurisdiction. Once a union entity had been granted an AFL charter, it could use the charter for whatever purposes it wished. The jurisdictional entitlement remained fully valid even if the owning union made no effort to organize the workers, and even if the workers themselves preferred to join a different union.[40]

Nearly all of the AFL's charters were framed on trade or craft rather than industrial lines. In the auto plants, for example, machinists fell under the jurisdiction of the Machinists' Union, electricians under the Electrical Workers' Union, and so forth, leaving the UAW with the semi- and unskilled remainder. Thus, the GM sit-downers, with their demand that the UAW be recognized as the exclusive representative for all trades, were in flagrant violation of AFL law. John P. Frey, leading AFL legalist and president of the AFL Metal Trades Council, angrily condemned the sit-down as a ploy of "militant minorities" that was "deliberately intended to destroy self-government by unions." In late March, AFL President William Green followed suit, repudiating the "illegal" sit-down tactic on the ground that the negative public reaction would eventually lead to repressive legislation affecting not only the sit-down, but also the core rights to strike and picket.[41]

Sit-down opponents gleefully quoted the AFL leaders to show that "American" unionists—as opposed to the "Communist" sit-downers—rejected the tactic. They escalated their campaign for government intervention. Chrysler bought a full-page advertisement condemning the capture of its plants as "a form of revolution." A Gallup poll reported that most Americans favored outlawing the sit-down, with the principal reason being its nature as an illegal seizure of employer property.[42]

Labor's Freedom Constitution: The Right to Stage a Sit-Down Strike

The growing law-and-order drive confronted union leaders with a difficult problem. Thus far, CIO officials had avoided taking a clear position on the legality of the sit-down. Fearing that an open endorsement of the tactic would anger both employers and the public, they tried to capitalize on sit-downs to win union recognition without accepting responsibility for the tactic. Now, however, the law-and-order campaign threatened to unleash the National Guard against the sit-downers. In this crisis, UAW President Homer Martin took the lead in asserting and justifying the existence of a legal right to stage a sit-down strike.

As described by one reporter, Martin delivered his defense of the sit-down "in thunderous tones," resorting frequently to backwoods phrases. By the time of the showdown in Detroit, he had pieced together a multi-pronged case. He did not invent the arguments; rather, he wove together justifications developed by labor activists and a few legal intellectuals. On March 22, Martin laid out his arguments in an open letter urging Michigan Governor Frank Murphy to refrain from deploying National Guard troops against the Chrysler strikers.

---

40. See Christopher Tomlins, *The State and the Unions: Labor Relations, Law, and the Organized Labor Movement in America, 1880–1960,* 172 (Cambridge: Cambridge University Press, 1985); *AFL EC Minutes,* 42–43 (Feb. 8–19, 1937); *Proceedings of Conference of Representatives of National and International Unions Affiliated with the American Federation of Labor,* 17–20 (May 24–25, 1937).

41. *DN,* 2 (Feb. 3, 1937); *DLN,* 5 (March 5, 1937); *NYT,* 1 (Mar. 29, 1937).

42. *CR,* Mar. 17, 1937, 2338 (Sen. King); *DN,* 3 (March 13, 1937) (advertisement); *DN,* 1 (March 14, 1937); *DN,* 1 (Mar. 18, 1937); Carlos A. Schwantes, "'We've Got 'em on the Run, Brothers': The 1937 Non-Automotive Sit Down Strikes in Detroit," 56 *Michigan History,* 179,195 (1972); *DN,* 1 (Mar. 19, 1937); *DN,* 5 (Mar. 20, 1937); *DN,* 1 (Mar. 23, 1937); George Gallup, "America Speaks: Majority Would Outlaw Sit-Down Strikes," *DN,* 10 (Mar. 21, 1937).

The effective right to strike. "First, it is our contention that the sit-down strike as such is a strike intended to stop production," wrote Martin. "The stoppage of production through strike has been recognized for years as legal in the United States." Here, Martin continued the labor movement's struggle to transform the legally recognized right to strike—a narrowly circumscribed right of individual workers to combine in withholding labor—into an effective right to veto production. As A. F. Whitney of the Railroad Trainmen explained, the notion that employers were entitled to operate during strikes led inevitably to the "absurd and futile proposition that a working man's right to strike means nothing more than his right to give up his job to a 'scab.'" On this view, there was no need to formulate a new right to stage a sit-down strike. "If there is any validity in strikes at all," reasoned Martin, "the sit-down is perfectly legal."[43]

Why was the sit-down necessary to make the right to strike effective? Because a strike could succeed only by stopping production, and the only other way for unskilled workers—who could easily be replaced—to halt production was the mass picket line, which was too vulnerable to suppression. "Should a worker leave his job behind and depart from a plant and his skill is not such that his absence stops production," explained one union journal, "then the corporation brings in guards, strike-breakers, poison gas and machine guns."[44] With the picket line broken, the "strikers are just men out of jobs" and the "strike staggers on awhile, collapses and the union dies," complained the *Summit County Labor News.* "Out of this fact has grown the sit-down strike." Far from a novel and radical tactic, then, the sit-down was an incremental response to changed conditions—"merely the transfer of the picket line into the plant."[45]

Just as the sit-down was nothing more than an updated version of old tactics, so was the employers' property argument against it merely a new iteration of old ideas. "[T]he same argument has been used against OUTSIDE PICKETING also," observed the *Flint Auto Worker,* "and has frequently been given as an excuse for the issuance of strike-breaking injunctions!" Unionists suspected that employers opposed the sit-down not because of some special affront to their property rights, but because "the strikes were so effective and they were unable to operate their plants with strike-breakers." Indeed, if property were the real concern, then employers "should feel grateful for the technique of the sit-down strike [because] the worker is protecting his job and consequently will protect the appliances that make that job possible." As for the charge of sit-down violence, it made no sense in light of the alternative. "Society owes it to itself to bring before its eyes in sharp contrast," urged CIO organizer Leo Krzycki, the "bitter, bloody conflict" on picket lines in the coal fields and around the steel mills compared to the automobile sit-downs, "where no property has been damaged and no lives have been lost."[46]

---

43. "Text of Martin Letter to Murphy on Chrysler Strike," *NYT*, 16 (Mar. 23, 1937); A. F. Whitney, President, Bro. of Railroad Trainmen, "Thinking Clearly on Property Rights," *Railroad Trainman*, 136–37 (March 1937); *DN*, 10 (Mar. 21, 1937) (quoting Martin); see also *NYT*, 1, col. 2 (Feb. 27, 1937).
44. *Paper Makers' Journal*, 25 (Feb. 1937); see also *Flint Auto Worker*, 8 (Jan. 12, 1937); Wyndham Mortimer, "History of the Sit-Down Strike," *United Auto Worker*, 3 (Jan. 22, 1937).
45. *SCLN*, 1 (Feb. 12, 1937); *PP* no. 8(1), n.d. [c. late Jan. 1937], 2; *American Teacher*, 26 (May–June 1937); *UNS*, 1 (Feb. 17, 1936); *The Hosiery Worker*, 2 (Mar. 10, 1939); *NYT*, 1 (Feb. 27, 1937); Martin's Speech at Newark, New Jersey, Feb. 26, 1937 (typescript), Homer Martin Collection, Box 3, at 6.
46. *Flint Auto Worker*, 8 (Jan. 12, 1937); *see also SCLN*, 1 (Feb. 12, 1937); Substitute For Resolutions Nos. 203 and 238 Sit-Down Strikes, *UAW Proceedings 1937*, 189–90; *DLN*, 8 (March 12, 1937); *The Lamp Maker* (newspaper of UAW Local 146), April 15, 1937, 4; Letter from Raymond McCoy to Editor, *DN*, 22 (Jan. 31, 1937); *UAW Proceedings 1937*, 10–11 (quoting Krzycki).

As the sit-down controversy escalated, it became apparent that unionists could not derail the employers' property rights argument merely by downplaying it. Politicians, the daily press, and other participants in public debate increasingly accepted the employers' claim that the sit-down constituted an illegal trespass. In his second argument, Martin embraced the concept of property and turned it against the employers.

The workers' communal property right to sit down. Martin wrote Murphy that the "right to strike involves the property right of the worker's job, which is, in our opinion, the most vital property right in America." He predicted that courts and legislatures would soon recognize the right of workers to defend this property right by occupying the job site. This argument reflected the traditional strikers' view that people who worked during strikes were "stealing" their jobs.[47] After visiting Flint, *New York Times* reporter Louis Stark joined other observers in reporting a hazily defined but deeply embedded property rights consciousness among the workers: "Talks with the sit-down strikers made it clear to me that they felt they had a property in their jobs. They did not use legal terms in giving expression to their views but their meaning was unmistakable. 'Our hides are wrapped around those machines,' was the way one man in the Fisher Body plant expressed it."[48]

At the same time that they claimed a "property" right to sit down, however, unionists argued that "human rights" should take precedence over property rights. "Clearly, the issue involved in this whole controversy," declared Martin, "is whether or not pure property and profit rights shall supersede and preclude the consideration of human rights," namely "the inalienable rights of all workers, to life, liberty and the pursuit of happiness." Angrily responding to the Chrysler injunction, the *Dodge Main News* roared: "'Plaintiff's valuable property rights!!! — The United Auto Workers say, 'HUMAN RIGHTS OVER PROPERTY RIGHTS!!!'"[49] Goodyear Committeeman F. L. Howard invoked the ultimate human right, claiming that the freedom to sit down was "my constitutional right, that no man shall be held in slavery or against his will."[50]

The *New York Times* pointedly observed that the property rights justification for the sit-down was "most aggressively asserted by precisely those persons who used to regret the very existence of 'property rights as opposed to human rights.'" But to unionists, there was no inconsistency in claiming property rights while simultaneously trumpeting the superiority of human rights over property rights. The worker's property right to his job was a *"human* property right," explained A. F. Whitney. "Unfortunately, in the past, the resources of the state have been too largely employed to protect, as against human property rights, an entirely different kind of property right — those of the so-called 'propertied classes.'" Unionists disaggregated the concept of property into distinct functions or origins, some of which had "human" value while others did not. First, unlike corporate property rights, the worker's property right concerned an asset that was essential to human survival. "It's

47. "Text of Martin Letter," 16; *NYT*, 1, col. 2 (Feb. 27, 1937). On the roots of this claim, *see* John Fitch, *The Causes of Industrial Unrest*, 221–23 (New York: Harper & Bros., 1924); Sidney and Beatrice Webb, *Industrial Democracy*, 559–63 (London: Longmans, Green & Co., 1902).

48. Louis Stark, "Sit-Down," *Survey Graphic*, 316, 320 (June 1937); *see also* William Allen White, "Sit-Down: Harbinger of a New Revolution?" *DN*, 1 (April 5, 1937).

49. *NYT*, 13 (Mar. 30, 1937); *Dodge Main News*, 3 (March 11, 1937); *see also* J. B. Livengood, "Human Rights Have Precedence," *Typographical Journal*, 338 (April 1937); *Paper Makers' Journal*, 20–21 (April 1937).

50. United Rubber Workers, *Proceedings of the First Convention*, 425 (Sept. 15–20, 1936) [hereafter *URW Proceedings 1936*]. On the role of the thirteenth amendment in labor's constitutional thinking, *see* William A. Forbath, *Law and the Shaping of the American Labor Movement*, 136–39 (Cambridge: Harvard University Press, 1991; Pope, "Labor's Constitution of Freedom," 962–66; Pope, "Thirteenth Amendment," 15–24.

worth more than stocks and bonds and machinery; it's the only right that he has, by which he feeds his family, takes care of his children, provides income to take care of his home," explained Martin. "Anybody who takes his job takes his home and deprives him of his very life." Prefiguring arguments that would later be accepted by courts and legal scholars in other contexts, unionists pointed out that—as a practical matter—a worker's job was his most valuable asset: "Is it any wonder then that the worker who has no un-mortgaged tangible property, who does not own stocks or bonds, and who may have a few household possessions, an insurance policy, or even a small savings account, will fig-ure that his 'job' is his property and his only title to economic income?"[51]

Next, unionists noted that workers, unlike corporate magnates or imported strike-breakers, were immediately and personally connected to the machines that they operated and the jobs they performed. In response to the charge of trespassing, the *Punch Press* snarled: "SO? THE WORKERS WHO SPEND HALF THEIR LIVES IN THE PLANTS, SWEATING OUT THE PROFIT FOR SLOANS WHO NEVER COME NEAR A SHOP, HAVE NO RIGHT TO BE IN THE SHOPS!" Echoing Hegel and prefiguring modern scholarship on property and personhood, unionists argued that by using the machinery productively, workers earned a property right: "After all, the property may belong to the company, but there is something else inside these plants that the workers have earned by years of sweat and toil—and that is THEIR JOBS!" Moreover, the requirements and the experience of performing his job adapted the worker and his conditions of life to that particular job. "These workers, in the great majority of cases, have spent years in train-ing their hands and minds to their work," observed the *United Auto Worker*, "and in short, have so arranged their lives in order that the plants and machinery of an employer can yield the owner a profit and a living for themselves."[52] This "investment in industry" at a minimum elevated the claims of striking workers over those of imported strikebreakers. "It is the height of absurdity to contend that a worker who may have traveled hundreds of miles in quest of the job, or sustained disfigurement or injury in the course of it, or even contributed a substantial part of his strength and energy to his employers enter-prise," inveighed one local union resolution, "has the same status as a mischievous stranger or interloper."[53]

While pumping up the property rights of workers, unionists did their best to deflate those of employers. A. F. Whitney found it "astounding" that opponents of the sit-down were analogizing GM's property rights to those of a homeowner. "Mr. Sloan's property right in his own home, which the common law has always held as his castle, is a prop-erty right of the highest order of human value," he wrote. Corporate property, on the other hand, could be no one's "castle" because the exclusion of others would render it

---

51. *NYT*, 22 (Mar. 30, 1937); Whitney, "Thinking Clearly on Property Rights," 136–37; *Flint Auto Worker*, 8 (Jan. 12, 1937); Speech Given by Mr. Martin to the Sit-Down Strikers in the Dodge Plant, Detroit, March 15, 1937, Homer Martin Collection, Box 3, at 3–4; "Text of Martin Letter," 16; *United Automobile Worker*, 5 (May 8, 1937); *Paper Makers' Journal*, 20 (April 1937); cf. *O'Brien v. O'Brien*, 66 N.Y.2d 576, 489 N.E.2d 712, 498 N.Y.S.2d 743 (Ct. App. 1985) (marital property interest in pro-fessional education); C. Edwin Baker, "Property and Its Relation to Constitutionally Protected Lib-erty," 134 *University of Pennsylvania Law Review* 741, 745–46 (1986).

52. *PP* No. 8(1), n.d. [c. late Jan. 1937], 2; *Flint Auto Worker*, 8 (Jan. 12, 1937); *SCLN*, 1 (Feb. 12, 1937); *American Teacher*, 26 (May–June 1937); *CR*, Mar. 23, 1937, 2642 (Rep. Bernard); *United Automobile Worker*, 5 (May 8, 1937; cf. Joseph Singer, "The Reliance Interest in Property," 40 *Stan-ford Law Review* 611, 711–18 (1987); Margaret Jane Radin, "Property and Personhood," 34 *Stanford Law Review* 957 (1982).

53. Local 157, UAW, Resolution on Sit-Down Strike Legislation (typescript), FMCS Records, RG 280, Entry 14, Box 419; *see also DLN*, 1 (April 9, 1937); *United Automobile Worker*, 5 (May 8, 1937).

useless: "His corporation's property rights in the factory have value only as the worker's property right in the job is preserved and respected." This argument shaded into old-style producerism. Sit-down supporters quoted Lincoln on the priority of labor over capital and pointed out that stockholders and bondholders created no value while the workers' labor made their property right the one "which produces wealth and which means more to national prosperity than any other property right in existence."[54]

The workers' claimed property right was triggered solely by collective action. Nobody claimed the right to "strike" as an individual and then return to the job. Though framed as a property right, then, it bore little relation to traditional notions of individual property rights. On the contrary, it belonged to the class of "communal rights"— rights "to act together, to engage in activity commonly and most effectively undertaken by groups."[55]

The sit-down as statutory and constitutional self-help.

Finally, Martin reminded Murphy that the Chrysler workers had occupied their factories only after the company violated the Wagner Act by refusing to recognize and bargain with their union, which—unlike the Flint local two months previously—actually represented a clear majority of the company's employees. Thus, the workers had "used the sit-down method of strike in an effort to establish what was their legal, constitutional and civil right, and to eradicate the impossible working conditions from which they suffered." Here, Martin echoed arguments made by John L. Lewis and other adherents of labor's progressive constitution. Unlike Lewis, however, Martin and other open proponents of the sit-down accepted responsibility for factory occupations and publically defended the right of workers to engage in statutory and constitutional self-help. "You[r] threat of violence would be better directed against violators of the national labor relations act," wrote Chrysler Local 3 to Murphy. "We mean to stay until they observe the law."[56]

Despite all these arguments, the few courts that had ruled on the sit-down issue by the time of the Chrysler confrontation had emphatically pronounced the tactic illegal.[57] In the short run, at least, the fate of the sit-down movement would hinge less on argument than on action.

III. Establishing and Shaping the Right to Sit Down

By mid-February 1937, there was a growing gap between official law and social practice. On the 11th, the General Motors strike was settled on terms favorable to the union, triggering an exuberant celebration in Flint. One week later, about one hundred sit-down strikers at the Fansteel Metallurgical Corporation in Waukeegan, Illinois, repulsed an attack by

---

54. Whitney, "Thinking Clearly on Property Rights," 136–37; *DN*, 22 (Feb. 11, 1937); *DN*, 8 (April 4, 1937); "Text of Martin Letter," 16; *Paper Makers' Journal*, April 1937, 20.

55. Staughton Lynd, "Communal Rights," 62 *Texas Law Review* 1417, 1423–24 (1984).

56. "Text of Martin Letter," 16; *NYT*, 13 (Mar. 30, 1937); Local 3, UAW to Frank Murphy (n.d., c. March 22, 1937), Kraus Papers, Reel 5, Wayne State Archives; Pope, "Thirteenth Amendment," 78–80 (citing additional sources).

57. *See The Oakmar*, 20 F. Supp. 650 (D. Md. 1937); *The Losmar*, 20 F. Supp. 887 (D. Md. 1937); *Plecity v. Local No. 37, International Union of Bakery and Confectionery Workers of America*, Superior Ct., Los Angeles County, Cal., 4 U.S.L.W. 898, C.C.H. 16357; *General Motors Corp. v. International Union, United Automobile Workers of America*, Cir. Ct. Genesee County, Mich., 4 U.S.L.W. 678 (1937), C.C.H. 16354; *Chrysler Corp. v. International Union, UAW*, Cir. Ct., Wayne County, Mich., 4 U.S.L.W. 858 (1937), C.C.H. 16358; *Apex Hosiery Co. v. Leader*, 90 F.2d 144 (3d Cir. 1937), *appeal dismissed*, 302 U.S. 656 (1937).

one hundred forty police officers after a two-hour battle despite the officers' extensive use of tear gas bombs.[58] The police had yet to clear an occupied factory against resistance.

Despite these successes, the sit-down movement was in a dangerous position. The workers' justifications for the right to sit-down had yet to prevail either in a single court or before the bar of public opinion, leaving them in the position of openly defying the law. Moreover, the sit-down tactic caused problems for unionists as well as corporations. A few sit-downers in a key department could force thousands of their co-workers out on strike. While staving off the police at the factory gates, workers struggled to solve these problems and shape a viable right to sit down.

Defiance of Old Traditions, of Legal Restraints, and a Hostile Judiciary

The first problem was how to sustain resistance in open defiance of law. Local union activists turned to history for inspiration. "It was once unlawful to picket," recounted one. "Every right, every liberty, every privilege ... has been won ... by men who dared to defy some law—by men who dared to be 'illegal.'" It was workers like the sit-down strikers who "in defiance of old traditions, of legal restraints and a hostile judiciary, established the right for labor to organize, to strike, to boycott and to picket," and would "yet establish their right to sit down, stand up or roll over, as suits their fancy, in the plants which the brain and brawn and genius of the working class have brought into being." These stories served not only to justify defiance, but also to stiffen workers' resolve. "Destroy fear of jail," the UAW advised its organizers, "by recalling the prison terms of William Penn, John Brown and other famous Americans."[59]

Since law was dynamic, disobedience of the law as it existed at any particular moment carried no necessary connotation of disrespect for law. "[I]f we are *lawless elements*, as you have falsely whined—Then we are such, only, in the progressive sense that we are determined to revolutionize the present law standards of conventions." Workers' rights, including the right to sit down, invariably "must be established outside the courts before they will be recognized within the courts." Official law might deny that a worker had a property right in his job, but "government, management and workers, dealing with a practical problem, act as if he did," and sooner or later the law would come into line with the practice. After factory occupations helped the UAW win contracts with auto makers and parts manufacturers, Flint strike leader Kermit Johnson claimed that the right to sit down had been "already established in the struggle of auto workers during the past year."[60]

A Recognized Weapon of Last Resort in Industrial Controversy

In the spring of 1937, Johnson's claim did not appear entirely far-fetched. It was true that polling results indicated broad public disapproval of the tactic. But by demonstrating their determination to hold the occupied factories, the strikers had tested the intensity of that sentiment. And according to a poll conducted by *Fortune* magazine, a large

---

58. *PP* No. 16, Feb. 12, 1937, 2; *Chicago Daily News*, 1,4 (Feb. 19, 1937); *In re Matter of Fansteel Metallurgical Corporation*, 5 N.L.R.B. 930, 942–43 (1938).

59. *Voice of Labor* (newspaper of UAW Local 206), 4 (March 27, 1937); Livengood, "Human Rights Have Precedence," 338; Brookwood Labor College, *Pointers for Organizers* (brochure), reprinted in Barclay, "We Sat Down with the Strikers," 48; *see also DN*, 10 (Mar. 21, 1937).

60. Draft of Plymouth Local 51 Strike Bulletin, Kraus Papers, Reel 5, Wayne State Archives (1st quotation); *Paper Makers' Journal*, 20 (April 1937); Local 157, UAW, Resolution on Sit-Down Strike Legislation (typescript), FMCS Records, RG 280, Entry 14, Box 419 (second and third quotations); *Typographical Journal*, 103 (Feb. 1937); Luigi Antonini, "Apropos 'Sit-Downs,'" *Justice*, 6 (April 15, 1937); Resolution No. 238, Submitted by Kermit Johnson, Local No. 156, Flint, Mich., *UAW Proceedings 1937*, Appendix III, 97.

majority of the American people was not prepared to countenance the suppression of sit-down strikes if bloodshed were involved. Even business executives were divided on the question.[61] This posed a dilemma for the forces of law and order. There was strong public support for action against sit-downers in the abstract, but the only method that could reliably break a determined occupation was violent eviction, and violent eviction ran the risk of bloodshed.

As workers repeatedly demonstrated their willingness to risk bodily harm defending occupied plants, some mainstream commentators and government officials began to admit the possibility that the sit-down was destined to become an accepted tactic in the new industrial order. Three prominent legal realists, Dean Leon Green of the Northwestern University School of Law, SEC Chairman James Landis, and Yale Law Professor Abraham Fortas, went the farthest. Green—a Texan who, like Homer Martin, had been trained as a preacher—defended the sit-down as the workers' way of protecting their interest in what he called the "common enterprise" of labor and capital. Landis predicted that the fate of the workers' claimed property right to sit down might depend "on the capacity of our law to devise new concepts and mechanisms to meet the needs out of which this type of economic pressure has been born." Fortas agreed, opining that—in view of the adaptability of law—the sit-down might not be illegal.[62]

After months of inveighing against sit-downs, the Republican *Akron Beacon Journal* suddenly shifted gears and included sit-downs along with strikes and lockouts among the "recognized weapons of last resort in industrial controversy." The problem with the sit-down "epidemic," editorialized the *Journal*, lay simply in the fact that "none of the sit-downs have been authorized in a regular business meeting" of the union. By early 1937, sit-downs had become so routine and so peaceful in Akron that, according to Daniel Nelson, the residents were no longer "particularly perturbed" at the phenomenon. Even in Detroit, after weeks of broadside attacks on the tactic by Mayor Couzens, Assistant Detroit Corporation Counsel James R. Walsh found himself charged with the task of developing policies to distinguish "legitimate" sit-downs from those that were ploys in a "muscle game."[63] This task would not be easy, but tentative solutions were already emerging from practice.

Democracy Means Majority Rule

The sit-down strike posed difficulties for unionists as well as employers. Because most segments of the mass production process were interconnected, a sit-down in one department could idle other departments whose workers had neither been consulted nor even informed of the protesters' objectives. Every unionist to leave a written record of thoughts on this issue agreed that the key to solving this problem was the imposition of majority control on sit-downs. "Democracy means majority rule, not minority rule," explained UAW Vice President Wyndham Mortimer. "And when a small minority of workers disrupt production by a departmental sit-down, they are in effect determining the welfare of many thousands of their fellow workers who were not consulted."[64]

---

61. See *Fortune*, 96 (July 1937) (reporting that only 20.1 percent of all respondents and 32.9 percent of executives expressed the opinion that sit-downs "should be stopped, even if bloodshed is necessary").

62. Leon Green, "The Case for the Sit-Down Strike," *New Republic*, 90 (Mar. 24, 1937); *NYT*, 18 (Mar. 21, 1937); *NYT*, 19 (June 15, 1937) (paraphrasing Fortas).

63. *ABJ*, 4 (July 16, 1936); Nelson, *American Rubber Workers*, 214; Eisenberg, Government Policy, 67, citing *NYT*, 4 (Mar. 20, 1937).

64. *URW Proceedings 1936*, 440 (resolution submitted by Goodyear Local 2); W. Mortimer, "Need of Caution in Sit-Downs," *United Auto Worker*, 3 (April 7, 1937).

There was disagreement, however, about whether to place the decision at the local or international level. At the URW convention in September 1936 this issue sparked a sharp controversy. Goodyear Local 2 argued that requiring authorization by the International Executive Board "involves too much red tape and undue delay for best results" and there-fore proposed "giving the authority to the Executive Board of a Local Union to sanction a sit-down where, in their opinion, it is justified." But URW Vice President Thomas Burns argued forcefully against the entire enterprise of legislating about the sit-down strike. Like John L. Lewis and other CIO leaders, he viewed the sit-down as a public embar-rassment. "The amount of adverse publicity we would get over taking any resolution and passing it should be avoided," he argued. E. L. Howard, an influential Goodyear com-mitteeman, responded. What Burns saw as an issue to be swept under the rug, Howard saw as a historic turning point for the labor movement. "The sit-downs today, if prop-erly authorized and supported, are as effective in proportion to a strike as a Thompson machine gun is to an old musket," he charged, "and you don't have the courage to take hold and lead." But the sit-down resolution—already watered down in committee—was defeated by a margin of 35 to 27.[65]

The issue also sparked sharp debate in the UAW. At the 1937 convention, local activists complained that the existing requirement of national approval for all strikes involved too much "red tape" and proposed resolutions placing control at the local level. UAW Vice President Wyndham Mortimer agreed that local authorization would solve the problem, but failed to support the resolution. Homer Martin opposed the resolution, arguing that because the union had been called upon to pay large legal fees on behalf of arrested sit-downers, it must be given a veto. He and UAW Secretary-Treasurer George Addes promised that authoriza-tion would be promptly granted under the current expedited procedure, which allowed for approval by the president pending board ratification. After these assurances, the existing procedure was retained on a voice vote. In place of the failed proposal for local control, the delegates adopted a resolution endorsing the stay-in strike as "an effective weapon against employers who refuse to recognize the moral and legal rights of the workers to collective bargaining" and as "labor's most effective weapon against the autocracy of industry."[66]

While the unions debated issues of procedure, workers began to define the scope of their new right on the ground.

Scope of the Emerging Right

Some limiting principles flowed directly from the justifications advanced in support of the claimed right. If, as unionists argued, the sit-down was merely an exercise of the workers' right to strike, then employers should suffer no more injury than they would in the event of an effective (meaning effective at withholding labor, but not necessarily vic-torious) traditional strike. Although workers never formally enacted this principle in union law, it was evident in a number of practices and shop rules. First, in contrast to the Italian factory occupations of 1920, American workers never attempted to operate em-ployer facilities for their own gain.[67] This comported with their claim that sit-down strikes

---

65. *URW Proceedings 1936*, 440 (resolution submitted by Goodyear Local 2); *ibid.*, 422 (Burns); *ibid.*, 424 (Howard); *ibid.*, 429; James Keller, "The Rubber Front in Akron," *The Communist*, 241, 242 (Mar. 1937).

66. *See UAW Proceedings 1937*, 225; *ibid.*, Appendix III, 87 (Resolution submitted by Local No. 217); *ibid.*, Appendix III, 97 (Resolution submitted by Kermit Johnson, Local No. 156); *ibid.*, 226–28 (Mor-timer, Addes & Martin), 189–90 (text of enacted resolution).

67. In rare cases, sit-downers did run machinery. On one occasion, striking power plant workers operated the plant in order to supply what they considered to be an essential service. Jones, *Life, Lib-erty, and Property*, 358–59. On another, striking printers and type-setters published a strike bulletin

were "merely the transfer of the picket line into the plant." Likewise, sit-downers gener-ally stood ready to evacuate occupied plants on a credible promise by the employer to re-frain from re-starting production until collective bargaining was concluded.[68] In the meantime, employer property was protected by the promulgation and enforcement of strike rules prohibiting sabotage.

The property-rights justification for the sit-down implied an additional limitation. Only the employees of the struck employer could claim a property interest in their jobs. Accordingly, unionists never contested Governor Murphy's charge that a sit-down con-ducted by outsiders was not a legitimate strike, but a kind of banditry. When the Detroit Police conducted a series of eviction raids against facilities that they charged were occu-pied by outsiders, unionists disputed only the charge, not the propriety of evicting non-employees. And when Murphy ordered a food blockade of Flint Chevrolet No. 4, where outsiders made up a significant proportion of the sit-downers, the UAW promptly with-drew all nonemployees from the plant. Had there been a threat of attack, the union might have insisted on the right to invite outsiders in to assist in defense, but Murphy had or-dered the National Guard to protect the occupied plants.[69]

On the question of defining the acceptable purposes of sit-downs, not all of the three justifications yielded the same answer. If the sit-down were merely an exercise of the right to strike, then the law governing the acceptable purposes of strikes in general would seem to control sit-downs as well. The property-right theory of the sit-down pointed in the same direction and harked back to the labor movement's tradition of voluntarism. "Since labor thus possesses property rights as well as capital and these rights are essentially of a similar nature...," resolved one UAW local union, "then it certainly ought to follow that the two contestants should be permitted to settle their differences without the intervention by the courts and the armed forces of the state on the side of one of them."[70] Many unionists, however, renounced the use of the sit-down for ordinary labor disputes and tailored the scope of the claimed right to some form of the self-help justification. Some drew the boundary narrowly to encompass only sit-downs "against an employer who has defied all of the laws set up to protect and aid and equalize the rights of the workers."[71] Others took a broader view, approving all sit-downs for the purpose of making the regime shift from the individual labor market—which amounted to "industrial slavery" or "autocracy"—to collective bargaining.[72]

As long as the constitutionality of the Wagner Act remained doubtful, these differ-ences of opinion had little salience. With the National Labor Relations Board tied up by constitutional challenges, it was clear to unionists that the only way to enforce workers' rights was through strike action. Those who supported the sit-down tactic only for self-help purposes still had a stake in its continued viability. But the constitutional issue was moving rapidly toward a resolution, and the sit-down strikers were to have a decisive im-pact on the outcome.

---

using the employer's printing press. They claimed that they were "keeping a strict account of the ma-terials used, and will pay back the company when the strike is settled." *DLN*, 1 (March 19, 1937).

68. *See, e.g., DN*, 1 (Mar. 25, 1937) (Chrysler); Fine, *Sit-Down*, 209 (Janesville Fisher Body); *DN*, 1 (April 14, 1937) (Yale & Towne).

69. *See DN*, 1 (Mar. 23, 1937); Fine, *Sit-Down*, 272–73; *DN*, 1 (Feb. 3, 1937).

70. Local 157, UAW, Resolution on Sit-Down Strike Legislation (typescript), FMCS Records, RG 280, Entry 14, Box 419.

71. *Paper Makers' Journal*, 20, 22 (April 1937); *see also* Luigi Antonini, "Apropos 'Sit-Downs," 6.

72. Resolution Adopted By Goodrich Local # 5, U.R.W.A., c. April 17, 1937, Lewis CIO Files, Part I, Reel 11, Frame 353; Substitute For Resolutions Nos. 203 and 238 Sit-Down Strikes, *UAW Proceed-ings 1937*, 190.

IV. Making Constitutional Law

At the time that GM workers commenced their historic strike, virtually no one expected the Supreme Court to uphold the Wagner Act. Every one of the twenty-four federal judges who had ruled on the issue agreed that the Act could not be applied to manufacturing companies. Lawrence Lucey summed up the prevailing view when he reported with "icy certainty" that the federal government lacked power to regulate labor relations.[73]

But workers and unions persistently declared the Act constitutional and proceeded to enforce it through strikes and factory occupations. "Labor demands," thundered John L. Lewis on the second night of the Flint sit-down, "that congress exercise its constitutional powers and brush aside the negative autocracy of the federal judiciary."[74] On February 5, 1937, President Roosevelt proposed a method for accomplishing this result: packing the Court with new appointees. The CIO promptly endorsed the president's bill as its top legislative priority.[75] In terms of lobbying and political mobilization, however, the movement's activity did not differ in kind from that of other groups. Labor's unique contribution came in the form of the sit-down strikes. By seizing hundreds of factories and demonstrating their willingness to risk injury or death defending them, the sit-downers tested the commitment of judges and other public authorities to the defense of corporate property rights. What follows describes how the various levels and branches of government, from municipalities to the Supreme Court of the United States, responded to the workers' challenge.

The Criminal Jury: Divided on the General Issue of the Strike

The first attempt to deploy official law against sit-down strikers came in Akron in May 1936. On the night of May 19, tire room workers had downed tools to protest the assignment of a non-union man to lead a crew. Not content to halt production, they imprisoned supervisors and non-union workers in a makeshift enclosure called the "Bullpen" for nearly twelve hours until the company agreed to rescind the non-union man's appointment. Thirty-one participants were charged with violating Ohio's anti-riot act, which required only a showing that the defendants had combined with the intent of committing some unlawful act.[76] In the ensuing proceedings, nobody contested the fact that the sit-downers had combined with the intent of seizing the facility and imprisoning their opponents.

But unionists argued that the real issue in the case was the right to organize or, as the head of the Goodyear local's defense committee put it: "Can the rubber companies break the unions through the use of legal trickery?" At the first trial, of a tire builder named Jimmy Jones, union attorney Stanley Denlinger relayed this argument to the jury. "You have no right to take the taxpayers' money to fight the battle for the Goodyear company," he asserted. "This was within the four walls of the Goodyear factory [and t]here was nothing here but a dispute between the company and the workers—something that we shouldn't be concerned about." Denlinger's associate followed up by comparing the bull pen sit-down to the Boston Tea Party and John Brown's raid on Harper's Ferry.[77]

The judge charged the jurors that they were to disregard their personal views on strikes and unionism and focus solely on the question of whether there was a riot as defined by

---

73. *See* Pope, "Thirteenth Amendment," 71–72 (collecting cases); Lawrence Lucey, "Labor and Law," *The Commonweal* 347 (July 3, 1936).

74. *United Mine Workers Journal*, 3 (Jan. 15, 1937); *see also* Pope, "Thirteenth Amendment," 78–81 (collecting additional quotations).

75. E. L. Oliver, Vice President, Labor's Non-Partisan League, to Congressmen and Senators, Feb. 17, 1937, Lewis CIO Papers, Reel 26, Frame 1096; *UNS*, Mar. 15, 1937, 1.

76. *ABJ*, 1, 6 (May 25, 1936); *ABJ*, 1, 6 (June 25, 1936); *ABJ*, 1, 6 (June 29, 1936).

77. *ABJ*, 1, 6 (May 25, 1936); *ABJ*, 1, 6 (July 1, 1936).

the statute. Nevertheless, the jury deadlocked six to six, and the prosecutors and defense attorneys all agreed that "evidently the jury is divided on the general issue of the strike, and not the evidence in the case." Charges against the remaining thirty defendants were quietly dropped several months later.[78]

The bull pen case demonstrated the limited value of criminal proceedings in controlling sit-downs. Despite the unusual abuses committed by the sit-downers, half of the jurors had refused to vote for criminal penalties. Later, a number of sit-downers would be successfully prosecuted for trespass and conspiracy—but not in movement centers like Akron and Detroit, where jurors tended to have considerable exposure to industrial workers and unions.[79] Although the U.S. Supreme Court had yet to recognize a federal constitutional right to jury trials in state criminal proceedings, the states generally honored that right. As in the labor wars at the turn of the century, then, employers would have to find a way to nullify or circumvent the jury requirement.

Lower Court Judges: Fearlessly Disregarding the Popular Mandate

Employers turned to the labor injunction—their traditional tool for controlling workers. While strikers could not be punished for trespass or other criminal offenses without a jury trial, state court judges could finesse that requirement by enjoining the crime and then punishing the strikers for contempt of court, which required no jury trial. In Flint, General Motors wasted no time seeking an injunction ordering the sit-downers to depart its plants. At the hearing, the issue centered on the relative weight to be given employer property rights as against the workers' right of self-organization. GM's attorneys argued that if property rights "can be challenged, all rights are gone." Union lawyers countered by invoking the principle that equitable relief cannot be granted to a supplicant with "unclean hands," meaning one that had engaged in unlawful activity related to the suit. They spent several hours presenting evidence that GM had discharged workers for unionism, hired detectives to spy on and intimidate workers, and fostered a company union—all in flagrant violation of the Wagner Act.[80]

Judge Paul V. Gadola promptly granted the injunction. Acutely aware of the public attention focused on the case, he issued a lengthy opinion that supplied the substantive justification for many of the anti-sitdown injunctions that were to follow. Ignoring the Wagner Act, which expressly provided that strikers remain employees, he held that when the workers struck they forfeited their status as employees and thus any right they might have had to remain on their employer's property. Hence, the sit-down amounted to a straightforward trespass. He disposed of the union's unclean hands argument by restating it as the claim that "one wrong could be righted by another wrong" and then pointing out that the "falsity of that position is apparent by merely the stating of the position." With this bold distortion, Gadola simply bypassed the fact that the unclean hands doctrine centered not on the relationship of the parties to each other, but on the role of the courts in the dispute. Courts sitting in equity, the doctrine held, should not assist one wrongdoing party against another; both parties should be left to their ordinary, legal remedies. By ignoring this basic feature of the doctrine, Gadola spared himself the necessity of considering GM's alleged violations of the Wagner Act. As critics were quick to point

---

78. *ABJ*, 1, 6 (July 1, 1936); *ABJ*, 1, 6 (July 2, 1936); *ABJ*, 1, 5 (July 3, 1936); *United Rubber Worker*, 5 (Dec. 1936).

79. *See* Eisenberg, "Government Policy," 107–11.

80. *See* Felix Frankfurter and Nathan Greene, *The Labor Injunction,* 106-8 (New York: MacMillan,1930); *DN*, 1, 23 (Feb. 2, 1937).

out, however, his reformulation of the unclean hands doctrine amounted to "a denial that there is any such doctrine," at least "when [the unclean hands] were the employer's."[81]

Judge Gadola's opinion stood out from other lower court opinions addressing the sit-down issue mainly in its temperate tone and its effort to address labor's arguments. By contrast, other judges fulminated against the "un-American" and "destructive revolutionary" sit-down that, if tolerated, would "strike down American institutions" and "destroy the foundations of government itself."[82] And when workers protested that they were engaging in self-help to counter employer violations of the statutory right to organize, courts only became more hostile. One court charged that such claims were "the hand-maid of crime and anarchy," while another referred to a self-help sit-down as a "horrible and dishonorable mess and rape upon law and order."[83] After arguing the unclean hands point before several judges, UAW counsel Maurice Sugar concluded that "their minds have been completely closed" so that even judges "with no mean local reputations as 'legal minds' simply do not hear you when you argue."[84]

Judge Gadola gave the workers until 3:00 pm on February 3 to evacuate the Fisher Body plants, with the union to be fined fifteen million dollars in the event of noncompliance. UAW leaders responded by calling on union locals across the midwest for volunteers to reenforce the picket line. Hundreds answered the call, including more than a thousand auto workers from Toledo, coal miners from Pittsburgh, and a contingent of rubber workers from Akron. Six days later, the strike was settled, with GM agreeing to drop all charges against the sit-downers and union officials.[85]

This experience underscored the problem with judicial injunctions as a means of controlling sit-downs. Though easy to obtain, injunctions were of little practical use unless there was a government agency with the will, the personnel, and the equipment necessary for enforcement.

Local and State Government: Not Enough Force to Evict

Impressed by the ignominious defeat of the Flint police in the Battle of Bulls Run, most local officials adopted a cautious approach toward sit-downs. Experts urged police to consider the destruction that would result from an eviction attempt, to delay as long as possible, and to refrain from action unless a force could be assembled that would clearly be sufficient for the job. Instead of attacking, urged one critic, the Flint police should have engaged in action just aggressive enough to demonstrate that outside assistance was required.[86]

On February 19, 1937, sit-down strikers at the Fansteel Metallurgical Corporation repulsed an attack by one hundred forty Waukegan police, apparently confirming the wisdom of caution. This time, however, the defeated officers rose to the challenge. On the

---

81. *DN*, 32 (Feb. 3, 1937) (reprinting text of decision); *I.J.A. Bull.* 101–02 (Mar. 1937).

82. *See, e.g, Apex Hosiery Co. v. Leader*, 90 F.2d 144, 158 (3d Cir. 1937), *rev'd as moot*, 302 U.S. 656 (1937); *The Losmar*, 20 F. Supp. 887, 891 (D. Md. 1937); *Ohio Leather Co. v. De Chant, Ohio*, 4 U.S.L.W. 951 (Court of Common Pleas, Trumbull County, Ohio 1937); *I.J.A. Bull.*, 103 (Feb. 1938).

83. *The Losmar*, 20 F. Supp. 887, 890 (D. Md. 1937); *Fansteel Metallurgical Corp. v. Lodge 66, Amalgamated Ass'n of Iron Workers* (Lake County Circuit Court, No. 37551, June 8, 1937), reprinted in Transcript of Record, *NLRB v. Fansteel Metallurgical Corp.*, 306 U.S. 240 (1939), 1724, 1726, 1732.

84. Maurice Sugar, "Is the Sit-Down Legal?," *New Masses*, 19, 21 (May 4, 1937).

85. *DN*, 1 (Feb. 3, 1937); Art Preis, *Labor's Giant Step*, 60 (New York: Pathfinder, 1964); Fine, *Sit-Down*, 207–08, 293; *DN*, 1, 18 (Feb. 11, 1937); *DN*, 1 (Feb. 12, 1937).

86. *See* Eisenberg, "Government Policy," 60; Miles Arnold, "What a Strike Means to a Police Department," 19 *City Manager Magazine* 44 (Feb. 1937); Donald C. Stone, "What Is the City's Role in Labor Disputes?" 19 *Public Management* 40 (Feb. 1937.

advice of Fansteel's attorney, they rigged a two-story assault tower mounted on a ten-ton truck. Arriving before sunrise, the police found the sixty defenders asleep. Officers positioned in the assault tower blasted tear-gas canisters through the factory windows at point-blank range. Within minutes, the plant was filled with gas. A picked force of between forty and sixty police officers battled strikers wielding fire hoses and hurling projectiles. After about an hour, the strikers were driven out and the facility secured.[87] A few days later, Connecticut state police evicted striking workers from the Electric Boat shipyard at Groton and some three hundred forty sit-downers evacuated the Douglas Aircraft factory in Santa Monica, California, after police equipped with machine guns surrounded the plant.[88] In the space of a week, law enforcement officers had succeeded in ending three major sit-downs, and they had done so without creating any martyrs.

In Detroit, police had yet to conduct a successful eviction. On March 15, the Chrysler Corporation obtained a court order compelling the evacuation of its eight Detroit-area plants and setting 9:00 a.m. March 17 as the deadline. On that day, between 30,000 and 50,000 workers guarded the plants—10,000 each at the Dodge Main and Chrysler Jefferson Avenue plants, with smaller lines elsewhere. The day passed with no attempt at enforcement. Governor Murphy explained that there was not "enough force here to evict the sit-down strikers in a strike of such magnitude."[89]

Blocked at Chrysler, the police turned their attention to smaller facilities. Between March 18 and March 21, police evicted small contingents of sit-downers from a number of retail stores and lumber yards. Following up on these successes, three hundred police assaulted the Bernard Schwartz Cigar Company where women strikers battled police with heavy wooden molds before succumbing. That same day, forty-nine men and fifteen women at the Newton Packing Company initially shouted defiance but surrendered without a fight after a force of one hundred sixty police broke into the plant under authority of an injunction.[90]

The police evictions tested the labor movement's commitment to the sit-down tactic. In Chicago, where the city Federation of Labor was led by conservatives, the movement failed to respond and the police offensive was largely successful.[91] But in Detroit, the UAW moved promptly to defend sit-downers in all industries, and the local Federation of Labor, led by the socialist typographer Frank Martel, backed it up. First, Homer Martin telegraphed all Detroit-area auto locals to prepare for a general strike in protest of the "unlawful" police raids on sit-down strikers. Next, the union called a mass demonstration to be held in Cadillac Square on Sunday, March 23. Finally, the union announced the formation of a force of "minute men" to be on alert around the clock to "protect strikers and the right to strike."[92] Meanwhile, Governor Murphy raised the level of tension by announcing, in what the press called an "ultimatum," that the state government would "employ all necessary and available means in this and similar cases to

---

87. *Chicago Daily News*, 1,3 (Feb. 26, 1937); *Chicago Daily News*, 1 (Feb. 26, 1937); *DN*, 4 (Feb. 26, 1937); *NYT*, 1 (Feb. 27, 1937).

88. *DN*, 4 (Feb. 26, 1937); *I.J.A. Bulletin*, 85 (Jan. 1938).

89. See *DN*, 1 (March 15, 1937); *DN*, 1 (Mar. 17, 1937); Brecher, *Strike!* 227; Steve Babson, *Building the Union: Skilled Workers and Anglo-Gaelic Immigrants in the Rise of the UAW*, 186 (New Brunswick: Rutgers University. Press, 1991); Norwood, *Strike-breaking and Intimidation*, 214; Eisenberg, "Government Policy," 82–83 (quoting Murphy).

90. Schwantes, " 'We've Got 'em on the Run,' " 194; *DN*, 1 (Mar. 18, 1937); Eisenberg, "Government Policy," 67; *DN*, 1, 12 (Mar. 21, 1937); *NYT*, 1 (Mar. 21, 1937).

91. *Chicago Daily News*, 1, 2 (Mar. 24, 1937); *Chicago Daily News*, 5 (March 30, 1937).

92. Russell B. Porter, "6,000 Chrysler Sit-ins Defy Gov. Murphy to Use Troops," *NYT*, 1 (Mar. 21, 1937); *DN*, 1 (Mar. 22, 1937); *Daily Worker*, 3 (April 14, 1937).

uphold public authority in this state and protect property rights in the interest of the general public."[93]

On March 23, a crowd estimated by police at 60,000 and by unionists at more than twice that assembled at Cadillac Square. Speakers called for drastic action to stop "police brutality" and the eviction of sit-downers. "From this time on the constitutional rights of this community are going to be respected in the City Hall, the police station and the courts," warned Frank Martel, "or we'll turn them wrongside up." By acclamation, the rally passed resolutions condemning the police and determining that "for every eviction, there be two sit-down strikes." Homer Martin drew cheers when he accused the Supreme Court of going "on a sit-down strike for the last six years" and announced that he was "squarely behind the President in his efforts to put those boys in their proper places!"[94]

After the rally, both Governor Murphy and the Detroit Police abruptly abandoned their law-and-order crusade against the sit-downs. Local and state government had been neutralized. Baffled by the difficulties of dealing with sit-downs, many local government officials now looked to intervention by the federal government as their "dream of heaven."[95]

The Federal Executive: No Words of Counsel

President Roosevelt greeted the advent of the sit-down strikes with a determined silence. At press conferences, he nimbly dodged reporters' questions about the tactic. As public opinion polls showed increasing hostility to sit-downers, the President's reticence began to cost him politically. A. Lawrence Lowell, President emeritus of Harvard University, joined with six prominent Bostonians to charge that Roosevelt could have ended the sit-down wave early on with just "a few words of counsel," but that it had now escalated to an "[a]rmed insurrection" challenging "the supremacy of government itself." In cabinet meetings, Vice President Garner—who considered the sit-downs to be "mass lawlessness"—engaged the President in shouting matches so violent that on one occasion Secretary Perkins was driven to tears, while on another Senate Majority Leader Joe Robinson was forced to impose silence. Meanwhile, in Congress, the sit-down issue threatened to split the New Deal coalition in two, as southern Democrats joined conservative Republicans in pressing for anti-sit-down legislation.[96] Yet, the President remained mute.

Why this hush? According to Secretary Perkins, Roosevelt shared the widespread view that the sit-down amounted to an illegal trespass, but believed that "shooting it out and killing alot of people" was a punishment that did not fit the crime.[97] This stance, which accorded with popular sentiment as reported in public opinion polls, might explain why Roosevelt did not take action against the sit-downers, but it cannot explain why he did not make his views public. Most likely, the President's silence was dictated by considerations of constitutional politics. Supporters of his court packing plan had seized on the sit-down wave to dramatize the costs of the Supreme Court's intransigence. Meanwhile, in Court, government lawyers were highlighting the sit-downs as proof of the need for na-

93. *Daily Worker*, 3 (April 14, 1937); *DN*, 1 (Mar. 23, 1937).

94. *See NYT*, 1 (Mar. 24, 1937); *DLN*, 1 (March 26, 1937); *DN*, 4 (Mar. 24, 1937); Mr. Homer Martin's Speech in Cadillac Square, March 23, 1937, UAW Local 9 Collection, Box 3, Wayne State Archives.

95. Eisenberg, "Government Policy," 56.

96. *Ibid.* at 88–89; *DN*, 1 (Mar. 27, 1937) (quoting Lowell telegram); James T. Patterson, *Congressional Conservativsm and the New Deal: The Growth of the Conservative Coalition in Congress 1933–1939*, 135–36 (Lexington: U. Kentucky Press, 1967); David Plotke, *Building a Democratic Political Order: Reshaping American Liberalism in the 1930s and 1940s, 128, 148* (New York: Cambridge U. Press, 1996).

97. Frances Perkins, *The Roosevelt I Knew*, 321–22 (New York: Viking Press, 1946).

tional labor legislation.[98] Had Roosevelt announced his view that the tactic amounted to an illegal trespass, he might have discouraged worker activists from occupying factories, thus depriving his supporters of what they considered to be one of their strongest arguments in favor of constitutional change.

With local authorities overwhelmed and the Roosevelt administration tacitly accepting the tactic, sit-down opponents turned to Congress.

Congress: In a Rather Ridiculous Position

On Capitol Hill, southern Democrats took the lead in proposing legislation declaring the sit-down illegal. Representative Martin Dies of Texas launched the effort by offering a resolution for a thorough investigation of the sit-down phenomenon. A few days later, Senator James Byrnes of South Carolina moved to amend the Guffey coal bill to outlaw sit-downs in the coal industry—a proposal later expanded to include all industries.[99]

Despite the growing unpopularity of the sit-down, the proponents of suppression quickly ran into trouble. While Roosevelt himself remained silent, his supporters in Congress explicitly demanded a favorable Supreme Court decision on the Wagner Act as a pre-requisite to action against the sit-down. "At present we are in the rather ridiculous position of being called upon to take some action with regard to strikes," complained Representative Voorhis, "when the action already taken by this body is itself rendered of no effect by the action of the judicial branch of Government." Representative Engel of Michigan, who had voted against the Wagner Act because he thought it was unconstitutional, now opposed legislation against sit-downs on the same ground: "Should I vote for this resolution I would be taking the position that a man who stands up and works in a factory comes under the intra-state commerce clause of the Constitution, while that same man sitting down in the same factory and refusing to work would immediately come under the interstate commerce clause."[100]

In an "uproarious session" on April 8, the House voted down the Dies resolution 236-150. Three days before, the Senate had rejected the Byrnes amendment 48-36, but only after Majority Leader Joe Robinson promised that the issue would be addressed in another form. Soon afterward, the Senate adopted a nonbinding resolution simultaneously condemning both the sit-down and employer violations of the Wagner Act.[101]

The Supreme Court: After Labor Pains, Quintuplets

With President Roosevelt silent, Congress standing by the Wagner Act, and local government lacking the force necessary to suppress sit-downs, all eyes turned to the Supreme Court. If the Court were to strike down the Wagner Act, it would validate continued employer resistance to unionism, leave CIO leaders with no choice but to continue supporting factory occupations, and—perhaps most important—corroborate Roosevelt's claim that the Court must be packed in order to prevent it from overturning essential legislation. But if the Court were to uphold the Act, it would—at one stroke—undercut employer resistance, put John L. Lewis to his promise that a "C.I.O. contract is adequate protection against sit-downs," and leave Congress with no excuse for failing to address the problem.

---

98. *CR*, Mar. 24, 1937, 2728; *NYT*, 1 (Mar. 21, 1937); Hansen, "The Sit-Down Strikes and the Switch in Time," 50, 109–10.

99. Patterson, *Congressional Conservativism*, 136–37, 167–68.

100. *CR*, Mar. 30, 1937, 2922 (Rep. Voorhis); *CR*, Mar. 23, 1937, 2639 (Rep. Harlan); *CR*, Mar. 18, 1937, 2379 (Sen. Brown); *CR*, Apr. 8, 1937, Appendix, 829–30 (Rep. Ellenbogen); *CR*, Apr. 8, 1937, Appendix, 758–59 (Rep. Engel).

101. Patterson, *Congressional Conservativism*, 137, 168; *CR*, April 7, 1937, 3248; Turner Catledge, "Senate Denounces Sit-Ins and Spies," *NYT*, 1 (April 8, 1937).

On April 12, 1937, a bare five-judge majority of the Supreme Court upheld the Wagner Act as applied to the Jones & Laughlin Steel Corporation. Chief Justice Hughes distinguished recent precedents striking down New Deal legislation on the ground that the impact of a strike at the giant steel corporation "would be immediate and might be catastrophic."[102] Almost unnoticed, however, the Court also upheld the Act as applied to a trailer company and a clothing company, neither of which could conceivably spawn a strike with "immediate" or "catastrophic" consequences. While Jones & Laughlin Steel employed 22,000 workers in an industry that, in Hughes' words, had a history of strikes with "far-reaching consequences," the trailer company and the clothing Company employed 900 and 800 respectively in industries not known for strikes with national consequences.[103] Yet, after declaring in *Jones & Laughlin* that the constitutional reach of the Act would depend upon the particular facts of each case, Chief Justice Hughes provided no reasoning whatever in either of the other cases except for a terse citation to *Jones & Laughlin*.

What explains the results in these cases? And what could induce the majority to announce a rule calling for fact-specific determinations in one case, and then fail to apply it in two other cases decided the same day? The best answer is that the Court was plainly and simply yielding to pressure from the sit-down strikers.[104] Judging from the lack of reasoning in the trailer company and clothing company cases, the Court would have been more comfortable drawing the line at *Jones & Laughlin*. But in the face of the sit-down crisis, even the dramatic concession of crossing the line from commerce to manufacturing in *Jones & Laughlin* would not have been enough to defuse the court-packing threat. The median sit-down strike involved about 100 workers, far fewer even than the 800 employed by the clothing company. As NLRB General Counsel Charles Fahy recognized, the viability of the NLRB — and thus of Congress' attempt to solve the industrial crisis — "would stand or fall" on cases like this. Thus, anything short of a Board sweep would have defeated Congress' attempt to resolve the labor crisis and, conversely, only a sweep could have deflated the pressure for court-packing as a means of freeing Congress to resolve that crisis. As a quip circulating in the Labor Department had it, "after some labor pains the Court gave birth to quintuplets."[105]

V. Constitutional Trade-Off

While labor leaders and activists celebrated *Jones & Laughlin* and the other Wagner Act cases as a "new day" of industrial freedom and democracy, the Detroit Police set out to establish a new era of law and order. On April 12, the day of the Wagner Act rulings, one hundred seventy-five sit-down strikers at the Yale & Towne Manufacturing Company, scene of a previous confrontation between police and UAW minute men, defied a court order commanding them to evacuate the premises by 9:00 that morning. Two days later, after last-minute peace efforts failed, two hundred police officers and deputy sheriffs appeared at the plant. The UAW again mobilized its minute man network, and workers from nearby shops began arriving just as the officers moved to the attack. The strikers,

---

102. Hansen, "The Sit-Down Strikes and the Switch in Time," 131–32; *NLRB v. Jones & Laughlin Steel Corp.*, 301 U.S. 1, 41 (1937).

103. *NLRB v. Fruehauf Trailer Company*, 301 U.S. 49 (1937); *NLRB v. Friedman-Harry Marks Clothing Company*, 301 U.S. 58 (1937); *Jones & Laughlin*, 301 U.S. at 43; *ibid.* at 85 (McReynolds, J., dissenting) (reporting the number of workers employed by each company).

104. For a more detailed argument on this point, *see* Pope, "Thirteenth Amendment," 85–97.

105. *Detroit Police Sit-Down List* (providing data on size of sit-downs); Peter Irons, *The New Deal Lawyers*, 263 (Princeton: Princeton U. Press, 1982), (quoting Fahy); Letter from Charles Wyzanski, Labor Solicitor, to Felix Frankfurter (Apr. 14, 1937), John Knox Papers, Harvard Law Library Manuscript Div., box 1.

nearly all of whom were women, barricaded themselves in the plant. While deputies pumped tear-gas shells through windows and skylights, strikers and minute men rained locks, radiator caps, and other projectiles down from the roofs and windows. After a sharp, half-hour battle, the officers took possession of the plant and arrested seventy-nine women and twenty-five men.[106]

The Yale & Towne eviction was the first in Detroit since the Cadillac Square rally three weeks before, and the first ever to be successfully conducted against UAW strikers in the Motor City. This new boldness on the part of police was the flip side of labor's victory in *Jones & Laughlin*. As soon as the Wagner Act decisions were announced, a chorus of commentators and political leaders proclaimed that the Court had eliminated the justification for the sit-down strikes. "Undoubtedly these decisions will serve to transfer the scene of conflict expressed by the sit-in strike," summarized the Socialist lawyer Louis Waldman, "from the factories and mills to the trial rooms of the Labor Relations Board."[107] CIO leaders declared that along with labor's new power came "a new responsibility" to honor contracts and eschew "revolutionary methods." The combination of *Jones & Laughlin* and the police offensive dampened labor militance. After 47 sit-downs of one day or more in February and 170 in March, there were 52 in April, 72 in May, and an average of 16 per month through the end of the year.[108] The overnight sit-down had declined from a standard to an exceptional tactic.

Now that the Wagner Act had been upheld by the Supreme Court, however, the reasoning of the early court decisions outlawing the sit-down was called into question. Its legal status would be determined not under the property-friendly common law but under the far more labor-friendly statutory law. Moreover, the initial determination would be made not by courts, which had exhibited such a deep affinity for employer property rights, but by the National Labor Relations Board, an administrative body appointed by President Roosevelt to enforce the workers' new statutory rights.

The NLRB: An Important National Policy against Industrial Strife

The landmark sit-down case arose out of the Fansteel strike. Ninety-five workers had occupied the plant after the corporation planted a labor spy within the union, isolated the union president from other workers, attempted to establish a company-dominated union, refused to bargain with the union after it represented a majority of workers in the shop, and maintained an official policy of refusing to negotiate with any "outside" union (meaning any national union) — all unfair labor practices under the Wagner Act. The company fired many of the sit-downers, and they sought reinstatement to their jobs with back pay.[109] At the hearing, Board attorneys made no effort to solicit justifications from the strikers and stood by while Fansteel's lawyers cut them off.

---

106. *See DLN*, 1 (April 16, 1937); *DN*, 4 (April 12, 1937); Lichtenstein, *Most Dangerous Man*, 81; Fred W. Cousins, "Girls of Cleared Plant Are Dubbed 'Gas Eaters,'" *DN*, 1 (April 15, 1937); *DN*, 1, 4 (April 15, 1937); *Local 205 Union Action*, 4 (April 17, 1937).

107. *NYT*, 20 (April 13, 1937); see also Arthur Krock, "Wagner Act Decisions Viewed from Political Angle," *NYT*, 24 (April 13, 1937); Louis Stark, "Sit-Down," *Survey Graphic*, 316, 320 (June 1937). For additional quotations, *see* Hansen, "The Sit-Down Strikes and the Switch in Time," 125–26.

108. *See* Charles P. Howard, CIO Secretary, "President's Page," *Typographical J.*, 435 (May 1937); *NYT*, 20 (April 13, 1937); Brecher, *Strike!*, 225–26; Bernstein, *Turbulent Years*, 481–97; *Monthly Lab. Rev.*, 360–61 (Aug. 1938).

109. *NLRB v. Fansteel Metallurgical Corp.*, 306 U.S. 240, 247–48 (1939); *Fansteel Metallurgical Corp.*, 5 N.L.R.B. 930, 931, 942 *enforcement denied, Fansteel Metallurgical Corp. v. NLRB*, 98 F.2d 375 (7th Cir. 1938), *reversed in part*, 306 U.S. 240 (1939).

Though uninterested in the workers' justifications, the Board did order them reinstated with back pay. This result was grounded not on any theory that the sit-down strike was legal or that the employer had violated the law by discharging the strikers, but on the theory that reinstatement was necessary to restore the status quo prior to the employer's unfair labor practices. Ironically, the Board — established as a substitute for the courts' use of equity powers to govern industrial relations — finally brought the equitable doctrine of unclean hands to the law of labor disputes. Responding to the argument that the strikers' unlawful seizure of the factory freed the employer to fire them, the Board observed that Fansteel did "not come before the Board with clean hands" as it was "guilty of gross violations of law, violations which in fact were the moving cause for the conduct of the employees." On the central question of the relative priority of individual property rights and collective labor rights, the Board adapted its position to the commerce clause foundation of the Act. Employer property rights were counterposed not to labor liberty, but to the "important national policy" against disruptions of commerce.[110]

Although the Board's *Fansteel* decision did not, in theory, recognize a right to sit down in protest of serious unfair labor practices, it had that effect on the ground. In a series of cases, the Board reinstated strikers who had occupied their workplaces in response to employer violations of the Act. "Looking at the matter from a practical standpoint," one commentator noted, "the average employee does not know the technicalities of the Wagner Act, and when reinstated he is of the opinion that his past conduct has been given the stamp of approval."[111] It remained to be seen, however, whether reviewing courts would accept the Board's approach.

The Supreme Court: Coppage and Adair Unburied

While government lawyers transmuted labor's slogan of human rights over property rights into an expansion of the commerce power, employer lawyers faithfully advanced their clients' claims of constitutional liberty. Fansteel's lawyers focused on two points, both of which went to the relative priority of employer property rights and worker rights of collective action. First, they argued that the Wagner Act had taken only a small bite out of the employer's Fifth Amendment right to discharge workers for any reason or no reason at all. In *Jones & Laughlin* and *Associated Press v. NLRB*, the Supreme Court had held that the Act did not infringe the employer's liberty of contract only because it left him free to fire a worker "for any cause that seems to it proper save only as a punishment for, or discouragement of, such activities as the act declares permissible" and thus did "not interfere with the normal exercise of the right of the employer to select its employees or to discharge them." To restrict the employer's freedom to discharge workers for unlawful activity — a "normal exercise" of the right to discharge — would, then, transgress the employer's retained liberty of contract.[112]

Having elevated the employer's interest to the constitutional level, Fansteel's lawyers went on to downgrade the countervailing interest in reinstatement. They pointed out that the Act directed the Board to apply only such remedies as would "effectuate the policies of the Act" and that the central purpose of the Act was promoting industrial peace

---

110. 5 N.L.R.B. 945, 949, 952–53 (1938); Eisenberg, "Government Policy," 197–98.

111. *See In re McNeely & Price Co.*, 6 N.L.R.B. 800 (1938); *In re Kuehne Mfg. Co.*, 7 N.L.R.B. 304 (1938); *In re Electric Boat Co.*, 7 N.L.R.B. 572, 573 (1938); *In re Douglas Aircraft Co., Inc.*, 10 N.L.R.B. 242, 248 (1938); *In re Swift & Co.*, 10 N.L.R.B. 991 (1939); Note, "Termination of Relation of Master and Servant," 17 *Chicago-Kent Law Review* 290, 293 (1939).

112. Brief for Fansteel Metallurgical Corporation, *NLRB v. Fansteel Metallurgical Corporation*, 306 U.S. 240 (1939), 26 (quoting *Associated Press v. NLRB*, 301 U.S. 103, 132 [1937]); *ibid.*, 26 (quoting *Jones & Laughlin*, 301 U.S. at 45–46); *ibid.*, 34.

so as to facilitate interstate commerce. Thus, there was no need to discuss worker freedom except as a means of achieving industrial peace; not even the Board raised the possibility that remedying violations of workers' rights might have intrinsic value under the statute. Once on the terrain of industrial peace, the employer lawyers had a powerful argument that—far from promoting that objective—the reinstatement of sit-down strikers would encourage workers to resort to violent and disorderly self-help in place of the "orderly process" provided by the statute.[113]

The Supreme Court upheld the Court of Appeals' denial of enforcement by a 6–2 margin. Writing for the majority, Chief Justice Hughes embraced the Fansteel lawyers' approach. The issue, he wrote, was whether the Act abrogated "the right of the employer to refuse to retain in his employ" workers who had illegally seized his property. Both of the employer interests involved—its right to exclude its workers from its property and its right to discharge them—were of the highest magnitude. An intrusion on the corporation's right of possession was "not essentially different" from an assault on a person. And the corporation's right to discharge the "wrongdoers" received the respect due to a right of constitutional dimension. "Apart from the question of the constitutional validity of an enactment of that sort," wrote Chief Justice Hughes in an early version of today's clear statement rule, "it is enough to say that such a legislative intention should be found in some definite and unmistakable expression."[114]

The countervailing interests gave the Court no reason to find such an expression. The fact that the employer had repeatedly and openly violated the Wagner Act impressed the Court so little that it could describe the sit-down as "an illegal seizure of the buildings in order to prevent their use by the employer in a *lawful* manner." While describing the workers as "wrongdoers" who had forfeited their statutory rights, the Court never placed the corporation in that category. Although Fansteel's conduct was "reprehensible," there was "no ground for saying that it made respondent an outlaw or deprived it of its legal rights to the possession and protection of its property." The Court did not mention the effects of Fansteel's violations on the workers' right to organize; nor did it respond to the Board's argument that reinstatement was the only effective way to remedy those effects and restore the status quo. These omissions were especially significant in light of the fact that the workers' unfair labor practice charges, filed five months prior to the sit-down, had produced no action from the NLRB. With management continuing to violate the Act, the union had come under membership pressure to do something or lose support. Fansteel's spy in the union had attempted to foment a traditional strike, which would have enabled the company to replace the union workers. The sit-down was the union's response to this situation—apparently the only way to prevent the company from breaking the union. But the Court ignored these facts, instead pointing out that the purpose of protecting rights of self-organization was to promote industrial peace and thereby "remove obstructions to the free flow of commerce." Far from aiding in the accomplishment of this purpose, the reinstatement of sit-down strikers would encourage violent self-help in place of the orderly procedures established in the Act.[115]

In effect, then, *Fansteel* sealed the constitutional compromise that had been scripted by the Senate two years before—but with an added twist. At the height of the sit-down

---

113. *Ibid.*, 35, 35–52.

114. *NLRB v. Fansteel Metallurgical Corp.*, 306 U.S. 240, 252, 253, 255, 259 (1939); *ibid.*, 265 (Stone, J., concurring).

115. 306 U.S. at 256 (emphasis added); *ibid.*, 256–57; *ibid.*, 253; Henry M. Hart, Jr., and Edward F. Pritchard, Jr., "The Fansteel Case: Employee Misconduct and the Remedial Powers of the National Labor Relations Board," 52 *Harvard Law Review* 1275, 1280–81 (1939).

crisis, the Senate had refused to condemn the workers' tactic without issuing a simulta-neous condemnation of employer violations of worker rights, thus apparently placing the two on the same level of reprehensibility. The *Fansteel* Court affirmed that both were illegal, but also concluded that the employer could violate the workers' statutory rights with-out sacrificing its property rights, while the workers could not violate the employer's property rights without sacrificing their statutory rights—a return to the hierarchy of values that predated the Wagner Act.

It is a commonplace that the doctrine of economic due process, according to which fed-eral courts would strictly scrutinize legislation that infringed the liberty of contract, died in 1937 with the Supreme Court's decision in *West Coast Hotel v. Parrish*.[116] It is true that the Court has not invalidated a statute on economic due process grounds since *Parrish*. But *Fansteel* revived the doctrine in labor law. "The surreptitious burial believed by some to have been the fate of *Coppage v. Kansas* and *Adair v. United States*," commented J. Den-son Smith after *Fansteel*, "appears not to have been as enduring as suspected."[117] Others agreed. On the view that *Fansteel* reflected the pre-New Deal mentality, Arthur Krock confidently predicted that the dissenters' position—which was "eloquent of New Deal reasoning" in emphasizing the Board's statutory power to remedy unfair labor practices—would eventually prevail.[118]

But by the time of *Fansteel*, the sit-down's main public supporters had been silenced. Dean Leon Green of Northwestern and SEC Chairman James Landis, the most prominent members of the legal profession to defend the possibility that the sit-down might be law-ful, had succumbed to pressure from wealthy critics. Dean Green, who had written his defense of the sit-down while on leave, returned to an "icy reception." Alumni protested so vehemently that the school's board of trustees was prepared to demand his resigna-tion but for the opposition of two members, both clerics, who threatened to do likewise. Landis, who was preparing to take up the Deanship at Harvard Law School, received angry letters from alumni and urgent complaints from Harvard fundraisers.[119] Neither Green nor Landis went so far as to recant, but both fell silent on the issue.

Epilogue

By the time of the Supreme Court's ruling in *Fansteel*, factory occupations were infre-quent. From May 1938 to February 1939, the month that *Fansteel* was decided, there had been an average of only 3.2 sit-downs (defined as an occupation lasting one day or more) per month, constituting 1.4 percent of all strikes. Nevertheless, the decision had an effect. Until *Fansteel*, workers could claim that the legal status of sit-downs remained uncertain. But *Fansteel* removed all doubt. Henceforth, any unionist who participated in a sit-down would be engaging in open defiance of a legal prohibition that had been endorsed by the nation's highest tribunal. In the week following *Fansteel*, at least two employers took advantage of

---

116. 300 U.S. 379 (1937); Laurence H. Tribe, *American Constitutional Law*, 2d ed., 567 (Mineola, N.Y.: Foundation Press, 1988).

117. On the re-inscribing of *Coppoage* in employment law generally, *see* Kenneth M. Casebeer, "Teaching an Old Dog Old Tricks: *Coppage v. Kansas* and At-Will Employment Revisited," 6 *Cardozo L. Rev.* 765 (1985).

118. J. Denson Smith, "From Nose-Thumbing to Sabotage," 1 *La. L. Rev.* 577, 577, 580 (1939); *see also* Frank Thomas Miller, Jr., "Sit-Down Strikes—Reinstatement of Employees Under the Wag-ner Act," 17 *N. Car. L.Rev.* 438, 439 (1939; Note, "Power of the National Labor Relations Board to Order Reinstatement of Sit-Down Strikers," 27 *Cal. L.Rev.* 470, 473 (1939); Arthur Krock, "Implications in the dissents of Reed and Black," *NYT,* 20 (March 1, 1939).

119. Willard Wirtz, "Dean Green," 56 *Texas L.Rev.* 571, 574 (1978); Donald A. Ritchie, *James M. Landis: Dean of the Regulators,* 84 (Cambridge: Harv. Univ. Press, 1980).

the new ruling to discharge nearly three hundred sit-downers. The Labor Department reported only one sit-down for March 1939, the month after *Fansteel*, and zero sit-downs for each month from April through December 1939, the last month for which statistics were kept. Subsequent factory occupations were rare, although militant workers did manage to win a few as late as the mid-1950s.[120] While *Jones & Laughlin* had reduced the factory occupation from a routine to an exceptional but still usable tactic, *Fansteel* all but eliminated it.

Most sit-downs, however, were quickies—brief, usually departmentally based actions that rarely involved excluding management from the premises. These quickies shaded imperceptibly into other forms of shop-floor action. Workers staged slowdowns, for example, setting the pace of production at the level that they felt they were being paid for. They also conducted intermittent or "stop-and-go" strikes—short, repeated strikes intended to reduce production without providing the employer an opportunity to hire replacements. Using such tactics, industrial workers continued to enact and enforce production standards and other unilateral rules.[121] Early NLRB decisions held many such partial strike tactics protected. None of them violated the criminal law. Nevertheless, as recounted by Craig Becker, *Fansteel* was soon interpreted "to stand for the sweeping proposition that not all work stoppages—even those unaccompanied by other acts and otherwise lawful—were protected." Applying this approach, the courts and—later—the Board itself overturned early Board decisions protecting partial strikes.[122]

In the long run, *Fansteel* and its progeny contributed to the development of what labor historian David Brody has called "the workplace rule of law"—a regime characterized by detailed collective bargaining agreements, grievance procedures culminating in binding arbitration, and an obligation on the part of unions and workers to acquiesce in employer violations of the contract pending an arbitration award. In place of the open, union-backed production standards and shop rules that emerged in the late 1930s, workers were forced back to the kind of informal, shop-group rulemaking and enforcement that predated the rise of the CIO. As Brody points out, the contractualist rule of law "effectively forestalled the institutionalization of shop-group activity." By denying legitimacy to shop-floor legislation and action, this workplace rule of law "ate at the vitals of the shop-floor impulse." American workers might engage in pressure tactics, but, as Sumner Slichter remarked, they knew they were breaking the rules. It would be hard to imagine a more insidious check on so fundamental a phenomenon as the self-activity of the work group."[123] Along with the shop-floor impulse went the capacity of industrial workers to engage in unilateral lawmaking. And along with that capacity went the active participation, solidaristic spirit, and loyalty of rank-and-file union members. But that is a story for another time.[124]

---

120. Eisenberg, "Government Policy," 316–18; *NYT*, 18 (Mar. 3, 1939); *Federated Press*, 2 (Nov. 3, 1949); *Federated Press*, 2 (Jan. 8, 1954); *Federated Press*, 3 (Oct. 14, 1954); *Federated Press*, 2 (Nov. 17, 1954).

121. *See, e.g.*, Nelson Lichtenstein, "Life at the Rouge: A Cycle of Workers' Control," in Charles Stephenson & Robert Asher, eds., *Life and Labor: Dimensions of American Working-Class History*, 237, 242–43 (Albany: State U. of New York Press, 1986); Harold S. Roberts, *The Rubber Workers*, 254 (New York: Harper & Bros., 1944); Sumner H. Slichter, James J. Healy & E. Robert Livernash, *The Impact of Collective Bargaining On Management* 667, 670 (Washington: Brookings, 1960).

122. Craig Becker, "'Better Than a Strike': Protecting New Forms of Collective Work Stoppages under the National Labor Relations Act," 61 *U. Chic. L. Rev.* 351, 368–69 nn.77, 83 (1994).

123. Brody, *Workers in Industrial America*, 206, 199–207; see also Gartman, *Auto Slavery*, 268–80.

124. For one version of that story, and citations to others, *see* James Gray Pope, *Class Conflicts of Law I: Unilateral Worker Lawmaking versus Unilateral Employer Lawmaking in the U.S. Workplace*, 56 *Buff. L. Rev.* 1095–1127 (2008); *Class Conflicts of Law II: Solidarity, Entrepreneurship, and the Deep Agenda of the Obama NLRB*, 56 *Buff. L. Rev.* 653–84 (2009).

XII

The Duty to Obey:
Sit-Down at Sea, or Mutiny?

Southern Steamship Co. Warehouse and Docks.

Mutiny, Shipboard Strikes, and the Supreme Court's Subversion of New Deal Labor Law (1938)

Ahmed A. White*

I. Introduction

The National Labor Relations Act, or Wagner Act, of 1935 was by no means fundamentally radical; it did not in any way portend the destruction of private property, wage labor, or capitalism. At the same time, the Wagner Act was a remarkably progressive legal document, consistent with a genuinely reformist vision of labor relations. It could be read to support effective rights to organize, strike, and compel collective bargaining, to sanction a vibrant labor movement, and even to endorse a truly progressive regime of "industrial democracy."[1]

As Karl Klare states, the Roosevelt Court of the late 1930s and early 1940s took up "the task of plotting the contours of the nation's new labor law." As it carried out this funda-

* This chapter first appeared as a portion of an article in 25 *Berkeley J. of E. & L. Law* 275 (2004). It is reprinted with the permission of the Journal and the Regents of the University of California.

1. Karl E. Klare, *Judicial Deradicalization of the Wagner Act and the Origins of Modern Legal Consciousness, 1937–1941*, 62 MINN. L. REV. 265, 284–85 (1978).

mentally political project, the Court "shaped the ideological and institutional architecture of the modern capitalist workplace."[2] In a handful of decisions, the Court essentially purged the Act of its more reformist tendencies.[3] *Southern Steamship Co. v. NLRB*,[4] helped to define the meaning of post-New Deal labor law.[5]

On the morning of July 18, 1938, just as the *City of Fort Worth* prepared to embark from the Port of Houston bound for its home in Philadelphia, thirteen crewmen, all members of the radical and militant National Maritime Union (NMU), struck to protest their employer's unfair labor practices: its refusal to recognize and bargain with their union. The strikers remained aboard ship throughout and their refusal to work successfully prevented the ship from sailing. But the strike was free of any violence and did not entail any threat to the ship's safety or any interference with its primary functions. Indeed, the whole affair was rather tame; by the end of the day, the dispute was temporarily resolved and the ship was under way. Although the ship had no further labor troubles of any kind during the voyage, when the *City of Fort Worth* reached Philadelphia, the ship's officers discharged five crewmen who had played an active role in the strike. This, it seemed at the time, constituted another violation of the Wagner Act and in the view of the union, the Board, and the Third Circuit Court of Appeals, clearly warranted the standard remedies of reinstating the fired strikers and awarding them back pay. But when the matter was finally decided by the Supreme Court, the Court found against the Board and the seamen.[6] It held that a shipboard strike constituted an act of mutiny, a felony under federal law, that the strike aboard the *City of Fort Worth* was illegal and unprotected, and that the Board therefore could not remedy the discharges by ordering that the seamen be reinstated and provided back pay.[7]

---

2. Klare, *supra* note 1, at 291–92.

3. *Ibid.* at 297–99. For example, in the very case in which it upheld the Act's constitutionality, the Court broadly affirmed a traditional doctrine of freedom of contract. *NLRB v. Jones & Laughlin Steel Corp.*, 301 U.S. 1 (1937). Elsewhere, it confirmed the prerogative of employers to permanently replace so-called "economic strikers" and generally to resort freely to their economic advantages over workers in labor disputes. *NLRB v. Mackay Radio & Tel. Co.*, 304 U.S. 333 (1938). The Court declared the sit-down strike illegal and unprotected by the Act. *NLRB v. Fansteel Metallurgical Corp.*, 306 U.S. 240 (1939). It declared unprotected by the Act a strike undertaken during the term of a collective bargaining agreement, where the strike could be characterized as an attempt to modify the agreement. *NLRB v. Sands Mfg. Co.*, 306 U.S. 332 (1939). And in a particularly confused opinion, the Court limited the authority of the National Labor Relations Board (Board) to afford workers remedies under the Act. *Phelps Dodge Corp. v. NLRB*, 313 U.S. 177 (1941).

4. 316 U.S. 51 (1942).

5. Most recent references to *Southern Steamship* concern the important role it played in the *Hoffman Plastic Compounds* decision. 585 U.S. 137 (2000). Even these references, though, are uniformly brief and say little about the substance of *Southern Steamship* itself. See, e.g., Michael J. Wishnie, "Emerging Issues for Undocumented Workers," 6 *U. Pa. J. Lab. & Emp. L.* 497, 500 (2004); Christopher David Ruiz Cameron, "Borderline Decisions: *Hoffman Plastic Compounds*, The New Bracero Program, and the Supreme Court's Role in Making Federal Labor Policy," 51 *UCLA L.Rev.* 1, 9–10 (2003).

6. An important point about the term "seamen" should be made at the outset. Seamen is a term of art, albeit one subject to somewhat varied definition. As I use the term here, it denotes shipboard workers generally, but so-called "unlicensed" personnel in particular. Through the Great Depression, this class of shipboard workers included members of the deck crew, including "deck boys," able-bodied seamen, and boatswains; members of the engine department, including "trimmers," "oilers," "stokers," and engineers; and the catering crew, meaning mainly stewards and cooks. Not included are the so-called "executive departments": the chief engineer; the chief steward; the mates; and the captain, or "master." I avoid the term "sailor," as it usually denotes only those seamen who are part of a vessel's deck crew. *See* James C. Healey, *Foc'S'Le and Glory-Hole: A Study of the Merchant Seamen and His Occupation*, 6–10, 18–38 (1936). As we shall see, the strike aboard the *City of Fort Worth* involved unlicensed personnel, who were the mainstay of the NMU's membership.

7. *S. S.S. Co. v. NLRB*, 316 U.S. 51 (1942).

Prior to capitalism's penetration of the maritime world in the seventeenth and early eighteenth centuries, medieval shipboard life was dominated by norms of paternalism, reciprocity, and stability. As in other contexts, the rise of capitalism displaced these medieval norms with a dynamic, profit-driven logic of commodification and accumulation. This transformation was at its most salient with respect to labor relations. While medieval norms often encouraged enduring and mutually supportive relationships between a seaman and his captain, capitalism replaced this with a system of anonymous and transitory contracts, mediated by money wages, and largely devoid of any kind of security against loss or injury.[8] As this transformation unfolded, the seaman's worth was radically recast in terms of the relationship between the costs of maintaining him in wages and accommodations, on the one hand, and the value of his work to a commercially successful voyage, on the other.[9] A hard-driven crew and a hard-driven ship, which would likely have constituted serious transgressions of medieval workplace norms, now appeared as legitimate — in fact, from the vantage of ship owners, desirable—methods to achieve a more profitable voyage.[10]

As a result of these constructions, any seamen who collectively refused the captain's orders were subject to conviction of mutiny.

A. The Strike Aboard the City of Fort Worth

Southern Steamship Company was one of the fifty or so companies named by the ISU in its fatal petition to the NLRB to hold representation elections.[11] The company, a Delaware corporation based in Philadelphia, operated seven ships, all of which sailed regular routes between Houston and Philadelphia.[12] Prior to the Board election, which was held in October 1937, the ISU held a contract with Southern Steamship. But in the Board's opinion the ISU had waived any rights of incumbency under the contract by filing the petition.[13] In any case, the NMU's victory over the ISU among Southern Steamship em-

---

8. I do not mean to idealize the condition of medieval shipboard labor, which was characterized by its own kinds of unpleasantness: social immobility, material poverty, parochialism, and the like. Rather, in drawing the contrast between the modern and the medieval, I mean to show the unique ways in which the penetration of capitalism made the condition of shipboard labor not only unpleasant, but unpleasant *and* immersed in class conflict. All the same, the cooperative moral economy of medieval seafaring is clearly suggested in the *French Laws of Oleron* and the *Barcelona Maritime Code*, both of which emerged in the Thirteenth Century. They provided, among other things, for the captain to submit important decisions to crew for approval, for the distribution of risks and gain between captain and crew, for the captain to care for lost or injured seamen, and for mutual defense and support generally.

9. With very few exceptions, the modern maritime world from its advent through the mid-twentieth century was composed entirely of men. For this reason alone, I use male pronouns throughout this article.

10. On the contradictory social structure of the modern ship and its origins, *see* Peter Linebaugh & Marcus Rediker, *The Many-Headed Hydra: Sailors, Slaves, Commoners, and the Hidden History of the Revolutionary Atlantic,* 149–53 (2000) [hereinafter Linebaugh & Rediker].

11. *Am. France Line*, 3 N.L.R.B. 64 (1937).

12. In 1937, these vessels carried 341,581 tons of cargo. They were not large. All seven totaled only 18,382 gross tons (a measure of cargo capacity by volume)—compared to over 7,000 gross tons for a single Second World War "Liberty Ship' and over 80,000 gross tons for the passenger liner *Queen Elizabeth*, launched the same year as the strike aboard *the City of Fort Worth*. This information emerges from the Board's fact-finding for decisions involving the company. *S. S.S. Co.*, 12 N.L.R.B. 1088, 1089 (1939); *S. S.S. Co.*, 23 N.L.R.B. 26, 29 (1940). The *City of Fort Worth* itself was apparently a general cargo vessel constructed in 1919 by the McDougall-Duluth Company at Duluth, Minnesota, for the United States Shipping Board. Originally named *La Crosse*, it was renamed in 1925.

13. *Am. France Line*, 3 N.L.R.B. at 71.

ployees was decisive. Out of 134 eligible voters, 132 cast ballots; of the 128 ballots that were counted, 73 were for NMU representation, 51 for neither the NMU nor the ISU, and only 4 for the ISU.[14]

Southern Steamship immediately challenged the results of the election on the grounds that its representative was not present for the vote on one of its ships, the *City of Houston*.[15] Despite the fact that the Board rejected this claim out of hand, the company refused to recognize the union. Between late January 1938, when the Board affirmed the NMU's representative status, and August 1938, after the strike aboard the *City of Fort Worth*, the NMU's Philadelphia business agent, Paul Palazzi, made repeated attempts by letter and phone, and in person, to initiate bargaining with Southern Steamship officials and to obtain shore passes. The company either ignored or refused each request.[16]

The decision to strike Southern Steamship in order to force it to recognize the NMU and to grant the shore passes was made on July 17, 1938, by thirteen crewmen from the *City of Fort Worth* who had met in a Houston union hall to discuss the matter. They represented over half of the "unlicensed" seamen—the non-officers over whom the NMU enjoyed representative status—of the crew. At 8:00 a.m. the next morning, one of these men, John J. Tracey "failed to turn on the steam" to the machinery needed to load the ship's cargo. When the ship's assistant engineer turned it on himself, Tracey had another crewman "throw the pumps." Eventually the ship's officers and the six seamen who did not strike got the steam up. But in the meantime the thirteen strikers gathered on the poop deck, which served as the crew's "general meeting place" when not on duty, and refused to do any further work.[17]

While the *City of Fort Worth's* officers managed to load its cargo, they could not get the ship under way as long as the strike continued. At 10:30 a.m. the captain recited a copy of the *strikers'* shipping articles and demanded that they return to work. Their spokesman, Joseph Warren, responded by reiterating the strikers' demands and pointing out to the captain that the law—the Wagner Act—was actually in the strikers' favor. Later that morning, the captain summoned to the ship the deputy United States Shipping Commissioner, who also recited the articles, but to no avail.[18] The strike continued through the afternoon, during which time the strikers were allowed to remain on board the ship. In fact they were all allowed their lunch and some of them were permitted to go ashore to con-

---

14. *Am. France Line*, 4 N.L.R.B. 1140, 1141 (1938).

15. The Board found that Southern Steamship had no right to observe the election. In any case, both the ISU and NMU consented to the presence of company representatives at subsequent elections aboard the other ships. *Am. France Line*, 4 N.L.R.B. at 1141. In 1939, the Board found that Southern Steamship had unlawfully discharged and refused to reinstate the chief engineer of the *City of Philadelphia*, who was a member of the Marine Engineers Beneficial Association, which was allied with the NMU, for his participation in one of the strikes of 1936. The employee, one Max Starke, had an exemplary service record and was recommended by the captain of the *City of Philadelphia* for reinstatement. He was also the last of the crew to go out on strike, having remained on board for several days after the strike commenced. *S. S.S. Co.*, 12 N.L.R.B. at 1090–91.

16. *S. S.S. Co.*, 23 N.L.R.B. at 31–32; Transcript of Record at 90–121, *S. S.S. Co. v. NLRB*, 316 U.S. 31 (1942) (No. 320).

17. *S. S.S. Co.*, 23 N.L.R.B. at 33. Tracey and the other four seamen, who would be discharged when the ship reached Philadelphia, were delegates or otherwise active in the union's organizing campaign. Transcript of Record at 127–29, *S. S.S. Co. v. NLRB*, 316 U.S. 31 (1942) (No. 320).

18. *S. S.S. Co.*, 23 N.L.R.B. at 33–34 (1940); Transcript of Record at 162–63, 436–40, *S. S.S. Co. v. NLRB*, 316 U.S. 31 (1942) (No.320). Warren did not testify; but according to fellow striker John Pfuhl, Jr., Warren told the captain, "We realize we are under articles, but we are alongside the dock of an American port, safely moored, and we are on strike, and we have a right to strike." Transcript of Record, at 220, *S. S.S. Co. v. NLRB*, 316 U.S. 31 (1942) (No. 320).

fer with the union's shore delegates.[19] During the meantime, negotiations began between the attorneys of Southern Steamship and the NMU. By 7:00 p.m., Southern Steamship's attorney had promised that if the strike were ended, collective bargaining would begin the following week and shore passes would be granted. As soon as this information was communicated to the strikers, they returned to work and at 9:00 p.m. the *City of Fort Worth* set sail for Philadelphia.[20]

According to subsequent findings by the Board, "the officers on board admitted that the strike did not delay the [ship's] sailing and that the vessel was in no danger during the period of the strike."[21] In fact, the strikers had conceived the strike such that it would not result in violence or danger to the ship.[22] Moreover, during the passage to Philadelphia, the strikers "conducted themselves in a competent manner." The captain had no complaints to make about them. Other officers admitted that the crew was "good" and "safe" during the trip. Indeed, one officer proposed to the "boys" that they "forget all about what happened." Unbeknownst to the strikers, who nonetheless anticipated trouble, Southern Steamship's attorney had given them a promise which he had not cleared with either the company's marine superintendent or its president and which the company had no intention of fulfilling. Moreover, the captain and his officers were not inclined to "forget all about" the strike. Before the ship reached Philadelphia, the ship's officers decided to refuse to re-ship five of the strikers, which they carried out as soon as the ship arrived on July 25. Acting on a prior agreement, all but one of the original strikers then struck the ship in protest; they too were discharged.[23]

B. The Southern Steamship Case: From the Board to the Supreme Court

The very next day, July 26, the NMU filed unfair labor practice charges against Southern Steamship.[24] The charges alleged that by refusing to bargain with the NMU, Southern Steamship violated 8(5) of the Wagner Act, that by discharging and refusing to reinstate the strikers, it violated 8(3) of the Act, and that by interfering with the workers' right to organize and bargain collectively the company violated 8(1) of the Act.[25] On November 23, 1938, the NLRB's Regional Director for the Fourth Region issued a formal complaint based on these charges. In December 1938 and January 1939, several days of hearings were held on these charges, first in Philadelphia, then in Houston, before a trial examiner. In February 1939, the trial examiner ruled against Southern Steamship on all charges and recommended that it be ordered to cease and desist from its unfair labor practices, that upon application, it reinstate four of the five seamen[26] discharged for their partici-

19. Transcript of Record, at 1142–42, *S. S.S. Co. v. NLRB*, 316 U.S. 31 (1942) (No. 320).

20. *S. S.S. Co.*, 23 N.L.R.B. at 33–34.

21. *Ibid.* at 33–34.

22. According to Tracey, the seaman whose actions initiated the strike, "It was to be conducted very orderly, no violence whatsoever, just tell them what we want [recognition], and if we didn't get it, we were going to sit down. We were going to keep steam in all of our auxiliaries, and if they put steam on the deck, we were going to shut down on them, we were not going to give them no steam." Transcript of Record at 130–31, *S. S.S. Co. v. NLRB*, 316 U.S. 31 (1942) (No. 320).

23. *S. S.S. Co.*, 23 N.L.R.B. 26, 34–35 (1940). *See* also Transcript of Record at 60–85, 150–58, 244, *S. S.S. Co. v. NLRB*, 316 U.S. 31 (1942) (No. 320).

24. These charges were amended on November 22, the day before the Board issued a formal complaint. (The changes mainly added factual information. They did not alter the basic substance of the ULP claims.)

25. *S. S.S. Co.*, 23 N.L.R.B. 26, 27 (1940). These provisions now constitute 8(a)(1), (3), and (5) of the National Labor Relations Act, 49 Stat. 499 (1935), as amended; 29 U.S.C.A. 158(a) (1988).

26. The trial examiner agreed with Southern Steamship's contention that the fifth seamen, John Pfuhl, Jr., was unfit for reinstatment because he was a "slow worker" and had a petty larceny record. The Board, citing Pfuhl's long and apparently effective service with the company, rejected this con-

pation in the July 18 strike and offer all five of them back pay, and that it also reinstate with back pay those discharged for the July 25 strike.[27] Southern Steamship promptly filed exceptions and the Board granted a full hearing with oral arguments, which was held on November 2, 1939.

Southern Steamship's arguments before the Board, which would frame the later litigation of the case, essentially consisted of the following contentions. First, regarding its refusal to recognize and bargain with the NMU, Southern Steamship claimed that the NMU had made no demand to bargain before the July 18 strike, that the strike, because unlawful, negated any obligation to bargain, and that in any case it had no obligation to bargain pending a judicial hearing on its earlier objections to the representation election. Second, regarding the discharges, the company argued that the discharged seamen's shipping articles, which like most articles[28] expired upon the vessel completing its voyage, terminated the seamen's employment, so that there could be no claim of unfair discharges. Third, again regarding the discharges, Southern Steamship argued that the July 18 strikers engaged in a sit-down strike by which they "took possession" of the ship, trespassed upon it, and stirred up disobedience among the crew; by so doing, the company claimed, the strikers forfeited any right to continued employment. With this, the company clearly hoped to invoke the rule just announced by the Supreme Court in *Fansteel* casting sit-down strikers outside the protection of the labor law.[29] As to its discharge of the July 25 strikers, the company raised no clear defense, although it would subsequently suggest that they had not been discharged but had simply "voluntarily left the ship" and not returned.[30] Finally, Southern Steamship claimed that the July 18 strikers violated the terms of their shipping articles, thereby committing a breach of contract that justified the company's refusal to re-ship them.[31]

In a unanimous decision released April 23, 1940, the Board rejected each of these contentions.[32] On the issue of recognition, the Board noted that it had already resolved the

---

clusion and ordered that Pfuhl also be offered reinstatement. *S. S.S. Co.*, 23 N.L.R.B. at 41–42, 44–45, 47–48.

27. *S. S.S. Co.*, 23 N.L.R.B. at 28. *See also* "NLRB Aide Backs Ship Crew's Strike," *N.Y. Times*, S9 (Mar. 5, 1939).

28. Shipping articles, which are statutorily required of all seamen, may be of two types: continuous articles, which continue over a definite time period, and voyage articles, which describe a particular voyage. *See* Norris, *supra* note 71, at 6:11. Most seamen in the 1930s, including those aboard the *City of Fort Worth*, sailed under voyage articles.

29. *NLRB v. Fansteel Metallurgical Corp.*, 306 U.S. 240 (1939). The Court decided *Fansteel* on February 27, 1939.

30. Brief of Petitioner at 6, *S. S.S. Co. v. NLRB*, 316 U.S. 31 (1942) (No. 320). It is possible that Southern Steamship also felt that the status of the July 25 strikers was contingent on that of the July 18 strike. This was apparently the Board's view as well. Although it is nowhere entirely clear on this question, the Board seemed to hold that if the July 18 strike was legal, then the July 25 strike was as well, and the discharge of the July 25 strikers an unfair labor practice. *S. S.S. Co.*, 23 N.L.R.B. at 44–45. In any case, the status of the July 18 strike was throughout the most important question for all involved.

31. *S. S.S. Co.*, 23 N.L.R.B. at 38–39. Southern Steamship also alleged that it had alternative reasons, unconnected to the strike, to discharge each of the July 18 strikers. But these reasons were not taken seriously by the trial examiner (except with respect to one striker, John Pfuhl, Jr.), the Board (which reversed the trial examiner on that one striker), or the courts. *Ibid.* at 40–43; *S. S.S. Co. v. NLRB*, 120 F.2d 505, 508 (3d Cir. 1941). The matter was not raised by Southern Steamship before the Supreme Court. *See* Brief of Petitioner, *S. S.S. Co. v. NLRB*, 316 U.S. 31 (1942) (No. 320); Transcript of Record at 68–75, *S. S.S. Co. v. NLRB*, 316 U.S. 31 (1942) (No. 320).

32. "NLRB Rules Sitting on Deck Not a Sit-Down; Orders Pay for Five Seamen From July, 1938," *N.Y. Times*, 14 (Apr. 24, 1940).

representation issue in an earlier decision in which it emphasized that the company had no right to participate in representation proceedings. Furthermore, the Board held, the NMU's agent had made repeated efforts before the *City of Fort Worth* strike to bargain with the company.[33] Moving to the issues regarding the strikes, the shipping articles, and the subsequent discharges, the Board, citing an earlier decision upheld by the Supreme Court, held that the shipping articles did not conclusively define seamen's tenure of employment. Indeed, it noted that the *City of Fort Worth* crew, including all the discharged strikers, had worked under a clear presumption of continuous employment and that relative to employment tenure, the articles were therefore an irrelevant formality.[34] The Board was also firm in its view that the July 18 strike was not illegal. Noting first that the strike was caused by Southern Steamship's own illegal act, its refusal to bargain, the Board also emphasized that the strike was not actually a sit-down strike. The July 18 strikers did not seize, take possession of, or otherwise jeopardize the ship; they were not violent and were apparently never ordered to leave the ship;[35] and in remaining on board during the strike they were, in a very real sense, simply retiring to their home.[36] Accordingly, the Board construed the July 18 strike as a lawful protest of Southern Steamship's continuing unfair labor practice, its refusal to bargain with the NMU. Likewise, the July 25 strike was a lawful protest of that unfair labor practice as well as another, the discharge of the July 18 strikers.[37] Finally, the Board rejected Southern Steamship's breach of contract argument. The Board acknowledged that the July 18 strike contravened a covenant of the shipping articles but pointed out that this would often be the case with any kind of individual employment contracts and that—consistent with the anti-yellow dog contract provisions of the Wagner and Norris-LaGuardia acts—such contracts must necessarily yield on many occasions to a meaningful right to strike. Because the July 18 strike in this case was legal, a contractual promise not to strike would not control.[38]

After rejecting all of Southern Steamship's arguments, the Board upheld the trial examiner's findings that the company had committed several violations of the law. It held unequivocally that Southern Steamship violated 8(5) of the Wagner Act by its persistent refusal to recognize and bargain with the NMU. The Board held further that both the July 18 and July 25 strikes were legal and "protected" within the meaning of 7 of the Act. As such, the company's discharges, because motivated by the workers' participation in those protected strikes, were unfair labor practices under 8(1) and (3) of the Act and,

---

33. *S. S.S. Co.*, 23 NLRB at 29–31.

34. It was customary for Southern Steamship to have its seamen sign new articles at the conclusion of a voyage at the same time that they signed off on the old articles. Even if for some reason this did not happen, the seamen considered themselves employed for the next voyage unless specific notice to the contrary was given. *Ibid.* at 36. The Supreme Court upheld the Board's view of this issue in a very similar case. *NLRB v. Waterman S.S. Corp.*, 309 U.S. 206 (1940).

35. The Board's finding that the strikers were never ordered to leave the ship remained a matter of minor controversy throughout the litigation. There was some testimony from one of the strikers —Tracey—that they were asked to leave the ship. Transcript of Record at 140–42, *S. S.S. Co. v. NLRB*, 316 U.S. 31 (1942) (No. 320). No other striker testified to this effect. And Tracey's testimony, while not overly contradictory, is inconsistent with the other strikers on less controversial issues—including Warren's response to the Captain's demand to get back to work, which Tracey alone did not recall occurring. *Ibid.* at 138–39. In any case, the Board was not swayed by his reference to the command to leave the ship.

36. *S. S.S. Co.*, 23 N.L.R.B. at 37–38.

37. *Ibid.* at 34–35, 44–45.

38. *Ibid.* at 38–39. The Board's view of the relationship between statutory rights and individual employment contracts was inherent in depriving yellow dog contracts of any legal effect, which was clearly a major aim of the Act.

along with the 8(5) violation, subject to remedy under 10(c). With only minor alterations, the Board then upheld the trial examiner's remedies ordering Southern Steamship to cease and desist from its unfair labor practices, to recognize and bargain with the NMU, and to reinstate all of the discharged strikers with back pay—all standard remedies for the unfair labor practices the company was found to have committed.[39]

In April 1940, Southern Steamship appealed the Board's decision to the Third Circuit.[40] A year later the court issued a ruling on the matter in which it not only agreed with the Board on every important point, but substantially followed the Board's reasoning.[41] On the issue that would be central to the Supreme Court—the legality of the July 18 strike—the court admitted that the issue was "still an open one," with the law's traditional prohibition of shipboard strikes running up against an expanding regime of labor rights from which seamen were not obviously excluded. Other courts, the majority noted, had recently decided the issue in seemingly conflicting ways.[42] But upon closer analysis the court discerned a consistent theme in these cases that clearly supported the Board's decision. While shipboard strikes that were violent, that involved taking possession of the ship or otherwise substantially interfering with its operations, that occurred at sea or in a foreign port, or that otherwise put the ship in jeopardy, had all been found illegal and unprotected—and in the court's view, quite properly so—strikes such as the one aboard the *City of Fort Worth*, which were in every way different, were treated very differently by the courts.[43] Furthermore, although the court took note of *Fansteel*, it followed the Board in refusing to declare the *City of Fort Worth* strike a sit-down strike within the meaning of that decision. Instead, it referred to the *Fansteel* decision only for the proposition that "[i]f the strikers had been guilty of criminal acts of violence or of forcible detainer of the vessel" their discharge would be warranted.[44] Inasmuch as the *Fansteel* strikers had taken control of their factory for over a week, had held off the police in open combat, and were eventually convicted of various crimes of violence, this distinction seems quite apt.[45] Further, the court held, if the July 18 strike had indeed taken place in a manner that imperiled the vessel—for example at sea or in an "unsafe port"—then perhaps the strike "might well have transcended the bounds of action in a labor dispute and have constituted a revolt or mutiny."[46] In the absence of this or any other reason to deem the strike illegal, the court upheld the Board's unfair labor practice findings as well as its remedies.

The company's brief candidly challenged seamen's right to strike altogether and did so by invoking a traditional view of shipboard authority. Appealing to tried and true notions of shipboard paternalism, the company argued that seamen enjoy a "special relationship"

---

39. *Ibid.* at 44–45. The most important change made by the Board was to order that the fifth seaman, John Pfuhl, Jr., whom the trial examiner had denied reinstatement because of his alleged inefficiency, be offered this remedy as well.

40. Transcript of Record at 1–13, *S. S.S. Co. v. NLRB*, 316 U.S. 31 (1942) (No. 320).

41. *S. S.S. Co. v. NLRB*, 120 F.2d 505 (3d Cir. 1941).

42. *Ibid.* at 510.

43. *Ibid.* at 509–11. In particular, the court contrasted the results in *Weisthoff v. Am. Hawaiian S.S. Co.*, 79 F.2d 124 (2d Cir. 1935) and *Black Diamond S.S. Corp. v. NLRB*, 94 F.2d 875 (2nd Cir. 1938), with *Rees v. United States*, 95 F.2d 792 (4th Cir. 1938) and *Peninsular & Occidental S.S. Co. v. NLRB* (5th Cir. 1938).

44. *S. S.S. Co. v. NLRB*, 120 F.2d 505, 509 (3rd Circuit 1941).

45. On the events that led to the *Fansteel* decision, see, for example, Henry M. Hart, Jr. & Edward F. Prichard, Jr., "The Fansteel Case: Employee Misconduct and the Remedial Powers of the National Labor Relations Board," 52 *Harv. L. Rev.* 1275, 1289–91 (1939).

46. *S. S.S. Co.*, 120 F.2d at 509.

to their "master," one that "has not materially changed notwithstanding the vast changes in industrial pursuits on shore."[47] As a natural reflection of this relationship, the ship must be a "disciplined organization." And discipline must be maintained "at all times wheresoever the ship may be — in port or at sea."[48] For this reason a strike aboard ship could never be countenanced, except possibly in the vessel's home port.[49] Even more remarkably, Southern Steamship specifically described mutiny law as designed to preserve traditional authority against the threat of shipboard strikes and the expansion of worker rights in the workplace generally.[50]

The Board, as well as the NMU, which had intervened in the case, focused their arguments on countering the notion that the strike was illegal.[51] Both took issue with Southern Steamship's paternalistic premise that seamen are a group deserving this kind of special treatment. In their briefs, the Board and the NMU pointed out that Congress had every opportunity to incorporate such an exceptional view of seamen into the Wagner Act — for example, by excluding them from coverage, as it had done with several other categories of workers — and obviously declined to do so.[52] This suggested a broad intent to give seamen the same labor rights as other, shoreside workers.[53] Turning to the notion that the July 18 strikers had committed mutiny and that this negated their right to strike, the respondent parties raised several very plausible arguments. The Board noted that recent case law revealed a growing reluctance among courts to treat peaceful, safe shipboard strikes aboard dockside ships as mutinies.[54] This contention was advanced with even more force by the NMU, which observed that every one of the cases cited by Southern Steamship for the notion that peaceful, dockside shipboard strikes are mutinous — or at least every one that clearly supported this notion — was not only distinguishable on the facts but also was an archaic decision decided before labor of any kind enjoyed meaningful rights of protest.[55]

The Board also observed that while the law once contained provisions that did seem explicitly to criminalize peaceful, dockside strikes — the "willful disobedience" provisions of the 1872 Shipping Commissioners Act — Congress in 1898 had amended these provisions in such a way that they clearly no longer applied to the strike in question.[56] If Congress had intended the mutiny law to apply to strikes like the one aboard the *City of Fort*

---

47. *Ibid.* at 12.

48. *Ibid.* at 25.

49. *Ibid.* at 23–24 & n.21.

50. For good measure, the company also suggested that shipboard strikes would undermine the country's vital interest in a strong merchant marine, a matter whose importance was underscored by the country's entrance into the Second World War. *Ibid.* at 9–27.

51. No doubt appreciating the weakness of Southern Steamship's claims on these issues, neither the Board nor the NMU focused much on the representation question or the shipping articles. Their arguments essentially repeated those made before the Board and the Third Circuit. Brief of Respondent at 59–61, *S. S.S. Co. v. NLRB*, 316 U.S. 31 (1942) (No. 320); Brief of the Nat'l Mar. Union at 13–21, *S. S.S. Co. v. NLRB*, 316 U.S. 31 (1942) (No. 320).

52. Brief for the Nat'l Mar. Union at 42, *S. S.S. Co. v. NLRB*, 316 U.S. 31 (1942) (No. 320).

53. *See* Brief of Respondent at 23–24, *S. S.S. Co. v. NLRB*, 316 U.S. 31 (1942) (No. 320).

54. *Ibid.* at 41–52.

55. Brief for the Nat'l Mar. Union at 26–40, *S. S.S. Co. v. NLRB*, 316 U.S. 31 (1942) (No. 320).

56. Section 51 of the Shipping Commissioners Act had created several crimes of "willful disobedience," including one that specifically referred to willful disobedience by "combining with others." *See supra* note 40. The Maguire Act of 1898 eliminated the last of these altogether and amended the other provisions such that they applied only to conduct occurring "at sea." Brief of Respondent at 28–29, *S. S.S. Co. v. NLRB*, 316 U.S. 31 (1942) (No. 320).

Worth, the Board argued, there would have been no need to enact these provisions of the Shipping Commissioners Act in first place—let alone to repeal them.[57]

Litigating in the wake of *Fansteel*, the Board and the NMU were also keen to show that the July 18 strike was not a sit-down strike and was not as a matter of course illegal under that ruling. In their briefs, both emphasized the points they and the Third Circuit had raised below in distinguishing this strike from *Fansteel*: that the strike was non-violent and did not involve taking possession of the ship; that the ship was never endangered; that the ship's interests were not substantially prejudiced; and that the strikers were never even ordered to leave the ship.[58] Indeed, as the Board's brief was especially concerned to underscore, the real issue in *Fansteel* had little to do with the workers sitting down as such and instead involved the "illegal seizure and retention of the plant by force and violence and the refusal of the strikers to permit the owner to enter its property."[59] In essence, both the union and the Board argued, all that the *City of Fort Worth* strikers did was refuse to work at a time not critical to the well-being of the ship or its crew; and rather than sitting down on the job, let alone seizing control of the workplace, what they really did was tantamount simply to staying home.[60] On the other hand, they noted that if such a strike was illegal under the mutiny law, and if Southern Steamship's argument that the shipping articles alone determine tenure of employment prevailed, seamen would be left with no meaningful right to strike at all.[61] Moreover, even if the strike was illegal under *Fansteel* or the mutiny statute, the issue here was whether it was nonetheless protected—and technical or minor violations of the law need not be taken to cause strikers to forfeit their rights under the labor law.[62]

The Supreme Court decided *Southern Steamship* by a five-to-four vote, with the majority opinion written by Justice James Byrnes, a Franklin D. Roosevelt appointee from South Carolina who served only one term on the Court.[63] Byrnes began his opinion by summarily rejecting Southern Steamship's argument that it had a right to be present during voting and that the denial of that right vitiated the election results. He just as quickly dispensed with the company's claim that the shipping articles established the seamen's tenure of employment. On each point, Byrnes refused to set aside the Board's and the Third Circuit's rulings.[64] Indeed for Byrnes, the only real question was whether the Board had exceeded it remedial authority under 10(c) in ordering the reinstatement of the July 18 strikers. As Byrnes understood the case, reaching an answer to this question required the Court to determine first, whether the strike was legal and protected under 7, and second, whether the discharges were therefore violations of 8(1) and (3).

---

57. Brief of Respondent at 36–38, *S. S.S. Co. v. NLRB*, 316 U.S. 31 (1942) (No. 320). The Board also noted that 20 of the Clayton Act seemed to express the intent by Congress that mutiny law not be applied in labor disputes in the first place. *Ibid.* at 36 & n.21.

58. *Ibid.* at 9–21, *S. S.S. Co. v. NLRB*, 316 U.S. 31 (1942) (No. 320); Brief for the Nat'l Mar. Union at 22–28, *S. S.S. Co. v. NLRB*, 316 U.S. 31 (1942) (No. 320).

59. Brief of Respondent at 20, *S. S.S. Co. v. NLRB*, 316 U.S. 31 (1942) (No. 320).

60. Indeed, the Board pointed out that had the seamen left the ship they would have committed the offense of desertion and that Southern Steamship had conceded this would have been far worse for its interests than the strike. *Ibid.* at 21 & n.12.

61. Brief of the Nat'l Mar. Union at 21–22, *S. S.S. Co. v. NLRB*, 316 U.S. 31 (1942) (No. 320).

62. Brief of Respondent at 52–58, *S. S.S. Co. v. NLRB*, 316 U.S. 31 (1942) (No. 320).

63. Byrnes, who served only a year on the court (from October 1941 to October 1942), is little known as a Justice. Before taking a seat on the Court he was a Congressman and then Senator from South Carolina. After leaving the court he served as Director of Economic Stabilization and Director of War Mobilization under Roosevelt, Secretary of State under Truman, and, finally, Governor of South Carolina. *See* David Robertson, *Sly and Able: A Political Biography of James Byrnes* (1994).

64. *S. S.S. Co.*, 316 U.S. at 37–38.

Byrnes began his analysis of that issue by expressing a view of seamen that might have come straight from Justice Story a century earlier and that left little doubt as to the way the Court would rule.

> Ever since men have gone to sea, the relationship of master to seamen has been entirely different from that of employer to employee on land. The lives of passengers and crew, as well as the safety of ship and cargo, are entrusted to the master's care. Every one and every thing depend on him. He must command and the crew must obey.[65]

For Byrnes, as for Story and indeed many other Nineteenth Century jurists, this obligation to obey was justified by the fundamentally paternalistic notion that "workers at sea have been the beneficiaries of extraordinary legislative solicitude, undoubtedly prompted by the limits upon their ability to help themselves."[66] "It is in this setting of fact and law," he continued, "that we must test the validity of the Board's order of reinstatement."[67] That part of this "extraordinary legislative solicitude" might include the Wagner Act, which was being flouted by Southern Steamship in this very case, was of no apparent concern to the Justice. Neither was the fact that the ability of seamen to "help themselves" under the Wagner Act was precisely the issue at hand.

Byrnes turned from here straight to the question of mutiny and promptly concluded that the strike aboard the *City of Fort Worth* on July 18 constituted both mutiny as such as well as conspiracy to commit mutiny. Again begging a key question, Byrnes concluded that "It may hardly be disputed that each of the strikers resisted the captain and other officers in the free and lawful exercise of their authority and command, within the meaning of 293, or that they combined and conspired to that end, within the meaning of 292."[68] In his view, the strikers "undertook to impose their will on the captain and officers."[69] And while he acknowledged that the strike may not have been violent or otherwise interfered with the ship's functions, he saw no grounds to draw a distinction along these lines. The strike prevented the ship from sailing, and this was sufficient.[70]

Citing the Board's concession that if the strike had taken place on the high seas it would no doubt be mutinous, Byrnes allowed his analysis of the mutiny question to focus on only one additional issue: the propriety of distinguishing between a shipboard strike such as this one, and other situations already deemed by the courts mutinous.[71] Although Byrnes cited a number of Nineteenth Century cases (including several authored by Story), as well as two Twentieth Century cases, for the proposition that shipboard strikes on the high seas, "in harbor," or in foreign jurisdictions were properly deemed mutinous, he admitted that no authority spoke to the issue of a strike on a ship tied to the dock in domestic waters.[72] In order to contend with this ambiguity, he then pointed to recent, unsuccessful attempts to amend the mutiny statutes that they might clearly permit shipboard strikes as evidence of prevailing legislative purpose.[73] Finally, summoning up var-

---

65. *Ibid.* at 38.
66. *Ibid.* at 39.
67. *Ibid.*
68. *Ibid.* at 40.
69. *Ibid.* at 41.
70. *Ibid.* at 40–41.
71. *Ibid.* at 41.
72. *Ibid.* at 42 & n.14.
73. *Ibid.* at 43–44. The bills to which Byrnes refers, H.R. 3427, 76th Cong. 1st Session (1939) and H.R. 3428, 76th Cong. 1st Sess. (1939), were not introduced until January 30, 1939. 84 Cong. Rec. H967 (1939).

ious speculative scenarios, Byrnes argued that a ship is never safe, even in port, and that therefore the same considerations that rendered at-sea strikes mutinous should also apply to in-port strikes.[74] For Byrnes, these were more than sufficient reasons to hold that all shipboard strikes, except perhaps those occurring in the vessel's home port, are mutinous and illegal.

There remained the Board's alternative argument that even if the strike were mutinous, it should still be protected by 7 and the discharges subject to Board remedy. The Board had raised two interconnected reasons to support this position: first, that the employer had engaged in a serious unfair labor practice; and second, that the mutiny, if one existed at all, was merely "technical." To the first reason, Byrnes responded that, "the Board has not been commissioned to effectuate the policies of the Labor Relations Act so single-mindedly that it may wholly ignore other and equally important Congressional objectives."[75] The Board, he continued, had undertaken what must be a "careful accommodation of one statutory scheme to another" in an incorrect way; it had placed "excessive emphasis on its immediate task."[76] To the Board's second reason, which referenced the strike's placid, unthreatening nature, Byrnes again speculated widely as to the possible dangers posed by the strike. He suggested that the strike's lack of violence was but a "fortunate feature of the affair" and that "as a practical matter, the *City of Fort Worth* was definitely wrested from the control of its officers."[77] Indeed, Byrnes not only rejected the idea that strikes should remain protected when merely technically violating other laws, he actually held that where the Board's use of its remedial power impinged on any other federal statute or policy which the Board itself—in the Court's view—had insufficient expertise to interpret, the Board's remedial power must yield completely.[78]

As a final matter, Byrnes attempted to address the concern so clearly raised by the NMU that the majority's ruling would deprive seamen of any real right to strike. Articulating one of *Southern Steamship's* more important themes, Byrnes steered the seamen away from the strike to the courts. He proposed that "[a]t any time following the certification of the NMU in January, 1938, the union and the Board could have secured the assistance of the courts in forcing petitioner to bargain." Had the union done this, he surmised, the "unfortunate occurrence at Houston might have been averted."[79]

Justice Stanley Reed authored a brief dissent, in which he was joined by Justices Hugo Black, William O. Douglas, and Frank Murphy.[80] Perhaps the most notable feature of Reed's dissent is that it does not challenge the majority's view that the strike was an act of mutiny. Instead Reed assumed this to be true and focused his entire argument on criticizing the majority's notion that such an unlawful act negates the Board's remedial au-

---

74. *Ibid.* at 46. Byrnes argued that "it is by no means clear that a ship moored to a dock is "safe" if its crew refuses to tend it."

75. *Ibid.* at 47.

76. *Ibid.*

77. *Ibid.* at 47.

78. *Ibid.* at 48–49.

79. *Ibid.*

80. As Governor of Michigan, Frank Murphy had refused to evict the United Auto Workers' sit-down strikers, thus assuring their momentous victory over General Motors Corporation. On Murphy's role in the sit-down strikes, see, for example, James Wolfinger, "The Strange Career of Frank Murphy: Conservatives, State-Level Politics, and the End of the New Deal," 65 *Historian* 377 (2002); J. Woodward Howard Jr., "Frank Murphy and the Sit-Down Strikes of 1937," 1 *Lab. Hist.* 103 (1960).

thority. By so ruling, he argued, the majority "unduly expands judicial review of the Board's discretionary power."[81] To bolster this point, Reed also emphasized that *Fansteel* was concerned with violent seizure of the plant, not with a peaceful, non-possessory strike; it dealt with a serious criminal act of which strikers were actually convicted, not a technical violation of the law that featured no attempt at prosecution. For that reason, there was "no justification for an iron rule that a discharge of a striker by his employer for some particular, unlawful conduct in furtherance of a strike is sufficient to bar his reinstatement as a matter of law."[82]

C. Critiquing the Supreme Court's Decision

The majority's decision in *Southern Steamship* rests on rather questionable legal grounds, only one or two of which are mentioned by the dissent. Perhaps the most important shortcoming in the Court's reasoning is its determination that mutiny law continued to apply in this case as it did in the nineteenth century, unchanged by the Wagner Act. In reaching this conclusion, on which depended the characterization of the strike as illegal, the Court discounted completely the dramatic changes in labor policy that had occurred since the interpretation of mutiny law that it cited was established. As was noted not only by the Board and the NMU, but also by several commentators in the late 1930s who anticipated this issue, when the law of mutiny was developed along these lines, so favored by Justice Byrnes, it was essentially illegal for *all industrial workers* to organize unions, to demand collective bargaining, or to strike.[83] The Wagner Act, as well as the Norris-LaGuardia and Lafollette acts, had transformed the law in this area, suggesting the need to re-conceptualize and subordinate mutiny law, not labor law. At the same time, as the Court itself admitted, the application of mutiny law to a strike such as the one aboard the *City of Fort Worth* had not been endorsed by appellate courts.[84] In combination, these points call very much for the subordination of mutiny law to labor law, not vice versa.

A similar point can be made about the obsolescence of the Court's view of contract. While the Court did not allow the shipping articles to determine the tenure of employment question, it did specifically rest its determination that the strike was mutinous, and therefore unprotected, on the promise made by the seamen in the articles to obey lawful commands.[85] In so doing, the Court in effect construed the articles as a waiver, by individual contract, of the right to strike. This, which the Board had criticized in its brief, is problematic in at least two ways. For one thing, 8(3) of the Wagner Act on its face outlaws yellow dog contracts—precisely because such contracts are inconsistent with the meaningful exercise of labor rights.[86] For another, this use of the articles seems to have also violated 3 of the Norris-LaGuardia Act, which specifically prohibits federal courts to

---

81. *S. S.S. Co.*, 316 U.S. at 50–51.

82. *Ibid.* at 51.

83. *See* Aaron Saprio & Eugene H. Franks, "Mutiny at the Dock," 25 Cal. L. Rev. 41, 44 (1936–1937).

84. *S. S.S. Co.*, 316 U.S. at 42.

85. *Ibid.* at 38–39.

86. Section 8(3) of the Wagner Act provides, in relevant part, that it shall constitute an unfair labor practice for an employer "by discrimination in regard to hire or tenure of employment or any term or condition of employment to encourage or discourage membership in any labor organization." Wagner Act, ch. 372,8, 49 Stat. 449 (1935); 29 U.S.C.S. 158(a)(3), as amended. The Board's view of the Wagner Act on this issue would be authorized by the Supreme Court one year later in a case involving the relationship between individual contracts and union representation. *J.I. Case Co. v. NLRB*, 321 U.S. 332 (1944).

rely on any contractual promise not to join a labor union or not to strike as a "basis for granting legal or equitable relief."[87]

A related problem with the Court's reasoning is that it did not invoke anything resembling a traditional rule for constructing conflicting statutes. The only thing in the way of statutory construction in Byrnes' opinion is the reference to an unsuccessful effort in Congress to amend the mutiny law to specifically allow dockside strikes. For Byrnes the failure of this legislation—which was proposed, in 1939, after the *Southern Steamship* controversy commenced, and which sought to craft a broader exception than the one at issue in this case—tended to prove Congressional intent to prohibit all shipboard strikes.[88] This exercise, though, did not confront the obvious, facial conflict between mutiny law and the labor law. If the seamen's conduct was indeed mutinous as the Court believed, it was also, without question within the apparent protections of 7 and 8 of the Wagner Act. And the general rule for interpreting such conflicting statutes—that in the absence of clear legislative intent (which was certainly true in this case), the latter of two conflicting statutes should prevail—would clearly have supported the Board's position. Of course, this doctrine should apply only when the statutes are in actual conflict; but it seems this is precisely what the Court thought to be the case.

Even if the Court were correct in its view that mutiny law had remained unchanged and that the strikers were in effect mutineers, it is not at all clear that this fact alone justified denying the Board the power to remedy the strike. This was the dissent's major argument and it is one the majority hardly acknowledges. In fact, this issue once again presented the Court with a conflict between the mutiny law and the labor law. And once again, the Court was satisfied simply to subordinate the terms and policies of the Wagner Act, passed by Congress only seven years before, to archaic judicial interpretations of a vague statute enacted exactly 100 years before the Wagner Act.[89] Even more problematic is that it rendered this as a general rule that labor law should *never* be enforced in a way that conflicts with other federal statutes or policies.

It is also critical to note in this connection that the accommodation sought by the Board did not in the Board's view foreclose application of the mutiny law. The Board specifically recognized a scenario under which mutiny law would remain available to punish the seamen—who in this case, it should be noted, were not even charged—at the same time that the employer remained liable for its unfair labor practices. From this vantage, it is not at all clear that a genuine conflict actually existed between mutiny law and labor law in the first place—much less a conflict requiring subordination of labor law. It is not clear either that what the Board proposed to do in this connection actually involved a derogatory "construction" of the mutiny statute so much as an acknowledgement of its significance.

Another difficulty with the Court's decision inheres in its attempt to identify this case with *Fansteel*. This maneuver, which is implicit in Byrnes' view of *Southern Steamship* as an appropriate extension of *Fansteel*, is unfounded. The Court does not really engage arguments by the Board, the NMU, and (to some extent) the dissenting justices that tend

---

87. Section 3 of the Norris-LaGuardia Act, 29 U.S.C.A. 101, 103, 47 Stat. 70 (1932).

88. *S. S.S. Co.*, 316 U.S. at 43–44. The opinion refers to Sections 292 and 293 of the federal mutiny statutes, as originally enacted in 1835 and amended in 1909. Act of March 3, 1835, ch.40, 1, 4 Stat. 775, 776; Act of Mar. 4, 1909, ch. 321, 292–293, 35 Stat. 1088, 1146 (1909).

89. The mutiny statute that prevails over the Wagner Act in the Court's analysis was enacted in 1835. Act of Mar. 3, 1835, ch. 40, 1, 4 Stat. 775, 775. Minor amendments were made in 1909. Act of Mar. 4, 1909, ch. 321, 292–293, 35 Stat. 1088, 1146 (1909).

to distinguish the *City of Fort Worth* strike in a fundamental way from the true sit-down strike in *Fansteel* and the unique concerns raised by that strike. The ship, unlike the *Fansteel* factory, was without any doubt the crew's home. The crew of the *City of Fort Worth*, unlike the *Fansteel* strikers, engaged in no violence, made no attempt to seize the ship or displace the captain, did not defy orders in remaining aboard, and were never actually charged with, let alone convicted of, any crimes at all. By the same token, the *Fansteel* majority had been careful to avoid holding that any unlawful conduct would prevent the Board from remedying a discharge, particularly where the underlying strike was motivated by the employer's unfair labor practices.[90] The *Southern Steamship* majority was not so discerning. Moreover, while *Fansteel* focused on the unlawfulness of the sit-down strike as part of a broader analysis of its unprotectedness—one attuned to the strike's violence and the like—the *Southern Steamship* Court took unlawfulness as such, combined with a brief speculation on the risks of such strikes, as a sufficient basis to leave the strikers unprotected.

Even to the extent that couching *Southern Steamship* in the logic of *Fansteel* was appropriate, this only raised the larger question whether *Fansteel* itself was rightly decided. The most trenchant critique of that decision remains one offered in 1939 by Henry Hart and Edward Prichard.[91] In *Fansteel* as in Southern Steamship the primary cause of the strike was the employer's violation of 8(5): its refusal to bargain with a union that enjoyed representative status. The *Fansteel* Court, per Justice Charles Evans Hughes, recognized this as "reprehensible" conduct, but nonetheless upheld the employer's property rights and deferred to the general virtues of law and order.[92] This, in turn, cast the strike as illegal and unprotected, and put the discharges of the strikers beyond the power of the Board to remedy. For Hart and Prichard, the main defect in this reasoning was its shortsighted, overly formalistic, and altogether unrealistic view of the Act's aims. The Court's reasoning, they observed,

> converts the actual problem of the effect of misconduct as a qualification upon the Board's remedial power to correct actual wrongs by employers into a hypothetical problem of the employer's punitive power to obtain redress for hypothetical wrongs by employees. The Court's approach omits from consideration the provocation to the employees. It omits from consideration the effect of reinstatement upon the future of collective bargaining in the plant. It omits from consideration, finally, the importance of discouraging unfair labor practices which is the prime function of the Act.[93]

In these respects, *Fansteel*, in the guise of discouraging serious labor unrest, actually left unremedied the very causes of such unrest and unfulfilled the Wagner Act's main purpose: to rely on the prospect of a strike as a way of compelling collective bargaining. On the other hand, had the Court allowed the Board's remedies to stand, the *Fansteel* employer would have "felt the full deterrent effect of the federal remedies provided for violation of

---

90. *NLRB v. Fansteel Metallurgical Corp.*, 306 U.S. 240, 255–56 (1939). Before *Southern Steamship* was decided, lower courts had been quick to draw on this limiting language to avoid overturning Board reinstatement orders in cases involving violent conduct by strikers. This was particularly true of the Third Circuit. *See, e.g., NLRB v. Stackpole Carbon Co.*, 105 F.2d 167 (3d Cir. 1939) (fist-fighting striker); *Republic Steel Corp. v. NLRB*, 107 F.2d 472 (3rd Cir. 1939) (multiple, mainly minor, acts of violence and other criminal behavior); *NLRB v. Elkland Leather Co.*, 114 F.2d 221 (3d Cir. 1940) (throwing stones).

91. *See generally*, Hart & Prichard, *supra* note 234.

92. *Fansteel*, 306 U.S. at 253.

93. Hart & Prichard, *supra* note 45, at 1316.

federal law." By this route, the Wagner Act's aims would have been better achieved and any serious misconduct could still be dealt with by the criminal law.[94]

For reasons we have already touched on, the very same criticisms can made with even more effect of *Southern Steamship*. Like the strike in *Fansteel*, the *Southern Steamship* strike was in protest of an egregious unfair labor practice that struck at the heart of the Wagner Act's legislative agenda. Having unsuccessfully appealed to their employer and then taken equally unsuccessful steps to enforce their right to recognition and collective bargaining before the Board, the seamen resorted to a logical and effective fall back. And unlike the *Fansteel* strikers, they conducted themselves in an altogether non-threatening, non-violent fashion. Still the Court found their actions unprotected and beyond the Board's remedial powers. In so doing, it seriously weakened the Board's ability to enforce the Act and dramatically diminished the Act's meaning for workers.

In fact, as this very case also well illustrates, the law—and with this the meaning of unlawfulness—has a deeply contingent meaning which is dependent on precisely the kinds of contextual analysis that the Board is so much better suited than any court to perform. The Board's interpretation of the law and the facts was at least as reasonable as the Court's, and considerably more grounded in the peculiarities of this dispute.

By invoking such risks, Byrnes reveals his commitment to a particular kind of formalist bias: that the law, *as defined by the courts*, provides a legitimate indicator of acceptable levels of social risks and, overall, a legitimate index of acceptable social order. Just as problematically, this speculative appeal to risks conjures up a key theme in pre-New Deal labor jurisprudence—the theme on which the most notorious exercises in anti-labor judicial activism were based.[95]

This doctrine, with its intensely derogatory view of labor law and labor policy, has become an important precedent of *Southern Steamship*.

In *Hoffman Plastic Compounds Inc. v. NLRB*, decided in 2002, the Court called on *Southern Steamship* to limit the protections of the labor law to undocumented alien workers.[96] In *Hoffman Plastic*, the Court took up the question whether the Board could order an employer to pay back pay to an undocumented worker under any circumstances. Relying primarily on *Southern Steamship*, the Court, per Chief Justice William Rehnquist, ruled that a back pay award was beyond the Board's authority because it would conflict with the policies reflected in the Immigration Reform and Control Act of 1986 (IRCA).[97]

---

94. *Ibid.* at 1320.

95. Speculative appeals to the risks that supposedly inhered in labor protests are fundamental to the reasoning of a number of infamous labor injunction cases. *See, e.g., Plant v. Woods*, 176 Mass. 492, (1900); *Vegelahn v. Gunter*, 167 Mass. 92, (1896).

96. *Hoffman Plastic* was anticipated to some degree by *Sure-Tan Inc. v. NLRB. Sure-Tan* involved an employer who reported undocumented workers to an immigration official in retaliation for their support of the union, which caused them to leave the country. The issue for the Court was whether the Board's remedies for such clear violations of 8(a)(3), as modified by the Seventh Circuit, were legal. In particular, the Seventh Circuit had ordered that in order to effectuate the aims of the labor law in the case of such workers, the workers should be allowed four years in which to claim reinstatement and six months of back pay. While a majority of the Court endorsed the Board and the Seventh Circuit's position that undocumented workers are properly considered employees under the labor law, it also invoked *Southern Steamship* to reject the remedies as modified. *Sure-Tan, Inc. v. NLRB*, 467 U.S. 883 (1984).

97. *Hoffman Plastic Compounds, Inc., v. NLRB*, 535 U.S. 137 (2002).

According to Rehnquist, "[s]ince *Southern S.S. Co.*, we have … never deferred to the Board's remedial preferences where such preferences potentially trench upon federal statues and policies unrelated to the NLRA."[98]

Strikes at the point of production, which had proven so effective in the mid and late 1930s at revitalizing the labor movement and giving real meaning to the labor law, would no longer be tolerated, regardless of whether they were non-violent or justified by employer unfair labor practices. For all these reasons *Southern Steamship* should be seen as one of the clearest expressions of the Court's refusal to allow of any truly reformist agenda of workplace democracy — or, as it was so often expressed in the 1930s, industrial freedom — to follow from the Wagner Act.

But it is certainly useful to wonder whether the normalization of militant, point of production labor protest, which a different outcome in *Southern Steamship* would have entailed, would have offered the NMU and other unions much more effective ways to fight runaway shops, to sympathize in meaningful ways with other strikers, perhaps most importantly to assert a limited right of property in their jobs and right of control over their workplaces.

---

98. *Ibid.* at 144.

President Franklin D. Roosevelt

Economic Bill of Rights for the American People
January 11, 1944

In our day these economic truths have become accepted as self-evident. We have accepted, so to speak, a second Bill of Rights under which a new basis of security and prosperity may be established for all—regardless of station, race, or creed. Among these are:

The right to a useful and remunerative job in the industries, or shops or farms or mines of the Nation;

The right to earn enough to provide adequate food and clothing and recreation;

The right of every farmer to raise and sell his products at a return which will give him and his family a decent living;

The right of every businessman, large and small, to trade in an atmosphere of freedom from unfair competition and domination by monopolies at home or abroad;

The right of every family to a decent home;

The right to adequate medical care and the opportunity to achieve and enjoy good health;

The right to adequate protection from economic fears of old age, sickness, accident, and unemployment;

The right to a good education.

Interlude

The Duty of Fair Representation

Charles H. Houston arguing *Steele v.* Locomotive, Library of Congress.
Louisville and Nashville Railroad Co.

Steele v. Louisville and Nashville Railroad Company (1944)
Eric Arnesen*

In December 1944, the U.S. Supreme Court's ruling in *Steele v. Louisville and Nashville Railroad Company* squarely addressed the issue of the discriminatory treatment of African-American railroad workers by the all-white railroad brotherhoods that both excluded them from union membership and used their institutional power to negotiate contracts that were explicitly harmful to blacks' job rights. Although failing to overturn the brotherhoods' whites-only membership policy, the Court found an implicit "duty of fair representation" in labor law that accorded formal, legal recognition on the unions, requiring them to represent black workers covered by their "craft or class" without prejudice.

The context for the decision was the long-standing tradition of racial exclusion and discrimination in the railroad industry and its dominant unions. For decades before World War II, African-American workers in the railroad-operating trades (firemen, brakemen, and switchmen, in particular) had confronted a sharply discriminatory labor market as well as considerable hostility from their white counterparts. Allowed access to these positions only in the South, they were everywhere excluded from membership in the all-white railroad brotherhoods, which used their strength and legal recognition as trade unions to negotiate contracts that favored white employees at black workers' expense. "For the past fifty years," civil rights attorney Charles Hamilton Houston observed in 1949, the white rail-

* This article was first published as, Eric Arnesen, "Steele v. Louisville and Nashville Railroad Company (1944)," in Eric Arnesen, ed., *Encyclopedia of U.S. Labor and Working Class History*, 1324 (New York: Routledge, 2007). It is reprinted by permission of the publisher, Routledge Publishing Company.

road brotherhoods "have been using every means in their power to drive the Negro train and engine service worker out of employment and create a 'racially closed shop.'" Whites' hostility toward blacks assumed a variety of forms, including strikes calling for the dismissal of black employees and outbreaks of violence, particularly in hard economic times. During the 1910s and especially after World War I, contracts became whites' most effective technique for limiting blacks; access to key jobs and fixing their percentage in the workforce.

In the years following World War I, it was evident that many black railroaders were losing ground in the labor market, and by the Great Depression, their status in the industry had reached a crisis point. Black firemen and trainmen had decreased in number from their historic high in 1920 of about 6,505 and 7,609, respectively, to 2,356 and 2,857 in 1940. So bad did the situation appear that John T. Clark of the St. Louis Urban League privately admitted in 1934 that the "story of the Negro in the railroad and transportation industry is most pathetic." There was little question that by the start of World War II, racial discrimination in the operating sector of the railroad industry, a long-established fact of life, was increasing. Despite growing shortages of labor, the white brotherhoods refused to relax their staunch opposition to the employment of black firemen and brakemen; for their part railroad managers and officials of the federal War Manpower Commission and Office of Defense Transportation responsible for labor procurement maintained an anti-black stance as well.

The plight of black railway firemen particularly deteriorated under the Southeastern Carriers' Conference Agreement of 1941, which one federal investigator later called the "ultimate in all discriminatory agreements" aiming at the "total elimination of colored men as firemen." The previous year the all-white Brotherhood of Locomotive Firemen and Enginemen (BLFE) informed some 21 railroads of its intention to negotiate even more restrictions for black workers. Their proposed agreement would reserve all diesel jobs for promotable men, a category restricted to whites; in addition promotable men would be given preference on all new or changed runs, and the percentage of non-promotable men would be limited to 50% on each railway division. With officials of the National Mediation Board (NMB)—the federal agency overseeing railroad labor relations playing a key role, the parties signed a contract in February 1941. Almost overnight black workers found themselves confronting demotions and furloughs.

Southern black firemen turned to the courts for redress. In the late 1930s, two southern, independent railroad associations, the International Association of Railway Employees (IARE) and the Association of Colored Railway Trainmen (ACRT), had retained noted civil rights attorney Charles Hamilton Houston to represent them in legal matters. Houston was not a labor law specialist when he began his legal work on their behalf, but he needed little introduction to southern black railroaders' plight: His father, the prominent Washington, DC, attorney, William Houston, had served as general counsel for the independent Railway Men's International Benevolent Industrial Association after World War I. After graduating from Harvard Law School, Charles worked with his father in the firm of Houston & Houston and joined the Howard University Law School faculty, where he would serve as the vice-dean. In that capacity he transformed legal education with the aim of training a new generation of black attorneys committed to social activism in the legal realm. From 1935 to 1938, Houston served as special counsel for the National Association for the Advancement of Colored People before returning to private practice. Although he had only occasionally addressed labor issues before, the ACRT and the IARE retained him in 1939. Houston would now launch a campaign against employment and union discrimination that would engage a good portion of his energy until his death in 1950. The 1941 Southeastern Carriers' Conference Agreement, which Houston believed to have been "born in iniquity and conceived in sin," made for a convenient target.

Bester William Steele, a 54-year-old veteran employee of the Louisville and Nashville Railroad in Birmingham, Alabama, put himself forward as a plaintiff for the IARE. As a result of the new agreement, Steele lost a desirable job in the passenger pool in 1941, replaced by a white fireman who possessed less seniority. Out of work for 16 days, he was next assigned to a more difficult and less-remunerative position in local freight service, where he was again displaced by a junior white fireman and assigned to work on a switch engine. Angered by the unfair treatment, Steele turned to his union, the Birmingham chapter of the IARE, of which he was general chairman. For Steele and other IARE officers, the 1941 agreement and the subsequent legal challenge to it became an organizing tool to generate publicity and enthusiasm among black railroaders. Over the next decade of legal maneuvering, Steele remained a committed activist, representing his men not just in court, but in negotiations with company and white brotherhood officials as well.

Houston filed suit in Alabama court in August 1941. Over the next 3 years, the Steele case made its way through the judicial system. On January 13, 1944, only months after Steele and other black railroaders had publicized their plight by testifying at the federal Fair Employment Practice Committee hearings on discrimination in the railroad industry, the Alabama Supreme Court upheld a lower court's dismissal of Steele's suit. As in earlier rulings, the Alabama court found no constitutional questions or federal action involved. Where Steele's attorneys argued that the white brotherhood "was under a duty to give the minority employees, non-members of the Brotherhood, notice of any action to be taken which would in any manner detrimentally affect their seniority rights," the court found no such duty at all.

Then in December 1944, the U.S. Supreme Court dramatically reversed the lower court's decisions, as well as its own previous stance in cases of racial discrimination under the 1934 Railway Labor Act. In two related cases concerning railway trade unions and racial discrimination in employment—*Steele v. Louisville & Nashville Railroad Company* and *Tunstall v. Brotherhood of Locomotive Firemen and Enginemen*—the court held that the Railway Labor Act that governed union-management relations in the railroad industry implicitly imposed a "duty of fair representation" on the exclusive bargaining agent—in this case, the BLFE. Under the provisions of the Railway Labor Act, the BLFE had been "clothed with power not unlike that of a legislature which is subject to constitutional limitations on its power to deny, restrict, destroy or discriminate against the rights of those for whom it legislates and which is also under an affirmative constitutional duty equally to protect those rights." As the exclusive bargaining agent, the union had to serve as the representative of all members of its craft or class (in this instance locomotive firemen), the minority as well as the majority, nonmembers as well as members. That means that like it or not, the BLFE had to represent fairly the black workers in the class or craft of firemen that it excluded from membership. The court made it clear that the Railway Labor Act did not require the union to admit blacks to membership; indeed it could legally establish its own membership guidelines that explicitly prohibited African-Americans from joining. Yet the act imposed "upon the statutory representative ... at least as exacting a duty to protect equally the interests of the members of the craft as the Constitution imposes upon a legislature to give equal protection to the interests of those for whom it legislates." The U.S. Congress had "seen fit to clothe the bargaining representative with powers comparable to those possessed by a legislative body," the court argued, but it had also "imposed upon the representative a corresponding duty ... to exercise fairly the power conferred upon it in [sic] behalf of all those for which it acts, without hostile discrimination against them." Congress had not intended to "confer plenary power upon the union to sacrifice, for the benefit of its members, rights of the minority of its craft." Discrimination "based on race alone" was "obviously irrelevant and invidious." Such reasoning led the court to conclude that the 1941 contract was unquestionably discriminatory.

The ruling was widely hailed by supporters of civil rights. "[E]very single proposition we have advocated for five years was adopted by the United States Supreme Court," Houston privately but enthusiastically declared. For the black weekly the *Pittsburgh Courier,* the decisions had forever outlawed the nefarious practices of the "unholy alliance of reactionary employers and prejudiced rail unions." The decision was "another milestone in the legal struggle to break down discrimination against Negro Americans," declared NAACP special counsel Thurgood Marshall. The white head of the Fair Employment Practice Committee (FEPC), Malcolm Ross, insisted that the Steele case would in time "be recognized as a *Dred Scott* decision in reverse," while the white director of the FEPC's San Francisco Office, Harry Kingman, concluded that Houston's accomplishment was "worth many hundreds of the individual cases with which we deal in field operations." As a consequence Houston should be considered "one of the most famous and respected attorneys in the nation."

These assessments and predictions overstated the impact of these decisions. Houston himself realized that considerable legal effort would be required to make the ruling a reality. Moreover he understood clearly the limitations of his victory: The white brotherhoods were still legally free to bar black railroaders from union membership. The issue of racial exclusion in unions had been consciously left off Houston's legal agenda on the grounds that it "may be best that we do not bite off too much at one time." His purpose rather was to lay the groundwork for future challenges. But for Houston's clients—the IARE and the ACRT—the membership issue was hardly a priority; they exhibited little interest in merging into the much larger, more powerful, and hostile white brotherhoods, instead preferring an approach that would allow them to bargain for themselves.

Through the *Steele, Tunstall,* and numerous other cases over the next 15 years, black workers won tangible if limited gains. As the court toppled barriers to employment and representation, the white railroad brotherhoods erected new ones, although they took pains to disguise their discriminatory intent. Following the *Steele* decision, Houston predicted accurately that there would be a rush to the courts by the remaining several thousand black firemen who were still suffering under the 1941 contract. Houston, still representing the ACRT and IARE, filed multiple suits, while the Provisional Committee to Organize Colored Locomotive Firemen—an organization formed by A. Philip Randolph in 1941 and supported heavily by his Brotherhood of Sleeping Car Porters—followed an identical path, similarly seeking injunctive relief against the 1941 contract and subsequent revisions. After considerable legal effort, black firemen had emerged more-or-less victorious in their legal struggles against the white brotherhood and various southern railroads to preserve their jobs and respect their seniority by 1952. An internal study conducted for the Provisional Committee in 1954 concluded that, "the anti-discrimination injunctions are effective in practice" and found "No over-all patterns of discrimination." The cases of discrimination uncovered, Provisional Committee Attorney Joseph Rauh concluded with satisfaction, were "more or less isolated incidents rather than a pattern of systematic discrimination."

In effectively overturning discriminatory contracts, black railroaders achieved their occupational preservation: They held onto their jobs and secured respect for their seniority rights. But their judicial victories did not address hiring discrimination or the overall loss of jobs brought about by the contraction of the railroad industry. Given the decline in railroad employment in this period, few new black workers replaced their retiring predecessors. Black railroaders were "rapidly passing out of the operating departments of the railroad industry," Randolph testified before congress in 1962. "In the South today, most of the railway yards have been practically transformed from black to white."

The final and ultimately insurmountable barrier to full black rights was union membership. Over the course of the 1950s, Randolph and his Provisional Committee spearheaded an unsuccessful legal effort to open the firemen's brotherhood and force the admission of African-Americans on the straightforward grounds that the BLFE could not, by definition, represent blacks fairly — that is, exercise its duty of fair representation — if it continued to exclude them from membership. In *Oliphant et al. v. BLFE, et al.*, the Provisional Committee's attorneys argued that the BLFE continued to discriminate through its exclusion of blacks from membership. But the court accepted the white union's assertion that no discrimination had taken place, only "legitimate practices used by unions for reasons other than discrimination." The intent of Congress in passing the Railway Labor Act was the promotion of industrial peace, a goal that would have been undermined had Congress required the admission of blacks into white unions. The white brotherhood was, it concluded, a private association, not a governmental agency. "To compel by judicial mandate membership in voluntary organizations where the Congress has knowingly and expressly permitted the bargaining agent to prescribe its own qualification for membership would be usurping the legislative function," it reasoned. Black workers who continued to feel that union exclusion undermined fair representation needed to look to Congress, not the courts, for change. The Sixth Circuit Court of Appeals upheld the district court's ruling, resolving any doubt about the BLFE's status as a "private association, whose membership policies are its own affair." The following year the Supreme Court denied certiorari. The Provisional Committee's test case in its long campaign to mandate union desegregation through the law had failed. Throughout the mid-1960s, the Supreme Court refused to address the issue of railroad union integration, effectively resolving one of the most significant remaining issues in favor of the white brotherhoods. Only with the passage of the 1964 Civil Rights Act would union membership exclusion and segregation become illegal under federal law.

References:

Arnesen, Eric. *Brotherhoods of Color: Black Railroad Workers and the Struggle for Equality.* (Cambridge, MA: Harvard University Press, 2001).

Chick, C. A. "Some Recent United States Supreme Court Decisions Affecting the Rights of Negro Workers." *Journal of Negro Education* (Spring 1947).

Eberlein, E. Larry. "Judicial Regulation of the Railway Brotherhoods' Discriminatory Practices." *Wisconsin Law Review* 516–536 (May 1953).

Herring, Neil M. "The 'Fair Representation' Doctrine: An Effective Weapon against Union Racial Discrimination?" *Maryland Law Review* 113–165 (Spring 1964).

Klare, Karl E. "The Quest for Industrial Democracy and the Struggle against Racism: Perspectives from Labor Law and Civil Rights Law." *Oregon Law Review* 61 (Dec. 1982).

Malamud, Deborah C. "The Story of Steele V. Louisville & Nashville Railroad: White Unions, Black Unions, and the Struggle for Racial Justice on the Rails." In Laura L. Cooper and Catherine L. Fisk, eds., *Labor Law Stories*, 55–105 (New York: Foundation Press, 2005).

McNeil, Genna Rae. *Groundwork: Charles Hamilton Houston and the Struggle for Civil Rights.* (Philadelphia: University of Pennsylvania Press, 1983).

Cases Cited:

Bester William Steele v. Louisville & Nashville Railroad Company, Brotherhood of Locomotive Firemen and Enginemen, et al., December 18, 1944 (323 U.S. 192, 65 S.Ct. 226).

Lee Oliphant et al. v. Brotherhood of Locomotive Firemen and Enginemen, et al., U.S. Court of Appeals, Sixth Circuit (Cincinnati), No. 13387, November 26, 1958, cited in 9 *FEP Cases 446–449.*

Tom Tunstall v. Brotherhood of Locomotive Firemen and Enginemen, Ocean Lodge No. 76, Port Norfolk Lodge No. 775, December 18, 1944 (323 U.S. 210, 65 S. Ct. 235).

XIII

Slowdowns and Worker Control

Loading Dock, Elk Lumber Co., Copyright Forest History Society.

Elk Lumber,* Slowdowns, and the Suppression of Worker Solidarity (1950)

James Atleson

Sec. 7. [§ 157.] Employees shall have the right to self-organization, to form, join, or assist labor organizations, to bargain collectively through representatives of their own choosing, and to engage in other concerted activities for the purpose of collective bargaining or other mutual aid or protection, and shall also have the right to refrain from any or all such activities except to the extent that such right may be affected by an agreement requiring membership in a labor organization as a condition of employment as authorized in section 8(a)(3) [section 158(a)(3) of this title].

Sec. 13. [§ 163. Right to strike preserved] Nothing in this Act [subchapter], except as specifically provided for herein, shall be construed so as either to interfere with or impede or diminish in any way the right to strike or to affect the limitations or qualifications on that right.

---

* In Re Elk Lumber Co. and Lumber and Sawmill Workers Union, Local No. 3063 (AFL) 91 NLRB 33 (1950).

When workers are confronted by working conditions they believe are unfair, unsafe or violative of their sense of personal integrity, they act in collective ways. Such solidarity actions occur throughout history despite hostile law or administrations, in democratic or oppressive regimes. The responses of the state vary, but the human need to express unhappiness is a universal response. Thus, solidarity actions are just as likely to occur in current China as in the US or Europe.

Often, the state, like the US, responds to collective action by repressive means, that is, via the use of force or judicial restrictions. Many believed that the National Labor Relations Act (NLRA) of 1935 altered this historic antipathy to worker actions. After all, collective action was specifically protected, not once, but twice.

Nevertheless, from an early date courts began to drastically reduce the scope of protection seeming provided by the statute. Courts have employed a number of strategies to accomplish these restrictions. First, for instance, the decision might be to simply state that the action is not "concerted" or not for "mutual aid or protection," that is, the activity involves only individual action or, alternatively, is not a "strike" within section 13. Second, the court might hold that the action is indeed concerted but is not one falling within the scope of section 7 or, if it seems obviously a "strike," not the type of strike meant to fall within either of the above sections. Generally, no statutory language, legislative history or policy is asserted to justify the limitations imposed.

These type of decisions are the focus of this chapter, although two other common devices for narrowing the reach of the statute could be mentioned. Thus, without focusing on sections 7 or 13 that create the rights protected by the statute, courts might insert procedural or substantive limits into the unfair labor practice provisions themselves, the provisions which are designed to prohibit distinct violations of the rights granted in section 7. Thus, the need to prove employer "motive" might be required to demonstrate an unfair and illegal discharge despite the absence of any support in statutory language or legislative history. Finally, the court might hold that a purported violation can be established only if it violates a specific unfair labor provision instead of the all-encompassing prohibition in section 8(a)(1). In none of the judicial or administrative examples one might cite to reflect these actions do tribunals feel the need to cite clear legislative policy objectives, legislative history or statutory language. Indeed, there usually is none.

By the early 1950s courts were already restricting the kinds of collective actions permitted by the NLRA. Of course, restrictive opinions occurred earlier. For instance, *Mackay Telegraph*[1] in 1938, only three years after the act's passage, made it clear that although strikes were "protected," and thus strikers could not be discharged for the act of striking, the strikers could nevertheless be permanently replaced, a decision which overshadows all of labor law. One year later the Supreme Court in *Fansteel*[2] held that the NLRB did not have the authority to protect and reinstate sitdown strikers irrespective of the fact that the sitdown is obviously a "strike" and despite the statutory violations of the employer. Added to this list is *Elk Lumber*, one of the shortest decisions ever written by the NLRB but clearly one of the most revealing. Prior to *Elk* and relied upon by the Board, judicial decisions had refused to enforce reinstatement orders by the NLRB for workers who had refused to work overtime without premium pay and who had refused to handle orders from

---

1. *NLRB v. Mackay Radio & Tel. Co*, 304 US 333 (1938).
2. *NLRB v. Fansteel Metallurgical Corp.*, 306 US 240 (1939). For a penetrating analysis, *see* A. White, "The Depression Era Sit-down Strikes and the Limits of Liberal Labor Law," 39 *Seton Hall L. Rev.* 1 (2010).

a struck plant. *Elk,* thus, may reflect the Board's capitulation to the judicial narrowing of the statute, concluding that that even without illegal activities, collective direct action affecting the work process or production details were not to be "protected" activity.

The basic facts, as per the record, are scanty, largely because the complaint was dismissed by the Trial Examiner after the presentation of the General Counsel's case. Interestingly, the first witness, called by the General Counsel, was George Flanagan, the vice president of Elk Lumber Company. The Company had been formed in Medford, Oregon in 1910, although the then current plant was operational in 1946. A lumber manufacturing operation, the case concerned only the car loaders who picked up boards placed alongside box or flat cars and loaded them into the car. The lumber is moved to the cars via a "straddle carrier," a vehicle that straddles the unit of lumber. Previously, the carloaders had been paid on the "gyppo" or piecework basis, and Flanagan estimated their average hourly wage under the piecework basis at $2.71 an hour. The production process meant that as soon as a boxcar was loaded, the planer stopped, and the loaders moved the boxcar with an electric winch so as to make room for an empty car. Flanagan noted: "So, actually, the men were working only part-time, and yet it was necessary to pay on a gyppo basis because no man would work as hard as they had to work when the planer was running, on a day-labor basis. In other words, they worked intermittently very hard, and then stood around." [tr. 20]

A new covered dock meant, according to Flanagan, that car loaders could now load four and a half cars at a time at the dock instead of one car at the dock and one outside. Since it was no longer necessary to load off the end of the inconsistent planer chain into the cars, the employer moved on January 3, 1948 to an hourly rate of pay for the carloaders, an amount of $1.52. On January 5, the vice president was informed that the carloaders had "had all absented themselves from the job to the smoke house, and stayed there for twenty-five minutes." [tr. 23]. Flanagan stated that the loaders could perhaps load two or three cars a day, assuming the planer operated consistently, under the gyppo basis, but, given the uncertainties of the planer machine, the average was more like a car and a half a day. [tr. 23–24]. For the month of January, however, under the newly established hourly pay, the average was somewhat less than a car a day.

Although the car loaders were apparently represented by a union local of the AFL's Lumber and Sawmill Workers' Union, there is no evidence of a regional or national involvement in the dispute, but there was implicit, workplace bargaining going on.[3] For instance, at a dinner sponsored by the employer, Flanagan stated that the workers indicated that more lumber would be loaded if the carloaders were paid either $2 an hour or if the employer returned to the piecework system. [tr. 30] Flanagan responded that other mills were on the hourly system and, given the new operational changes, the men could work steadily rather than the prior work hard—stand around situation. Presumably, Flanagan believed the workers would prefer to work steadily, albeit for considerably less pay. Since the loaders were now averaging only $1.52 an hour at straight time instead of $2.71 under the previous piecework or "gyppo" system, they felt they would give a "dollar and a half's worth of work for a dollar and a half."[4] As Ellen Dannin notes, the cut amounted

---

3. The lack of union involvement is not mentioned in either the transcript or the Board's opinion. Since the workers were represented, however, the unilateral decrease in pay would seem to have violated the employer's obligation to bargain under section 8(a)(5).

4. Nothing in the record indicates that the northwest lumber industry was a hotbed of organizing in the 1930s and 1940s, and, indeed, a conflict raged between an AFL and a CIO lumber union. *See Inland Empire District Council Lumber and Sawmill Workers Union, Lewiston Idaho v. Millis,* 325 US 697 (1945); The jurisdictional battles over sawmill workers was fierce and, according to *Time* in 1940, in one three-month period 900 men went to the hospitals as a result of inter-union battles."

to about $61 a week, and the loaders "did not simply decide they were going to change their wages . . . , they were responding to their employer's unilateral change in their rate of pay by keeping the ratio of their pay to amount of work in status quo." It was the employer, Dannin notes, "that altered the terms of the "parties' wage-effort bargain," and "the employees were trying to keep their work effort in line with the new pay arrangement."[5]

Once the workers learned about the change in pay, "we [the loaders] talked it over among ourselves and decided we would not work as hard. . . . We thought one carload was a good day's work at a dollar and a half." [tr. 40]. Another said "it was all everybody else loads in this valley." [tr. 76] Ordinarily, said one of the terminated carloaders, James Johnson, "other outfits that go by the hour, one carload is their quota." At one car a day, he said, it was not a hard, steady pace, by a long shot," although he allowed that under the gyppo rate they "worked pretty hard," as fast as they could. Johnson denied that the work was lighter in the present new planer shed than previously: "as far as handling lumber is concerned, it takes just much muscles to do it on an hourly basis as it does to do it on piece time work. The only difference between piece time work and an hourly wage, to my own idea, is that piece work is faster work production." [tr. 47] Another loader, H.W. Coltts conceded that they could load more cars a day, but their output was clearly related to the new pay rate. "Well, because you get $3 an hour for loading it gyppo, and you load two cars a day. Okeh. Half of that is about $1.50." [tr. 78].

The loaders never received any formal notice, oral or written, about the change in pay, learning of the change only when they picked up their pay checks. One testified that he had not known about the change until he picked up his check about 23 days after the change went into effect. Moreover, no loading quota was ever set by the employer, and, although the employer clearly expressed unhappiness with the loaders' output at the dinner, no supervisor apparently ever explicitly said the loaders had to work harder or faster. Indeed, there was testimony, ignored both by the Trial Examiner and the Board, that at least one manager viewed the workers' actions as reasonable. Two of the car loaders testified that the yard superintendent explicitly agreed that a car a day was fair at the established hourly rate, and one loader was told that, if finished with his work, he should "make yourself look busy doing something. . . ." [tr. 71].

Prior to the luncheon break in the hearing, the Trial Examiner, Wallace E. Royster, noted the direction in which he was leaning:

> So far it seems that the carloaders were dissatisfied with their rate of pay, and so decided they would do a somewhat limited amount of work each day in return for that pay, which is in a sense a strike, I suppose, or species of strike, a form of it. What is an employer to do in a case like that, if he feels that he is entitled to more work from the men for the wages he is paying? [tr. 67]

Hubert Merrick, for the NLRB, responded, consistent with prior Board decisions, that the loaders were engaged in a form of concerted activity for their own mutual aid and

---

www.time.com/time/printout/0,8816,884222,00.html. Much has been written about the contentious and turbulent life in many timber communities in Northern California, the northwestern states, and British Columbia. See, e.g., Robbins, "Forestry workers and their communities," www.entrepreneur.com/tradejournals/article/print/180029149.html. Robbins notes that "boom-or-bust production cycles, seasonal employment, and the industry's unrelenting efforts to force labour to bear the burden of the instabilities of capitalism were constant points of reckoning for resident working-class populations. In each of those settings, 'working stiffs' sold their labour for daily wages or piecework production." (Spring, 2008.)

5. E. Dannin, *Taking Back the Workers' Law*, 113 (Cornell U. Press, 2006).

protection, using the language of section 7, and they had a right to engage in such action whatever it might be called. Moreover, "they had a right to tell the employer that they will give him a dollar and a half worth of work for a dollar and a half." [tr. 68] Royster's response set out what was to be his final judgment later in the day: "I have no doubt you do have the right to do just that. But don't they run the risk of having their employment terminated? Because I don't think the employer is required to continue them on the payroll." In addition, "Must it forever permit that situation to continue if they can't persuade their employees differently? Or are they allowed to say, "Well, we disagree with you, and since we do, we will hire people who will be content to work for their wage." [tr. 96].

Such is the peculiar view of "rights" under the NLRA. What does it mean to call an action a "right," if that means it can lead to termination of employment, permanent at that? To Merrick, "the whole question probably is whether or not it [the slowdown] is protected." [tr. 94]. Citing other decisions, Merrick argued that so long as the action was for the loaders "mutual aid or protection," is was protected even if "no union activity is involved," and, interestingly, "even though the thing which they are attempting to get action on is a prerogative of the management ..." [tr. 94]. Conceding that the speed of work or the amount of labor expended is a "prerogative of management," however, concedes an issue that has historically been a serious conflict area between labor and ownership. A prerogative of management suggests, as later decisions affirm, that the area has been totally set aside for unilateral management concern, an area over which labor is to have no role, and certainly no ability to alter by economic action such as a slowdown. The amount of work and working conditions are apparently part of the employers' realm, limited only by collective bargaining.[6]

However, given the statute, the Trial Examiner conceded that a strike would have to be treated differently:

> I think the only remedy left to employees when they find the wages not to their liking, or in their opinion inequitable, is either to accept the wage for a full day's work and try by processes of bargaining to persuade their employers to increase the wage, or to resort to a strike which take place off the employer's property. Here the employees are occupying the working place but are not doing the amount of work which the employer says they should. [tr. 98].

So, although a strike would indeed be protected, the offense committed by the carloaders was their remaining at work and expending less effort than the employer desired. Of course, even strikers, under *Mackay*, could be "permanently replaced," albeit not "fired." Still, the notion is that the pace of work, the amount of effort to be expended, is solely to be set by the employer, despite mounds of sociological studies showing worker efforts to control the pace of work. It was not sufficient that in the language of the statute the carloaders were engaged in a strike or concerted action, but other values existed that could be used to restrict the scope of the act. Thus, not only slowdowns, but subsequently also intermittent strikes and support for strikers elsewhere were not to be protected despite their collective nature.[7]

---

6. The Board's representative conceded that the General Counsel had decided not to bring a refusal to bargain charge given uncertainty over whether the carloaders could be an appropriate bargaining unit.

7. The impetus to cease working, especially when faced with abusive or dangerous conditions is strong, even among unorganized workers. A recent and remarkable work stoppage occurred at Case Farms in Morganton, North Carolina, when 150 out of 500 nonunion and mostly immigrant workforce stopped work to protest long-held grievances. *Labor Notes*, (7/27[2010]). See www.labor notes.org/print/2010/07/immigrant-workers-non-union-chicken-plant-stop-work.

The Board's affirmance of the dismissal of the action added little to the opinion of the Trial Examiner. Like the Trial Examiner, the Board relied upon prior circuit and Supreme Court opinions to find that even collective action could be punished if the activity "is so indefensible as to warrant the employer in discharging the participating employees. Either an unlawful objective or the adoption of improper means of achieving it may deprive employees engaged in concerted activities of the protections of the Act." The test reflects the 18th-century criminal conspiracy test, later applied in tort and injunction cases, that permitted courts to determine what was actually in the union's interest. As I noted many years ago,

> Despite an act designed to free labor activity from the legal regulation and to modify common-law restrictions, the Board's test focused on "improper" means, a test not defined by criminal law or the act, but, rather, the views of the decision makers. The result is painfully ironic, for common-law judges were most criticized for reading their own political and economic predilections into the law, and the improper means-ends test was criticized as permitting arbitrary, unbounded judicial discretion. The repeated use of such a test despite changes in formal law may indicate that no better doctrine is available, relevant, or appropriate or that the underlying notions of American labor law have not significantly been altered by the passage of the Wagner Act."[8]

In this case, the "means" was the slowdown, and it was determined to be improper because it "constituted a refusal on their part to accept the terms of employment set by their employer without engaging in a stoppage but to continue rather to work on their own terms." If that was not sufficiently clear, the Board cited *Montgomery Ward*, in which workers at one of the employer's plants refused to process orders from another plant which was on strike:

> It was implied in the contract of hiring that these employees would do the work assigned to them in a careful and workman-like manner: that they would comply with all reasonable orders and conduct themselves so as not to work injury to the employer's business; that they would serve faithfully and be regardful of the interests of the employer during the term of their service ... While these employees had the undoubted right to go on a strike and quit their employment, they could not continue to work and remain at their positions, accept the wages paid them, and at the same time select what part of their allotted tasks they cared to perform of their own volition, or refuse openly or secretly, to the employer's damage, to do other work."[9]

With the omitted language included, the above set of obligations eerily parallels the language and diction of 18th-century indentured servant agreements.[10]

The three Montgomery Ward workers believed, perhaps erroneously, that the increase in orders they were processing was due to the rerouting of orders from the now struck Chicago facility. The Trial Examiner, as well as the Board, had no apparent trouble finding that by refusing to process the orders the workers were providing legal assistance to their union. That is, in the words of the statute, the workers were engaged in concerted action to support collective bargaining or other mutual aid or protection. Again, they could completely

---

8. James B. Atleson, *Values and Assumptions in American Labor Law*, 52 (1983).

9. *Montgomery Ward v. NLRB*, 157 F. 2d 486 (8th Cir. 1944). Although the employees' work did not seem related to war production, the fact that this action took place in wartime may have influenced the court. *See, generally*, Atleson, *Labor and the Wartime State* (U.Ill. Press, 1998).

10. *See, generally*, R.Morris, *Government and Labor in Early America* (Harper Torchbooks, 1946).

strike, at least theoretically, removing themselves completely from the workplace, a right even judges could not finesse given the statute, but they could not partially strike or partially withhold their labor.[11] A full strike, of course, could conceivable injure the employer more significantly, although it might hire replacements—which, in American law, means "permanent replacements." This approach, however, gives no respect to the workers' sense of dignity or the values of solidarity. Moreover, it permits judges to decide that a strike is not a strike within the statute or, alternatively, that actions of solidarity, despite being concerted and for mutual aid, are not protected even despite the language of the act. Even if the employees' action was "protected," of course, employer countermeasures were possible. Thus, a statute designed to remove from the judicial branch the ability to make policy judgments on the wisdom or appropriateness of collective action becomes the vehicle for just this type insertion of values.

What, then, might be the value used by the courts or Board to narrow the seeming broad language of the statute?[12] The courts are fairly clear: "If they [the workers] had a right to fix the hours of their employment," the 7th circuit said in *C.G.Conn, Ltd v. NLRB*,[13] "they could prescribe all conditions and regulations affecting their employment." Since the workers in none of these cases were attempting to "prescribe all conditions" of their employment, the courts must see the risks of a slippery slope leading to something like worker control. The courts, therefore, see themself as the last bastion before worker control, a fear traditionally underlying the judicial hostility for secondary and sympathy strikes. Of course, the car loaders in *Elk Lumber* were not dictating their working conditions, but, in contrast, they were setting a work effort level different than the one apparently desired by the employer in an attempt to secure a higher rate of pay.

Efforts by workers to limit or regulate production have a long history which long predates unions, and the conflict in *Elk Lumber* represents the classic workplace battle over work levels. If employees are unwilling to strike, risking permanent replacement, they must, according to the Board and these circuit courts, work at the terms proscribed unilaterally by their employer. In other words, the employers control over the production process is paramount, and, although it was apparently unreasonable for workers to respond to a huge cut in pay by reducing effort, the reasonableness of the employer's enormous cut in pay was irrelevant to the ultimate judgment.[14] More importantly, the statute would be used to limit effective devises of economic pressure and restrict collective action to formal strikes. Given *Mackay*, however, even this grudging albeit very limited acceptance of the NLRA seems inconsistent with the spirit and even language of that statute.[15]

---

11. The solidarity action in *Montgomery Ward* might now be deemed a secondary boycott, violating section 8(b)(4) of the NLRA. Yet, it is difficult to justify treating any secondary action from nominally protected primary actions. In *Ward*, for instance, why is a worker's refusal to handle "hot cargo" or "hot goods" not seen as a primary dispute. Is this refusal not a dispute with his or her own employer who insists that the worker weaken the effect of worker actions elsewhere? *See, e.g.*, Atleson, "The Voyage of the Neptune Jade; The Perils and Promises of Transnational Labor Solidarity," 52 *Buff. L.R.* 85, 158–162 (2004).Atleson, "the Voyage of the Neptune Jade: Transnational Labour Solidarity and the Obstacles of Domestic Law, 379, 395–396 in Conaghan, Fischl and Klare, eds., *Labour Law in an Era of Globalization* (Oxford, 2002).

12. I have previously written about the hidden values in American labor law. Atleson, *Values and Assumptions in American Labor Law* (1983).

13. *C.G.Conn, Ltd. V. NLRB*, 108 F. 2d 390 (7th. Cir. 1939).

14. For a penetrating analysis of *Elk Lumber* and other decisions restricting actions of worker solidarity, *see* James G. Pope, "Class Conflicts of Law I: Unilateral Worker Lawmaking versus Unilateral Employer Lawmaking in the U.S. Workplace," 56 *Buff. L. Rev.* 1095 (2008).

15. These decisions are also inconsistent with the ILO's international labor law conventions. The basic right to strike has been assumed by the ILO's Freedom of Association Committee and the Com-

To avoid the notion that courts are reading the statute in light of their own values or assumptions, some have tried to find justifications for the holdings noted above. One argument is that the employer, facing a slowdown for instance, is disabled from taking any action in response. This purported justification has at least two significant flaws. First, it is far from clear that actions, of either party, are to be evaluated in light of the availability or effectiveness of possible responses. Second, Elk Lumber's management indeed had responses to the slowdown. It could, for instance, have reduced the workers' wages in light of the slowdown or it could have set a work quota.

A similar justification for these judicial outcomes is that certain actions, such as the slowdown or intermittent strike, give workers "too much power" in relation to the employer. What is "too much" is, of course, in the eye of the beholder. What about imbalances of power or wealth on the employer's part. Should employer weapons, such as permanent replacement, lockouts, threatened moves, or pre-strike stockpiling be deemed to give employers too much power vis-à-vis workers.

Moreover, there is nothing in the act suggesting that the amount of power gained by an economic pressure devise is relevant to its legal propriety. Indeed, in at least two cases the Supreme Court has made it clear that neither the Board nor the courts are to employ their own judgment on the appropriate balance of economic weapons.[16] As the Court stated in *Lodge 76*, quoting in part from *Insurance Agents*, "... the economic weakness of the affected party cannot justify state aid contrary to federal law for "as we have developed, the use of economic pressure by the parties to a labor dispute is not a grudging exception [under] ... the [federal] Act; it is part of parcel of the process of collective bargaining.'" The avenue of choice under the statute, after all, is collective bargaining, a process whose result mirrors the power differences between the respective parties. Thus, there is no review of the results or terms of collective bargaining.

The reason for the slowdown in *Elk Lumber* is clear, but in other cases the motivation might be more subtle. Slowdown actions, like wildcat strikes, are usually rational responses to work frustrations which either might not justify a full-scale strike or which only affect a portion of the workforce. A complete walkout, after all, leads to the possibility of permanent replacement or picket line violence. The union may be uninterested as, apparently, the union representing the lumber workers in *Elk*. Nor is it easy to draw lines between various kinds of labor withholding. For instance, a recent, remarkable one-hour stoppage of work by immigrant workers in Morganton, North Carolina, exemplifies the importance of safety issues to workers and the fact that a short stoppage is little different that a slowdown in effect.[17] In addition, a slow down invokes the basic dignity interest of the worker, that is, how he or she disposes of her own labor or seeks to demonstrate solidarity with workers elsewhere. While freedom to work or not, for pay, is obviously not advocated, solidarity actions should be protected since "protected" under the NLRA does not prohibit employer responses.

---

mittee of Experts, although not explicitly expressed in ILO documents. Nevertheless, the Freedom of Association Committee, for instance, has taken a broad, though not unlimited, view of the right, including sit-ins and slowdowns. *See* Gernigon, et al., "ILO Principles Concerning the Right to Strike," 137 *Int'l Lab. Rev.* 441, 444 (1998).

16. *NLRB v. Insurance Agents International Union*, 361 US 478 (1960) (holding that a union could not be charged with bad faith bargaining under the statute for engaging in a slow down); *Machinists, 76 v. Wisconsin Employment Relations Commission*, 427 US 132 (1976) (holding that state agencies are preempted from enjoining action like a refusal to work overtime even if not protected by the NLRA.). The ironic result of these two decisions is that a union that engages in unprotected actions may not be found in violation of the NLRA nor may a state enjoin the actions, yet workers are subject to the greatest and most harmful result—termination.

17. *Labor Notes*, July 15, 2010 (see www.labornotes.org).

Disputes over "a fair days work" and "a fair days' pay" are endemic to the employment relationship. This classic conflict emerges from the employer's attempt to force the worker to expend the greatest amount of labor possible while the worker's is obviously different. An employer's view might be closer to that of Frederick Taylor that a worker should perform all the work he or she can do without injury to health. Fairness, then, tends to be defined as physiological maximum output and effort, while a worker's view might more closely equate the amount of labor to be expended as an amount "necessary to add to the product a value equal to the worker's pay ..."[18] Yet, as my grandmother might have said, albeit not in English, "where is it written" that workers must work up to their physical, emotional, and psychological maximum? Indeed, sociologists and historians have recorded the ever-present attempt by workers to control the pace of work.[19]

Moreover, cases like *Elk* reflect the conflict of cultural norms which is present in many areas of work. Management's view of efficiency is generally seen in terms of the lowest per-unit cost of production, but worker perceptions of fairness and justice is generally quite different. Workers, when possible, try to maintain their own work norms and work customs which effectively undercut management conceptions of production. As David Montgomery noted in relation to the mostly successful effort by early 20th century employers to break the last vestiges of artisan independence, "the small informal work group persisted, not as an agency of explicit control, as it had been under craft unionism, but as a submerged, impenetrable obstacle to management's sovereignty."[20] Decisions like *Elk*, therefore, represent a choice among conflicting cultural norms.

---

18. D. Rodgers, *The Work Ethic in Industrial America: 1850–1920*, 165–68 (U. Chi. Press, 1979). *See also*, Atleson, *Values and Assumptions in American Labor Law*, ch. 3, n. 33. (U. Mass. 1983).

19. To cite only one study, see J.S. Peterson, "Auto Workers and Their Work, 1900–1933," 22 *Labor History* 213, 231–32 (1981). A more scatological and humorous view is presented by Ben Hamper, *Rivethead* (Warner Books, 1986). The classic study is Donald Roy, "Restriction of output by Machine Operators in a Piecework Machine Shop: A Preliminary Analysis," U. Chi. PhD (1952) (sincere thanks to Professor James Wooten for sending me Roy's dissertation).

20. D. Montgomery, *Workers' Control in America*, 101–102 (Cambridge U. Press, 1979).

XIV

Public Workers Strike and Racial Justice

I AM A MAN, Memphis Sanitation Strike, Copyright Ernest C. Withers.

Martin Luther King, Jr., the Crisis of the Black Working Class, and the Memphis Sanitation Strike (1968)

Michael K. Honey*

Martin Luther King's radicalism became especially apparent during his later career from 1965 to 1968 and particularly during the Poor People's Campaign and the Memphis sanitation workers' struggle in the last months of his life. From this context, King must be understood more fully, as a minister to the poor and the working class, as well as a civil rights leader, if his legacy is to be useful to new generations struggling with blatant disparities between rich and poor.

---

* This chapter is a modification of Michael K. Honey, "Martin Luther King, Jr., the Crisis of the Black Working Class, and the Memphis Sanitation Strike," in Robert H. Zieger, ed., *Southern Labor in Transition 1940–1995*, 205–223 (Knoxville: U. of Tenn. Press, 1997). It is reprinted by permission of the publisher, University of Tennessee Press.

By the time of the sanitation strike in1968, King believed that movements by those at the bottom, allied with unions and middle-class people of good will, could regenerate what seemed to be a flagging struggle for freedom and equality. Since the mid-1950s, he had put his life on the line repeatedly to end southern segregation, but increasingly he had come to believe that desegregation by itself could not end black oppression. The Watts rebellion and other uprisings of the urban black poor after 1965 forced King to focus on questions of economic justice. In numerous speeches and writings of this period, he repeatedly warned of economic trends throwing black workers into crisis, even as they strode toward legal and civic freedom. He spoke of the deep roots of black economic distress in slavery and segregation. He probed the effects of a global economy which increasingly mechanized and marginalized people of color, the uneducated, and the poor; and he criticized unions for failing to address the needs of African Americans. He saw trends creating a crisis of the poor and the black working class that neither civil rights organizations nor the established labor unions by themselves could address. King hoped that poor people's movements would focus renewed energy on reforming an oppressive racial and economic order that placed disproportionate numbers of African Americans on the bottom. He saw the Memphis sanitation strike as one such movement.[1]

King's focus on economic and class issues did not emerge during the sanitation strike, nor during the Poor People's Campaign. As a graduate student, King recalled his firsthand experience of the Depression as one source of his "anti-capitalist feelings," and in his early graduate school papers he displayed some sympathy for Karl Marx's critique of capitalism, while opposing Marx's moral relativism and historical materialism. As a minister, King certainly empathized with the working class and the poor, despite his Ph.D. and relative affluence. As a civil rights leader, King had a long-standing concern for economic issues. Civil rights legislation, he repeatedly wrote and said, was but a down-payment on, and not a fulfillment of, the American dream of economic security and civic equality.[2] In 1957, he told civil-rights activists at Highlander Folk School: "I never intend to adjust myself to the tragic inequalities of an economic system which will take necessities from the masses to give luxuries to the classes." At that early date, King said that he sought the

---

1. I have developed these themes in unpublished papers drawing upon King's speeches before unions in the 1950s and 1960s: Michael K. Honey, "Coalition and Conflict: Martin Luther King, Civil Rights, and the American Labor Movement," paper presented at North American Labor History Conference, Detroit, Mich., Oct. 1992; and Michael K. Honey, "Labor and Civil Rights Movements at the Crossroads: Martin Luther King, Jr., Black Workers, and the Poor People's Campaign," paper presented at Annual Meeting of the Organization of American Historians, Atlanta, Ga., Apr. 1994. For details of King's later development, see David J. Garrow, *Bearing the Cross: Martin Luther King, Jr., and the Southern Christian Leadership Conference,* 357–624 (New York: William Morrow, 1986); Adam Fairclough, *To Redeem the Soul of America: The Southern Christian Leadership Conference and Martin Luther King, Jr.,* 253–384 (Athens: Univ. of Georgia Press, 1987); Adam Fairclough, *Martin Luther King, Jr.,* 105–22 (Athens: Univ. of Georgia Press, 1990). Charles H. Cone, *Martin and Malcolm and America: A Dream, or a Nightmare?* 219–27 (Maryknoll, N.Y.: Orbis Books, 1991), also discusses King's commitment to the poor. On King's heartbreaking struggles in Chicago, *see* James R. Ralph, Jr., *Northern Protest, Martin Luther King., Jr., Chicago, and the Civil Rights Movement* (Cambridge, Mass.: Harvard Univ. Press, 1993).

2. *See* Martin Luther King, Jr., "I Have a Dream," text in James M. Washington, ed., *Testament of Hope: The Essential Writings of Martin Luther King, Jr,.* 217–30 (New York: Harper and Row, 1986); Clayborne Carson et al., eds., *The Papers of Martin Luther King, Jr.,* vol. 1: *Called to Serve, Jan. 1929–June 1951,* 31, 41, 54, 359, 435–36 (Berkeley: Univ. of California Press, 1992); and Taylor Branch, *Parting of the Waters: America in the King Years, 1954–63,* 79–87 (New York: Simon and Schuster, 1988). *See also* Martin Luther King, Jr., *Stride Toward Freedom: The Montgomery Story,* 164–67, 183 (New York: Ballantine, 1958); and Martin Luther King, Jr., *Why We Can't Wait,* 130–33, 140–43, 146–55 (New York: Penguin, 1963).

"complete realization" of democratic principles in the United States, emphasizing that "we must not rest until segregation and discrimination have been liquidated in every area of our nation's life." King initially may have hoped that civil rights gains themselves would rectify economic inequalities, but later in his career he increasingly called for national economic compensation for centuries of slavery and segregation, as well as for a continuing moral commitment to ending racism.[3]

Nor did King's relationship with unions evolve only later in his life. During the Montgomery Bus Boycott and after it, King gained from unionists some of his knowledge of organizing and considerable financial support. He drew support not only from the AFL-CIO and the United Auto Workers (UAW), but also from smaller activist unions with leftist leaders and sizable black memberships, among these the United Packinghouse Workers, headquartered in Chicago. Throughout the 1960s, he continued to go to these unions and to others, such as Local 1199 Hospital Workers Union in New York City, for funds and organizational support. By observing the active civil-rights programs of these unions and using his own creative analysis, King early in his career developed a positive advocacy of organized labor that might be described as "civil-rights unionism." This form of unionism saw equal rights struggles and labor struggles complementary and mutually reinforcing, rather than as antagonistic and divisive.[4]

Although King spent most of his time working in the top-down organizational style of the Baptist Church, via the Southern Christian Leadership Conference (SCLC), his Ghandian understanding of the role of masses in history caused him to view both labor and the civil rights movements, at their best, as grassroots rebellions evolving from the bottom up. Long before the 1968 sanitation strike, King had made speech after speech to unions, pointing to the common methods and goals of labor and civil rights movements, and calling for a grand alliance of the two. He presumed not only that civil rights and voter registration would break segregation, but also that black and white workers' votes would combine to end state restrictions on union organizing and replace reactionary

---

3. Martin Luther King, Jr., "The Look to the Future," an address delivered at the 25th Anniversary of the Highlander Folk School, Monteagle, Tenn., Sept. 2, 1957, Box 6, Folder 28, Sanitation Strikers' files, Mississippi Valley Collection, Brister Library, Univ. of Memphis, Memphis, Tenn. (hereafter cited as SSFMVC/UMT). Labor organizer and southern Communist Party activist William E. Davis rode in a car with King and Anne Braden from the Highlander meeting, and he recalled that King seemed quite aware of the economic aspects of racism and of the Leftist critique of capitalism. William E. Davis, interview by Michael Honey, Memphis, Tenn., May 21, 1989, notes in author's possession. In *Where Do We Go From Here*, 93, and in speeches, King pointed out that, in the process of emancipation, the nation never created an economic base for African Americans.

4. Union supporters such as E. D. Nixon, Jack O'Dell, Stanley Levison, Bayard Rustin, A. Philip Randolph, Myles Horton, Carl and Anne Braden, and Ralph Helstein all had a good deal of early contact with King. In 1957, Helstein turned over to King $11,000 created as a "fund for democracy" in the South, raised by UPWA locals across the country. The UPWA already had launched one of the most impressive efforts of any union to root out racism from within the ranks of its members and their communities, and was one of the earliest and most persistent financial supporters of the Montgomery Bus Boycott and of King's subsequent work in the South. King supported the union when some called it "Communist," and in a 1962 speech before the UPWA, he declared that, had other unions followed the example of the Packinghouse union, "the civil rights problem would not be a burning national shame, but a problem long solved." *See* King's addresses at 4th Biennial Wage and Contract Conference, 3rd National Anti-Discrimination Conference, and 3rd National Conference on Women's Activities, all United Packinghouse Workers of America, AFL-CIO, Sept. 30–Oct. 4, 1957, Chicago; in UPWA Conferences, Box 526, as well as other items, UPWA Collection, Wisconsin Historical Society, Madison. *See also* his "Address Before the United Packinghouse Workers of America," May 21, 1962, in Martin Luther King, Jr., Papers, Martin Luther King, Jr., Institute for Nonviolent Social Change, Atlanta, Ga. (hereafter cited as MLK Papers).

southern legislators with liberals. The high point of his own alliances with unions came in June 1963, with a mass freedom march in Detroit, co-sponsored with the UAW, with over 125,00 participants; and with the August 28 March on Washington, to which the UAW and many other unions (although not the AFL-CIO) gave crucial support. By 1965, King and SCLC even went so far as to propose to UAW President Walter Reuther that unionists collaborate with SCLC to train a new generation of southern organizers for placement in the field, to "bring Unions into every sphere of labor activity here in the South w[here] Unions do not now exist."[5]

King relished the glowing promise of a civil rights-labor alliance, but he also expressed growing unease with its limitations, which became more apparent as the 1960s wore on. Unions and the civil rights movement needed each other but often had separate and competing concerns. Like other black leaders, King saw unions as fundamental allies in the freedom struggle, but he also recognized clearly the role white unionists frequently played in marginalizing blacks economically. Moreover, in the second half of the 1960s, King increasingly worried that a growing economic crisis among black workers would continue to drive ghetto rebellions in the cities. These uprisings forced King's attention to the North and in 1966–67 drew him into a frustrating and largely fruitless campaign for black economic advancement and open housing in Chicago. In speeches to union gatherings, he repeatedly described the cause of black economic crisis as rooted partly in automation, which in the 1950s and 1960s eliminated hundreds of thousands of unskilled jobs. After a long history of employer and union discrimination, these positions had only begun to provide accessible, high-wage, unionized employment for black workers; racism still blocked African-American advancement into more skilled production and craft jobs. In his speeches, King stressed the vulnerability of the black working class and called upon unions to do away with all vestiges of discrimination within their own organizations.[6] If the unions did not find a way to raise the living standard of all workers, and not just those under union contract, the proportion of unionized workers would continue to shrink; black workers would continue to be impoverished; and the strength of both labor and civil-rights organizations would ebb.[7]

The growing inequality of blacks in the 1960s that King highlighted in his labor speeches was starkly documented in economic statistics. These figures showed that, since the mid-1950s, black economic fortunes had declined. In the 1940s, the access of black workers, both male and female, to industrial employment had increased dramatically compared to previous decades, giving rise to a generally higher standard of living and greater black

---

5. King's speeches to unions are collected in Martin Luther King, Jr., Papers, Series 3, speech files, Martin Luther King, Jr., Institute, Atlanta. They are analyzed in Honey, "Coalition and Conflict." See also Branch, *Parting of the Waters,* 842–43; and King to Walter Reuther, May 23, 1962, on black-labor voting, in Walter P. Reuther Papers, Box 523, Folder 1, Archives of Labor History and Urban Affairs, Wayne State Univ., Detroit, Mich. (hereafter cited as WRP); and King to Reuther, July 19, 1965, enclosing a proposal, "To All Union Representatives," in WRP, Box 523, Folder 2. For material on the March on Washington, *see* WRP, Box 494, Folders 8–10.

6. Honey, "Coalition and Conflict." *See also* King's only speech to a national AFL-CIO convention, "If the Negro Wins, Labor Wins" (1962), printed in Washington, *Testament of Hope,* 201–7. *See also* King, *Why We Can't Wait; 129.*

7. Manning Marable, "The Crisis of the Black Working Class: An Economic and Historical Analysis," 66 *Science and Society* 130–61 (Summer 1982), describes many of the characteristics of the crisis also described by King. King made his most critical statements about unions in "Civil Rights at the Crossroads," an address to the shop stewards of Local 815 of the Teamsters, New York, May 2, 1967, and in "The Other America," a speech before Local 1199 at Hunter College, New York, Mar. 10, 1967, both in King Speeches, MLK Papers, Atlanta.

longevity.[8] But the Korean War was the last period of relatively low unemployment for black males (4.4 percent). Since then, relative economic decline had characterized the plight of black male workers. Their income had averaged 37 percent of the level for white males in 1939, 54 percent in 1947, and 62 percent in 1951; by 1962, though, it had dropped to 55 percent, about where it had been in 1945. Between 1959 and 1964, the most rapid job growth occurred in professional, technical, and clerical work; but these white-collar jobs remained largely closed to blacks. Throughout the 1950s, while some black males did gain semiskilled and skilled jobs as factory operatives, most black male workers remained in the constricting sector of unskilled labor.[9] In the 1940s and 1950s, black women also had made advances as factory operatives, and in the 1960s, to a greater extent than black men, some of them also made their way into the lowest-paid white-collar workers as teachers, clerks, and office workers. Still, most employed black women remained stuck in domestic, laundry, and restaurant work.[10]

Constricted job opportunities not only drove down black income levels relative to those of whites; lack of employment opportunity, too, contributed to massive black unemployment. Males suffered most, with an unemployment rate two to three times that of whites and rising rapidly by the mid-1960s. In 1947–48, black unemployment had been 5 percent, relative to a white rate of 3 percent; by 1964, the respective rates were 10 percent and 5 percent. Counting hidden unemployment, however, the gap between white and black was much wider. These conditions especially irritated the youngest and best-educated blacks, concentrated in the North, who had great difficulty finding jobs to match their training. Northern working-class blacks increasingly fell into two broad categories: a unionized group, who in the period 1940–53 had gotten and, protected by seniority provisions, for the most part kept industrial jobs classified as semiskilled and unskilled; and a younger and often better-educated group of workers, who after the Korean War could find no such employment security.[11]

Black workers in the South suffered grievously as well. Millions of African Americans had left the region in search of work, but a reverse flow also had begun, as industries were fleeing unionized areas of the North for the non-unionized South. Between 1940 and the 1960s, manufacturing employment in the latter region increased by 80 percent, and during World War II blacks had gained an increasing share of these jobs. But after the war, industrial employers increasingly "whitened" their workforce, seeking workers who were better educated and less willing to organize than blacks. At the same time, agricultural employment declined by 60 percent, as the percentage of cotton harvested by machines went from 5 percent in 1950 to 50 percent by 1960 and 95 percent by 1970. Mechanization of cotton production gutted rural employment in the Mississippi Delta surrounding Memphis, forcing black farm laborers to flee to the city or to remain behind in

---

8. According to Charles Killingsworth, between 1900 and the 1960s, life-expectancy for blacks doubled, with the largest change in the white-black health differential occurring in the 1940s. This development coincided not just with employment in manufacturing but also with a movement of rural people to the cities. Killingsworth, "Negroes in a Changing Labor Market," in Arthur M. Ross and Herbert Hill eds., *Employment, Race, and Poverty,* 55 (New York: Harcourt, Brace and World, 1967).

9. Arthur M. Ross, "The Negro in the American Economy," in Ross and Hill, *Employment; Race, and Poverty,* 18–19, and Killingsworth, "Negroes in a Changing Labor Market," 51–52, 57–71; William H. Harris, *The Harder We Run: Black Workers Since the Civil War,* 82 (New York: Oxford Univ. Press, 1982).

10. Harris, *The Harder We Run,* 159–60; Jacqueline Jones, *Labor of Love, Labor of Sorrow: Black Women, Work and the Family, from Slavery to the Present,* 260–62, 277 (New York: Random House, 1986).

11. Killingsworth, "Negroes in a Changing Labor Market," 59, 58, 62, 60, 69.

unrelenting poverty. Although the rate of industrial growth in the South exceeded that in the North, most of the new jobs were nonunion and concentrated in white, suburban areas. Partly as a result of these trends, the 1959 median income of black men in the South remained half that of black men in other regions. And in contrast to the 1940s, when southern blacks' income rose relative to that of whites, in the 1950s it fell by ten percentage points. Whereas growing industrial employment once had engendered hope, contracting rural employment and stagnant urban manufacturing employment in the 1960s aroused anger and frustration among southern African Americans. Moreover, their declining fortunes came during a period in which many white southerners, and white Americans generally, were doing better than ever.[12]

Vast and growing economic disparities between African Americans and whites came into high relief in the Mississippi Delta and in its urban capital, Memphis. Always grim, life for black migrants to the city deteriorated in the 1960s. Those escaping mechanization in the cotton fields had little education and few marketable skills to bring to Memphis, at a time of slack demand for unskilled labor. Entrenched barriers of racial discrimination and poor education in the city barred most African Americans from white-collar jobs, although a few black men and women worked as teachers, while a thin stratum of professional and business people provided political and social leadership. But most employed black men continued to work in the declining labor-intensive cotton and wood-related extractive and manufacturing industries, or in service work that paid equally poorly; the lucky ones worked at Firestone Tire, International Harvester, and a few other unionized industrial plants. Most employed African-American women continued to work as domestics and laundresses or in other lowly occupations, as this group made only token advances into white-collar employment. To avoid paying the higher wages required by federal minimum-wage laws, labor-intensive industries eliminated many unskilled positions normally filled by blacks and replaced these workers with machines, usually tended by whites. African-American men, the mainstay of unskilled factory employment in Memphis, suffered especially: as late as 1969, an astounding 86 percent of black men in Memphis still performed unskilled and service work. African Americans as a whole remained, worse off by occupational distribution in Memphis than in many other parts of the urban South, to say nothing of the rest of the country.[13]

As a cumulative effect of these conditions, 57 percent of the black population lived below the poverty line in Memphis in the 1960s, compared to 13.8 percent in the white

---

12. On percentages of agricultural and industrial employment, *see* Vivian W. Henderson, "Region, Race, and Jobs," in Ross and Hill, *Employment, Race, and Poverty,* 80. On the disparity in median black income North and South as of 1959, *see* Killingsworth, "Negroes in a Changing Labor Market," 68. *See* Gavin Wright, *Old South, New South: Revolutions in the Southern Economy since the Civil War,* 243, 247, 255 (New York: Basic Books, 1986), on the mechanization of southern agriculture. *See* F. Ray Marshall, "Industrialization and Race Relations in the Southern States," in Guy Hunter, ed., *Industrialization and Race Relations: A Symposium,* 91 (New York: Oxford Univ. Press, 1965), on the decline in black median income relative to that of whites.

13. *See* Bruce Williams, Michael Timberlake, Bonnie Thornton Dill, and Darryl Tukufu, "Race and Economic Development in the Lower Mississippi," Research Paper No. 15, Center for Research on Women, Univ. of Memphis, Memphis, Tenn., 1992; John M. Brewster, *Labor and Power Utilization at Cotton Seed Oil Mills,* U.S. Dept. of Agriculture Marketing Research Report 218 (Washington, D.C.: USGPO, 1958); James E. Fickle, *The New South and the "New Competition": Trade Association Development in the Southern Pine Industry,* 314–35 (Urbana: Univ. of Illinois Press, 1980) (on mechanization in extractive industries); and Arvil Van Adams, "The Memphis Labor Market," in F. Ray Marshall, ed., *Negro Employment in the South,* Manpower Research Monograph no. 23, 2:9–18 (Washington, D.C.: USGPO, 1971). On the industrial configuration, *see* Michael Honey, *Southern Labor and Black Civil Rights: Organizing Memphis Workers,* 13–64 (Urbana: Univ. of Illinois Press, 1993).

community. Although African Americans comprised less than 40 percent of the Memphis population, they made up 86 percent of the residents of the city's poverty areas. Other statistics showed disproportionately high rates of death, malnutrition, and family disorganization among African Americans. One of the greatest gaps between white and black Memphians remained in education, the single most telling index of discrimination and unemployment. Twenty-four percent of the people in poverty areas were functionally illiterate; fewer than 17 percent of them had finished high school (compared to 45 percent for white Memphis); fewer than 7 percent of them, compared to a 17.5 percent rate for whites, went on to college. Schools remained highly segregated, and white males generally obtained nearly four years more schooling than black males, while an eighth-grade education in African-American schools was roughly equivalent to a sixth-grade education in white schools. Inferior, segregated education continued to block the movement of African Americans into the growing sector of white-collar employment, even though significant desegregation of public places had occurred after numerous protests in the early 1960s.[14]

These devastating conditions fit easily into the history of a place that, like other southern cities, had a long record of virulent white supremacy. Slavery and then segregation had inculcated in most whites a deep belief in black inferiority. In Memphis, a small number of elite families had built a racial and economic order based on commerce, land ownership, extractive and processing industries, cheap labor, and unreconstructed white supremacy. Cemented into place by the poll tax and by political boss E.H. Crump, who ran the town on behalf of these families from before World War I until his death in 1954, the racial-economic system of white supremacy insured wealth for a few and poverty for the many. From the late 1930s on, black and white workers had contested their common victimization through industrial unions. Yet Memphis also had a long history of craft union exclusion, while its industrial unions, though interracial in membership for the most part remained firmly controlled by whites. In some cases, as at the International Harvester plant, White Citizens Council and Ku Klux Klan influence remained strong. White workers resisted efforts of black workers to break down segregation in factory facilities, in seniority lines, and in union halls. "Massive resistance" to desegregation and the post-World War II Red Scare combined to defeat organizing drives and to drive progressives from the unions. In the 1960s, the unions still failed to reach beyond the core of organized industries and into the service sector to organize the least skilled, lowest-paid workers, most of them black and many of them women.[15]

The union movement once had promised much more, but by the 1960s the labor movement was in decline in Memphis. Although blacks composed about one-third of

---

14. F. Ray Marshall and Arvil Van Adams, "Negro Employment in Memphis," 9 *Industrial Relations: A Journal of Economy and Society* 308–23 (May 1970); Donald D. Stewart, *Poverty in Memphis: Report of a Preliminary Study,* 23, 40 (Memphis, Tenn.: Dept. of Sociology and Anthropology, Memphis State Univ., 1964); David M. Tucker, *Memphis Since Crump: Bossism, Blacks, and Civic Reformers, 1948–1968,* 118–42 (Knoxville: Univ. of Tennessee Press, 1980).

15. *See* Honey, *Southern Labor and Black Civil Rights,* 245–91; Michael Honey, "Industrial Unionism and Racial Justice in Memphis," in Robert H. Zieger, ed., *Organized Labor in the Twentieth-Century South,* 135–57 (Knoxville: Univ. of Tennessee Press, 1991); Michael Honey, "Operation Dixie: Labor and Civil Rights in the Postwar South," 45 *Mississippi Quarterly* 439–52 (Fall 1992); and Michael Honey, "Labor, the Left, and Civil Rights in the South: Memphis during the CIO Era, 1937–1955," in Judith Joel and Gerald M. Erickson,eds., *Anti-Communism: The Politics of Manipulation,* 57–87 (Minneapolis, Minn.: MEP Publications, 1987). See also Alan Draper, *Conflict of Interests: Organized Labor and the Civil Rights Movement in the South, 1954–1968,* 29 (Ithaca, N.Y.: ILR Press, 1994), on the segregationist and right-wing movement among white workers in the South, and in Memphis.

the city's union members, and by the 1950s the AFL and CIO unions had combined memberships of some 50,000 to 60,000, this total represented only about 23 percent of potential union membership, in a city with 540,000 people. Black influence in union leadership remained marginal, while the percentage of all workers organized into unions had begun to decline. Indeed, the situation in Memphis provided an archetypal example of how racism, mechanization, and a flagging labor movement combined to keep African-American workers poor, powerless, and exploited.[16]

Memphis exhibited all the racial and economic problems which King had pointed to in his speeches before union audiences. It is not surprising, then, that in the winter and spring of 1968 the mounting socioeconomic grievances of African-American workers erupted into a dramatic and far-reaching confrontation. In February, more than thirteen hundred black sanitation men launched what became a sixty-four-day strike, seeking nothing more than what many other workers had gained long before: union recognition, decent conditions, improved wages and benefits. The uprising of such men shocked white Memphians, as even those older workers who presumably had resigned themselves to their condition rose *en masse* to support the strike. The strike quickly developed into a stark confrontation, pitting supporters of the old racial-economic order against practically the entire Memphis African-American community and major portions of the city's organized labor Movement.[17]

The condition of the thirteen hundred sanitation men who worked for the city epitomized the plight of the black urban poor. Many sanitation workers lived below the poverty level, even as they worked two or more jobs. A large portion of them came from rural Fayette County, Tennessee, where control of the cotton economy had shifted from planters using black unskilled labor to corporations using machines. There black unemployment reached nearly 70 percent, and 80 percent of the housing lacked plumbing. According to one of the men who moved from Fayette County to become a sanitation worker in Memphis, "There is no worst job. I would take anything." Such individuals usually obtained sanitation work through friends or family members already employed. At one time, rural blacks had used low-wage jobs in Memphis as stepping stones to jobs in Chicago or elsewhere in the North. But as employment opportunities in northern cities slackened, those who remained in Memphis were locked into dead-end jobs. They soon discovered that, no matter how long they might work as sanitation men, they remained classified as unskilled day laborers and could not become foremen or supervisors. Only whites held these positions, and most of them had little more than contempt for African Americans, who did backbreaking work compensated by low wages, few benefits, and no job security. Forty percent of sanitation workers were so poor that they qualified for welfare to supplement their salaries. In the 1960s, conditions worsened, as successive city governments economized by sending them home without pay on rainy days (it typically rained 60 inches a year in Memphis), refusing to replace obsolete and dangerous trucks and other equipment, and refusing to increase wages even to keep up with the cost of living.[18]

---

16. Earl Green, Jr., "Labor in the South: A Case Study of Memphis—The 1968 Sanitation Strike and Its Effect on an Urban Community" (Ph.D. diss., New York Univ., 1980), 79, 90, 94; Joan Turner Beifuss, *At the River I Stand: Memphis, the 1968 Strike, and Martin Luther King,* 54 (Memphis, Tenn.: Band W Books, 1985); and Richard P. Schick and Jean J. Courtier, with Thomas W. Collins, "Memphis, Tennessee: Sanitationmen's Bargaining Climate in 1975 Compared with 1968," in Richard P. Schick and Jean J. Courtier, eds., *The Public Interest in Government Labor Relations,* 69–104 (Cambridge, Mass: Ballinger Publishing Co., 1977).

17. For a dramatic account of the situation in 1968, *see* Beifuss, *At the River I Stand, passim,* and also Garrow, *Bearing the Cross,* 575–624.

18. Thomas W. Collins and L. B. Brooks, "Regional Migration in the South: A Case Analysis of Memphis," paper presented at the Annual Meeting of the American Anthropological Association, New

Unionization for these men represented a break from their past of peonage and share-cropping in the countryside and urban poverty and caste-system status in the city. Their organizing efforts also directly conflicted with long-entrenched anti-union policies of the city government. True, the Crump machine always had used craft unions as a vehicle for patronage and as a political auxiliary, and the machine had allowed whites to organize in the building trades and other areas where the city let contracts. Even then, however, it had made its agreements with the white unionists orally. It had violently resisted industrial unions, encouraging and even organizing beatings and expulsion of organizers. It also totally opposed public employee unions, and city officials repeatedly had vowed never to sign an agreement with a labor organization. In the 1930s and 1940s, when city employees, including teachers, firefighters, and police, tried to organize, the municipal authorities fired and blacklisted them. From the 1930s into the 1960s, municipal judges issued injunctions freely, crippling organizing campaigns and disrupting even the most militant strikes of white workers. Given this history, the idea that poor black sanitation workers would breach the barriers to form a public employee union seemed unthinkable.[19]

Union organizing among sanitation workers reflected the heroic and dogged efforts of a few individuals. In 1947 and again in 1960, outsiders had attempted to unionize sanitation workers, but both times city authorities had scared them off. However, with help from the Retail Clerks International Association, garbage worker T.O. Jones, a Memphis native who had returned to the city in 1958 when a recession in West Coast shipyards had eliminated his job, began another attempt to help the sanitation workers. In 1963, acting on the basis of tips from informants, the Public Works Department fired Jones and thirty-three other workers. Over the next several years, however, Jones continued to meet with workers in their homes and to collect union dues. By 1964, aided by ministers and a black businessman and civic leader, O.Z. Evers, Jones and a number of workers had formed an Independent Workers Association of Memphis. With help from Secretary-Treasurer Bill Ross of the Memphis Trades and Labor Council, Jones succeeded in getting several of the dismissed unionists rehired. Ross said Jones' dedication and humility won over other sanitation workers. They believed in him "because he understood their problems. He had a certain amount of charisma with them. He talked their language. He was just another tub toter."[20]

The American Federation of State, County, and Municipal Employees (AFSCME) put him on its payroll as an organizer, and he soon succeeded in gaining a charter for Local 1733. The Trades and Labor Council supported this initiative and called on the city to grant a written contract and dues check-off. City Commissioners rejected the council's demand, claiming that the city charter forbade formal recognition of any union.[21]

Orleans, La., Nov. 30, 1973, in author's possession; and Thomas W. Collins, "An Analysis of the Memphis Garbage Strike of 1968," in Johnetta B. Cole, ed., *Anthropology for the Eighties: Introductory Readings,* 353–62 (New York: Free Press, 1982).

19. Strike incidents led by white workers included a six-month walkout of Dixie Greyhound bus workers in 1946, the American Snuff factory strike in 1950, and construction strikes in the 1950s involving confrontations on picket lines and even bombings and shootings. However, the city resorted to injunctions to break unions, no matter who inspired the violence or, indeed, whether or not violence was involved. *See* Honey, *Southern Labor and Black Civil Rights,* 72–73, 75–78, 93,149,181, 208–9, on AFL and Crump, and 260–63 on the American Snuff strike; and Green, "Labor in the South," 70–73, on the Greyhound strike.

20. Michael Honey, *Going Down Jericho Road: The Memphis Strike, Martin Luther King's Last Campaign,* 63 (New York: W.W. Norton & Co., 2007).

21. Green, "Labor in the South," 102–24.

City politics also helped the sanitation workers to press their case. Unlike their counterparts in most of the South, Memphis's African-American citizens never had been disfranchised, although for decades the poll tax and the Crump machine had controlled their vote. Civil rights protesters had made modest gains in desegregating the downtown stores, and in 1964 black voters provided the winning margin in the election of racial moderate William Ingram as mayor, giving Jones encouragement to press on. Hoping for a reasonable response, in August 1966, the workers were on the verge of a strike. But even during Ingram's regime, the courts issued a severe injunction, and the Public Works Department threatened to replace the workers if they ignored it. At this point, black community leaders remained reluctant to endanger that progress toward desegregation that had been made during Ingram's regime and took little action to support the union.[22]

By 1968, however, things had changed dramatically. By now, many blacks no longer viewed the sanitation workers' struggle as simply a labor dispute. Organizing among sanitation workers had become a struggle of African Americans as a group for the right to be treated with human dignity by the white power structure. But which side one took in this struggle depended a great deal upon perceptions of the past, and these perceptions differed dramatically for whites and blacks.[23] Prior to 1968, many whites, and even some blacks, had held that Memphis had no race problem. In the 1950s and 1960s, these people pointed out, blacks had voted in significant numbers. Desegregation of public facilities had occurred earlier and more peacefully there than in any other major city in the Deep South. Yet, beneath a veneer of civility and white paternalism, brutality at the hands of an overwhelmingly white police force was a fact of daily life for blacks; so was widespread poverty and exclusion from any of the real centers of economic power or political decision making. In the mid-sixties, racial progressives saw signs of real change under Mayor Ingram. The 1966 shift from a commission to a mayor-council form of municipal government would, they believed, facilitate Ingram's progressive reforms. And in 1967 three blacks gained seats on the new city council. At the same time, however, the 1967 mayoral election split black and working-class white voters. Previously they had joined to elect Ingram, but now the black vote divided between incumbent Ingram and black mayoral candidate A.W. Willis, while Henry Loeb won by campaigning openly as a white supremacist, gaining virtually no support from the eighty thousand African-American voters. Loeb's election hardened white resistance to further black gains and especially frustrated and angered the city's historically moderate black middle class and religious

22. On the city's civil rights history, *see* Green, "Labor in the South"; Gerald D. McKnight, "The 1968 Memphis Sanitation Strike and the FBI: A Case Study in Urban Surveillance," 83 *South Atlantic Quarterly* 138–56 (Spring 1984); and Tucker, *Memphis Since Crump*, 118–42.

23. For accounts of the strike and its meaning, *see* J. Edwin Stanfield, *In Memphis: More Than a Garbage Strike*, (Atlanta, Ga.: Southern Regional Council, Mar. 22, 1968); Beifuss, *At the River I Stand*; Schick and Courtier with Collins, "Memphis, Tennessee"; and Green, "Labor in the South." *See also* the sparest and most direct account: Philip S. Foner, *Organized Labor and the Black Worker, 1619–1973*, 378–85 (New York: International Publishers, 1974). A good short account is in Joseph Goulden, *Jerry Wurf: Labor's Last Angry Man*, 142–82 (New York: Macmillan, 1982). *See also* Anne Trotter, "The Memphis Business Community and Integration," in Elizabeth Jacoway and David R. Colburn, eds., *Southern Businessmen and Desegregation*, 282–300 (Baton Rouge: Louisiana State Univ. Press, 1982); and one of the most pointed and thorough accounts, F. Ray Marshall and Arvil Van Adams, "The Memphis Public Works Employees Strike," in W. Ellison Chalmers and Gerald W. Cormick, eds., *Racial Conflict and Negotiations, Perspectives and First Case Studies*, 75–216 (Ann Arbor, Mich.: Institute of Labor and Industrial Relations et al., 1971).

leaders. "After all these years of being cooperative citizens, there were not enough white people to join with us to give us a decent mayor," recalled Rev. Benjamin Hooks.[24]

Under Loeb, a fiscal conservative who vowed to cut the city's costs, conditions worsened considerably for both the sanitation workers and the African-American community. The city's refusal to provide modern equipment meant that workers had to carry leaking tubs of garbage on their heads. White residents considered these workers "garbage men," not hard-working fellow citizens providing essential services. In the neighborhoods, they were treated as servants who should be grateful for gifts of cast-off clothing as a "fringe benefit" of the job. City authorities refused to entertain the idea that their work might be worth more than $1.60 an hour. To save money, Loeb's administration reduced the workforce in the sanitation division of the Public Works Department, an act that vastly increased the workloads of those who remained and forced them to toil extra hours without compensation. Loeb also appointed as Director of Public Works his political crony, Charles Blackburn, a man with little tact and few negotiating skills, who repeatedly affronted the workers' sense of dignity. In one episode at the end of January, the sanitation division sent black workers home without pay during a rainstorm, while allowing the few white supervisors and drivers who worked for the division to remain on the job and collect wages. Such behavior by white bosses was typical, as was their refusal to allow blacks to take shelter during storms. On February 1, this disdain for black workers' safety and comfort had tragic consequences, when two African-American sanitation workers took refuge from a storm in a truck's compactor, which malfunctioned and crushed them to death. Having no insurance, the men's families were left destitute, while the city took more than a week to pay for their burial expenses. Meanwhile, the deeply racist Loeb regime continued to scorn—when it did not simply ignore—black sanitation workers' efforts to organize and thus seek to ameliorate their condition.[25]

Following a chain of accumulated grievances, the deaths of the two black workers and the failure of the Public Works Department to pay wages to the men sent home in January set off a spontaneous walkout by outraged workers on February 12. "You got home you had to take your clothes off at the door 'cause you didn't want to bring all that filth in the house. We didn't have no decent place to eat your lunch. You didn't have no place to use the restroom. Conditions was just terrible. We didn't have no say about nothing. Whatever they said, that's what you had to do: right, wrong, indifferent. Anything that you did that the supervisor didn't like, he'd fire you, whatever. You didn't have no recourse, no way of getting' back at him. We just got tired of all that."[26]

Almost immediately, the local chapter of the National Association for the Advancement of Colored People (NAACP) and many black ministers voiced their support for the job action. In response, for the next two months, Loeb's government refused to bargain with the men as long as they were on strike and hauled out every means at its disposal to break the union. Its methods included an injunction that prohibited union leaders from almost all public activities, continual police intimidation of strikers and their supporters, permanent replacement of many strikers by scabs of both races, and refusing to talk to union representatives or to recognize the right of city workers to organize. The city's two

24. *See* Trotter, "Memphis Business Community," 286–89; Sandra Vaughn, "Memphis: Heart of the Mid-South," in Robert D. Bullard, ed., *In Search of the New South; The Black Urban Experience in the 1970s and 1980s*, 98–120 (Tuscaloosa: Univ. of Alabama Press, 1989); and Stanfield, *In Memphis: More Than a Garbage Strike*, 3. Hooks is quoted in Beifuss, *At the River I Stand*, 57.

25. Green, "Labor in the South," 119, 127–40, and Beifuss, *At the River I Stand*, 28–31.

26. Michael Honey, *supra* note 20, at 62

daily newspapers supported these policies and ignored the perspectives of the strikers and the black community. The press failed to explain the underlying causes of the strike and ran racist cartoons and headlines that further offended black sensibilities. Powerful city elites saw the dispute as an opportunity to teach lower-class blacks that while their counterparts in other places, such as Detroit and New York, might demonstrate and strike, this could not happen in Memphis. White citizens seemed to Support Loeb's hard-line stance, helping with garbage collection and applauding the city's intransigent stance. The city government even gave the impression that those who interfered with strike-breakers might be shot in the streets, as newspapers pictured white replacement workers carrying guns while they picked up garbage.[27]

Confusion on the part of the city council heightened tensions. Its Committee on Public Works first told strike supporters that it would recommend a settlement to the council, but instead the council, on February 23, without permitting public comment, adopted a hostile substitute resolution. Finding the council meeting closed, strikers and their supporters flooded from the City Hall into the streets for a march, only to be attacked by truncheon-wielding, mace-spraying police. This incident, more than any other, demonstrated the limits of the black political empowerment and civil rights victories that had been achieved in Memphis. It demonstrated in a visceral way that black economic powerlessness remained the main fact of life, and it fused festering economic grievances with fundamental questions of civil and human rights.

On Saturday, February 24, the city obtained an injunction against AFSCME national President Jerry Wurf, other union staff, and local organizers, blanketly prohibiting any of them from marching, picketing or making public speeches, under threat of arrest. Chancellor Robert Hoffman declared, "No principle of law is more firmly established than the principle that public employees do not have the right to strike ... it is illegal for any person to authorize, induce or engage in a strike against the city of Memphis."[28]

The blatant racism of the city administration now galvanized black ministers, politicians, and civil rights leaders and energized a hitherto somnolent local labor movement. On the day after the police attacks, black community leaders and organizations, long at odds with each other, put aside their divisions and organized a group called Community on the Move for Equality (COME). Over the next six weeks, this organization proceeded to unite the African-American community behind the strikers with mass meetings, daily picketing, and a boycott of downtown businesses (particularly targeting the Loeb family's laundries), and the newspapers. Whites and blacks from the Memphis Trades and Labor Council and the United Rubber Workers and other Industrial unions joined to support the strike.[29] Rev. James Lawson declared to reporters, "[Mayor Loeb] treats the workers as though they are not men, that's a racist point of view. For at the heart of racism is the idea that a man is not a man, that a person is not a person." Thereafter, marchers, particularly the sanitation workers carried signs, "I Am a Man."

All in all, the walkout triggered a degree of mobilization of both the African-American community and progressive whites rarely seen in Memphis or anywhere in the South. As the conflict in Memphis became both more dramatic and more desperate, the strug-

---

27. Green, "Labor in the South," 140–64; Beifuss, *At the River I Stand, passim*; Garrow, *Bearing the Cross*, 575–624; and Goulden, *Jerry Wurf.*

28. In *City of Alcoa v. Electrical Workers Local 760*, 308 S.W. 2d 476 (1957), the Tennessee Supreme Court shakily reasoned that since the National Labor Relations Act did not cover public workers, strikes by public workers must be illegal.

29. Green, "Labor in the South," 190–93, 197; *Memphis Union News*, Mar. 8, 1968.

gle drew in Roy Wilkins of the NAACP, Bayard Rustin of the AFL-CIO's A. Philip Randolph Institute, and AFSCME President Jerry Wurf, as tacticians and speakers at huge mass rallies. On March 14, a crowd variously estimated at between nine thousand and twenty-five thousand Memphians attended a rally featuring Wilkins and Rustin. Behind the scenes, debates whirled over whether to emphasize the strike as a workers' struggle, with hopes of drawing in more white unionists, or as a civil rights struggle, in order to solidify the black community behind it. For AFSCME, the outcome of the struggle represented the success or failure of its efforts to organize blue-collar public workers, especially in the South. For national civil rights leaders, the struggle in Memphis provided a crucial test of white America's willingness to come to grips with black economic demands or to recognize the dignity of African Americans in a more general sense. Many local people concluded that the strike was *both* a labor and a civil rights struggle and that the two could not be separated. With this perspective in mind, on March 17, Rev. James Lawson, a long-time Memphis religious and civil-rights leader, called his friend and colleague Martin Luther King, Jr., for the second time to ask him to come to the city and speak on behalf of the workers.[30]

King's labor perspective led him naturally to support the Memphis union struggle. His staff at SCLC, in the midst of frenzied preparations for the Poor People's Campaign, opposed his involvement in Memphis, while King identified the situation as emblematic of the dilemmas facing poor people and especially poor blacks. As workers, the sanitation men fought for union recognition; for the right to vacations, decent wages and benefits, rest breaks, and health and safety precautions; and for recognition of their right to belong to a union. King commented that these men, like most of the working poor, had none of the benefits that made a job worthwhile. Yet, more than that, he realized, black sanitation workers fought for dignity and respect as human beings. King understood that the conditions of the Memphis strikers typified the harsh realities facing the black working poor and unemployed all over America.[31]

On March 18, when King made his first speech to the workers and the Memphis community, the strike already had been under way for five weeks. King's role was to break the national news blackout of what was developing into one of the most dynamic labor and civil-rights struggles of the 1960s. He proceeded to put the situation into a context that could help people understand the strike as something with larger implications. Thereby the support of both unions and civil rights organizations across the country might be mobilized.

King used Memphis as an example of how the nation had devalued the labor of the working poor. "You are reminding the nation that it is a crime for people to live in this rich nation and receive starvation wages ... this is our plight as a people all over America," King said. "We are living as a people in a literal depression," but one unrecognized by most whites or the government. "Do you know that most of the poor people in our country are working every day?" he asked the crowd. "And they are making wages so low that they cannot begin to function in the mainstream of the economic life of our nation. These are the facts which must be seen, and it is criminal to have people working on a full-time basis and [in] a fulltime job, getting part-time income." It was the

---

30. Green, "Labor in the South," 190–93, 197. For a dramatic account of how the issues around the strike developed into broader concerns, see the film version of Beifuss, *At the River I Stand,* as shown on the Public Broadcasting System, Apr. 2, 1993, and distributed by California Newsreel.

31. Garrow, *Bearing the Cross,* 616; and "Address of Rev. Martin Luther King, Jr., on Mar. 18, 1968, at Mason Temple Mass Meeting in Memphis," Box 6, Folder 29, SSFMVC/UMT.

powerlessness of workers and the unemployed, especially people of color, said King, that accounted for the widespread poverty in America. "We are tired of being at the bottom," he said; we are tired of "wall-to-wall rats and roaches" instead of wall-to-wall carpeting; "We are tired of smothering in an airtight cage of poverty in the midst of an affluent society. We are tired of walking the streets in [a] search for jobs that do not exist."[32]

King also explained the sanitation strike as emblematic of the freedom movement's evolution from civil-rights demands to more systemic demands. According to King, the struggle for black equality logically had brought the movement to Memphis. While the Selma march and the Voting Rights Act of 1965 had brought to an end one phase of the struggle, "now our struggle is for genuine equality, which means economic equality. For we know that it isn't enough to integrate lunch counters. What does it profit a man to be able to eat at an integrated lunch counter if he doesn't earn enough money to buy a hamburger and a cup of coffee?" Civil rights gains had been only a down payment on the fulfillment of the American Dream. Returning to a theme of his 1963 "I Have a Dream" speech, King demanded payment on the "promissory note" for life, liberty, and happiness that originated in the documents of the American Revolution. "We are saying now is the time," King told Memphians, "to make real the promises of democracy."[33]

King's plea for African-American racial unity in support of working class demands resonated deeply in Memphis; his call for the "haves" to join hands with the "have-nots" already had become a central theme of the strike. Even before his appearance, the confrontation between ill-treated workers and a racist city administration had lessened divisions based upon conflicting political loyalties and organizational turf battles among African-American leaders in Memphis, particularly among black ministers. As Rev. Ralph Jackson, a key leader and negotiator in the conflict, later told interviewers, he and other members of the black middle class had been distant from black workers and had not understood their plight at all. His eyes had been opened by thirteen hundred sanitation strikers carrying placards proclaiming "I Am a Man" and demanding to be treated not as "boys" or as servants but as citizens with rights equal to those of the wealthy and White. Moreover, the experience of being maced by the police had brought Jackson and other better-off blacks sharply up against the racial system and taught them how it felt to be both black and poor. The strike drew ministers and professionals away from a focus purely on civil-rights concerns and into the daily lives of poor people, where economic and racial injustice went hand in hand. Thus, a struggle that the poorest of the poor had initiated became central to the achievement of intraclass black unity in the Memphis of the late 1960s.[34]

The March 18 mass meeting validated King's poor people's strategy and released him from the brooding depression, anxiety, and exhaustion that increasingly had weighed him down. Rev. Lawson, the leading minister organizing support for the strikers, pointed out that, despite the "sardine atmosphere" in Mason Temple and the rising militancy of younger black activists who rejected nonviolence as an absolute principle, the Memphis crowd showed complete support for King's mission of nonviolent mass struggle. "Martin was visibly shaken by all this," said Lawson, "for this kind of support was unprecedented in the Movement. No one had ever been able to get these numbers out before."

---

32. "Address of Rev. Martin Luther King, Jr., on Mar. 18, 1968, at Mason Temple Mass Meeting in Memphis," Box 6, Folder 29, SSFMVC/UMT.

33. *Ibid.*

34. H. Ralph Jackson, interview by F. Ray Marshall and Arvil Van Adams, July 21, 1969, in Marshall and Van Adams, "Memphis Public Works Employees Strike," 169–79.

King became so inspired by the rally that he vowed to return to lead a mass march and called for a one-day general strike in support of the sanitation workers. At this point, the Memphis strike seemed to offer powerful testimony supporting King's belief that movements of the working poor and the unemployed represented the next phase of the freedom struggle.[35]

King had placed the sanitation strike not only into the context of the movement for black unity, but into an almost classic labor context. King's presence in Memphis awoke the national media to the importance of the strike there and brought many international unions into the picture. More than any other group, AFSCME, whose future in the South, if not nationally, hung on the outcome of the strike, provided care and support. In addition, however, once King and other civil rights leaders had made the strike a national issue, the AFL-CIO and its member unions sent substantial financial support—well over one hundred thousand dollars by the end of the strike. Fifty union officials from ten southern states meeting in Memphis for an AFL-CIO Social Security conference backed the strike and called the conduct of the city government "a throw-back to the Dark Ages."[36]

At the local level, attention from the national AFL-CIO galvanized many white union leaders to take a stronger position in support of the strike. The white-led Memphis Trades and Labor Council, the local AFL-CIO coordinating body, backed the strike with donations of funds and by mobilizing a March 4 march of some five hundred white unionists. The *Memphis Union News,* edited by Bill Ross, sharply and repeatedly denounced Mayor Loeb and "the ultra-conservative community leaders" he represented and supported the boycott of downtown stores and "the labor-hating press." The Labor Council and its Amalgamated Meat Cutters and Butcher Workman's Union President Tommy Powell called for a petition drive to recall Loeb. And some local white leaders challenged white workers' racism. George Clark, white president of United Rubber Workers of America Local 186, responded to criticism from white members of his union with a ringing denunciation of "the right-wing people in our plant that are supposed to be union members," stating that they "will not prevent this union from supporting this, or any other group of workers, in their efforts to have a union."[37]

Black unionists also were forthright in their support of the strike. Leroy Clark, president of Local 282 of the United Furniture Workers of America, and other African-American trade unionists encouraged community and union picketing and support, while black members of the rubber workers' local provided space for meetings and moral support to the sanitation workers from the beginning. William Lucy played a key role as an international AFSCME organizer. George Holloway and a few other black members of UAW Local 988 at the International Harvester plant supported the strike wholeheartedly, despite the disapproval of whites at the plant. One perspective, then, held that a labor-civil rights coalition had in fact been created in Memphis. Labor economist F. Ray Marshall, for example, concluded that the support of organized labor, black and white,

---

35. On King's state of mind, *see* Garrow, *Bearing the Cross,* 570–610. James Lawson, interview by F. Ray Marshall and Arvil Van Adams, July 21, 1969, in Marshall and Van Adams, "Memphis Public Works Employees Strike," 179–85, quotation on 181.

36. *Memphis Union News,* Jan. through May 1968, carried heavy supportive coverage of the strike. The quoted views are in the Mar. 1968 issue. *See also* an article in the national periodical of the American Federation of State, County and Municipal Employees, 33 *Public Employee* 12 (Apr. 1968), on union contributions.

37. *Memphis Union News,* issues of Mar. and Apr. 1968.

combined with an aroused civil-rights community, provided "a significant element leading to the [eventual] settlement of the dispute."[38]

However, at the same time that labor and civil rights solidarity seemed to be growing, white workers' responses were ambivalent, even contradictory. While some white unionists engaged in arms-length solidarity, others expressed outright hostility to the strike. The AFL-CIO's regional political organizer Dan Powell recalled that African American workers could win only when their strike became a racial issue, making it possible to mobilize the African-American community behind them. Yet, as he and AFSCME leader Lucy noted, while white union leaders supported the strike as an economic issue, as soon as it became a racial struggle, many rank-and-file whites abandoned it. AFSCME organizer Jesse Epps and Rev. Lawson both observed that white workers generally stayed out of the struggle. On March 4, when they did march in support of the sanitation workers, white workers began their march separately from blacks, took a different route, and stayed to themselves when the groups came to a common destination. Worse, the building trades and many craft unions, always a conservative force in Memphis, took no official position on the sanitation strike but unofficially sided with Mayor Loeb. Many white workers did not want to pay the increased taxes that wage increases for sanitation workers would have necessitated. Nor did national union support necessarily translate into support at the local level. Although the national UAW had a strong record of support for Dr. King, for example, whites in UAW Local 988 had a long history of militant racism and largely opposed the sanitation workers' struggle. In short, the resistant racialized consciousness of the white working class surfaced clearly during the strike.[39]

The schizophrenic character of organized labor in Memphis reflected a growing racialization of white worker consciousness in the late 1960s which had become apparent to King, who found himself increasingly at odds with many white union members and much of the established union leadership. The 1955 merger of the AFL craft unions and the CIO industrial unions may have strengthened organized labor but, as Lucy later commented, its leadership, starting with AFL-CIO President George Meany, "was not vested in the more progressive side of labor." King wanted labor leaders to take up the challenge of poverty in America, but he felt that, for the most part, they had not done that. King's opposition to the Vietnam War and his unwillingness to condemn Black Power also distanced him, and many grassroots activists, from mainstream liberals, especially many top union leaders with institutional ties to the American foreign-policy establishment.

At the same time that King struggled with these contradictions between the "movement" and the labor bureaucracy, Black Power advocates criticized him for his ties to liberals and integrationists. In 1967, when King spoke in Chicago of a "Negro-Labor alliance," blacks booed him. Such responses forced King to speak less about alliances with labor

38. Leroy Clark, recorded interview by Michael Honey, Mar. 27, 1983, Memphis; George Clark, recorded interview by Michael Honey, Oct. 30, 1984, Memphis; Clarence Coe, recorded interview by Michael Honey, May 28 and 29, 1989, Memphis; and George Holloway, recorded interview by Michael Honey, Mar. 23, 1990, Baltimore; all in author's possession. Clark quotation in "A Report to Members of Local 186 from G.W. Clark, President," mimeographed, ca. Mar. 1968, in Box 5, Folder 12, SSFMVC/UMT. Marshall and Van Adams, "Memphis Public Works Employees Strike," 100.

39. Concerning the depth of the problem of white union racism, see Honey, *Southern Labor and Black Civil Rights, passim*. William Lucy, recorded interview by Michael Honey, Apr. 2,1993, Memphis, in author's possession; and Holloway, interview by Honey, Mar. 23, 1990. Epps, interview by Marshall and Van Adams, July 8, 1969, 165–69; James Lawson, interview by Marshall and Van Adams, July 21, 1969, 179–83; and Dan Powell, interview by Marshall and Van Adams, June 11, 1969, 183–85.

and more about independent black action. Thus, while King assumed the role of a labor militant in Memphis, his ties to many of the international unions, and certainly to the AFL-CIO, increasingly frayed.[40]

Long before the Memphis strike, King had realized that the coalition he sought between the civil rights movement and the unions was problematical. At the same time, King lacked a real grounding in the labor movement, making it difficult to conceive or execute the Poor People's Campaign, which included few unions in the coalition of the poor. Neither King nor his lieutenants had built a strong working-class base for the campaign, nor did they seem to know how to do so. King's conception of the campaign rested on the idea of an alliance among poor whites and poor people from racially oppressed minorities, few of whom belonged to unions and many of whom were without jobs. Most unions in high-wage sectors of the economy, on the other hand, long since had opted out of poor people's politics.

Even more worrisome to King, the ability of such racial polarizers as George Wallace to stimulate "backlash" among white voters had increasingly come to define two-party politics. In a May 1967 speech titled "Civil Rights at the Crossroads," delivered to shop stewards of the Teamsters Union, which in the past had pledged funds to SCLC, King identified the racial undercurrents eroding potential coalitions. Few whites, unionized or not, said King, recognized or welcomed the new phase of the movement that had opened after the passage of the Voting Rights Act in 1965. Once basic civil rights had been won, blacks began to look for the second phase, which King called "the realization of equality," meaning economic and social equality as well as civil rights. King realized that his effort to end widespread economic disparities had no guarantee in the Constitution or Bill of Rights and would cost billions of dollars in taxes, at a time when many in the white population, including many white workers, increasingly saw their interests as being in conflict with those of the poor and people of color. "To put it in plain language," King told the Teamsters, "many Americans would like to have a nation which is a democracy for white Americans but simultaneously a dictatorship over black Americans."[41]

King's move into the second phase of the civil rights revolution had elicited hostility toward him from many quarters, particularly the media and the federal government. The Federal Bureau of Investigation long had orchestrated a smear campaign against him in the press, and during the Memphis campaign its surveillance of King and all his associates escalated.

On March 28, media hostility climaxed after black Memphis teenagers began breaking store windows on Beale Street during an attempted mass march led by King. Within

---

40. On the waning of the CIO and its merger with the AFL, *see* Robert H. Zieger, *The CIO, 1935–1955*, 333–56 (Chapel Hill: Univ. of North Carolina Press, 1995). In the turmoil within the civil rights movement in 1966 and 1967, Bayard Rustin and other liberals and unionists remained silent about the war in Vietnam and became increasingly vocal in criticizing movement radicalism, thus discrediting themselves in the eyes of militants. King, on the other hand, refused to condemn the more militant wing of the movement, even while he criticized the Democratic party for its failure to provide a real vehicle for change. *See* Fairclough, *To Redeem the Soul of America*, 327, and Foner, *Organized Labor and the Black Worker*, 366, 376. *See also* King's speech, "Civil Rights at the Crossroads, an Address to the Shop Stewards of Local 815," and Honey, "Coalition and Conflict."

41. King, "Civil Rights at the Crossroads, an Address to the Shop Stewards of Local 815." During the Chicago struggles, Teamsters President James Hoffa had pledged $50,000 to SCLC, but it is unclear whether he came through with the funds. Garrow, *Bearing the Cross*, 536.

a block, King took the lead, linked arm in arm with CME Bishop Julian Smith, Ralph Abernathy, Bernard Lee, and John Lawson. It was 11:05. King's admirers continued to charge up from the back and push ministers out of the way.

March organizers had strategically placed L.C. Reed and other sanitation workers right behind King. The workers had gone from Clayborn Temple to City Hall and back many times, and they could lend a great deal of discipline to this march. But as the workers passed W.C. Handy Park, said Reed, "Well, we got mixed up some kind of way. And they had a lot of youngsters in there, and they were running up through the crowd hollering, 'Let me get by, I want to get to the front.'" Youngsters moved ahead of the workers and cut them off from the march's leadership, and then, "They really got unruly."

As the crowd moved down Hernando to Beale, marchers grew more confident and strode down the street singing, "We shall overcome" and chanting, "Down with Loeb." A mass work stoppage had not occurred that morning, but they estimated that 10,000 to 15,000 people marched.

Before they got to Main, Lawson, King, and others at the front of the march heard the resounding crack of storefront windows behind them on Beale Street. Lawson sent marshalls back to see what was going on, but the frightening sound of shattering glass continued. Others in the march exclaimed, "Windows! They're breaking windows!" Someone shouted, "Damn it! They're ruining the march!"

Reverend Starks and several others surrounded King, putting their arms through his to lead him down McCall, a side street. Using this disorder as their excuse, Memphis police unleashed an indiscriminate and violent attack against all marchers and citizens in the area of the march.

As they tried to get marchers to retreat, the police kept moving in on them. At 11:18, Police Chief McDonald used a bullhorn to order the march to disperse, while his officers put on gas masks and began moving south from their blockade across Main Street. "The police somewhere got their word to get tough, and believe me they did," said Reverend Jackson. Patrolmen and motorcycle police waded into the crowd, using clubs and mace, shooting tear gas or rolling tear gas grenades on the ground.

Looting and police attacks escalated. Police actions, far from stopping violence, spread it. A flying wedge of policemen came through the area, and the young people started throwing rocks and bottles at them. Their resistance infuriated police.

Most of the sanitation workers managed to stay in a group and turned back toward the church under their own discipline. They had their own marshals and mostly avoided police assaults. "We didn't have trouble with the tub toters," one of the police remarked.

When police started swinging clubs and spraying mace, people scattered in every direction, as the police seemed to make no distinction between marchers and looters. In the pandemonium, children lost their parents, older people who could not run became trapped, people ducked into doorways or into people's homes for refuge. Fear surged through the crowd. "The police seemed slightly reluctant about apprehending the group that was doing the damage and dashed head-long into the peaceful marchers."

At the rear of the march, Kay Pittman Black had made her way to Clayborn Temple and Ralph Jackson's adjoining AME Minimum Salary Building. "Inside the AME building was a horror show," she wrote. "I saw a man with a mangled bloody arm. People's eyes were streaming and red from the effects of mace. I saw an 8- or 9-year old child with a bloody head and a woman on the floor moaning and crying. The skin across her forehead looked like bloody pulp."

The interior of Clayborn Temple looked like the aftermath of a war. The church held 1,500 people, who filled every seat and space in the aisles, as ministers read the names of lost children and instructed people on how to get treated for tear gas. A little boy took tissues to people, and a Southwestern College student took a bucket of water around to bathe people's faces. Reverend Blackburn, Clayton Temple's pastor, found a man in the chapel beaten into a semi-conscious state, a girl with asthma suffering terribly from tear gas, and, on the trunk of a car in the alley, a man that he feared had a broken back. People sick from gas or wounded by broken glass lay everywhere. Reverend Starks pleaded, "All of you that are on our side, we are asking you to go home. Tonight we are asking you to go home and prepare for this weekend." But until things calmed down outside, they couldn't leave. When people tried to leave Clayborn Temple, police attacked them with mace and clubs. Police entered the Temple, clubbing people and shooting tear gas canisters onto the floors and against the walls, leaving stains that remained many months later. People ran from the canisters, but as the gas spread through the sanctuary, they were forced to the floor to get air—eyes watering, gasping for breath.

By 2:00 pm, police lifted the state of siege at Clayborn Temple. For leading the march, the City sued Dr. King, *City of Memphis v. Reverend Martin Luther King, Jr., et al.* C-68-80, 1968.[42]

Later in their enthusiasm to repress the gathering, police killed black youth Larry Payne with a shotgun and beat scores of others. Following this incident, the mayor placed the African-American community under curfew, and the state brought in four thousand members of the National Guard, while the courts enjoined King from leading any more marches. With FBI encouragement, both federal officials and national news media barraged the public with unfavorable images of King's abilities and character. The events in Memphis now brought King's national leadership into question. This onslaught convinced King that he must defy the court order against him and return to Memphis to lead a massive and nonviolent public demonstration, even under the most unfavorable of circumstances. Failure to do so, he feared, would destroy the Poor People's Campaign and his own status as a national leader.[43]

The Memphis strike thus brought King, and in many ways the movements of the 1960s, to a point of crisis that entailed both opportunity and danger. On the night of April 3 at Mason Temple in Memphis, King, on the verge of complete exhaustion, offered the world his last speech. In it he offered both a pessimistic and an optimistic vision of the future. King still believed that the direction of events favored the freedom movement. "Something is happening in our world. The masses of people are rising up" all over the world in a "human rights revolution." He saw this rising up as a positive thing, not as something to be repressed, and the sheer force of numbers involved in the revolution meant that people did not need violence to bring about change if they were united. But he also warned that Pharaoh had prolonged slavery by keeping the slaves fighting each other, whereas in truth "either we go up together or we go down together." King reviewed the great history of achievements and change the freedom struggle had wrought in his lifetime; and his own life flashed before him, as he more or less predicted his death at the hands of some of "our sick white brothers." In a climax of emo-

---

42. Descriptions of March 28 taken from Michael Honey, *supra* note 20, at 343–355.

43. *See* McKnight, "The 1968 Memphis Sanitation Strike," on the role of the FBI; and Beifuss, *At the River I Stand,* 211–42, on the Mar. 28 altercations. The film *At the River I Stand* graphically depicts these events. See also Garrow, *Bearing the Cross,* 611–16; and David Garrow, *The FBI and Martin Luther King, Jr.: From "Solo" to Memphis,* 173–203 (New York: Norton, 1981). The clippings files in SSFMVC/UMT make clear the role of the media in exacerbating King's difficulties.

tionalism, King issued his last testament before the black poor and dispossessed of Memphis, saying, "I may not get there with you, but I want you to know tonight that we as a people will get to the promised land."[44] The next day he was dead, victim of an assassin's bullet.

King's death led to massive bad publicity for Memphis and to rapid defeat for Mayor Loeb, who had resisted or sabotaged every effort by the city council or citizens to resolve the sanitation strike. On April 2, white business leaders already had begun to pressure Loeb to soften his opposition to collective bargaining; after King's death, a delegation of them came to him and demanded that he settle the strike. Meanwhile, cities all over the U.S. went up in flames in response to King's death. In Memphis alone, nearly a million dollars in property damage (including 275 stores looted) and three deaths resulted from turmoil in the streets. On April 7, some eight thousand Memphians, most of them white, held a "Memphis Cares" memorial. Then, on April 8, thousands of labor, civil rights, and religious leaders converged on the city from around the country for a completely silent march by between twenty and forty thousand people. Some one hundred thousand people marched the next day at King's funeral procession in Atlanta. At the Memphis rally, the UAW's Walter Reuther pledged fifty thousand dollars to the sanitation workers, and the AFL-CIO's Meany set aside twenty thousand dollars as the first installment in a special fundraising drive among unions to support the sanitation strike. President Lyndon B. Johnson sent Undersecretary of Labor James Reynolds to impress upon local officials the urgency of the need for a strike settlement; Tennessee's Gov. Buford Ellington likewise pressed for resolution of the dispute. Although unrepentant to the end, Loeb finally removed himself as an obstacle to negotiations, and on April 16 union members ratified a proposed settlement in which the city capitulated to virtually all of the union's demands, including union recognition and dues check-off. The union had won.[45]

At the national level, however, King's death destroyed whatever chance the Poor People's Campaign had had for success, and removed from national life the one figure who still had the capacity to unite progressives in America. In a real sense, it brought to an end one phase of the movements of the 1960s. American history indeed turned in a direction that King had greatly feared. Mass uprisings in urban ghettoes, the assassination of Robert Kennedy, police riots in the streets of Chicago, and the election of Richard Nixon as U.S. president all followed on the heels of King's murder. Subsequent years saw the creation not of a progressive coalition of black and white workers, but the Republican party's "southern strategy" to split white workers and the white middle class away from the Democratic party, using racism to rationalize growing racial-economic inequality. White racial identity, forged through centuries of propaganda and white economic advantage over people of color, continued to undermine both unions and larger political coalitions, turning "Populism" into a rhetorical prop for business interests.

Twenty-five years after King's death, participants at observances in Memphis noted some of the consequences of failing to attend to the agenda he laid out in 1968. In pre-

---

44. *See* the film *At the River I Stand* and King, "Mountaintop Speech," Apr. 3, 1968, in SSFMVC/UMT, Box 6, Folder 29.

45. Beifuss, *At the River I Stand,* 333–42; Trotter, "Memphis Business Community and Integration," 295–97; *Memphis Union News* 9 (Apr. 1968), on donated union funds; and Goulden, *Jerry Wurf,* 181.

dominantly black cities such as Memphis, African Americans continued to lose ground in a disintegrating economic order on which they had a slippery foothold at best. Employers and the state have repressed, discouraged, and in other ways whittled away the gains of both unions and the organized black freedom movement, while the economic fortunes of many African Americans have sunk to the lowest level since the Great Depression of the 1930s. These conditions remain nowhere more apparent than in the American South.[46]

On the other side of the historical ledger, King's struggles in the last year of his life have left an important and positive legacy. Black leader Rev. H. Ralph Jackson recalled that bringing King into Memphis was the key to the strike's outcome; the strike would have remained lost "as long as it was a local affair." In the aftermath of the strike victory, the black community and civil rights forces in Memphis surged forward. AFSCME 1733 became the largest single local in the city, consolidating nearly six thousand members, 90 percent of them black. In 1969, Local 1733, along with other Memphis unions, the NAACP, and the black community went on to instigate support of union organizing at Saint Joseph's Hospital. Although this drive failed, the city eased its opposition to collective bargaining; and in 1972 and 1973, white fire fighters and, ironically, the police (the vast majority of them white) created officially recognized unions. In 1978, both groups won strikes. In the early 1970s, an aroused African-American community elected blacks to the school board and elected the first black congressmen from the Mid-South since Reconstruction. By virtue of their prestige and the size of their union, the lowly sanitation workers became power brokers of a sort. In 1975, according to scholar Thomas Collins, "Local 1733 was the largest and by far the most powerful black political organization in town." As late as 1982, he felt that "the sanitation workers are in a position of power capable of making demands on the city political system quite independent of the black middle class," although the union's political power weakened in subsequent years. The racial divide in Memphis remained deep, and intraclass unity among blacks dissipated as well. Yet the strike victory and its aftermath brought a significant change in power relations in Memphis, leading in the 1990s to the election of an African American, Willie Herrenton, as mayor and also to a degree of black-white power sharing.[47]

The 1968 strike victory had ramifications beyond Memphis as well. "A new kind of respect and a new kind of recognition" of the role of garbage workers in municipal economies emerged after the Memphis strike, according to William Lucy. An upsurge of sanitation-worker organizing in several southern cities followed the Memphis struggle, and public-employee unionism became the fastest-growing sector of the union movement in the 1970s. According to Lucy, "a new enthusiasm to organize really went across sanitation workers across the country." The Memphis formula of maximum community involvement in union battles, the "Memphis spirit," as Lucy called it, also inspired other efforts to build labor-civil lights coalitions, most notably in the dramatic struggle between black hospital workers organized into Local 1199B Hospital Workers Union, joined by King's

46. *See* Honey, *Southern Labor and Black Civil Rights,* 279–91; and Michael Honey, "King's Unfinished Agenda: Economic Justice," paper delivered at conference on "Twenty-Five Years Since Martin Luther King, Jr.: Rebuilding Movements for Social Change," at National Civil Rights Museum, Memphis, Tenn., in author's possession, Apr. 2–4, 1993.

47. Jackson quotation from Marshall and Van Adams, "Memphis Public Works Employees Strike," 176; Trotter, "Memphis Business Community and Integration," 298; Schick and Courtier with Collins, "Memphis, Tennessee," 69–72, 75, and quotation on 80; second quotation is from Collins, "An Analysis of the Memphis Garbage Strike," 361.

Southern Christian Leadership Conference, and white city leaders in Charleston, South Carolina, in 1969.[48]

By the end of the 1970s, the upsurge in civil-rights unionism had receded, along with the SCLC itself. The Charleston strike, for example, led to no consolidation of union power. The model of a labor-civil rights coalition and of maximum community involvement in strikes remained, but their implementation seemed uncertain. Nonetheless, the death of King amid a labor struggle in Memphis left an ideological imprint on history which is an important legacy of the 1960s. Memphis and the Poor People's Campaign represent the culmination of King's search for a means to shake the foundations of Americanism and economic injustice. No one mounted as ambitious an effort to deal with the deep-seated ills of society or provided as universalistic a response to the forces of economic fragmentation and the disintegration of community. King sought to turn the civil rights movement toward an economic agenda that finally would address black economic demands that the United States had neglected ever since Reconstruction. At the same time, he tried to bring together the economic grievances of poor whites, blacks, and other people of color. The legacy of civil rights unionism remained uncertain in a subsequent era in which Republican and corporate strategies of divide-and-rule dominated the American landscape. Nonetheless, King's struggle to counter such strategies with coalition politics aimed at uniting poor and working people with other potential allies continued to offer an alternative road map for labor, civil rights, and reform movements, one based on King's admonition to striking sanitation workers in Memphis: "We can all get more together than we can apart ... and this is the way we gain power."[49]

---

48. William Lucy, interview by Honey, Apr. 2, 1993, in author's possession. See the positive assessment of the strike's outcome in Marshall and Van Adams, "Memphis Public Works Employees Strike," 83, 106–7. *See also* Foner, *Organized Labor and the Black Worker,* 378–96; Leon Fink and Brian Greenberg, *Upheaval in the Quiet Zone: A History of Hospital Workers' Union Local 1199,* 128–58 (Urbana: Univ. of Illinois Press, 1989); and Leon Fink, *In Search of the Working Class: Essays in American Labor History and Political Culture,* 51–85 (Urbana: Univ. of Illinois Press, 1994).

49. "Address of Rev. King," Mason Temple Mass Meeting, Mar. 8, 1968.

"I Have Been To the Mountaintop," Memphis Speech, April 3, 1968

Rev. Martin Luther King, Jr.

Something is happening in Memphis; something is happening in our world. And you know, if I were standing at the beginning of time, with the possibility of taking a kind of general and panoramic view of the whole of human history up to now, and the Almighty said to me, "Martin Luther King, which age would you like to live in?" I would take my mental flight by Egypt and I would watch God's children in their magnificent trek from the dark dungeons of Egypt through, or rather across the Red Sea, through the wilderness on toward the promised land. And in spite of its magnificence, I wouldn't stop there.

I would move on by Greece and take my mind to Mount Olympus. And I would see Plato, Aristotle, Socrates, Euripides and Aristophanes assembled around the Parthenon. And I would watch them around the Parthenon as they discussed the great and eternal issues of reality. But I wouldn't stop there.

I would go on, even to the great heyday of the Roman Empire. And I would see developments around there, through various emperors and leaders. But I wouldn't stop there.

I would even come up to the day of the Renaissance, and get a quick picture of all that the Renaissance did for the cultural and aesthetic life of man. But I wouldn't stop there.

I would even go by the way that the man for whom I am named had his habitat. And I would watch Martin Luther as he tacked his ninety-five theses on the door at the church of Wittenberg. But I wouldn't stop there.

I would come on up even to 1863, and watch a vacillating President by the name of Abraham Lincoln finally come to the conclusion that he had to sign the Emancipation Proclamation. But I wouldn't stop there.

I would even come up to the early thirties, and see a man grappling with the problems of the bankruptcy of his nation. And come with an eloquent cry that we have nothing to fear but "fear itself." But I wouldn't stop there.

Strangely enough, I would turn to the Almighty, and say, "If you allow me to live just a few years in the second half of the 20th century, I will be happy."

Now that's a strange statement to make, because the world is all messed up. The nation is sick. Trouble is in the land; confusion all around. That's a strange statement. But I know, somehow, that only when it is dark enough can you see the stars. And I see God working in this period of the twentieth century in a way that men, in some strange way, are responding.

Something is happening in our world. The masses of people are rising up. And wherever they are assembled today, whether they are in Johannesburg, South Africa; Nairobi, Kenya; Accra, Ghana; New York City; Atlanta, Georgia; Jackson, Mississippi; or Memphis, Tennessee — the cry is always the same: "We want to be free."

And another reason that I'm happy to live in this period is that we have been forced to a point where we are going to have to grapple with the problems that men have been trying to grapple with through history, but the demands didn't force them to do it. Survival demands that we grapple with them. Men, for years now, have been talking about war and peace. But now, no longer can they just talk about it. It is no longer a choice between violence and nonviolence in this world; it's nonviolence or nonexistence. That is where we are today.

And also in the human rights revolution, if something isn't done, and done in a hurry, to bring the colored peoples of the world out of their long years of poverty, their long years of hurt and neglect, the whole world is doomed. Now, I'm just happy that God has allowed me to live in this period to see what is unfolding. And I'm happy that He's allowed me to be in Memphis.

I can remember—I can remember when Negroes were just going around as Ralph has said, so often, scratching where they didn't itch, and laughing when they were not tickled. But that day is all over. We mean business now, and we are determined to gain our rightful place in God's world.

And that's all this whole thing is about. We aren't engaged in any negative protest and in any negative arguments with anybody. We are saying that we are determined to be men. We are determined to be people. We are saying—We are saying that we are God's children. And that we are God's children, we don't have to live like we are forced to live.

Now, what does all of this mean in this great period of history? It means that we've got to stay together. We've got to stay together and maintain unity. You know, whenever Pharaoh wanted to prolong the period of slavery in Egypt, he had a favorite, favorite formula for doing it. What was that? He kept the slaves fighting among themselves. But whenever the slaves get together, something happens in Pharaoh's court, and he cannot hold the slaves in slavery. When the slaves get together, that's the beginning of getting out of slavery. Now let us maintain unity.

Secondly, let us keep the issues where they are. The issue is injustice. The issue is the refusal of Memphis to be fair and honest in its dealings with its public servants, who happen to be sanitation workers. Now, we've got to keep attention on that. That's always the problem with a little violence. You know what happened the other day, and the press dealt only with the window-breaking. I read the articles. They very seldom got around to mentioning the fact that one thousand, three hundred sanitation workers are on strike, and that Memphis is not being fair to them, and that Mayor Loeb is in dire need of a doctor. They didn't get around to that.

Now we're going to march again, and we've got to march again, in order to put the issue where it is supposed to be—and force everybody to see that there are thirteen hundred of God's children here suffering, sometimes going hungry, going through dark and dreary nights wondering how this thing is going to come out. That's the issue. And we've got to say to the nation: We know how it's coming out. For when people get caught up with that which is right and they are willing to sacrifice for it, there is no stopping point short of victory.

We aren't going to let any mace stop us. We are masters in our nonviolent movement in disarming police forces; they don't know what to do. I've seen them so often. I remember in Birmingham, Alabama, when we were in that majestic struggle there, we would move out of the 16th Street Baptist Church day after day; by the hundreds we would move out. And Bull Connor would tell them to send the dogs forth, and they did come; but we just went before the dogs singing, "Ain't gonna let nobody turn me around."

Bull Connor next would say, "Turn the fire hoses on." And as I said to you the other night, Bull Connor didn't know history. He knew a kind of physics that somehow didn't relate to the transphysics that we knew about. And that was the fact that there was a certain kind of fire that no water could put out. And we went before the fire hoses; we had known water. If we were Baptist or some other denominations, we had been immersed. If we were Methodist, and some others, we had been sprinkled, but we knew water. That couldn't stop us.

And we just went on before the dogs and we would look at them; and we'd go on before the water hoses and we would look at it, and we'd just go on singing "Over my head I see freedom in the air." And then we would be thrown in the paddy wagons, and sometimes we were stacked in there like sardines in a can. And they would throw us in, and old Bull would say, "Take 'em off," and they did; and we would just go in the paddy wagon singing, "We Shall Overcome." And every now and then we'd get in jail, and we'd see the jailers looking through the windows being moved by our prayers, and being moved by our words and our songs. And there was a power there which Bull Connor couldn't adjust to; and so we ended up transforming Bull into a steer, and we won our struggle in Birmingham. Now we've got to go on in Memphis just like that. I call upon you to be with us when we go out Monday.

Now about injunctions: We have an injunction and we're going into court tomorrow morning to fight this illegal, unconstitutional injunction. All we say to America is, "Be true to what you said on paper." If I lived in China or even Russia, or any totalitarian country, maybe I could understand some of these illegal injunctions. Maybe I could understand the denial of certain basic First Amendment privileges, because they hadn't committed themselves to that over there. But somewhere I read of the freedom of assembly. Somewhere I read of the freedom of speech. Somewhere I read of the freedom of press. Somewhere I read that the greatness of America is the right to protest for right. And so just as I say, we aren't going to let dogs or water hoses turn us around, we aren't going to let any injunction turn us around. We are going on.

We need all of you. And you know what's beautiful to me is to see all of these ministers of the Gospel. It's a marvelous picture. Who is it that is supposed to articulate the longings and aspirations of the people more than the preacher? Somehow the preacher must have a kind of fire shut up in his bones. And whenever injustice is around he tell it. Somehow the preacher must be an Amos, and saith, "When God speaks who can but prophesy?" Again with Amos, "Let justice roll down like waters and righteousness like a mighty stream." Somehow the preacher must say with Jesus, "The Spirit of the Lord is upon me, because he hath anointed me," and he's anointed me to deal with "the problems of the poor."

And I want to commend the preachers, under the leadership of these noble men: James Lawson, one who has been in this struggle for many years; he's been to jail for struggling; he's been kicked out of Vanderbilt University for this struggle, but he's still going on, fighting for the rights of his people. Reverend Ralph Jackson, Billy Kiles; I could just go right on down the list, but time will not permit. But I want to thank all of them. And I want you to thank them, because so often, preachers aren't concerned about anything but themselves. And I'm always happy to see a relevant ministry.

It's all right to talk about "long white robes over yonder," in all of its symbolism. But ultimately people want some suits and dresses and shoes to wear down here! It's all right to talk about "streets flowing with milk and honey," but God has commanded us to be concerned about the slums down here, and his children who can't eat three square meals a day. It's all right to talk about the new Jerusalem, but one day, God's preacher must talk about the new New York, the new Atlanta, the new Philadelphia, the new Los Angeles, the new Memphis, Tennessee. This is what we have to do.

Now the other thing we'll have to do is this: Always anchor our external direct action with the power of economic withdrawal. Now, we are poor people. Individually, we are poor when you compare us with white society in America. We are poor. Never stop and forget that collectively—that means all of us together—collectively we are richer than all the nations in the world, with the exception of nine. Did you ever think about that? After you leave the United States, Soviet Russia, Great Britain, West Germany, France, and I could name the others, the American Negro collectively is richer than most nations of the world. We have an annual income of more than thirty billion dollars a year, which is more than all of the exports of the United States, and more than the national budget of Canada. Did you know that? That's power right there, if we know how to pool it.

We don't have to argue with anybody. We don't have to curse and go around acting bad with our words. We don't need any bricks and bottles. We don't need any Molotov cocktails. We just need to go around to these stores, and to these massive industries in our country, and say, "God sent us by here, to say to you that you're not treating his children right. And we've come by here to ask you to make the first item on your agenda fair treatment, where God's children are concerned. Now, if you are not prepared to do that, we do have an agenda that we must follow. And our agenda calls for withdrawing economic support from you."

And so, as a result of this, we are asking you tonight, to go out and tell your neighbors not to buy Coca-Cola in Memphis. Go by and tell them not to buy Sealtest milk. Tell them not to buy—what is the other bread?—Wonder Bread. And what is the other bread company, Jesse? Tell them not to buy Hart's bread. As Jesse Jackson has said, up to now, only the garbage men have been feeling pain; now we must kind of redistribute the pain. We are choosing these companies because they haven't been fair in their hiring policies; and we are choosing them because they can begin the process of saying they are going to support the needs and the rights of these men who are on strike. And then they can move on town—downtown—and tell Mayor Loeb to do what is right.

But not only that, we've got to strengthen black institutions. I call upon you to take your money out of the banks downtown and deposit your money in Tri-State Bank. We want a "bank-in" movement in Memphis. Go by the savings and loan association. I'm not asking you something that we don't do ourselves at SCLC. Judge Hooks and others will tell you that we have an account here in the savings and loan association from the Southern Christian Leadership Conference. We are telling you to follow what we are doing. Put your money there. You have six or seven black insurance companies here in the city of Memphis. Take out your insurance there. We want to have an "insurance-in."

Now these are some practical things that we can do. We begin the process of building a greater economic base. And at the same time, we are putting pressure where it really hurts. I ask you to follow through here.

Now, let me say as I move to my conclusion that we've got to give ourselves to this struggle until the end. Nothing would be more tragic than to stop at this point in Memphis. We've got to see it through. And when we have our march, you need to be there. If it means leaving work, if it means leaving school—be there. Be concerned about your brother. You may not be on strike. But either we go up together, or we go down together.

Let us develop a kind of dangerous unselfishness. One day a man came to Jesus, and he wanted to raise some questions about some vital matters of life. At points he wanted to trick Jesus, and show him that he knew a little more than Jesus knew and throw him off base....

Now that question could have easily ended up in a philosophical and theological debate. But Jesus immediately pulled that question from mid-air, and placed it on a dangerous curve between Jerusalem and Jericho. And he talked about a certain man, who fell among thieves. You remember that a Levite and a priest passed by on the other side. They didn't stop to help him. And finally a man of another race came by. He got down from his beast, decided not to be compassionate by proxy. But he got down with him, administered first aid, and helped the man in need. Jesus ended up saying, this was the good man, this was the great man, because he had the capacity to project the "I" into the "thou," and to be concerned about his brother.

Now you know, we use our imagination a great deal to try to determine why the priest and the Levite didn't stop. At times we say they were busy going to a church meeting, an ecclesiastical gathering, and they had to get on down to Jerusalem so they wouldn't be late for their meeting. At other times we would speculate that there was a religious law that "One who was engaged in religious ceremonials was not to touch a human body twenty-four hours before the ceremony." And every now and then we begin to wonder whether maybe they were not going down to Jerusalem—or down to Jericho, rather to organize a "Jericho Road Improvement Association." That's a possibility. Maybe they felt that it was better to deal with the problem from the causal root, rather than to get bogged down with an individual effect.

But I'm going to tell you what my imagination tells me. It's possible that those men were afraid. You see, the Jericho road is a dangerous road. I remember when Mrs. King and I were first in Jerusalem. We rented a car and drove from Jerusalem down to Jericho. And as soon as we got on that road, I said to my wife, "I can see why Jesus used this as the setting for his parable." It's a winding, meandering road. It's really conducive for ambushing. You start out in Jerusalem, which is about 1200 miles—or rather 1200 feet above sea level. And by the time you get down to Jericho, fifteen or twenty minutes later, you're about 2200 feet below sea level. That's a dangerous road. In the days of Jesus it came to be known as the "Bloody Pass." And you know, it's possible that the priest and the Levite looked over that man on the ground and wondered if the robbers were still around. Or it's possible that they felt that the man on the ground was merely faking. And he was acting like he had been robbed and hurt, in order to seize them over there, lure them there for quick and easy seizure. And so the first question that the priest asked—the first question that the Levite asked was, "If I stop to help this man, what will happen to me?" But then the Good Samaritan came by. And he reversed the question: "If I do not stop to help this man, what will happen to him?"

That's the question before you tonight. Not, "If I stop to help the sanitation workers, what will happen to my job. Not, "If I stop to help the sanitation workers what will happen to all of the hours that I usually spend in my office every day and every week as a pastor?" The question is not, "If I stop to help this man in need, what will happen to me?" The question is, "If I do not stop to help the sanitation workers, what will happen to them?" That's the question.

Let us rise up tonight with a greater readiness. Let us stand with a greater determination. And let us move on in these powerful days, these days of challenge to make America what it ought to be. We have an opportunity to make America a better nation. And I want to thank God, once more, for allowing me to be here with you.

You know, several years ago, I was in New York City autographing the first book that I had written. And while sitting there autographing books, a demented black woman came up. The only question I heard from her was, "Are you Martin Luther King?" And I was looking down writing, and I said, "Yes." And the next minute I felt something beating on my chest. Before I knew it I had been stabbed by this demented woman. I was rushed to Harlem Hospital. It was a dark Saturday afternoon. And that blade had gone through, and the X-rays revealed that the tip of the blade was on the edge of my aorta, the main artery. And once that's punctured, you're drowned in your own blood—that's the end of you.

It came out in the New York Times the next morning, that if I had merely sneezed, I would have died. Well, about four days later, they allowed me, after the operation, after my chest had been opened, and the blade had been taken out, to move around in the wheel chair in the hospital. They allowed me to read some of the mail that came in, and from all over the states and the world, kind letters came in. I read a few, but one of them I will never forget. I had received one from the President and the Vice-President. I've forgotten what those telegrams said. I'd received a visit and a letter from the Governor of New York, but I've forgotten what that letter said. But there was another letter that came from a little girl, a young girl who was a student at the White Plains High School. And I looked at that letter, and I'll never forget it. It said simply,

Dear Dr. King,

I am a ninth-grade student at the White Plains High School."

And she said, "While it should not matter, I would like to mention that I'm a white girl. I read in the paper of your misfortune, and of your suffering. And I read that if you had sneezed, you would have died. And I'm simply writing you to say that I'm so happy that you didn't sneeze."

And I want to say tonight—I want to say tonight that I too am happy that I didn't sneeze. Because if I had sneezed, I wouldn't have been around here in 1960, when students all over the South started sitting-in at lunch counters. And I knew that as they were sitting in, they were really standing up for the best in the American dream, and taking the whole nation back to those great wells of democracy which were dug deep by the Founding Fathers in the Declaration of Independence and the Constitution.

If I had sneezed, I wouldn't have been around here in 1961, when we decided to take a ride for freedom and ended segregation in inter-state travel.

If I had sneezed, I wouldn't have been around here in 1962, when Negroes in Albany, Georgia, decided to straighten their backs up. And whenever men and women straighten their backs up, they are going somewhere, because a man can't ride your back unless it is bent.

If I had sneezed—If I had sneezed I wouldn't have been here in 1963, when the black people of Birmingham, Alabama, aroused the conscience of this nation, and brought into being the Civil Rights Bill.

If I had sneezed, I wouldn't have had a chance later that year, in August, to try to tell America about a dream that I had had.

If I had sneezed, I wouldn't have been down in Selma, Alabama, to see the great Movement there.

If I had sneezed, I wouldn't have been in Memphis to see a community rally around those brothers and sisters who are suffering.

I'm so happy that I didn't sneeze.

And they were telling me—. Now, it doesn't matter, now. It really doesn't matter what happens now. I left Atlanta this morning, and as we got started on the plane, there were six of us. The pilot said over the public address system, "We are sorry for the delay, but we have Dr. Martin Luther King on the plane. And to be sure that all of the bags were checked, and to be sure that nothing would be wrong with on the plane, we had to check out everything carefully. And we've had the plane protected and guarded all night."

And then I got into Memphis. And some began to say the threats, or talk about the threats that were out. What would happen to me from some of our sick white brothers?

Well, I don't know what will happen now. We've got some difficult days ahead. But it really doesn't matter with me now, because I've been to the mountaintop.

And I don't mind.

Like anybody, I would like to live a long life. Longevity has its place. But I'm not concerned about that now. I just want to do God's will. And He's allowed me to go up to the mountain. And I've looked over. And I've seen the Promised Land. I may not get there with you. But I want you to know tonight, that we, as a people, will get to the promised land!

And so I'm happy, tonight.

I'm not worried about anything.

I'm not fearing any man!

Mine eyes have seen the glory of the coming of the Lord!!

XV

Plant Closing

Demolition of Closed U.S. Steel Mill, Youngstown,Ohio, April 28, 1982. UPI. © CORBIS Film Preservation Facility.

Local 1330 v. U.S. Steel (1977–1980)

Staughton Lynd*

Background

Youngstown, Ohio[1] had the unusual experience that in each of three successive years — 1977, 1978, and 1979 — the closing of a major steelmaking complex was announced. By the summer of 1980 steel was no longer being made in what had been, at one time, the second or third largest steelmaking community in the United States.[2]

---

* A version of the following remarks was offered at a gathering to celebrate the thirtieth anniversary of the lawsuit *Local 1330 v. U.S. Steel* held at the Harvard Law School on February 25, 2011.

1. "In the 1980 census the city of Youngstown numbered approximately 115,000 persons, about 45,000 of them members of minority groups. The Youngstown-Warren metropolitan statistical area contains more than 500,000 inhabitants.

Manufacturing employment represents close to half of the employment in the Youngstown-Warren area, compared to about one quarter in the United States as a whole. Steel has been the dominant industry." Staughton Lynd, *The Fight Against Shutdowns: Youngstown's Steel Mill Closings*, 4–5 (San Pedro, Ca: Singlejack Books, 1982).

2. "Most of us have come to feel that factories are permanent fixtures. Our jobs in them create a kind of conservatism which has now been attacked at the root. As one Youngstown steelworker

With each shutdown announcement the community's understanding deepened. When the closing of the Campbell Works was announced in September 1977, popular sentiment blamed the federal government for imposing unreasonable environmental standards and for letting foreign steel into the country. Announcement in 1978 that Brier Hill would be shut down caused local public opinion to target the Lykes Steamship Company, a corporate conglomerate that had acquired Youngstown Sheet & Tube and, so it was said, used the steel company as a "cash cow" for additional acquisitions. The final closings, announced by U.S. Steel in November 1979, resulted in dramatic direct action, and in litigation in which I served as lead counsel.

In law school I had been fascinated by the concept of "promissory estoppel." The idea was that if A made a promise to B, and B, with A's knowledge, relied on that promise to his detriment, this course of conduct gives rise to an enforceable legal contract.

I was accordingly delighted when, after U.S. Steel announced the closing of all its Youngstown area facilities, my Legal Services colleague Jim Callen remarked: "The newspaper says the workers believe they had been promised that the mill would stay open. Isn't that promissory estoppel?"

Tape recorder in hand, I set off to interview steelworkers up and down the Mahoning Valley to find out exactly what they had been promised, and whether U.S. Steel had broken that promise when it closed the mills.

Had U.S. Steel made a promise? David Roderick, CEO of the corporation, had stated on local television in June 1979, less than six months before the company announced the shutdown, "We have no plans for shutting down ... Youngstown." More specifically, Youngstown area superintendent William Kirwan had promised members of the local unions that so long as the Youngstown facilities made a profit they would not be closed. On the eve of trial I was able to take a deposition from Superintendent Kirwan. He confirmed that he had offered that assurance on the mill "hot line."

Next, had the workers relied on U.S. Steel's promise to their detriment? Frank Georges, a 37-year-old machinist at U.S. Steel's Ohio Works, told me that after hearing Mr. Roderick and Mr. Kirwan he and his wife had decided to buy a larger house so as to be able to invite his wife's parents, who were ill, to live with them. Mr. Georges had spent most of November 27 at a local bank completing the "closing" on the new house. As he drove home from the bank Mr. Georges was obliged to stop at a railroad crossing. He turned on the car radio and heard that the mill was to be closed.

At his deposition Mr. Kirwan also shared with us a glossy brochure he had prepared for his corporate superiors outlining plans to make the Youngstown mills more profitable. The existing situation was that in its Ohio Works, across the Mahoning River from downtown Youngstown, U.S. Steel made molten steel in open hearth furnaces. The hot metal was then put in railroad cars and transported seven miles upstream to the company's Mc-

---

put it to me, 'You felt as if the mill would always be there.' Because steelworkers felt this way they put up with boredom, and danger, and humiliating harassment from supervisors every day, trading off these indignities for the fringe benefits which would come to them from long service at a particular plant. . . .

A plant closing affects more than the workers at the plant. City income from industrial property taxes goes down, schools start to deteriorate and public services of all kinds are affected. Layoffs occur in businesses which supplied raw materials for the shutdown plant and in businesses which processed the product, retail sales fall off. All the signs of family strain — alcoholism, divorce, child and spouse abuse, suicide — increase." *Ibid.* at 3–4.

Donald Mills where it was reheated and rolled into finished coils. Superintendent Kirwan's idea was to build electric furnaces next to the finishing mills. Beside making it possible to produce the steel more efficiently, this strategy would eliminate the costly transportation and re-heating of the semi-finished steel. The brochure had a red light and a green light on its outside cover. The idea, so said the brochure, was to press the green light on the electric furnaces at the same time that the company pushed the red button on the open hearths, continuing production and filling orders "without missing a beat."

Newly armed with this exciting information, we proceeded to trial. The plaintiffs were six local unions, several dozen individual steelworkers, an "ecumenical coalition" of local religious bodies, and the incumbent Republican Congressman. In addition to the main claim of promissory estoppel, the suit alleged a community property right had been infringed—a kind of public easement to prevent the wasting of other property—and an antitrust claim over the refusal of U.S. Steel to sell the plant to the workers.

Trial was held in the old courthouse near the river in early March. Every day at lunchtime, lawyers for workers and the supportive crowd of those in attendance would meet in a church across the street. We made plans to ring the church bells of Youngstown if we won.

We lost. I stayed up all night before final argument working on my remarks. As I presented them the next morning there was a hush in the courtroom, and when I returned to the table around which sat the presidents of the plaintiff local unions, I could feel their support. Even the judge, as we met on the way to the men's room during a bathroom break, said to me: "Great closing, Staughton." Then, after lunch, he read a long typewritten opinion that had to have been written the night before.

An appeal followed. The opinion of the federal appeals court began with the words, "This appeal represents a cry for help from steelworkers and townspeople in the City of Youngstown, Ohio who are distressed by the prospective impact upon their lives and their city of the closing of two large steel mills...."[3] The Court went on to quote from appellants' amended complaint the many representations by U.S. Steel officials to the work force at its Youngstown mills that the facilities would remain open so long as they were "profitable." There followed an arcane discussion of the meaning of the word "profit" in which the Court followed the definition offered by U.S. Steel executives at trial rather than that which Mr. Kirwan, the corporation's highest-ranking officer in the Youngstown area, had communicated to the local unions and their members. A community property claim was likewise found wanting on the ground that only a legislature, not the courts, could formulate public policy "on the great issues involved in plant closings and removals." Finally the appeals court, acting out of "perhaps an excess of caution," remanded the antitrust claim to the District Court, where it, too, died.

Analysis

There is a tendency to look back on events like the Local 1330 law suit as beads on a long string of labor struggles, some of them won, most of them lost, all of them inspiring.

Let me suggest a different conceptual framework. I believe that the shutdown of steelmaking in Youngstown and then in Pittsburgh illustrates the catastrophic failure of the CIO model of trade unionism. It is a failure comparable to the collapse of European Social Democracy in August 1914 when labor parties in nation after nation voted to support taxes for the war efforts of their various governments.

3. *Local 1330, United Steel Workers of America v. U.S. Steel*, 631 F. 2d 1264 (6th Cir. 1980).

From the 1970s onward, industrial trade unions in the United States with hundreds of thousands of members have stood by helplessly as corporations shut down manufacturing and moved their operations to other countries. This is not the typical recession followed by the return of manufacturing to previous levels. Corporations are hiring again, but overseas. Thus more than half the 15,000 workers that Caterpillar, Inc. hired in 2010 were hired outside the United States.[4] Corporations are expanding markets, but in other countries. Thus in 2010 General Motors sold 2.2 million vehicles in the United States but 2.4 million vehicles in China.[5] And the percentage of American workers in trade unions declined to 11.9 percent in 2010, "the lowest rate in more than 70 years."[6]

We in the law tend to think of any defeat as a failure to pursue the appropriate legal theory. However, we had good legal theories in Youngstown and Pittsburgh. In Youngstown we pursued a contract theory, promissory estoppel, articulated in Restatement of Contracts 2nd section 90. In Pittsburgh close to a dozen municipalities in the Monongahela Valley, including the City of Pittsburgh, created a new regional entity similar to the Tennessee Valley Authority and sought to acquire, reopen, and operate shutdown steel mills by using the power of eminent domain.

We failed, not because our legal theories or our lawyering were inadequate, but for several more fundamental reasons.

First, the United Steelworkers of America sabotaged our efforts. The USWA was suspicious of any initiative that it did not control. In Youngstown, the so-called international union left the battle to its local unions, disavowed the idea of worker-community ownership, and failed even to file a requested amicus brief when we appealed to the Sixth Circuit Court of Appeals. In Pittsburgh, the international relied on feasibility assessments by the Wall Street firm Lazard Freres and failed to inform embattled rank and filers until long after it had ceased to believe in and support their cause.

Second, without the support of the Steelworkers, we failed to obtain from the federal government an indispensable component of any legal strategy for reopening facilities as capital-intensive as steel mills, namely, money. A Democratic Party administration abandoned Youngstown. At the time it would have cost perhaps twenty million dollars to acquire any of the closed facilities in the Mahoning Valley. But every ton of steel in Youngstown was made in antiquated open hearth furnaces. It would have made no sense to reopen any of the area's steel mills without the capacity to rebuild the "hot end," that is, to install Basic Oxygen or electric furnaces in place of open hearths, and substitute continuous casters for blooming mills to semi-finish the steel. In any of the three mills that shut down in Youngstown between 1977 and 1980 necessary new investment would have cost at least two hundred million dollars. But the Carter Administration had set aside loan guarantees to assist steelmakers amounting to only one hundred million dollars for the entire country. As John Barbero observed in the documentary film "Shout Youngstown," decisionmakers in government and private industry were not interested in worker-community steel operations in what they considered their private preserve.

In Pittsburgh, the struggle unfolded during the first years of the Reagan Administration. The exercise of eminent domain has two prerequisites. The first is a public purpose. The second is cash in the amount of fair market value. Where were the TriState Confer-

---

4. "Where are the Jobs? For Many Companies, Overseas," *Associated Press*, Dec. 28, 2010.

5. "GM Sells More in China than in U.S.," *USA Today*, Jan. 25, 2011.

6. Steven Greenhouse, "Union Membership in U.S. Fell to a 70-Year Low Last Year," *New York Times*, Jan. 22, 2011.

ence on the Impact of Steel or the newly-minted Steel Valley Authority to find that kind of money in the early 1980s?

Finally, the union reform movement, even had it been more successful, would not have prevented this Rust Belt catastrophe. That movement has focused on the internal government of unions; hence, between 1970 and 2000, the campaign of Arnold Miller and Miners for Democracy in the United Mine Workers, of Ed Sadlowski in the United Steelworkers of America, of Ron Carey and Teamsters for a Democratic Union in the International Brotherhood of Teamsters.

None of these reformers said anything about two features of the standard CIO collective bargaining agreement that made our task in Youngstown and Pittsburgh almost impossible.

The first such feature is the management prerogative clause. One day during the summer of 1980 I stopped by the Local 1330 union hall. This was the meeting place from which Ed Mann had led a mass meeting of outraged steelworkers "down that hill" to occupy the U.S. Steel administration building. Six months later, defeat was visibly evident. The now empty building with its big glass windows had become a natural target for neighborhood kids, and several windows and the glass front door had been smashed.

Bob Vasquez, president of Local 1330, was alone in the building, sorting papers. He looked up as I came in and said, "I understand that you're a historian." Then he gave me several typewritten drafts of the first collective bargaining agreement between the Steel Workers Organizing Committee and U.S. Steel.

One clause was the same in all these drafts, and remains virtually unchanged today, seventy-five years later. It reads:

> The management of the works and the direction of the working forces, including the right to hire, suspend or discharge for proper cause, or transfer, and the right to relieve employees from duty because of lack of work or other legitimate reasons, is vested exclusively in the Corporation.[7]

Having thus given management a free hand to make unilateral investment decisions, including the right to close a facility "because of lack of work or other legitimate reasons," the new CIO unions also took away from their members the ability to do anything about such decisions by direct action. A second feature of the standard CIO collective bargaining agreement, for example in the contracts with General Motors and U.S. Steel in early 1937, was the clause prohibiting strikes and slowdowns for the duration of the contract.

The no-strike clause violated the explicit legislative intent of the Wagner Act, expressed in Section 13 of the statute. The principal draftsperson of the National Labor Relations Act, Leon Keyserling, was asked by an interviewer years later whether "there was some specific reason for putting that residual guarantee of the right to strike in the Act?" Keyserling responded:

> There was a definite reason. First, because Wagner was always strong for the right to strike on the ground that without the right to strike, which was labor's ultimate weapon, they really had no other weapon. That guarantee was a part of his thinking. [And it] was particularly necessary because a lot of people made the argument that because the government was giving labor the right to bargain collectively, that was a substitute for the right to strike.

---

7. *See* Staughton Lynd, *supra* note 1, at 219–20.

Keyserling added: "We didn't want to interfere in any way with that basic weapon. We never interfered with the right of the employer to close his plant."[8]

Keyserling's apprehension proved altogether correct. Proceeding on the fiction that rank-and-file union members had somehow voluntarily surrendered or "waived" their statutory right to strike during the duration of a collective bargaining agreement, unions, the NLRB, the courts, and professors of labor law have acquiesced in this dramatic departure from legislative intent.

So what is to be done? Let me suggest a radical tactic and a radical strategy.

The radical tactic is an extension of management's duty to bargain embodied in Section 8(a)(5) of the Act to encompass what have been called "members-only" or "minority" unions, that is, any group of workers numerically fewer than half the potential voters in an appropriate bargaining unit. Professor Charles Morris, in his book, *The Blue Eagle at Work*,[9] demonstrates that this was the original conception of union recognition in the 1930s and recommends a duty to bargain with members-only unions as a way to reclaim meaningful democratic rights in the American workplace.

An important ambiguity remains, however. Existing unions have at all times, in Professor Morris' words, "looked upon these membership-based agreements as merely a temporary means" to the end of exclusive representation, "useful stepping-stones on the path to majority membership and mature collective bargaining."[10]

This was spectacularly true of the CIO's Founding Father, John L. Lewis. Lewis, while apparently endorsing a members-only approach as a preliminary objective in newly organized workplaces like the Denver tramway system or the nation's steel mills,[11] fought it bitterly within his own union, the United Mine Workers. Indeed Lewis' hostility toward members-only unionism for coal miners was the reason the American Civil Liberties Union opposed the Wagner Act.

Cletus Daniel tells the story in his book, *The ACLU and the Wagner Act*.[12] The ACLU's misgivings sprang from deep involvement in a bitter jurisdictional dispute between two rival unions in the bituminous coalfields of southern Illinois. In late 1932, dissident local unions had bolted District 12 of the UMW to form the Progressive Miners of America. When the National Industrial Recovery Act (NIRA) was enacted in June 1933, Baldwin feared

> that Lewis would succeed in having included in the bituminous coal code labor
> provisions giving the UMW exclusive bargaining rights, employer checkoff of
> union dues, and a closed shop. Baldwin was convinced that such a development
> would surely threaten the destruction of the Progressive Miners and thereby,
> deny the right of thousands of miners in Illinois to be represented by a union of
> their own choosing.[13]

---

8. Kenneth M. Casebeer, "Holder of the Pen: An Interview with Leon Keyserling on Drafting the Wagner Act," 42 *University of Miami Law Review*, 353 (Nov. 1987).

   9. Charles J. Morris, *The Blue Eagle at Work: Reclaiming Democratic Rights in the American Workplace* (Ithaca and London: Cornell University Press, 2005).

   10. *Ibid.*, p. 85.

   11. *Ibid.*, at 36–37, 82–83.

   12. Cletus E. Daniel, *The ACLU and the Wagner Act: An Inquiry into the Depression-Era Crisis of American Liberalism* (Ithaca and London: Cornell University Press, 1980).

   13. *Ibid.*, pp. 33–34. The Progressive Miners championed by Roger Baldwin opposed John L. Lewis' support for mechanization, and proposed the alternative of "job sharing or equalization of work" as a means of controlling the mechanization of the workplace and keeping operating mines in production. Carl D. Oblinger, *Divided Kingdom: Work, Community, and the Mining Wars in the Cen-*

One concludes that members-only unionism as a stepping stone to exclusive representation would be unlikely to usher in the new day imagined by Professor Morris. But what about members-only unionism as a permanent arrangement, that is, a situation as in Europe where different unions exist in the same workplace?

I recently experienced a moment of enlightenment in this regard. The very first labor activist with whom I did oral history was John Sargent, three-time president of the 18,000 member local union at Inland Steel in East Chicago, Indiana. Labor historians generally describe the Little Steel strike of 1937 as a defeat in contrast to the agreement with U.S. Steel earlier that same year. John Sargent, however, called the end of the Little Steel Strike "a victory of great proportions" as a result of which "we secured for ourselves ... working conditions and wages ... that were better by far than what we have today." How could this be? What in the world was John talking about?

John Sargent was describing members-only or minority unionism that, in his experience, was more effective than the exclusive representation that superseded it during World War II. As John explained at a community forum in 1970, the Little Steel strike was settled by an agreement through the governor's office

> that the company would recognize the Steelworkers Union and the company union and any other organization that wanted to represent the people in the steel industry. And we went back to work with this governor's agreement signed by various companies and union representatives in Indiana.

As a result, according to Sargent, without a contract, and hence, without the restrictions of a management prerogative and a no-strike clause,

> a tremendous surge took place.... The union organizers were essentially workers in the mill who were so disgusted with their conditions and so ready for a change that they took the union into their own hands.... [A]s a result of the enthusiasm of the people in the mill you had a series of strikes, wildcats, shut-downs, slow-downs, anything working people could think of to secure for themselves what they decided they had to have.[14]

Nick Migas, grievance committeeman in the critical open hearth, recalled an incident when the company refused to settle a grievance for the charging car operators.

> So that night it started to slow down, and by the next morning there were two furnaces where they had to shut the heat off. They settled the grievance in a hurry. Nobody told anybody to strike. There was just that close relationship, working with the people, where they knew what was necessary.[15]

So what would a workplace be like if members-only unionism became a permanent way of life? It would be interesting to find out. Rank-and-file workers would presumably retain the right to protest an unjust discharge or a shutdown decision when, where, and how they thought best. There would be no deduction of dues from a worker's paycheck unless authorized by that member, and so, as Morris writes, the union's accountability to

---

tral Illinois Coal Fields During the Great Depression, 20–21 (Springfield: Illinois State Historical Society, 2004).

14. "Your Dog Don't Bark No More," in Alice and Staughton Lynd, eds., Rank and File: Personal Histories by Working-Class Organizers, 107 (Boston: Beacon Press, 1973). See also "Guerrilla History in Gary," in Andrej, Grubacic, ed., From Here to There: The Staughton Lynd Reader (Oakland, CA: PM Press, 2010), based on conversations with "John Smith" (John Sargent) and "Jim Brown" (Jim Balanoff).

15. "How the International Took Over," in Rank and File, supra note 14, at 168.

its voluntary members would be governed by ordinary principles of agency.[16] Finally, that which outside the workplace is viewed as a prerequisite to democracy, an opposition party or parties, would be available if desired.

But this radical tactic remains a tactic. Like other radical tactics such as working to rule or occupation of the plant,[17] except in an unusually favorable context and after life-and-death struggle it would not have prevented U.S. Steel from shutting down its Youngstown mills at will. We need a strategy.

This is where Pittsburgh, not Youngstown, and Local 1397, not Local 1330, came forward as pioneers and showed the way. The Pittsburgh movement in the first half of the 1980s fought tooth and nail for worker-community ownership, just as Youngstown had. But Pittsburgh pursued a strategy based on eminent domain. I want to stress two things about that strategy.

First, we didn't say: "We are socialists who believe in public ownership, and therefore, U.S. Steel, get out of the way." Instead we said: "If U.S. Steel won't make steel here in [whatever community it was], we will." And: "If [facility X] cannot return a rate of profit acceptable to U.S. Steel shareholders, we'll run the plant so long as we can cover our expenses."

And second, it is pure fiction to suggest that American workers threatened with the alternative of a plant shutdown would reject such an approach. Frank O'Brien was president of the local union at the big Jones & Laughlin steel mill on the north side of the Monongahela River. He also served in the Pennsylvania legislature, where he saw the way employers used the eminent domain power. Let me close with these words of Frank's:

> When you work in a mill, and you see all these guys with the know-how, all together right there, then you see that you have the ability to operate the mill no matter what top management does.
>
> The company says, "Hey, it's not profitable for us any more to produce steel here." But we still need jobs. Companies like J&L are making money. They are moving because they don't make **enough** money to suit them. They've let their plants run down like an old automobile: you run it into the ground, and then you take the license plate off and walk away from it.
>
> So we should think about forming an Industrial Development Authority and running the mills ourselves....
>
> The companies have used this [eminent domain] ... for their own purposes. In the 1950s J&L used it to evict people from their homes in Scotch Bottom in Hazelwood. They said they needed the land to expand, but when they had evicted the people and gotten the land they didn't expand. They just let the land sit there and stored raw materials on it.

---

16. *The Blue Eagle at Work, supra* note 9 at 219.

17. For lockout as an effective response to working to rule, *see* Steven K. Ashby and C.J. Hawkins, *Staley: The Fight for a New Labor Movement*, chapter 4 (Urbana and Chicago: University of Illinois Press, 2009), Similarly, after the dramatic occupation of the Moss 3 coal preparation plant of the Pittston Coal Company in 1989, Rev. Jim Sessions candidly acknowledged: "The settlement was not perfect. Months after the settlement ... some miners are still laid off. Some may never return to work. The company won more 'flexibility' on work rules, thus eroding hard-fought union victories and shifting more control over the work process back to management." Jim Sessions and Fran Ansley, "Singing Across Dark Spaces: The Union/Community Takeover of the Pittston Coal Company's Moss 3 Coal Preparation Plant," Staughton and Alice Lynd, eds., *Nonviolence in America: A Documentary History*, 396 (revised edition; Maryknoll, NY: Orbis Books, 1995).

So I'm thinking the law can be used in reverse.

I think back to the time when the Port Authority was born. Pittsburgh Railways was the big operator transporting people in the City of Pittsburgh. They ran into a financial bind. So the Port Authority was formed, taking in all the bus companies in Allegheny County as well. It bought up the railway and the bus companies because people still had to be transported.

Recently they decided to close down the J&L hot strip mill. A thousand people lost their jobs.

A couple of Sundays later the Mayor was out to our father-and-son communion breakfast at St. Stephens in Hazelwood. He made a little speech and then he opened it up for questions.

So I got up. I said the Mayor had better start worrying now about the U.S. Steel mills. . . .

He said, "Well, what would you do?" I told him: "You, and the County Commissioners, sit down and form an authority, like the Port Authority. We can run the plants ourselves."[18]

---

18. Frank O'Brien, "Introduction" to Tri-State Conference on the Impact of Steel, What Can We Do About Plant Closings?, quoted in Staughton Lynd, *supra* note 1, at 216–17.

XVI

Communities on Strike

Miners Blocking Coal Trucks, Pittston, Copyright Dickinson Star.

"Tying the Knot of Solidarity"
The Pittston Strike of 1989–1990

*James Green**

The new UMWA-BCOA national agreement, signed on January 30, 1988, gained some job security, won a modest 6.8% wage increase and established an unprecedented Education and Training Trust Fund to pay for educating unemployed miners and their dependents. The rank and file ratified the contract and UMWA President Richard Trumka secured another agreement without a strike. But Pittston rejected the new pact and the UMW had to continue frustrating negotiations while trying to penetrate the corporation's "baffling web of subsidiaries."[1] With the old contract due to expire on January 31, 1988, a strike seemed inevitable.

---

* This chapter first appeared as a chapter in John H.M. Laslett, *The United Mine Workers of America: A Model of Industrial Solidarity?* 513–44 (University Park: The Pennsylvania State Univ. Press, 1996). It is reproduced by permission of the publisher.

1. United Mine Workers of America, "The United Mine Workers' Strike Against the Pittston Coal Company," (1989), Background Briefing Paper, unpublished manuscript in author's possession.

The Pittston Coal Group withdrew from the BCOA and stopped paying into the industry wide health insurance fund for retirees. Pittston's new coal division President Mike Odum said he wanted a contract like Massey's because his firm, unlike most BCOA members, needed to compete in international markets where it sold a great deal of low sulphur coal, used to make coke for steel producers. The company intended to shave five to six dollars a ton from the costs it incurred under the BCOA agreement.[2]

The mines Pittston owned were concentrated in the southwestern corner of Virginia in some of the most beautiful country in the Appalachians, mainly in Buchanan and Dickenson counties wedged up against the West Virginia and Kentucky borders. These mines had been working under a UMW contract since 1939 and labor relations had been stable. The company earned a bad name, however, after the Buffalo Creek tragedy in 1972 when waste from one of its mines caused a dam to burst, flooding a hollow and drowning 125 people in West Virginia. In 1984 a new management team took over headed by CEO Paul W. Douglas and Coal Operations Vice President Joseph Farrell. Douglas had spent thirty-one years with Freeport-McMoran in New York where he had risen through the ranks to become chairman and chief executive. In Douglas's first year Pittston lost $26 million and accumulated $104 million in debts. In 1987, when Pittston left the BCOA, it took a $133 million loss.[3]

Pittston had acquired other companies, including Brinks Security where it eliminated the Teamsters Union, but coal accounted for more than half the corporation's profits. The demand for Pittston's metallurgical coal rose, especially among Japanese steelmakers who bought 57% of the company's fuel. Productivity had increased 72% in the union mines. Still, Douglas wanted a much higher return on investment from coal operations. He developed a corporate restructuring plan that created a "complex web of over 50 coal mining subsidiaries, holding companies and land companies" designed to cut down dependence on coal reserves mined by UMW members and to move work to Pittston's nonunion subsidiaries. Through restructuring and cost cutting Douglas reduced the union mining force by four thousand. But he wanted more. Specifically, he wanted out of the BCOA agreement and he wanted concessions in a new contract that would cut labor and health care costs. The company also wanted to run coal seven days a week and to escape from the costly health care fund.[4]

If Paul Douglas represented a new breed of managers who wanted to push up returns on investment and break unions to do it, Richard Trumka represented a new brand of union leader. Well-educated and well-spoken, sophisticated in public relations and legal affairs, he broke new ground in 1988 when he negotiated an innovative contract with Island Creek Coal Company that emphasized labor-management cooperation and enhanced productivity incentives in return for access for UMW members to new mines that had employed only nonunion workers. By then even A. T. Massey's CEO praised Trumka as a progressive labor leader who had reduced strikes and increased productivity in the industry. *Business Week* touted him as a future head of the AFL-CIO. But those who thought Trumka

---

2. On Pittston *see Betraying the Trust: The Pittston Company's Drive to Break Appalachia's Coalfield Communities* (Washington, D.C.: United Mine Workers of America, 1989); and Martha Hodel, "The Pittston Company," *Charleston Gazette* (August 29, 1989).

3. "In Midst of Strike, Pittston Chairman Plans for Future," *Journal of Commerce* (August 7, 1989); and Alecia Swasy, "Pittston Chief Digs In Against UMW," *Wall Street Journal* (August 22, 1989). On The Buffalo Creek tragedy *see* Kai T. Erikson, *Everything in its Path: Destruction of Community in the Buffalo Creek Flood* (New York: Simon and Schuster, 1976).

4. *Ibid.*; James Green, "Corporate Culture's Failure in Dealing with Coal Miners," *Boston Globe* (June 21, 1989), and Moe Seager, "One Day Longer Than Pittston," *Z Magazine,* 14 (October 1989).

had left behind the UMW's militant traditions were mistaken. Still a vigorous young man with the build of a fullback and a striking dark complexion, Trumka talked often of the stories his Polish father, a miner, and his Italian mother told him of growing up in a poor Pennsylvania coal patch called Nemacolin. He retold stories of striking families being put out of their houses, described the Catholic Church as the only place in town where miners felt equal to the foremen and remembered eating nothing but government cheese in hard times.[5]

Trumka had been tracking Pittston's corporate strategy for three years and he feared another Massey strike in which the employer would try to break the UMWA as it had the Teamsters. On January 27, 1988, Pittston confirmed his suspicions when it announced that it would hire permanent replacements in the event of a strike. The union offered to work under an extension of the old contract, but Pittston refused. When the existing agreement expired on January 31, 1988, the company ended pension contributions for working miners; eliminated arbitration of disputes; stopped the check off of union dues; and cut off health benefits to fifteen hundred widows, retirees, and disabled miners.[6]

This last action would later become a central moral issue in the strike, arousing deep anger in the coalfields and moral condemnation from churches; at the time, however, it attracted little attention. Pittston was confident that a strike could be isolated, that many of its union employees would cross the picket lines and come back to work and that the courts and police would limit pickets and protect replacement workers.

But the company had misread the lessons of the Massey strike and underestimated the union's leaders. Though steeped in labor history and UMWA tradition, Trumka was not a prisoner of the past. He was enormously popular with the members, having won re-election to a second term in 1987 without opposition, and he believed they would follow him even if he broke with tradition. Contrary to UMW custom, which required members to strike immediately after a contract expired, Trumka decided to keep the Pittston miners on the job working without a contract. He surprised the company's managers who had hoped to goad the UMW into a strike for which it was unprepared.[7]

The UMW needed a new strategy to avoid a repeat of the Massey strike. Together with Vice President Cecil Roberts and a remarkably gifted staff, Trumka planned an ambitious, multifaceted strategy. Since it would be difficult to win the strike on the picket line (though quite possible to lose it there), the union planned what Trumka called a "sophisticated" corporate campaign against Pittston on a national level and, because of the company's export business, on an international scale as well. Unions had waged corporate campaigns and boycotts before, but the ambitious Shell Boycott against Massey's owners had not produced a victory in that bitter strike. Nor had the corporate campaigns against Hormel and International Paper earlier in the 1980s prevented striking employees from losing their unions and their jobs.[8]

5. "Today, the Mine Workers, Tomorrow the AFL-CIO," and author's interview with Richard Trumka, Nemacolin, Pennsylvania, July 12, 1990.
6. "The United Mine Workers Strike Against Pittston," 3; and *Betraying the Trust*.
7. Dwayne Yancey, "Thunder in the Coal Fields: The UMW's Strike Against Pittston," a special report of the *Roanoke Times & World News*, 2 (April 29, 1990).
8. *Ibid.* Other information on strike strategy is from an interview with strike coordinator Ron Baker, July 15, 1993. For an overview of concessionary bargaining in this period, *see* Kim Moody, *An Injury to All: The Decline of American Unionism* (London: Verso 1988). On the International Paper and Hormel strikes, *see* Jane Slaughter, "Corporate Campaigns: Labor Enlists Community Support"; and Peter Rachleff, "Supporting the Hormel Strikers," in Jeremy Brecher and Tim Costello, eds., *Building*

The brutal concessionary strikes of the eighties also convinced Trumka that nothing less than a total mobilization of UMW members and their allies could win. He believed the union had been too isolated from its allies in the Massey strike. That conflict also demonstrated that even aggressive UMWA picket lines could be decimated by court orders and violated by heavily guarded strike-breakers, who could become permanent replacements. Trumka knew that unless he was willing to take big risks, defeat would be certain. He drew two lessons from recent movement history. From the 1980s he learned that playing by the rules meant defeat for striking unions and from the 1960s he learned that nonviolent movements could mobilize and energize ordinary people and win support from the public and the media. All this pointed toward civil disobedience, toward building something like a 1960s protest movement around the strike.[9]

But Trumka, a creative labor lawyer and student of military as well as union history, also wanted to use laws when they could help the union. If the UMW struck Pittston over the contract, the courts would regard it as an economic strike (that is, a conflict over contract issues, not over violations of labor law) and therefore would allow Pittston to hire permanent replacements for the strikers. With disastrously high unemployment in Appalachia, the company could easily find those replacements and if it held out long enough, it could break the union. So UMWA lawyers immediately filed unfair labor practice charges against Pittston with the NLRB. If the board ruled against the company, then, in a strike over unfair labor practices, Pittston would not be allowed to hire replacements permanently. On March 23, 1989, the National Labor Relations Board agreed to hear the union's unfair labor practices charge.[10]

During the fourteen months Pittston miners worked without a contract (from January 1988, to April 1989) they suffered various kinds of harassment from company managers trying to provoke a strike. The union attempted an inside strategy trying to slow production while its members were still on the job, but these efforts failed to bring Pittston to the bargaining table. While the inside strategy bogged down, the union's outside strategy patiently prepared miners and their families for a new kind of strike, the likes of which the UMWA had never seen. In late 1988 and early 1989 the union "braintrust" grappled with how to avoid another Massey strike, which had remained an isolated conflict publicized mainly for its violence. Marty Hudson, the executive assistant to Vice President Cecil Roberts, was appointed strike coordinator with strict orders from the president to keep the strike nonviolent.[11]

But the strike strategists had more in mind than avoiding violence. They wondered if they could use a campaign of civil disobedience to defy the courts but still gain public support and mobilize the masses of people it would take to win the strike on the picket line. Vice President Cecil Roberts thought so. Though he was a devoted student of labor's past whose family had helped make working-class history in West Virginia, he drew on a different history now. The civil rights movement, he argued, taught lessons that could help win the impending strike. He had devoured *Parting the Waters*, Taylor Branch's book on Martin Luther King, and he carried a dog-eared copy with him to staff meetings where

---

Bridges: The Emerging Grassroots Coalition of Community and Labor, 47–69 (New York: Monthly Review, 1990).

9. Trumka later said that he was attracted to what Harris Wofford wrote on Gandhi in the 1950s, writings that had influenced Martin Luther King; Trumka interview, January 19, 1994. *Also see* David Moberg, "Envisioning a New Day for the Labor Movement," *In These Times* (August 30–September 5, 1989).

10. Yancey, "Thunder in the Coal Fields," 2–3.

11. *Ibid.*, 3.

he insisted that everyone read it until they could quote easily from the words of both King and Gandhi. Trumka agreed fully. He later recalled the lessons of the violent Massey strike: that unless the top leaders gave strong direction to a strike the "infinite number of clashes" that would take place on the picket lines could lead to violence. But if members were to follow their leaders' nonviolent strategy, the union would have to develop in "a continuous process of education and re-education."[12]

UMWA attorney Judy Scott and corporate campaign director Ken Zinn proposed a training program in nonviolent protest tactics. Another staffer, Gene Carroll, who had worked for the nuclear freeze campaign, brought in two peace activists who met with UMW leaders in Washington and told them how civil disobedience could involve entire families and communities, even children and the elderly, and how it could win allies. They talked about ways of occupying offices and blocking roads. On February 18 they conducted training in Charleston, West Virginia, for seventy union field reps from the eastern coalfields. The leaders had to be convinced that civil disobedience would work and that the strikers would not reject it as being "unmanly." Some union leaders thought civil disobedience would seem too timid to Appalachian miners accustomed to violent picket-line struggles. Nonetheless, UMW staffers and officers, impressed by the training in Charleston, fanned out to preach the new gospel of nonviolence in the union halls and homes of Pittston's miners in southwest Virginia, West Virginia, and Kentucky.[13]

While union leaders expounded the ideas and tactics of the civil rights and peace movements, others adopted the approaches of the women's movement and community-organizing struggles. The union hired Cosby Totten and Catherine Tompa, who had been underground miners, to organize miners' wives, daughters, and other women in the community to raise consciousness about what was at stake. Together with UMW organizer Marat Moore, they drove hundreds of miles through the coalfields to talk with union members about setting up local women's auxiliaries and then linking them up in district organizations. "They held fund raisers, staged convoys, and established a regular presence at local company headquarters" in Lebanon, Virginia, that started in July 1988 and lasted for the whole strike. Even before the strike began "the knot of solidarity had been tied."[14] The stage was now set.

Pittston's managers wanted a strike all along and on April 5, 1989, they got one. But as Cecil Roberts said later, "it wasn't the one they were looking for."[15] Officially, the union began an "unfair labor practices" strike against the company's alleged violations of federal labor law. But the enthusiastic response of the strikers showed that much more was at stake: the health and welfare of their elders on retirement; the survival of their communities, which depended on union wages; and even the future of their union. In the fourteen months the Pittston miners worked without a contract the union had made an extraordinary effort to educate the coal communities about these grave stakes. It paid off almost immediately.

On the first day of the strike the battle lines were drawn at McClure mine No.1, the company's biggest operation. Vance Security guards in blue jump suits and sun glasses guarded

12. *Ibid.*, 3, and Trumka interview, January 19, 1994.

13. Yancey, "Thunder in the Coal Fields," 3.

14. Marat Moore, "Ten Months That Shook the Coal Fields: Women's Stories from the Pittston Strike," unpublished manuscript, n.p. An edited version appeared as "Women's Stories from the Pittston Strike," *Now and Then*, 6–12, 32–35 (Fall 1990).

15. Roberts quoted in "Out of Darkness: The Mine Workers' Story," Video produced by Barbara Kopple, directed by Bill Davis (New York: Cabin Creek Films, 1990).

the mine and heard curses rain down on them from the massive crowd of pickets; they were denounced as "gun thugs," like the Baldwin-Felts who had terrorized the Appalachian coal camps in Sid Hatfield's day. Across the road a detail of Virginia state troopers looked on warily at a large group of miners all dressed alike in camouflage. This uniform had become popular during the Massey strike and it served a useful purpose. During that strike scab truck drivers whose rigs had been stoned identified alleged assailants by describing their dress. So from day one, the Pittston strikers wore camouflage as their uniform for tactical reasons; but the fatigues came to have rich symbolic meaning as well. The uniform signified a state of mind, a feeling of solidarity among people ready to wage an all-out war—a war without firearms—to defend their way of life.[16]

From Civil Disobedience to Civil Resistance

The strike's first day passed peacefully, but organizers were tense. Pittston's lawyers went to court to stop the mass picketing. On April 12, Donald McGlothin Jr., the circuit court judge for Dickenson and Russell counties, issued his first order limiting pickets to ten. In the meantime, other supporters took action. Someone shot out a transformer at Lambert Fork, cutting off power to the mine. A scab truck convoy headed for Pittston's Moss 3 coal preparation plant came around a bend in the road and "ran into a barrage of rocks that hit us like a hailstorm," according to one truck driver. "Jackrocks" turned up on mountain roads, puncturing the tires, of coal trucks, Vance security vans, and state police cars. For those unfamiliar with jackrocks in the state capitol, the Richmond paper described these objects, often called "mountain spiders" by miners, as "nails welded together so they puncture truck tires." "Miniature versions" were "fashioned into ear rings," and were worn proudly by female strike supporters.[17]

It was time to begin civil disobedience in order to discourage violence, maintain discipline, and boost morale. The women of the strike moved first on this front perhaps because the strike organizers thought wives and sisters of the miners would be more willing to experiment with nonviolent protest than the men. On April 18, thirty-seven women occupied the Pittston offices in Lebanon where they had maintained a tent site picket for months. These wives, widows, and daughters of miners confronted a startled receptionist; after a moment of silence they started singing "We Shall Not Be Moved," the old CIO-civil rights song. They expected to be arrested by the police and, if that occurred, they had decided not to cooperate by giving their names: they would all say they were "Daughters of Mother Jones."[18] The sit-in lasted all night, and the next morning it made headlines across the state. When the women left at 4:00 P.M., Marty Hudson was delighted. "It let me know what you can do with civil disobedience," he recalled. After this, the women "became the backbone of the strike."[19]

When the women's occupation ended, civil disobedience began on a mass scale. On April 24, three hundred strikers in full camouflage sat down in front of the McClure mine. They locked arms, so that when the state police waded in to make arrests they had to pull people apart. There were injuries. James Gibbs, the only black miner, suffered a broken arm. The actions of the police at McClure angered and, according to one report, "radicalized" many citizens in the area. Next day the community mobilization expanded. To

16. Moore, "Ten Months That Shook the Coal Fields," 13; Yancey, "Thunder in the Coal Fields," 4; and Nicolaus Mills, "Solidarity in Virginia: The Mine Workers Remake History," *Dissent*, 238 (Spring 1960).

17. Yancey, "Thunder in the Coal Fields," 4.

18. *Ibid.*, and Moore, "Ten Months That Shook the Coal Fields."

19. Yancey, "Thunder in the Coal Fields," 4.

protest the arrests and the brutalities at McClure a crowd of students from three area high schools walked out and over a hundred gathered at Dickenson County courthouse wearing camouflage uniforms. The school superintendent ordered a three-day suspension for those absent without leave.[20]

The next morning nearly five hundred pickets gathered at the Moss 3 coal preparation plant. Violating Judge McGlothin's order, they sat down in front of a convoy of replacement workers. Again, police waded in and hauled off sit downers as the crowd's anger swelled. John Cox, an international organizer, took the bullhorn and persuaded people to submit to arrest. He kept a scary moment from exploding in violence. When the crowd started rocking the buses, UMWA District 28 President Jackie Stump ordered them to stop. State police arrested 457 people at Moss 3 that day, including Stump, "whose strong lungs and stern countenance probably prevented a riot that day."[21]

One of the miners told the reporters who had gathered: "They talk about violence and all, but look who's getting hurt." The strikers had begun their campaign to win hearts and minds to their cause. A few days later the strike made the *New York Times*. It was a short story on the inside pages, but it reported on the seriousness of the strike, and it attracted other media to the remote coalfields of southwestern Virginia.[22]

At this moment the union organized its biggest demonstration to celebrate and legitimatize the new resistance movement. On April 30, some ten thousand people braved a driving rainstorm and crowded into Wise County Fairgrounds on an old strip mine near Norton, Virginia, to hear the Reverend Jesse Jackson and the strike leaders. Two separate car caravans, each one with four hundred vehicles, arrived from West Virginia and Kentucky. Traffic backed up for miles on the roads leading to the fairgrounds. Echoing the themes of his 1988 presidential campaign, Jackson urged the wet sea of people, in forest green and earthy brown, to "keep hope alive" even in the hardest times, and to unify across all boundaries, including race. When miners went down in the mine every day, everyone looked alike. These workers learned to "live together eight or nine miles underground." If they could do this deep below the ground, he said, "we must learn to live together above ground." Celebrating the fusion of the labor movement and the civil rights movement, Jackson proclaimed: "When we look around today we see the tradition of John L. Lewis and Martin Luther King have met together, and we will not go back." Aware that civil disobedience had led to many arrests, Jackson glorified the defiance of unjust laws. He did so not only as a black civil rights leader but as a preacher who could speak in familiar Baptist idiom to a throng of faithful Christians. Ever since his first presidential campaign in 1984 Jackson had aroused an almost religious fervor among hard-pressed union workers, who thrilled to his jeremiads against corporate greed and his exciting appeals for radical change.[23]

Jackson also stressed the wider significance of the strike. "This is not just your strike; it's the people's strike. Workers everywhere identify with this strike." Then Trumka spoke,

---

20. *Ibid.*, 4–5; John Clarks, "Students protest for UMWA," *Cumberland Times* (April 26, 1989), and Moore, "Ten Months."
21. Yancey, "Thunder in the Coal Fields," 5.
22. *Ibid.*, 5.
23. McKelway, "Jackson Makes Pledge to Miners," *Richmond Times-Dispatch* (May 1, 1989); "The Message Comes to the Mountains," *Herald-Courier* (Bristol, Va.) (May 1, 1989); and Greg Edwards, "Jackson to Miners: Don't Go Back," *Roanoke, VA Times and World News* (May 1, 1989); and Tracy Wimmer, "Miners Lifted by Jackson Magic," *Roanoke, VA Times and World News* (May 1,1989). On Jackson's appeal to white union workers in the 1980s see James Green, "Campaign '88: For Jackson Populism is a Class Act," *Boston Sunday Globe* 63–64 (April 3, 1988).

calling Pittston a "turning point for labor" in the United States. In his best stem-winding style, he took aim at Democratic Governor Gerald Baliles who had earlier won labor's political support but then had sent in state police to occupy the coalfields. Trumka joined Jackson in emphasizing the power of nonviolent protest. It was working. He also took pains to distinguish civil disobedience from "civil resistance." The strike involved more than disobeying unjust laws; the strikers were resisting wrongs caused by corporate greed.[24]

The strikers dramatized their cause by attending the Pittston stockholders meeting in Greenwich, Connecticut, on May 10, where union members who had been given small shares of stock introduced resolutions to embarrass management. One proposal, to allow for secret ballot voting, actually won significant support, and suggested that some of Pittston investors might be vulnerable to the union's corporate campaign aimed at the company's executives in Connecticut, and its board members around the country.[25]

The union explained the strike as a moral defense of decency and tradition, a struggle for community survival, not for wages. Cutting off the benefits became a key issue in the UMWA's public campaign against Pittston. In 1988 Pittston had reported $59 million in profits yet, the union charged, it was breaking "a delicately forged social pact" with coalfield communities just to make more money. Demanding Sunday work and scorning the traditions of a churchgoing people, it had become "just one more megacorporation with micro-vision."[26]

But Trumka knew the crusade to win the moral high ground would fail if the strikers acted violently. He also knew however that the courts would make peaceful civil resistance a costly strategy to pursue. On May 16 Judge McGlothin fined the UMW more than $600,000 for violating his order banning mass picketing. He also threatened to add $200,000 for each day union members violated his order and $100,000 for every rock-throwing incident or other act of violence. Trumka knew what to do. The UMW might lose its treasury but it would not lose this strike by caving in to court orders.[27]

In the Massey strike the union responded to court orders by limiting mass picketing and ending civil disobedience, but it would not make that mistake now. It would mobilize all strikers, their families, and their supporters to circumvent or to directly challenge court orders. The picket lines at Moss 3 and other Pittston operations remained jammed with strikers and their families. The union's tactics allowed thousands of people to "discover the democratic potential in their own power to say 'No' to corporate power," Richard Couto observed. The actions of April and May involved people who had never been activists but were now "mesmerized by their newly discovered power to stand up for what they thought was right."[28]

The strikers created a new sense of community in their region. An exciting "culture of solidarity" emerged in defense of traditional rights and standards. The strikers spoke of these things in plain language with the moral clarity of evangelical Protestantism. Initially, they drew upon their "deep bonds" as coal-mining families with common stories and tragedies, and with shared religious traditions and moral values. In these ways, Marat Moore recalled, "people were harmonically tied with one another." You could feel it, she

24. Dana Priest, "Jesse Jackson Joins Forces With Striking Miners in Va.," *Washington Post* (May 1, 1989); and Wayne Barber, "Westmoreland Workers Will Remain Off Jobs," *Bristol Herald Courier* (May 1, 1989).

25. Yancey, "Thunder in the Coal Fields," 7.

26. *Betraying the Trust.*

27. Yancey, "Thunder in the Coal Fields," 7.

28. Couto, "The Memory of the Miners," 179, 180.

said, when people would spontaneously sing "Amazing Grace" when someone was being arrested. But there was also something new in how people expressed this "spiritual commonality." The union borrowed an idea from the civil rights movement and organized weekly evening rallies on a ball field in St. Paul. Like civil rights activists inspired by black preachers, these strike activists expressed their religious values on the new terrain dictated by social struggle and civil resistance. In defending a way of life the UMW had earlier created, the strikers crossed the boundaries between work and community, established novel associations and allies, experimented with alternative roles and relationships, and clarified the meaning of values like solidarity.[29]

The strikers also created their own heroes and found their own leaders in Marty Hudson and Jackie Stump, two men who spoke in the idiom of mountain evangelicals using the words of Martin Luther King. Their leadership would soon face its toughest test. On May 24 Federal Judge Glen Williams issued an order to the strikers at the request of the Republican-dominated National Labor Relations Board: stop blocking Pittston gates, and end the new tactic of impeding coalfield roads with slow-moving vehicles. When the union ignored the order, Williams was incensed. A Republican schooled in the hard-edged politics of southwestern Virginia, the judge called Hudson, Stump, and strike coordinator C. A. Phillips into court to face contempt charges on June 5. When they refused to order their members to end civil disobedience and invoked their Fifth Amendment rights to avoid self-incrimination, Williams sent them off to jail in handcuffs and leg-irons. The *Roanoke Times* report suggested later that the fines and jailings had hurt Pittston's cause because the court had created martyrs and turned the strike into a conflict "like no other in the Virginia coal fields."[30]

Expanding The Strike

It would soon become one of the most unusual strikes in recent U.S. history. Ever since the air traffic controllers' strike of 1981, labor people had bemoaned a lack of union solidarity that helped employers isolate and defeat unions. Trumka shared this bitter memory, and reflected on it often during the strike. "If we play by their rules," he would say, "we lose." On June 11 he spoke to a militant rally of fifteen thousand UMW members in Charleston, West Virginia, and called on them to "rise up and fight back."[31]

The next day ten thousand union miners in West Virginia started a wildcat strike to protest the jailing of the Pittston strike leaders and to show sympathy with the strikers. Mingo and Logan counties, the battlefield in the 1921 civil war, reported 98% of the miners on strike. David Evans of Logan County said the workers walked out to protest "the excessive fines and the jailings of three union officers down in Virginia. They're going to shut down all the union and non-union mines by the end of next week…, whatever it takes to get this settled." Before the week ended the wildcat had spread to six more states involving another twenty thousand miners.[32]

The union now risked even more astronomical court fines; it also jeopardized relations with BCOA members, who had just negotiated a new contract. When questioned,

---

29. Yancey, "Thunder in the Coal Fields," 8–9. Author's interview with Marat Moore, Washington, D.C., December 15, 1993. For a discussion of this process in other strikes, see Rick Fantasia, *Cultures of Solidarity: Consciousness, Action and Contemporary American Workers*, 218–19, 230–31, 236–37 (Berkeley and Los Angeles: University of California Press, 1988).

30. Yancey, "Thunder in the Coal Fields," 8.

31. "Wildcat Strikes Break Out in West Virginia," *Bristol Herald Courier* (June 13, 1989).

32. "Miners Defiant," *USA Today* (June 14, 1989); and "Wildcat Coal Strike Continues Despite Order," *New York Times* (June 15, 1989).

Trumka said he had met his legal duty by asking the thousands of miners to return to work. He said the rank and filers simply refused. "They believe their union is threatened and they walked off their jobs because of that," he said. "They genuinely believe the rules are written for them to lose every time."[33]

It was not clear at this point that the UMWA would win its battle with Pittston, but "It had taken a local strike in Southwest Virginia and stirred up a national ruckus." Important media began to cover the story. The prime-time television program 48 *Hours* aired a segment on the dispute, and one of the strike's most eloquent philosophers, a preacher and retired miner named Harry Whitaker, appeared on the *Donahue* show.[34] At first, civil disobedience seemed necessary to ensure a nonviolent strike, but it soon became apparent that such tactics also attracted the media. At an early training for strike organizers, peace activists "suggested the union cultivate local heroes, who could personalize the strike for the public so it wouldn't be just another anonymous dispute between the company and the union." The media, struck by the romance of mountain life, readily focused on the spectacle of law abiding rural folk sitting down in front of gigantic coal trucks and kneeling down on a roadside with troopers holding shotguns to their heads.[35]

Some reporters exaggerated strike violence and blamed it on the union, but many media people reported favorably on the strikers' commitment to nonviolence.[36] However, the positive media coverage and public support the UMW won through civil disobedience could have ended with just a few rounds of gunfire. The union prohibited alcohol, firearms, and strangers in picket shacks, and it put a picket captain on duty twenty-four hours a day. Top leadership was crucial. One reporter wrote that miners on "the picket line say their new style of conducting a strike has percolated down from the union president Richard Trumka who has brought them a sense of dignity and pride not felt since the glory days of union founder John L. Lewis."[37]

The union's strike strategy seemed to be winning favorable media attention and public support, but tension and anxiety still gripped the strikers and their leaders. Eddie Burke, coordinator of the Massey strike who had come over from West Virginia to help, worried that history would repeat itself. The month began with Pittston breaking off negotiations, strike leaders jailed, the coalfields occupied by state police and another Massey strike on people's minds. But "it ended with the entire labor movement rallying behind the UMW" and Pittston hurting.[38] The wildcat strikes had even begun to affect those operators who supplied Pittston's overseas customers with metallurgical coal.[39] A Wall Street investment firm's report expressed surprise that the UMW, thought to be weakened over the 1980s, had fought Pittston to a standstill for two months. "After more than 2,200 ar-

---

33. Martha Hodel, "Wildcat Walkout: Trumka Not Doing Enough to Get Miners Back, Companies Say," *Sunday Gazette Mail* (July 9, 1989).

34. Yancey, "Thunder in the Coal Fields," 8.

35. *Ibid.*, 2–3.

36. For reports unfavorable to the strikers see James Buchan, "A Marriage of Coal and Violence," *Financial Times of London* (July 10, 1989), Wayne Barber, "Explosion Rocks Pittston Building," *Bristol Herald Courier/Virginia-Tennessean* (July 6, 1989); and the discussion in William J. Puette, *Through Jaundiced Eyes: How the Media View Organized Labor,* 117–39 (Ithaca: ILR Press, 1992).

37. Jules Loh, "UMW Now Negotiates from a Position of Civility," *Allegheny Journal* (July 23, 1989).

38. Yancey, "Thunder in the Coal Fields," 9.

39. Richard Trumka, speech at Harvard Trade Union Program, March 4,1990, and Ken Zinn, "International Labor Solidarity and the Pittston Strike," presentation at International Confederation of Free Trade Unions Conference, Elsinore, Denmark, March 26, 1990. Manuscript in author's possession.

rests and $3 million in fines for civil disobedience, the UMW's perseverance is starting to payoff where it counts most — in the financial community which could pressure Pittston to compromise."[40]

As the sympathy strikes postponed shipments to foreign customers and threatened the industry's export market, Federal Judge Williams got the two sides back to the table. For the first time since the UMW and Pittston began negotiations in 1987 the top people from both sides attended the talks. They refused to sit at the same table, however, and a federal mediator took messages between labor and management teams sitting in separate rooms.[41]

Building a Movement

As wildcat strikes rolled across the midwestern coalfields, the imprisoned strike leaders Hudson, Stump, and Phillips were released. However, they had to promise the judge not to advocate illegal strike tactics, and so they could no longer take the lead in directing the civil resistance movement. A crisis of leadership loomed, because no one in Virginia enjoyed their moral authority with the miners. But there was someone in Washington who did. In modern labor history few top national officers had ever taken leadership of a strike on the ground. But on this occasion Vice President Cecil Roberts boldly assumed command. No one could have been better suited to do so. Born in Cabin Creek, West Virginia, Roberts had been one of the young militants in the turbulent 1970s when conflict raged through those mine fields. His father had been a coal miner who remembered seeing airplanes drop bombs on the miners' army as it marched to free Mingo County from the gun thugs in 1921. His great uncle was Bill Blizzard, the UMW commander who led that historic march. Cecil grew up hearing stories about Mother Jones sitting on his family's front porch and about Baldwin-Felts guards shooting up strikers' tent colonies. He was a crack negotiator who knew the industry inside and out and he was an old-fashioned radical orator — one of the few national labor leaders who still used the words "working class" and "class war." It was a class war that he came down to fight that June.[42]

Roberts arrived in the nick of time. "The strikers weren't losing their resolve but some were starting to lose their patience," said a local attorney. The UMW vice president took on the difficult task of escalating militancy while keeping the strike activity nonviolent. He constantly told the strikers they were part of something much bigger than a strike against Pittston and a fight with scabs. Like Trumka, he made the whole legal system an issue. In one speech, on June 17 in Norton, Virginia, Roberts declared: "It's the system that's really at issue here as much as the contract. The country desperately needs labor law reform that will at least level the playing field."[43]

Roberts boldly defended direct action tactics as wildcat strikers poured into the area from the other coalfields; they escalated the "rolling road blocks," which cut the haul to Pittston Moss 3 coal treatment plant by one-third. Speaking to a crowd of three thousand including many wildcatting midwestern miners, Roberts stood in the bed of a flatbed truck and looked out over a muddy field at the men and women in fatigues. "It's not just

---

40. *Roanoke Times* (June 7, 1989); and Richard Phalon, "Mis-Calculated Risk?" *Forbes* 142 (June 12, 1989).

41. Yancey, "Thunder in the Coal Fields," 9; and "Producers Fear Lengthy Strike, Loss of Sales," *Journal of Commerce* (June 7,1989).

42. Author's interviews with Cecil Roberts, April 22, 1990, on the road from Norton, Virginia, to Welch, West Virginia, and December 15, 1993, Washington, D.C.

43. Yancy, "Thunder in the Coal Fields," 9; and Wayne Barber, "UMW Official Calls for Law that at Least Levels Playing Field," *Bristol Herald Courier* (June 18, 1989).

a strike any more, it's a movement," he said. "Everybody has been wanting to rally around something for years and this is it."[44]

At a big Fourth of July rally in St. Paul, the UMW introduced the last union leader to arouse the labor movement and the national conscience. Joining the hundreds who now came to be arrested on the region's back roads, United Farm Workers President Cesar Chavez declared that with nonviolence social struggles took on a transcendent, spiritual dimension. "Your commitment to nonviolence and the use of passive resistance has captured the attention of organized labor," he declared. "People are attracted to nonviolence. They want to come and help you. If the judge likes to put people in jail, let him. He can't put the whole world in jail."[45]

Judge Williams had already fined Roberts $200,000 for refusing to take responsibility for the road-blocking effort. On July 5, he added another $800,000 to the union's fines which, it now seemed, would bankrupt the UMWA. The judge blamed Roberts and UMW leaders for threatening the legal system and creating a situation "bordering on anarchy." On his orders federal marshals were dispatched to aid state police in enforcing court injunctions. Roberts said the courts were threatening to fine the union out of existence because members refused to give up their jobs to other men. But still the resistance grew. The *Richmond Times-Dispatch* reported that UMW strike supporters who said they were "tourists" were clogging the region's coal-hauling roads with their cars, "defying federal court orders against the practice and subjecting the union to $500,000 in daily penalties."[46]

By now the union's stakes in the Pittston strike were enormous. Federal court fines against the UMW had reached $960,000 which, when combined with state court fines, equaled a total of $4 million. Still, the union's leaders did not waver. As Trumka later said, "we did what we thought we had to do to win the strike." On July 9 he spoke in Charleston and said he was willing to go to jail. "They've done everything they can to me except take away my personal freedom." "It's win this fight or be stampeded to death in the very near future." If the fight bankrupted the union, then so be it, Trumka declared "If we aren't successful," he added, "if justice and legal redress are totally denied here, I submit to you that from the crumbled blocks will arise a movement" as it had in the past when the UMW faced hard times with no money.[47]

At this point, 2,265 felony charges had been filed against strikers and their supporters, many of them out-of-state sympathy strikers. The arrest of law-abiding citizens for blocking traffic aroused special concern. Some had to post $10,000 bonds for minor violations and others were forced to sit in hot buses for long periods of time. The most sensational case came on July 12 when police arrested Sister Bernadette Kenney for impeding traffic. She was a nurse driving a mobile unit for dispensing medication. Sister

---

44. 48. David Reed, "UMW: Pittston Strike is More than Labor Dispute," (AP) *Williamson Daily* (June 29, 1989), and Yancey, "Thunder in the Coal Fields," 4.

45. Martha L. Hall, "NLRB Ruling May Protect Union Jobs," *Kingsport Times-News* (July 5, 1989); and Deborah Rouse, "Striking UMWA Miners Hear Encouraging Words from Cesar Chavez of United Mine Workers," *Coalfield Progress* (July 6, 1989).

46. Jonathan Gill, "Union Leaders Stress Merits of Non-violence," *Williamson Daily* (June 30, 1989); "U.M.W. Fines Again in Virginia Coal Fight," *New York Times* (July 6, 1989); Bill McKelway, "Defiant Miners Clog Roads," *Richmond Times-Dispatch* (July 7, 1989), and "Extra Police Sent to Coalfields as Acts Spread to West Virginia," *Richmond Times-Dispatch* (July 14, 1989).

47. Mike Wright, "49 Strike Related Cases Dismissed by Greenwalt," *Dickenson Star* (July 13, 1989); and "Union Set for Memorial Period, President 'Willing' to Go to Jail," *Bristol Herald Courier/Virginia-Tennessean* (July 10, 1989); and Harry E. Stapleton, "It Was Old Men That Made This Union," *New York Times* (July 9, 1989).

Kenney's arrest received national publicity and aroused even greater support for the strike among religious people.[48]

Kenney's story also added weight to the union's charge that Governor Baliles had sent one-fourth of the state police to "occupy southwestern Virginia." One of the most photographed picket signs, nailed to a shack outside Moss 3, read: "Governor Baliles! This is Southwest Virginia not South Africa!" The governor had won the region's traditionally Democratic vote with the support of the UMWA, but, according to one report, "Sentiments have run so high against Baliles in the coal fields that the governor has cancelled at least one visit" and had made no plans to tour the strike zone. A frustrated Baliles wrote to Pittston's Douglas expressing disappointment about his failure to bargain and asking him to return to the table because the strike was hurting the growing foreign market for Virginia coal.[49]

"The nation's worst coal strike since the mid-1970s arrives at a crossroads," a July 10 article in *Journal of Commerce* observed. "The great majority of the coal hauling" had reportedly ceased in West Virginia where one company laid off ten drivers who refused to cross picket lines. At this point, the Pittston strike had become even more than a survival struggle for the UMWA. Sympathy strikes and massive civil resistance helped accomplish what Roberts and Trumka had hoped: turning a local strike into a national cause for the labor movement. After extending the national walkout several days, Trumka called the wildcat strikers back to work. He then joined Senator Jay Rockefeller in a New York meeting with Japanese steel officials to assure them that the West Virginia coal supply was not in jeopardy. Trumka appealed to their respect for the elderly. "We're fighting for the health care of our parents and grandparents," he told them. "Would you have me turn my back on them?" He thought that this particular appeal touched the Japanese and that they in turn put some pressure on Pittston to settle the strike.[50]

Later that month Trumka issued a "national call of conscience" inviting the entire labor movement to come to support the strikers in Southwest Virginia. The response was surprising. All through July, reported the *Washington Post*, "Miners and their supporters from around the country continue[d] to pour into Camp Solidarity, the strike's makeshift headquarters in a lush meadow outside Castlewood, Virginia." Many activists traveled to the war zone to witness what one local journalist called the "Appalachian Intifada." They went to be arrested for the cause, to bear witness for justice and against corporate greed. Besides the attractiveness of the strikers' civil resistance campaign, other unionists plunged in because, Trumka suggested, the UMWA was still a symbol of militancy and solidarity— still seen as the group most willing to take on the toughest fights, the first group to be targeted by anyone "who wanted to kill the labor movement." Thousands of supporters came to believe that if the miners lost at Pittston, the labor movement might lose its vanguard.[51]

---

48. "U.S. Marshals Halt Strikers' Convoys," *Bluefield Daily Telegraph* (July 7, 1989); and Jeff Moore, "Nun Arrested; Community Angered," *Coalfield Progress* (July 13, 1989).

49. "Baliles' Appearance Postponed," *Bristol Herald Courier* (July 7, 1989); and Jeff Moore, "Export Clients told Shipments Can't be Filled," *Coalfield Progress* (July 11, 1989). Also see "Baliles Calls for New Bargaining," *Bristol Herald Courier/Virginia-Tennessean* (July 11, 1989).

50. "Coal Miners Strike Reaches Critical Point," *Journal o/Commerce* (July 10, 1989); and Trumka interview, January 19, 1994.

51. "Miners' Union Cooling-Off Period Starts With Gunfire and Explosion," *New York Times* (July 11, 1989); David Reed, "UMW: Pittston Strike Is More than Labor Dispute," *Williamson Daily* (June 29, 1989); Dana Priest, "Striking Coal Miners Fear End Of Union, Way of Life in Va.," *Washington Post* (July 6, 1989); and Moberg, "Envisioning a New Day for the Labor Movement"; Trumka interview, January 19, 1994. Also see Denise Giardina, "Coal Field Violence: Myths and Realities," *Christianity & Crisis* (August 14, 1989), and "Strike Zone: The 'Appalachian Intifada' Rages On," *Village Voice*, 31–36 (August 29,1989).

To accommodate the wildcat strikers motoring into the region, the union opened Camp Solidarity on a ten-acre parcel of land near the Clinch River. While the wildcat strikers rolled into the camp with convoys hundreds of cars long, other unions began sending delegations from all over the country. The strikers, emotionally drained from their confrontations with scabs and police, at first seemed overwhelmed by the flood of visitors who needed a place to eat and sleep. But then seeing "people from all over the country with different accents and different license plates, gave the miners and their families renewed determination."[52]

The women of the strike rose to the challenge and spent every day at the camp cooking for the pilgrims. "They spent their own money to come here and help us," organizer Cosby Totten recalled. "Could we let them down?" The women had already been mobilized by the auxiliaries and the Daughters of Mother Jones to feed and care for the local strikers at the Binns-Counts Community Center. The Daughters started "as a traditional UMW women's auxiliary and 'just caught on fire.'" For months they had prepared for the strike as a struggle for community survival. Linda Adair, a hairdresser in St. Paul who gave up her business and devoted all her time to the strike, explained that the Daughters wanted to avoid slipping back into the "powerlessness" that "ruined the lives" of their grandparents — into what she called "the days of slavery." The group included a core of fifty women willing to be arrested and at least two hundred more who acted as supporters. Like the Ladies' Auxiliary in the Flint sit-down strike of 1937, which transformed itself into an emergency brigade, the Daughters wanted to take direct action in the strike.[53]

They did take direct action and in the process they "helped transform the strike into a movement of wider dimensions." Despite all they seemed to have in common, most did not know each other because they lived in isolated rural areas. The Daughters of Mother Jones brought them together literally and symbolically. Being arrested gave some a common experience and "had become pretty much a badge of honor among people." Wearing camouflage gave them all a uniform, "a fashion of discontent" in Marat Moore's words. As more women became more involved in the strike "camouflage underwent a sex change" as the colors worn by hunters and soldiers appeared on cakes, quilts, afghans, umbrellas, bathing suits, and baby clothes. The women made one thing clear, Moore wrote: "In the coal fields camouflage would never again be simply military, or simply male."[54]

---

52. Yancey, "Thunder in the Coal Fields," 9; Jenny Burman, "The Daughters of Mother Jones," Z Magazine (November 1989); Fred Brown, "Striking Miners Gather to Relax at Camp Solidarity," Knoxville News-Sentinel (July 22, 1989); and Gene Caroll, "Camp Solidarity: The Heart of the Pittston Strike," 100 UMWJ 15 (November 1989).

53. Quotes from Moore, "Ten Days"; Burman, "Daughters of Mother Jones"; and Yancey, "Thunder in the Coal Fields," 9.

54. Quotes from Moore, "Ten Months that Shook the Coal Fields." Women's role in the Pittston strike remains to be studied in more detail. It seemed as though the Daughters might emerge as a kind of autonomous organization that would not only break down female isolation but create a real public role for women in the strike beyond the supportive role women's auxiliaries had played in the past. This happened earlier in the 1980s for women in the British coal miners' strike and in the Arizona copper strike. See Jill Evans, Clare Hudson, and Penny Smith, "Women and the Strike: It's a Whole Way of Life," in Bob Fine and Robert Miller, eds., Policing the Miners' Strike, 18:203 (London: Lawrence and Wishart, 1985), and Barbara Kingsolver, Holding the Line: Women in the Great Arizona Mine Strike of 1983 (Ithaca: ILR Press, 1989). The Daughters certainly overcame their isolation during the strike, emerged as highly public activists, and experienced empowerment, but they did not act on their own advice or command their "own ship" like the highly effective Morenci Miners Women's Auxiliary did during the 1983 Phelps-Dodge strike; 140.

"The Daughters have made this [strike] a people's movement," said Linda Adair. They did this in part by making Camp Solidarity "the heart of the strike," and before it was over, a point of contact for the strikers and thousands of supporters who visited during the summer. "This strike could really be depressing, but our people have been brought together like never before because of the spirit that comes from what goes on in the camp," said Peggy Dutton, the spouse of a striking miner. "It's a place where we demonstrate how much we care about one another — not just the families on strike at Pittston but all working people." In this free space the union staked out in Carterton Hollow strikers created a culture of solidarity that touched supporters who came from far and wide to bear witness and offer help. Camp Solidarity gave them all something to remember, a taste of movement experience to carry back home. "On summer evenings, as the heat soaked into the hills, the smell of burning charcoal and the twang of banjos drifted across the wild field," wrote reporter Dwayne Yancey. "Kids chased a stray dog named Jackrock. A garbage-bag effigy of Judge Williams swung from a branch. An Alabama coal miner brought his bride on their honeymoon." "It was like a hillbilly Woodstock," Eddie Burke remembered. By midsummer forty thousand people had already visited the camp. Not even the mass strikes of the early 1930s had attracted this many allies to participate directly in strike support.[55]

Politicizing The Strike

Although the Pittston strike took place in an isolated part of Appalachia, its leaders not only insisted on its national significance; they placed it in an international context as well. They compared the striking miners to those striking for democracy in South Africa, Poland, and the USSR. They even compared their struggle with the pro-democracy movement in China, which generated intense interest and concern after the Army massacred protesters on Beijing's Tiananmen Square early in June. By bringing international attention to the violations of labor law and the anti-union use of court injunctions arising from the strike, the union hoped to embarrass the Bush administration, which claimed to support the Chinese students, the striking Soviet coal miners, and the Polish Solidarity movement, but opposed trade unions back at home. The passionate protest Pittston strikers made against their oppression by the U.S. legal system helped make the Bush administration vulnerable to the charges of hypocrisy in its defense of democracy abroad. It was deeply ironic, Trumka often said, that our officials protested the treatment of workers in the USSR but ignored workers' rights violations in the United States. Only two industrialized countries, allowed employers to replace workers when they struck, South Africa and the United States. "To tell a worker you have the right to strike and then replace him in the next breath is a cruel hoax," he charged.[56]

---

55. Quotes from Burman, "Daughters of Mother Jones"; Brown, "Striking Miners Gather"; and Yancey, "Thunder in the Coal Fields," 9. See also James Green, "Camp Solidarity: The United Mine Workers, The Pittston Strike, and the New People's Movement," in Brecher and Costello, eds., *Building Bridges,* 15–24.

56. Greg Edwards, "UMW Chief Faults Labor Law," *Roanoke Times & World News* (July 9, 1989). Author's interview with Ken Zinn, December 15, 1993. Local miners wrote many letters to local papers and gave many interviews to local media putting their struggle in an international context. See, for example, letter to editor likening the strike to protests of Beijing students for democracy, *Coalfield Progress* (July 6, 1989). These points also appeared in media outside the state. The Charleston, West Virginia, paper quoted an editorial by radical journalist Alexander Cockburn comparing the favorable press coverage of the Soviet miners' strike with the union slurs in the Pittston media coverage. Alexander Cockburn, "Their Miners and Ours," *The Nation* (August 21, 1989), quoted in "Wrong Strike Site," *Charleston Gazette* (August 12, 1989).

Trumka believed that U.S. unions had failed to use international labor organizations effectively. He asked staff lawyers to file charges with the International Labor Organization against the U.S. government for failing to stop labor law violations during the strike. The UMWA had already been more involved in international solidarity work than most unions, especially in South Africa, where black workers supported its Shell boycott in the mid-eighties. Trumka wanted to build on this work. In July he addressed an international conference to "tell the miners' story" and promote "global labor solidarity." Heads of unions all over the world pledged their help. The Australian miners' union persuaded employers not to supply excess metallurgical coal to Japanese steelmakers hurt by the strike. The International Confederation of Free Trade Unions pledged its support. The International Metal Workers Federation urged its affiliates to demand support for a settlement from those of their employers who were Pittston customers. The steel company Italsider telexed Paul Douglas on June 20 from Italy threatening legal action if Pittston's intransigence continued to reduce its coal supply.[57]

For three months pressuring the state and national, political systems had seemed totally ineffective. Then, on July 11, the NLRB found Pittston guilty of unfair labor practices. The company had violated federal labor law twenty-eight times and was "failing and refusing to bargain in good faith." The board's ruling made the walkout an "unfair labor practices strike" and thus prohibited Pittston from offering permanent jobs to replacement workers.[58] This decision eliminated a key element of Pittston's strike-breaking strategy and gave the union an important legal victory.

A day later Congressman William Clay (D-Mo.), chair of the House subcommittee overseeing labor law, announced an investigation of the dispute, stating that "the Pittston strike and the sympathy strikes by thousands of other UMW workers have raised concerns about the administration of labor laws, the involvement of Virginia state and federal courts in the conflict and the increasing threat to the national economy."[59]

In early August, a report for Clay's subcommittee criticized the federal government's inaction in prosecuting Pittston for violating labor law. While it could be years before a court ordered the company to correct unfair labor practices, the report said, "the striking miner has seen union leaders jailed and is confronted each day with a massive display of state police and company security forces who are present for the express purpose of assuring that the company can continue to operate." So the strikers and their families "are understandably perplexed and frustrated by this apparent discrepancy in how the legal system is working."[60]

While the union gained in making labor law reform and court bias a national issue, its leaders also worked to increase national concern over the matter of miners' health care.

57. Zinn, "International Labor Solidarity and the Pittston Strike"; and John F. Harris, "Trade Unions Pledge Support to Striking Miners," *Washington Post* (July 9, 1989); and "World Wide Support for Miners," *Free Labour World*, no. 13 (August 31, 1989); and "Foreign Miners Chief Supports UMW," *Washington Times* (August 23, 1989).

58. "Labor Ruling Finds Coal Company Guilty in Strike," *New York Times* (July 12, 1989). Also see, Phil Primack, "UMW Chief to Drum up Hub Support," *Boston Herald* (July 12, 1989). Two years later, the NLRB published an opinion in *Simmons Bros. Coal Corp. and Middle Creek Energy, Inc., Alter Egos, and Covenant Coal Corporation and United Mine Workers of America, District 28*, NLRB, Case 11-CA-12779, JD 281–91, (1991).

59. Bill McKelway, "Pittston Mum on Plea for New Talks," *Richmond Times-Dispatch* (July 12, 1989); "Report on the Strike at the Pittston Coal Company," prepared by the Majority Staff Subcommittee on Labor-Management Relations, August 31, 1989, 22.

60. Martha L. Hall, "Report Questions Aspects of Strike," *Kingsport Times-News* (August 5, 1989).

Pittston had followed other major employers in demanding reduced health care costs. When it cut off health benefits to retirees the company unwittingly provoked the most publicized of many health-care related strikes. It also gave the union an opportunity to take the moral high ground, and its leaders pressed the advantage in Washington. Senator Jay Rockefeller introduced a bill that would force Pittston to contribute to industrywide health funds. Later in the summer a *New York Times* article on the strike featured health care as an emerging national crisis, especially in labor relations.[61]

Whatever the long-term hopes the strike inspired, the short-term costs reached intimidating levels. Pittston's lawyers presented Judge McGlothin with new evidence that strikers were violating his orders and on July 27 he fined the union another $4.5 million-one hundred times what Pittston had been fined after the 1983 explosion that killed seven miners at McClure. In early August the UMW announced it was spending $4 million each month on strike support (while taking in about $500,000 per month from miners not on strike).[62]

In response to a request by Federal Judge Glen Williams, strike talks resumed on August 6, but again the two sides met in separate rooms. The union offered a new proposal to discuss more flexible hours but the company stood on its last offer. Chief union negotiator Roberts emerged "disappointed and disillusioned." *Coal Outlook* worried about the possibility of a national strike.[63]

The union's resistance took on a more defiant tone. In August Cecil Roberts made news all over the coalfields when he directly challenged court authority and dared Judge Williams to jail him for contempt. As he came to appear before the federal judge on August 21, Roberts gave a rousing speech before six hundred people at the courthouse. "I don't fear going to jail because when you're right, going to jail is okay. Regardless of what happens today, you keep your heads up, keep your hearts beating like they've been beating and stay on fire for this cause because this is a class struggle between the working class and the very rich."[64]

Roberts's confident words and bold actions heightened a mood of militant engagement but discouraged violent acts of revenge. During the weeks he had been in command Roberts showed an unabashed affection for the people on strike. He seemed as moved by their courage as they were by his eloquence. "I've never felt this way about any group of people in my entire life," he declared before facing the court. "I think you are the finest group of people in the entire world. The solidarity movement in Poland has nothing on you people here today." The affection and admiration was returned. Strikers told the media that if the courts put Cecil Roberts in jail, there would be hell to pay. Judge Williams shrank before Roberts's challenge and dismissed the contempt charges against him.[65]

---

61. Michael Freitag, "The Battle Over Medical Costs," *New York Times* (August 17, 1989). Also see "Health Care, Pensions Key Issues in Strike Against Pittston Group," *Washington Post* (July 6, 1989).

62. Wayne Barber, "More than $4 Million in UMW Fines Imposed," *Bristol Herald Courier-Bristol Virginia/Tennessean* (July 28, 1989).

63. "UMW official pleads innocent in Virginia," *Charleston Gazette* (August 4, 1989); "Efficiency Panel Proposed by UMW," *Richmond Times-Dispatch* (August 9, 1989); "UMW Makes New Proposal to Pittston in Coal Strike," *Washington Post* (August 9, 1989); and "UMW Officials 'Is a National Strike in the Offing?'" *Coal Outlook* (August 7, 1989).

64. "UMW Vice President Arrested," *Kingsport Times-News* (July 26, 1989); "Mine Workers Officers, Others Are Arrested," *Wall Street Journal* (July 26, 1989); Yancey, "Thunder in the Coal Fields," 9; Tim Sansbury, "Pittston Coal, Miners' Union To Resume Talks Today," *Journal of Commerce* (August 1, 1989); and "UMW Vice President Dares Federal Judge to Jail Him," *Charleston Gazette* (August 9, 1989).

65. "Labor in America, 'We Won't Go Back': The UMWA/Pittston Strike, 1989–90," *Dickenson Star*, 69, 98 (Clinchco, Va.), 1990.

The continuing defiance of state and federal courts politicized the strike in one way; the all-out attack on Governor Baliles did in another way. Citizen anger grew because the state police had arrested so many people, including many nonstrikers. One merchant erected a sign: "We respectfully refuse to serve troopers during the course of the strike." According to a federal report, hundreds of state police, along with the federal marshals, had created "a sense that the coal fields" were "occupied by a massive security force from outside the ... region."[66]

Trumka blasted Baliles on many occasions, and he questioned the Democratic Party's commitment to working people. In an article headlined "Miners' Discontent gets Political," the *Washington Post* reported: "Sentiments against Baliles have run so high in the coalfields that the governor has cancelled at least one appearance in the region and has not visited the region at all since the strike began." The Dickenson County Sheriff even criticized the governor's use of state troopers and complained about "unofficial martial law."[67]

Governor Baliles's role in the strike fueled labor's discontent with conservative Democrats. Although the union endorsed the Democratic ticket in 1988, many had supported Jesse Jackson and others favored a labor party. When the fall political campaigns began in Virginia, strikers wanted to take political action. Don McGlothin Sr., the incumbent Democratic representative from Buchanan County to the Virginia House of Delegates, stood unopposed for re-election. A conservative who had held that seat for over two decades, McGlothin was a power in the House, but he was the father of the judge who had fined the union $31 million during the strike. Trumka wanted a union candidate to run against the elder McGlothin. Strike leader Jackie Stump reluctantly agreed, announcing his candidacy on September 18 at the John L. Lewis Building in Oakwood. No one thought Stump had a chance of upsetting a powerful incumbent like McGlothin with a last minute write-in campaign, but the strike and the civil resistance movement had shaken up the status quo in southwest Virginia, and within a few weeks people were talking about a UMW leader going from the jailhouse to the state house.[68]

"Stirring up the Labor Movement"

The union exerted surprising power against Pittston in the coalfields, but it could not win the strike on the picket line, at the ballot box, or in the courts. The company seemed willing to lose millions of dollars to break the union. To crack Pittston, the union had to hit its directors and investors with a corporate campaign more effective than those conducted by other striking unions in the eighties.[69]

When the strike began the union launched an intense campaign against the company where its executives lived—in Greenwich, Connecticut, and in other cities where its board of directors resided.[70] The union hired Pat Speer to run its campaign in Greenwich. A

---

66. *Ibid.*, 69; House Subcommittee Report on the Strike at Pittston, 17; and Mike Wright, "Trumka's 'Call To Conscience' Answered."

67. "The Strike at Pittston," *Trade Union Advisor* 2, no. 15 (July 25, 1989); Ken Jenkins Jr., "Coal Miners' Discontent Gets Political," *Washington Post* (August 6, 1989); and "Sheriff Blasts Coalfield Troopers," *Roanoke Times and World News* (September 24, 1989).

68. Yancey, "Thunder in the Coal Fields," 4, 17–20.

69. Zinn, "International Labor Solidarity and the Pittston Strike."

70. Two months before the strike started in April the union targeted the Crestar, a major Pittston lender. The campaign cost Crestar money, according to the union staffer who directed the campaign, and put the bank in frequent communication with Pittston about the strike's negative effects. "Mine workers vs. Manny Hanny," *ABA Banking Journal* (August 1989); author's interview with Ken Zinn, December 15, 1993.

devout Catholic and community organizer involved with the Campaign for Human Development in Appalachia, Speer roused the religious community in Connecticut against Pittston. In late June twelve local clergy sent a letter to CEO Douglas protesting the company's efforts to blame strike violence on the union; the twelve boldly suggesting that he was "like the Pharaoh" who had enslaved people, and wondered why a pestilence stalked his land. The company dismissed the letter as "absolutely ridiculous." It was harder to dismiss another letter, signed by eighty-six area clergy, calling for a fair contract and condemning Pittston's decision to cut off health benefits because it was "not the will of God ... that ... persons should be used this way."[71]

The strikers and their supporters haunted the Pittston executives in Greenwich. "When they went to church, some heard sermons from their priests and ministers against their company," wrote one reporter. "When they commuted to and from work, they ran into strikers passing out leaflets." The minister of the Methodist Church in Greenwich thought the moral campaign "jarred the Pittston Company people who just kind of assumed this would be a safe haven from the strike. There was just no escape. They just couldn't get away from it."[72]

The union also pressured the board of directors in cities across the nation dispatching striking miners and their families to work with local supporters. Along with investors and lenders these directors were principal targets of the corporate campaign headed by UMW staffer Ken Zinn. He came to Boston in April to begin an effort against board member William Craig, a vice president of Shawmut Bank. Craig was a good target because his bank had extensive dealings with the public, including unions and city governments. A strike support committee formed to carry on the campaign. The feuding labor factions in Massachusetts buried their hatchets, not deeply but long enough to unify behind the strikers.[73]

On July 12 Trumka came to Boston for a spirited rally at the Shawmut's downtown bank and testified before the Boston City Council urging that municipal funds be withdrawn from the bank unless Craig agreed to work for a settlement. On July 26 the City Council passed a resolution to remove $20 million from Shawmut Bank because of Craig's links to Pittston and his refusal to work for a fair strike settlement. The resolution passed unanimously and made headlines. Boston Mayor Ray Flynn did not act on the resolution immediately, but he was sympathetic to the strikers, so much so that he visited the coalfields and made a controversial statement comparing the use of state police in Virginia to their use against Solidarity in Poland. Encouraged by these developments, the Boston support committee put added pressure on Craig by picketing his home and encouraging the cities of Somerville and Cambridge, along with several unions, to withdraw their funds from the Shawmut Bank. Within a few weeks $280 million had been withdrawn and the political phase of the corporate campaign began to take its toll on one of Pittston's directors. Meanwhile, protest mounted against Shawmut's subsidiary in Connecticut when several unions announced major withdrawals to protest Craig's connection with that bank. The union also targeted the firms of other board members and some parent companies reportedly complained that Pittston's hard-nosed tactics were hurting them and "stirring up the labor movement."[74]

71. Charles Isenhart, "A Coal Strike Comes to Affluent Greenwich, Conn.," *National Catholic Register* (August 1989); and Yancey, "Thunder in the Coal Fields," 10; and "A Letter to Paul Douglas, Chairman the Pittston Company," by Religious Leaders of Fairfield County, leaflet in author's possession.

72. Yancey, "Thunder in the Coal Fields," 10.

73. Paul Cannon, "Miners Reach Out for Our Help," *New England Labor News* & *Commentary* (July–August 1989); and Green, "Camp Solidarity."

74. Joe Sciacca, "Council Votes to Close Its Shawmut Accounts," *Boston Herald* (July 27, 1989); "Flynn Remarks Anger Mass. Cops," *Boston Herald* (July 22, 1989); "Flynn Visits Miners," *Boston Her-*

The Pittston strike had stirred up a labor movement deeply frustrated and angered by the series of defeats that began when President Reagan broke the PATCO strike in 1981. The UMW's willingness to risk everything in a final confrontation aroused deep sympathy in union ranks. Trumka received boisterous responses wherever he spoke, often in tandem with Jesse Jackson. He called upon "people across the country to visit southwest Virginia and see 'a system that doesn't have room for workers in it.'" National AFL-CIO leaders took note of the grounds well of support for Pittston strikers and for the use of civil disobedience. They also recognized that their affiliates and major media organs like the *Washington Post* had come to see the Pittston strike as a last stand for the UMWA and even for the labor movement itself. On August 30, just before Labor Day, AFL-CIO President Lane Kirkland and Secretary-Treasurer Thomas Donahue, joined Trumka and eighteen other top labor leaders in blocking Dickenson County courthouse as a crowd of more than one thousand miners and supporters cheered. Their arrests received national media coverage. Kirkland, who had never been arrested in a strike, hoped the UMW would reaffiliate with the AFL-CIO and he wanted to show that federation could offer real support to the miners' strike. Trumka and Roberts were convinced, partly by the example of Martin Luther King, that a civil resistance strategy could work only if the rank-and-file activists knew that their leaders would also disobey the law and take the penalty.[75]

After five months, the striking miners remained united, according to the *Baltimore Sun,* and Pittston continued to take a beating in the press and from politicians like Senator Rockefeller, who demanded government prosecution of Pittston for unfair labor practices. But as the summer waned, a settlement still seemed to be remote. With court fines still mounting, some experts began to doubt the UMWA's chances for victory or even for survival. This was a fight the union had to win, but it might not, said the *Los Angeles Times.* The strike had become a "cause célèbre of organized labor" but it now attracted a lot less attention than it had when tens of thousands of miners had wildcatted earlier in the summer. "[T]he strike is bogged down," the report said, "attracting few headlines outside the coal country." The Pittston miners now stood in isolation, clustering in wooden shacks they built at each Pittston mine entrance. The arrest of Lane Kirkland and other labor leaders appeared to the *Times* to be just a "desperate" attempt to keep the issue alive.[76]

Indeed, after mobilizing an entire region, creating a powerful resistance movement and hurting Pittston's production, the UMW seemed no closer to reaching an agreement. The union needed to do something to keep the pressure on Pittston, to keep morale strong

---

ald (July 21, 1989); "Boston Council Cites Pittston-Bank Link," *Journal of Commerce* (July 28, 1993); and "AFL-CIO Threatens to Sever Tie with CNB," *Greenwich Time* (August 23, 1989). Zinn quoted in Yancey, "Thunder in the Coal Field," 10.

75. Mike Wright, "Trumka's 'Call To Conscience' Answered," *Dickenson Star* (August 31, 1989); Frank Swoboda, "Organized Labor Toughens Its Stance," *Washington Post* (September 3, 1989); "Labor Leaders Arrested at Rally Held to Support Striking Union," *New York Times* (August 25, 1989); Dana Priest, "Labor Leaders Arrested in Va.," *Washington Post* (August 24, 1989); and author's interview with Cecil Roberts, Washington, D.C., December 15, 1993.

76. For critical news coverage of Pittston see Martha Hodel, "The Pittston Co.," Alexander Cockburn, "Their Miners and Ours," *The Nation* (August 21–28, 1989), and "Corrupt Firm," *Charleston Gazette* (August 18, 1989); Wayne Barber, "Religious Leaders Rally Behind UMW," *Bristol Herald Courier* (September 10, 1989); and Stephen Coats, "Churches Respond to the Pittston Strike," *Christianity and Crisis* (September 25, 1989). Quotes from Carol Schoettler, "After Five Months, Striking Miners remain United," *Baltimore Sun* (September 5, 1989); and Bob Baker, "Coal Strike a Fight Union Has to, but May Not, Win," *Los Angeles Times* (August 23, 1989).

and maintain nonviolence. Faced with this situation, union leaders made a bold plan to seize and occupy the Moss 3 coal treatment plant near Carbo, the site of the biggest resistance actions.

Eddie Burke, who organized the operation, was a keen student of labor history who knew what the sit-down strikers of the 1930s had accomplished. Burke and three team leaders spent nearly a month in secret meetings on the plan, code-named Operation Flintstone after the UAW occupation of a Fisher Body plant in Flint, Michigan, in 1937. The action was organized in military fashion and on September 16, 1989, ninety-nine carefully chosen miners and one clergyman, Jim Sessions, gathered at Camp Sol to receive their secret orders. They arrived at Moss 3 on schedule and Burke, his heart pumping wildly, led his teams through the gate toward the huge six-story structure as supporters cheered from the road. Anxious about the possibility of gunfire, Burke shouted over his bullhorn that the group was peaceful and unarmed and, rather audaciously, that it was a group of Pittston stockholders coming "to inspect their property."[77]

Surprisingly, only three troopers patrolled the area and only two private guards stood watch. The security men quickly fled as occupiers marched through the gates and clambered up the stairs of the huge facility. In twenty minutes they had locked themselves in the control room. Cecil Roberts assumed command of the crowd outside. He asked 2,000 supporters to stay all night to protect the occupation. By nightfall the crowd had grown much larger as state troopers arrived belatedly on the scene. Tension swelled as supporters worried about a police assault.[78]

On the second day, the miners, surprised that they had not been evicted, rigged makeshift showers and set up dorms in the processing plant. While the NLRB sought an injunction to end the illegal sitdown, Roberts dealt with the police and the large crowd that had gathered. On the third day U.S. marshals served subpoenas on Roberts and Burke, while Mike Odum, Pittston's chief in Virginia, denounced "this latest act of violence by the union," calling the occupiers "common terrorists." Federal Judge Williams, sitting in Abingdon, gave the sit-downers twenty-four hours to "walk out honorably." If they did not accept this offer of amnesty, the union would be fined $600,000 a day and the union leaders would face jail sentences. Meanwhile, state police made plans to storm the plant. Roberts met with the men inside and said there was an immediate possibility of a police attack on the plant and that they should probably leave. Judge Williams's 7:00 P.M. deadline passed and then the men came out at 9:00 P.M., cheered wildly by the big throng that had gathered to protect them.[79]

The union helped restore the strikers' militancy and tighten the knot of solidarity; and it had once again caught Pittston and the police offguard. Moss 3 was Mike Odum's crown jewel and he seemed stunned that the union could capture and hold it. The occupation did not get the national media coverage the union wanted, even though the UMW deluged papers and television news with information. The occupation had not delivered a

---

77. Author's interview with Eddie Burke, Norton, Virginia, April 20, 1990, video taped by Cabin Creek Films; Jim Sessions and Fran Ansley, "Singing Across Dark Spaces: The Union/Community Takeover of Pittston Moss 3 Plant," in Steve Fischer, *Fighting Back in Appalachia*, 199–222 (1993); Yancey, "Thunder in the Coal Fields," 10–11; and "Striking Coal Miners Hold Pittston Processing Plant," *Washington Post* (September 19, 1989).

78. Yancey, "Thunder in the Coal Fields," 10–11.

79. *Ibid.*, 11–13, Dana Priest, "Miners Heed Court Order, End Va. Plant Takeover," *Washington Post* (September 21, 1989); and Priest, "Striking Miners Settle In At Va. Processing Plant," *Washington Post* (September 20, 1989); and Paul Kwik, "Pittston Power," *The Nation* (October 16, 1989).

knockout blow to Pittston, but it let the company know the union was still willing and ready to hit anywhere at any time without regard to legal constraints.[80]

Signs of Hope

As the Appalachian hills turned brilliant colors of crimson, brown, and yellow that October new signs of hope appeared. On October 2 a bi-partisan group of senators introduced a bill to take health benefits to retirees off the bargaining table, proposing that the federal government assume responsibility for two debt-ridden health funds covering 161,000 retired miners. Two days later the Senate Finance Committee endorsed the plan, which Senator Rockefeller succeeded in attaching to the budget bill, thus ensuring its quick passage.[81]

On October 12 a delegation of international labor leaders arrived in the coalfields. The group, which included a Solidarity member newly elected to Poland's Senate, denounced the Pittston's violations of labor law, promised to file a complaint with the International Labor Organization, and to work through the International Confederation of Free Trade Unions to discourage Pittston's customers and allied suppliers.[82]

The next day the international delegation visited Secretary Elizabeth Dole and made a forceful presentation about the violations they had witnessed. Dole then announced that she would go to the coalfields herself. International scrutiny was beginning to make a difference. On October 14 Dole convened the first meeting attended by both Trumka and Douglas and announced she would soon appoint a supermediator to put federal pressure on the parties to settle. After returning from an "emotionally wrenching" tour of the coalfields, she said, "I saw families against families, brothers against brothers. This is tearing entire communities apart." Dole's comments seemed newsworthy if only because they represented the most sympathetic words unions had heard from a federal official in nearly nine years. In a few days Dole appointed William Usery as her supermediator. He had worked for both Republicans and Democrats, and had "earned a reputation as one of the nation's top labor dispute troubleshooters." If anyone could wrench an agreement out of the warring adversaries, Bill Usery could. But he soon found this strike to be one of his toughest assignments because, he said, the parties found themselves stuck in a "deep hole full of animosity."[83]

On October 20 the corporate campaign claimed a victory when William Craig announced in Boston that he would resign as a vice president of the Shawmut Bank. Ken Zinn recalled later that Craig's resignation marked a turning point. "It sent a very strong message to the board of directors that there was a personal cost" to the strike. "What we did in this campaign was to take the coal mines to him in Boston and it cost him."[84] In-

---

80. Author's interview with Ron Baker, Washington, D.C., July 15, 1993; and with Trumka, January 19, 1994.

81. Dana Priest, "Senate Bill May Settle Big Issues in Coal Strike," *Washington Post* (October 3, 1989); "Coal Accord?" *Charleston Gazette* (October 5, 1989); Pamela Porter, "Panel OKs Plan to Salvage Miners' Fund," *Bluefield Daily* (October 10, 1989); and Joel Chernoff, "Miners Fighting for Health Plans," *Pensions & Investment Age* (October 30, 1989).

82. "Secretary Dole to Visit Site of Pittston Strike," *Daily Labor Report* (October 13, 1989); "ICFTU tour Appalled at Pittston, U.S. Law," *AFL-CIO News* (October 14,1989); and William Keesler, "Foreign Unions Pressure Firms to Cut Purchases from Pittston," *Louisville Courier Journal* (October 13, 1989).

83. Yancey, "Thunder in the Coal Fields," 14; "Dole Leads Cole Strike Summit," *Washington Post* (October 15, 1989); and "Ex-Labor Secretary Usery to Mediate Va. Coal Strike," *Washington Post* (October 25, 1989).

84. Joe Battenfeld, "Mine workers Applaud as Shawmut Exec Resigns," *Boston Herald,* 10 (October 20, 1989); Doug Bailey and Bruce Butterfield, "Shawmut Boycott Off as Craig Quits," *Boston Globe* (October 20, 1993).

vestors wondered about the costs of the strike too. Pittston's income had fallen by 79% in the third quarter of 1989 from $14.7 million to $3.1 million.[85]

By late October Jackie Stump's write-in election campaign against incumbent House Delegate Don McGlothin began generating some excitement in the strike zone. The energy mobilized for civil resistance had been redirected into the campaign, just at a time — "crunch time" Trumka later called it — when the strike strategists had exercised nearly all their tactical options. "People told me they'd gotten four phone calls prior to the election," a McGlothin supporter said with amazement. It was one of the best orchestrated campaigns he had ever seen.[86] All of the movement-building energy that Cecil Roberts and his zealous followers had generated in the spring and summer powered Stump's insurgent campaign against the senior McGlothin. It was the clearest expression of how political the strike had become.

Campaign manager Eddie Burke was surprised and delighted when his phone banks reported that 75% of the people called said they would vote for strike leader Stump. On November 7 the miners' write-in candidate won every precinct except the incumbent's home town. "It was a landslide beyond anyone's imagination: Stump 7,981; McGlothin 3,812," wrote an observer. As Stump said to a rally of supporters: "The work has just started because now people throughout the United States have realized that if the politicians that are supposed to help working people don't help working people then we can take them out of office."[87]

Two days later, after news of Stump's election "hit like a storm," Supermediator William Usery reopened contract talks in the Washington area with Cecil Roberts and Joseph Farrell heading the union and company teams. Usery began by declaring a news blackout for both sides and insisting on a cease-fire in the war zone. The mass picketing and road blocking ended. No trucks were stoned. Most of the state troopers left and nearly all of the hated Vance security guards departed.[88]

Now, time seemed to be on the union's side. In November a UPI story predicted that Pittston could lose up to $60 million by the end of the year. One expert said: "Douglas believed the law would take care of everything" in what should have been a "small strike." But "Pittston apparently misread how fast the courts could move" and it "underestimated the union's resolve." UMW officials and other union leaders had "targeted the Pittston strike as a place to take a stand" and now that they had forced government intervention, the corporation could not expect "a clear-cut victory."[89]

After a week of intensive negotiations that lasted late into the evening, Usery declared a week's suspension to talk independently with both sides. When the parties returned, a

---

85. "Pittston New Earnings Plunged 79% in 3rd Quarter, Coal Strike is Cited," *Wall Street Journal* (October 23, 1989); and "Pittston Income Falls 79%," *Greenwich Time* (October 21, 1989). Six weeks later the UMW won a suit against Pittston when a federal district judge ruled that the company had violated securities regulations when it conducted votes on three proposals submitted by striking miners at the annual stockholders' meeting in May. "Judge Says Pittston Co. Violated Securities Rules," *New York Times* (November 30, 1989).

86. Trumka, speech at Harvard Trade Union Program; and Yancey, "Thunder in the Coal Fields," 14.

87. Yancey, "Thunder in the Coal Fields," 15; and "Labor in America: 'We Won't Go Back,'" 90, 91.

88. Dana Priest, "Va. Coal Miner Strikes Gold in Politics," *Washington Post* (November 20, 1989); and Yancey, "Thunder in the Coal Fields," 15.

89. "Pittston Company Misread Strike," UPI, *Charleston Gazette* (November 21, 1989); Dana Priest, "Big Machines, Ready Replacements and the Strike's Bottom Line," *Washington Post* (November 26, 1989).

more cooperative atmosphere developed. After eight months on strike and great financial losses on both sides, the two parties realized that this might be their last chance to settle and avoid a struggle to the death. The sticking point remained Pittston's withdrawal from the health care fund. Usery talked to Elizabeth Dole and she said that the government might be able to look into the problem; this possibility opened up new progress in the talks. Usery set a Christmas deadline to create a sense of urgency and Trumka joined the talks, a sign of progress.[90]

As Christmas in the coalfields approached, union caravans arrived bringing toys and clothes to the strikers and their families. But the holiday was a somber one. The hatreds stirred up by the strike hung over the region like the coal dust stirred up by giant trucks still hauling "scab coal" to Moss 3. Judge McGlothin, no doubt angered by his father's stunning defeat by Jackie Stump, handed out $33.4 million more in fines in the eighth, ninth, and tenth rounds of criminal contempt hearings and called UMWA members "thugs" and "terrorists." A spokesman for Usery criticized these fines and said they might hurt negotiations.[91]

After a Christmas break the parties reconvened in Washington at the Capitol Hilton and on New Year's Eve, just before midnight, Trumka and Roberts reached across the table and shook hands with their enemies, Douglas and Farrell. On New Year's Day 1990, the union and company announced a tentative agreement. Trumka, "who had staked his reputation and the future of the union on the strike's outcome, called the settlement 'a victory for the entire labor movement.'" The miners appeared to "score a major victory," U.S. News said, "leaving the company with relatively meager gains won only at great expense."[92]

Other reporters saw losses for both sides in the settlement that gave the company some of the flexibility it wanted in work rules including two alternatives to the conventional eight-hour, five-day week and the freedom to run coal twenty-four hours a day except Sunday during daytime. On the other hand, the company agreed to maintain the 100% health care coverage the union insisted on. On the difficult issue of the trust funds, the employer agreed to pay $10 million into the funds that covered those who retired before 1976 if it could then drop out. To address the long-term problems of the troubled funds, Secretary Dole agreed to appoint a commission, chaired by Usery, to explore other solutions. On the critical union issue of job security Pittston and its subcontractors agreed to hire laid-off union miners for four of the first of every five job openings at Pittston's new operations; subcontractors would provide the first nineteen of every twenty jobs to UMW miners. It also agreed to limit but not end transfers of coal reserves from union to nonunion subsidiaries.[93]

Union leaders discussed the contract proposal with strikers intensively and on February 20, 1990, the Pittston miners ratified it by a 60% majority. Trumka announced the results at the AFL-CIO meetings in Florida and a celebration erupted. "One line of labor leaders after another at meetings in Bal Harbor said they saw the accord as a break in the

---

90. Yancey, "Thunder in the Coal Fields," 15.
91. Yancey, "Thunder in the Coal Fields," 15; *Camo Call* (December 8 and 29, 1989), and "Union 'Santas' Aid Striking Miners," *Bridgeport Post-Telegram* (December 10, 1989).
92. Yancey, "Thunder in the Coal Fields," 15, and "A Healthy Settlement for Mine Workers," *U.S. News & World Report* (January 15, 1990).
93. "A Healthy Settlement," Yancey, "Thunder in the Coal Fields," 16; Peter Kilborn, "Pittston and Miners in Accord to Resolve Bitter Coal Strike," *New York Times* (January 2, 1990); and Dana Priest, "Light at the End of the Tunnel," *Washington Post* (February 26, 1990).

long decline of trade union membership." Critics of the labor establishment also saw the strike as a great victory and a turning point for labor.[94]

Trumka, who knew the strike's costs, said the results were "bittersweet." There had been great suffering, hard feelings, millions of dollars lost, thousands of people arrested, but Pittston's union busting drive had been stopped and the UMWA had been saved. The strike "caught fire" and became a movement that inspired union workers all over the United States, he recalled. The strikers even "twanged the nation's conscience." Moreover, Trumka concluded, "the union had convinced the public that it spoke for the working people of America and that the UMW's defeat would have weakened the position of all working people." Few labor leaders in the modern era could have made such a claim with so much credibility.[95]

From the seeds planted by the Pittston strikers, Trumka hoped, would spring "nothing less than a movement for the overhaul of U.S. labor law." He thought the strike demonstrated the futility of abiding by existing laws and that it highlighted an "outrageous" contradiction: corporations made products that killed people but suffered no fines while UMW people went on strike, sat down in the roads, or drove slowly on the highway "and they ended up getting fined 64 million bucks." Trumka believed it was so outrageous that many unions began pushing harder for labor law reform and making it a number-one priority for the AFL-CIO.[96] In addition, the attention the strike drew to the health care crisis led to a very surprising outcome: the passage of legislation recommended by Elizabeth Dole's commission on miners' health care and sponsored by Senator Jay Rockefeller to guarantee health benefits for 120,000 UMW people covered by the bankrupt funds. It was, Trumka said, the "greatest victory the Mine Workers have had in fifty years." It also gave impetus to the move for "national health care" reform with full coverage.[97]

However, the massive court fines levied against the union lingered like a dark cloud into 1994. In the strike settlement Pittston agreed to drop most of the charges that led to fines. Others would be appealed. But the courts insisted on holding the UMW accountable for over $60 million in fines. In 1993 the union's legal appeal went all the way to the Supreme Court. The case is still undecided. If the Court ruled against the union, Trumka said in early 1994, it would discourage the use of civil disobedience as a peaceful form of protest. The Court will be saying to unions, "Don't you ever sit in the street to protect health care of elderly people because we will fine you into oblivion."[98]

In 1994, the Supreme Court in a unanimous opinion by Justice Blackmun struck down the fines as criminal rather than civil contempt penalties, thus requiring foregone jury trials: "[T]he Virginia trial court levied contempt fines for widespread, ongoing, out-of-court violations of a complex injunction. In so doing, the court effectively policed petitioners' compliance with an entire code of conduct that the court itself had imposed. The

---

94. Dana Priest, "Striking Miners Vote on New Contract," *Washington Post* (February 19, 1990); "Labor in America: 'We Won't Go Back,'" 98, 99; David Reed, "Pittston Miners OK Contract," *Greenwich Times* (February 21, 1990); Dana Priest, "Contract Approved By Miners," *Washington Post* (February 21, 1990); Lionel Barber, "Miners' Settlement May Herald New Era," *Financial Times* (January 3, 1990); Greg Tarpanian, "Pittston: Rebirth of the Unions?" *Wall Street Journal* (November 20, 1989); and Jane Slaughter, "Is the Labor Movement Reaching a Turning Point?" *Labor Notes* (January 1990).

95. Trumka interview, January 19, 1994. *Also see* Richard L. Trumka, "On Becoming a Movement," *Dissent*, 57–60 (Winter 1992).

96. Marianne Lavelle, "The New Coal Wars," *National Law Journal*, 28 (November 20, 1989), and Trumka interview, January 19, 1994.

97. "Keeping the Commitment," *UMWJ*, 4–9 (February 1992).

98. *Ibid.*

union's contumacy lasted many months and spanned a substantial portion of the State. The fines assessed were serious, totaling over $52 million. Under such circumstances, disinterested factfinding and evenhanded adjudication were essential, and petitioners were entitled to a criminal jury trial."[99] The Court did not decide that per se the level of the fines were illegitimate.

Even a short time after the settlement in early 1990 it is difficult to re-create the mood of anger and passion the Pittston strike aroused in union labor across the land. It came in the context of antiworker Republican rule and an anti-union onslaught organized labor had not seen since the 1920s; it also came after a series of defeats in which top labor leadership had failed to support local strikers or to mobilize fully against the employer. Strikers from Arizona to Minnesota felt abandoned and betrayed by their national leaders and this feeling produced a bitterness far deeper and more destructive to the labor movement than the tough opposition of the employers, the courts, and the Republican administrations in Washington. Although local cultures of solidarity blossomed in many of these desperate strikes, at the national level "legal strategies predominated over strategies for mass mobilization."[100] The United Mine Workers, led and inspired by their national leaders, shattered this discouraging trend in 1989 and thus renewed hope in the union movement. They retied the knot of solidarity between local strikers and national unions.

In the struggle with Pittston the UMWA demonstrated how old forms of struggle could be blended with new ones. The union had organized ladies' auxiliaries, community allies, and local officials before, but it had never mobilized churches and the rest of the labor movement so effectively. It perfected strategies used in the 1970s and 1980s, like corporate campaigns, and it expanded them to the international scene with unusual effectiveness. It returned to the sympathy strike rank-and-file miners used in the wildcats of the 1970s and it reached back to the 1930s to resurrect another illegal maneuver: the plant occupation. But it also added new tactics like civil disobedience, borrowed from the civil rights movement, and renamed them civil resistance to harmonize nonviolent tactics with the militant traditions of coalminer protest in Appalachia. It relied on familiar forms of political influence with remarkable success at a national level (notably in the form of Secretary Dole's intervention) and returned to an old practice of running a union miner for state office. But it also politicized the conflict in unprecedented ways so that it became much more than a strike. What began as a contract fight became a people's movement against corporate greed and an oppressive legal system, a movement many hoped would provide a model for the revival of organized labor in the United States.

---

99. *International Union, United Mine Workers of America v. Bagwell*, 512 U.S. 821, 837–838 (1994).

100. On the problems of local strikers with their international unions, *see* Fantasia, *Cultures of Solidarity*, 218–25; quote, 242. On the failure of national unions to support Phelps Dodge miners on strike in Arizona and Hormel packinghouse workers in Minnesota, *see* 278–79, and Peter Rachleff, *Hard Pressed in the Heartland: The Hormel Strike and the Future of the Labor Movement* (Boston: South End Press, 1993).

XVII

Market Fragmentation: Service Workers in the Home

Organizing Home Care: Low-Waged Workers in the Welfare State (2002)

*Eileen Boris & Jennifer Klein**

Commemorating the death of Martin Luther King Jr. on April 4, 1988, a hundred Los Angeles home care workers marched to demand union recognition. "This is Memphis all over again," civil rights leaders addressed the mostly female and minority crowd. "We are saying again today, 'We are somebody.' We're men and women who deserve to be treated with dignity."[1] For over a decade, all across the nation, these caretakers of the frail elderly and the disabled had been asking for "respect, dignity and an increase in our wages."[2] They were a hidden workforce, located in the home and confused with both the labor of domestic servants and the care work of wives and mothers.[3] After 74,000 entered the Service Employees International Union (SEIU) in 1999, media celebrated these minimum-waged, predominantly Latina, Black, and immigrant women, who pulled off the largest gain in union membership since the sit-down strikes of the 1930s.[4] This organizing, however, depended on the welfare state location of the labor—that is, on the prior organizing of home care through law and social policy during the last quarter of the twentieth century.

---

* This chapter is a portion of an article by the authors first published in 34 *Politics & Society* 81 (March 2006). It appears here by permission of the publisher, Sage Publications.

1. Bob Pool, "Faithful Rally Across U.S. to Keep King Dream Alive," *Los Angeles Times*, April 5, 1988; Victor Merina, "Home-Care Workers Rally, Gain Support in Pay Issue, "*Los Angeles Times*, December 23, 1987.

2. Charisse Jones, "Providers of Home Care in Budget Pinch," *Los Angeles Times*, March 22, 1989.

3. *See* Linda Delp and Katie Quan, "Homecare Worker Organizing in California: An Analysis of a Successful Strategy," 27 *Labor Studies Journal* 17, 4.

4. Steven Greenhouse, "In Biggest Drive Since 1937, Union Gains a Victory," *New York Times*, February 26, 1999.

These front-line care workers enable aged, blind, and disabled individuals to remain in their own homes by performing a range of duties, depending on the needs of clients, such as assisting with personal hygiene, cooking, cleaning, and shopping and helping with medication.[5] Despite such socially necessary labor, their average hourly wage is lower than that of all other jobs in health care with the exception of janitors. In 2000, hourly rates ranged from $5.74 to $10.13, with nearly half at $7.50 an hour or less.[6] Workers in nursing homes received 30–60 percent more for identical labor, while the annual earnings of hospital aides and orderlies were 70 percent greater. Thus, despite earning wages, home care workers remain poor, with one-quarter having family incomes below $10,000 per year and a third at the poverty line. Rarely employed full time, they also have lacked health insurance, paid sick leave, paid vacations, or even workers' compensation.[7] Most have been middle-age women of color or immigrants, though the exact mix of race, ethnicity, and citizenship status has depended on the region of the country.[8] Both the state and the long-term care industry have shared the presumption that "women would always be willing to provide care and companionship for our loved ones—despite jobs that kept them working but poor."[9]

Since the 1980s, home care has emerged as one of the fastest growing sectors of the health care industry. It can be secured through public and private social welfare agencies, county welfare departments, Medicare-certified home health agencies, private employment agencies, and independent workers directly hired by clients, or through families. These workers may labor in "private homes" and perhaps for a nongovernmental agency, but in most cases the public sector provides or pays for their services. By the 1990s, Medicaid accounted for 43% of all long-term care expenditures, a percentage that persisted into the next century. While spending for institutional services predominated, government pay-

5. Katherine Ricker-Smith, "An Historical and Critical Overview of the Development and Operation of California's In-Home Supportive Services Program," San Francisco Home Health Service, Grant HEW-100-78-0027, December 31, 1978.

6. Table D-3, "Personal and Home Care Aides Employment and Wages in 2000 by Industry Group," in National Center for Health Workforce Analyses, Bureau of Health Professions, Health Resources & Services Administration, *Nursing Aides, Home Health Aides, and Related Health Care Occupations: National and Local Workforce Shortages and Associated Data Needs*, 92 (February 2004), available at http://bhpr.hrsa.gov/healthworkforce/reports/nursinghomeaid/nursinghome.htm (accessed October 9, 2005). Compare this with nursing aides, orderlies, and attendants whose average was over a dollar more, 91.

7. William Crown, Dennis Ahlburg, and Margaret MacAdam, "The Demographic and Employment Characteristics of Home Care Aides: A Comparison with Nursing Home Aides, Hospital Aides, and Other Workers," 35 *The Gerontologist* 163–169; Lyn C. Burbridge, "The Labor Market for Home Care Workers: Demand, Supply, and Institutional Barriers," 33 *The Gerontologist*, 41–46; Steven Dawson and Rick Surpin, "Direct Care Health Workers: The Unnecessary Crisis in Long-Term Care," Report Submitted by the Paraprofessional Health Care Institute to Aspen Institute 11–12 (Jan. 2001), at http://www.paraprofessional.org/publications/Aspen.pdf (accessed October 14, 2005).

8. Grace Chang, *Disposable Domestics: Immigrant Women Workers in the Global Economy*, 133 (Boston: South End Press, 2000), has 80 percent women, 60–70 percent people of color, and 40 percent immigrants in the mid-1990s for California. Using Alameda County data, Candace Howes, Howard Greenwich, Laura Reif, and Lea Grundy found that in 2000, 43 percent were African American, 24 percent white, 13 percent Chinese, 7 percent Latino, 13 percent other persons of color. Fifty-five percent were age forty or older and 80 percent were women, with 52 percent serving family members. East Bay Alliance for a Sustainable Economy, *Struggling to Provide: A Portrait of Alameda County Homecare Workers*, 4–5 (Berkeley: Center for Labor Research and Education, May 2002). In New York and Connecticut, in contrast, the workforce is predominantly people of African descent, including immigrants from Ghana and the Caribbean. Interview by J. Klein with Griswold Homecare Associates, May 2002.

9. Dawson and Surpin, "Direct-Care Health Workers," 8.

ments made up over half of all monies for home care. Over two million people receive home and community-based care through Medicaid.[10] State and local governments additionally have drawn on other federal, state, and county funds. Consequently, government social policies and reimbursement rates directly have shaped the structure of the industry and the terms and conditions of work. Indeed, the contracting out of labor and services by states maximized the uncertainties of the work, the employment status of home care workers, and hence, the service itself.[11]

New Deal labor law refused to recognize the home as a workplace. Nurse-companions and other in-home care workers hired directly by clients became classified as domestic servants. Localities treated home care workers as independent contractors rather than employees, thus denying the status of worker and their own responsibility for working conditions and compensation.[12]

Home care organizers began within the confines of New Deal labor law, signing up members workplace by workplace, with the aim of a positive National Labor Relations Board (NLRB) election. But they found themselves doubly stymied: by the industrial union model, premised on all employees laboring at the same worksite, and by the NLRB representation system, which assumed an unambiguous employer-employee relationship. They needed, instead, a form of unionism that could encompass the service provider-client relationship, as well as maneuver around the dispersed location of the labor. They required, as Dorothy Sue Cobble has argued, unions that offered "portable rights and benefits" and a means to "improve the image and standing of the occupation."[13]

The caregiving relationship itself has generated obstacles to unionization. Caregivers could not imagine neglecting their charges or going on strike. "Sure, there are a lot of times I'd rather spend a little more time out shopping or whatever," confided one Contra Costa, California attendant. "But I always think … He can't do it by himself. Besides, I want to be here." This sense of devotion has kept nonrelative providers from quitting.[14] A 1998 report commissioned by SEIU concluded that many saw "their work more as service than as employment." Those attending family preferred better wages but downplayed compensation, such as an Armenian respondent who confessed: "We were doing it anyway…." Latinas, tending nonrelatives, had more of a worker consciousness; so did African Americans who remained keenly aware of the association with domestic service—"we are cooks, we are chauffeurs, we are nursemaids, we are hazels. We are everything," one proclaimed in pride and disgust.[15]

The question of empowering care workers within their own organizations persists. All the reasons that bring women to home care in the first place, such as low-income, poverty,

---

10. Ellen O'Brien and Risa Eliasm, "Medicaid and Long Term Care." Report prepared for the Kaiser Commission on Medicaid and the Uninsured, 2–3, 6 (Washington, DC: Henry J. Kaiser Family Foundation, May 2004).

11. Burbridge, "The Labor Market for Home Care Workers," 41, 44; Margaret MacAdam, "Home Care Reimbursement and Effects on Personnel," 33 *The Gerontologist*, 55–62.

12. Phyllis Palmer, "Outside the Law: Agricultural and Domestic Workers Under the Fair Labor Standards Act," 7 *Journal of Policy History* 416–40; Molly Biklen, "Note: Healthcare in the Home: Reexamining the Companionship Services Exemption to the Fair Labor Standards Act," *Columbia Human Rights Law Review* 113 (2003).

13. Dorothy Sue Cobble, "The Prospects for Unionism in a Service Society," Cameron L. McDonald and Carmen Sirianni, eds., *Working in Service Society*, 348, 345 (Philadelphia: Temple Univ. Press, 1996).

14. Joe Garofoli, "Recognizing Caregivers' Hard Work," *Contra Costs Times*, A03 (September 4, 1998).

15. Feldman Group Inc., "Focus Group Homecare Workers," Heinritz Canterbury Papers, 2, 7, 8 (April 1998).

family responsibility, immigrant status, lack of training, and social instability, inhibit their ability to participate fully in unions. Given the large ethnic workforce, many still look at the job as family duty rather than as employment. Political unionism needs its members for campaigns, and the unions have brought their membership to city, county, and state halls. But to the extent that the home care unions become providers of services rather than educators and mobilizers, to the extent that they stop the effort to revalue caring labor, they can fall into a kind of bureaucratic unionism that reinforces the old racialized gender distinctions of care work and stymies the advancement of rank and file women.

Transforming Labor Law: The California Case Study

California became a recognized leader in consumer-directed home care services, but only after a political struggle that involved a coalition of unions, seniors, and the disabled. From the start, the state had one of the largest home care caseloads from a combination of demographic and political factors, including a large elderly population and a robust social movement of the disabled that created Centers for Independent Living in the 1970s. It was well poised, as we have argued, to take advantage of federal funding. Its solution to the ambiguous status of the workforce became the public authority, an old form used for new purposes.[16]

Created in 1973, In-Home Supportive Services (IHSS) developed out of previous attendant and homemaker/chore programs that often sought to employ those on welfare to care for others on public assistance. Over the years the program experienced underfunding (from state, federal, and county sources) relative to the demand, uneven administration, local financial shortfalls, and bureaucratic red tape. Charges of fraud and abuse periodically accompanied calls for reorganization. With the poor elderly and disabled as its clients, and a minimum-wage workforce, Republican governors especially attempted to balance budgets by cutting appropriations, despite the fact that those eligible were entitled to the service.[17]

Trying to provide "on the cheap" exacerbated the already confused employment status of the workforce. County attempts to have other levels of government pay for the service joined with denials of employer responsibility. Beginning in 1960, under the state attendant care program for severely disabled persons on public assistance, the consumer of services — the client — acted as the employer. After social workers assessed their needs and ability to supervise aides, consumers received state monies to pay for attendants. When funding and levels of expenditures increased in the mid-1970s, attendants earned enough to qualify for Social Security, but consumers lacked the income to pay the employer share of taxes, as mandated by the California Department of Social Welfare.[18]

The fiction nevertheless developed that the home aide was an independent contractor working for the consumer/client. After passage of MediCal, California's equivalent of Medicaid, in 1966, home health aides joined homemakers and attendant care workers among the services offered to the poor. The expectation was that the MediCal would cover most attendant care cases, displacing costs to the federal level. Meanwhile, while the legislature directed the State Department of Social Welfare to recruit and train women on AFDC for home care, county welfare departments in 1969 gained the ability to contract with proprietary as well as voluntary agencies to provide services. Such contracts speci-

---

16. Gail Radford, "From Municipal Socialism to Public Authorities: Institutional Factors in the Shaping of American Public Enterprise," 90 *Journal of American History* 863–90.

17. State of California, Little Hoover Commission, "Elder Care at Home," Recommendations, November 6, 1991, at http://www.lhc.ca.gov/lhcdir/113rp.html (accessed October 14, 2005).

18. Ricker-Smith, "An Historical and Critical Overview," 12.

fied that for-profit contractors give preference to welfare recipients. Still, certain conditions encouraged the retention of individual providers, such as isolated location, relative availability, or a preexisting long-term caregiver relationship. In 1973, with IHSS, the method of reimbursement changed again when the state paid the home care provider rather than their clients, most of who continued to hire attendants directly.[19] Rarely were deductions taken for Social Security or taxes, since such payments came out of the overall IHSS appropriation, indirectly lessening the number of care hours funded.[20]

Under IHSS, counties could organize the service in one of three ways. The Individual Provider or IP mode emphasized consumer direction. Under this option, the consumer hired, trained, supervised, and terminated the attendant and the worker was considered an independent contractor. While this option met demands of independent living activists to control their own care, it obscured the role of government in service provision since the state cut the check and issued payment of an hourly wage to providers of care, the County Department of Social Services ran the program and its social workers allocated hours. But not all consumers were capable of acting like employers. Other options more clearly defined the employment relationship. Under the County mode, the care provider became a government employee, but most counties, concerned with keeping costs down, hired few workers directly. With the Contract mode, the county contracted with a for-profit or nonprofit company, which became the employer.[21]

Disability rights activists wanted more control over their arrangements; others wanted to hire family members, which was more difficult to do when having to go through a contractor. Counties sometimes reimbursed relatives only for tasks beyond expected routines and sometimes they would pay only relatives who left other employment to engage in home care. Investigating one minimum-waged rural county, the Western Center on Law and Poverty found that "when the worker came to the premises and saw what had to be done, she put in extra hours which would lower her low minimum wage even worse."[22] Contractors thus took advantage of the relational and intimate nature of carework, which rarely could be dropped in the middle of a task just because compensated time ran out.[23]

Located in isolated homes, IHSS workers had no mechanism to bring themselves together to challenge the conditions of their labor. Defining this labor became crucial to who would organize this workforce. Were they public sector employees and therefore under the jurisdiction of a union such as AFSCME (American Federation of State, County, and Municipal Employees)? Were they domestic service workers, thus the constituency of United Domestic Workers of America (UDW), or movements of household employees? Did they belong to the service workforce, rapidly being organized by the growing SEIU in commercial and non-profit sectors? Policy changes, especially Medicare and its

---

19. *Ibid.*, 33, 46, 48.

20. *Ibid.*, 85.

21. County Welfare Directors Association of California, In-Home Supportive Services: Past, Present, and Future, January 2003, 8–10, at http://www.cwda.org/downloads/IHSS.pdf (accessed October 14, 2005).

22. Testimony of Dorothy Lang, Assembly Committee on Human Resources, Hearing on Administration of Homemaker/Chore Services Program.

23. Deborah Stone, "Caring by the Book," in Madonna Harrington Meyer, ed., *Care Work: Gender, Labor, and the Welfare State*, 93, 110 (New York: Routledge, 2000); Jane Aronson and Sheila M. Neysmith, "'You're Not Just in There to Do The Work': Depersonalizing Policies and the Exploitation of Home Care Workers' Labor,' 10 *Gender & Society* 59–77. For specific complaints of the Department of Social Services against one major contractor, Tamara Webb, "State Faults In-Home Care," *Visalia Times-Delta*, April 28, 1993.

subsequent amendments, had pushed home attendants and aides into the expanding health care sector, and so some unions began to see them as health care workers. Indeed, given both the structural ambiguities and the blurred nature of the labor itself, union activists spent well over a decade experimenting with organizing strategies, navigating the shifting legal terrain and modes of service delivery, and competing with each other to define a viable unionism for home care. In every case, no matter the union, organizers found their task complicated by the service provider-client relationship, not just by the worker-boss relationship — particularly in California, where consumers were already well organized themselves. To succeed, unionization of home care workers would have to rally all those impacted by the welfare nexus and create a viable base of employment within the state itself. Union strategy hinged on emphasizing the welfare state location of IHSS labor.[24]

Civil rights unionism shaped UDW from the start. With financial aid from the United Farm Workers of America (UFWA) and the Catholic Church, the new group sought to form "a poor people's union in an urban setting" for and by domestic laborers who fared even worse than those who toiled in the fields.[25] It envisioned a membership that also would include private household, hotel maids, and nursing home workers. Reaching a scattered constituency proved daunting, even though organizers chatted with women waiting for early morning busses, crossing the border when necessary; set up house meetings; established neighborhood committees; and planned a service center to aid with housing and other problems.[26] In April 1979, 150 delegates attended the first convention at a time when San Diego County had about 15,000 domestics. But even then the union had targeted local government. IHSS was under persistent scrutiny for mismanagement and, with a constituency of the poor, elderly, ill, and disabled, it increasingly became caught in the vise of state budget negotiations and county attempts to pay as little as possible for the service. UDW founder Ken Seaton-Msemaji understood that organizing home care workers required political clout because "you really end up negotiating with the supervisors on the wages."[27]

Over the next eighteen months, the union's staff, grown to ten, put the house-meeting and community-oriented UFWA model into high gear, training eighty homemakers, who then organized their co-workers. Information from SEIU 250 led UDWA to focus on the county's home attendant contract up for renewal.[28] One breakthrough occurred in March, 1980 when organizers met Claudia Bowens, a fifty-ish black woman; Margaret Insko, a Chicana and domestic for over a decade; and Carol Leonard, a twenty-something white woman, who were leaving an employer-training session. Like other home care providers, these women suffered from underpayment and lack of sick days. Instead of the adversarial relationship emphasized by industrial unionism they sought a movement that valued the care relationship, an exchange that could and should have multiple

---

24. We discuss these strategies in "'We Were The Invisible Workforce:' Unionizing Home Care," in Dorothy Sue Cobble, ed., *The Sex of Class: Women and America's New Labor Movement* (Ithaca: ILR Press, 2007).

25. Lynn Eldred, "United Domestic Worker: Power and Pride," *San Diego Newsline* (November 26–December 3, 1980; Greg Gross, "Homemakers Union to Sign Its 1st Pact," *San Diego Union*, 1 (November 20, 1980); H. G. Reza, "Organizing Still a Labor of Love," *Los Angeles Times*, 2-1 (August 14, 1989).

26. Eldred, *supra* note 25.

27. Paula Parker, "Domestics' Union Makes Gains," *Los Angeles Times*, A1 (November 22, 1980); Eldred, *supra* note 25; Gross, *supra* note 25; Ken Seaton-Msemaji, "He Believed Every Human Being was Valuable," *The Sacramento Observer*, (May 27–June 2, 1993).

28. Parker, *supra* note 27.

benefits for each side and could foster and reward employee-employer relations that were more collaborative than bureaucratic. They cared "about people and, in return, we think someone should care about us.... We are not just objects."[29]

These women became central to the effort while the newly formed Domestic Workers Service Center mobilized local support for hearings before the Board of Supervisors.[30] Thorough lobbying and testifying, the UDWA helped block the award of the contract to one company by getting the supervisors to throw out the original bids.[31] Members began to learn the lesson of unionization: "In unity we have *strength*," roared Bowens.[32] Msemaji emphasized that "the biggest thing in their (union members) lives is that they've learned ... they don't have to settle for working conditions if they're not fair, that they can change things.... The contract is secondary to that."[33]

The San Diego based UDW, now affiliated with AFSCME, initially promoted contract home care. Founded under the influence of Cesar Chavez, this black and Latino union discovered in home care providers a type of domestic worker they could locate. SEIU had been engaged with organizing health care workers in more traditional workplaces and saw the expanding home care labor force a logical extension of its activity. Both SEIU and AFSCME had benefited from earlier changes in labor law that facilitated public sector unionism, while SEIU mobilized immigrant workers through direct action militancy. UDW began to focus on the county contracts with proprietary firms; such contracting concentrated the workforce, facilitating organization and providing a terrain of struggle. In April 1980 UDW blocked the San Diego County Board of Supervisors from awarding the IHSS contract to a firm that "promised no improvements" in wages or working conditions.[34] Instead, San Diego gave its $7.2 million contract to Remedy Home and Health Care Corporation, which signed a union agreement two months later, covering over 2,000 attendants. Workers gained a small hourly raise, paid vacation, sick leave, and their own health plan as well as a grievance procedure system and union security.[35] Nearly a decade later, Remedy would be the site of a Ford Foundation demonstration project on improving the conditions of home care workers. Guaranteed hours, subsidized health insurance, and increased training, this project revealed, facilitated worker retention. But soon afterward, the county moved its contract to a lower bidder.[36] UDW, however, became committed to the county mode of service delivery, which also put the union in the position of supporting privatized corporate management of IHSS. Through the California In-Home Care Council, UDW worked closely with contractors. This collusion did not sit well with prominent consumer groups, deeply opposed to the contract mode.

In other parts of the state, SEIU locals chose a different tack: they sought to reach the more numerous independent providers. This focus entailed the additional legal challenge of defining the employment relationship. The Ninth Circuit court in 1983 held the state and counties liable for purposes of the FLSA—that is, for wage and hour regulations—

29. *Ibid.*

30. Eldred, *supra* note 25.

31. Parker, *supra* note 27.

32. Eldred, *supra* note 25.

33. Parker, *supra* note 27.

34. Lynn Eldred, "United Domestic Workers: Power and Pride," *San Diego Newsline* (November 26–December 3, 1980).

35. "Domestic Workers Union Born in San Diego," *The Economic Democrat*, December 1980; Paula Parker, "Domestics' Union Makes Gains," *The Los Angeles Times*, November 22, 1980.

36. Penny Hollander Feldman, "Work Life Improvements for Home Care Workers: Impact and Feasibility," *The Gerontologist* 33 (1): 52; personal communication with E. Boris, e-mail, March 25, 2003.

for the Department of Social Services and county welfare agencies "controlled the rate and method of payment, and … maintained employment records." Particularly important was their assignment of hours, even though consumers supervised home workers on a day-by-day basis. The court noted that "these services have been traditionally performed by domestic employees in the private sector," but as a federally funded and regulated program, administered by the state, home care was not immune from FLSA.[37] Similarly, the California Court of Appeal two years later said of the direct payment option, in which the county gave funds to the recipient, that the county's "*sufficient control over the IHSS provider*" made the State an employer.[38]

In 1985, California's attorney general determined that IHSS attendants came under state workers' compensation and other labor laws. "For purposes of collective bargaining … the IHSS workers (under the IP mode) may be considered the employees of the counties," but not of the state because they were not civil service employees. This ruling worried counties, which sought to end liability by contracting out services. SEIU Local 250, in fact, had joined with UDW to push for legislation favoring the contract mode. It convinced San Francisco County to move all of its caseload to the unionized Remedy over a three-year period. In this situation, support of community groups dissatisfied with the IP mode was crucial.[39] By 1987, when SEIU began its "massive campaign" to organize home care in Los Angeles, in which it poured $285,000 for nine months in 1988 alone and hired over twenty full-time workers, legal rulings existed that claimed government as the employer of IHSS workers, rather than the thousands of program recipients.[40]

Yet SEIU's Los Angeles Homecare Organizing Committee faced a number of hurdles, including which "employer definition … suits our organizing needs." Primarily it had to identify the workers. Elsewhere it had obtained lists of names "through co-opting an inside source of the targeted company" or it had circulated a petition on "a popular issue (e.g., minimum-wage increase)" at the site where workers picked up paychecks. In Los Angeles, it planned to use its members in other government employee locals: caseworkers could get names from microfiche, and data and payroll processors could compile a list, while other county contacts could pilfer the program's "referral list." So, even when counties formally refused to hand over the names of workers, the sectoral strength of SEIU provided alternative routes.[41] That social workers and home care workers belonged to the same union, although usually in separate locals, proved a benefit for organizing. This advantage UDW used to attack the ability of SEIU to truly represent the best interest of at-

---

37. *Bonnette v. California Health and Welfare Agency* 704 F.2d 1465 (1983) at 13–14, 19–21.

38. *In-Home Supportive Services v. Workers' Compensation Appeals Board* 152 Ca. App.3d 720, 731 (1984).

39. Memo, n.d., with notation, "File: Home Healthcare Organizing," c. 1986, 2–3, in SEIU Organizing Department, General Organizing, 1984–1992, Box 42, folder "California Home Care," SEIU Papers, Walter Reuther Library, Wayne State University, Detroit [hereafter SEIU papers]; Opinion No. 84-308 — July 23, 1985, Subject: "State Employee' Status of Employee of In-Home Supportive Services Program Aid Recipient," opinion by John K. Van De Kamp, Attorney General, *Attorney General's Opinions,* 68 (July 1985) at 194.

40. Andy Stern to Bob Welsh, "Healthcare Organizing Subsidies," Feb. 10, 1988, in SEIU Organizing Department, Organizing Files A-N, Box 1 of 3, folder "Healthcare Organizing 1988," SEIU Papers. On number of organizers, *Service Employees International Union, Local 434 v. County of Los Angeles,* "Complaint for Declaratory Relief," Superior Court for the State of California in and for the County of Los Angeles, December 29, 1987, 4.

41. Memo, n.d., with notation, 3, 4; Peter Rider to Health Care Organizing Team et al. on 5/25 Meeting Assignment, 2, SEIU Organizing Department, Box 1, folder "Healthcare Organizing, 1988," SEIU Papers.

tendants, since social workers supervised them, in contrast to its unitary focus on home care.[42]

Los Angeles County initially opted for designating itself as the employer. SEIU built a citywide organizing committee through home visits and direct mail, trying in the mid-1980s to reach 40,000 attendants, whose numbers kept on growing even as individuals dropped out of the work. Based on its experience in Boston and Chicago, it believed on-the-ground organizing would look like a political canvass. No matter if the employer was public or private, organizers concluded "that the more the organizing is based on public events and grounded in public issues, the better our chances of winning and the stronger the organization will be at the other end."[43]

This strategizing assumed that the employer question soon would "be resolved in ways that will allow for successful organizing."[44] SEIU launched its campaign in October 1987, but by December was requesting the courts to determine whether in fact Los Angeles County was the employer under the Meyers-Milias-Brown Act, the law governing collective bargaining for government employees. Apparently the Deputy Director of Labor Relations Services had advised that Los Angeles County reject this reasoning. The union argued that if the county was not the employer, IHSS workers would have "no legally-sanctioned opportunity for collective representation." They did not meet the requirements for state employees and the National Labor Relations Act excluded those "in the domestic service of any family or person at his home" from the definition of "employee," thus making it impossible to have recipients serve as employers for collective bargaining—even if that was logistically possible.[45] As International President John Sweeney told a rally of 1,500 home care workers in 1988, "When these officials won't even acknowledge they are your employer, they bring dishonor on this county," especially since "if it were not for you, 83 percent of your clients would have to be placed in an institution at an astronomical financial cost."[46]

When the State Court of Appeals ruled two years later, the union met legal defeat. In *Service Employees International Union, Local 434 v. County of Los Angeles*, the court found IHSS workers to be "independent contractors" because the counties did not control their activities on the job. Yet, as SEIU later argued in defense of the public authorities, "Even under a common law test, these unskilled workers, with no capital, who have their tasks detailed in work plans specifying the number of minutes they may spend on each task, and who are paid an hourly wage—are not independent contractors, but employees jointly employed by the recipients and the public authorities."[47]

Los Angeles County would not negotiate with the union because it claimed that it was not the employer. But neither was the state Department of Social Services, the IHSS program, MediCal, or individual clients. This uncertain legal status led SEIU to develop the

---

42. Glenda Ponder to Tulare County UDW Members, "Our Response to SEIU!!!," 9-14-93, including "Facts About SEIU" and "Facts About United Domestic Workers—UDW," in Edward V. Roberts Papers, Box 7, folder 37, Bancroft Library, University of California-Berkeley, Berkeley, California.

43. Memo, n.d., with notation, 3–7.

44. Memo, n.d., with notation, 3.

45. *Service Employees International Union, Local 434 v. County of Los Angeles*, "Complaint for Declaratory Relief," 5–6.

46. "Rallying homecare workers," *Update: Healthcare Division* II(1): 10.

47. *See* Memorandum in Support of SEIU Local 434B's Motion to Dismiss in *Hummel v. SEIU Local 434B*, Case No. 01-10826 CAS (FMOX) (C. D. Cal), 1; and Reply Memorandum, 5, both in possession of E. Boris from Craig Becker.

public authority, for someone to bargain with, as the state already had granted voluntary dues check off, thus providing a stable financial base for future campaigns.[48] By Fall 1990, a task force within the union, led by its chief representative in Sacramento Maury Kealey and with UCLA Law Professor Craig Becker, began sketching the contours of such an authority, its legal basis and political effectiveness. SEIU envisioned that representatives from the local area and disability entities would have seats on the authority's advisory committee. Equally important for the disabled community, recipients would "retain the authority to hire, fire, and direct the personnel." In crafting the legislation, SEIU sought to place IHSS workers within the meaning of public employee without defining them as civil servants both to maximize flexibility for bargaining and ease enactment.[49]

SEIU's chief lobbyist then joined with others from organized groups of seniors and the disabled to spearhead the effort to amend the state welfare code governing IHSS. The California Senior Legislature went on record for the public authority concept in 1991, the year when the union initially tried to have its bill passed as a rider to the state budget. In the midst of proposed cuts by Governor Pete Wilson and public outcry over elder abuse and fraud documented by the Little Hoover Commission, in 1992 the legislature permitted counties to develop authorities. The next year Assemblywoman Gwen Moore (D-Los Angeles), whose election the union had supported, introduced further legislation that saved IHSS from a 12 percent reduction by transferring some services to Medicaid's personal care option. Other amendments provided start-up funds for the authorities. Alameda, San Francisco, and other Bay Area counties immediately created mechanisms to reclassify home care workers as employees; Los Angeles only followed after a five-year struggle. This legal change, gained from political lobbying by the union, the Congress of California Seniors, the California Senior Assembly, the California Foundation of Independent Living Centers, and various local disability groups and commissions, created an employer to bargain with—as well as a central registry to locate the home care workforce. At least half of the members of the authorities were mandated to be current or past IHSS recipients.[50]

The union alliance with disability activists was not necessarily a natural one. The union had approached the Oakland-based World Institute on Disability, an activist think tank, as early as 1986. The Institute's 1987 report, "Attending to America: Personal Assistance for Independent Living," had endorsed unionization to enhance attendant wages. The organized independent living centers by the summer of 1992 agreed to support collective bargaining for the union if disabled people would retain consumer control over the authorities. Indeed, the centers and the union apparently shared the same lobbyist for a

48. Memo from Jennifer Fleming to Dan Stewart, "Homecare Transition," March 11, 1992, on Los Angeles County, in SEIU Organizing Department, General Organizing, 1984–1992, Box 42, folder "California Home Care," SEIU Papers; Jess Walsh, "Creating Unions, Creating Employers: A Los Angeles Home-Care Campaign," in Mary Daly, ed., *Care Work: The Quest for Security*, 224 (Geneva, 2001.

49. Memo to Dan S., Ophelia M., Jennifer F., Amado D. from Wilma C., "Attached Memos Re: Authority," December 13, 1990, in SEIU Organizing Department, General Organizing, 1984–1992, Box 42, folder "California Home Care," SEIU Papers.

50. On the public authorities, see Memorandum in Support of SEIU, 5–12; Janet Heinritz-Canterbury, *Collaborating to Improve In-Home Supportive Services: Stakeholder Perspectives on Implementing California's Public Authorities*, 9–13 (New York: Paraprofessional Healthcare Institute, 2002); Delp and Quan, "Homecare Worker Organizing," 9; on the seniors, Alan Toy, "L.A. County Public Authority: An Empowering Solution," 7 *New Mobility* 55 (November 1996); Lynn May Rivas for the World Institute on Disability, "A Significant Alliance: The Independent Living Movement, The Service Employees International Union and the Establishment of the First Public Authorities in California," draft pamphlet, 2005, in authors' possession.

time. This cooperation came out of an informal group that worked closely together in Sacramento on legislative issues.[51] Even though SEIU gained credit for opposing an attempted managed care "takeover" of attendant programs, other militant activists feared that the interests between the two groups conflicted and subsequently sought to slow down implementation of the authorities, especially in Los Angeles.[52]

In 2000, the legislature provided additional monies for pay raises and training, while mandating that all counties establish public authorities by 2003. This followed the U.S. Supreme Court's Olmstead Decision, which upheld community-based treatment over institutionalization under the Americans with Disability Act.[53] Mobilization to pass these laws has helped to organize workers; in turn, these political victories provided institutional spaces for union organizing. As public sector employees, then, IHSS workers have found collective bargaining projected into the political arena.[54] By 2005, some 360,000 people received IHSS monthly, costing $3 billion annually.[55]

Despite this new recognition, most IHSS workers still earn less than a livable wage (though the unions have increased wages into the $8 per hour range.) IHSS worker Amanda Figueroa explained their plight before the Los Angeles County Board of Supervisors in March 2001 "as that of a 'ping-pong ball,' tossed between the state and county with neither willing to accept fiscal responsibility for wage increases or benefit coverage," as labor educators Linda Delp and Katie Quan observe.[56] Before Los Angeles County raised wages in 2004, SEIU Local 434B only could deliver on services for members, such as aid with immigration issues, housing, health care, and training. UDW long had run food banks and training centers. Dignity depended, then, on legislative victories. But, after the gubernatorial recall of union supporter Gray Davis in 2003, the political terrain became newly perilous with Republican Governor Arnold Schwarzenegger yearly proposing cutbacks.

SEIU and UDW also decided to end their rivalry. Plagued by jurisdictional disputes throughout the 1990s, the two unions agreed to divide up the counties so that only one would work in a given location. They formed the California Homecare Council in 2000 as a joint lobbying and organizing effort.[57] But, with SEIU leaving the AFL-CIO and AFSCME putting UDW into receivership for diverting dues to SEIU, among other charges, raiding each other began again during the summer of 2005. In late September, however, AFSCME and SEIU entered into a two-year pact, agreeing to form the California United Homecare Workers Union, to be affiliated with both, while maintaining their existing jurisdictions. The new entity would organize the twenty-six mostly rural counties that lacked bargaining agreements. Some viewed this as a first step toward one home care union in California.

---

51. Rivas, "A Significant Alliance," documents these events, 6–9.

52. Marta Russell, "L.A. County Public Authority: A Zero-Sum Game," 7 *New Mobility* 40, 50–51 (November 1996).

53. 527 U.S. 581 (1999).

54. Delp and Quan, "Homecare Worker Organizing," 7.

55. http://www.dss.cahwnet.gov/cdssweb/In-HomeSup_173.htm (accessed August 8, 2005).

56. Delp and Quan, "Homecare Worker Organizing," 16.

57. We have reconstructed this history from conversations with union leaders and visits to union Web pages, as well as intensive reading of the local newspapers. However, the UDW Web page was redesigned in late July 2005 and the history presented by its founders has been modified. See, http://www.seiu434b.org/docUploads/Union% 20History%20Dec04.pdf (assessed August 8, 2005); http://www.udwa.org/history.htm (accessed August 8, 2005).

Coda, 2011

While inter-union differences abated, an internal split rocked SEIU in the late 2000s. The fate of some 65,000 long-term home care workers became entangled in a bitter battle between the 150,000 strong United Health Workers West (UHW), the union's third largest local, and the International over national vs. local bargaining, health care reform, and, ultimately, union democracy. By Spring 2008, Stern not only sought to unilaterally transfer some 65,000 home care and nursing home members to the jurisdiction of the Southern California Long Term Care Local 6434, a merger of the old 434B with smaller units, but he also attempted to remove the elected leadership of UHW itself. The following January, the International put the defiant local into trusteeship and its leadership left to form a new union, the National Union of Hospital Workers—setting the stage for years of decertification battles and contested elections between rival unions just as it appeared possible that labor might gain new rights through the Obama administration.[58]

But that would not be. The union unsuccessfully had challenged the "elder companion" exemption of home care workers from the minimum wage and overtime protections of FLSA when the Supreme Court ruled against it in the 2007 case, *Long Island Care at Home v. Evelyn Coke*.[59] The union hoped that the new administration would change the regulations to include home care workers, but rather than find the political conditions in its favor, the union faced the worst recession since the 1930s that dropped state revenues. Faced with a united Republican Party that refused to raise taxes, governors from both parties began to cut welfare spending, including home care. Then, after the massive Republican victory in 2010, an all-out assault on public employee unionism placed home-worker collective bargaining in jeopardy. Indeed, in states where workers won this right through executive orders, like Wisconsin and Michigan, new conservative governors revoked it; in others, Republican majorities in legislatures ended it. Such top down political deals fell apart. In this context, the SEIU organizing model lost its luster. Some fifteen years after the massive victory in Los Angeles, the fate of home care unionism was uncertain and the legal innovations that it spawned under attack.

---

58. Steve Early, *The Civil Wars in U.S. Labor: Birth of a New Workers Movement or Death Throws of the Old?* (Chicago: Haymarket Books, 2011).

59. 551 U.S. 158 (2007). For a fuller discussion, Eileen Boris and Jennifer Klein, "Making Home Care: Law and Social Policy in the U.S. Welfare State," in *Intimate Labors: Cultures, Technologies, and the Politics of Care*, ed. E. Boris and R. Parreñas (Stanford: Stanford University Press, 2010), 187–203.

Contracting Out and Low-Wage, Immigrant Worker Voice

Serviceworkers Strike at University of Miami.

Of Service Workers, Contracting Out, Joint Employment, Legal Consciousness, and the University of Miami (2006)

Kenneth M. Casebeer*

On February 28, 2006, at the 10:00 p.m. shift change, the janitorial and groundskeeping staff at the University of Miami went on strike against their employer, UNICCO. UNICCO contracts with the University to provide these services. The strike was led by those workers assisted by the Service Employees International Union (SEIU) in an attempt to organize the workers. However, the strike itself occurred over unfair labor practices charged by the National Labor Relations Board (NLRB) during the organizational activities.

The strike and accompanying struggle were historic. And not just because it was rare that the workers won. Concepts of class appeared in a myriad of contexts. The victory rep-

---

* This chapter was first published in 56 *U. Buff. L. Rev.* 1059 (2008). It is used here with permission of the University of Buffalo Law Review.

resented the most basic way in which class enters discussion — the struggle of workers to organize and use their collective strength to obtain higher wages and better working conditions. However, class played a far deeper role. Before the strike was over, individual workers had been fired for union activities, students were undergoing disciplinary proceedings for protest activities, workers and students went on hunger strikes — some requiring hospitalization — and clergy were arrested. Thus, class consciousness became somewhat shared among workers, union activists, students, and faculty. Further, the strike became both a community and civil rights struggle attracting national figures and celebrities. The striking workforce was almost entirely Latin American, Haitian, or Black. Thus, class solidarity emerged around a low wage community and its ethnic identity. More mundane, but perhaps most important for class analysis, the strike setting represented the quintessential new world economy: a large corporation contracting out work done on its premises to another large service provider utilizing largely poor minority workers, most of whom were immigrants. Thus, the labor market structured the experience of class. This form of employment differs from an older, well-known practice of worker contracting for short-term needs.[1] It is the service, rather than the worker, that the end user wants for an indefinite long-term use.[2]

Also, raising the stakes even further, the strike represented the coming together of the living wage movement and the union movement in the first major test of the Change to Win Coalition of unions that had recently broken away from the AFL-CIO.[3] That schism basically turned on how to reinvigorate worker organization, especially in low wage occupations. Class is implicit both in terms of the conditions of organization and market wage segmentation. This is the present and future of mass service employment, and the University is the largest private employer in Miami-Dade County. Thus, the strike was about class and workers, class and consciousness, class and communities, class and labor markets, class and worker organization, and class as an entering wedge against the largest employer in area-wide struggles for advancement. All these issues are affected by the background of legal permissions, protections, and prohibitions, both inside and outside labor law proper.

While the NLRA was meant to empower the working class by protecting collective organization, the new reality of third party employment hiring across an area's labor force fragments potential class interests and makes organization under traditional procedures very difficult at any location of work. The concluding section, Section III, describes how contemporary legal doctrine structured the parties' description and perception of the strike. Law appears in the narrative as both doctrine and legal consciousness.

I. The Strike

In August 2001, *The Chronicle of Higher Education* reported that in a survey of 195 institutions, the University of Miami ranked second worst in terms of wages paid to jani-

---

1. According to Richard Belous, the contingent workforce increased approximately seventy-five percent faster than the overall workforce between 1980 and 1993. As of 1995, it was projected that the contingent workforce would grow to represent 50% of the U.S. labor force. Richard S. Belous, "The Rise of the Contingent Work Force: The Key Challenges and Opportunities," 52 *Wash. & Lee L. Rev.* 863, 864–67 (1995).

2. *See* Guy Davidov, "Joint Employer Status in Triangular Employment Relationships," 42 *Brit. J. Indus. Rel.* 727, 728 (Dec. 2004).

3. *See generally* Change to Win, *Who We Are*, http://www.changetowin.org/fileadmin/pdf/CTW2 Pager.pdf (last visited Oct. 31, 2008).

tors on campus, paying less than the federal poverty wage.[4] The University appointed a committee to study the question, which in turn recommended pay raises. Nothing happened. In 2005, the SEIU began to help organize the employees of UNICCO, which had won a contract to provide housekeeping and groundskeeping work. In 2006, the workers were being paid starting at $6.40 per hour with no health care benefits,[5] more than $4.00 per hour less than the Miami-Dade County living wage. The average wage was $7.53 per hour.[6] With the announcement of a strike vote on February 26, 2006, University President Donna Shalala formed another review committee to study market wages. Her statement read in part:

> It is in keeping with the mission and character of the University of Miami that we be responsive to questions raised by our constituents regarding the compensation and benefits of employees of outside contractors working on the University's campuses.
>
> … Because changes in wages and benefits during an organizing campaign can be unlawful if motivated by union considerations, the University has, to date, remained silent on those issues.
>
> The University has a responsibility and an obligation to be responsive to its community, however.… We have heard from virtually every constituent group in our University community, including students, faculty, staff, alumni, trustees, donors, civic leaders, the clergy, elected officials, and the SEIU, all of whom have called for — even demanded on occasion — an increase in resources from the University for employees of outside contractors.[7]

However, the strike called February 26, 2006, was neither over recognition of the union nor for higher wages. Rather, the strike was called over unfair labor practices by UNICCO during the organizing campaign. This status was important because, under the NLRA, unfair labor practice strikers cannot be permanently replaced by their employer as is the case with purely economic or organization strikes.[8]

In January, the NLRB issued charges against UNICCO that included interrogating workers about union activities, prohibiting workers from discussing the union at work, forcing them to sign a statement disavowing the union, accusing workers of disloyalty for off-hour activities, threatening reprisals against supporters, and illegally spying on union meetings.[9] Within a week before the beginning of the strike, UNICCO fired a union

---

4. Martin Van Der Werf, "How Much Should Colleges Pay Their Janitors?: Student Protests Force Administrators to Consider Issues of Social Justice and Practicality," *Chron. Higher Educ.*, A27 (Aug. 3, 2001).

5. Steven Greenhouse, "Walkout Ends at University of Miami as Janitors' Pact is Reached," *N.Y. Times*, May 2, 2006, available at http://www.nytimes.com/2006/05/02/us/02labor.html.

6. Posting of Faculty for Workplace Justice to Picketline, *Bishop Estevez Offers to Mediate Between President Shalala and the Striking Janitors*, http://picketline.blogspot.com/2006/03/bishop-estevez-offers-to-mediate.html (Mar. 7, 2006, 21:50 EST).

7. Statement from University of Miami President Donna E. Shalala, "New Work Group Formed to Study Compensation and Benefits for Employees of Outside Contractors," *E-Veritas*, Feb. 23, 2006, http://www6.miami.edu/news/everitas/2005-06/02-23-06Extra.htm.

8. *NLRB v. Mackay Radio & Tel. Co.*, 304 U.S. 333, 345 (1938) (finding that in reinstating employees after a strike, discriminating against striking employees for the sole reason that they had been active in the union was an unfair labor practice, and the permanent replacement of such workers was not permissible).

9. "See Labor Board Will Hear Union's Case," *Miami Herald*, 3C (Feb. 2, 2006).

leader, Zoila Mursuli, for talking with a newspaper reporter.[10] If the company could be forced to stop engaging in such behavior, of course, union organization would be more likely, and that would increase pressure for both recognition and better pay and working conditions. Worker Maritza Paz commented, "I feel good about what President Shalala said. But it only happened because we were working to form a union. But we can not stop our campaign until UNICCO stops retaliating against us when we stand up for our-selves."[11] Legal rights were a necessary predicate to economic rights.

> "I was here the first time the University formed a committee to talk about our wages. I was making barely over minimum wage then, and I still am now," said Nelson Hernandez who has worked at the University for 25 years and earns only $6.80 an hour. "I look forward to working with the committee and the union to make this real."[12]

Furthermore, economic advances were seen through a class-based frame:

> Zoila Garcia has the toughest job at the University of Miami. From 10 p.m. to 6 a.m., five nights a week, she washes windows, cleans desks and picks up the potato chip bags and used condoms that students leave behind in the library.

> "Ay mamita! And when they decide to draw on those tables, it's scrub scrub scrub," Garcia said.

> When she returns to her mobile home off Southwest Eighth Street just after dawn, she takes the pills she gets through a Jackson clinic. Some are for high blood pressure. One is for the pain in her arms.

> For now, there's nothing to be done about a blood clot that formed on her calf and blackened the leg from knee to ankle. She needs an operation. But when the doctor told her it would cost $4,000, she laughed. "Where do you get that kind of money?"

Garcia, who makes $6.70 an hour, has no health insurance.

> I have worked hard all my life, but the situation in this country has changed," Zoila said. "The cost of living is so high and no one can live with these salaries. These millionaires just don't understand the struggles of working people."[13]

Approximately fifty percent of the more than four hundred UNICCO workers went on strike. Many others were sympathetic but simply could not afford to go out.

The University administration immediately announced that since it was not the ac-tual employer, it would remain neutral in the labor dispute. Despite this stance, the SEIU filed an unfair labor practice claim alleging that the University had been allowing the company to speak out against the union to its workers on campus (legal activity) while prohibiting the union from accessing campus (illegal discrimination). This prohibition extended to preventing the union from soliciting workers on campus for Hurricane Wilma relief and providing food to workers with storm damages.

---

10. Maya Bell, "Fired University of Miami Janitor Leads Strike Over Benefits," *Orlando Sentinel*, D1 (Mar. 1, 2006).

11. Posting of Faculty for Workplace Justice to Picketline, *A Brief Documentary History: The Pres-ident's Statement of 2/23*, http://picketline.blogspot.com/2006/03/brief-documentary-history-presi-dents.html (Mar. 5, 2006, 09:34 EST).

12. *Ibid.*

13. Ana Menendez, "While Shalala Lives in Luxury, Janitors Struggle," *Miami Herald*, 1B (Mar. 1, 2006).

The University also immediately established a special gate several blocks from other campus activity, through which all UNICCO workers had to report and be assigned work, in order to arguably restrict picketing to that one location. This was a controversial legal position because of the common *situs* doctrine.[14] Workers in a labor dispute have the right to reach other workers of their employer in order to publicize their dispute and gain support. However, where, as here, the employer does all its work on the premises of another, the workers can only effectively protest at that worksite. If an outside contractor does work which is not part of the everyday operation of the workplace company, picketing can be restricted to a single gate in order to limit impact on the neutral employer.[15] Janitorial and groundskeeping work do not fit this exception. Further, UNICCO workers had to use company trucks on public roads to reach many parts of campus from their sign-in gate. It should therefore have been possible to picket at these other university entrances. Nonetheless, the SEIU respected this designation. Initially about one hundred workers picketed at the sign-in gate. Later on in the strike, when the union had evidence of non-striking UNICCO workers using other gates, picketing was briefly extended for two days to the main entrance of the University.

Finally, the University administration continuously and publicly called for a union election among UNICCO workers. In contrast, the union's position was that it wanted the faster card signing approach instead of the majority recognition method provided for under the NLRA.[16] Unions can demonstrate they have majority support to force bargaining in a number of ways, including: holding elections supervised by the NLRB; collecting signed representation cards; wearing union T-shirts; or calling a strike. Once an employer knows a union has majority support, a company is under a duty to bargain in good faith. The catch is that unless the company agrees to recognize the majority by other means, the company can at that time call for an election. During an election period, the employer can run an anti-union campaign during work hours, make hints of the consequences of unionization, and even utilize illegal tactics of threats and discharge knowing how long it will take to pursue remedies. Because of this time and events the union will have lost momentum. This would be a particularly relevant risk where the company was already facing charges of unfair labor practices. In such a situation, an election might not even be scheduled until after the unfair labor practices were resolved because those practices may have already tainted a fair election.[17] The estimated time to an election would be two to three years. President Shalala's continued calling for a secret election, therefore, had the rhetorical power of pro-democracy, but a hollow promise of actual current worker choice.[18]

Despite having several weeks notice of the strike vote, the initial reaction of the campus seemed to be shock. Many professors spontaneously moved their classes off campus, refusing to cross a hypothetical picket line. A loose faculty organization formed by pro-

---

14. *Sailors' Union of the Pac.* (Moore Dry Dock Co.), 92 N.L.R.B. 547 (1950). "When a secondary employer is harboring the *situs* of a dispute between a union and a primary employer, the right of neither the union to picket nor of the secondary employer to be free from picketing can be absolute. The enmeshing of premises and *situs* qualifies both rights." *Ibid.* at 549.

15. *See Local 761, Int'l. Union of Elec., Radio & Mach. Workers v. NLRB.*, 366 U.S. 667, 681–82 (1961).

16. *See* James J. Brudney, "Neutrality Agreements and Card Check Recognition: Prospects for Changing Paradigms," 90 *Iowa L. Rev.* 819, 824 (2004–2005).

17. It was rumored that UNICCO offered to waive the usual election period if SEIU agreed to an election. The union refused, perhaps believing an election was already tainted, or perhaps just preferring the card check procedure.

18. Seventy percent of private-sector workers organized (150,000) in 2005 were organized through card checks. Steven Greenhouse, "Employers Sharply Criticize Shift in Unionizing Method to Cards from Elections," *N.Y. Times*, A9 (Mar. 11, 2006).

fessors Traci Ardren, Michael Fischl, and Giovanna Pompele, Faculty for Workplace Justice, was joined by a student group, Students Toward a New Democracy (STAND).[19] Web sites were established by the company, as well as faculty and student groups. Through faculty volunteers and the faculty web site, rooms for classes were located off campus in area churches and community rooms. Many classes were conducted outside on a green adjacent to the University and visible to drivers.[20] After a few days, some classes met on the lawn in front of the Ashe Administration Building. In total, more than 200 classes moved off site.

On Friday, March 3, 2006, over three hundred and fifty faculty and students marched past the administration building and through the campus, to the corner of the campus, where they met more than one hundred strikers. More than five hundred marchers then crossed Miami's main thoroughfare, U.S. 1, chanting the strike's theme, "Si Se Peude!," "Yes, we can." This was the beginning of a publicity campaign that largely shunned traditional labor picketing in favor of community protests. The march was followed by a faculty letter to President Shalala, dated March 5, signed initially by 102 faculty.[21] On Monday, March 6, the Auxiliary Catholic Bishop of the Archdiocese of Miami offered to mediate the dispute between UNICCO and SEIU by including the University President.[22]

On Wednesday, March 8, the STAND organization held a meeting discussing peaceful civil disobedience. The SEIU announced plans to walk out at the medical campus and the airport, triggering a response of support from Miami Commissioner Joe Martinez. Striking workers issued a statement reflecting both class and ethnic/racial concern:

> **Announcement from striking UNICCO employees at UM:** Every Miami Worker Deserves A Chance for a Better Life. You Can Help UM Janitors Get That Chance. IT'S NEARLY IMPOSSIBLE TO MAKE ENDS MEET in Miami on $6.40 an hour. Yet that's all many contract cleaners at the University of Miami are paid. $51 a day with no health benefits. Less than half the county median wage. On these tiny salaries, we're forced to make choices we never thought we'd be faced with in the United States: Do we pay rent or buy groceries? Buy shoes for our kids or fill a prescription? UM's mostly Cuban-American janitors have been joining together to build a better life for ourselves, one where we don't have to make these choices. But the company we work for — UNICCO, the cleaning contractor hired by the university — has been punishing those who speak out by threatening, intimidating, and even suspending union supporters. So we've decided we must strike to make our voices heard. You can help send a message to UNICCO: **"Give Miami janitors a chance to live the American dream!"**[23]

---

19. *See generally* Richard Michael Fischl, "The Other Side of the Picket Line: Contract, Democracy, and Power in a Law School Classroom," 31 *N.Y.U. Rev. L. & Soc. Change* 517, 520 (2007); Posting of Faculty for Workplace Justice to Picketline, FAQ One, http://picketline.blogspot.com/2006/03/faq-one.html (Mar. 4, 2006, 4:03 EST).

20. *See generally* Nicholas Spangler, "U.M. Janitors' Strike Turns Park into Classroom," *Miami Herald*, 1B (Mar. 3, 2006).

21. Faculty for Workplace Justice Posting, *A Brief Documentary History: the President's Statement of 2/23, supra* note 13.

22. Posting of Faculty for Workplace Justice to Picketline, *Bishop Estevez Offers to Mediate Between President Shalala and the Striking Janitors, supra* note 8.

23. Statement, SEIU Local 11, Announcement from Striking UNICCO Employees at UM (Mar. 7, 2006) (on file with author).

At a student sponsored teach-in Wednesday night, the topic of worker health brought forth myriads of complaints from workers about the impossibility of obtaining health care, or debts incurred up to thousands of dollars. One woman had been turned away from a mammogram to check a lump in her breast.[24]

On Friday, three hundred to four hundred people rallied at the County Government Center Building in downtown Miami, as part of widening the conflict to the community. Significantly, the SEIU strategy throughout the strike centered on public demonstrations and events to bring attention to the strike, rather than traditional picketing at the job site gates. Most of the UNICCO strikers normally worked at night, so perhaps non-traditional public events would reach the same number of workers and a wider audience.

Strike activity on campus paused during the next week of spring break, although significant decisions were announced. First, the University's Living Wage Committee issued their report. The report acknowledged that university contractors were paying below market rates and that there were problems with recruitment and retention. The President responded by announcing that contractors would raise pay for food service employees to $8.00 per hour, janitors to $8.55, and landscapers to $9.30, with health insurance benefits to be provided within a month.[25] Although both UNICCO and the SEIU welcomed the announcement, it was not explained how the University, a supposed neutral, could have effectuated the increase during a current contract.[26] The University's announcement did include other labor contractors besides UNICCO, but maintaining job parity between union and non-union employees would still be considered an unfair labor practice if carried out by a direct employer during on-going strike negotiations. The union expected the strike to continue because the one-time pay increase still fell considerably short of the county living wage (one to over two dollars per hour), and because the workers continued to insist on unionization by means of a card signature demonstration of majority status, without which workers felt they would be fired. Worker Elsa Rodriguez said, "we're not going to stop just because we're getting more dollars. That's not the only thing that we want. We want to form a union to get respect and to not be humiliated."[27] Unsurprisingly, the workers' class consciousness included a demand for respect as well as wages. However, after approval from the union, the leaders of the Faculty for Workplace Justice called for those teaching off campus to return to their normal class rooms, and continue support by other means. This was a highly controversial call according to many faculty supporting the strike, but almost all faculty returned to the classroom.

---

24. Posting of Faculty for Workplace Justice to Picketline, *Teach-In Last Night,* http://picket-line.blogspot.com/2006/03/teach-in-last-night.html (Mar. 10, 2006, 7:34 EST).

25. Niala Boodhoo, *Striking Workers at UM to Get Raise,* MIAMI HERALD, Mar. 17, 2006, at A1.

26. According to the President's statement:

It is also important to point out that the University's position on the labor dispute has not changed. The University remains neutral and is not a party to those discussions. That is an issue to be decided between UNICCO, its employees, and the union.... I appreciate your input on this issue during the past few weeks. And I know that you support our decision to provide increased wages and health insurance for the hourly employees of our service contractors. I wish I could assure you that the next few months will be quiet, as the union, service contract workers, and their employer engage in a debate over representation. We need to respect the process. Democracy is messy. Donna E. Shalala, "A Message from President Shalala," *News Ibis* (Univ. of Miami Student Newsletter, Miami, Fl.), Mar. 19, 2006, *available at* http://www6.miami.edu/ibis-news/20060319se/.

27. Boodhoo, *supra* note 25, at 10A.

On March 22, the Faculty Senate passed two resolutions unanimously.[28] First, they insisted that all contract companies pay at least the Miami-Dade living wage, including affordable, employer-subsidized health insurance and other benefits and working conditions.[29] Second, they voted that if the UNICCO contract is not renewed, the successful bidder will be required to offer to any and all UNICCO employees currently assigned to the University of Miami positions comparable to or better than they now hold. In a third resolution, passed by a strong majority, the Senate urged that all parties involved in the union negotiations adhere to fair labor practices and labor law.[30]

On Monday, March 27, the union announced it had received signed membership cards from fifty-seven percent of the workers.[31]

> The [service workers] signed the cards despite threats from UNICCO over the past week that janitors would be fired for striking. "They called me over the weekend and said that if I didn't go back to work that they would fire me,' said janitor Elmis Loredo. "Their words were supposed to send a chill through the whole community. But we will not be intimidated any longer. We have won a great deal, not just for us, but for all the workers on campus. And now our success is spreading hope to other workers that they too can win better wages and affordable health insurance."[32]

Another worker, Eloy Morales, received seventeen calls in one day telling him to return to work or be fired.[33]

One of the pivotal events of the strike took place the day following the card check announcement. A rally was called for 11:00 a.m. at the Episcopal Chapel on campus (also serving as the workers' strike sanctuary). The rally was sponsored by faculty, students, and the Committee for Interfaith Worker Justice, a group of local clergy. Local clergy had opened their churches from the beginning for alternative class rooms and publicly supported the low wage workers. Now, they led a march from the chapel to the intersection of U.S. 1 and Stanford Drive at the main campus entrance and met a large group of strikers. As the light changed, protesters moved into the street from all corners. A group of seventeen clergy and workers sat down in the middle of the intersection. Thereupon, Coral Gables police, who had been previously notified, moved in and arrested the group.

At noon, while this protest was taking place, a group of nineteen students from STAND moved into the Ashe Administration Building, occupying the admissions office on the first floor. They were later joined by the Episcopal priest on campus, Father Frank Corbishly. University police immediately isolated the building. One hundred workers from the U.S. 1 protest surrounded entrances to the building, chanting support for the stu-

---

28. Posting of Faculty for Workplace Justice to Picketline, *Academic Senate: Three Cheers for Justice,* http://picketline.blogspot.com/2006/03/academic-senate-three-cheers-for24.html (Mar. 24, 2006 19:27 EST).

29. *Ibid.*

30. *Ibid.*

31. Posting of Faculty for Workplace Justice to Picketline, *Today's SEIU Press Release: A "Super" Majority,* http://picketline.blogspot.com/2006/03/todays-seiu-press-release-super.html (Mar. 27, 2006 21:54 EST).

32. Press Release, SEIU, Today's SEIU Press Release: A "Super" Majority (Mar. 27, 2006) (on file with author).

33. Posting of Faculty for Workplace Justice to Picketline, *Why a Hunger Strike: Statement from STAND,* http://picketline.blogspot.com/2006/04/why-hunger-strike-statement-from-stand.html (Apr. 10, 2006, 18:11 EST).

dents. Throughout the day, university police stayed inside the building and manned stairs and entrances. Coral Gables police stood a short distance from the building serving as back-up. Only a few faculty members with offices on upper floors were let in. People observing the students inside were permitted to leave but not return. In addition to the occupying students and Father Corbishly, three law students served as inside observers. An ACLU attorney who was on campus to speak to a class volunteered to provide counsel for the students, helping to establish communications with the administration. The administration responded to the occupation by denying the students inside access to bathrooms, water, and food, and by shutting off the air conditioning. The students had brought cat litter with them and were forced to use trash cans for bodily needs. Students were threatened with arrest, forced removal, and possible expulsion.

In mid-afternoon, University President Shalala, the Provost, and the Dean of Students agreed to meet with the students. Fearing they would not be allowed back into the admissions area, the students delegated negotiations to a small group of students and faculty, keeping in touch by cell phones. The students asked to have their lawyers take part, but were refused despite the fact that the University's outside counsel was present. Students demanded a living wage, and the increasing focal point for the strike — union recognition by the workers' preferred method of a card check. No agreement was reached. At 4:30 p.m., the administration cleared the building except for the occupying students. At 5:00 p.m. a vigil of students, workers, and faculty stayed at each entrance. Large numbers of police cars and a paddy wagon parked around them. President Shalala refused to meet with students with Father Corbishly present. He was only allowed to sit outside the door. Negotiations and the vigil continued until approximately 1:30 a.m., when the President agreed that the students would not be arrested and that a group made up of students, faculty, workers, UNICCO, and the University would meet within forty-eight hours to attempt to settle the strike. President Shalala issued a statement to university students stating the University administration's position:

> Why, then, did 15 students end up in the foyer of the Admissions Office at 1:00 am talking to me about their frustration with the university[?] Basically, they want the university to tell one of our contractors, UNICCO, to accept cards that the union, SEIU, has had UNICCO employees sign requesting union recognition. The union argues that collecting signatures as an indication of what the employees want is better and fairer than a secret, federal government (National Labor Relations Board) supervised vote. The contractor, UNICCO, has called for the secret ballot procedure supervised by the NLRB (it should be noted that recognizing a union on the basis of cards is optional under the law; recognizing a union under a secret ballot election is mandated by the law).

> Both sides have accused the other of intimidating the UNICCO employees to support or not support the union and to sign or not sign the cards. The students ... believe the NLRB process takes too long and is flawed.... I pointed out that the university simply could never take a position against a secret ballot procedure supervised by a federal government agency. Secret ballots are at the heart of our democratic system. In fact, many of the UNICCO employees in our community came to this country precisely because of our free (and secret ballot) elections....

> In addition, I want to repeat the university's policy on demonstrations, protests and free speech — all are welcome and are part of the fabric of American higher education. However, no one has the right to coerce or intimidate another member

of our community. Nor do they have the right to interfere with anyone's right to study, teach, do research, provide for our patients or do the university's other business.[34]

The group announced by President Shalala met twice. On Friday, March 31, the meeting was moderated and run by a University Vice-President. One worker present reported that at the beginning of the meeting the University brought up the issue of an NLRB election to decide on representation. It was not spoken about by either the company or the union before that time. Another worker present reportedly banged a hand on the table stating, "I already voted. My signature is my word." The second meeting was run by an outside labor law mediator and was more productive, producing the outlines of the eventual agreement. Predictably, neither party moved their positions at either of the two meetings held. By now the strikers were convinced that they would be picked off over time and fired without union representation, and further convinced that card check recognition was the best strategy.

At this point, the strike gathered more national attention. It had become a University community affair, then a South Florida test of the living wage movement and a test for raising wages and unionization in the non-union era of service employment. A striker, Clara Vargas, said, "the Mayor has been here along with commissioners, Congress members.... They have all promised to try to solve this problem. I do hope they will be able to do something."[35] Author and activist Barbara Ehrenreich headed a letter sent to President Shalala. Nova University UNICCO employees voted to authorize a strike over similar unfair labor practices there. Meetings were reported at the University of Virginia and the State University of New York at Buffalo.

Complicating the local strike support was the ethnicity of the strikers. Three faculty members, Elizabeth Aranda (Sociology), Elena Sabogal (Latin American Studies), and Sallie Hughes (Communication), explained what their research on labor and immigration revealed regarding the workers' strike support:

> We have been researching the immigrant/Latino communities here for a couple of years now. In the course of our research, we have spoken to UNICCO workers on campus. One of the things we have learned is that many are part of a vulnerable population — more than earning poverty wages, these workers share an immigrant background that places them at an additional level of disadvantage. We speculate that some of them cannot afford to engage in civil disobedience because they know this could jeopardize their immigrant status. It's not just about losing their jobs or missed wages — they could put in danger the right to be in this country. One thing we have consistently heard in our interviews is that life as an immigrant has become harder to endure since 9/11 due to increasing fears of deportation in spite of being in the country legally. So, they lay low — something that is incompatible with a public demonstration. We feel this makes their fight even more courageous. In speaking to some of the workers in the past week, they have expressed to us how much they appreciate that students and faculty are fighting their fight. Even though some who we have spoken to do not plan to picket, rather than interpret this as a sign of ambivalence or non-support, in our view, it is part of their strategies for survival that involve remaining "in-

---

34. Press Release, Donna E. Shalala, President Shalala's Message to Students (Mar. 27, 2006) (on file with author), *available at* http://picketline.blogspot.com/2006/03/president-shalalas-message-to-students.html.

35. Abby Goodnough & Steven Greenhouse, "Anger Rises on Both Sides of Strike at U. of Miami," *N.Y. Times*, A18 (Apr. 18, 2006).

visible." The legal community could probably speak more on this issue than we can, but many immigrants feel that even if they are here legally, they are subject to deportation if they are arrested. This underscores their vulnerabilities as a population marginalized by multiple structures of inequality, something we should keep in mind as the strike unfolds.[36]

On April 5, against the muted advice of the SEIU, workers began a hunger strike. Clara Vargas, Maria Ramirez, Isabel Montalvo, Victoria Carbajal, Maritza Gonzalez, Pablo Rodriguez, Odalys Rodriguez, Feliciano Hernandez, Elsa Rodriguez, and Reinaldo "el loco" Hernandez comprised the original group of ten. They built a tent enclave where the hunger strikers lived called "Justice City" or "Freedom City," across from the University and adjacent to the mass transit elevated tracks along U.S. 1. The tent city became a gathering place for media and strike supporters daily, creating closer ties between workers and supporters.

On April 9, Isabel Montalvo, one of the hunger strikers, was taken to the hospital, suffering from heat exhaustion and elevated blood pressure. Feliciano Hernandez, who was also suffering from elevated blood pressure, adamantly said, "there are two ways in which I'll leave this place ... either President Shalala recognizes our right to be treated like human beings, or they can bring me away dead."[37] The hunger strikers wrote to President Shalala:

> Today, April 7, 2006, is the fourth day that UNICCO janitors have been on a hunger strike, after a month and a half of being on strike asking that they be treated like people, humanely. All they ask is that the university respect their human rights like citizens of this country and most of all they ask this under the representation of a union to defend the workers interests.
>
> Today, after the fourth day of the hunger strike for the workers, they had to call the ambulance because one of the workers (Isabel Montalvo) had problems with blood pressure. The ambulance arrived silently, so as not to show the world what is happening at the University of Miami.
>
> Another worker was also having problems with high blood pressure, but this worker, Odalys Rodriguez, decided to stay while she has the strength to show everyone that "yes, it is possible" (*si se puede!*) and we have to win, because we are only asking for liberty and respect, which is what we all hoped to find when we get to this country.
>
> Because of this, we cannot conceive of this attitude that the hunger strike hasn't been given the appropriate press by the TV channels, now that each of these workers is risking their life to achieve what every person who lives and works in this country should have anyway.
>
> This is why we are writing this short and thoughtful letter, so that everyone will know what is going on at the University of Miami and so that Donna Shalala, the president, will know she is responsible for whatever happens, seeing as though she is the one putting the brakes on the solution to these problems.
>
> *—Clara Vargas, elected representative of*
> *UNICCO workers and hunger striker*

---

36. Posting of Faculty for Workplace Justice to Picketline, *Why Are All the Workers Not on Strike?*, http://picketline.blogspot.com/2006/04/why-are-all-workers-not-on-strike.html (Apr. 7, 2006, 16:40 EST).

37. Posting of Faculty for Workplace Justice to Picketline, *Yesterday at Justice City: One Striker is Evacuated*, http://picketline.blogspot.com/2006/04/yesterday-at-justice-city-one-striker.html (Apr. 10, 2006, 15:20 EST).

(Odalys was taken to the hospital since this letter was written).

This letter is signed by the remaining hunger strikers:

> Feliciano Hernandez, 60
> Reinaldo Hernandez, 52
> Victoria Corbajal, 50
> Maria Leonor Ramirez, 25
> Pablo Rodriguez, 34
> Martiza Gomez, 44
> Clara Vargas, 32[38]

On April 12, one week after the hunger strike began, seven students joined the hunger strike. After a rally, twelve students again tried to enter the admissions office but were dragged outside by University police. The students then linked arms with others to block the entrance. The building was locked down by the administration, with no one allowed in or out. The administration employed professional photographers to take pictures of the protesters. President Shalala claimed in a letter to the University that outside protesters were entering campus and interfering with the dispute. In her strongest support for UNICCO's position, President Shalala said that pressure was being brought to "bully" the University to force UNICCO to accept unionization without a single vote by a worker. She implied union opposition by stating that seventy-five percent of the workers were at work.[39] This opposition to card checks came despite the fact that, according to the SEIU, ninety percent of UNICCO's 8000 unionized workers organized through card checks.[40]

Another hunger striker, Feliciano Hernandez, who spent nine years in a Cuban prison for dissent, was rushed to the hospital with an advanced heart rate.

The seven student hunger strikers who were denied a meeting with the President set up a second "Freedom Village" in tents outside the Ashe Building entrance. The University administration responded by turning on the water sprinklers in that area of the campus, leaving them on overnight and for the next several days. The water was briefly stopped when actor and activist Ed Asner visited "Freedom City" and tried to speak with President Shalala.

On Friday, April 14, Mayor Alvarez of Miami and former Congressman David Bonier visited "Freedom City." On Saturday, a fourth worker, Maritza Gomez, was hospitalized with tachycardia and a weak pulse. By Tuesday, a fifth worker, Pablo Rodriguez, was hospitalized shaking and with a weak pulse, and the first student, Tanya Aquino, went to the hospital. On the fourteenth day of the hunger strike five strikers remained at "Freedom City." The hunger strike finally changed on Friday, April 21, after seventeen days, when numerous faculty and community leaders substituted for the hunger strikers for up to seventy-two hour stints of fasting. SEIU President Andrew Stern and Vice-President Eliseo Medina, who had been a veteran organizer earlier with Caesar Chavez, began fasts after meeting with strikers.

On Monday, April 24, UNICCO announced health insurance employee premiums: only $13.00 per month for the worker alone, but $241 for the worker and one child,

---

38. Posting of Faculty for Workplace Justice to Picketline, *Message from the Hunger Strikers*, http://picketline.blogspot.com/2006/04/message-from-hunger-strikers.html (Apr. 10, 2006 17:59 EST).

39. Donna Shalala, Letter to the University of Miami Community, Apr. 12, 2006.

40. Posting of Faculty for Workplace Justice to Picketline, *What About Card Check Versus NLRB Elections?*, http://picketline.blogspot.com/2006/04/what-about-card-check-versus-nlrb.html (Apr. 7, 2006 16:48 EST).

and $493 for a family of four (thirty-six percent of pre-tax pay).[41] The next day a rally at "Freedom City" brought Rev. Charles Steele, President of the Southern Christian Leadership Conference, John Edwards, Democratic Vice-Presidential candidate in 2004, James Hoffa III, President of the Teamsters, and others to town. Meanwhile, the students camping at the Ashe building feared arrest by university police. Rev. Steele announced that if any student went to jail, he would be arrested too. Senator John Edwards said:

> None of you, no American, should be working full time and be living in poverty. That's what this struggle is about.... Your struggle is my struggle ... If a Republican can join the Republican Party by signing their name to a card, then any worker in America should be able to join a union by signing their name to a card.[42]

Each day from April 25 to April 28, the University took out full page advertisements in the Miami Herald, presumably to counter the outside publicity. On April 25, the advertisement proclaimed: "We Provided Higher Wages. We Provided Health Insurance. We Have Done Our Part."[43] The wage/benefit increases indeed were applauded but, as noted, did not measure up to the county living wage, and did not address the main point of contention—a card check election.

On April 26, the advertisement stated: "Outside Protesters Trespass On Our Campus. Our Students, Faculty, Staff Are Harassed. The Union Has Gone Too Far."[44] No incidents of harassment were ever publicly reported. The only incidents were of university police confronting students. The University administration repeatedly locked down the Ashe Building when luminaries like Ed Asner, Charles Steele, David Bonier, or John Edwards spoke on or near the campus or tried to see President Shalala. A few "outsiders" from the community, including the organization ACORN, were briefly on campus, although not directly connected to the strike. However, once the strike became a community matter the distinction between those who were and were not of the strike blurred. The University administration seemed to play both sides of the community issue, first saying they had done their part to bring wages to community or market standards, and then insisting the community had nothing to do with the strike.

On April 27, an advertisement stated: "They Stage Daily Publicity Stunts. They Disrupt Our Academic Mission. The Union Needs To Stop Its Tactics."[45] On the issue of publicity, many national leaders visited the hunger strike and spoke to workers and students. This was a matter of free speech. Again, there was no evidence that anyone other than the administration, which at times prevented students from reaching teachers' offices, caused academic disruption.

Finally, on April 28, the advertisement took sides and stated: "They Don't Want Workers To Vote. They Argue Against Freedom And Democracy. Does The Union Think Work-

---

41. Posting of Faculty for Workplace Justice to Picketline, *And What About Health Insurance,* http://picketline.blogspot.com/2006/04/and-what-about-health-insurance.html (Apr. 7, 2006, 16:47 EST).

42. Posting of Faculty for Workplace Justice to Picketline, *Help Is on the Way,* http://picketline.blogspot.com/2006/04/help-is-on-way.html (Apr. 25, 2006 11:57 EST) (quoting Senator John Edwards, Address at the Freedom Village Rally (Apr. 25, 2006)).

43. Advertisement, "We Provided Higher Wages. We Provided Health Insurance. We Have Done Our Part," *Miami Herald,* 13A (Apr. 25, 2006).

44. Advertisement, "Outside Protestors Trespass On Our Campus. Our Students, Faculty, and Staff Are Harassed. The Union Has Gone Too Far," *Miami Herald,* 6A (Apr. 26, 2006).

45. Advertisement, "They Stage Daily Publicity Stunts. They Disrupt Our Academic Mission. The Union Needs To Stop Its Tactics," *Miami Herald,* 20A (Apr. 27, 2006).

ers Are Second-Class Citizens?"[46] This ignored the fact that the majority of workers had signed cards. Tellingly, the advertisement put the University publicly on the side of management in the dispute. Real questions exist about the unfairness of NLRB elections, which the University never addressed, hiding behind the rhetoric of elections. The advertisements indicated to the workers and the community that the University was aligned with UNICCO, if not bargaining for it.

Almost paradoxically, on May 1, 2006, the union and UNICCO announced a settlement agreement to allow a card check process to determine a bargaining representative. The basics of the agreement formed a clear victory for the union and set forth the following provisions: (1) a code of conduct for both the union and management during the campaign; (2) verification of the result by the independent American Arbitration Association; (3) agreement by UNICCO to recognize the union the same day that a supermajority of sixty percent of the workers signed cards; (4) the union would have until August 1, 2006, to succeed; (5) the workers would return to work May 3; and (6) the union leader who was fired, Zoila Mursuli, would be rehired with back pay.[47] On May 2, the workers took down their "tent city."

The strike was over, but the University administration was not over it. In the first week of May, twenty student activists were given administrative subpoenas, many handed out during classes. They were charged with "major" violations of University rules subjecting them to potential expulsion or suspension including: disorderly conduct; failing to follow University directives; and "distributing literature." The ACLU immediately found lawyers for all twenty students. In their administrative hearings, those lawyers counseled silence when administrators asked charged students to identify other students from pictures.

By May 30, the charges had been reduced to "minor" violations of the same charges. This had two effects: the students were no longer able to have lawyers or other representatives at their hearings, and since the hearings could be scheduled during the summer, no students or faculty needed to be part of the summary process used by the University. The procedure would be before a single Dean. One student's attorney, Lida Rodriguez said:

> This is about punishing these students for having the nerve to stand up for what they believe in and sending a message to other students not to do the same. Even for a private institution, this is the height of unfairness. I'm sure there are parents of UM students that do not know who (sic) their hard-earned dollars are going to a system that's unfair.[48]

Just before the mid-May graduation, the University obtained an injunction in state court preventing the union or its members from entering the campus, ostensibly to prevent any demonstrations at graduation ceremonies.

On Thursday, June 15, the results of the card check were announced: the union had collected more than seventy percent of the workers' signatures. Also in mid-June most of the charged students, faced with a fait-accompli, pleaded no contest to the charges. They were sentenced to two semesters probation, a five hundred word essay, and ironically, community service. They also lost housing privileges in newly constructed Univer-

---

46. Advertisement, "They Don't Want Workers To Vote. They Argue Against Freedom And Democracy. Does The Union Think Workers Are Second-Class Citizens?," *Miami Herald*, 5A (Apr. 28, 2006).

47. Posting of Faculty for Workplace Justice to Picketline, *In Case You Haven't Heard ... We've Won !!!!!*, http://picketline.blogspot.com/search?q=we%27ve+won (May 1, 2006, 19:32 EST).

48. Jessica M. Walker, "UM Dean to Run Hearing, Decide Student's Fate," *Palm Beach Daily Bus. Rev.*, 253 (June 9, 2006).

sity student apartments. A faculty protest signed by a hundred and ten professors, despite dispersal for the summer, claimed:

> 1) Students who pleaded not guilty were denied postponement of their hearings to the Fall, at which time they would appear before a University Disciplinary Hearing Panel including their peers. Instead, Associate Dean Singleton, who is a witness in some of the cases, now serves simultaneously as investigator, prosecutor, judge and jury....

> 2) Some students have now seen added to their previous charges the further charge of unauthorized distribution of printed material.... The policy refers specifically to advertising....[49]

The University administration responded with an unsigned letter to the Daily Business Review, claiming that the 2000 plus members of the faculty who had not signed the letter all supported the administration on the proceedings, despite the fact the letter only reached five hundred and fifty professors, many of whom no doubt never saw the overnight petition.[50]

One of the students who pleaded no contest is suing the University for breach of contract for failing to follow student handbook procedures.

On August 23, the new SEIU local ratified a new contract, the main highlights of which include:

Wages: $0.25 per hour raise on Sep 1, 2006, $0.40 Sep 1, 2007, $0.50 Sep 1, 2008, $0.50 Sep 1, 2009.

Health Insurance: any increases in the premium up to 10% to be absorbed by UNICCO. Increases beyond that will trigger a committee to investigate further ways of reducing costs.

Personal Days: Increase from 2 to 3 paid personal days.

Vacations: 1 year—1 week, 5 years—2 weeks, 10 years—3 weeks.

Holidays: Three extra paid holidays: Christmas Eve, New Year's Eve and the day after Thanksgiving.

Funeral Leave: 3 paid days.

Seniority: Workers with more years get more benefits.

Safety: A committee of workers and management will meet every month to address any safety issues.

Union Rights: The union will have the right to post materials, to speak to new hires and to investigate abuses on job time.

Immigration: Workers will be allowed time off to deal with immigration issues.

Job Security: Basic structures will be put in place to deal with harassment, favoritism and improper dismissal.[51]

---

49. Letter from University of Miami Faculty to Patricia A. Whitely, Vice President for Student Affairs, University of Miami, and William W. Sandler, Jr., Dean of Students, University of Miami (June 27, 2006) (on file with author).

50. *See* Posting of Faculty for Workplace Justice to Picketline, *Dear Colleagues*, http://picketline.blogspot.com/2006/07/dear-colleagues.html (July 14, 2006 09:16 EST).

51. Posting of Faculty for Workplace Justice to Picketline, *The Contract We Fought For Has Been Ratified!*, http://picketline.blogspot.com/2006/08/contract-we-fought-for-has-been.html (Aug. 23, 2006 at 18:22 EST).

The workers had won recognition, health benefits, and a living wage scheduled over the next three years.[52] Shortly after the University of Miami workers ratified their new contract, Nova University workers won their own union recognition from UNICCO. Nova University responded by not renewing UNICCO's contract.[53] The workers lost their contract and their jobs, and only some of them were rehired by the replacement contractors. Only a few new contractors hired sufficient numbers of former employees necessary to require successorship negotiations with the union.[54] Furthermore, the number of smaller contractors replacing UNICCO's services will make organizing the same number of workers improbable because each employer would have to be separately organized. The contrast between the University of Miami and the Nova University outcomes underlines the challenge by the tri-partite employment form of employee, labor contractor, and end user to collective bargaining as a statutory policy.

II. Joint Employment and the Low-wage Service Sector

Although many legal issues have been raised by the Miami strike, one issue permeates the actions and structural relationships among affected parties: who is the real employer of the janitors and landscapers at the University? Is the University a joint employer with UNICCO? There are potentially two legal issues here. First, should the University be jointly liable for the alleged unfair labor practices committed by UNICCO? Second, should the University be considered the real employer required to negotiate wages and conditions of employment? The latter situation would represent a difficult labor-management negotiating arrangement since the end user would be part of determining the direct employer's labor costs.[55] Perhaps ironically, the University held more control over the latter issue than the labor practices of UNICCO.

Several interests are at stake in answering these questions. First, although there is very little settled law under the NLRA, the issue of joint responsibility is a profoundly important legal question as worker-management relations in a new global economy depend increasingly on the three-way relationship created by the work's end user. This is important both for organization initially and for determining whether the purpose of promoting collective bargaining under the NLRA can be feasibly pursued. Even a remedy of an unfair labor practice against the direct contractor may depend on the actions and interests of the end user. As attorney Jonathon Axclrod has stated:

> As ... leased employees turn toward unions, they will realize that a union's effectiveness is limited by the very predicament that caused them to seek a union.... Unions representing leased employees are ineffectual unless the recipient of the leased employees is a joint employer.... Absent joint employer status, the recipient is not a party to negotiations and is immune to a union's economic strength.[56]

Second, the third-party contract relationship also explains the shape of bargaining and public relations among those interested. In this case the main public protagonists were the University (the end user) and the workers. Less publicly visible was the direct employer, UNICCO.

---

52. Niala Boodhoo, "Pay Day," *Miami Herald*, 1C (Aug. 24, 2006).

53. *See* Ana Menendez, "Better Wages, Health Care Not Enough," *MIAMI HERALD*, 1B (Feb. 18, 2007).

54. *See generally, Fall River Dyeing & Finishing Corp. v. NLRB*, 482 U.S. 27, 42–43 (1987).

55. Although a simultaneous negotiation between the labor contractor and the end user, or a contract which automatically included the labor costs of the contract between the labor contractor and the workers, would be possible.

56. Jonathan G. Axelrod, "Who's the Boss? Employee Leasing and the Joint Employer Relationship," 3 *Lab. Law* 853, 871–72 (1987).

Third, the three-party relationship also invites turning the labor organization question into a community struggle, which the end user usually will not admit exists. This is not only significant in terms of the dynamics of the dispute, but again in terms of how the basic policies of our labor statute are characterized and fulfilled.

The definition of an "employer" under the NLRA is very broad; "the term 'employer' includes any person acting as *an agent* of an employer, directly or indirectly...."[57] Also, the question of whether one is an employer is to be interpreted broadly as the act is a remedial statute. The formal contract arrangements and the characterizations of the parties are not significant in finding a joint employment relationship.[58] Under many federal labor statutes, the issue in the joint employment doctrine is whether, as a matter of economic reality considering the totality of circumstances, the worker is economically dependent on the entity. This is initially a question of whether the putative employer has a right of control over the work or worker in question.

Under the NLRA, early influential cases refer to whether the contracting employer "shares or codetermines" labor relations or employment decisions.[59] In *Boire v. Greyhound Corp.*, the Supreme Court found sufficient control in the following situation:

> The Board NLRB found that while Floors hired, paid, disciplined, transferred, promoted and discharged the employees, Greyhound took part in setting up work schedules, in determining the number of employees required to meet those schedules, and in directing the work of the employees in question. The Board also found that Floors' supervisors visited the terminals only irregularly — on occasion not appearing for as much as two days at a time — and that in at least one instance Greyhound had prompted the discharge of an employee whom it regarded as unsatisfactory.[60]

The Third Circuit found joint employment in *NLRB v. Browning-Ferris Industries.*[61] In that case *Browning-Ferris Industries* (BFI), the end user waste processing plant, used brokers who hired truck drivers daily to haul waste to landfills.[62] BFI paid the brokers biweekly, had the work at its location, provided uniforms, approved hired drivers, assigned deliveries, and, on occasion discharged an employee, while the brokers hired the truckers, directed the routes, scheduled and supervised the truckers daily, paid their wages on a per load basis, and provided their own insurance.[63]

---

57. 29 U.S.C. § 152(2) (2000) (emphasis added).

58. The joint employer doctrine must be distinguished from two distinct doctrines: Single Employer, where two entities are in fact one business for the purpose of bargaining unit determination and negotiation; and Alter Ego, where an employer formalistically alters corporate form to attempt to avoid collective bargaining. *See* Walter V. Siebert & N. Dawn Webber, "Joint Employer, Single Employer, and Alter Ego," 3 *Lab. Law.* 873 (1987). The Sixth, Eighth, and Seventh Circuits have collapsed single employer and joint employer tests together, discussing the four factors of single employment: (1) some functional integration of operations; (2) centralized control of labor relations; (3) common management; and (4) common ownership or financial control. *Ibid.* at 875. This test, by examining ownership and management, makes a finding of joint employment more difficult than the majority rule. The two doctrines of single and joint employer are distinguished and the majority rule is established in *NLRB v. Browning-Ferris Industries*, 691 F.2d 1117, 1124 (3d Cir. 1982).

59. *See Browning-Ferris Indus.*, 691 F.2d at 1117; *Clinton's Ditch Coop. Co.*, 274 N.L.R.B. 728 (1985), *cert. denied*, 479 U.S. 814 (1986).

60. *Boire v. Greyhound Corp.*, 376 U.S. 473, 475 (1964).

61. 691 F.2d at 1117.

62. *See ibid.* at 1119.

63. *See ibid.* at 1119–20.

Under the common law of agency, right of control includes but is not limited to the location of work, provision of tools and processes, direct supervision of tasks, skill level, control over wages and hours, distinct occupation or business, length of employment, and intent of the parties.[64] These factors often point in differing directions or are blurred.

In the Miami situation, the location of work is on the premises of the University, and the work done is necessary to the regular course of University business. Tools are supplied by UNICCO, but other supplies are not always provided. The University makes decisions of what trees to plant and where, but direct daily supervision is by UNICCO. Skill levels are low and the workers do not own or manage their business. Employment is open-ended. The intent of the University is, however, to create a contractual relationship only with UNICCO. If these factors are considered alone it is arguable that the University would not be a joint employer.

Where joint employment was found in a recent Court of Appeals case, *Dunkin' Donuts v. Mid-Atlantic Distribution Center, Inc.*, the end user, Dunkin' Donuts, was involved in employment tenure, assignment of work and equipment, recognition and awards, and day-to-day direction of its leased drivers, who also did some warehouse work.[65] While in Miami's case, location, supplies, task-planning, the use of low-skill labor, and the management of the regular course of business all indicate the University's joint employment status, there seems much less direct supervision than in *Dunkin' Donuts*.[66]

In addition to the right to control, perhaps more significantly in the Miami situation, is the potential importance of economic dependence between the employees and the end user. The UNICCO contract was low bid partly because the University assumed low-wage costs. The University knew, or should have known, that they were not paying enough for UNICCO to pay living wages. Although joint employer doctrine is formally the same under the NLRA, it seems to be found more easily in cases brought under the FLSA.[67] For example, in *Bureerog v. Uvawas*, marketers of clothing apparel were potentially liable under the FLSA for past minimum wages where they paid clothing manufacturers at a product price they should have known was too low to allow payment of minimum wages to the manufacturers' workers.[68] Plaintiffs were accorded leave to amend to state a claim based on the FLSA.[69]

Further, if the entity controls another company's labor-management negotiations, they are per se joint employers.[70] In *Rivera-Vega v. ConAgra, Inc.*, a holding company controlled negotiations of a local plant with its union.[71] The holding company sent a representative to negotiations between the union and the subsidiary. The representative set the parameters of what was acceptable to the holding company and served as a conduit for approval or disapproval of offers made by the union.[72] In Miami, the University did conduct at least two negotiation sessions including UNICCO and the strikers and the union. The settlement

---

64. Restatement (Second) of Agency, § 220 (2000).
65. 363 F.3d 437, 440 (D.C. Cir. 2004).
66. *Ibid.*
67. *See, e.g., Bureerong v. Uvawas*, 959 F. Supp. 1231 (C.D. Cal. 1997).
68. *See ibid.*
69. *See ibid.* at 1238.
70. *Rivera-Vega v. ConAgra, Inc.*, 70 F.3d 153, 163 (1st Cir. 1995).
71. *See ibid.*
72. *See ibid.*

adopted was first proposed during one of these sessions, but the University was never asked by UNICCO to approve those conditions or work on the substance of a collective bargain.

In *Greenhoot, Inc.*, not only did the property management company and the building owners share decisions about hiring and firing, but owner consent was required for wage budgets and wage increases.[73] In *Shultz v. Falk*, building owners and rental agents were joint employers given owner approval of long-term budgets and setting of wages for building workers.[74] But, in *International Longshoreman's Ass'n v. Norfolk Southern Corp.*, the fact that the railroad paid all operating costs of the subsidiary was insufficient.[75] In *Clinton's Ditch Coop. Inc. v. NLRB* no joint employment was found despite the fact that Fairfield Transportation Corporation required consultation by its only customer, Clinton's Ditch, during the negotiation of employment contracts.[76] In Miami, the University unilaterally *raised* the wage rates of the contracted employees showing economic dependence of the employee on the University. Furthermore, if the University had promised these wage increases to their own employees during a strike, it would have been an unfair labor practice (like a bribe to avoid unionization).

Should the University-UNICCO combination be allowed to potentially circumvent the intent and provisions of the NLRA? Considering the totality of the circumstances, including: some control of employees, the conduct of negotiating sessions, making proposals, and running ads to side with the direct employer, whether the University would be held liable is uncertain. However, the point is that the University could be held liable without changing existing law. This would be the easiest, if not a final solution, for new labor markets. The doctrine of joint employment and its variables is capable of broader application than the lower federal courts and NLRB have held thus far. Also, most of the case law in all circuit courts of appeal was decided before 1987. Since then, the practices of leasing employees and contracting out services have exploded.[77]

From both a plain language view of an employer being an agent of another employer, and a purposive view of the need to fully carry out the intent of the statute, a broader reading of joint employment is more contemporary with the changing market and supportive of collective bargaining. Even more appropriate to economic reality as a test of joint employment would be an analysis of the power relationship of the end user, the direct employer, and the workers. A new test should find joint employment: (A) if the end user wants to substitute an "outside" workforce for; (B) a function the business would otherwise have to employ itself; in (C) a situation where the employees are economically or in their work conditions partially dependent on the financial influence of the end user; or (D) the worker is under the end user's ultimate supervision or control of employment status or relations, or a combination of some of these variables. Joint employment should be found for both bargaining and resolution of unfair labor practices. Perhaps a more attenuated additional variable of indirect approval or facilitation should be added for unfair labor practices liability.

Such a power-centered decisional test has a common sense connection to the right to "share or codetermine" employment relations.[78] Such a test is certainly not new or for-

---

73. *Greenhoot, Inc.*, 205 N.L.R.B. 250, 251 (1973).

74. *Shultz v. Falk*, 439 F.2d 340, 345 (4th Cir. 1971).

75. *Int'l Longshoremen's Ass'n v. Norfolk S. Corp.*, 927 F.2d 900, 903 (6th Cir. 1991).

76. *Clinton's Ditch Coop. Co.*, 274 N.L.R.B. 728 (1985), *cert. denied*, 479 U.S. 814 (1986).

77. *See* Kenneth G. Dau-Schmidt, "The Labor Market Transformed: Adapting Labor and Employment Law to the Rise of the Contingent Workforce," 52 *Wash. & Lee L. Rev.* 879, 880 (1995).

78. For a partial critique of a case-by-case approach, *see* Davidov, *supra* note 2, at 743.

eign to interpretations of the NLRA in its applicability to changing markets.[79] If either doctrinal approach were adopted, the NLRB would be the primary applier of the test, presumably with deferential *Chevron* review of the factual basis of the determination.[80]

In order to promote effective collective bargaining for such employees, ultimately a change in the NLRA is necessary.

Although admittedly politically very unlikely, a more market realistic unit for representing such workers would allow either party to choose mandatory, regionally sectoral bargaining, including joint bargaining with end users and contractors. A union might choose to bargain only with the labor contractor in order to create pattern settlements as is the present setting, but if either party insisted, end user or multi-site bargaining could take place. Such sectoral bargaining voluntarily occurs in retailing between employer councils and unions.[81] Adding end users would be more complicated but also has taken place voluntarily in other settings.[82]

III. The Parties' Positions and Economic Reality

By legal consciousness this Essay means simply the way the parties publicly portrayed legal power during the dispute.[83] The University administration maintained throughout that they were a "neutral" third party to the dispute between UNICCO and its workers. This public stance served two instrumental purposes. It allowed the administration not only to avoid liability for the unfair labor practices of UNICCO, but also to manage the visibility of the strike to others in the University by confining picketing to a remote special contractor's gate. Many actions beyond the gate decision — siding with management on the election position, unilaterally raising wages, disparaging strike supporters without evidence, etc. — raised substantial doubts about neutrality. However, relying on contractual formality allowed the administration to suggest that strike supporters were unwanted outsiders and downplayed the claim that the events were of significance to the University community and to the Miami low-wage working community. This strategy played upon class divisions and attempted to alienate potential solidarity with the workers. Strikingly, aside from a polemical web site, UNICCO itself was almost publicly invisible, as the workers and the University administration fought out the issues in the media.

The workers and the union sought from the beginning to characterize the strike as a civil rights and even a community event and they used the unfair labor practices characteristic of the strike to their direct legal advantage. This was partly meant to mobilize the workers who were almost entirely immigrants, mostly Latinos and Haitians, as part of a class-wide response to exploitation of such workers by many employers. Partly, the stance reflected the organizing strategy of the SEIU, working with groups of workers who are low wage and often employed by many small employers. The corporate organization of the service worker market through third-party contractors all but required the union to target many end users simultaneously to make the organizing economically effective and feasible. The aim was to organize the labor market in parallel to the contractor-employers.

---

79. *See, e.g., First Nat'l Maintenance Inc. v. NLRB*, 452 U.S. 666 (1981) (examining whether the power to decide issues of entrepreneurial control is subject to mandatory bargaining); *Fibreboard Prods. Corp. v. NLRB*, 379 U.S. 203 (1964).

80. *Chevron U.S.A., Inc. v. Nat'l Res. Def. Council*, 467 U.S. 837, 842–43 (1984).

81. *See, e.g., Emporium Capwell Co. v. W. Addition Cmty. Org.*, 420 U.S. 50 (1975).

82. *See, e.g., Greenhoot, Inc.*, 205 N.L.R.B. 250, 250 (1973); *Schultz v. Falk*, 439 F.2d 340, 345 (4th Cir. 1971).

83. Compare the more rigorous description of legal culture in essays such as, James L. Gibson & Gregory A. Caldeira, *The Legal Cultures of Europe*, 30 *L. & Soc'y Rev.* 55 (1996).

This strike was part of the initial organizing done under the banner of "Change to Win," and was part of a growing living wage movement nationwide. It also reflected the problems of working poverty levels in Miami and the increasingly detrimental impact of a labor market more dependent on third-parties to manage contracted service work for multiple end users. Such end-users are seeking to avoid publicity and save costs through low wage rates.

In terms of community orientation, the strikers from the beginning welcomed and were emotionally moved by student and faculty support on the campus. They saw the strike as against the University and the place that they worked, and they felt, by virtue of the University administration's public statements, that the University had the final say on an agreement. Furthermore, the largest meetings and demonstrations started on campus and moved to public settings where large numbers of pedestrians or vehicle traffic were visible. The parading through South Miami, the sitting-in at the intersection on U.S. 1, and the pamphleteering at the airport were all aimed at instigating a reaction from the South Florida community. Few demonstrations in recent Miami history have so clearly identified participants by class. Miami city commissioners, clergy, and media figures responded by calling on the University to end the strike. The action expanded to both public and private area universities, with workers supporting the other actions. Even workers at universities in other cities started organizing drives based on the living wage movement.

From the beginning, strikers spoke of the importance of the strike in terms of obtaining a voice in the workplace and securing fairness for individual worker treatment. A union was, for them, a mechanism of government for the workplace. It was a substantial miscalculation that the University administration thought a unilateral wage increase during the third week of the strike would lead workers to cross the picket line or end the strike. In fact, at that point the strike intensified.

Strikers began speaking more about the connection between low wage work and recent immigration of families to the U.S. Nationally known speakers addressed workers about low wage work, putting class issues before the public's notice. Most significantly, the strikers went on a hunger strike and built Freedom City adjacent to the University. By doing so, the workers bypassed traditional picketing of employer gates and created a visible presence in the community itself. Workers compared the power held by the University over their lives in response to the strike as a result of low wages as akin to imprisonment in Fidel Castro's jails for pro-democracy protests. They insisted that they came to the U.S. to avoid both economic and political oppression. Pressure was on the University to do something. The national publicity was not bothering UNICCO.

The hunger strike was definitely aimed at community support. Recognizing community backlash, the University felt it necessary to take out four full-page newspaper advertisements. This was the same week UNICCO and SEIU were agreeing to a settlement first proposed by the union at the sessions overseen by the University following the Administration building occupation.

Consciousness of the strike on the part of the University was driven by the doctrine of labor law. This could be seen in its claims of neutrality, support for elections, and restriction of picketing to a single gate. On the part of the strikers, it was driven by a larger vision of the connection of law or rule of law and political and economic power. The workers perceived their class position as created by power relations that were subject to the spirit of democracy in the economy, not just black letter doctrine. State and society were linked rather than separated. These conflicting visions doubtlessly protracted the strike. Direct negotiation between the union and UNICCO was overshadowed by the public antagonism of the workers and the University. The University was believed to be the real power behind the throne.

More importantly for class analysis, the workers' consciousness mapped well on the economic structure of the work—low wage immigrants doing service work which could be organized by labor contractors on behalf of and indirectly through contracts with end users. Consciousness mapped structure. The structure of the labor market also undoubtedly led to ethnic solidarity among immigrant groups that transferred to workforce mobilization.[84] Structure mapped consciousness.

---

84. *See* E.P. Thompson, *Whigs and Hunters: The Origin of the Black Act,* 258–69 (1975) (explaining that law, and therefore consciousness of which law is a part, both reflects and shapes social conditions).

XIX

Plant Occupation in a Corporate Campaign

Congressman Luis Guitierrez at Republic Windows and Doors, Copyright A.P., Brian Kelly.

Revolt on Goose Island:
The Chicago Factory Takeover and
What It Says about the Economic Crisis (2008)

*Kari Lydersen**

> *When it comes to the situation here in Chicago with the workers who are asking for the benefits and payments that they have earned, I think they are absolutely right.... What's happening to them is reflective of what's happening across this economy.*

> President-Elect Barack Obama

In early, December 2008, headlines around the world focused on the workers of the Republic Windows & Doors factory in Chicago, Illinois. There, 250 workers had been

* This chapter is a highly condensed version of the book, *Revolt on Goose Island: The Chicago Factory Takeover, and What it Says About the Economic Crisis*, (New York: Melville House, 2009). It is reprinted by permission of the publisher.

laid off after the abrupt shutdown of their factory. The closing wasn't unusual—it came in the midst of the largest economic collapse since the Great Depression, at a moment when every day brought news of more job losses. Just days before the closing, the U.S. Labor Department announced more than a half million job cuts.

But the company's workers did something unusual.

Represented by Local 1110 of the United Electrical, Radio, and Machine Workers of America labor union (UE), they occupied the factory, located on Goose Island in the Chicago River, and refused to leave until they were paid for accrued vacation time and 60 days of federally-mandated severance.

According to Reverend Jesse Jackson, the takeover represented "the beginning of a larger movement for mass action to resist economic violence."

Those involved point out that far from being a spontaneous act, it was the result of finely-tuned and tireless organizing and strategizing, by an independent union that has forged a path separate from most organized labor and with a workforce largely comprised of Latino immigrants. Most of the Republic employees had been there for 10 years or more. The most senior employee had 34 years at the plant. And almost three-quarters of them, had come to the United States from Mexico, leaving families and homes behind. Some might have paid thousands of dollars to "coyotes" to lead them across the border, may have walked for days through the stifling heat of the desert, trudging through a seemingly endless landscape of barren, rocky hills and deep arroyos where feet sunk into the soft crumbly dirt.

"Turn out all the lights right now," a supervisor at Republic Windows & Doors told Armando Robles as he was wrapping up the second shift at the factory on Goose Island, a small hive of industry sitting in the middle of the Chicago River. It was about 10 p.m. on November 5, 2008. Robles thought the order strange, as other employees were still finishing up. "Everyone has to leave right now," the supervisor said. For a while Robles and other workers had been suspicious about the health of the company and strange occurrences at the factory. They knew business had been bad for the past two years. The housing crash meant not many people were in the market for new windows and doors, neither Republic's higher-end ornate grooved, wood-framed glass panes nor their utilitarian vinyl- and aluminum-framed windows. At monthly "town hall meetings" that the company had started holding over the past year, managers were constantly bemoaning how much money they were losing. And the workforce had been nearly cut in half in the past few years, from about 500 to 250. Something seemed to be up, and Robles felt sure it wasn't good.

He alerted fellow worker Sergio Revuelta, a union steward with eight years at the company. The two left the building as if nothing was amiss, then huddled outside the plant. They watched as the plant manager and a former manager came out and looked around carefully. Five cars drove up. That was strange. "It was all faces and cars we recognized, former employees and former supervisors," said Revuelta later. Robles and Revuelta watched as the men began removing boxes and pieces of machinery from the low-slung, inconspicuous warehouse. They crept around to the back, where they saw a U-Haul truck waiting with its lights off. Over the next few hours, they watched a parade of objects being loaded into the truck. They were shivering by this time, as they had been sitting in Revuelta's car, and he had sold the car's ailing heater to a junkyard. The only illumination came from the light on a forklift. They stayed all night; it wasn't until almost 5 a.m. that they finally headed home to their families. "We knew something was going to happen, we wanted to watch and see if we were right," remembered Revuelta, 36. "When we saw the stuff coming out, I said, 'Bingo!'"

The news of the suspicious night quickly spread to other workers. Robles' friend Melvin "Ricky" Maclin later heard a similar story from a distraught secretary who said most of the office furniture had been removed. In the following days, Robles and other workers were ordered to load heavy machinery from the factory onto semi-truck trailers. Sometimes, they were first told to replace components on the machinery with new ones. They saw deliveries being unloaded at Republic that weren't intended for their plant. One time, a brand-new and mysterious piece of machinery was dropped off after a plant engineer's mother said it could not be stored in her garage, Robles remembers. The workers knew this equipment wasn't going to be used at Republic, so what was the company up to?

Union representatives started filing written requests for information; under their collective bargaining agreement with the company, the union had the right to be advised of major operating decisions or changes.

"I asked my supervisor, 'How can I work when I don't even know if you can pay me?'" said Rocio Perez, a single mother of five and union steward. She felt like the managers viewed them as gullible and naive since they expected them to keep working as the factory was obviously being dismantled under their noses. "It was like they were mocking us."

The workers organized a surveillance team that would keep watch outside the factory after hours and on weekends, when the plant was closed. One Saturday, Robles and Revuelta were lurking in the parking lot north of the factory, Robles with his wife Patricia and their young son Oscar in tow. They could see the plant's front entrance on Hickory Street, where boxes were being loaded onto two trailer trucks. They hopped into their cars: Revuelta drove out after the first trailer, and Robles followed the second one. He wasn't frightened or intimidated, only determined to see what the company was up to. The union's contract covers any activity within a 40-mile radius of the plant, and rumors were circulating that the equipment was being moved to Joliet, an industrial town exactly 40 miles outside Chicago.

The two men took note of the trucks' license plates and followed them for about 15 miles to a truckyard on the southwest side of the city, an industrial, grimy swath of land next to the highway. They parked just outside the yard and, keeping their eyes on the now-stationary trailers, Robles called international union representative Mark Meinster, a 35-year-old Philadelphia native who had been, an activist since high school.

Meinster asked Robles if they could hold tight for an hour. Robles wasn't planning to go anywhere.

They hit upon another idea, one with a long and glorious history in union lore: they could occupy the plant. Robles immediately liked the idea. In other countries, including his native Mexico, factory occupations are fairly common. But in the United States the tactic had not been used other than in a few scattered cases since organized labor's heyday in the 1930s, when auto workers brought the industry's top companies to their knees with sit-down strikes. Occupying the factory would likely mean that people would be arrested, Robles realized, and there was no guarantee it would work or even gain popular support.

Some workers were not citizens, on probation for minor criminal offenses, or had no one to take care of their children, so they couldn't risk it. But most everyone who heard about the idea was enthusiastic and vowed to be outside picketing if a takeover started. "I said, 'Let's do it!' We had to do something to get some respect," said Revuelta. "We don't know why some bosses just treat the workers like nothing, but we can't let them do that."

Meinster had never undertaken anything like this before, so he began to do his homework. This included logistics—how to get food into the plant, how to bail people out in case of arrests—and strategy: What would their demands be? Who would be their target?

In 1965, William Spielman formed Republic Windows & Doors, a small family business on the southwest side of Chicago making low-cost storm windows and doors. Spielman's business grew quickly, and he moved it to a larger location in Lincoln Park on the north side of the city, which was then a hardscrabble neighborhood home to many working-class Puerto Rican residents and with a smattering of heavy industry. Spielman's nephew Richard Gillman started working as a salesman for the company in 1974.[1] During the 1980s, the business expanded by leaps and bounds. For its first two decades the company had largely targeted home-improvement contractors, selling them relatively small orders of windows and doors specifically tailored to their residential projects. Many of these contractors were small, often family-run operations. Then, in the mid '80s, Republic began producing vinyl replacement windows and patio doors, expanding their market to include businesses, factories, and large apartment complexes and subdivisions across the region.[2]

Goose Island is the Chicago River's only island, a 160-acre chunk formed in 1853 by the building of a canal. Irish immigrants who moved onto the island coined its name. They raised livestock, farmed, and worked in small factories. Soon Polish and German immigrants joined them in worker housing built on the island. No bridge connected it to the mainland until after the Chicago Fire of 1871. By the late 1800s, the island was packed with heavy industry, including two grain elevators, 11 coal yards, many leather tanneries, various other factories ... and plenty of taverns. Chicago at this time was a commercial and industrial hub for the whole country, thanks to its position on Lake Michigan and at the crux of rail lines, and Goose Island was right in the heart of it all. It was called "Little Hell" for the billowing smoke and soot, and people began to move away from the island. Over time, so did much of the industry.[3] But history-obsessed Chicagoans remained fond of the island; the Goose Island brewpub located just north of the island spread its name to beer lovers around the country. In the 1980s, as professionals who had fled the city for the suburbs gravitated back to newly trendy lofts and apartments downtown, there was a debate over Goose Island's future. Some developers envisioned it hosting prime luxury riverfront housing, even though the sluggish river was still relatively polluted. But Mayor Richard M. Daley and other politicians wanted Goose Island to return to its industrial roots, and Daley instituted a plan in 1990 to further this goal, giving subsidies to industry and making it illegal within a certain zone to turn factories into housing.[4] Hence Republic and its neighboring factories were part of a larger municipal vision for revitalizing Chicago's legacy as the "city of big shoulders."

Goose Island itself is now home to various light manufacturing facilities and warehouses.

In 1996, the city committed almost $10 million to help Republic establish the new site and to grow. The money came out of tax increment financing (TIF) funds, a controversial program wherein an area is designated as "blighted" and then property taxes are diverted to fund development meant to revitalize the neighborhood.

---

1. Statement by Richard Gillman at bankruptcy creditors meeting, Jan. 18, 2009.
2. Slate.com "The Fray" chat room; posting by "Schmutzie," Dec. 8, 2008.
3. *Encyclopedia of Chicago History,* see www.encyclopedia.chicagohistory.org.
4. Martha Bayne, "Wheels of Industry," *The Chicago Reader,* June 29, 2001.

Republic's TIF funding came with the stipulation that the factory maintain 549 jobs for at least eight years and make "reasonable commercial efforts" to maintain more than 600 jobs until 2019.[5]

The new Goose Island facility was spacious, sterile, and state-of-the-art, with the latest in machinery, comfortable cafeterias and break rooms, even a gym. A building contractor who was a longtime customer was impressed during a tour of the factory. But he thought the company was in over its head. He said the quality of their products had declined after the move and he stopped buying from Republic in 2000. He felt that the needs of small contractors like himself were no longer a priority for the company, saying, "They wanted to sell semi-truck loads, not pickup-truck loads" to developers of subdivisions all over the Midwest.[6]

In May 2004 Republic began supplying windows to Pacesetter, an Omaha-based home improvement company that had recently closed its own window factory, laying off 70 union members. But by summer 2005 Republic cut off sales to Pacesetter, and later that year Pacesetter began bankruptcy proceedings. Republic lost $4 million in the debacle, which prompted Spielman to step aside and turn the company over to his cousin, Richard Gillman.[7] Gillman took majority ownership without paying a penny but rather by assuming a debt load of about $30 million.[8]

In early 2007, Dubin recruited JPMorgan Chase & Co. to take a 40-percent equity stake in the company as a flagship of its newly launched Chase Capital investment program for "alternative capital solutions to middle market companies."

In January 2007, Gillman also got a $5 million line of secured credit from Bank of America. Such a credit line is based on formulas determining the borrower's ability to repay, and it is backed by collateral and assets that will essentially revert to the lender if the borrower defaults.

This new investment seemed to mean a new beginning for the company. But any optimism about Republic's prospects soon turned out to be misplaced. In the summer of 2007, a mortgage crisis began to mushroom out of control, quickly infecting the whole housing market and the rest of the economy. But the downward spiral continued. The widespread practice of banks bundling mortgage-backed securities and selling them off to investors had exploded like a balloon. Banks panicked and clamped down on offering new credit, which of course put a big chill on consumer spending, housing rehabs, and construction, new businesses, and, in a domino effect, almost every market sector.

In this climate, it didn't take long for Republic to burn through its $5 million line of credit, according to Bank of America Mid-west government relations manager Pat Holden. The company lost the equivalent of the credit line, about $5 million, in 2007.[9] In February 2008, Bank of America, officials told Gillman that they were concerned about his company's situation and advised him to find new investors and lenders or consider shutting the business down.[10]

Holden emphasized that Republic's woes went beyond the expected effects of the housing crisis followed by the larger economic crisis. It was simply a badly run company, in

---

5. *City Council Journal of Proceedings,* pp. 27849–27928: Redevelopment Agreement enacted Sept. 11, 1996.

6. Slate.com "The Fray" chat room; posting by "Schmutzie," Dec. 8, 2008.

7. Steve Jordon, "Pacesetter windows were once among Omaha's best known products ..." *Omaha World-Herald,* Sept. 17, 2006.

8. Comment from Richard Gillman, in person, March 19, 2009.

9. Interview with Bank of America Midwest government relations manager Pat Holden, Jan. 14, 2009.

10. *Ibid.*

the view of bank officials, and financial troubles that had plagued it for years were only exacerbated by the housing collapse. Given the fact that Republic had lost almost $10 million in less than two years as of the summer of 2008, Holden said there was no way the bank could continue, to give them credit.

In October 2008, Bank of America was granted $25 billion in bailout funds as part of the $700 billion federal bailout, otherwise known as TARP, or the Troubled Assets Relief Program. The bank used the funds in part to acquire Merrill Lynch, the once mighty brokerage firm then facing collapse as part of the larger Wall Street meltdown. (In January, the U.S. Treasury would grant Bank of America an additional $20 billion in TARP funds to help with the rocky Merrill Lynch takeover.)

When Armando Robles started working at Republic, the workers were represented by a union called the Central States Joint Board (CSJB) that was well known in Chicago labor circles for ties to organized crime.

This was late 2003, about a year before the CSJB's union contract would expire. The UE launched its typical organizing drive, holding meetings to inform workers of their rights, providing stickers and flyers, and pointing out all the things the CSJB was not doing for them. Robles remembers that for the first time, CSJB union officials actually showed up and attempted to convince workers they were helping them. Most weren't buying it. Meanwhile, company officials launched an aggressive campaign against the UE. Advised by an anti-union law firm, they held public meetings decrying unions. Meinster said they displayed large photos of the workers leading the UE drive, and said, "If you join the union, this person will control your life for the next three years." He also felt company officials tried to pit Latino and Mexican American workers against each other, a common tactic in anti-union campaigns.

Republic managers utilized a typical carrot-and-stick approach to try to thwart the UE's efforts: along with intimidating key organizers and disparaging the UE, the company suddenly stocked the lunch room with Xbox video games and ping pong tables, built a basketball court outside, and even hosted cookouts for the workers. Robles' said company officials begged the workers to give them a year to prove that workers could be happy without a union. They referred to the workers' well-known disillusionment with the CSJB and insinuated all unions were the same. Robles was afraid that many workers were buying the company's spiel, so he went into overdrive, talking to co-workers about the merits of the UE. He held meetings for the second-shift workers, often at St. Pius Church and the Casa Aztlan community center in Pilsen, the heart of the city's Latino activist scene, where many workers lived. He cornered co-workers for one-on-one talks in the cafeteria. Every week he handed out flyers. Getting a crash course in workers rights, he was surprised and elated to learn they had the right to wear pro-union stickers and buttons and pass out literature on the job.

When the vote came around on November 10, 2004, the UE won by a landslide. The UE got 340 votes, the organizers remember; the CSJB got 8 or 9, and just over 100 workers voted for no union. UE Local 1110 was born.

Negotiations for a new contract began immediately. The UE drove a hard bargain, and it paid off. They obtained a nearly unheard-of average $3-an-hour raise over the course of three years, with $1.75 in the first year. They overhauled a subpar bonus system. And they won the right to have 19 union stewards on the shop floor, compared to five before.[11] This meant more power for the union and more ability to file and win grievances.

---

11. Interviews with UE organizers.

In contrast to the CSJB, which, was run by officials who most union members never saw, the UE Local 1110 leadership was elected from among the workers themselves, who continued to work on the shop floor. For the first time, workers began to feel like they were equals to their supervisors. Robles was thrilled. When co-workers would come to him asking if the union could help them, he would say, "You are the union, I am the union, we are the union."

Melvin Maclin, by contrast, was not initially glad to be part of the UE. But then he saw UE representative Leah Fried at work. Fried, a 36-year-old with fiery brown eyes and Betty Page bangs, had grown up learning about labor history from her own family. She grew up in Rogers Park, an eclectic lakeside neighborhood on Chicago's far north side known as a haven for activists and rabble-rousers. The nation's oldest labor press, Charles H. Kerr & Co., founded in 1886, is run out of a cluttered, sagging Rogers Park three-flat. Fried's father was the editor of his local union newsletter (AFSCME Council 31, which represents government employees from teachers to prison guards), and her mother helped organize a union at a large non-profit Organization that serves refugees and immigrants. Before joining the UE 11 years earlier, Fried had worked a smorgasbord of jobs including truck driver, farm laborer, temporary office worker, social-service agency case manager, and community organizer. She married into a family of Guatemalan labor and human-rights activists, and her husband is a prominent organizer of workers centers nationwide. They would spend long nights debating and arguing about labor history and strategy. So when the idea for the occupation was hatched, Fried was ready. "She was on fire. The company hated her, which made us love her more," Maclin said. "I've always been a fighter. So I listened to Leah."

The UE was formed in 1936 at a conference in Buffalo, New York, attended by independent local unions and non-unionized workers in radio and electrical manufacturing who had come together seeking to form a larger, progressive organization. They asked the American Federation of Labor (AFL) to recognize them, but the AFL turned them down. So the UE became the first union chartered by the newly-formed CIO.[12]

The CIO often reached out to black workers, seeing this partly as a way to increase their ranks while the AFL generally backed white (including ethnic Irish and Italian) workers who were terrified and irate at the prospect of competing with blacks for jobs.

Given the breadth of the deindustrialization, some Chicagoans are now surprised to see factories like Republic remain, inconspicuously, in their midst.

And it is these small prizes that the UE has focused on, allowing the union to grow modestly during the 1990s, adding relatively small groups of workers here and there for a slow but steady gain in overall membership.

At this writing, the UE represents about 35,000 workers nationwide in private- and public-sector jobs, including a continued high concentration in manufacturing and specifically electrical manufacturing, metalworking, and plastics. Hence their base is still the type of manual labor that built strong unions of the past, and it continues to be an important though shrinking sector of the American workforce. The union's website says, "UE members work as plastic injection molders, tool and die makers, sheet metal workers, truck drivers, warehouse workers and custodians. We build locomotives, repair aircraft engines, assemble circuit boards, manufacture metal cabinets, produce industrial scales and make machine tools."

Like most unions, the UE has also branched out to workplaces beyond their traditional jurisdictions, and represents teachers, speech pathologists, nurses, clerical workers, graduate instructors, librarians, day-care workers, and even scientists.

---

12. UE website: www.ranknfile-ue.org/uewho5.html.

In many cases these members chose to organize with the UE because of its progressive and independent nature, which makes it a good fit for workers who feel they don't fit into the traditional unions or who want their union to be part of a larger social movement.

As Andrew Dinkelaker, president of the UE eastern region, which covers the GE factories, notes:

> Most union's are top down—you have union bosses who can nix it if workers want to do a strike. The UE is set up democratically, so if its membership is interested and willing to take on a fight, the whole organization backs them and consults about the best way to achieve victory. It's not seen as the workers needing approval from the national organization. You hear these reports at other workplaces of members wanting to do something revolutionary but leadership stopping them. That's not the case within our organizational structure. We don't have union bosses who have the power to stop the workers. We try to figure out, if there's motivation to fight, how do we become successful rather than telling them no.

It was also one of the first unions to embrace undocumented immigrant workers, who in decades past faced (and still face to some extent) outright hostility from organized labor who saw them as "stealing jobs" and as potential scabs. Furthering the relationship with Latino workers, the UE has a strategic partnership with Mexico's independent FAT *(Frente Autentico del Trabajo)*, or Authentic Labor Front.

In tough economic times, xenophobia historically rears its head and right-wing groups play on public fear and insecurity to stoke hatred of immigrants, who some see as taking jobs. But the truth is that immigrants are a huge and inextricable part of the U.S. labor force, so unions have stepped up organizing efforts of immigrant worksites, and also have realized it is in their interest to support struggles of workers' centers and other non-union groups of immigrant workers.

But the UE has found a particular niche with smaller immigrant workplaces, especially light manufacturing like Republic, largely because of their close ties with immigrants' rights activism. Another of UE's major campaigns in Chicago was winning the right to represent workers at the Azteca tortilla factory in Pilsen, the heart of the city's Mexican community.

In late November, there was some interesting news in the Midwestern window and door industry. Someone had purchased a window and door factory called TRACO (for Three Rivers Aluminum Company) in Red Oak, Iowa, a town of 6,200 in the southwest corner of the state, 50 miles from Omaha. The new owner was Echo Windows & Doors LLC, a company incorporated in Illinois on November 18, by Sharon Gillman, the wife of Republic owner Richard Gillman.

Now it seemed clear where the machinery mysteriously leaving the Republic factory was headed. This development added insult to injury for the UE workers. Not only was the company apparently shutting down without giving them the benefit of an explanation; it appeared that the assets were being spirited away to continue business as usual somewhere else, and somewhere without a union.

On Tuesday, December 2, plant operations manager Tim Widner called Republic workers to a meeting in the cafeteria. He gave them the news that most had been expecting to hear for some weeks now: the plant was closing, and in just three days. They would not get severance pay, nor pay for their accrued vacation time. Many workers had deferred vacations specifically at managers' request, since fall is a busy season in the window industry. In all, the company owed almost $150,000 in vacation pay, with as much as $6,000 due some individual workers.[13] Widner blamed the closure on Bank of America "cutting off credit" to the company, and then made a quick getaway, telling workers they'd get their final paychecks on Friday, December 5, and would have health insurance through December 15.

Many of the workers headed directly over to the UE hall about two miles away to decide how to proceed. Their anger and anxiety over the prospect of losing their jobs—in such a harsh economy and so close to Christmas—was tempered by a rising sense of determination and excitement about what they were about to do. Workers were angry that owner Richard Gillman had not even ventured down from his office to break the news himself.

The workers had been planning for a month to occupy the factory; now was the time to act on that plan. Maclin decided he would be part of it. It wasn't a decision he made lightly. As a young man he had made some bad choices and ended up in jail, an experience he never wanted to repeat. Now he was consciously making a move that could put him back behind bars. It wasn't easy convincing himself, and convincing his wife was even harder. "She thought I had lost my mind!" he said later. With six adult children and 16 young grandchildren looking forward to the holidays, Maclin felt like his family was on the line. "If we fight and lose, at least we'll know we fought," he told his wife. "It's about our dignity." By the end of the meeting, at least 30 other workers agreed with Maclin and promised to physically occupy the factory. Almost everyone else was ready to picket outside.

As soon as the meeting finished, union organizers began to strategically get word out to their allies and trusted advisers. C.J. Hawking, a minister connected to Interfaith Worker Justice, was one of the first to hear. Interfaith Worker Justice has a long history of tapping ministers, rabbis, imams and other spiritual leaders to persuade or shame the powers that-be into doing the right thing. Hawking and solidarity organizers got on the phones and pulled together a rally and prayer vigil outside Bank of America's headquarters for the very next day. This would be the public launch of the strategy that had been germinating behind closed doors: they had been told Bank of America was to blame for the factory closing, so they would take their demands not to Gillman, but to the bank.

Meanwhile, UE western region president Carl Rosen was also busy spreading the news. He and U.S. Congressman Luis Gutierrez had been friends and fellow activists since the days of Harold Washington, Chicago's first African American mayor, whose 1983 election not only broke racial barriers but also was a historical upset of Chicago's Democratic machine. Since then Gutierrez's and Rosen's paths had crossed often in various movements and struggles. Since 1992, Gutierrez has represented the horseshoe-shaped congressional district that encompasses both Pilsen, the city's most prominent Mexican neighborhood, and Humboldt Park, the heart of the Puerto Rican community. Gutierrez, who is Puerto Rican, is well known for his advocacy for immigrants' rights and not afraid to take a stand.

Rosen also called another longtime ally and fellow activist, Chicago city councilman Ric Munoz, who represents the Little Village neighborhood, a vibrant southwest-side barrio of recent immigrants. Little Village's main drag, 26th Street, could easily be mistaken for a street in Mexico. Mariachis stroll from restaurant to restaurant, *norteño* music blares

---

13. Schedules filed in bankruptcy case 08-34113, Dec. 12, 2008, U.S. Bankruptcy Court for the Northern District of Illinois.

out of small record stores; vendors sell corn on the cob and pork skins from pushcarts, and at night men dressed to the nines cruise the streets in big cars as gang members throw menacing gestures at each other from the corners. Munoz grew up in this neighborhood and knows well the struggles and spirit of hardworking Mexican immigrants.

On Wednesday, December 3, after the first shift, the union bussed Republic workers downtown to the rally outside Bank of America's headquarters.

Rosen, Gutierrez, Muñoz, and a few other allies spent Wednesday strategizing and researching. As the workers were planning their occupation, they were trying to determine what laws might have been broken by closing the factory and what political pressure points might be probed. They gave themselves a crash course in the Worker Adjustment and Retraining Notification Act (WARN).

During the waves of plant closings in the 1980s, unions, even in their weakened state, demanded laws preventing or regulating plant closings. The WARN Act was passed in this period as something of a compromise, backed by Republicans and Southern Democrats who wanted Northern and Midwestern plants to be able to close and send the jobs south.[14] The law basically says when an employer with more than 100 employees is going to close or make significant layoffs, the employer must give the workers 60 days' notice.[15] Theoretically, government agencies or other parties would also step in to offer retraining—the R part of WARN—for the employees, though labor experts say this rarely happens. If the employees are not given 60 days' notice, they are owed up to 60 days' severance pay. But there are exceptions to the law, including for unforeseeable business occurrences, natural disasters, or a "faltering company."

Another exception to the law allows the employer to avoid giving notice if an announcement would hurt the business, with lenders or customers fleeing a sinking ship. (This would apply mainly in the case of mass layoffs, when the business doesn't actually plan to close). If an employer claims this exception, workers must prove that the business was already doomed or that customers would have been lost regardless of the WARN Act notice. The Act also offers employers a "Get out of jail free" card, as one attorney described it, if they claim they tried in good faith to comply with the act and somehow were prevented from doing so. The law is often described by labor lawyers as toothless, since employers who break it face only minimal punitive damages of up to $500 a day until workers are paid.[16] The law is routinely broken, and employers often get away with violations without facing legal action. Any litigation is likely to be lengthy and financially draining for the workers, ending with at most a slap on the wrist, for employers.

Problematic as the WARN Act might be, Gutierrez, Rosen, and the local union leaders seized on the law as an important part of their strategy. They said that Republic had clearly violated the WARN Act, though in court Republic could easily have claimed it was a "faltering company" and probably would have invoked "unforeseeable business circumstances." In keeping with their larger strategy, Gutierrez and Rosen would connect Bank of America with the WARN Act violation. Gillman himself was doing as much. He had already told union leaders that he asked Bank of America to authorize him to give the employees WARN Act notice, and, he said, bank officials said no.[17] In a statement to the media, he said he asked Bank of America in October for permission to begin WARN Act compliance,

---

14. Stephen Franklin, *Three Strikes: Labor's Heartland Losses and What They Mean for Working Americans.* (Guilford Press, 2002).

15. U.S. Department of Labor fact sheet: www.doleta.gov/programs/factsht/warn.htm.

16. *Ibid.*

17. Interview with UE international rep Mark Meinster, Feb. 2009.

and was denied.[18] Bank of America's Pat Holden later said no such conversation ever took place, and she stressed that the bank had neither authority nor obligation to "authorize" any of the company's actions or in any way tell the company what to do.[19]

While two years ago citizens might have scorned an action that seemed to violate a company's rights or the sanctity of private property, now many were disgusted with corporations and banks and longing for an underdog willing to stand up to them. A factory takeover would be just the thing.

The UE members frequently invoked the UAW sit-down strikes in relation to their occupation. But in reality the parallel was a stretch, and the UE workers actually had a much bigger challenge ahead of them. The UAW strikes were not related to plant closings, but rather were militant strikes demanding better wages, security, benefits, and the right to unionize.[20] Ford, General Motors, Chrysler, Bendix, and the other auto plants needed to keep their production lines running in the 1930s; feeding the market and reeling in their profits depended upon it. The same was true for the 1989 Pittston mine strike in Virginia, where union miners and supporters essentially took over and prevented scabs from working by blocking company coal trucks and mine entrances.[21]

The miners and auto workers exerted great leverage by taking over the mines or plants and withholding their labor. But at Republic, the owner and creditors did not want the workers to work, and they had no immediate use for the factory or machinery (except in the Iowa facility). The Republic situation actually had more in common with the famous factory takeovers in Argentina following the country's 2001 economic collapse. Tens of thousands of workers took over idle factories that had made everything from auto parts to leather to chocolate and ran the companies themselves, raising money to fix broken equipment and finding eager customers in a country enamored of populist struggle.[22]

So the Republic workers' factory occupation would only really have leverage in relation to their taking temporary possession of the assets in the building—the finished windows and doors and raw materials stacked there, and the machinery that had not yet been removed. More importantly than this leverage, though, they would have the power of spectacle and opinion.

In a sense, they would be running what is known as a "corporate campaign," a specific strategy that became popular in the 1980s as unions got increasingly desperate and when the traditional methods like strikes and work slowdowns either weren't working or top union bureaucrats were unwilling to deploy them. During a corporate campaign, an employer is targeted on multiple fronts through its board of directors, shareholders, customers, and contractors. The corporate campaign brings the labor struggle into the community, with the union courting public support and pressuring the employer through its public image and consumer base.

Company officials had told the workers to report at 9 a.m. on Friday, December 2, three hours after their normal start time. Gillman and other executives met with union leaders at 8 a.m. The union had urged workers not to have any contact with management until after they had a chance to huddle with the union. The company had the workers'

---

18. Republic statement to media, Dec. 10, 2008.

19. Interview with Pat Holden, January 14, 2009.

20. Henry Kraus; *Heroes of Unwritten Story: The UAW, 1934–39.* (University of Illinois Press. 1993).

21. Eric Arnesen, *Encyclopedia of US Labor and Working Class History.* 1090 (CRC Press, 2006).

22. Sources including *The Take,* documentary film by Avi Lewis and Naomi Klein, 2004; and "Here's the chocolate factory; but where has Willy Wonka gone?" by Rory Carroll. *Guardian,* 2007.

paychecks ready, but they also had more bad news: health benefits, which they had said would last until December 15, had actually already been cut off, not even giving workers a chance to squeeze in a last doctor's visit.

When Robles, Meinster, Fried, and the other union leaders met with the full workforce, they quickly called for a vote on whether to enact their plan: the factory occupation. Hands shot up enthusiastically and people cheered and shouted "Si se puede." It was unanimous. Young Republic COO Barry Dubin was given the task of handing out personalized folders to workers: each folder contained a letter of recommendation, information on unemployment benefits, and a few inconsequential pieces of paper; a painful parting gift after years of service.

By late afternoon, Congressman Gutierrez and the union members had returned from the meeting at the bank, made fruitless by the company's absence. Now came the moment of truth. The handful of Republic supervisors who were in the office Friday had told the workers they had to be out by 5 p.m. Would they disobey these orders and push on to a full-blown factory occupation? They took the final vote. Again, it was unanimous, and the cheers and chants were even louder than before. While previously about 30 people had vowed to occupy the plant, suddenly everyone wanted to do it, arrest risk be damned.

Journalists swarmed around Congressman Gutierrez as he exited the factory that Friday evening. One called out to ask whether the occupation was illegal. After all, the workers were camped out on private property without the permission of the owner. Gutierrez didn't miss a beat. He shot back that the workers had ownership of the assets as the fruits of their labor. "It takes two things to make that window—parts and labor," he explained later. "To the extent the labor hasn't been paid for, those windows belong to the workers. If a plumber fixes my toilet and I don't pay him" he can take out a lien. The workers don't trust the courts, so their lien is their bodies."

The workers swung into action, forming committees and making plans. Their occupation would be a strictly nonviolent and orderly one, aimed at protecting the assets that they viewed as their own, as Gutierrez had explained. They decided that only 30 to 40 workers would actually be inside the factory at any given time, and they would rotate in and out in shifts. Only workers and union staff and some family members would be allowed on the shop floor. Keeping the place safe and tidy was important to both their public image and their hopes of reopening the plant. Several workers posted themselves as guards at the doors between the shop floor and the lobby, holding back eager reporters and activists trying to finagle a peek inside. One reporter convinced Robles' young son Oscar to take her camera inside and snap photos. "She brainwashed my son!" joked Robles' wife, Patricia. The workers organized teams to do everything from cleaning the bathrooms to providing security to shoveling snow.[23]

"People were just excited to be doing what it took," remembers Meinster. "They had been working there for decades, and to be thrown out in the cold without a job right before Christmas, it was a slap in the face. We couldn't have gotten people out of there if we'd wanted to."

That evening, factory managers did call the police demanding that the workers be forcibly removed. But the union was one step ahead. City Councilman Munoz had called his friend Scott Waguespack, the city councilman representing Goose Island and the surrounding area. Waguespack, formerly a Peace Corps volunteer in Kenya, had been re-

---

23. Interviews with UE workers, including Armando Robles and Melvin Maclin.

cently elected with a platform of revitalizing local industry. At Munoz' urging he had called the local police commander that morning to give him a heads-up, and to explain that this was a labor-management dispute in which the police should not intervene. Waguespack said the local beat cops, union members themselves, were happy to comply.

One of Mead-Lucero's first calls was to minister C.J. Hawking at a gala for the Illinois Labor History Society, titled appropriately "New Deal for Workers: Past, Present, Future." She jumped up to the microphone; she couldn't have asked for a more enthusiastic audience. "You have a room full of labor historians, and labor history is being made," she remembers. "There was a collective gasp of excitement."

Mead-Lucero also called his wife, Claudia, an organizer in the immigrants' rights movement, to get the word out to the Mexican hometown federations, the social and political clubs in Chicago and other U.S. cities that represent people from certain towns or states in Mexico. Then he rushed over to meet Claudia at a benefit dinner for the Latino Union grassroots organization, which was taking place on the second-floor ballroom of a bedraggled but grand old building on the city's northwest side. As a Mexican band was setting up for a dance later that night, he and Claudia climbed onto the stage, to break the news about the factory occupation. A ripple of bewilderment and excitement spread through the room.

On Saturday, December 6, a hastily organized support rally attracted several hundred people. Donations of food, blankets, pillows, sleeping bags, and other necessities poured into the factory. Over the weekend, Congressman Gutierrez returned to the factory several times, watching the occupation blossom into an international news story. He got a lot of media time, so people called him with updates and tips. He felt like a reporter breaking a big story. Though he declined to give names or details, he later said that various people approached him with documents that shed light on the Republic situation. One of these documents, he said, was a report from an independent financial consultant present at an October meeting at which Bank of America representatives and Gillman discussed options for liquidating the company. Several possible scenarios were proposed, Gutierrez said, and one of the items on the agenda was whether or how to comply with the WARN Act. This revelation irked the congressman. He recognized that Bank of America did not have a legal responsibility to make sure Gillman complied with the WARN Act, but he was angered by the fact that the bank was aware of the impending liquidation and the WARN Act and didn't somehow push Gillman to comply. At that, point, Gutierrez noted, WARN Act compliance would have been as simple as notifying the workers that the factory was closing, so they would have 60 days to find another job. The Act doesn't explicitly mandate severance pay; only 60 days' notice—or severance pay if notice is not given. And of course Gutierrez was well aware that Bank of America had just received $25 billion in TARP bailout funds, the specifics of which were publicly hammered out in Congress. He explained:

> While not sanctioned in law, certainly from a public opinion standpoint and a corporate citizen point of view Bank of America had not fulfilled its responsibility to the workers. And then with the bailout, those workers and all Americans became shareholders in Bank of America. While I understand they didn't have a legal responsibility, the issue of the WARN Act was raised and they didn't do anything about it. If you are taking the public's money, you should do a better job.

Gutierrez was a member of the House Financial Services Committee in Congress, and he had no qualms about throwing this weight around. He called committee chair Barney

Frank (D-Mass.) asking for advice and staff resources, and, he says he threatened to sub-poena various witnesses and documents regarding that October meeting and other financial dealings if bank officials did not cooperate. And Gutierrez was far from the only politician or public figure taking an interest in Republic. A labor expert from the Illinois Attorney General's office kept tabs on the situation over the weekend and reported back to his boss, Attorney General Lisa Madigan, who said she was eager to help the workers. On Sunday, she launched an investigation into whether Republic had broken state laws in regard to its workers or customers with unfilled orders. Her staff soon realized workers had not been paid for their last week of work, and it was unclear whether the company planned to pay them. "It looked like Gillman was going to worm out of it," said UE organizer Meinster. This could have been a serious and possibly criminal matter which the attorney general's office was investigating, though it became a moot point later when Gillman agreed to spend $117,000 of his own money to pay the workers.[24]

Then they got an endorsement that made all the others pale.

A TV in the factory cafeteria where the workers were gathered was tuned to a press conference given Sunday afternoon by President-Elect Barack Obama. A reporter asked Obama what he thought of the factory occupation. "When it comes to the situation here in Chicago with the workers who are asking for the benefits and payments that they have earned, I think they're absolutely right," he said. "These workers, if they have earned these benefits and their pay, these companies need to follow through on their commitments."

A wild cheer went up. Robles thinks Obama's support was a turning point. During Friday's meeting, he had felt that Bank of America representatives and other powerful people "treated us like we were nobody, like we were stupid, like we stink." By Monday, it was a different story. The most respected man in the world had spoken up for them, and now Robles felt like the people in suits and high-rise office buildings saw them in a new light.

Governor Blagojevich teased Munoz for losing $100 on an Oscar de la Hoya boxing match. Then he called boldly upon state agencies to stop any business with Bank of America until it "gave back" some of the bailout money to the Republic workers. The crowd cheered and erupted in chants of "Save more jobs" and *"Si se puede."*

City councilman Joe Moore, a longtime progressive and antiwar activist from the north-side neighborhood of Rogers Park, matched Blagojevich and raised him one. He promised to introduce a city council ordinance not only ending city business with Bank of America, but also denying zoning changes requested for any Bank of America or subsidiary branch and preventing the bank from selling city bonds. Moore described the bailout funds as "money that was intended to" jump-start the credit system and increase the number of loans to companies like Republic. But Bank of America, like other banks, is using that money not to increase loans but buy other assets.

Meanwhile that same day county commissioner Mike Quigley, who would later be elected to the U.S. Congress in a special election to fill the seat vacated by Obama's new chief of staff Rahm Emanuel, also promised to cut off county business with Bank of America until they did right by the Republic workers.

Meanwhile, as the sun set Monday evening and a frigid slushy rain began to fall, a semi-truck pulled up outside the factory and disgorged bags of food, an effort Gutierrez had coordinated. He considered his donation more appropriate than the turkeys brought

---

24. Interviews with a representative of Illinois Attorney General Lisa Madigan and with UE organizer Mark Meinster.

by Reverend Jackson. "You need something you can freeze, turkeys are too big," he noted. "And these are mostly Latinos, they don't eat a lot of turkeys. I got together chicken, rice, beans, tortillas, tomatoes, onions, the things in my refrigerator."

As fires blazed out of several trash drums, workers and supporters formed a line to throw the bags of food hand to hand from the truck up the sidewalk through the crowd into the factory, a lively exercise accompanied by much chanting and cheering. The workers' moods were balanced on a precipice between elated at the attention and grim, given the harsh reality they could be facing. Worker Apolinar Cabrera was surprisingly upbeat and hopeful, given his family's situation. His wife was pregnant, due sometime around Christmas day. Now they could be without health insurance, not to mention money for Christmas dinner and gifts for their children.

Friends William Lane and Donte Watson had thought they would spend their lives working at the company and retire from it. They had been reading and hearing about layoffs around the country but always felt that their jobs were safe. After all, people will always need replacement windows. Watson, wearing a brown White Sox ball cap and puny coat with a furry collar, was not very involved in the union and rarely went to· meetings; he said he'd been shocked when they got the news. He depended on his wages to support his six-year-old son. "My son knew there was a problem when I wasn't going to work in the morning," says Watson, 30. "It was hard to tell him, I had to break it down for him in a way he could understand."

Lane, 33, said his 11-year-old daughter didn't understand what was going on. "She's still asking for money and talking about Christmas," he said. "I had to say there will be no Christmas. We are truly shocked and scared. With this economic crisis there is nowhere to turn. I have extensive bills, a car note that I can't pay now, all the daily expenses. If they don't do the right thing I don't know what I'll do."

Watson felt betrayed by the company because he was proud of all the effort he had put into this job for eight years. He was angry that the company had closed with orders still to fill, because he didn't want customers to be let down. "People put their blood, sweat and tears into this company, it was our company too, not just the owners," he said. "They knew this was coming and they didn't say a word to us. They owed us more respect than that. We don't want anything extra, we just want what we are owed."

Forty-one-year-old Dagoberto Cervantes ruefully noted that a solution must be reached soon, or never. He was encouraged and elated by all the public support and media attention, but he worried it would fade as the holidays approached. "It's now or never," he said in Spanish, grabbing the jacket hood of his five-year-old son, who was hopping precariously around on a small brick wall holding a picket sign. *Es muy feo* — "it's very ugly," — said his son in a sweet little voice. Cervantes also has a 13-year-old daughter and was worried he wouldn't be able to get another job to support them if Republic remained closed. "We need money to pay the rent, to support our kids, all the things you need to survive," he said. "With this economic crisis and unemployment, there are no other jobs."

That's also how Jose Ornelas felt. An immigrant from Jalisco, Ornelas, 47, said his kids and wife were proud of him for taking part in the sit-in; though when his daughter first heard about the situation on the news, she thought her father had been kidnapped. "It's bad," he said. "A lot of companies are laying off—I don't know where we will get other work." He had only worked at one other factory in the United States in his three decades here, and that was only for two months.

"I hope we get some justice," said Ron Bender, a 55-year-old worker with 14 years at the plant and a laid-back, nonchalant attitude despite the drama around him. He hadn't seen anything like this since the protests of the 1960s and '70s that had defined his youth. "We have worldwide support, workers have been stepped on for so long ... maybe this will set a precedent that corporate America can't just take advantage of regular people."

Elisa Romo, 46, was nervous about speaking to reporters but wanted to get the story out. Wearing fragrant perfume and a warm, shy smile, she described how her son in the Army was so proud of his mother taking part in this struggle. She is a single mother of four sons, though only one, age eight, still lives at home. "They all studied and went to college, so they'll have a better life than me," she said proudly of her older sons. Her eight-year-old spent two nights at the sit-in with her, telling press, "I'm here to help my mom." She felt like she was fighting for him. "They give all this money to banks, but they won't help the regular people," added Romo, her shyness giving way to anger. We don't want anything that isn't ours, we just want what's owed us."

As the crowd dispersed, the exhausted workers staying for the "night shift" retreated onto the shop floor, followed by a priest carrying purple vestments and a plastic container of communion wafers for an impromptu mass. Officials at Bank of America still seemed blindsided by the whole situation. They avoided talking to media, just putting out a terse written statement saying that the bank had no role in telling the company how to run its business. "The bottom line is that TARP or no TARP, we have to remain firm in prudent stewardship of our resources," said Bank of America spokesperson Julie Westermann later. "Our shareholders, which now include taxpayers (thanks to the bailout), would not be served by throwing money at a company that can't repay the loan."

Meanwhile, over at Republic, the workers who had cheered Blagojevich less than 24 hours earlier heard news of his arrest but had more immediate things to worry about. The day started badly, as police had towed all the cars along Hickory Street in front of the factory. An officer told the union it was to make room for media vans, but the union suspected that wasn't the real story. There was hardly a reporter in sight anyway, since Blagojevich's arrest was making headlines worldwide. Workers noticed people they didn't recognize lurking around; they didn't like the looks of it. With people getting exhausted and increasingly nervous about the outcome of that day's negotiations and the actions of police, it was shaping up to be a rough day. The union sent out e-mails and text messages asking supporters to come out in force, and luckily many answered the call. That helped lift flagging spirits.

At 1 p.m., negotiators gathered again around a large table in a Bank of America conference room: politicians and government agency reps, Bank of America officials, the union leaders, Gillman, and a slew of lawyers. Robles remembers it as a big marble table, with at least 40 chairs. The talks were freewheeling and by turns conciliatory and contentious.

Maclin got the distinct impression that Bank of America officials were not so much concerned about the money being demanded of them as they were by the precedent-setting potential of the whole situation. "It's like they thought if we are fighting back and we win, then everyone will want to fight back," he said. "You could read that on their faces and hear it in their little, comments. They were trying to make it sound like this was all *our* fault, complaining about how much money they had lost."

Gillman was already not the most popular person in the room, needless to say. But that afternoon he managed to turn the crowd even more steadfastly against him. According to various participants, he asked Bank of America that any new loan include severance pay for himself ... and funds to pay the leases on two luxury cars.

By this time, JP Morgan Chase's 40-percent equity in the company had come to light. Gutierrez said he had received an unsolicited call from Bill Daley, JP Morgan Chase's director of social responsibility, offering to come to the table. (The attorney general's office indicated that calls from both their office and Gutierrez summoned Chase to the negotiations). Daley is also the brother of Mayor Richard M. Daley, a nemesis-turned-ally of Gutierrez'. Bill Daley was a special counsel on trade issues and later commerce secretary under President Clinton and a member of Obama's transition team—just one more high-profile and powerful supporting actor in the factory occupation drama.

Things were moving forward. The Bank of America officials agreed they would indeed extend a loan to cover the money due the workers. Though it was called a loan, it would be essentially a donation, since there was little hope it would ever be paid back.

The union was adamant about giving the workers the chance to approve any offer. "During the meetings they kept asking us if we would accept different things," said Fried. "They were having trouble understanding we had to bring every decision back to the workers. That's how we operate."

Patricia Robles and the couple's five kids were sitting in their kitchen wrapped in blankets and snacking that night, watching TV for news of the occupation, as they had been almost every minute they weren't actually at the factory. "We would eat and watch, eat some more," remembers Robles. A reporter announced the settlement. The family looked at each other in confusion and dawning giddiness, but Robles knew it couldn't be true, since she knew the workers would have had to approve a settlement and that Armando would have called her. They finally went to bed knowing another day of the occupation was still ahead of them.

But if President-Elect Obama happened to look out the window of his office on Wednesday, December 10, he would have gotten a reminder. Nearly 1,000 people were marching in circles around the Bank of America building, with the march passing right in front of the federal building, past the Secret Service, police, and journalists. A plethora of picket signs, hand-painted fabric banners, homemade posters, and flags waved and bounced happily above the throng. There were an abundance of rainbow flags; a gay-rights march protesting the passage of anti-gay-marriage Proposition 8 in California had merged into the Republic rally. Anarchists with bandannas tight over their faces waved black-and-red flags; union members jabbed the air with their respective placards, and affiliates of Interfaith Worker Justice carried signs invoking spirituality and fairness. "They got bailed out, we got sold out!" shouted the crowd. In San Francisco, New York and numerous other cities nationwide, people were also picketing outside Bank of America branches in protests organized by Jobs with Justice. In Little Village, Chicago's heavily Mexican neighborhood where many workers lived, people picketed at a storefront Bank of America branch.

As Robles, Maclin, and the other union reps arrived downtown for the meeting, they could hear the protest chants from three blocks away. The meeting started at 1 p.m. and dragged on for hours. Finally, in the evening, a proposal was put together combining a $1.35 million loan from Bank of America and $400,000 from Chase. "I've never seen a bank lend $1.3 million when they know they won't get it back," marveled Congressman Gutierrez. "And JP Morgan Chase gave the four hundred thousand knowing they'd be second in line to Bank of America as creditors, meaning they would never see the money. But we got them to lend it. It was uncharted territory, it was a wonderful thing."

The workers were thrilled to be getting their pay and to have won such a victory. But it wasn't all they had hoped for. Was there still a way to keep the plant open? What about all the work they had put into keeping the company alive for so many years—was that all reduced to 60 days' severance and vacation pay? As part of the agreement, Bank of America had demanded that the company file for Chapter 7 bankruptcy, a process that entails liquidation. This could greatly complicate a bid to keep the place open. All things considered, the workers decided to accept the offer but to continue their fight to keep the plant running. They didn't waste any time: that very night, they christened a new trust fund "the Window of Opportunity Fund," to raise money to acquire the plant themselves or find a new buyer. But tonight they would accept the banks' offer as a partial victory, and celebrate.

"This is about more than just money," added UE regional president Carl Rosen. "It's about what can be achieved when workers organize and stand up for justice. It's also a wake-up call to corporate America that the rules have changed in this country, and there needs to be a greater measure of economic justice for working people."

Back in the factory cafeteria, hidden from the press, the workers, union organizers, and their families began a celebration. A Bank of America official even joined them, with everyone putting the past week's hard feelings and antagonistic statements aside. It was December 10, Gutierrez's fifty-sixth birthday, and the celebration doubled as a birthday party. There were at least three birthday cakes and several cards signed by the workers, he remembers. He took a chocolate cake home and left the other confections for the happy crowd to devour.

One of the people who heard the Republic story loud and clear was Kevin Surace. He is a socially conscious, technologically savvy, San Francisco Bay Area denizen who made out quite well in the dot-com boom and decided to parlay his earnings, along with healthy support from other venture capitalists, into the green economy. He got a slight jump on the market, launching a company called Serious Materials in 2002 before "green" was the hot catchphrase of marketers and consumers everywhere. Serious Materials manufactures energy-efficient residential windows and commercial glass, said to keep in warm or cool air three to four times better than competitors' products. The company also makes ecologically friendly drywall, called Ecorock, using a process that consumes less water and produces less waste than standard drywall. Traditionally, drywall is made out of gypsum, which requires large amounts of heat and hence emits greenhouse gases. Ecorock is made largely from waste diverted from landfills, and it is heated through a chemical reaction rather than fossil-fuel burning, so the company calls it "zero-carbon drywall." They say if it was adopted nationwide, carbon dioxide emissions would be reduced by 25 billion tons. The product has won them significant media attention and awards for green entrepreneurship.

During the occupation, the union and their supporters touted Republic's ENERGYSTAR products, describing their windows as "green" investments that should grow in demand with expected national greenhouse-gas reduction mandates and weatherization incentives.[25] In reality, Republic was making high-quality but relatively traditional windows that weren't necessarily market leaders in energy efficiency or green innovation. Surace figured the machinery and workers' expertise could be adapted to make Serious Materials' various energy-efficient window and glass lines. He had been planning to open a Midwestern factory in the future, and with Republic he could fill this goal while also helping the workers and playing the good guy in a drama unfolding on the national stage.

Surace tracked down Robles' cell phone number and called him to express his interest in buying the company. A few days after Christmas, he flew to Chicago and took a

---

25. ENERGYSTAR is a label awarded as part of a joint U.S. Environmental Protection Agency and U.S. Department of Energy program to increase energy efficiency and reduce greenhouse gases.

tour of the factory with city councilman Scott Waguespack. (At this point, the factory was empty of workers but still lighted, heated, and guarded around the clock on Bank of America's tab). Waguespack was encouraged by Surace's interest. The city councilman saw Goose Island and the surrounding banks of the Chicago River as an increasingly forlorn island of industrial holdouts in an otherwise upscale, residential and retail-oriented swath of the city. The sight of the Finkl & Son's fiery forges and massive machinery behind sliding doors flung wide open on summer nights is quite an incongruous sight in the otherwise tony neighborhood. But the city's last working steel mill is slated to be moved to the city's south side, and other nearby industries have also closed. Waguespack thinks light industry and commercial and residential areas should be able to coexist, and he wants to turn his ward into a hub of green technology. He envisions wind turbines and other ecologically friendly technologies being built there. To make this a reality, he plans to lure companies by substantially increasing the internet bandwidth, paying for newcomers' architectural drawings, and offering other tax breaks or subsidies for green manufacturing projects. He's been discussing this in the city council's finance committee and bringing in professors to pick their brains. Surace was just his kind of man.

In early January, Surace officially announced his interest in buying the factory and rehiring all the workers. Union members were excited by the suggestion, and a press release was quickly put out. But the process would not be fast or easy. By this time bankruptcy proceedings were in full swing. A bankruptcy trustee was overseeing meetings of creditors, which is standard practice, going through a painstaking accounting of all the company's assets, debts, and possible future income. Meanwhile, a bankruptcy judge was holding hearings and ready to rule on disputes. The bankruptcy judge would have to okay the sale to Surace, and that would mean Bank of America, the major secured creditor, would also have to agree. Selling the company—or actually, just its physical assets since the company itself no longer existed—might not be the most obviously attractive solution for the bank.[26] The bank's quickest way out of the whole thing would be to liquidate all the assets and recoup as much as possible of the nearly $8 million debt owed them. When asked if Serious Materials' purchase could be profitable for the bank, Surace said, "Profitable? Those days are probably over. But this is likely to be an outstanding opportunity for everyone involved to do the right thing."

On January 6, 2009, the union filed Unfair Labor Practice charges against Republic with the National Labor Relations Board (NLRB), charging that the moving of the equipment, the failure to give WARN Act notice, and other issues preceding the closing violated their right to collective bargaining.

Meanwhile, the city was also asking Republic for its money back: the nearly $10 million in tax increment financing funds it had given the company. Various city councilmen and the mayor himself were demanding that Republic repay the funds, since it had not fulfilled its promise of keeping jobs. At a January 12 city council meeting, they ripped into the company. City councilman Joe Moore, who had previously called for the freeze on Bank of America business, said, "They accepted city tax dollars on the basis that they were going to remain in the city of Chicago. To accept these city tax dollars and do an about face and run to Iowa to pay workers there less wages and fewer benefits, runs contrary to the whole purpose of tax-increment financing."

---

26. "Secured" means the money owed to the creditor is actually backed up by assets, and they are first in line to be paid with whatever can be squeezed from the liquidated company. When a company closes, employees are usually not secured and are at the end of the line for any due payment.

The Republic case became a notorious one within the mazelike confines of Chicago's bankruptcy court, a warren of meeting and hearing rooms on the eighth floor of the Dirksen federal building downtown, just a stone's throw from Bank of America's headquarters. In bankruptcy cases, a bankruptcy judge essentially takes control of a company's or individual's assets and decides how debts will be paid. In most Chapter 7 bankruptcy cases like that of Republic, in which the company is being liquidated, the judge appoints a bankruptcy trustee who oversees most of the process administratively, with the judge hearing any disputes. The trustee holds creditors' meetings where the trustee and creditors ask questions to compile information about the bankrupt party's finances.[27] Administrative staff in Chicago's bankruptcy court knew all about the Republic case, which seemed to have hearings constantly. Bankruptcy trustee Phillip Levey's lead attorney, Scott Clar, got tired of wearing a suit every day because of it.

The facts outlined in the "schedules" filed by Republic with the bankruptcy court were not pretty. In all, Republic owed $32.3 million, not counting "unknown" amounts owed to some creditors and liens on equipment. The debt included $23.7 million in secured debt, meaning debt backed up by assets and first in line to be paid; $1.6 million in unsecured "priority claims"; and almost $7 million in unsecured debt, which is unlikely ever to be paid. The company listed $8.2 million in assets, including equipment, a pending patent, accounts receivable (payments due from other companies, and not necessarily likely to be collected) and even White Sox tickets and 39 pictures (both of unspecified value).[28]

The secured debtors were Bank of America for $7.45 million in loans, Chase for $11.1 million, GE Capital Solutions for $1.2 million, a Pittsburgh window company called VEKA for $3.4 million, a man named Larry Fields for $230,000, and Gillman himself for $320,000; plus several companies with liens on equipment. The unsecured debtors included about half a million dollars owed in state taxes to Illinois; tens of thousands in taxes owed to other state treasuries; $590,000 owed to the Wrigley company, Republic's landlord; and many tens of thousands owed to a slew of companies for metal, lumber, screws, machines, uniforms, delivery, trucking, molding, paper, and other goods and services. Workers with unpaid vacation time were also listed as unsecured creditors, since the schedules apparently had not been revised since the banks paid the workers this money. There was a $300 bill for the window-and-door industry magazine, and even a debt of more than $12,000 to the Bellagio Hotel in Las Vegas, the tab for the "dealers incentive meeting" that Gillman and Dubin attended after securing investment from Chase.[29]

At the first creditors' meeting January 18, Gillman got a grilling. The attorney representing the bankruptcy trustee, Scott Clar, confirmed that Gillman owned about 60 percent of the company, since essentially taking it over by assuming the outstanding debt of about $30 million from his cousin Ron Spielman in 2006. But Gillman stressed that even though he had the majority ownership, once COO Barry Dubin brought in JP Morgan Chase the bank had gotten "super powers, super control" over company decisions. Clar seemed to delight in repeating Gillman's "superpowers" phrase, invoking it repeatedly over the lengthy meeting.

When asked why the company closed, Gillman said, "The business could no longer raise capital, it was insolvent. Bank of America pretty much had been squeezing us to get

---

27. Creditors are those individuals, companies or other parties who are owed debts. U.S. Courts website: Bankruptcy Basics. See www.uscourts.gov/bankruptcy.

28. Schedules filed in bankruptcy case 08-34113, Dec. 12, 2008, U.S. Bankruptcy Court for the Northern District of Illinois.

29. *Ibid.*

the doors closed." When asked whether the workers had gotten any advance notice of the shutdown, Gillman said there had been discussions in the week or two before the closing. He had been at home at the actual moment the plant closed.

Clar walked them painstakingly through the company's tattered finances, ascertaining any outstanding payments that might still be due them, wondering if they'd tried to get back security deposits and what utility bills might still be owed. He seemed constantly annoyed that Gillman appeared unfamiliar with the details of the bankruptcy schedules he himself had signed. Clar repeatedly asked Gillman if he knew what was in the documents and if he had read them. When the attorney asked pointedly about any trailers that might be in the truckyard on the southwest side of Chicago, "or anywhere else," Gillman deferred, "Not that I know of." Then the attorney pointed out mention in the schedule of machinery at "an Iowa facility," including a frame notch saw, an end mill, a sash welder, a sash corner cleaner, and other saws and tools.

"I don't remember hearing an Iowa facility mentioned … does the debtor have an Iowa facility?" asked Clar, seemingly with mock innocence given the publicity around the whole situation. "No it does not," answered Gillman.

Gillman went on to say that the equipment in Iowa was actually owned by GE Capital, and Republic had been trying to buy it from GE. The attorney wanted to hear more. The equipment had been moved in November after Bank of America had told the company to shut down, Gillman said.

"Did Bank of America tell Republic to move the equipment?" Clar asked. "Are you saying that based on Bank of America's request you shut down, you moved the equipment?"

"Well it was clear the facility was shutting down," Gillman said evasively. "At that point the equipment would just be useless."

"You referred to Chase as being in super control—what does that mean?" asked Clar, returning to his pet phrase.

"They ultimately had voting power," said Gillman.

"Alright, was there any vote authorizing the movement of the equipment?"

No.

The equipment moved was worth $92,000, Gillman said, and it was now sitting idle at the manufacturing facility in Red Oak, Iowa, formerly owned by the TRACO company, which Gillman said had about $14 million in revenue. Then the history of Echo Windows, the company that the union thinks was meant to take Republic's business and break the union, came out.

Clar: "Okay, what company operates from that facility now?"

Gillman: "A company called Echo, E-C-H-O."

"When was that formed?"

"It was formed I believe the latter part of November."

"By whom?"

"Well, there were several entities."

"Okay, who are the shareholders?"

"It's a trust held in my wife's name."

"Your wife decided to go in the windows and doors business?"

"Well there's another entity that has an interest …"

"Who are the other directors and officers?"

"None."

"Is Echo Windows and Doors engaged in substantially the same business as Republic?"

"Yes."

Clar went through Republic's four window product lines—Builders, Contour, Allure, and Premier Enhancement Classic—and determined where the equipment that had been used to make each now sat. Gillman said that the equipment used to make the Builders and Contour lines was still at Republic, while the machinery used to make Allure windows was "sitting on trailers on the south side."

"Tell me again why you moved the machinery equipment for the Allure line onto trailers?" pressed the attorney. "It was clear the business was closing, and there was an attempt to purchase the equipment from GE," responded Gillman.

"Did GE know?"

"We had tried to communicate that with G E … we had been trying to contact GE to notify them of what was going on."

Meanwhile, Clar pushed for more details. He ascertained that seven trailers holding equipment were sitting in the south-side truckyard, in addition to machinery that was sitting idle in Iowa. The equipment had been fastened to the floor at Republic and had had to be unfastened for the moving; the work at least in some cases was done by Republic union members. Gillman said he himself did not authorize or supervise the moving, and he said his wife's company, Echo, paid for it. UE regional president Carl Rosen wanted to know if Echo had reimbursed Republic directly for the workers' labor; Gillman could not say. The bankruptcy attorney circled back to the moving of the equipment again.

Eventually Clar opened the floor to other creditors in the room who wanted to question Gillman. Carl Rosen wanted to know what happened to the computers that had been moved out under cover of night. The computers likely contained employees' social security numbers' and other personal information, he said. Gillman had no idea where the computers were but told Rosen he had nothing to worry about. They're in a closet somewhere in the suburbs, he eventually offered. "Were all federal laws related to identity theft followed to make sure employees won't be subject to damages?" pressed Rosen. Gillman appeared ready for the meeting to be over. But there were more questions, from the IRS, from the Department of Labor, from a trucking company, from a non-union employee who wanted severance pay. Rosen and Clar were still very interested in who had paid for the shipping of the equipment to Iowa. "Echo!" Gillman said. "How did Echo know what equipment Republic had?" Clar asked, continuing the charade that Echo was a company totally separate and independent from Gillman or Republic.

Brian Shaw, Republic's attorney, still seemed shocked by the whole situation. He said it might be precedent-setting. "This could completely change the future of lending, completely! You hear about this happening in other countries, but not in the U.S., at least not in the last few decades." If a public campaign can force a bank to lend—or essentially give, since there was little prospect of being paid back—money to a company, what's to say banks won't consider that a serious risk in deciding whether to lend or not in the future, he asked. "It does change the playing field, it brings the specter of other group activities. Bank of America had the screws turned on them by the public and by the state. It throws another element of risk into lending, all of a sudden there's this public relations element."

On Wednesday, February 25, two days after the Iowa plant closed, the Republic workers got the news. The bankruptcy judge had indeed approved the sale to Serious Materials, for $1.45 million. Serious Materials would pay the bankruptcy trustee, who would dole out the money to secured creditors after subtracting costs associated with the bankruptcy process. Serious Materials would be relieved of any future liability to the creditors or for any fines resulting from the Unfair Labor Practice charges, WARN Act violations or other results of Republic Windows' conduct.[30] A lease with Wrigley was signed, and the company finalized a collective bargaining agreement with the union. After a longer and more complicated process than anyone had expected, things were ready to fall into place. "There's no question some people, certain banks, weren't interested" in the sale, Kevin Surace said. "But you had the union, the city, the mayor's office, an awful lot of people who wanted to get this done."

The plant's official reopening was slated for May or June. Serious Materials managers were determining what Republic workers still wanted their jobs back and who to hire first. The union contract guarantees they will all be hired before any new employees can be considered.

Surace expects to profit significantly from the vaunted stimulus package, the American Recovery and Reinvestment Act (ARRA), which provides various subsidies and funds for reducing greenhouse gases. Among other things, it offers $16 billion worth of incentives for weatherization, which should theoretically fuel the market for energy-efficient windows and glass.[31] Surace said the prospect of stimulus dollars was what sealed the deal in his mind. After the Republic sale was announced, Vice President Joe Biden called it "an excellent example of how the money in the Recovery Act is targeted to spur job creation quickly. These workers will not only earn a paycheck again, they will go back to work creating products that will benefit our long-term future."[32]

Labor experts and union leaders all say the long-term impact of the Republic struggle and organized labor's prospects in this economic crisis remain to be seen. They point out that the Great Depression was perhaps the most vibrant, militant and innovative era of labor organizing, and they say that if people have the creativity and courage, the current crisis could present similar opportunities. Labor organizers and academics are in nearly unanimous agreement that the Republic victory would not have been possible even a year earlier: workers would not have been willing to take such risks, the larger public would not have been as sympathetic, and the banks would not have been as vulnerable to pressure. Despite much media spin portraying the factory occupation as a spontaneous action by workers who just couldn't take it anymore, labor experts and the workers themselves say the occupation was by no means spontaneous, but rather the confluence of painstaking strategy, tireless organization, perfect timing, and a dollop of luck. They say parlaying the Republic victory and future struggles into a larger sea change will take hard work, fearlessness, selflessness, and intelligence on all fronts.

The UE members and their supporters say creating public solidarity and pressure is key to revitalizing the labor movement, and, in the modern global economy, perhaps the only way to deal with employers with transient and transnational workforces.

---

30. "Order authorizing the sale of the purchased assets of Republic Windows ... :" Filing in U.S. Bankruptcy Court for the Northern District of Illinois Eastern Division. Feb. 24, 2009.

31. ARRAUpdate.com, March 3, 2009.

32. White House press release, March 1, 2009.

Postlude

Disappearing Public Sevices

Public Workers Mass in Wisconsin Capitol, Copyright Getty Images.

"Don't Buy Koch," Dismantling Public Workers Unions and Government Services in Wisconsin (2011)

Kenneth M. Casebeer

In the 2010 election, Wisconsin elected a new Republican Governor and a Republican majority of both state legislative bodies. The new Governor, Scott Walker, had been directly and indirectly financially supported by the Koch Brothers, often referred to as the bankers of the Tea-Party conservative political movement. Within six weeks of taking office, Gov. Walker announced that a looming state budget deficit required state employees to substantially increase their contributions for health insurance and pension funding. The new requirements would amount to a 7% reduction in pay. But the budget issue also provided the excuse for the Governor to introduce a bill to curtail virtually all legal rights of public workers to bargain collectively. In spite of the unions' acceptance of the increased payments on condition of public workers being allowed to continue bargaining through unions, the Governor refused and has demanded passage of the union-gutting legislation.

Workers responded immediately in two ways. First, they mounted large demonstrations outside the capitol in Madison, many camping overnight in freezing winter temperatures. Second, they gained support from a number of Democratic legislators who voluntarily left the State to prevent the necessary quorum to enact a new budget.

Starting February 11, 2011, workers representing both public and private unions poured by the thousands into the Statehouse seeking admittance to legislative hearings. The Governor's office was under siege, "As four game wardens awkwardly stood guard, protesters, scores deep, crushed into a corridor leading to the governor's office here on Wednesday, their screams echoing through the Capitol: 'Come out, come out, wherever you are!'"[1]

> They piled off of buses and out of cars, filling the streets of Madison, Wisconsin, and surrounding the towering Capitol. Thousands crowded inside the building's beautiful rotunda, their cheers echoing throughout the domed structure. An estimated 100,000 people had descended on frigid Madison to protest Republican Governor Scott Walker's "budget repair bill," a sweeping piece of legislation that would strip 170,000 public-sector workers of their right to collectively bargain.

> Last Saturday's "Rally to Save the American Dream" [February 26, 2011] was the culmination of two weeks of protests and a 24-7 sit-in inside the Capitol. Not for 30 or 40 years have unions and progressive groups come together in such an outpouring of support for workers' rights. What makes the Madison protests even more incredible is how spontaneous they have been: There has been no master plan, no long-anticipated strategy to turn Madison into ground zero for a reenergized labor movement.[2]

The remaining Republicans in the Senate approved a "resolution declaring Democrats—who've been holed up in Illinois—to be in contempt of the Senate, authorizing state troopers to arrest any senators they find back in Wisconsin. The move is mostly symbolic, reports the Wisconsin State Journal: 'The state constitution prohibits the arrest of legislators while in session unless they're suspected of committing felonies, treason or breach of the peace.'"[3] In the first week of March, Gov. Walker announced that if Democratic lawmakers did not return and vote on his "budget reform" bill that includes doing away with collective bargaining rights, he would issue more layoff notices than the 1500 thus far, a number that could reach 12,000. Without Senate action by March 20, Walker will begin sending termination notifications. Recall petitions against eight Republicans and six Democrats have been started.

The same tactics of worker resistance subsequently occurred in Indiana and Ohio upon introduction of similar legislation. Protests became nationwide. The long somnolent labor movement sounded a call to action for all union members:

> In the past, labor leaders have been hesitant to call militant actions in part because they're afraid they won't have the support and energy of union members. But after the massive outpouring of rank and file support in Wisconsin during the last eight days—triggered by proposed GOP legislation that would gut organizing rights for public-sector workers—today's leaders are starting to see things differently.

> I think for our generation of labor leaders, this is our "PATCO moment," said United Steelworkers International Vice President Jon Geenen. "We learned the lessons of PATCO and know that we need to instead engage in the type of militant direct action like the type we see in Wisconsin."

> "Governor's Walker decision to eliminate organized labor ... marks the end of an era of labor relations. We have now entered the era of organized labor extermination," says UE Political Action Director Chris Townsend. "There are no more negotiations, no more making concessions. Walker wants us to accept our death.

---

1. Monica Davey and Steven Greenhouse, *New York Times*, A1 (February 17, 2011).
2. Andy Kroll, "How Big Labor and Progressive Groups Pulled Off the Biggest Protests in 40 Years," *Mother Jones* (March 4, 2011).
3. Brad Knickerbocker, *Christian Science Monitor* (March 5, 2011).

Nobody in organized labor is willing to do that. Nothing quite motivates people like extermination."

Furthermore, they have been pleasantly surprised by the massive community support they have received in this fight from people not traditionally affiliated with organized labor. The protests initially tightly organized by organized labor are now essentially community-driven affairs.[4]

But on March 9, Wisconsin Republican State Senators split the union-busting bill from the budget bill and passed it as a non-revenue bill anyway. The House followed suit, and the Governor signed. The legislation restricts both state and municipal workers who are not public safety employees to collective bargaining over "wages;" limits all collective bargaining agreements to one year with no renewals; prohibits dues checkoffs for members of bargaining units, and requires periodic votes to determine if majority support continues for the union, or any union. The law is currently in state constitutional limbo (recently upheld by the Wisconsin Supreme Court, 4–3), although it's larger aim no mystery when split from budget "reform."

Despite saying time and again that the GOP budget was all about righting Wisconsin's fiscal ship, it turns out this was little more than a ruse. The words of senate leader Scott Fitzgerald should be enough to prove that once and for all:

Well if they flip the state senate, which is obviously their goal with eight recalls going on right now, they can take control of the labor unions. If we win this battle, and the money is not there under the auspices of the unions, certainly what you're going to find is President Obama is going to have a much difficult, much more difficult time getting elected and winning the state of Wisconsin. (In the recall, the Republicans retained the Senate by one seat.)

This is what the union-busting bills across the country are about. In Michigan, in Indiana, in Ohio, in Wisconsin, and elsewhere. Meanwhile Republicans in Arizona are trying to cut hundreds of thousands of people from the Medicaid rolls, while Republicans in Florida are enacting sweeping plans to privatize the state's schools and cut public services.[5]

As of early 2011, public workers comprised over one-half of all union members. Whether a new era of struggle and collective action will in fact be precipitated by the public services crisis, there can be little doubt that the union movement in the United States is fighting for its life. Since the beginning in Wisconsin, in Indiana a bill would forbid forcing private sector workers to pay union dues or fees. Ohio would end public sector bargaining and allow hiring replacements during a strike. Idaho restricted collective bargaining to salaries and benefits and eliminated teacher tenure. Four bills, each with part of the Wisconsin program, have been introduced in Florida. "We need to get off our duffs and fight for our futures and our children's futures."[6] The battle will depend on mobilizing the larger communities within which workers live. Perhaps it has always been this way.

---

4. Mike Elk, "Labor Leaders Say Wisconsin Signals 'New Era of Labor Militancy," *In These Times* (February 23, 2011).

5. Ezra Kain, "Wisconsin Republicans Sneak Through Union-Busting Bill Without Democrats," *Forbes* (March 9, 2011).

6. Tim Swanson quoted in Andy Knoll, *supra* note 2.

Frances Fox Piven

Big employers launched a campaign against unions, which they claimed made them uncompetitive in the new international economic environment. New union organizing efforts were fiercely resisted, and some employers even filed for decertification of unions that existed. Contract negotiations became occasions for demanding worker givebacks instead of ceding pay or benefit increases. Union-busting firms that had disappeared after the 1930s were reinvented, now staffed by lawyers and public relations experts instead of detectives and goons. Meanwhile, employer exit threats escalated, and this too was facilitated by globalization, as illustrated by the fabled corporate ploy of hiring trucks labeled "Mexico" to pull up to the loading docks of plants where unionization was afoot. Or workers in one production site were "whip-sawed" against workers in another. Then there was the restructuring of work associated with lean production, which in practice often meant increased reliance on insecure or precarious employment, including part-timers, temporary workers, and contracting out, all of which contributed to the employer clout gained from the threat or reality of exit. Business leaders also became increasingly aggressive and successful in enlisting government in their battle against unions.

Can American workers recover? Could a movement comparable to the upsurge of the 1930s arise again in the wake of the Great Recession. After all, the provocations are certainly similar. Once again, inequality is soaring, along with unemployment rates, foreclosures, and evictions. Of course, much else has changed, and a workers' movement today would reflect those changed circumstances. In the 1930s, mass production workers were the backbone of the protest movements. Now much of America's manufacturing has moved abroad; the factories, mines of the industrial era, and the neighborhoods they nourished are emptying; and even the infrastructure that once supported manufacturing has been allowed to decay. Most Americans work in service-sector jobs, and many of those workers are women. Still, do these changes mean that workers no longer have power?[1]

Eugene Victor Debs

No strike is ever lost.

---

1. Frances Fox Piven, "Introduction," Irving Bernstein, *The Turbulent Years,* (Chicago: Haymarket Books, 2010).

Index